PSYCHOLOGICAL AND BIOLOGICAL APPROACHES TO EMOTION

PSYCHOLOGICAL AND BIOLOGICAL APPROACHES TO EMOTION

Edited by

NANCY L. STEIN
BENNETT LEVENTHAL, M.D.
TOM TRABASSO
University of Chicago

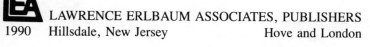

LAWRENCE ERLBAUM ASSOCIATES, PUBLISHERS
1990   Hillsdale, New Jersey   Hove and London

Lawrence Erlbaum Associates, Inc., Publishers
365 Broadway
Hillsdale, New Jersey 07642

Library of Congress Cataloging-in-Publication Data

Psychological and biological approaches to emotion / edited by Nancy
  L. Stein, Bennett Leventhal, Tom Trabasso.
      p. cm.
    "Outgrowth of a conference on the psychological and biological
  bases of behavior, held at the University of Chicago, in September
  of 1986"—Overview.
    Includes bibliographical references.
    ISBN 0-8058-0149-9 — ISBN 0-8058-0150-2 (pbk.)
    1. Emotions—Physiological aspects—Congresses. 2. Affective
  disorders—Physiological aspects—Congresses. 3. Neuropsychology-
  -Congresses. I. Stein, Nancy L. II. Leventhal, Bennett.
  III. Trabasso, Tom.
    [DNLM: 1. Affective Disorders—congresses. 2. Behavior-
  -congresses. 3. Emotions—congresses. 4. Emotions—physiology-
  -congresses. WL 103 P97354 1986]
    QP401.P79 1990
  152.4—dc20
  DNLM/DLC
  for Library of Congress   89-25829
                                                                      CIP

Contents

PART IV: COPING AND PSYCHOPATHOLOGY

PART V: SYSTEM APPROACHES TO EMOTION

Overview

This book is the outgrowth of a conference on the psychological and biological bases of behavior, held at the University of Chicago, in September of 1986. The major goal of the conference was to allow investigators in different areas of emotion to meet and exchange ideas with other scholars who were not directly in their own area of expertise. We wanted to integrate the biological consideration of emotion with current psychological approaches, and we wanted to include studies of the coping process associated with emotion as well as those that focus on the appraisal process that gives rise to emotion. Furthermore, we wanted to approach emotion from both developmental and psychopathological perspectives. Thus, the conference papers are organized around five major themes: (a) relationships between cognition and emotion, (b) biological approaches to emotion, (c) developmental perspectives on emotion, (d) coping and psychopathology, and (e) systems approaches to emotion.

The Relation between Cognition and Emotion

The chapters in this section are primarily focused on describing the process of experiencing emotion from the appraisal process that occurs before emotion to the consequences that ensue once an emotion is experienced. **Lazarus, Mandler, Stein, and Levine** focus primarily on the process of experiencing an emotion. The thrust of these contributions is to describe the components of the different processes related to the experience of emotion, discuss how emotion is continually influenced by the cognitive evaluation of the eliciting event, and illustrate how emotional reactions influence subsequent action.

Lazarus focuses on three constructs of mind-motivation, emotion, and cognition, and shows how they are related to action and to the way in which the structure of events are perceived. He points out that all theories of emotion have directed attention to these concepts, coming up with diverse ways of interrelating them. In particular, the relationship between thought and emotion serves as a dividing issue for understanding some of the primary differences among current approaches to emotion. Lazarus takes the position that, for all intensive purposes, cognition and emotion are inseparable. They cannot be studied separately, even in young children and animals other than humans. Lazarus then calls for a more systematic analysis of the appraisal and coping process, and indeed, in another chapter included in the **Coping and Psychopathology** section, Folkman and Lazarus describe some of the more detailed processing associated with coping.

Mandler also focuses on the cognition–emotion relationship, but from a slightly different perspective. He contrasts the constructivist position with that deriving from a fundamentalist theory of emotion. To Mandler, a constructivist theory (which he adopts) is defined as emphasizing the processes and mechanisms that generate emotional experience and behavior. The theory emphasizes the role of discrepancies and interruptions as a major source of autonomic (sympathetic) nervous system arousal and emotional intensity. In laying out the importance of these concepts, Mandler discusses the function that cognitive schemata play in determining the quality of emotional experience with an emphasis on describing some of the processes underlying the generation of emotion. In particular, Mandler focuses on the experience of positive emotion and the varieties of schemata that operate in emotional construction. Like Lazarus, Mandler rejects the view that cognition and affect can be separated and reduced to specific entities. Moreover, Mandler takes issue with researchers (e.g., Zajonc, 1980) who argue that affective responses need no cognitive input. As evidence for the hypothesis that cognitive processes continually regulate affective experience, Mandler demonstrates that cognitive analyses are prior to and faster than affective judgments. He elaborates on his model by showing how the problems of stress, close relationships, and music appreciation can be discussed within a constructivist framework.

Stein and Levine also focus on the cognition and emotion relationship, but their emphasis is directed more toward a specific description of the appraisal and coping process. They focus on the content-specific knowledge used to make inferences during appraisal and planning. In addition to discussing the conditions that elicit emotions in general, Stein and Levine are interested in the conditions that are specific to different emotions, and the planning process that follows from different emotional reactions. These investigators contend that emotional reactions occur when the status of valued goals change, and therefore they attempt to describe what happens when people recognize that changes have occurred in their ability to maintain a goal. Learning from success and failure is an important emphasis in their chapter as are the changes in value assigned to a goal before and after success or failure. Stein and Levine also show that when people succeed or fail at attaining one goal, other goals are directly affected. Thus, an important problem in predicting what emotion will be experienced is knowing what goal will be most salient. And finally, these investigators discuss what happens when people cannot immediately succeed at attaining a valued goal. A detailed process analysis of happiness, anger, and sadness is then presented to illustrate how changes in the status of goals affect thinking and planning subsequent to an emotional experience.

Isen is primarily interested in the impact that feelings have on cognitive structure and organization. In particular, she focuses on the different effects that happiness and sadness have on memory. She is also interested in exploring the relationship between happiness and creativity. Isen's major thesis is that positive affect leads to a broad, flexible, cognitive organization defined by certain measures of creativity. On the other hand, negative emotion often leads to a narrowing of focus and processing. She cites evidence in favor of each of these hypotheses and discusses the impact of positive and negative mood states on long-range development and problem-solving skills. Isen, however, is careful to point out that more research is needed to clarify whether the consequences of emotion states are general in that all negative states lead to a narrowing of thinking or whether some negative states might lead to a more creative way to approach a problem. In this sense, Isen's comments are similar to Stein and Levine's contention that, in specifying the effects of positive versus negative emotion, the specific situations that generate an emotion must be considered as well as the intensity of the specific emotional reaction.

Biological Perspectives on Emotion

This section begins with a chapter by **Heilman and Bowers,** who are interested in exploring and describing the emotional changes seen in patients with left and right hemisphere disease. These changes may result from interferences with specific neocortical emotion functions or with cognitive processes necessary for the evaluation of events that lead to emotion. Left and right hemispheric disease can also interfere with the expression of emotion or may even interfere with the expression of subjective feeling states. In exploring the effect of different hemispheric diseases, Heilman and Bower attempt to formulate a model that describes the mechanisms that control both the evaluation and the expression of emotion. These investigators reject the James Lang theory of emotion and partially support the Maranon–Schacter theory of emotional experience. The main thesis here is that the combination of bodily arousal and cognitive evaluation interacts to produce an emotion, similar to the basic assumptions of Mandler, Lazarus, Stein, and Levine. However, Heilman and Bower also cite data that on the surface go against the Maranon–Schacter model. Specifically, fear and anger are thought to be aroused without cognitive evaluation. These investigators also argue that feeling an emotion is distinct from expressing an emotion. Thus, they call for a more detailed study of emotion that focuses on exploring whether processes related to emotional arousal can be separated from those processes that are involved in the cognitive evaluation of an eliciting event.

Kolb and Taylor explore the role that the neocortex plays in emotion by examining the effects that discrete unilateral cortical lesions have on behavior. These investigators contend that the location of the lesion is critical in determining which aspect of emotional functioning is disrupted. In particular, lesions to the frontal lobe have marked effects on spontaneous facial expression, facial praxis, and spontaneous talking, whereas temporal lesions, particularly those in the right hemisphere, interfere with the perception of facial emotional expressions. A second avenue of exploration for Kolb and Taylor is the examination of certain psychiatric disorders on emotional functioning. These disorders deserve attention because of the disturbances that occur to different areas of the neocortical regions of the brain. Indeed, the central hypothesis of Kolb and Taylor's chapter is that damage to different areas of the neocortex has very different effects on emotional behavior much like damage to different hemispheres of the brain. Because each type of damage seems to produce disruption of specific components of emotional behavior, a more detailed analysis must be sought that compares the hemispheric systems to the neocortical systems in terms of their differential influence on emotional behavior.

Tucker, Vannatta, and Rothlind discuss the role of the two hemispheres in regulating modes of cognition that structure emotional processes. In particular, they are interested in the unique functioning of the two hemispheres in regulating emotion. However, their chapter also focuses on the importance of primitive emotional processes in regulating higher order functioning like memory and attention. They review evidence suggesting that the left and right hemisphere operate on different principles of neurophysiological self-regulation in regard to activation and arousal. The cognitive effects of these control mechanisms may help to explain how emotional states restrict or expand the breadth of attentional access to different types of information. These investigators also argue that in its regulation of memory functions, the neomamalian limbic system applies controls to human cognition, operating in parallel to more cortical, semantic representational functions. These limbic-system emotion controls involve special access routes for information that is hedonic or threatening. In this sense, Tucker et al. take a similar position to that of Heilman and Bower. More than cortical input must be considered in the elicitation of emotion, and convergent evidence as well as a theory that specifies how emotional experience is integrated must be considered.

Heller focuses on a neuropsychological theory of emotion that integrates both cognitive and biological perspectives. The model has several features. Heller first makes a distinction between feeling an emotion and the ability to think about an emotion. The ability to think about an emotion is a specialized function of the right hemisphere. The experience of a feeling, in contrast, is mediated by modulation in cerebral activation. Second, Heller focuses on the importance of cortical mechanisms in the control of arousal, removing focus from the autonomic nervous system. Third, she illustrates that pleasure/displeasure and the degree of arousal are dependent on different neurological systems. These dimensions can be used to explain more psychological theories of emotion. Heller then discusses the development and integration of these mechanisms from both a biological and a psychological perspective.

Developmental Approaches to Emotion

The four contributions in this section represent different approaches to the study of emotion. **Bloom** is interested in the relationship between the expression of speech and affect. Given that many aspects of affect are already in place before language development begins, does the expression of affect facilitate the emergence of speech in the second year. Bloom is also interested in the way in which the two systems come together so that infants say words with positive or negative emotional valence. To answer these questions, she carried out a longitudinal study on a group of 12 infants during the period from 9 to 26 months of age. The results from four studies are then considered. In the first one, individual differences in language achievement were correlated with the frequency and amount of time spent expressing neutral and non-neutral affect. In the second study, different developmental trends in affective expression were found for infants who differed in their profiles of language expression. The third study examines the words that children produce, along with the affect and valence of affect. And the fourth study focuses on the meaning attributed to children's words and affective expressions at two different times: (a) at the end of the first word period, when expression is predominantly affective, and (b) at the end of a period when children were saying words as often as they were expressing affect. The results are discussed in terms of a developmental interaction between affect expression and the cognition required for language learning.

Stenberg and Campos focus on the development of anger expression in infants from the ages of 4 to 7 months. In their studies of anger they conclude that the facial response pattern associated with anger develops between 1 and 4 months of age. Responding to restraint situations, infants by the age of 4 months were capable of expressing the critical dimensions associated with anger expressions. Stenberg and Campos then present evidence to illustrate the nature of anger expressions during the 4 to 7 month period of time. They also raise several interesting theoretical questions regarding anger. Given that they found full-blown anger expressions by 4 months of age, can these infants be said to experience the feeling of anger? Stenberg and Campos discuss the differences in positions regarding the evocation of anger and ask whether infants experience anger similar to that of older children. They consider the possibility that anger expressions are somewhat independent of emotion states and through development become associated with the more classical concepts of anger responses. Stenberg and Campos discuss the emergence of different anger expressions, with one form being more primitive than the other. They also include a discussion of the cross-cultural significance of anger expressions.

Huttenlocher and Smiley present a series of studies exploring the development of person concepts in young children. Word meanings are used as an index of children's understanding of concepts related to the self and other people. Parental use of person words is also considered because the absence of these words in the child's vocabulary may be due to the lack of exposure in the linguistic environment. Huttenlocher and Smiley's data support the hypothesis that children acquire a notion of a self with internal states before they acquire a notion of other people with internal states. In particular, children begin to use words for themselves around the age of 2 years, and they apply emotion words and verbs to the self just before 2 years of age. Words for other people are acquired earlier than words for the self, but Huttenlocher and Smiley argue that words for other people encode only the animate nature of others' action and not the intentional nature underlying the action. The critical age for understanding and using words referring to internal states of others appears to be around 2½. Huttenlocher and Smiley then discuss the relationship between parent use of internal states and the expression of these words in young children.

Radke-Yarrow and Kochanska, like Stenberg and Campos, focus on the development of anger in children from the ages of 1 to 8 years. Developmental changes, gender differences, and family-context variables are considered in relation to children's experience and expression of anger. When confronted with an anger episode, toddlers show patterns of both flight and fight. Their efforts to comprehend the anger of others are manifested in imitation and self-referential gestures and comments. Frequent exposure to anger, especially in the home, is associated with heightened expressions of anger in the child, increased emotionality, distressing feelings about the self, and negative images of their families. The amount of anger expressed by children was consistent over several days, suggesting a characteristic affective approach to experience. Overt anger was expressed more fully by toddlers than by their school-aged siblings, and mothers were more tolerant of anger in their toddlers than in their 5- to 8-year-old children. Radke-Yarrow and Kochanska then discuss pertinent issues related to the development and expression of anger.

Coping and Psychopathology

This section is devoted to discussions that range from the presentation of models of the general coping process to discussions of depression, helplessness, and psychopathology. **Folkman and Lazarus** begin by presenting a theoretical account that speaks to the flow that is established between coping and emotion. The behavioral flow begins with a transaction that is appraised as significant to a person's well-being. The appraisal influences coping, which in turn changes the person–environment relationship and hence the emotional response. The key question is: How do various forms of problem- and emotion-focused coping thoughts and acts alter the person–environment relationship, and hence the emotional response? Folkman and Lazarus consider three possibilities: cognitive activity that influences the deployment of attention, cognitive activity that alters the subjective meaning or significance of the encounter for well-being, and actions that alter the actual terms of the person–environment relationship. The effects of each type of coping on the quality and intensity of emotional response in a particular stressful encounter are considered.

Abramson, Alloy, and Metalsky then consider the status of the hopelessness theory of depression. A major tenet of their discussion is that the research strategies used over the course of the last 10 years do not provide an accurate test of a hopelessness theory of depression. Moreover, they contend that if investigators use the robustness of the findings that supposedly support the theory, they may be seriously misled regarding the validity of the phenomenon of hopelessness. Abramson et al. then discuss some of the major methodological difficulties associated with the studies on hopelessness and depression. Rather than end on a negative note, however, these investigators contend that it is critical to provide an accurate test of the theory, and they discuss ways of beginning the research.

Cicchetti and White attempt to provide an assessment of how emotion, cognition, and language interact and play a role in the etiology and course of psychopathology. They provide an historical summary of the ways in which emotion–cognition relationships have been characterized in psychiatric disturbances. Moreover, they look at psychopathology from a developmental point of view by focusing on children with Down Syndrome, maltreated children, and the offspring of parents with a manic–depressive disorder. Drawing on data gathered in multiple contexts, they discuss the role of emotion and the affective environment in the course of developmental deviation and psychopathology. Cicchetti and White underscore how the study of emotion in a psychopathological environment can enhance understanding of emotion in general, and they suggest future areas of research that would interface the study of development and psychopathology.

Systems Approaches to Emotion

The final section is devoted to a more general consideration of constraints that influence the development and expression of emotion. **Averill** begins by showing just how broadly based emotion is. To him, emotion is directly related to the evolution of the species, emotions reflect the values and norms of a culture, and they are critical in the development and growth of an individual. The first half of

Averill's chapter is devoted to an examination of the way emotions can be accounted for in terms of underlying structures (abstract systems of behavior) organized on biological, psychological, and social principles. In the second half of the chapter, the relation of emotion to social systems is examined in some detail, using anger and similar emotions in other cultures for illustrative examples. It is argued that social institutions have become the major vehicle for establishing and maintaining emotional syndromes. Conversely, emotional expression is one of the major ways in which individuals renew and sustain the social order. Emotions thus provide a vital link between the individual and society. Averill's contention is that socialization, to a large degree, is one of educating the emotions.

Brown attempts to then provide a model of the affective process in terms of indicating how affective systems play a role in adapting action and constructing knowledge. He uses Piaget's theory as a base, incorporating work by Pugh and Cellerier, and then shows how his model pertains to problem solving, decision making, and the evolution of scientific thought. In essence, Brown's theory not only incorporates Piaget's theory but directly parallels the approaches of Lazarus, Mandler, Stein, and Levine, who attempt to integrate different processes underlying the experience of emotion.

Nancy L. Stein

This book is dedicated to Irving R. Harris, who underwrote and supported the conference from which this volume emerged. His support and wisdom have served us well in bringing together an outstanding group of individuals to discuss and share ideas on the topic of emotion. He has also generously supported the Harris Center for Developmental Studies at the University of Chicago. Without his support, we would not be able to train as many students as we do, nor would the students working in the area of emotion have gotten a chance to discuss and exchange ideas with the scholars who attended this conference.

Nancy L. Stein
Bennett L. Leventhal
Tom Trabasso

RELATIONSHIPS BETWEEN
COGNITION AND EMOTION

1 Constructs of the Mind in Adaptation

Richard S. Lazarus
University of California, Berkeley

Some years ago, when I was thinking about cognitive appraisal as a central process in emotion, I realized that the cognitive revolution in psychology did not create new constructs with which to understand the human mind but only changed the definition and arrangement of old constructs. The basic theoretical entities of psychology have always consisted of *motivation, emotion,* and *cognition,* each of which describes different functions of mind. In an interesting discussion of the origins of faculty psychology, Hilgard (1980) has referred to these as the "trilogy of the mind." To these constructs we must add two other sets of variables, namely, *actions* and the *environmental stimulus* array, making a total of five concepts to juggle in our theories of emotion and behavior.

This presentation is an attempt to discuss the relationships among these constructs within a cognitive and relational approach to emotion and human functioning, and to elaborate somewhat on what I have said previously about the cognition–emotion relationship (Lazarus, 1966, 1980, 1982, 1984; Lazarus & Folkman, 1984; Lazarus, Kanner, & Folkman, 1980; Lazarus & Launier, 1978.

In the 1940s and 1950s Freudians and reinforcement learning theorists emphasized drives and placed them early in the stimulus–organism–response (S–O–R) sequence. These theories also gave relatively little attention to cognitive mediation. Drives that were in conflict or blocked from discharge produced tension or anxiety that was reduced by adaptive or ego-defensive behavior learned through the principle of reinforcement. Ego psychologists came along later to once again give prominence to cognition.

3

WHAT IS A COGNITIVE-RELATIONAL THEORY
OF EMOTION?

Renewed interest in cognition returned us to a position that had been well articulated as long ago as Aristotle (1831), who suggested that people are made angry by the thought that they have been insulted or demeaned. Mainstream psychology has once again resurrected cognition—like the Biblical Lazarus—in the form of judgments, expectations, attributions, or appraisals of the significance of what is happening for well-being. German Action Theory, which Frese and Sabini (1985) define as a conception of human behavior directed toward the accomplishment of goals, governed by plans that are hierarchically arranged, and responsive to feedback from the environment, is a good example.

Psychology has also turned from structural S–R and complex S–O–R formulations toward a *systems approach* that focuses on temporal relations and the flow of behavior involving many interdependent variables and processes (see also McGuire, 1983). A systems arrangement of variables and processes in emotion is portrayed in Fig. 1.1 (cf. Lazarus, DeLongis, Folkman, & Gruen, 1985; Lazarus & Folkman, 1984). Here the stimulus is buried in a person–environment transaction, still important but only in relationship with person characteristics. Cognitive appraisal and coping are the key mediators of emotion. Motivation, which comprises means, ends, and cognitive concerns, as well as drives, is identified as goals in this system. They are antecedent variables that interact with personal beliefs and environmental events in shaping appraisal and coping. The system is in constant flux, and because it is recursive (see also Bandura, 1977) any variable is capable of being either an antecedent, a mediating process, or an outcome, depending on the point in time at which one enters the flow.

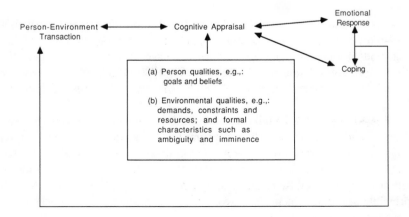

FIG. 1.1.   Cognitive and Relational Theory.

Very briefly stated, this approach to emotion contains two basic themes: First, emotion is a response to evaluative judgments or *meaning;* second, these judgments are about ongoing *relationships with the environment,* namely, how one is doing in the agenda of living and whether an encounter with the environment is one of harm or benefit. One's goal hierarchy, or what is most and least important to the person, and the specific external conditions of an encounter determine the potential for harm or benefit.

Acute emotions such as anger, fear, joy, and pride are reactions to specific encounters of the moment. The term acute means they are short-lived and can be distinguished from longer term emotions called moods. *Moods* too are based on judgments about the significance of the person–environment relationship, but their concerns are broader, longer term, and more existential than acute emotions. Each emotion, whether acute or a mood, expresses the particular harm or benefit that is cognized to be at stake in an ongoing relationship with the environment, and the action impulse such as attack or flight that addresses the harm or benefit.

The transactional themes of meaning and relationship are expressed theoretically in the concepts of cognitive appraisal (cf. Lazarus, 1966, 1981; Lazarus & Folkman, 1984; Lazarus & Launier, 1978) and coping (Folkman & Lazarus, 1980, 1985; Folkman, Lazarus, Dunkel-Schetter, DeLongis, & Gruen, 1986a; Folkman, Lazarus, Gruen, & DeLongis, 1986b; Lazarus & Folkman, 1984). *Primary appraisal* concerns whether what is happening in a relationship is relevant for one's well-being. This is assessed as the stakes one has in an encounter. *Secondary appraisal* concerns the options and resources for coping with problematic relationships.

Coping is important in the emotion process because it can change the significance for well-being of what is happening in the encounter in one of two ways: (1) by actions that alter the actual terms of the person–environment relationship, or (2) by cognitive activity that influences either the deployment of attention (e.g., by avoidance) or the meaning of the encounter (e.g., denial or distancing). The second process (2) has also been referred to as emotion-focused coping, whereas the first (1) is problem-focused coping (e.g., Folkman & Lazarus, 1980; Lazarus & Folkman, 1984). Throughout the remainder of this presentation I use the term *cognitive coping* for the latter because emotion-focused coping is essentially a cognitive process.

Many theorists and researchers accept the premise that adult human emotion can best be understood in cognitive terms. There is now what could be said to be a family of theories that have a cognitive-relational emphasis. Explicitly cognitive formulations of emotion theory have been offered by Arnold (1960), Averill (1982), Bandura (1977, 1982), Epstein (1983), Leventhal (1984), Mandler (1984), Roseman (1984), Scherer (1984), Solomon (1980), Weiner (1985), and in the clinical context, Ellis (Bernard & DiGiuseppe, in press) and Beck (1976). Most of these provide limited and incomplete statements of the details of the emotion process. Although they vary in emphasis and detail, all accept the idea of cognitive mediation in emotion. This is not the place to examine the overlaps and variations among them or to explore the historical origins of the cognitive theme in emotion theory.

The term appraisal has been adopted by a large number of writers, though it is often used imprecisely. My colleagues and I distinguish between *information* and *appraisal,* which refers to an evaluation of the significance of information for personal well-being and action (cf. Kreitler & Kreitler, 1976).

The task of cognitive appraisal is to assimilate two sometimes contradictory sets of forces operating in a person's transactions with the environment: the goals and beliefs brought to the scene by the person *and* the environmental realities that affect the outcome of the transaction. This process of assimilating these two sets of forces must not go overboard in either direction: To overemphasize personal agenda is autism and to overemphasize the environment is to abandon one's personal identity. Survival would be impossible if appraisals were constantly in a bad fit with the environmental realities. It would be equally in jeopardy if we failed to take personal stakes into account in our appraisals. As Ellis (Ellis & Bernard, 1985; see also Lazarus, in press-a) and other cognitivists (e.g., Beck, 1976) have long maintained, consistently faulty ways of thinking (or appraising) lead to persistent emotional distress and social dysfunction.

CURRENT CONTROVERSIES

Although few seem to challenge that appraisal can affect emotional quality and intensity, current controversies tend to focus on two closely intertwined questions: (1) Is appraisal necessary for emotion, which means that if appraisal of a harm or benefit does not occur, emotion does not occur? Connected with this we must consider whether there are exceptions to the principle that appraisal is always necessary, for example, in the case of infants or animals; (2) regardless of how the issue of whether appraisal is a necessary or sufficient condition of emotion is resolved, should cognition and emotion be regarded as separate processes, or as indissolubly bound together and only separated with difficulty or in psychopathology? This is quite a different matter than the status of appraisal, though those who tend to separate emotion from cognition seem also to favor a "no" answer to the claim that there is no emotion without appraisal.

Are Emotion and Cognition Separate Systems?

Beginning with the second issue, the separatist position has recently been debated by Zajonc (1980, 1984) and by me (Lazarus, 1982, 1984). Zajonc's position appealed to many because of the argument, which I regard as erroneous, that cognitive theories leave emotion bloodless and cold by subsuming it under thought. As Tomkins (1981) put it using the images of Shakespeare: "a remedy [is needed] for affect 'sicklied o'er with the pale cast of thought' " (p. 306). The notion that cognitive theories take the heat out of emotion is encouraged by the imprecise equation of emotion and cognition as illustrated by Solomon's (1980) comment that "emotions are akin to judgments" (p. 271), or Sartre's (1948) statement, taken out of context, that "Emotion is a certain way of apprehending the world" (p. 52).

Perhaps the best reply to Zajonc on this, and to those who share his view, is that emotion is both based on and contains cognitive activity, but it also includes other hot components such as action impulses and physiological changes that these action impulses generate when there is temporary or sustained mobilization to deal with harms, threats, challenges, or benefits. To emphasize cognitive activity in the generation of an emotion is not to equate emotion with cold cognition.

Zajonc argued that there are separate anatomical brain structures for emotion and cognition and, therefore, that emotion could precede cognition as well as the other way around. This position is especially appealing to those who think of emotion as a hard-wired, innate process. Separatists also tend to reduce mental activity to neurophysiological processes. Reduction leaves an unresolved mind–body problem in which key mental concepts such as appraisal and coping are not adequately mapped by concepts at the body level. This lack of parallelism makes the two levels of analysis, neurophysiological and psychological, difficult to connect in a meaningful way. It is also risky to make a decision about psychological concepts on the basis of what we currently know about the anatomy and physiology of the brain (see also Burghardt, 1985).

Although thought and emotion are normally conjoined, they can, of course, be kept apart, as in what is clinically referred to as defenses such as distancing, isolation, depersonalization, repression, denial, or dissociation. I like the term disconnection. We think of defensive processes as pathological or pathogenic, the result of intentional effort at regulating distressing emotions. When people use them, they are said to be out of touch with their emotions and with the environmental conditions influencing them. However, it is one thing to say that separation is *possible* under certain conditions and another thing to say that it is *normative*.

Dissociation theories of hypnosis, for example, imply the splitting of sensory and other mental processes, suggesting that a single, central, cognitive control process is not always firmly in the saddle (cf. Ahsen, 1985). However, when splitting occurs there is still some degree of mutual awareness of interaction among split thoughts and images in the normal waking state. Thus, all such dissociations are relative rather than absolute if care is taken to detect interactions (Hilgard, 1975, 1977).

To give the separation between motivation, cognition, and emotion the status of a biological principle is to turn the mind, which is usually coordinated and directed, into an uncoordinated arrangement in which each function operates on its own. This can also be a dysfunctional arrangement. Instead we should be seeking the *organizing principle* or principles that make the components of the mind a unit, operating in harmony with the adaptational requirements of the environment and the personal agenda that create the story lines of our lives.

The case for the normal integration of the constructs of the mind requires qualification. For example, mental development involves gaining gradual freedom from the concrete environmental stimulus and from the tyranny of drives or impulses in action. At the same time, however, development brings with it increasing integration of the components of the mind. Cognition, emotion, and motivation become welded into a system that, though under tension, must remain in touch with the environment and in control of actions in the interests of allowing the person to survive and flourish. The links between action and the demands, constraints, and resources of the environment, as well as the structure of the mind, are forged and changed developmentally and dialectically by continuous adaptational transactions (Block, 1982; Fischer & Pipp, 1984; Piaget, 1952). This is, of course, a Piagetian or formal structural view, but the appraisal process also depends on content in the form of information about how things work and on-the-spot evaluations of the significance for well-being of what is happening. What children know about social relationships and the consequences of their actions is crucial to an understanding of their appraisal processes in emotional encounters.

Disconnection refers to a condition in which the components of the mind are responsive to divergent influences and generate contradictory actions. For example, what the person thinks may be out of touch with the emotions that are experienced or the motives that shape action. Epstein (1985) makes a similar point in citing cases in which "the person does not 'feel' like doing what intellectually he or she 'thinks' should be done; the person may state . . . 'I made myself do it' " (p. 288). Epstein emphasizes that an overall self attempts to integrate various subselves, but when there is complete insulation among the subsystems there is psychopathology. Schwartz (1979) seems to mean something similar by his term disregulation to refer to the loss of communication among the parts of the brain, which allows the normally integrated system of feedback loops to go out of control.

For the opposite of disconnection to occur, short-term goals must be in harmony with long-term goals and contribute to them as means to ends. Conflict among goals is obviously disruptive of harmony and results in the system components pulling apart rather than working together. Motivation must accord with (cognitive) understandings of what is possible, likely, reasonably safe, properly timed, properly sequenced. Emotions must be accurate reflections of the significance of encounters for well-being. All conflict theories of psychopathology treat this as a basic assumption. Integration is a common term for harmony and fragmentation or ego-failure for disharmony (cf. Haan, 1969, 1977; Menninger, 1954).

Is Appraisal Necessary?

I favor a yes answer to the first question (1), which asks whether appraisal is necessary to emotion. For the garden variety of human emotions, no other principle of emotion-generation is necessary. Given what evidence is available, the burden of proof of another mechanism rests on anyone who would so claim. A statement by Sartre (1948) points up the essential connection of emotion and cognition as convincingly as any I have seen:

> It is evident, in effect, that the man who is afraid is afraid *of* something. Even if it is a matter of one of those indefinite anxieties which one experiences in the dark, in a sinister and deserted passageway, etc., one is afraid *of* certain aspects of the night, of the world. And doubtless, all psychologists have noted that emotion is set in motion by a perception, a representation-signal, etc. But it seems that for them the emotion then withdraws from the object in order to be absorbed into itself. Not much reflection is needed to understand that, on the contrary, the emotion returns to the object at every moment and it's fed there. For example, flight in a state of fear is described as if the object were not, before anything else, a flight *from* a certain object, as if the object fled did not remain present in the flight itself, as its theme, its reason for being, *that from which one flees*. And how can one talk about anger, in which one strikes, injures, and threatens, without mentioning the person who represents the objective unity of these insults, threats, and blows? In short, the affected subject and the affective object are bound in an indissoluble synthesis. Emotion is a certain way of apprehending the world. (pp. 51–52)

Expanding on Sartre, I offer the following manifesto for cognitive theorists that sums up the issue: *Emotion and cognition are inseparable.* If the personal meaning, however primitive or inchoate it might be, vanishes, so does the emotion. Emotion without cognition would be mere activation, without the differential direction that exists in the impulse to attack in anger or to flee in fear. What would motivation be without cognition? It too would be merely a diffuse, undifferentiated state of activation, as in a tissue tension that doesn't specify the consumatory goal or the means required to attain it (cf. Gallistel, 1980, 1985; Klein, 1958; Stadler & Wehner, 1985; White, 1960). Integration of behavior would also be impossible without cognitive direction (Miller, Galanter, & Pribram, 1960); there could be no possibility of the feedback control of behavior without the ability to take cognizance of what is happening. Cognition is thus the key to emotion and integrated human functioning.

Schachter (1966; Schachter & Singer, 1962; see also Reisenzein, 1983) points to two factors, activation and direction, in the generation of an emotion, but in my opinion he does not show how the activation, which in his view must precede an emotion, arises; unlike Mandler (1984), who also has a two-factor theory, Schachter does not see clearly that activation can be aroused merely by an idea; in addition, he externalizes the cognitive mediation by treating it as a process of labeling the social atmosphere of the emotional encounter. Thus, although he was an early cognitivist, his approach to emotion is not fully cognitive in that it does not rest entirely on the meaning of an encounter.

Because there is so much misunderstanding here, I emphasize that cognition and emotion are overlapping concepts but not the same. Cognition generates the emotion and continues as part of the emotional experience, as in my earlier quote from Sartre. One has the alternative of saying, as Epstein (1983) does, that the cognitive activity that generates the emotion ends with the arrival of the emotion, but I fail to see the advantage of this elementalism because the emotional experience is not adequately described without the cognitive component. The experience of an emotion includes the cognitive appraisal that produced it.

Moreover, a certain kind of cognition is indispensable to emotion, namely, the appraisal of the significance of what is happening for well-being. Information that one has been threatened or insulted does not per se produce an emotion, say, fear or anger. To feel fear or anger one must also appraise the information as signifying harm. If the person who insults us is believed to have no power to harm, the insult will probably not result in anger. Similarly, if the potential danger is totally within our power to neutralize or avoid, we are not apt to react with fear. In other words, the environmental information must be seen as relevant to our well-being to generate involvement in the transaction (Singer, 1974). Detached knowledge is not enough to generate emotion; a personal evaluation is required. This view has a parallel in Arnheim's (1958) analysis of ansthetic emotions. To feel emotion one must be actively engaged in appreciating a painting or a piece of music, not merely looking at it in a detached fashion.

There are many who more or less agree with the preceding view yet still question the principle that emotion is *always* a response to meaning. As Hoffman (in press) puts it, "we gain very little by postulating in advance, as Lazarus does, that cognitive evaluation is always necessary." Doubt is expressed by many that a single cognitive principle holds for simple animals and infants as well as for adult human beings. Leventhal (1984; Leventhal & Tomarken, 1986) speaks of a sensory-motor level of emotional processing and regards as innate the newborn's receptivity to emotional cues such as voice tone and facial expression. Leventhal and Tomarken (1986) write, for example, that "The variety of expressive reactions produced just hours after birth provide strong evidence to the preprogrammed nature of expression and its associated set of emotional experiences, though evidence for the latter half of the assumption is lacking" (p. 275). Therefore, even though infants grow into adults for whom cognitive activity mediates emotional responses, the nay-sayers argue that infants are unable to engage in the meaning-building activity on which emotions later depend.

The evidence on which to resolve this issue is not easy to obtain. Cognitively oriented developmental psychologists (e.g., Emde, 1984; Fischer & Pipp, 1984; Izard, 1978, 1984; Sroufe, 1984) appear to believe that this evidence does not favor the idea that infants express basic emotions at birth, but that they emerge from about 2 to 4 or 5 months of age. The earliest expressions seem to be "upset," followed by "wariness" or "interest," then "happiness," "joy" and "anger," and later "fear." It is quite possible that internal physiological states are directly responsible for emotion-like expressions in the newborn and young infants. Emde's (1984, p. 82) observation that smiling in the newborn is uncommonly related to external events should make us wary of statements that infants display emotions before they are capable of making even the most primitive kind of appraisals. Because infants do not attend to external stimuli until several weeks, the claims that they experience emotions are probably quite suspect.

On this issue, research by Campos and his colleagues (Bertenthal, Campos, & Barrett, 1984) suggests that an infant's appraisal of the dangers of height depends on experience with locomotion (crawling), and that such appraisals could develop very early. Other research (e.g., Harris, 1985; Harter, in press; Ridgeway, Bretherton, & Barrows, 1985; Schwartz & Trabasso, 1984; Stein & Levine, 1987) suggests that young children understand much more about the significance of social relations underlying emotions than has hitherto been assumed. The development of the concept of self (cf. Lewis, in press) appears relevant here too. In sum, we may well be understating an infant's appraisal capacities and also mistaking very early expressive activity as evidence of emotion. Therefore, it may not be so intemperate to propose that emotion is "always" (a high-risk word) a response to meaning, and that no other mechanism of emotion-generation is required.

The case for emotion in infrahuman animals may be similar. Animals have the cognitive capacity to make rough categorical appraisals at the very least. Griffin's (1984) remarkable descriptions of complex and flexible patterns of adaptive behavior in relatively simple creatures such as birds makes a strong case for goals, plans, and goal-directed actions in animals, particularly those kinds of behaviors that previously would have been called instinctive. For example, a mother bird's "broken wing" displays are directed toward distracting a predator away from her offspring. During this feigned injury in which she appears badly impaired, the mother is (Griffin, 1984):

> clearly controlling its behavior and modifying it in detail according to what the intruder does. It looks frequently at the intruder, continues in one direction if the intruder follows, but flies in a well-coordinated fashion back to the intruder's vicinity if he does not. Furthermore, if the intruder comes too close, the bird always recovers its coordinated locomotion. There are many well-orchestrated complexities to the behavior, and its adjustment to the circumstances strongly suggests intentional reaction to the situation rather than crippling confusion. (p. 90)

Thus, even so-called instincts or released behavior can be interpreted to be purposive and goal directed, implying the capacity for emotions, though the jump to emotion is, of course, inferential.

Some might argue that I made a tactical error in my argument with Zajonc (1980, 1984) by seeming to overextend the meaning of cognition to include inborn discriminations between dangerous and benign stimulus configurations. Such discriminations, especially in very simple animals such as the fowl and fish studied by Tinbergen (1951), could be hard wired and therefore not subject to learning or cognitive mediation, but I remain impressed by Beach's (1955) famous admonitions about "either/or" treatments of genetics and learning in trying to understand adaptive behavior. I had intended this to be an analogy to, not an example of, cognitive activity. The danger is that in including hard-wired processes in the definition of cognitive appraisal, what constitutes cognition might get confused (cf. Ellis, 1985; Kleinginna & Kleinginna, 1985).

It is difficult to evaluate the limits of cognitive activity in simple animals, as well as in human infants. To argue that meaning is necessary to emotion is to presume, by definition, that when an animal or infant is not capable of generating meaning of the most elementary kind until some months after birth—if this could ever be demonstrated—it is also unable to experience an emotion, except perhaps wariness or interest, even when it acts expressively (e.g., with a smile) as though an emotion is taking place.

Even if one accepts the preceding concept as tenable, the issue about how meaning arises—via appraisal—in the generation of an emotion remains unsettled. The initial appraisal is often hasty, incomplete, and even inaccurate, in which case a judgment that one is in danger or safe can be changed by further input or deliberation (Folkins, 1970), a process I have called reappraisal. Zajonc was correct in arguing that recognition of danger, and hence emotion, can be instantaneous and contain very little in the way of complex information processing. But this is not to say that emotion is entirely free of cognitive activity. Cognitive psychology stresses the acquisition and use of knowledge, and recognition depends on stored representations in which appraisal involves an interaction of what is stored with what is perceived in the stimulus array.

The approach to appraisal that I have just advocated seems to have a parallel in Buck's (1985) concept of *syncretic cognition,* which is analogous to Gibson's (1966, 1979) view of perception as the analogue detection of ecologically significant information. *Analytic cognition,* on the other hand, draws on an analogy of the mind as a computer, which works by building up meaning from originally meaningless bits in a stimulus display through linear scanning and digital analysis.

Buck's distinction provides two possibilities about how meaning is generated in any encounter, one instantaneous and without reflection, the other complex, deliberate, conscious, and reasoned. LeDoux (in press) has suggested that there is a neural pathway for affective processing from the thalamus to the amygdala, which can function independently of the neocortex. This pathway permits rapid, crude, and even hasty judgments of danger in the environment, a defensive reaction that later can be aborted on the basis of more detailed cognitive analysis. It is tempting (see Lazarus, in press) to think of this thalamo–amygdala neural circuit as the analogue of a primitive, instantaneous, and perhaps unconscious stimulus evaluation process. This can be contrasted with appraisals and reappraisals that are complex, deliberate, conscious, and reasoned, and which must therefore involve the neocortex (see also Lazarus, in press-b).

Although my position is that the personal significance of an encounter is a necessary condition for emotion, and although I have emphasized a holistic process of appraisal akin to Buck's syncretic cognition, I need not take a stand on which meaning-generating process is involved in any particular encounter. Both could be involved, and the process could vary with the type of creature (human vs. nonhuman), the stage of human development, and the temporal stage of the encounter when the observations are made.

This might be a good place to observe that there are occasional expressions of unease about the isolation of cognitive activity, as it is presently being studied by cognitive scientists, from the social, cultural, and emotional processes so important in human adaptation in nature. Norman (1980), for example, has written most trenchantly about what is wrong in this regard with the existing cognitive models. Among the many issues he takes up, those of interest here concern the importance of prior beliefs or knowledge, motivation, and emotion in cognitive processing. What he writes is welcome and there is considerable overlap in the way Norman views cognitive activity in nature (as distinct from laboratory experimentation) and the account I have presented here.

There is, however, one very important difference between us, which concerns his use of the term emotional system. Norman diagrams the emotional system in his flow charts as though it were separate from though interactive with cognition (and motivation). I have emphasized, alternatively, that one cannot speak of an emotional system without including cognitive and motivational activity. Therefore, it is something of a tautology to say that emotions affect cognition, or vice versa, unless in so doing one is willing to treat emotion merely as intentless or directionless activation, physiologically or psychologically. In the theoretical position I have taken, appraisal, and the network of memories, beliefs, short- and long-term goals, and other thoughts that are part of it, is an integral feature of the emotional experience and process. To say that emotion affects cognition, which it surely does, requires that we recognize that such emotion includes some of the very cognitive activity that is being affected in the "causal" relationship between emotion and cognition. One cannot truly speak of an emotional system as an entity separate from the cognitive system, as Norman and most others have, and to do so tests the logical limits of what we might mean about cause and effect.

A COGNITIVE-RELATIONAL DEFINITION OF EMOTION

What I have been suggesting in this chapter points to a *conception of emotion,* which could help with the task of considering cognition–emotion relationships. Emotions are organized psychophysiological reactions to good news and bad news about ongoing relationships with the environment. "News" is colloquial for information about the significance for well-being, harmful or beneficial, of the person–environment relationship. The quality (e.g., anger vs. fear) and intensity (degree of mobilization or behavioral-physiological change) of the emotional reaction depends on subjective evaluations—I call these cognitive appraisals—of the information about how we are doing in the short- and long-run agenda of living. Emotions are thus organized and complex motivational–cognitive–psychophysiological–behavioral configurations in adaptation to particular environments. Because that is such an unwieldy phrase, we can get by with the simpler term cognitive–motivational–emotional configurations, thereby emphasizing the three traditional constructs of mind. Emotional reactions themselves include three components: (1) strong impulses to act in certain ways, for example, to attack or flee, to shout with joy, to express warmth to another person, to hide, and so on; (2) these impulses are usually coupled with some degree of psychological and bodily disturbance that in harm or threat emotions probably involve mobilization for some adaptational end; and (3) there is always a cognitive-evaluative component, often referred to as an affect, which is the subjective or experiential side of the emotion.

The issues I have discussed in this chapter, and the systems chart of interdependent variables in emotion, do not make a complete theory of emotion because some of the necessary chapter and verse is still missing. Rather, I have tried to set forth some of the key principles, implicating motivation and beliefs as generative conditions and appraisal and coping processes as mediators. A full theory must not only be a general set of statements about emotion, but also a series of statements about specific emotions that are consistent with what is said about emotion in general. At the very least, this means stating the core person–environment relational themes and the cognitive appraisals for each specific emotion. In addition, we must address how cognitive activity, that is, beliefs, information about the encounter, and appraisals, operate in the emotional encounter and produce changes as the encounter unfolds. These cognitive–emotional processes must be addressed in detail if we are to have a fully elaborated theory of emotion.

I end my discussion with a restatement, for emphasis, of the principle that emotion is always a response to meaning, however primitive and vague or complex and abstract. I draw here on Oliver Sacks, a neurologist who describes numerous examples of brain-damaged patients struggling as best they can to retain a serviceable sense of the world, and who, like Kreitler and Kreitler (1976), distinguishes meaning from information. Picking here and there from Sacks's (1987) report of one patient points up the essence of what I have been saying about appraisal and emotion:

A judgment is intuitive, personal, comprehensive, and concrete—we 'see" how things stand, in relation to one another and oneself. . . . Neurology and psychology, curiously, though they talk of everything else, almost never talk of 'judgment'—and yet it is precisely the downfall of judgment . . . which constitutes the essence of so many neurophysiological disorders. . . . Judgment must be the *first* faculty of higher life or mind—yet it is ignored, or misinterpreted, by classical (computer) neurology . . . Of course the brain *is* a machine and a computer— everything in classical neurology is correct. But our mental processes, which constitute our being and life, are not just abstract and mechanical, but personal, as well—and, as such, involve not just classifying and categorizing, but continual judging and feeling also. If this is missing, we become computer-like. . . . And by the same token, if we delete feeling and judging, the personal, from the cognitive sciences, we reduce *them* to something as defective as [the patient he has been describing]—and we reduce *our* apprehension of the concrete and real. (pp. 19– 20)

Appraisal is about personal meaning, an evaluation of the significance of what is happening for one's well-being. Each kind of emotion reflects and includes as part of the experience a different kind of appraisal that contains a distinctive core relational theme, for example, insult in anger, imminent danger in fear, actions that expose one to social criticism in shame, escape from or avoidance of harm in relief, appreciation of favors in gratitude, and so on. Without the concept of appraisal emotion ceases to make psychological sense, both as an experience and as a feature of mammalian adaptation. Future research on the generation of emotions must center on how appraisal works in the emotion process.

REFERENCES

Ahsen, A. (1985). Image psychology and the empirical method. *Journal of Mental Imagery, 9*(2), 1–40.
Aristotle (1831). Bekker (Ed.), *Rhetorica II*. Berlin: Academica Regia Borussica.
Arnold, M. B. (1960). *Emotion and personality* (2 vols.). New York: Columbia University Press.
Arnheim, R. (1958). Emotion and feeling in psychology and art. *Confinia Psychiatria*, vol. 1, pp. 69–88.
Averill, J. R. (1982). *Anger and aggression: An essay on emotion*. New York: Springer–Verlag.
Bandura, A. (1977). *Social learning theory*. Englewood Cliffs, NJ: Prentice–Hall.
Bandura, A. (1982). Self-efficacy mechanism in human agency. *American Psychologist, 37*, 122–147.
Beach, F. A. (1955). The descent of instinct. *Psychological Review, 62*, 401–410.
Beck, A. T. (1976). *Cognitive therapy and the emotional disorders*. New York: International Universities Press.
Bernard, M. E., & DiGiuseppe, R. (Eds.). (in press). *Inside rational emotive therapy*. Orlando, FL: Academic Press.
Bertenthal, B. I., Campos, J. J., & Barrett, K. C. (1984). Self-produced locomotion: An organizer of emotional, cognitive, and social development in infancy. In R. N. Emde & R. J. Harmon (Eds.), *Continuities and discontinuities in development* (pp. 175–210). New York: Plenum.
Block, J. (1982). Assimilation, accommodation, and the dynamics of personality development. *Child Development, 53*, 281–295.
Buck, R. (1985). Prime theory: An integrated view of motivation and emotion. *Psychological Review, 92*, 389–413.
Burghardt, G. M. (1985). Animal awareness: Current perceptions and historical perspective. *American Psychologist, 40*, 905–919.

Ellis, A. (1985). Cognition and affect in emotional disturbance. *American Psychologist, 40*, 471–472.

Ellis, A., & Bernard, M. E. (1985). What is rational-emotive therapy (RET)? In A. Ellis & M. E. Bernard (Eds.), *Clinical applications of rational-emotive therapy* (pp. 1–30). New York: Plenum.

Emde, R. N. (1984). Levels of meaning for infant emotions: A biosocial view. In K. R. Scherer & P. Ekman (Eds.), *Approaches to emotion* (pp. 77–107). Hillsdale, NJ: Lawrence Erlbaum Associates.

Epstein, S. (1983). A research paradigm for the study of personality and emotions. In M. Page (Ed.), *Personality: Current theory and research. Nebraska Symposium on Motivation, 1982.* Lincoln: University of Nebraska Press.

Epstein, S. (1985). The implications of cognitive-experiential self-theory for research in social psychology and personality. *Journal of the Theory of Social Behavior, 15*, 283–310.

Fischer, K. W., & Pipp, S. L. (1984). Development of the structures of unconscious thought. In K. Bowers & D. Meichenbaum (Eds.), *The unconscious reconsidered* (pp. 88–148). New York: Wiley.

Folkins, C. H. (1970). Temporal factors and the cognitive mediators of stress reaction. *Journal of Personality and Social Psychology, 14*, 173–184.

Folkman, S., & Lazarus, R. S. (1980). An analysis of coping in a middle-aged community sample. *Journal of Health and Social Behavior, 21*, 219–239.

Folkman, S., & Lazarus, R. S. (1985). If it changes it must be a process: Study of emotion and coping during three stages of a college examination. *Journal of Personality and Social Psychology, 48*, 150–170.

Folkman, S., Lazarus, R. S., Dunkel-Schetter, C., DeLongis, A., & Gruen, R. (1986a). The dynamics of a stressful encounter: Cognitive appraisal, coping, and encounter outcomes. *Journal of Personality and Social Psychology, 50*, 992–1003.

Folkman, S., Lazarus, R. S., Gruen, R., & DeLongis, A. (1986b). Appraisal, coping, health status, and psychological symptoms. *Journal of Personality and Social Psychology, 50*, 571–579.

Frese, M., & Sabini, J. (Eds.) (1985). *Goal-directed behavior: The concept of action in psychology.* Hillsdale, NJ: Lawrence Erlbaum Associates.

Gallistel, C. R. (1980). The organization of action: A new synthesis. In M. Frese & J. Sabini (Eds.), *Goal-directed behavior: The concept of action in psychology* (pp. 48–65). Hillsdale, NJ: Lawrence Erlbaum Associates.

Gallistel, C. R. (1985). Motivation, intention, and emotion: Goal-directed behavior from a cognitive-neuroethological perspective. In M. Frese & J. Sabini (Eds.), *Goal-directed behavior: The concept of action in psychology* (pp. 48–65). Hillsdale, NJ: Lawrence Erlbaum Associates.

Gibson, J. J. (1966). *The senses considered as perceptual systems.* Boston: Houghton–Mifflin.

Gibson, J. J. (1979). *The ecological approach to visual perception.* Boston: Houghton-Mifflin.

Griffin, D. R. (1984). *Animal thinking.* Cambridge: Harvard University Press.

Haan, N. (1969). A tripartite model of ego functioning: Values and clinical research applications. *Journal of Nervous and Mental Disease, 148*, 14–30.

Haan, N. (1977). *Coping and defending: Processes of self-environment organization.* New York: Academic Press.

Harris, P. L. (1985). What children know about the situations that provoke emotion. In M. Lewis & C. Saarni (Eds.), *The socialization of affect.* New York: Plenum.

Harter, S. (in press). Cognitive-developmental processes in the integration of concepts about emotions and the self. *Social Cognition* (special issue on social-cognitive theory from a developmental perspective).

Hilgard, E. R. (1975). Neo-dissociation theory: Multiple cognitive controls in hypnosis. In L. Unsestahl (Ed.), *Hypnosis in the seventies.* Orebro, Sweden: Veje Forlag.

Hilgard, E. R. (1977). *Divided consciousness: Multiple controls in human thought and action.* New York: Wiley Interscience.

Hilgard, E. R. (1980). The trilogy of mind: Cognition, affection, and conation. *Journal of the History of the Behavioral Sciences, 16,* 107–117.

Hoffman, M. L. (in press). Affect, cognition, and motivation. In R. Sorrentino & E. T. Higgins (Eds.), *Handbook of motivation and cognition.* New York: Guilford.

Izard, C. E. (1978). On the ontogenesis of emotions and emotion–cognition relationships in infancy. In M. Lewis & L. Rosenblum (Eds.), *The development of affect* (pp. 389–413). New York: Plenum.

Izard, C. E. (1984). Emotion–cognition relationships and human development. In C. Izard, J. Kagan, & R. Zajonc (Eds.), *Emotions, cognition, and behavior.* New York: Cambridge University Press.

Klein, G. S. (1958). Cognitive control and motivation. In G. Lindzey (Ed.), *Assessment of human motives.* New York: Holt, Rinehart, & Winston.

Kleinginna, P. R., Jr., & Kleinginna, A. M. (1985). Cognition and affect: A reply to Lazarus and Zajonc. *American Psychologist, 40,* 470–471.

Kreitler, H., & Kreitler, S. (1976). *Cognitive orientation and behavior.* New York: Springer.

Lazarus, R. S. (1966). *Psychological stress and the coping process.* New York: McGraw–Hill.

Lazarus, R. S. (1980). The stress and coping paradigm. In L. A. Bond & J. C. Rosen (Eds.), *Competence and coping during adulthood* (pp. 28–74). Hanover, NH: University Press of New England.

Lazarus, R. S. (1981). The stress and coping paradigm. In C. Eisdorfer, D. Cohen, A. Kleinman, & P. Maxim (Eds.), *Models for clinical psychopathology* (pp. 177–214). New York: Spectrum (Medical & Scientific Books).

Lazarus, R. S. (1982). Thoughts on the relations between emotion and cognition. *American Psychologist, 37,* 1019–1024.

Lazarus, R. S. (1984). On the primacy of cognition. *American Psychologist, 39,* 124–129.

Lazarus, R. S. (in press a). Cognition and emotion from the RET viewpoint. In M. E. Bernard & R. DiGiuseppe (Eds.), *Inside rational emotive therapy.* Orlando, FL: Academic Press.

Lazarus, R. S. (in press b). Comment on LeDoux's "Sensory systems and emotion: A model of affective processing." *Integrative Psychiatry.*

Lazarus, R. S., DeLongis, A., Folkman, S., & Gruen, R. (1985). Stress and adaptational outcomes: The problem of confounded measures. *American Psychologist, 40,* 770–779.

Lazarus, R. S., & Folkman, S. (1984). *Stress, appraisal, and coping.* New York: Springer.

Lazarus, R. S., Kanner, A. D., & Folkman, S. (1980). Emotions: A cognitive-phenomenological analysis. In R. Plutchik & H. Kellerman (Eds.), *Theories of emotion.* New York: Academic Press.

Lazarus, R. S., & Launier, R. (1978). Stress-related transactions between person and environment. In L. A. Pervin & M. Lewis (Eds.), *Perspectives in interactional psychology* (pp. 287–327). New York: Plenum.

LeDoux, J. E. (in press). Sensory systems and emotion: A model of affective processing. *Integrative Psychiatry.*

Leventhal, H. (1984). A perceptual motor theory of emotion. In K. R. Scherer & P. Ekman (Eds.), *Approaches to emotion* (pp. 271–291). Hillsdale, NJ: Lawrence Erlbaum Associates.

Leventhal, H., & Tomarken, A. J. (1986). Emotion: Today's problems. In M. R. Rosenzweig & L. W. Porter (Es.), *Annual review of psychology.* Palo Alto, CA: Annual Reviews.

Lewis, H. B. (1971). *Shame and guilt in neurosis.* New York: International Universities Press.

McGuire, W. J. (1983). A contextualist theory of knowledge: Its implications for innovation and reform in psychological research. In L. Berkowitz (Ed.), *Advances in experimental social psychology* (Vol. 16, pp. 1–47). New York: Academic Press.

Mandler, G. (1984). *Mind and body: Psychology of emotion and stress.* New York: Norton.

Menninger, K. (1954). Regulatory devices of the ego under major stress. *International Journal of Psychoanalysis, 35,* 412–420.

Miller, G. A., Galanter, E. H., & Pribram, K. (1960). *Plans and the structure of behavior.* New York: Holt.

Norman, D. A. (1980). Twelve issues for cognitive science. In D. A. Norman (Ed.), *Perspectives on cognitive science: Talks from the La Jolla Conference.* Hillsdale, NJ: Lawrence Erlbaum Associates.

Piaget, J. (1952). *The origins of intelligence in children.* New York: International Universities Press.

Reisenzein, R. (1983). The Schachter theory of emotion: Two decades later. *Psychological Bulletin, 94,* 239–264.

Ridgeway, D., Bretherton, L., & Barrows, L. (1985). Children's knowledge and use of emotion language. *Paper presented at the Biennial Meeting of the Society for Research in Child Development,* Toronto, April, 1985.

Roseman, I. (1984). Cognitive determinants of emotion: A structural theory. In P. Shaver (Ed.), *Review of personality and social psychology* (Vol. 5, *Emotions, relationships, and health,* pp. 11–36). Beverly Hills, CA: Sage.

Sacks, O. (1987). *The man who mistook his wife for a hat.* New York: Harper & Row.

Sartre, J. P. (1948). A sketch of a phenomenological theory. *The emotions: Outline of a theory.* New York: Philosophical Library.

Schachter, S. (1966). The interaction of cognitive and physiological determinants of emotional state. In C. D. Spielberger (Ed.), *Anxiety and behavior* (pp. 193–224). New York: Academic Press.

Schacter, S., & Singer, J. E. (1962). Cognitive, social and physiological determinants of emotional state. *Psychological Review, 69,* 379–399.

Scherer, K. R. (1984). On the nature and function of emotion: A component process approach. In K. R. Scherer & P. Ekman (Eds.), *Approaches to emotion* (pp. 293–317). Hillsdale, NJ: Lawrence Erlbaum Associates.

Schwartz, G. (1979). The brain as a health care system. In G. C. Stone, F. Cohen, & N. Adler (Eds.), *Health psychology* (pp. 549–571). San Francisco: Jossey-Bass.

Schwartz, R. M., & Trabasso, T. (1984). Children's understanding of emotions. In C. E. Izard, J. Kagan, & R. B. Zajonc (Eds.), *Emotions, cognition, and behavior* (pp. 409–437). Cambridge, England: Cambridge University Press.

Singer, M. T. (1974). Engagement-involvement: A central phenomenon in psychophysiological research. *Psychosomatic Medicine, 36,* 1–17.

Solomon, R. C. (1980). Emotions and choice. In A. O. Rorty (Ed.), *Explaining emotions* (pp. 251–281). Berkeley: University of California Press.

Sroufe, L. A. (1984). The organization of emotional development. In K. R. Scherer & P. Ekman (Eds.), *Approaches to emotion* (pp. 109–128). Hillsdale, NJ: Lawrence Erlbaum Associates.

Stadler, M., & Wehner, T. (1985). Anticipation as a basic principle in goal-directed action. In M. Frese & J. Sabini (Eds.), *Goal-directed behavior: The concept of action in psychology* (pp. 67–77). Hillsdale, NJ: Lawrence Erlbaum Associates.

Stein, N. L., & Levine, L. J. (1987). Thinking about feelings: The development and organization of emotional knowledge. In R. E. Snow & M. Farr (Eds.), *Aptitude, learning and instruction* (Vol. 3: *Cognition, conation, and affect*). Hillsdale, NJ: Lawrence Erlbaum Associates.

Tinbergen, N. (1951). *The study of instincts.* London: Oxford University Press.

Tomkins, S. (1981). The quest for primary motives: Biography and autobiography of an idea. *Journal of Personality and Social Psychology, 41,* 306–329.

Weiner, B. (1985). An attributional theory of achievement motivation and emotion. *Psychological Review, 92,* 548–573.

White, R. W. (1960). Competence and the psychosexual stages of development. In M. R. Jones (Ed.), *Nebraska Symposium on Motivation* (pp. 97–141). Lincoln: University of Nebraska Press.

Zajonc, R. B. (1980). Feeling and thinking: Preferences need no inferences. *American Psychologist, 35,* 151–175.

Zajonc, R. B. (1984). On the primacy of affect. *American Psychologist, 35,* 151–175.

2 A Constructivist Theory of Emotion

George Mandler
Center for Human Information Processing, University of California,
San Diego

INTRODUCTION

A cognitive theory of emotion (in this case discrepancy/evaluation theory) is concerned with the representations and processes that construct emotional experience. Its main focus must be on problems of representation, on the way emotion-relevant information is processed, and on the way unified emotional conscious contents are constructed. The intent of this chapter is to amplify an approach to emotional experience that has been in the process of development for over 25 years—and still is (Mandler, 1962, 1964, 1975, 1980, 1984).

I start with a short summary of the constituents of emotional experience, with special emphasis on evaluative knowledge as the source of "affective" information. I also discuss some ideas about the functions of consciousness (the "constitutive problem of psychology"; Miller, 1985). I then discuss some possible (and actual) criticisms of discrepancy/evaluation theory. The following sections are concerned with extensions of the theory. I present some new data on "affective" processing, showing once more that the inclusion of "affect" *slows* processing of simple informational tasks. In addition, data are presented on the supposed separability of cognitive and affective processes. Next, I briefly discuss extensions of discrepancy theory and conclude with some speculations about evolutionary aspects of human emotion.

Before I start on this journey, a brief word about the use of the word *affect*. Unfortunately it has meant many things to many people, ranging from hot to cold interpretations. At the hot end it has been used coextensively with emotion, implying an intensity dimension; at the cold end it is frequently used without passion at all, referring to preferences, likes and dislikes, and choices. I use the term as appropriate to the context, trying to assure that its specific use is as clear as possible.

Much contemporary cognitive theory seems to leave human beings unable to feel. Until recently, conventional wisdom in cognitive science has painted people without passions—thinking and acting rationally and cooly. Such coolth has been most obvious in the investigation of problem solving. On the other hand, psychologists and other humans typically are frustrated, angry, joyous, de-lighted, intense, anxious, elated, and even fearful when dealing with complex problems, whether these involve dealing with a recalcitrant computer program, an exasperated customer, a difficult bridge hand, an unassembled toy, or a mathematics problem. If cognitive psychology aspires to an understanding of human thought and action, it can ill afford to leave out their emotional aspects. And I should add that it is not enough for cognitive models to have nodes or even processors labeled *fear* or *joy* that are to be accessed whenever appropriate (e.g., Bower & Cohen, 1982). That simply acknowledges theoretical agnosticism; it does nothing to solve the problem.

Emotion is not only anecdotally and phenomenally part of human thought and action; there is now a burgeoning body of evidence that emotional states interact in important ways with traditional "cognitive" functions. For example, Isen's work has shown that positive feelings determine the accessibility of mental contents in the process of decision making, serve as retrieval cues, and influence problem-solving strategies (e.g., Isen, Means, Patrick, & Nowicki, 1982). More generally, accessibility of mental contents is determined by the mood both at the time of original encounter and at the time of retrieval (Bower, 1981; Bower & Mayer, 1985).

There are essentially two different views of emotional phenomena. One con-siders emotions to be discrete patterns of behavior, experience, and neural ac-tivity, usually consisting of some few (5 to 10) such patterns—the fundamental emotions such as fear, joy, and rage. I refer to this as the fundamentalist position (e.g., Izard, 1977; Plutchik, 1980; Tomkins, 1962, 1963). Most of these theories are derived from Darwin (1872), and basic emotions usually are seen as having developed as a function of human (mammalian) evolution, with other emotions being some combination of the fundamental ones. Given the wide variety of human emotion, this latter postulate engenders complex analyses of and recipes for emotion—something like a cordon bleu school of emotion.

The other approach is cognitive and constructivist, which considers emotional experience (and behavior) to be the result of cognitive analyses and physiological (autonomic nervous system) response (e.g., Averill, 1980; Lazarus, Kanner & Folkman, 1980; Mandler, 1984). The constructivist approach has as its founding father William James (e.g., 1884), but his particular constructions depended entirely on patterns of visceral and muscular feedback and are no longer found acceptable.

There exists another argument in the field of emotion that concerns the character of emotional (or affective) reactions. This argument is related to, but somewhat different from, the division between fundamentalist and constructivist theories. The distinction here is between a constructivist view of emotional reactions (specifically subjective feelings) and one that makes a distinction between affective (emotional) and "cognitive" analyses. The foremost practitioner of the latter approach is Robert Zajonc. He has marshalled an impressive array of anecdotal and phenomenal evidence to argue that affective responses are unmediated and fast initial reactions to people and events (Zajonc, 1980). Affective reactions are said to occur without mediating "cognitive" analyses. The implication is that specific characteristics of events (so-called preferanda) force preferences. The response of a cognitive constructivist is that whatever the array of attributes and features in the environment might be, it needs analysis and processing by underlying representations. Specifically, the phenomenal evidence that many of our reactions to the world are initially affective is not, by itself, evidence for an unmediated affective response. Affective experiences are constructed conscious contents, just as any other such content. The indisputable observation that we frequently react affectively to events, before experiencing a more "analytic" knowledge of the event, speaks to the ubiquity of affective and evaluational constructions and intentions. We live in a world of value and affect, and the themes that determine our conscious constructions often require an affective content. This does not force an absence of other analyses and activations going on at the same time at the preconscious level. Which of these analyses will be used in conscious constructions will depend on the intentions and requirements of the moment—which happen to be "affective" in many cases. On the other hand, the assertion of "fast" affective reactions is an empirical one. If, in fact, affective, evaluative reactions are faster than those requiring only access to cognitions (knowledge), then one would have to reconsider the constructivist argument. However, the available evidence, reviewed below, suggests that affective reactions are actually *slower* than "cognitive" ones. Such a finding is consistent with the notion that questions about the familiarity or identity of objects or events require access to relatively fewer features of the underlying representation and can be quickly constructed, in comparison with more extensive analyses and constructions required by questions about the appeal, beauty, or desirability of the object or event.

A REVIEW OF DISCREPANCY/AFFECT THEORY

The theory views the construction of emotion as consisting of the concatenation in consciousness of some cognitive evaluative schema together with the perception of visceral arousal. This conscious construction is, as all other such constructions, a holistic unitary experience, even though it may derive from separate and even independent schematic representations. This is part of a view of the construction of conscious experience that suggests that the conscious contents of the moment are constructed out of two or more underlying structures and have the function of "making sense" of the current situation (Mandler, 1985a; Marcel, 1983). This attitude toward emotion only approximates the commonsense meaning of the term. To ask "what is an emotion?" is not, in principle, answerable. The term is a natural language expression that has all the advantages (communicative and inclusive) and disadvantages (imprecise and vague) of the common language. However, it is exactly for communicative purposes that one needs to approximate the common meaning as a first step.

I have focused on two dimensions out of the many available from analyses of common language "emotions": the notion that emotions express some aspect of value, and the assertion that emotions are "hot"—they imply a gut reaction, a visceral response. These two aspects not only speak to the common usage, but they also reflect the fact that such conscious constructions are frequent occurrences in everyday life. Thus, an analysis of the concatenation of value and visceral arousal addresses natural language usage as well as theoretically interesting problems. One of the consequences of such a position is that it leads to the postulation of a potentially innumerable number of different emotional states, because no situational evaluation will be the same from occasion to occasion. There are of course regularities in human thought and action that produce general categories of these constructions, categories that have family resemblances and overlap in the features that are selected for analysis and that create the representation of value (whether it is the simple dichotomy of good and bad, or the appreciation of beauty, or the perception of evil). These families of occasions and meanings construct the categories of emotions found in the natural language (and psychology). The emotion categories are fuzzily defined by external and internal situations and events as well as by some actions. In case any evidence were needed for the "fuzziness" of emotional concepts, Russell and Bullock (1986) have shown that judgments of facial expression are quite fuzzy, and they suggest that natural language concepts of emotion are best "thought of as overlapping and fuzzy, rather than as mutually exclusive and properly defined" (p. 309).

The commonalities found within the categories of emotions may vary from case to case, and they have different bases for their occurrence. Sometimes these commonalities are based on the similarity of external conditions (as in the case of some fears and environmental threats), sometimes an emotional category may be based on a collection of similar behaviors (in the subjective feelings of fear related to avoidance and flight), sometimes the common category arises from a class of incipient behavior (as in hostility and destructive action), sometimes hormonal and physiological reactions provide a common basis (as in the case of lust), and sometimes purely cognitive evaluations constitute an emotional category (as in judgments of helplessness that eventuate in anxiety). It is these commonalities that give rise to the appearance of fundamental or discrete emotions.

Emotions are usually situation specific, and subjective emotional states, however one defines their source, need to be tied to cognitive evaluations that "select" the appropriate emotion. The various indices that constitute an "emotion" are not haphazard collections of current conditions; they are organized by behavioral, cognitive, or physiological states and conditions of the individual. The source for the discreteness of the emotions can often be found in those conditions. It should be well understood, however, that even these "fundamental" emotional states require some analytic, "cognitive" processing. Even if it were the case that well-coordinated, innate neural/behavioral/cognitive systems are "elicited" as a unit, as single emotions, one would still have to analyze the eliciting conditions that produce one emotion or another.

The problem of *cognitive evaluation* seems therefore a common one to all emotion theories. Basically, cognitive evaluations require a theory for the representation of value. The task cannot be avoided if we are truly interested in the full range of human thought and action. What is the mental representation that gives rise to judgments and feelings of "good" or "bad" or of some affective nature in general? Surprisingly, psychologists have paid relatively little attention to problems of value, in the sense of developing a theory of the underlying structures that give rise to phenomenal experiences of value. My concern is with both accepting and explaining these phenomenal experiences.

A full discussion of the problem of value is precluded in this presentation (but see Chapter 9 in Mandler, 1984). In brief it involves the different external and internal sources that lead us to see some person or event as "good" or "bad," as evil or benign, as harmful or beneficent. Within the realm of learning and problem solving, for example, a wide range of sources of values operate and determine emotional reactions. Consider the valuative attitudes toward learning and schooling. On the one hand it is a "good thing" to do well in school; on the other hand school (and its tests) is a source of apprehension. Parents may value schooling highly or ignore it; children may look forward to school or fear it. School may be a place where intense positive or negative emotions are experienced, or it may be passively accepted and tolerated without any great affect being experienced. All these values and experiences will contribute to the way emotions in the learning context are constructed.

I suggest three general sources of value: The first is innate approach and withdrawal tendencies interpreted as value. The avoidance of looming objects, the experience of pain (and the avoidance of pain-producing objects), and the taste of sweet substances are all examples of events that produce approach and avoidance reactions. It is the secondary effects of these tendencies, such as our observations of our own approaches and withdrawals, that is one of the conditions that produces judgments of positive and negative values. I look here toward something like Bem's self-perception notions to produce the experience of value as a function of approach/withdrawal actions (Bem, 1967). It is equally possible, however, that approach and withdrawal themselves are the expressions of value (as Schneirla, 1959, suggested).

The second source of value can be found in cultural, social, and idiosyncratic predications that refer essentially to the learning process. The outcome of such a process is that events and objects—whether actually encountered or not—are predicated to have certain values as a result of social or personal learning experiences. Food preferences and aversions (such as frogs' legs and chocolate cake) are frequently acquired without any contact with the actual substances, as are likes and dislikes of people and groups of people. These predications, socially and idiosyncratically acquired, are judgments of value. Similarly constituted are the culturally acquired esthetic judgments of beauty, whether of people, landscapes, or paintings. There is a secondary issue involved, namely how these predications are acquired. A detailed discussion of that issue is beyond my scope here, but I assume that there are a variety of different learning mechanisms that generate these predications. One interesting approach to the acquisition of value involves the postulation of goal states and the evaluation of their satisfaction (e.g., Stein & Levine, this volume, but see also Mandler, 1985b, for a discussion of the complexities of the goal concept).

The third source of value is structural. This aspect of value resides in the cognitive structure of objects, in the relations among features, as in the appreciation of an object seen as beautiful or abhorrent as a function of a particular structural concatenation. Structural value, which differentiates patterns rather than mere identification of objects, arises out of our experience with objects and the analyses of their constituent features. One of the factors that influences judgments arising out of structural consideration is the frequency of encounter with objects and events, as, for example, in the experience of familiarity. I appeal to the notion of schemas and the fit between an experience and an existing schema to produce one aspect of value. If an experience fits an existing schema it is—ceteris paribus—positively valued. We generally prefer the known to the unknown. I need to stress the ceteris paribus part of this assertion, because unfortunately ceteris is rarely paribus. There are of course many situations where we do not seem to like or prefer the familiar. On analysis it is usually the case that other sources of value override the structural analysis. But when nothing but structural comparisons predominate in a situation, we will find the preference for the familiar.

Rare as modern psychological approaches to value are, there are some who have looked at the problem. For example, Toda (1982) suggests that "emotions reveal values and . . . we do evaluate, very often, the utility of a state by the emotions it may arouse" (p. 205). Whereas undoubtedly we anticipate outcomes in terms of their positive or negative (emotional) consequences, I argue that "emotions reveal values" not just by the consequences of events, but also as a function of their very structure.

Values can arise out of a number of different representations, ranging from given or acquired reactions to or predications of objects and events to being inherently generated by cognitive structures. The integration of such representations with arousal/intensity factors defines the quality of an emotion. I should add that I have not extensively engaged the intra and extrapsychic conditions that give rise to specific emotions—that has been done by many others in the analysis of both natural language usage and of the cognitive structure of affective judgments (see Mandler, 1984, pp. 209–214). My primary concern is to elucidate the general conditions and variables that generate emotional experiences.

If evaluative cognitions provide the quality of an emotional experience, then visceral activity provides its intensity and peculiar "emotional" feel. As a first approximation I assume that degree of autonomic (sympathetic) arousal can be mapped into the felt intensity of an emotion. On the other hand, some theorists, and some critics of my position, have argued that the autonomic, visceral component is not necessary for emotional experience. In reply, I argue that emotion is, of course, one of these great natural language concepts that can serve any and most arguments, depending on how you wish to use the language or the concept. The best one can do is to propose a definition that satisfies a reasonable portion of the common concept and produces some degree of social consensus. In part the denial of visceral activity as a necessary part of "real" emotions is related to such alternative terms as *affect*. Some writers, such as Zajonc, use affect more or less coextensive with my use of value. Affects then can obviously occur without visceral involvement. But to say that something is pretty or fine or awful or even disgusting may be said quite dispassionately and unemotionally. I believe that what we need to understand are the occasions when visceral activity (however slight) or even just autonomic imagery co-occurs with these judgments or affects.

In one version of the common understanding of emotion, the occurrence of some visceral or gut reaction is generally assumed. Emotions are said to occur when we feel "aroused," "agitated," when our "guts are in an uproar," etc. The reference is—properly—always to some autonomic nervous system activity, such as increased heart rate, sweating, or gastro–intestinal upheavals. The autonomic nervous system has been implicated in quasi-emotional activity ever since Walter Cannon (e.g., 1929) delineated the function of the sympathetic and parasympathetic systems in fight/flight reactions, giving them a function over and beyond energy-expending and energy-conserving in keeping the internal environmental stable. However, if one looks at the literature on the ANS, one is faced with a lack of any principled account of the sources of ANS activation.

I have argued that a majority of occasions for visceral arousal follow the occurrence of some perceptual or cognitive discrepancy, or the interruption or blocking of some ongoing action. However, discrepancies are only a sufficient, not a necessary, condition of sympathetic arousal. Other sources of sympathetic nervous system arousal can and do also play a role in emotional experience. Discrepancies and interruptions depend to a large extent on the organization of mental representations of thought and action. Within the purview of schema theory, these discrepancies occur when the expectations generated by some schema (whether determining thought or action) are violated. This is the case whether the violating event is worse or better than the expected one and accounts for visceral arousal in both unhappy and joyful occasions. Most emotions follow such discrepancies, just because the discrepancy produces visceral arousal. And it is the combination of that arousal with an ongoing evaluative cognition that produces the subjective experience of an emotion. I do *not* say that emotions are interruptions. Interruption, discrepancies, blocks, frustrations, novelties, etc. are occasions for ANS activity. Whether or not an emotional construction follows such arousal depends on the evaluative activity of the individual. It is only the concatenation of an evaluative process and ANS arousal that produces emotion. And I might note parenthetically that I am not talking about conscious appraisals of the situation when I call on evaluative processes. They may be conscious but typically appear in consciousness only as a component part of the holistic emotional experience.

We now have some rather convincing evidence that any kind of discrepancy produces autonomic arousal. One study by Yoshio Nakamura in our laboratory presented subjects with very simple (deliberately boring) stories and asked subjects to imagine how the stories would end. The stories were presented one sentence at a time and the last sentence was either consistent or discrepant with the preceding context. One story, for example, was about a little girl building sandcastles. The tide threatens to wipe out her castle, but eventually the tide recedes. In the consistent ending, she was happy that her castle was saved; in the discrepant one, she was happy that her castle was ruined. In all cases we obtained slight but significant increases in heart rate variability following discrepancy.

More evidence is accumulating in an ongoing study of Kathleen MacDowell's with an interactive compute game. Here we have obtained consistent and large heart rate responses of the order of 10 to 20 beats per minute, and equally so to positive and negative discrepant events. In addition, we are encountering data that suggest theoretical modifications in our ideas of the source of emotional intensity. Subjective intensity seems to depend, in some interactive fashion, on both the autonomic response to the discrepancy and the evaluation of the salience of the discrepancy. In other words, autonomic arousal is a necessary but not a sufficient condition for determining the intensity of an emotional experience.

The effects of situational or life stress are excellent examples of unexpected events producing visceral arousal, negative or positive evaluations, and emotional experiences. Berscheid (1983) has imaginatively described the conditions of interpersonal interactions that lead to interruptions and discrepancies and therefore to emotional reactions. When a relationship is meshed, when one individual's actions depend on the actions of the other, then the two people involved may become occasions for each other's interruptions. The actions of the other are essential for one's own action. Thus, emotional reactions are more likely in such meshed relationships than they are when the two lives are, in effect, parallel, when the actions of the two are not interdependent.

Finally, the construction of emotions requires conscious capacity. The experience of emotion is by definition a conscious state and thus preempts limited capacity. Limited capacity refers to the fact that conscious contents are highly restricted at any one point in time. Whenever some particular construction preempts conscious capacity, then other processes that require such capacity will be impaired. The best example is found in stress and panic reactions when emotional reactions prevent adequate problem-solving activities. Emotional experiences may inhibit the full utilization of our cognitive apparatus, and thought may become simplified (i.e., stereotyped and canalized) and will tend to revert to simpler modes of problem solving. However, the effects of emotion are not necessarily intrusive and deleterious. In part, it will depend on other mental contents and mechanisms that are activated by the emotional experience and that may become available for dealing with stressful situations. For example, stress tends to focus attention on the perceived central aspects of a situation, and such focusing may be useful; and previously acquired coping mechanisms may be invoked and reduce the stress. The relationship of "emotions" to discrepancies and autonomic nervous system recruitment also points to their adaptive function; emotions occur at important times in the life of the organism and may serve to prepare it for more effective thought and action when focused attention is needed.

AMPLIFYING THE THEORY

In this section I want to extend some theoretical notions but also take advantage of accumulated comments to clarify my position on a variety of issues. I address only a few specific issues. The critical reader who has questions about the necessarily very brief exposition given here will—alas—have to consult *Mind and Body* (Mandler, 1984).

Expectancies, Discrepancies, and the Variety of Schemas

The argument has been made that discrepancy is vacuous as an explanatory argument, that discrepancy, as usually defined, is practically always present. To some degree, all events are somewhat discrepant from what is expected; the world changes continuously. That is, of course, correct, and I would expect that there is some degree of arousal present in many, possibly most, day-to-day situations. But so is there some degree of feelings or moods. In fact, the criticism has been made that theories such as the cognitive/arousal theory are too discrete, that they do not account for the pervasiveness of moods and emotions, that human beings are characterized by some feeling or mood state much of the time. And it is the very pervasiveness of discrepancies and evaluations that accounts for the continuous feeling states. However, the degree of discrepancy is usually slight and the amount of arousal is small, which accounts for background feelings and moods. So-called "true" emotions occur typically with high degrees of arousal and are frequently associated with extreme discrepancies and interruptions.

The continuity of discrepancies in everyday experience also speaks to the fact that thought and action at any point in time are hardly ever determined by a single schema. Whereas I have made that point in the past, many of the illustrations I have used have appealed—for the sake of simplicity—to cases with a single operating schema. It must be obvious that everyday experiences, and everyday emotions, are the result of a number of different schemas and expectations that are continuously active, changing, and interacting. Even though phenomenal experience often has a rather singular and unitary appearance, various underlying processes that do not participate in the momentary conscious construction are, of course, still active. The reason for the seemingly single-minded nature of momentary experience lies in the nature of consciousness. Whereas I cannot go into detail to describe the nature of constructive consciousness, suffice it to say that momentary consciousness is constructed to take account of the regnant needs and interests of the individual, and in doing so makes use of a few limited active (preconscious) processes and structures. The limitation is a characteristic of consciousness, but it also has adaptive value by focusing on dominant concerns.[1]

A number of different schemas and expectations are preconsciously active at any one time. And discrepancies and values can occur with all or any of these active processes. Such a view takes into account that even expected events that may not appear to be discrepant can be followed by emotional episodes. Consider the person who experiences the loss of a loved one who has been ill and whose

---

[1]For an extensive discussion of constructive consciousness, see Chapter 3 of *Cognitive Psychology* (Mandler, 1985a).

death has been long anticipated. Clearly, the actual event will produce strong emotions, despite the expectation. The possible discrepancies that play into that emotion are numerous and I list just a few. The actual loss is always different than the anticipated one. After all, the other person is now truly absent, and it is unlikely that the grieving individual has rehearsed (anticipated) all the possible situations in which interactions with the living person have occurred. What has been anticipated is the actual death, and not most of its consequences. Furthermore, there is usually one anticipation that is violated and that is rarely absent (i.e., the hope that the person may not die after all). And as a final example, consider the events that occur following the death of the loved one (apart from the actual loss). Friends remind one of past interactions that cannot be recreated and thus generate discrepancies; actions and plans must be envisaged that are often discrepant with previous experiences and expectations; in short, one's life changes and the changes produce emotions. For a sensitive discussion of such interruptions, losses, and emotions see Berscheid (e.g., 1984).

A similar exposition is necessary with respect to discrepancies associated with some positive events. Many otherwise sympathetic consumers of discrepancy theory feel uncomfortable with the notion that discrepancies are the source of autonomic arousal for positive as well as for negative events. One of the reasons for this discomfort is due to the common notion that discrepancy is somehow by itself a negative event, associated with frustration and other similar concepts. It is not, of course, within the confines of this theory. I have illustrated this aspect of the theory in Mandler (1984) but marshall some additional illustrations. Consider the joys of young love. One has met the person of one's dreams and hopes, but reciprocity is not quite apparent. One is to meet again a few days hence, and as the object of passion appears at the designated time, joy floods the lover, ecstasy is near. What is discrepant? I argue that the anticipation of the event is never devoid of doubts and fears—will the loved one appear at the appointed time, is she or he at all interested, does she or he look as desirable as one has imagined? The world of romantic love is full of such ambivalences, and wherever there are ambivalences the actual event will be discrepant with some of them. There is no argument about the emotional quality, the "value" of the love; what is at stake here is the question whether there is in fact autonomic arousal generated by interruptions and discrepancies. In contrast, consider a positive event that is fully anticipated, in all its details and nuances. For example, a prize has been won and the check arrives in your mail. The value is still there, but the intensity will be relatively low. I believe that an appropriate analysis of positive events will disclose the operation of many ambivalent expectancies that are more than sufficient to explain the intensity of positive emotions. Similar ambivalences operate, of course, as I have already shown, for many negative events. For every expected "good" there are thoughts of disappointments and slip-ups, and for every expected "bad" there are hopes of redemption and relief.

There is an additional difference between positive and negative emotions that has tended to be overlooked. The result of experiencing a negative emotion is that one wishes to terminate, avoid, or leave the situation/conditions that produce it; the opposite is the case for positive emotions. The additional cognitive effort required in trying to change the conditions of negative experiences preempts conscious capacity and may explain, in part, why negative emotions (in contrast to positive ones) interfere with constructive and productive thinking.

Finally, some comments on the use and misuse of the term *cognitive*. In the natural language it refers to knowledge and knowing in the widest sense, and in psychology it has historically been distinguished from emotion and conation. In the contemporary sense, however, cognitive psychology was the successor name for information processing and came into general use around 1970. It is, in that use, not restricted to knowledge in the narrow sense but has been used instead for current American mainstream psychology with its emphasis on theories concerned with representations and processes. In no modern sense has it been equated with thinking with which it is often confused. In any case it is in terms of representational theory that I have used *cognitive*.

Some criticisms of a cognitive theory of emotion are based on a misinterpretation of the term cognitive. One critic has described cognitive approaches as limited in that they consider emotional development dependent on cognitive development. It is also claimed (Izard, 1986) that they see "emotion experiences as time limited (often brief) and transient phenomena," and as a result, emotion is relegated "to a minor role in human development" (p. 25). I would still claim that to develop mature value concepts children need to develop first their basic information-processing equipment. And emotional experiences are often brief, but they are certainly not time limited. Another commentator (Santostefano, 1986) claims that constructivist approaches present a "static picture of constructions imposed on situations." He calls for cognitive mechanisms that are not "primarily affective or cognitive or some combination, but all mechanisms participate in coordinating internal and external requirements" (p. 205). And I thought all along that a "cognitive" view of emotion is exactly one that makes no distinctions as to the mechanisms that construct different kinds of experience, and which does coordinate internal and external requirements. And because "situations" and "experiences" are both constructed, their mental interplay is exactly what a dynamic point of view requires.

Reductionism—Mind is not Brain, or Vice Versa

The increasing interest in brain/behavior relationships and the rise of neuropsychology have both contributed to a revival of reductionism, i.e., the view that complex [mental] phenomena can be understood [reduced to] more basic

---

[2]See Chapter 1 of *Cognitive Psychology* (Mandler, 1985a) for a discussion of the emergence of the "cognitive" movement.

[physiological] ones. This is in contrast to the prevailing view that mental phenomena cannot be reduced entirely to physical ones. I do not intend to review the
argument against the reductionist fallacy here. For illustrative purposes, a recent
illustration by Putnam (1980) is relevant. Putnam notes how ridiculous it would
be to "explain" why a cube of a certain size passes through a square but not a
round hole in terms of the atomic structures of the board and the cube. An
explanation in terms of the relevant geometric relationships (i.e., at a "higher"
level) has more generality and, in fact, an explanation at the "lower" atomic
level would conceal the geometric laws.

The point to be made is obvious. Explanations at the psychological level
cannot, in principle, be reduced to explanations of the same phenomena at the
physiological or hormonal level. This is not to say that the cooperation between
psychology and neurophysiology is either unnecessary or fruitless. On the contrary, it has created a new and budding field, and observations and hypotheses
have usefully gone in both directions. But, in general, it seems to be the case that
"explanations" in science in terms of more "basic" processes have occurred
after the more complex observations and theories were well established. This has
happened in biology where gene theory was a necessary precursor of molecular
explanations, in physics where an understanding of atomic and molecular functions preceded nuclear physics in the modern sense, and in psychology in both
vision and acoustics. At the present time, the burgeoning interest in neuropsychology as a productive and informative discipline *followed* the exploration of language and memory in psychology and linguistics. A similar chain of
events is to be expected in the field of emotion, but it has not quite happened yet.

I want to address some specific reductionist issues that have arisen with
respect to discrepancy/evaluation theory. Note that my theoretical interests are
entirely psychological. When I speak of "BODY," I explicitly refer to those
physiological functions that are mentally effective (i.e., perceivable by the person or incorporated into psychological structures such as schemata). The primary
physiological function of interest in that respect is the autonomic nervous system, which is important in the construction of emotion and may even at times
have the subsidiary function of directing attention. Autonomic arousal is incorporated in emotional constructions and is psychologically discriminable. The
autonomic nervous system is a bodily function that enters into psychological
functions, but that is quite different from seeking exhaustive physiological explanations for mental functions.

---

[3]For older critiques see Mandler (1969, 1985a), for more recent ones Eldredge and Tattersall
(1982) and Pippard (1985).

[4]In that context it is interesting that the emotion of lust and its physiological orchestration are
typically slighted by the theorists of fundamental emotions. Nor do they seem particularly interested
in the somewhat different (and possibly "fundamental") emotion of love.

I have no doubt that there are important lessons to be learned from our knowledge of the limbic system, the effects of lesions of the frontal lobes, of the brain stem activating system, hemispheric specialization, and the neurochemical pathways of the brain. But I do not know what that knowledge tells us about the construction of the subjective experience of emotions. Nor do observations, such as Cannon's classical 1929 critique of William James, that emotional *behavior* remains unchanged when adrenal discharge is constrained or blocked tell us how the absence of adrenalin affects emotional *experience*. The behavior (e.g., "rage" reactions) may be unaffected, but is experience affected by such interventions? A related set of phenomena (i.e., severing of the spinal cord; cf. Hohmann, 1966, and others) did however show us how experience may be afected by a physiological change, and we learned much from that instance. I was also delighted to hear in Dr. Heilman's presentation that current neurophysiological knowledge supports a distinction between arousal and cognitive evaluation. In general, I do not believe that the last word is in on the assertion that certain *emotions* are identified with specific localized brain functions. The function of the limbic system in the generation of emotional *experience* is vague, but the elicitation of specific actions (e.g., "rage" in cats) can be seen in the first instance as just that—actions. We do not know whether such elicited actions necessarily produce any accompanying subjective emotional experiences, or whether more than a cat brain is needed to do that.

AFFECT AND COGNITION: NEW DATA

The cognitive/constructivist positions that I have advocated imply that affective/emotional events are the result of general mechanisms and processes that operate within the mental system. There are no separate or privileged affective mechanisms or processes. Robert Zajonc (e.g., 1980) has been the primary advocate of the point of view that affect does operate separately from cognition. In particular, he has implied that affect bypasses cognitive processes (i.e., is accessed very rapidly) and that affective judgments arise independent of cognitive ones (i.e., that variables such as simple exposure generate affective products in the absence of cognitive judgments or effects).

In 1983, Shebo and I addressed the question of immediate and speedy access to affective judgments. It has been strongly implied by Zajonc (1980), and others, that the immediacy of affective access should make affective judgments more easily accessible than cognitive ones (i.e., they do not need any cognitive processing). In the Mandler and Shebo (1983) study we showed that liking judgments for words were about 200 msecs slower than lexical decision judgments, and in a study of judgments of paintings we showed that judgments of liking were 200 to 300 msecs slower than judgments of "knowing" (i.e., whether the painting had been seen before). In all cases we equated items for discriminability so that items were compared that were matched in cognitive and affective discriminability. These data have not fazed the defenders of affective speed. Shebo-Van Zandt and I now have new data on the same topic. In this case we collected 40 animal and 40 person instances, with 20 in each category being identifiable as being "good" or "bad." For example, DOVE and FRIEND are good animals and people, whereas VULTURE and MURDERER are bad ones. The intersubject consistency in judging the appropriateness of the "good" and "bad" labels was high: .835 for the animals and .903 for persons. We then asked subjects in one group to judge whether each of the 80 instances was "good" or "bad." Another group was asked to decide whether each of the items was a person or an animal. In comparing the speed with which these judgments were made, we found a significant 144 msecs advantage for the "cognitive" animal/person judgment over the "affective" good/bad judgment. I know of no evidence that shows the opposite effect.

The special noncognitive status of affective judgments was claimed to have been demonstrated by Kunst-Wilson and Zajonc (1980). They reported that very brief exposures of meaningless stimuli (irregular octagons) produced preferences for exposed over new stimuli in the absence of recognition of the old, exposed stimuli. Kunst-Wilson and Zajonc's claim was that affective judgments arise out of repeated exposure without any intervening cognitive processing, and that such data provided evidence for an assumed separation and independence of cognitive and affective judgments (Zajonc, 1980).

Studies of the differential and preferential accessibility of higher order information following minimal exposure have used pattern masks and have generally appealed to spreading activation as an explanatory mechanism. On the other hand, the Kunst-Wilson and Zajonc report also employed minimal exposure, but it was not masked, and it implicates an entirely different process of *direct* access to affective information without any cognitive processing.

Kunst-Wilson and Zajonc presented subjects with 10 irregular octagons each of which was exposed 5 times for 1 ms under conditions of lowered illumination and without a mask. In the test phase subjects were presented with 10 pairs of octagons for 1 sec each. One member of the pair was new and the other one came from the exposed set. Subjects were required to judge either which of the pair they liked better (or preferred) or which had been shown previously. Overall recognition judgments were close to chance (47% correct), whereas preference judgments showed a significant preference for previously exposed stimuli (60%). The Kunst-Wilson and Zajonc effect has been replicated and extended, for example by Seamon, Brody, and Kauff (1983) and Bonnano and Stillings (1986). The latter showed that subjects not only showed preference in the absence of recognition for the previously presented shapes, but that they also generated familiarity judgments for the presented stimuli that were equal in magnitude to the preference judgments.

We have explored these effects further in Mandler, Nakamura, and Shebo-Van Zandt (1987). Given that prior exposure can produce both preference and familiarity, we suggested that these effects are not specific to any feature of the stimulus but depend on the sheer activation of the representation of the random shapes. This goes beyond the suggestion that familiarity may mediate preference judgments. Prior exposure generates the representation of the stimuli, and these initially rudimentary representations are further specified and activated by successive presentations. Such activated representations may then apparently be related to any judgment about the stimuli that is stimulus relevant. The notion of relevance is introduced only to indicate that subjects are unlikely to attempt to relate the activation of the representation to questions about such irrelevant dimensions as, for example, taste or odor. We showed that judgments both of brightness and of darkness are equally facilitated by prior minimal exposures.

The procedure used followed the Kunst-Wilson and Zajonc experiments with minor modifications. Of 20 irregular octagons, 10 were randomly assigned to the exposure phase, and 10 test pairs were constructed by randomly pairing exposed and unexposed octagons. The octagons were presented for 2 ms, followed by a dark field. The subjects were instructed that during the first part stimuli would be presented in the tachistoscope at durations so brief that they might not actually see what was being presented, but that they were to pay close attention to the flashes. They were then presented with the 10 target octagons repeated 5 times in different random orders. Following the exposure phase, subjects were given the test phase in which pairs of exposed and unexposed (old and new) octagons were presented in the tachistoscope for 1 sec. The procedure was identical for all conditions, except for the test instructions. For the recognition test, subjects were instructed to choose the octagon that they recognized as having seen before. In the preference condition they were asked which shape they liked better; and in the brightness and darkness conditions they were instructed to report which of the two shapes seemed brighter or darker, respectively. Twelve different subjects were tested in each of the four conditions (recognition, preference, brightness, and darkness).

The results in Table 2.1 show mean percentages for recognition, and for identification of target shapes as preferred to, brighter than, or darker than the unexposed shapes. Recognition and preference results replicate the Kunst-Wilson and Zajonc experiment. Preference percentages were significantly greater

---

[5]The distinction between the experience of familiarity and contextual knowledge is central to recognition performance (Mandler, 1980) and can be derived from the distinction between activation/integration and elaboration (Mandler, 1979).

TABLE 2.1
Mean Percentages for
Four Experimental Groups

Recognition	46.7
Preference (Liking)	61.7
Brightness	60.0
Darkness	60.1

than recognition probabilities. The preference judgment is also significantly different from chance (.50), whereas the recognition judgment obviously is not. Values for preference, brightness, and darkness judgments are significantly different from the chance recognition results and do not differ significantly among each other.

The data are unequivocal in showing that judgments of brightness, as well as the opposite judgments of darkness, are generated with the same likelihood as preferences (liking) in the absence of stimulus recognition. We conclude that any relevant dimensions can be related to the activation of the stimulus representation. In contrast to Kunst-Wilson and Zajonc, these experiments do not permit any conclusion of unique, specific, affective discriminations. If preferences bias the stimuli toward brightness judgments—as might be argued—they should not equally bias the stimuli toward darkness judgments. In contrast, the results can be reasonably assimilated within the context of current information-processing theory, which stresses the activation of, and subsequent access to, underlying representations. No special affective processes need to be invoked.

The dissociation between lower (perceptual) and higher (conceptual) stimulus information demonstrated in the Marcel experiments (1983) requires that the stimulus be presented followed by a pattern mask. Marcel showed that for very short exposures it is possible to discriminate the conceptual information (e.g., category membership) but not lower level information such as stimulus identification (see also Warrington, 1975). It is assumed that the mask distorts the perceptual, visual information of the representation of the item but leaves unaffected other information such as category membership. In contrast, in a series of preliminary studies of the Kunst-Wilson and Zajonc exposure effect, we found that the effect was absent whenever a pattern mask was used. Thus, the exposure effect seems to depend on the integrity of the activated perceptual pattern, which is then related to any dimension of judgment (liking or brightness or darkness) imposed on it.

In short, there is no privileged access to affective information. The data are consistent with the notion that affective judgments are more complex than "cognitive" ones (they take longer), and that their emergence follows general principles of human information processing.

EXTENSIONS

Any theory of emotion deserving of the name should address issues that extend the usefulness of the theory to topics at the boundaries of the field, where emotions and other psychological topics interact. I have tried to do that in the past, for example with respect to the problems of stress and panic, anxiety and performance, the development of emotion, and the emergence of values. More recently, Bill Gaver and I (Gaver & Mandler, 1987) have expanded the application of discrepancy theory to the relation between affect and music. In that paper we explore inter alia the effect of familiarity on liking, the relation between familiarity and complexity, and the appreciation of musical structure. Others have extended our approach to problems of close relationships (Berscheid, 1983, 1984) and the development of emotion (e.g., Stein & Levine, this volume), and T. Purcell at the University of Sydney has applied discrepancy theory to problems of aesthetic judgments in architecture. The most recent extension has been on the interaction between emotion and learning (Mandler, 1989), which I now summarize briefly.

Discrepancies occur in the learning process whenever the interaction between the learner and the environment (teacher, materials) results in unexpected (unpredicted or unpredictable) outcomes. These fall into two classes: (a) errors and failures, and (b) successes. Errors and failures are by definition unintended; they are not expected, and they will have two consequences—autonomic arousal and negative evaluations. Successes may also be unexpected, either because they occur at unexpected times or because they are discrepant with the learners' evaluations of their likelihood of success. Whereas there is an extensive literature on school learning, there is relatively little on the specific emotional effects or errors, failures, and successes. A burgeoning literature on errors and action slips has explored the cognitive structure of errors (cf. Norman, 1980, 1981; Reason, 1977, 1979), but little if any attention has been paid to the emotional consequences of these slips and errors. Under the influence of Skinner (1961), the possibility of errorless learning was raised in the past but later shown not to have the proposed consequences of affectless learning (Rilling, 1977; Terrace, 1963, 1972). It can be argued that affectless learning would, in any case, not be a desirable state, because the world presents us frequently with unexpected and even unsolvable situations—we need emotional preparations for these events.

Some Speculations About the Evolution of Emotion

Even though many tales have been spun about the evolution and origins of the separate emotions (e.g., Izard, 1977; Plutchik, 1980), there is little agreement or consistency to be found. One of the difficulties that faces speculators about the origins of discrete emotions is that they have not yet agreed on what the discrete fundamental emotions are (see Mandler, 1984, p. 36). If there is an evolutionary basis to the primary emotions, should they not be more obvious? I find it intriguing, though, that there seems to be some agreement that interest and surprise are distinct and separate emotions. Surprise can be interpreted as a nice commonsense way of talking about the value-neutral consequence of interruption and discrepancy. Discrepancies are surprising and surprises may be positive or negative. And most theorists in the fundamentalist camp are uncomfortable with surprise; it is often described as a preliminary stage of emotion, a state that is followed by positive or negative states. One would expect people to be aware of an important aspect of the emotional sequence (i.e., surprise or discrepancy). But whether one wants to call surprise an emotion depends on one's interpretation of the common usage of emotion.

A problem that confronts us all when talking about behavioral evolution is that "there are no behavioral fossils." What needs to be done is to advance an argument that is plausible and that fits other knowledge about the evolution of human characteristics.

Discussions about the evolution of the emotions is often preceded by an argument that our emotions evolved to fit an environment that was wild, dangerous, and uncivilized (e.g., Toda, 1982), or, as Wald (1978) stated, that large portions of our animal heritage "have become inappropriate to civilized life" (p. 277). The focus is usually on the "violent" emotions, such as pain, fear, and rage, which are "out of place." But one tends to forget other violent emotions, such as the positive passions of love (whether of sexual partners or one's children) and lust, ecstasy, and joy. Are these too "out of place"?

The notion that specific emotions evolved somehow separately for different reasons requires repeated appeals to their adaptive origins. Whereas arguments have been advanced for the adaptive uses of emotions in general, frequently specific evolutionary stories have been advanced for different emotions. However, appeals to adaptation—the Panglossian argument—frequently ignore the fact that current advantages (or disadvantages) may have relatively unrelated evolutionary origins. More strongly: Current utility does not permit inferences about evolutionary history. And because it isn't quite clear how one is to use the term *emotion,* it seems somewhat futile to describe how it may have been selected and how it has evolved. If, on the other hand, one defines emotions as evaluative/autonomic conjunctions, then the role of the autonomic nervous system plays an important role. I add to the speculations about the evolution of emotion with a scenario that considers emotions to be the result of a number of different and somewhat independent evolutionary events.

I start with the generally agreed viewpoint that the autonomic nervous system developed for primarily economic reasons, first by the evolution of (parasympathetic) energy storage functions and followed by the (sympathetic) energy expenditure functions (Pick, 1970). At some later time (or even in parallel) there developed the discrepancy/interruption effect on sympathetic arousal (i.e., that interruptions of thought or action became sufficient occasions for sympathetic nervous system activity). It seems reasonable that unexpected situations should prepare the organism for action. Quite separately, and for quite different reasons, came the development of specific response tendencies and action syndromes. These include some vocal patterns, motor patterns such as reaching and avoiding/flinching, sexual behavior, and many others. The action patterns in turn have developed parallel mental representation that, in some cases, have become the source of value. Finally, we add the independent development of a facial expressive *language*, not to "express emotions" but rather to communicate evaluations—warnings, encouragements, etc.—in a nonverbal environment. One can argue that the combination of these initially separate and independent tendencies and characteristics eventually combined to produce the mechanisms and processes that construct the emotions. The ANS provided the intensity and the various reactions and expressions added the quality of the emotional concatenations. The "evolution" of emotions then becomes not a separate unique evolutionary event but rather the fortunate (or unfortunate) outcome of the independent evolution of its constituents, eventually combined in a conscious animal into holistic unitary phenomenal experiences. Emotions need not be seen as adaptive or selected for some contemporary reason or another; we have been bequeathed these outcomes as a result of a variety of evolutionary developments, just as we have been bequeathed a writing instrument when the hand developed.

CONCLUSION

I have tried to show that cognitive, constructivist approaches to emotion—and in particular discrepancy/affect theory—are alive and well and growing. The theory changes as it matures, but it also can be extended to take account of new and interesting phenomena. To a large extent it benefits from advances in information-processing theory and research. The theory also is useful in understanding such disparate phenomena as reactions to stress, the affective value of music, and affective interactions with learning.

Experimental research is usually only valuable when it is driven by, and drives, theory. Discrepancy notions make possible a wide variety of new experimental approaches to problems of emotion. I have indicated that we can manipulate the occurrence of emotions by working with controlled environments that produce specific interruptions and discrepancies on the one hand, and values on the other. As research on discrepancies and values continues to be pursued more extensively, we can look toward better specifications of the parameters of the theory, as well as toward new evidence that will change and improve the theoretical structure as such.

ACKNOWLEDGMENTS

Preparation of this chapter and the research reported have been supported by grants from the National Science Foundation and the Spencer Foundation. I am grateful to Kathleen MacDowell for comments on an earlier draft.

REFERENCES

Averill, J. R. (1980). A constructivist view of emotion. In R. Plutchik & H. Kellerman (Ed.), *Theories of emotion*. New York: Academic Press.

Bem, D. J. (1967). Self-perception: An alternative interpretation of cognitive dissonance phenomena. *Psychological Review, 74*, 183–200.

Berscheid, E. (1983). Emotion. In H. H. Kelley, E. Berscheid, A. Christensen, J. H. Harvey, T. L. Hudson, G. Levinger, E. McClintock, L. A. Peplau, & D. R. Peterson (Eds.), *Close relationships*. San Francisco: Freeman.

Berscheid, E. (1984). Emotional experience in close relationships: Implications for child development. In Z. Rubin & W. Hartup (Eds.), *The efffects of early relationships on children's socioemotional development*. New York: Cambridge University Press.

Bonnano, G. A., & Stillings, N. A. (1986). Preference, familiarity, and recognition after repeated brief exposures to random geometric shapes. *American Journal of Psychology, 99*, 403–415.

Bower, G. H. (1981). Mood and memory. *American Psychologist, 36*, 129–148.

Bower, G. H., & Cohen, P. (1982). Emotional influences in memory and thinking: Data and theory. In M. S. Clark & S. T. Fiske (Eds.), *Affect and cognition: The Seventeenth Annual Carnegie Symposium on Cognition*. Hillsdale, NJ: Lawrence Erlbaum Associates.

Bower, G. H., & Mayer, J. D. (1985). *In search of mood-dependent retrieval*. Unpublished manuscript.

Cannon, W. B. (1929). *Bodily changes in pain, hunger, fear and rage* (2d ed.). New York: Appleton–Century–Crofts.

Darwin, C. (1872). *The expression of the emotions in man and animals*. London: John Murray.

Eldredge, N., & Tattersall, I. (1982). *The myths of human evolution*. New York: Columbia University Press.

Gaver, W. W., & Mandler, G. (1987). Play it again, Sam: On liking music. *Cognition and Emotion, 1*, 259–282.

Hohmann, G. W. (1966). Some effects of spinal cord lesions on experienced emotional feelings. *Psychophysiology, 3*, 143–156.

Isen, A. M., Means, B., Patrick, R., & Nowicki, G. (1982). Some factors influencing decision-making strategy and risk taking. In M. S. Clark & S. T. Fiske (Eds.), *Affect and cognition: The 17th Annual Carnegie Symposium on Cognition*. Hillsdale, NJ: Lawrence Erlbaum Associates.

Izard, C. E. (1977). *Human emotions*. New York: Plenum Press.

Izard, C. E. (1986). Approaches to developmental research on emotion–cognition relationships. In D. J. Bearison & H. Zimiles (Eds.), *Thought and emotion: Developmental perspectives* (pp. 21–37). Hillsdale, NJ: Lawrence Erlbaum Associates.

James, W. (1884). What is an emotion? *Mind, 9*, 188–205.

Kunst-Wilson, W. R., & Zajonc, R. B. (1980). Affective discrimination of stimuli that cannot be recognized. *Science, 207*, 557–558.

Lazarus, R. S., Kanner, A. D., & Folkman, S. (1980). Emotions: A cognitive-phenomenological analysis. In R. Plutchik & H. Kellerman (Eds.), *Theories of emotion*. New York: Academic Press.

Mandler, G. (1962). Emotion. In R. W. Brown, E. Galanter, E. H. Hess, & G. Mandler (Eds.), *New directions in psychology.* New York: Holt.

Mandler, G. (1964). The interruption of behavior. In E. Levine (Ed.), *Nebraska Symposium on Motivation: 1964.* Lincoln: University of Nebraska Press.

Mandler, G. (1969). Acceptance of things past and present: A look at the mind and the brain. In R. B. McLeod (Ed.), *William James: Unfinished business.* Washington, DC: American Psychological Association.

Mandler, G. (1975). *Mind and emotion.* New York: Wiley.

Mandler, G. (1979). Organization and repetition: Organizational principles with special reference to rote learning. In L.-G. Nilsson (Ed.), *Perspectives on memory research.* Hillsdale, NJ: Lawrence Erlbaum Associates.

Mandler, G. (1980). Recognizing: The judgment of previous occurrence. *Psychological Review, 87,* 252–271.

Mandler, G. (1984). *Mind and body: Psychology of emotion and stress.* New York: Norton.

Mandler, G. (1985a). *Cognitive psychology: An essay in cognitive science.* Hillsdale, NJ: Lawrence Erlbaum Associates.

Mandler, G. (1985b). Scoring goals. *CC-AI: Journal for the integrated study of artificial intelligence, cognitive science and applied epistemology, 2,* 25–31.

Mandler, G. (1989). Affect and learning: Causes and consequences of emotional interactions. In D. B. McLeod & V. M. Adams (Eds.), *Affect and mathematical problem solving.* New York: Springer Verlag.

Mandler, G., Nakamura, Y., & Shebo-Van Zandt, B. J. (1987). Non-specific effects of exposure on stimuli that cannot be recognized. *Journal of Experimental Psychology: Learning, Memory, and Cognition, 13,* 646–648.

Mandler, G., & Shebo, B. J. (1983). Knowing and liking. *Motivation and Emotion, 7,* 125–144.

Marcel, A. J. (1983). Conscious and unconscious perception: An approach to the relations between phenomenal experience and perceptual processes. *Cognitive Psychology, 15,* 238–300.

Miller, G. A. (1985). The constitutive problem of psychology. In S. Koch & D. E. Leary (Eds.), *A century of psychology as science.* New York: McGraw–Hill.

Norman, D. A. (1980). *Errors in human performance* (Rep. No. 8004). San Diego: Center for Human Information Processing, University of California, San Diego.

Norman, D. A. (1981). Categorization of action slips. *Psychological Review, 88,* 1–15.

Pick, J. (1970). *The autonomic nervous system.* Philadelphia: Lippincott.

Pippard, B. (1985). Discontinuities. *London Review of Books, 7,* 8–9.

Plutchik, R. (1980). *Emotion: A psychoevolutionary synthesis.* New York: Harper & Row.

Putnam, H. (1980). Philosophy and our mental life. In N. Block (Ed.), *Readings in the philosophy of psychology.* Cambridge, MA: Harvard University Press.

Reason, J. T. (1977). Skill and error in everyday life. In M. Howe (Ed.), *Adult learning.* London: Wiley.

Reason, J. T. (1979). Actions not as planned. In G. Underwood & R. Stevens (Eds.), *Aspects of consciousness.* London: Academic Press.

Rilling, M. (1977). Stimulus control and inhibitory processes. In W. K. Honig & J. E. R. Staddon (Eds.), *Handbook of operant behavior* (pp. 432–480). Englewood Cliffs, NJ: Prentice–Hall.

Russell, J. A., & Bullock, M. (1986). Fuzzy concepts and the perception of emotion in facial expressions. *Social Cognition, 4,* 309–341.

Santostefano, S. (1986). Cognitive controls, metaphors and contexts: An approach to cognition and emotion. In D. J. Bearison & H. Zimiles (Eds.), *Thought and emotion: Developmental perspectives* (pp. 175–210). Hillsdale, NJ: Lawrence Erlbaum Associates.

Schneirla, T. R. (1959). An evolutionary and developmental theory of biphasic processes underlying approach and withdrawal. In M. R. Jones (Ed.), *Nebraska Symposium on Motivation: 1959.* Lincoln: University of Nebraska Press.

Seamon, J. G., Brody, N., & Kauff, D. M. (1983). Affective discrimination of stimuli that are not recognized: Effects of shadowing, masking, and cerebral leterality. *Journal of Experimental Psychology: Learning, Memory, and Cognition, 9,* 544–555.

Skinner, B. F. (1961). Why we need teaching machines. *Harvard Educational Review, 31,* 377–398.

Terrace, H. S. (1963). Discrimination learning with and without errors. *Journal of the Experimental Analysis of Behavior, 6,* 1–27.

Terrace, H. S. (1972). By-products of discrimination learning. In G. H. Bower (Ed.), *The psychology of learning and motivation* (Vol. 5). New York: Academic Press.

Toda, M. (1982). *Man, robot, and society.* Boston: Martinus Nijhoff.

Tomkins, S. (1962). *Affect, imagery, and consciousness: The positive affects* (Vol. 1). New York: Springer.

Tomkins, S. (1963). *Affect, imagery, and consciousness: The negative affects* (Vol. 2). New York: Springer.

Wald, G. (1978). The human condition. In M. S. Gregory, A. Silver, & D. Sutch (Eds.), *Sociobiology and human nature* (pp. 277–282). San Francisco: Jossey–Bass.

Warrington, E. K. (1975). The selective impairment of semantic memory. *Quarterly Journal of Experimental Psychology, 27,* 635–657.

Zajonc, R. B. (1980). Feeling and thinking: Preferences need no inferences. *American Psychologist, 35,* 151–175.

3
Making Sense Out of Emotion: The Representation and Use of Goal-structured Knowledge

Nancy L. Stein
Linda J. Levine
University of Chicago

This chapter focuses on the representation of emotional experience and the way in which emotion and thought are interrelated. We present a model that specifies the type of knowledge acquired about emotion, the way in which this knowledge is organized, and how it is used to regulate behavior. We describe the thinking that occurs during emotion episodes and the way in which thought and emotion influence each other. We also illustrate how emotional behavior is perceived and understood by both children and adults, and we show how differences in values and beliefs lead to variation in emotional responses. As such we address issues related to both learning and development.

Our model of emotion is based on a goal-directed, problem-solving approach to the study of personal and social behavior. We assume that much of behavior is carried out in the service of achieving and maintaining goal states that ensure survival and adaptation to the environment. A basic tenant underlying this belief (Stein & Levine, 1987, in press) is that people prefer to be in certain states (i.e., pleasure) and prefer to avoid other states (i.e., pain). A second assumption is that when people experience unpleasant states, they attempt to regulate and change them. One way of achieving this change is to represent a state, called a goal. A goal state can then be used to initiate action or thinking that results in the desired internal state change.

A critical dimension in defining and describing emotional experience, therefore, focuses on the concept of change. Representing and evaluating change with respect to how valued goals have been affected is seen as a necessary prerequisite for experiencing and regulating emotion. As such, our theory is oriented toward a specification of the process by which changes in goal states are detected and emotions are elicited. We also focus on the way in which emotion-eliciting events are represented and the type of thinking that occurs throughout an emotion episode. Thus, the encoding and retrieval processes that occur during emotional understanding become germane.

Given our focus on the importance of changing conditions, a distinguishing characteristic of emotional experience is an effort to assimilate some type of new information into current knowledge schemes (Mandler, 1975, 1984). We (Stein & Levine, 1987) contend that people constantly monitor their environment in an effort to maintain preferred states. To succeed at this task, pattern-matching procedures are used to analyze and compare incoming data to what is already known. When new information is detected in the input, a mismatch occurs, causing an interruption in current thinking processes. Attention then shifts to the novel or discrepant information. With the attentional shift comes arousal of the autonomic nervous system and a focus on the implications new information has for the maintenance of valued goals. Thus, emotional experience is almost always associated with attending to and making sense out of new information.

Consequently, learning almost always results during an emotional episode. In an attempt to understand the nature of changing conditions, people revise and update their beliefs about the conditions necessary for maintaining their goals. For example, people encode many different aspects of the conditions that cause a goal to be achieved or to fail. Furthermore, people often change the value associated with a set of particular goals; that is, in attaining or failing to attain a goal, the value associated with that and other goals may increase or decrease in strength. As a result, people often forfeit their goals as a function of failure or they may intensify their efforts to achieve their goal.

We assume that people have a built-in mechanism that allows them to represent action–outcome sequences in relationship to the maintenance of goals (Gallistel, 1985; Piaget, 1981; Stein & Levine, 1987, in press). Individuals are able to infer and represent the causal conditions that must be operative in order to produce actions that result in certain outcomes, and they are able to use this knowledge to achieve goals. Thus, when a change in goal maintenance occurs and emotions are experienced, plans become operative. Being able to access a plan that specifies the conditions necessary to achieve a goal provides an opportunity for coping with goal failure. Similarly, constructing and carrying out a plan enables the maintenance of a goal, once it has been achieved.

There are situations, however, where little planning occurs or where plans cannot be accessed and retrieved. Intense emotional experience often precludes access to certain types of information, and under these conditions, critical inferences about the emotion situation are not made. Thus, intensity of an emotional experience along with the sensory and physiological feedback associated with such responses become important dimensions in predicting the thinking, decision making, and quality of planning that occur during emotional experience.

Because we are dealing with very young children as well as adults, we discuss some changes that occur in emotional awareness as a function of development and learning. Approaching this issue is thorny at best, for often developmental differences are more a function of the type of knowledge acquired or the degree to which children have been exposed to a task rather than to any general process pertaining to development per se. With due respect to this potential confound, however, certain developmental differences in emotional processing must be considered.

The debates concerning development revolve around which aspects of emotion are innate and which are learned. A second issue concerns the nature of the changes that occur in children's knowledge of emotion and the way in which development affects the organization of emotion. We begin by considering some of the regulatory processes present at birth and some that develop as a function of maturation and experience. Then we present an analysis of the specific processes and types of knowledge that are acquired and used during emotional experience. Finally, we present data that bear on the validity of our model, with respect to both developmental and individual differences in emotion knowledge.

THE DEVELOPMENT OF EMOTIONAL EXPERIENCE

The first issue we consider is whether preferences are innate. At birth, the infant's repertoire includes a set of behaviors for responding to different types and intensities of stimulation. Many are reflexive in nature (i.e., the startle, orienting, blinking, and sucking reflex). Some involve an affective response to the nature of stimulation. For example, certain events precipitate distress responses, consisting of volatile activity, crying, and particular facial expressions. Other events elicit a quieting response, with the absence of volatile activity and expression. A few researchers have held that these responses are evidence for assuming that the infant has innate preferences for being in certain states and preferences for avoiding others. For example, Zajonc (1980) argues that initial preferences need no cognitive input for their elicitation and that they drive all other forms of emotional development.

We do not question the existence and importance of preferences, for they are critical to the experience and expression of emotion. But we take issue with the claim that newborns have acquired full-blown preferences such as desires to be in certain states or desires to avoid others. The fact that infants experience pleasure and distress does not mean that they prefer or desire to shift from one state to another. Having preferences requires the ability to represent, compare, and choose between two different states, where a desire to orient more toward one state than another is expressed. To carry out this type of thinking, a person must have acquired the ability to represent a state that does not currently exist. Although newborns can experience pleasure or distress in response to different events, they have yet to acquire the capacity to represent internal or external states different from those currently directing their behavior.

One reason that young infants experience difficulty in representing hypothetical states such as goals is that they have yet to acquire enough knowledge to construct stable representations of their environment. Being able to construct organized representations permits an infant to understand the causal constraints that make events predictable; that is, when infants have enough exposure to and experience with a specific situation such that they are able to construct a stable representation, they form expectations whereby they understand that certain actions and events result in certain outcomes. In other words, they learn that certain conditions must be present for specific actions and events to occur. In conjunction with this type of understanding, young infants also learn that their own actions can control or change the conditions that lead to certain outcomes. The result of acquiring an adequate knowledge of the world is that young infants engage in decision making about the value of particular experiences, and they can actually determine whether or not to pursue a particular objective.

Although much of this learning occurs rapidly, it does not appear to be present in the newborn infant. The critical period appears to be the first 4 to 5 months of life. During this time, several significant changes occur. First, the infant's ability to habituate to different classes of events increases. Evidence of habituation signals that infants can form predictable representations of a phenomenon and that they experience some type of discrepancy (or dishabituation) when novel stimuli are introduced. Second, infants attend more systematically to external events so that they appear to consciously engage in an appraisal process (Campos, this volume; Emde, 1980; Sroufe, 1979). In other words, these young children begin to evaluate an event in terms of how it will affect them. This evaluation requires that the infant understand that a given event results in a specific outcome and that the outcome results in a particular affective state. If the affective state is aversive or unpleasant, the infant must then be able to understand and represent a state that is not unpleasant. Third, children begin to construct plans that enable them to change their current affective state, and they become more skilled in regulating their motor behavior so that they can carry out and accomplish their plans.

From an analysis of current literature on infant development (e.g., Fernald, 1984; Mandler, 1988), these skills seem to cohere and become integrated somewhere during the 4th to 7th month of life. When infants can bring to bear all these skills, we would say that a true emotional reaction can be experienced. In making this claim, we are distinguishing between the more general class of affective versus the more specific class of emotional responses. Affective responses are those that include distress or quieting behaviors where changes in the level of autonomic nervous system arousal occur without an evaluative component being accessed. These types of reactions occur frequently in the young infant and less frequently in the adult. Emotional reactions are those that involve the autonomic nervous system as well as higher order thinking processes. In the following discussion, we lay out the processes and components involved in our model of emotional experience and understanding.

EVALUATION PROCESSES UNDERLYING EMOTIONAL EXPERIENCE

A necessary feature in our theory is the presence of a representational system that monitors subjective states and bodily reactions. Monitoring is carried out in the service of moving toward states that are beneficial for survival and moving away from environments that are harmful. The primary function of this system is to access knowledge that allows the evaluation of an event, action, object, or state in regard to its value (see also Mandler, 1982, 1984). This representational system must include information about states that are pleasurable and preferred and states that are aversive and to be avoided. The system also contains information about the conditions that lead to specific goal states, and it contains information about the relative ordering of goals in terms of their necessity for maintaining or avoiding certain states (i.e., preferences).

Given these properties, a value system has three primary characteristics. First, it is hierarchical in nature such that a series of goals can be represented with regard to the causal conditions that embed and connect one goal to another. Second, preference trees can be constructed such that certain goals are considered more valuable than others. And third, this system is dynamic in nature such that some preferences and some parts of a goal hierarchy (i.e., the conditions linking goals together) can be changed. As a result of incorporating new information about conditions leading to the attainment of valued goals, the structure of the hierarchy undergoes continued construction and reorganization. Goals that have a high value on one occasion often decrease in value on another, depending on the operating conditions. Similarly, goals that are unfamiliar or lacking in value often increase in worth as new connections are made between these new goals and other valued familiar goals. The important point is that, like all other schemata, value systems are both stable and dynamic. Some parts of the value system remain constant and other parts change.

The existence of a value system is fundamental to emotional behavior (Lazarus & Folkman, 1984; Mandler, 1984; Stein & Levine, 1987) because it alerts individuals to those situations that bring pleasure and pain. With such a system operating, two primary tendencies exist: the desire to attain or maintain a valued state and the desire to get out of or avoid an aversive state. As we previously stated, a value system becomes operative when an individual is in one particular state, can imagine the existence of another one, and has an understanding that the imagined end state leads to a more pleasurable outcome.

Thus, a second component critical to our model is the ability to detect change in the environment as well as in one's own internal states. Moreover, the change must be assessed with respect to maintaining current values and goals. Here, we describe the different processes that occur when emotional reactions are experienced. We begin by describing baseline activities that occur immediately before the onset of a precipitating event. Four are of interest: (1) the type of ongoing cognitive activity, (2) the level of physiological arousal, (3) the emotional state of the participant, and (4) the type of ongoing overt activity. These variables are important because our model assumes that an emotional reaction always causes a change in the first three processes and often causes a change in overt actions as well (Ekman, 1977). Thus, our model is a state change model where all properties change in some specific way when an unexpected precipitating event occurs.

Precipitating events emerge from three different sources: the environment (i.e., a physical event such as a rain storm, a fire, the formation of a rainbow, or the action of another person, such as the giving of a gift or the violation of a promise), one's own actions, or the result of memory retrieval of past events. For an emotional response to occur, the precipitating event must be encoded and accessed during the evaluation process. In the case of retrieving an event from memory, the initial encoding has already taken place, but the event must be accessed and placed in working memory. Then, a meaning analysis has to be performed on the focal information.

The meaning analysis can be broken down into different processes. Of primary interest are those that facilitate the integration of incoming information into current knowledge structures. Assuming that different pattern-matching procedures underlie most attempts to integrate new information into current knowledge stores, it is important to discriminate between those where a match results and those where a discrepancy occurs. If incoming information is congruent with information in existing knowledge stores, then it is readily assimilated into current knowledge schemes. Under these conditions, individuals are often unaware of the processes associated with encoding and understanding.

When a mismatch occurs, however, information cannot be immediately assimilated into current working schemes. By definition, some of this information is novel or unexpected; that is, some aspect of the incoming information is incongruent with what was expected, given the current state of a person's knowledge. Mismatches cause an interruption of ongoing thinking, give rise to subsequent evaluation processes, and cause subsequent changes in states of ANS arousal (Mandler, 1975, 1984). When both ANS arousal and cognitive evaluation occur, an emotional reaction occurs. As we stated before, precipitating events often cause ANS arousal leading to an affective or reflexive response. However, we do not consider these affective responses to belong to the class of emotional responses, because no evaluation of current goal states is made. It is when both autonomic arousal and evaluation occur that an emotional reaction occurs.

When the evaluation process is initiated, an assessment is first made as to whether an adequate representation of the precipitating event exists. Many instances occur where only part of an event is understood because the information is so novel. In these cases, surprise and a sense of curiosity is evoked. This indicates that the first cognitive activity of the individual is to form a representation of the event in the service of understanding the new information; that is, many precipitating events require that new categories get formed or that beliefs are updated so that the event can become known and predictable. Then an evaluation can be made as to whether the event has any significance with respect to changing, blocking, or facilitating the attainment of valued goals.

Separating the process of forming an adequate representation from the process of evaluation is difficult because frequently the two occur in close temporal proximity. However, the formation of a representation always precedes the evaluation process. Moreover, different affective reactions should occur when representations are being formed than when changes in goal maintenance are being assessed. Surprise, curiosity, and interest are indicative of the formation of new representations, whereas happiness, anger, sadness, and fear are indicative of those emotions that occur when an event is being assessed with respect to the maintenance of valued goals.

The fact that surprise is often reported in conjunction with happiness, anger, or distress lends support to the notion of separating the understanding process from the evaluation process. When surprise occurs in close proximity to other emotions, surprise normally precedes other emotions. As an example, we provide dialogue from a recent study we (Stein & Trabasso, 1989) have carried out with 5-year-old children. On one occasion, a kindergarten student was told that her teacher was going to let all the children paint as part of the normal course of activities in the classroom. The child was then told that painting would occur on a daily basis, and she was asked how she would feel if she were allowed to paint everyday in her classroom. Her responses to this question were that she really liked painting (value) and that she felt it made her really happy (emotional response), especially when she could paint whatever she wanted.

This child was then told that today when she got through painting, her teacher was going to give her all the paints to take home. As a result, she would be able to paint at home as well as in school. The child was then asked to describe her thoughts and feelings in response to this event. She began by saying: "Do you really mean that she (the teacher) is going to let me take all the paints home? Am I the only one who gets to do this? Is this a present for me? Does she want me to paint everyday?"

If we had videotaped the facial expression of this child, we would have seen a look of surprise followed by a look of concern as she began to talk. First, this child did not quite believe that the teacher would give her a gift. Thus, to respond to this event, she first had to change her belief about the relative improbability of the event occurring. If we had asked her whether or not she thought her teacher would ever give her a gift of paints, we would probably be able to show that this child judged the event as highly unlikely. Approximately 70% of all the children in this study (Stein & Trabasso, 1989) actually said: "I don't believe it. Can you believe it? Why would she do that?" Apparently, teachers are not thought of as givers of gifts, and the act of a teacher giving a child a gift to take home violated these children's conceptions of what a teacher does. For children to evaluate the event in terms of their own goals, however, they first had to accept the fact that the teacher was indeed giving them a gift with which they could do whatever they wanted. Once the children accepted this fact, almost all of them expressed extreme happiness.

Thus, in our example, children first attempted to discern the truth value associated with the occurrence of a precipitating event. They then attempted to understand exactly why the teacher was giving them a paint set and what she wanted them to do with the set. The general act of one person giving another a gift was not an unfamiliar event to these children. In fact, this transaction is highly familiar, and children considered it a very pleasant experience. Therefore, most of the children encoded the event correctly the first time they heard about it. However, disbelief was still expressed because of the ambiguity inherent in the event. A teacher could give children paint sets for many reasons other than the one expressed in the text. The children were not initially convinced that the stated reason was in fact the one that the teacher had in mind. For these children, teachers are not associated with gift giving as much as they are associated with setting up tasks that must be accomplished. Thus, the novel element for these children was the act of their teacher giving them a gift.

The familiar combined with a novel dimension is often the factor that causes the greatest surprise, shock, or horror when such an event occurs. Examples of tragedies are those instances where a horrible event occurs, such as a plane crash or an earthquake, where the victim loses a loved one and does not believe that such an event could ever happen to him or her. The familiarity of such an event (i.e., knowing that such an event could happen and perhaps witnessing the grim reality of others having to cope with such a disaster) allows the victim to experience horror or grief. Moreover, shock and an air of unreality set in almost immediately or often precede the feeling of terror and grief. The ability to accept the fact that the event really has occurred and cannot be changed is the critical variable that regulates whether or not the consequences of the event will be processed. If doubt surrounds the occurrence of an event, attention will be focused first on determining the certainty of the event. For if there is any doubt that such an event occurred, most likely all possible resources will be devoted to ascertaining the reality of the event.

Surprise and interest are different from emotional responses in that they indicate an effort to construct new representations of novel information in a precipitating event. These affective responses are not directly associated with an evaluation of how a precipitating event affects the accomplishment of goals. The degree to which a precipitating event is considered possible or understood will predict whether surprise or interest is expressed. If the implications of the precipitating event are not evaluated in terms of whether valued goals have been threatened, blocked, or attained, then surprise should be expressed. Attempting to understand how precipitating events affect valued goals should be associated with states of interest or curiosity. However, as soon as the event is understood in terms of a valued goal, specific emotional responses should be present.

We now turn our attention to a description of the process of thinking and planning associated with four emotional responses. Most investigators studying the conceptual organization of emotional knowledge have simplified the thinking processes associated with emotional responses. Although emotional responses can indeed be rapid, occurring almost in an automatic fashion (Ekman, 1977), the delay between a precipitating event and an emotional response can also be quite long. We know of few on-line processing studies that have actually documented the variations in the time delays of emotional responses, nor do we know of any studies that have described the multiple changes that occur during attempts to understand the meaning of a precipitating event. Although we illustrate how four different emotional responses occur, our focus is on the process of experiencing and thinking about emotion.

THINKING AND REASONING ABOUT HAPPINESS, ANGER, AND SADNESS

When we talk about happiness as opposed to pleasure, or when we refer to anger, sadness, and fear, as opposed to pain, distress, or a startle response, we need to include additional evaluative processes that focus on the recognition of changes in maintaining or attaining a valued state (see Sroufe, 1979, for a cogent analysis of this shift). Pleasure, pain, interest, distress, and startle can occur without many of the dimensions associated with the causes of happiness, anger, sadness, or fear. These latter emotions do not occur independent of a context. We are happy or sad about something that happened; we are angry at something, we are afraid of something. These emotions occur because evaluations have been made about how a particular event will affect valued goals.

Before presenting a process analysis of these emotions (see Stein & Jewett, 1986; Stein & Levine, 1987, for an extended analysis), we draw attention to three problematic issues associated with the study of emotion. The first concerns the belief that some type of novel information must be detected for any emotion to be experienced. The second focuses on the disruption of thought and the disorganized nature of thinking and behavior that supposedly occur as a function of experiencing an emotion. The third pertains to whether positive and negative emotions have differential effects on thinking, planning, and decision making (see Isen, this volume, for a review of this literature; see Schwarz, 1988, for a somewhat different analysis).

For some reason, the claim that emotional responses occur in response to processing new or discrepant information has been one of the more misunderstood assertions associated with cognitive theories of emotion (Isen, 1984; Scherer, 1984; Sroufe, 1979). Positive emotions, in particular, are seen as not requiring the processing of novelty and are thought not to result in the interruption of ongoing cognitive activity. Moreover, positive emotions are thought to differ from negative emotions in being facilitative rather than disruptive of ongoing thought and behavior (see Isen, this volume; or Averill, 1979; Sroufe, 1979; for a discussion of these claims).

In a recent theoretical paper (Stein & Levine, 1987), we argued that both classes of emotional responses result from the processing of novel information. Moreover, both positive and negative emotions could be seen as facilitative or disruptive of ongoing thinking, depending on the context in which the emotion is experienced. Some of the variables regulating thinking once an emotion has been experienced are: the importance of attaining or maintaining the goal under consideration, whether or not plans have been formulated to cope with goal failure or success, whether or not immediate action is required; whether or not all goal-related activities have been accomplished; and whether or not the full implications of the goal–outcome relationship have been understood. These dimensions not only regulate attention and thinking during emotional experience, but they also regulate the intensity with which an emotion is experienced.

To say that negative emotions disrupt thinking or that positive emotions facilitate thinking is to conclude that the class of positive emotions versus those of negative emotions have some general property in common that would serve to influence subsequent thinking and planning. Moreover, the experience of positive versus negative emotion would be independent of the context that evoked the emotion. Although positive emotions are associated with reactions to goal success whereas negative emotions are evoked in response to goal failure, the thinking and reasoning in positive and negative emotional episodes is significantly constrained by the importance of the goal being considered and by the quality of inferences made about a goal in relation to other goals.

We now describe the evaluation and planning processes associated with the emotions happiness, sadness, anger, and fear (a more detailed description can be found in Stein & Levine, 1987). We have chosen to focus on only four emotions in order to give an in-depth description of each emotion. Our goal is to advance a theory about the process of experiencing an emotion and to speak to issues concerning the thinking and reasoning during an emotional episode.

We begin with a description of happiness to illustrate how it depends on the recognition of discrepant information, and how different types of "happy" experiences can either disrupt or facilitate thought and behavior. Moreover, we discuss the somewhat contradictory claims of Isen (this volume) and Schwarz (1988), who on the one hand claim that happiness leads to more creativity (Isen, this volume) and on the other assert that happiness leads to mindless, less analytical behavior (Schwarz, 1988). Finally, we show how an analysis of goal hierarchies and goal conflict is essential to understanding the representation of this emotion.

HAPPINESS

For a person to experience happiness, four dimensions must be detected or inferred from a precipitating event: First, some aspect of the event must be perceived as novel with respect to the ability to maintain, attain, or avoid a particular goal state; second, the inference must be made that a valued state has been achieved; third, an inference must be made about the certainty of attaining or maintaining the goal; that is, the person must believe that goal attainment is certain or that goal attainment has already occurred such that no further obstacles can hinder goal success; and fourth, a person must believe that enjoyment of the goal state or goal maintenance will follow from the outcome.

A prototypical way of thinking about the experience of happiness is to envision the transition from a negative to a positive state. Before the precipitating event occurs, the baseline thinking and behavior of an individual must be described. If we take those situations where people begin an emotion episode in a negative emotion state, several dimensions characterize their state. First, they have not yet attained the valued goal under consideration or they believe that a valued goal is threatened. Moreover, they believe that the probability of attaining the goal is not high.

A precipitating event then occurs causing or enabling the goal to be achieved. Happiness results when the following inferences are made. First, the event is encoded and seen as discrepant from what is known or believed. When an individual begins the emotion episode in a negative state, the discrepancy occurs because of the belief that goal achievement was not very likely. The fact that the goal has been attained or that goal attainment is virtually guaranteed violates expectations; that is, something unusual or unexpected has occurred. Attention is then focused on two different dimensions. First, an assessment is made as to whether or not the event was encoded properly, and second an appraisal is made about the relative certainty that a particular goal has been attained.

An example from one of our studies (Stein & Trabasso, 1989) illustrates this point. Five-year-old children were initially asked to imagine that their mother was not going to be able to read them a story before bedtime. They were told that they would just have to go to bed by themselves. Children were then asked: (a) how they would feel if this happened to them, (b) how intense their feelings would be (rating intensity on a 5-point scale), and (c) how sure they would be that their mother would not read them a bedtime story. In 92% of the cases, children said that they would feel sad because they could not hear a story and would have to go to bed alone. Their feelings were very intense, 4.5 out of 5. In rating the certainty of the fact that they were not going to get a story read to them, the average score was 1.5, with 1 being certain that no story would be read and 5 being certain that a story would be read to them.

After answering these questions, children were then told that their mother had thought about it again and that she was going to read them a story because she was able to get more of her chores done than expected. Children were asked what their first thoughts were about this event. Approximately 96% of the children said they would feel really happy because they loved stories and were glad that their mother changed her mind. Thus, for the clear majority of children there was a rapid shift from believing that goal attainment was at a very low probability (1.5) to believing that they would really attain their goal (4.5).

The other 4% of the children did not experience as significant a shift in certainty ratings. Their scores went from 1.6 to 3.5 on the certainty scale. These children first focused on whether or not their mother would really be able to get her chores done in time for the story. Thus, once the uncertainty of goal attainment was established in the beginning of the episode, a few children did not automatically believe that goal attainment was certain. When explicitly asked about how they felt when their mother said she would read them a story, these children said they felt okay but would wait to see if she really read them a story. None spontaneously expressed happiness, and when pressed explicitly about their feelings, most said they felt nervous or "jittery" or didn't know how they felt.

These data illustrate that happiness is expressed when expectations about the probability of goal success are violated. However, children must also update their beliefs about the certainty of goal success if they are to experience happiness. If they are able to change their beliefs, then happiness will be expressed. And when they talk about being happy, children almost always focus on being able to enjoy the activities associated with goal fulfillment. If children do not believe that goal attainment is certain, then a low-level anxiety response is evoked. Thus, the perception of certainty appears to be a necessary component to the expression of happiness.

Happiness does not necessarily require that people initially be in a negative emotion state. Individuals can make the transition to a happy state by first being in a more neutral state or by experiencing surprise or interest, signaling the formation of a new representation. However, once the representation is constructed and inferences are made about the success and the certainty of goal attainment, happiness is experienced.

Situations also exist where the experience of happiness intensifies. For example, suppose a person has just achieved an important goal and experiences a state of happiness. Suddenly, another event occurs to ensure the achievement of other valued goals. In this case, the emotion of happiness should intensify. The increase in intensity is due to the unexpected attainment of additional desired goals, some of which may be more valued than those originally attained. For example, in one of our studies, (Stein & Trabasso, 1989), 5-year-old children were told that they were to imagine that their teacher brought a new toy to class every week and that they got an hour to play with it by themselves. Children responded to this initial situation by giving almost unanimously happy responses, with an average of 4.3 on a 5-point intensity rating scale.

The children were then told that the teacher decided that they could take the toy home and keep it, because she knew how much they liked the toy. After acknowledging their surprise at such an event, 94% of the children expressed happiness about being able to take the toy home. The average intensity rating rose to from 4.3 to 4.9. Moreover, when asked if they were just as happy after getting the toy to take home, more happy, or less happy, 96% responded with more happy. When asked whether or not they expected the teacher to give them a toy, 94% said that they never thought she would do such a thing.

What we have shown so far is that fulfilling goals unexpectedly is sufficient to evoke happiness. Accomplishing additional goals unexpectedly increases the intensity of happiness. The question remains, however, as to whether novelty is *necessary* to induce happiness once inferences have been made about the achievement of a valued goal. In an attempt to answer this question, we asked 5-year-old children to respond to situations where habitual positive activities were repeated. Children were probed about their feelings and expectations the first time the teacher brought a new toy, the second time, and the third time. In all these instances, the children were told to remember that each time the teacher brought a toy, it would be different from the one before. In these situations, 80% of the children gave the same emotional response (happiness) over all three situations, and their intensity ratings remained the same (4.5). When asked why they would feel happy, over 98% explained their emotion by saying they would get to play with a new toy. Thus, the introduction of a new toy each time served to maintain the initial intensity rating of these children.

Children were then asked how they would feel if their teacher brought the same toy to class the first week, the second week, and the third week. In collecting this data, we took care to introduce the events sequentially as they would occur in a real-world environment. Again, 92% of the children said they would be happy the first time, with a mean intensity score of 4.7. After trial two, 75% said they would be really happy, with a mean intensity score of 3.5. On the third trial, only 20% said they would be really happy, with a mean intensity score of 2.8. Those children who did not express happiness said that they wouldn't feel anything or that they would become bored. The reason given for these affective responses (or lack of a response) was that sometimes they got tired of playing with the same toy and they needed to switch to another one.

Thus, we propose that when continued exposure to an event results in an emotional response at the same intensity level as the initial response, some degree of novelty is still being processed. However, as people incorporate the novel aspects of a stimulus and build a more stable representation of the event (i.e., the event becomes predictable and responses to it automatic), the emotional response decreases in intensity, eventually resulting in a state where attention is no longer focused on the event. These changes are similar to those described in studies of habituation and adaptation to a stimulus, where subjects become immune and almost unaware of certain sensations. Although our studies are still in the preliminary stages of development, they speak to the necessity of considering more seriously the role of repeated exposure on ratings of novelty, predictability, pleasure or pain, emotion, and intensity of the felt emotion. It is in the further understanding of adaptation phenomema that we will be able to determine whether or not novelty is necessary for the evocation of an emotional response.

Positive emotions do not necessarily facilitate thinking any more than negative emotions. Many studies have attested to the fact that positive mood states provoke more divergent thinking than negative emotions (see Isen, 1984, 1987, this volume), but that negative mood states, such as anger, lead to a greater degree of vigilance and analytical thinking than positive emotions. Thus, both positive and negative moods have been shown to facilitate thinking, depending on the nature of the thinking processes measured.

Our interpretation of these findings, however, is somewhat different from those of Isen (this volume) and Schwarz (1988). Although both these investigators have established robust findings with regard to how mood state affects subsequent thinking, we argue that both positive and negative emotions can be used to induce divergent or analytical thinking, and both classes of emotion can facilitate or hinder subsequent processing of new information. The important variables are the understanding and decision-making processes associated with the event that caused an emotional response and the thinking focused on coping with the emotion (see Folkman & Lazarus, this volume, on emotion-focused coping). We argue that the contextual constraints surrounding the induced mood state are as important as the particular valence of the mood.

Recent studies exploring the effect of mood state on subsequent thinking and decision making have focused largely on determining the effects of mood on subsequent thinking (Isen, 1984, 1987; Johnson & Tversky, 1983), without describing the thinking and decision-making processes that occur as a function of experiencing a particular emotion. The thinking that precedes a particular emotion, along with the intensity of the emotional experience, are powerful determinants of the ability to shift attention to new incoming information. For example, certain classes of "positive" events, like winning 40 million dollars in a lottery, are truly disruptive, as well as exhilarating. The probability of ever attaining this goal is small, and the number of life goals affected is enormous. If this event occurred before the presentation of some other cognitive task, we doubt we would see any facilitative effects of the happy state, including divergent thinking. In fact, we doubt that an experimenter could even get a subject's attention were this event to occur. However, if the event resulting in a positive emotion did not relate to other important life conditions and did not require continued attention to the emotion-eliciting event, then the focus of attention could readily shift to a new task.

Similar comments can be made about negative emotions. Thinking about a newly introduced task will be facilitated or disrupted depending on the type of prior goal obstructed, the value of the goal, and the complexity of the planning activities that result as a function of goal failure. In fact, if the experimental task required finding a solution to the problem that elicited the emotion in the first place, negative emotions might well facilitate performance on the task, especially in regard to divergent thinking. For example, one of the first steps in a problem-solving sequence is often devoted to "brainstorming" or generating many possible alternatives that might lead to a solution. The activation of this strategy is often the direct result of goal failure on the first attempt at a solution.

The important point in regard to the effects of happiness on subsequent thinking is that individuals typically construct plans to maintain the goal that has been achieved. They also attempt to maintain the positive emotion state associated with the successful outcome. The structure and content of some positive outcomes, however, are simpler than others. Figures 3.1 and 3.2 illustrate the different planning sequences accompanying two different positive outcomes. The first example is taken from the Stein (1988) corpus of stories children have generated in response to different stems. The second is taken from several newspaper articles about the Chicago winner of the 40 million dollar lottery. In the first example (Fig. 3.1), the plan is simply to participate in an activity that ensures the maintenance of the accomplished goal. We see this type of plan generated by young children when we give them a toy that they really desire. Their primary plans are to play with the toys and keep them close by for future play. In these situations, the outcome does not lead to consideration of any other goal except one of enjoyment.

In other situations, the achievement of the first goal is simply the first step in achieving more important goals. There are times when a person must accomplish a series of subgoals to achieve the superordinate goal. Happiness may be associated with the attainment of each subgoal. However, knowledge that the positive state is transitory unless other conditions are fulfilled results in attention to the new conditions that must be fulfilled.

Figure 3.2 illustrates the complexity associated with winning a lottery. Discovering that you hold the winning ticket in a lottery is only the first step in receiving the money. Although hearing your number broadcast over the radio results in surprise and a shock-like response, intense happiness does set in. In fact, the feeling by a recent Illinois lottery winner was described as one of disbelief and then sheer joy, especially as the increasing number of goals that could be accomplished was reviewed.

However, soon after the initial expression of happiness, disbelief again sets in. The number is confirmed again by calling the radio station to verify that the number was heard correctly. Joy is again expressed but short-lived because instructions are then given about claiming the money. These procedures involve accomplishing certain subgoals, like not losing the ticket, meeting the deadline for turning in the ticket, and showing care in driving to the radio station. The

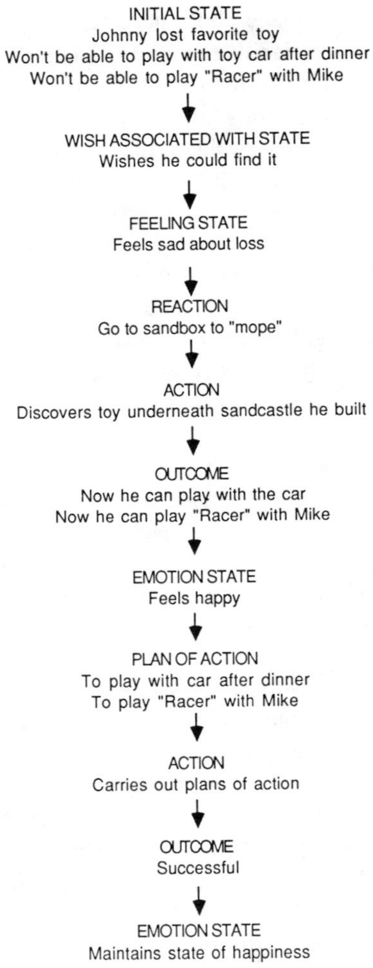

INITIAL STATE
Johnny lost favorite toy
Won't be able to play with toy car after dinner
Won't be able to play "Racer" with Mike

↓

WISH ASSOCIATED WITH STATE
Wishes he could find it

↓

FEELING STATE
Feels sad about loss

↓

REACTION
Go to sandbox to "mope"

↓

ACTION
Discovers toy underneath sandcastle he built

↓

OUTCOME
Now he can play with the car
Now he can play "Racer" with Mike

↓

EMOTION STATE
Feels happy

↓

PLAN OF ACTION
To play with car after dinner
To play "Racer" with Mike

↓

ACTION
Carries out plans of action

↓

OUTCOME
Successful

↓

EMOTION STATE
Maintains state of happiness

FIG. 3.1.   Simple episode.

effect of activating these subgoals is to evoke anxiety over losing the ticket or not making the deadline. The complexity of the scenario continues even when the ticket is handed in and the winner confirmed. The lottery winner's parents are contacted because they put up some of the money for the ticket, and decisions need to be made as to how the winnings will be divided. Again, happiness in interleaved with attention to other goals that need to be accomplished as a result of winning. Thus, the question of context or framing becomes an important concern in making predictions about the effect of different emotions or mood states on subsequent thinking.

INITIAL STATE
Mike bought lottery ticket
So did one million others
Does not expect to win

↓

WISH ASSOCIATED WITH STATE
Wants to win lottery
Would not have to work
Could go to college
Could get married
Could buy house for parents
Could start own business

↓

PLAN OF ACTION
To find out if he won

↓

ACTION
Listens to radio

↓

OUTCOME
Numbers match his ticket

↓

EMOTION STATE
Happiness, combined with surprise and startle

LIST OF GOALS AND EVENTS THAT ARE EMBEDDED IN LEARNING OF WIN

1. Check ticket again to make sure of accuracy
2. Find out how to claim money
3. Find out how ticket can be protected until money is claimed
4. Be careful driving to lottery site so you won't get into an accident
5. Check with parents and brothers to see how winnings will be divided
6. Decide how many of you are going to the lottery board to claim the money
7. Go down to board to claim prize

PROBLEMS ARISING AS A FUNCTION OF THE LOTTERY WIN

1. Discord between parents and brothers as to how money should be distributed
2. Arguments with IRS about legality of dividing lottery win
3. Arguments with lawyers about the necessity of a prenuptial agreement concerning lottery money
4. Discord at work because of status change and availability of new resources
5. Problems in starting a new business because of lack of skill in any particular area

GOAL COMPLETION AS A FUNCTION OF LOTTERY WIN

1. Got married
2. Split money with parents and brothers
3. Bought parents new house

FIG. 3.2.   Complex episode.

Our position also differs from that of Bower (Bower & Cohen, 1982), who proposed that the induction of specific mood states results in the activation of memories highly similar to the one induced by the emotion. From this point of view, when in a sad state, thinking reflects a series of associations related to the notion of sadness per se and not to the situation. Although we can think of instances where associative chaining occurs, a primary assumption underlying our model is that the experience of emotion is goal driven and problem focused. Moreover, when an emotion is experienced, attention is directed toward being able to maintain or reinstate a goal. Instead of running off an associative network that is driven by the emotion per se, people try to achieve a better understanding of the conditions that would lead to goal maintenance or reinstatement. Therefore, thinking subsequent to an emotional experience is likely to focus on the conditions that caused the emotional reaction, past experiences that allow predictions to be made about the probable consequences of the event, memories of successful strategies adopted in response to similar situations in the past, and an assessment of the outcome of those strategies.

We also assume that as people succeed or fail to attain valued goals, they learn more about the conditions that lead to the outcome. They also change their beliefs and feelings about the people who took part in their emotional experiences. For example, as a function of winning the 40 million dollar lottery, Mike changed his feelings about many of his friends. A few of them decided to ask Mike for backing in a financial venture. When Mike refused, they reacted by completely ignoring him. The result was that Mike learned that they did not consider him a friend unless he would support them financially. Moreover, they tried to harm him by rejecting him. Mike felt devastated at the loss of these friendships, but at the same time the value of these friendships decreased. Mike no longer trusted any of them.

From these newspaper and magazine accounts, we developed a scenario that explained Mike's feelings and reactions to the lottery in terms of the goals he wanted to accomplish before the lottery and after winning the lottery. The scenario contained the feelings Mike expressed and the plans that he actually carried out. Then we asked eight students to rank the importance of Mike's goals before and after the lottery. We predicted a significant change in almost all importance scores given before and after the lottery. Before winning the lottery, the average ratings assigned to each of five goals on a 10-point importance scale, with 10 being the most important, were as follows:

1. Get Married: 7
2. Go to college: 8
3. Stop work: 9
4. Buy a house for parents: 5
5. Start own business: 4

Once the lottery was won, however, certain goals became more important and others became less important. For example, our scenario included the fact that Mike decided that the first thing he wanted to do was to get married, so his rating of getting married went from 7 to 10. He then decided that he didn't have to go to college because he had enough money so that he didn't have to worry about education or his future. Thus, the rating of going to college went from 8 to 2. Buying a house for his parents became very important as did his concern about their general welfare. The importance rating went from a 5 to a 9. Before the lottery, he was so preoccupied with his own growth and survival that he rarely devoted the time or effort into thinking about his parents except in a rather automatic "caring" fashion. Starting his own business stayed at a medium low level because being accepted as a "regular" guy became more important as a function of winning the lottery. Mike perceived that people at work began to treat him differently. He now had access to resources that few of them did. Moreover, he received a great deal of publicity about his win, including being written about in "People" magazine and "Good Housekeeping." Thus, Mike felt a dramatic change in the feelings and attitudes people had toward him. His response to this change was to place a greater degree of importance on maintaining his present job, so the importance rating for stopping his job went from 9 to 3.

Thus, an event like winning a lottery changed the perceived importance attached to several different goals. Certain goals became more important in the sense that Mike really wanted to achieve these goals, and others became less important in that he did not have an immediate desire to see them accomplished. Some goals, like going to college, became very unimportant. In fact, for those goals that shifted dramatically in their level of importance, we must consider another issue: whether their value also changed.

Although the degree of importance and the degree of value overlap considerably, these dimensions are not isomorphic. In collecting our rankings, importance was defined by the question, "How much does Mike really want to accomplish this goal? How important is it that he accomplish this goal?" Although positive value would probably be imputed to most of Mike's goals (i.e., "How much does he like doing this?"), this does not always have to be the case. Accomplishing a subgoal can be very important in maintaining a higher order goal, but true displeasure can be expressed in terms of how much the subgoal is valued. For example, before winning the lottery, Mike asserted that he hated his job and would do anything he could to quit. After the lottery, winning the acceptance of his friends became very important to him, and he chose to do it by maintaining contact with them through his job. However, he still hated his job. The problem was that he could not generate any other plan of action that would accomplish the superordinate goals that were important to him.

Although we are just beginning to describe the nature of value construction and that of shifting values, both these factors are important for theories of emotional understanding. The value imputed to a goal and the importance of achieving it organize and determine in part whether an emotional response is experienced and the plan of action associated with the emotional response. As we turn now to a description of anger and sadness, we illustrate again the centrality of values, value construction, and learning from negative outcomes. Moreover, we again show that when people experience loss or aversive states, the number of goals affected can vary dramatically. Thus, the consequences can be major in that several different goals are affected, or they can be minor in that one or two goals are affected.

ANGER AND SADNESS

These two emotions are considered together because of the similarity in the types of events that elicit them. Anger and sadness can both be elicited by loss and aversive states. Loss states signal that a person has failed to attain or maintain a desired state, whereas aversive states signal that a person has not been able to avoid being put into an unpleasant state. The prototypic expression of either anger or sadness occurs when a person enters an emotion episode believing that a particular goal can be accomplished or believing that certain standards will be upheld. Anger and sadness also arise when people enter into a situation believing that they can avoid aversive states. To evoke either emotion, something about the ensuing loss or the onset of the aversive state must be perceived as novel or unexpected. Moreover, the loss or aversive state must be perceived as certain.

The certainty aspect attached to anger and sadness appears problematic at first. Many times we are alerted to a major loss that will occur, such as finding out that a loved one is terminally ill or being told that our job will no longer exist. Neither of these events have yet occurred, and yet when asked how we feel the answer is often extreme sadness. Two explanations for these responses exist. First, if people believe that nothing can be done about a situation (i.e., no plan of action can prevent the outcome) such that the event is a certain occurrence, then we would say that sadness is experienced. However, the experience is based on the belief that the occurrence of the event is certain.

The second possibility is that different affective responses are experienced rather than sadness, but the experiences are mislabeled as sadness. For example, the immediate response to the threat of a major loss is often one of startle or surprise much like the response to unexpected gains. The first step is often one of testing out the certainty that this event will occur. During this process, the most prototypic emotional response is one of high anxiety or fear. The event hasn't yet occurred, but the belief is that it will occur with a fairly high degree of certainty. Under these conditions, the feeling is not one of sadness, but as the person struggles to accept the loss (i.e., changing a belief from the possibility of a loss occurring to a belief that the event will almost certainly occur), the situation can easily be labeled as a sad one. The important component for the evocation of either sadness or anger is that a person must believe that certainty will exist. If this inference has been made and the loss or aversive state is unexpected, then anger or sadness will be experienced.

Given that anger and sadness are similar in this regard, what differentiates them? According to our model (Stein & Levine, 1987, 1989) anger occurs when a person responds to a loss or aversive state by inferring that the obstructed goal can be reinstated. More specifically, people firmly believe that they can some-how initiate a plan to restore the original conditions that existed before a loss or an aversive state occurred. In these circumstances, attention is often focused on understanding the cause of the loss or aversive state so that an effort can be made to change the conditions resulting in the undesired state. Thus, anger often carries with it a desire not only to reinstate the goal but also to remove or change the conditions that led to goal blockage in the first place.

Unlike many other analyses of anger (Averill, 1979; Roseman, 1979, 1984; Weiner, 1985), in our analysis the perception of intentional harm or the presence of an animate agent is not necessary to invoke anger. Anger is expressed because a person experiences an unexpected loss, failure, or aversive state and refuses to accept being in the resultant state. Refusal here means that the person believes that somehow the conditions surrounding the loss or aversive state can be changed so that the unpleasant state no longer exists. Thus, almost any type of loss or aversive state can evoke anger when a belief about goal reinstatement exists.

The intentional harm component associated with anger may be a function of socialization. In most societies, anger is not condoned because the plan accom-panying anger is often destructive and harmful to others. In some societies, actions carried out under the influence of anger are often thought to indicate insanity (Averill, 1979; Tavris, 1982) or the lack of the ability to reason. There-fore certain forms of anger are acceptable only in young children who have not yet been accorded the status of a reasoning and thinking person (Lutz, 1985a, 1985b). However, when children reach the age of 6 or 7, they are taught that anger is a permissible emotion, but only under certain conditions. The dis-tinguishing dimension that is used to teach children when anger can be expressed is directly associated with intentional harm (Lutz, 1985a, 1985b). In fact, in the Ifaluk society, two different words are used to talk about anger. One refers to anger evoked without reason, and the other refers to justifiable anger cause by an agent who meant intentional harm.

Although sadness and anger often occur in response to the same event, sad-ness is different from anger in two respects. Sadness is experienced when a person believes that a goal cannot be reinstated. Although people who experience sadness often desire to reinstate a failed goal (much like anger), the plan of action associated with sadness is one of goal abandonment or goal substitution. Here we make a distinction between the wishes that accompany an emotion and the plans of action that are activated by goal failure. When people suffer major losses such that they no longer have access to a valued state, such as the loss of a loved one, they soon recognize that no possibility exists for them ever to reinstate their goal (e.g., to regain the relationship in the literal sense). Under these conditions, however, the desire to reinstate the goal does not necessarily recede or become less important. Because a multitude of memories are associated with loved ones, the desire to have them back or to interact with them again often remains ever present. A good example of this desire was expressed by the comedian George Burns (1988), who confessed to the fact that once a month when he visited Gracie Allen's grave he sat and talked to her about everything that was happening to him. In fact, he admitted that he had been doing this for 24 years, since Gracie had died. This is not uncommon behavior on the part of many individuals (Worden, 1982). The social condemnation that goes along with it, however, inhibits most individuals from expressing their real desires and thoughts.

In many instances, the uniqueness of a love object determines whether the desire to reinstate the goal abates. If the love object is deemed irreplaceable, the desire to recreate the original conditions before the loss remains strong. Although this type of desire is deemed unrealistic (i.e., the focus of attention is on the recreation of conditions that are no longer possible), positive value can be attributed to this type of thinking. By recreating previous situations that were highly valued, an opportunity exists to examine exactly what it was about the situation that proved to be so important. By focusing on these critical features, wishes and plans can gradually be constructed to substitute a goal for the permanently blocked goal.

Wishes and plans to abandon the goal can also occur. Many times, goal failure results in such intense distress, as well as sadness, that the goal is abandoned without a desire to reinstate or substitute a similar goal. For example, in many athletic competitions, the athletes who lose will not try to compete again. They feel that they've given the competition their best shot and interpret their losing as irrevocable under any condition. Thus, the goal to become the top athlete is permanently abandoned, and no future attempts are made.

So far, we have described the evaluation and planning processes associated with anger and sadness. One more phenomenon with respect to these two emotions deserves discussion. Not only do the same events provoke these two emotions, but often both emotions are expressed in reaction to a loss or aversive state. In our model, the expression of more than one emotion to a precipitating event is not only feasible but increasingly likely, especially as a function of development. The reason for the occurrence of multiple emotions is that a precipitating event can change the probability of attaining or maintaining more than one goal. Anger can be expressed in regard to one goal and sadness to another.

The prototypic context in which both emotions are expressed is one of loss, where the loss is brought about by intentional harm (Stein & Levine, 1989). For example, when Johnny found out that his friend smashed his favorite toy to pieces, at least three different emotional responses could be expressed: Johnny could be sad, angry, or both sad and angry. On the one hand, Johnny is sad because his favorite toy has been destroyed, and he feels that it is irreplaceable. Thus, even though he would like the toy fixed, he knows that it's impossible to repair it, so sadness is expressed. On the other hand, Johnny feels really angry because he recognized that his friend intentionally destroyed his favorite toy. In doing this, his friend violated either an unwritten or explicit code about what friends are and are not allowed to do. Moreover, the violation of this code resulted in direct harm, and Johnny perceived this act as a threat to other important goals. He also felt that his friend could repeat the harmful act in other situations.

Thus, loss caused by an agent intending harm generates changes in the status of several goals. One set of changes focuses on the loss of a valued object and the goals associated with its reinstatement. Another set of changes focuses on the relationship between Johnny and his friend. The violation of the "friendship" code results in the realization that Johnny cannot trust his friend in other situations. Moreover, the fact that his friend was responsible for breaking the toy evoked a desire to have the friend recompensate him in some way. It is interesting to note that anger responses to irrevocable loss often involve getting the harmful agent to engage in some kind of behavior that promotes the substitution of a goal by the injured party. For example, Johnny's response to the loss of his toy was to demand that his friend reimburse him for the cash amount of the toy. According to Johnny, the only way the friendship could ever be restored was for his friend to pay for the broken toy. Moreover, his friend had to "promise" that he would never again engage in another harmful act directed toward Johnny.

There are many instances of anger where the primary goal of the injured party is simply to destroy the agent who caused intentional harm. However, this is not necessarily the prototypic anger response (Tavris, 1982). For revenge strategies to be initiated, specific inferences must be made about the aggressor. The first concerns the value the victim places on the aggressor, and the second focuses on the degree of harm the aggressor can still inflict on the victim. If the victim believes that the aggressor will actively seek to carry out harmful acts in the future and if the victim believes that the aggressor's behavior cannot be changed, then the solution of destroying the aggressor or destroying the aggressor's power might emerge. Indeed, we can generate many examples of these solutions by examining intense family conflict, where the majority of violent acts are committed. In the prototypic anger situation, however, the goal of the victim is to reinstate the original conditions that existed before the loss or aversive state occurred (Stein & Jewett, 1986). The restoration of conditions focuses on both those that pertain to the loss (if possible) and to the relationship that exists between the victim and the aggressor.

To test many of these ideas, we (Stein & Levine, 1989) carried out an empirical study with 3- and 6-year-old children as well as a group of college students. The task for all subjects was to respond to several different events by thinking out loud and by answering questions that focused on the causes of three different emotions: happiness, sadness, and anger. The events used to elicit these three emotions were constructed to mirror four different types of goal–outcome relationships: (a) the attainment of valued states; (b) the avoidance of undesirable states; (c) the loss of a valued state; and (d) failure to avoid an undesired state. The valued states focused on acquiring or losing a favorite toy car or a puppy. Unpleasant states focused on having to eat a disliked food (spinach) or having to be outside when it was very cold. The type of event that caused these states also varied such that the end states resulted as a function of: (a) another person intentionally causing the outcome, (b) another accidentally causing the outcome, or (c) a physical event causing the outcome.

All subjects were asked a series of questions regarding their feeling states, their first thoughts after the event occurred, the reasons for their feelings, the type of wish they would have in response to coping with the situation, the plans they would devise to carry out, and explanations for their choice of actions. In other words, each subject was guided through all the parts of an emotion episode related to a causal theory of emotional understanding. Although many investigators have described theoretical constructs for examining the process of emotional experience, the specific processes that are actually carried out with respect to the encoding, representation, and retrieval of information have yet to be described. Thus, we chose to structure our interview to reflect the various processes associated with the sequence of representing and understanding emotional experience.

Figure 3.3 contains the proportion of anger responses reported in each causal condition (physical event, animate agent causing intentional harm, animate agent causing unintentional harm) for each type of negative outcome (loss versus aversive state). Anger was chosen more frequently in all conditions when the

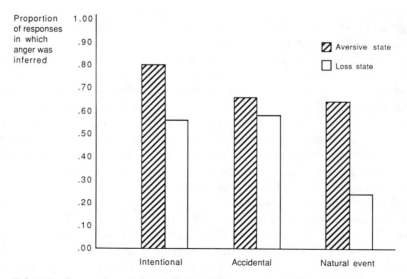

FIG. 3.3.   Proportion of responses in which anger was inferred in each causal condition and in episodes ending in loss and aversive states.

3. MAKING SENSE OUT OF EMOTION

episodes ended with an aversive rather than a loss state. The type of causal agent, however, did affect the proportion of anger responses. When an animate agent intentionally or unintentionally caused the story protagonist to suffer a loss, anger responses were more frequent than when a natural event caused the loss. Thus, the mere presence of an animate agent was enough to increase the frequency of anger responses in loss states. When an intentionally harmful agent put the story protagonist into an aversive state, the frequency of anger responses increased significantly in proportion to the frequency in aversive conditions where accidental harm resulted. Thus, the concept of agency is important in ascribing anger to others, but the type of goal failure is also a powerful predictor of anger. Thus, our results are similar to those of Berkowitz and Heimer (1989), who contend that aversive events indeed prime anger, irritation, and hostility across a variety of contexts.

If anger is elicited by the perception that harm has occurred and that an unpleasant state exists, then the immediate goal will be to focus on the removal of the unpleasant state. Desiring a change in the existing conditions should be especially true in situations of an aversive painful nature. In fact, our results supported this hypothesis. When aversive states resulted and the emotion inferred was one of anger, over 76% of all subjects desired to reinstate the goal. However, the plans of action adopted were often associated with abandoning the goal rather than reinstating it. For example, in one of our scenarios, subjects were told that a protagonist would have to eat spinach for dinner because there was no other food in the house. Under these circumstances, the clear majority of subjects expressed anger at having to eat a food that was intensely disliked. On the other hand, most adopted plans of action where the protagonist ate the disliked food. When spinach was all there was to eat in the house, many subjects stated that the thought of not eating anything was worse than eating the spinach. Thus, in actuality plans to abandon the goal were enacted.

These data strongly suggest that the planning process associated with specific emotions is more complex than originally described. Although anger and sadness carry definite wishes of goal reinstatement, the plans that accompany the two emotions are often constrained by an assessment of how the desired plan of action will affect the achievement of other goals. If the desired plan will result in a more general failure experience such that more goals become unattainable, then the normal plan associated with an emotion will not be enacted. Thus, reasoning about possible conflict among goals becomes an important concern in future work on emotional experience.

Furthermore, what needs to be examined is the effect of repeated anger in situations where the aversive state continues over time. In our study, subjects had to make predictions about other people's behavior when aversive states were experienced on a one-time basis. For example, our scenarios had protagonists having to eat spinach because of a snow storm or because one's mother forgot to buy a favorite food at the store. Although these aversive states were permanent, in the sense that, for the moment, subjects chose to tolerate them in order to avoid other unpleasant states, it is unclear what would happen if subjects were exposed to aversive states on a continual basis. If someone had to eat spinach everyday and initially disliked it, the ensuing response might change from one of toleration to one where specific action was taken to end the aversive state. If no action could be taken, the option of not maintaining other important goals might be made. Under these conditions, anger responses could easily become ones of sadness.

CONCLUSIONS

The approach we are advocating in the study of emotion is one where the achievement of specific goals are tracked over time in order to assess how success or failure of one goal affects the maintenance of other goals. Moreover, the way in which subjects react to repeated success or failure must be assessed. Something is learned each time a person attempts to achieve a goal and either succeeds or fails. If subjects succeed at attaining a valued goal, the initial focus of attention is typically on the positive consequences that ensue from success. Moreover, a feeling of relaxation often accompanies positive feeling states because effort is no longer needed to plan for successful goal attainment. In fact, Schwarz (1988) proposes that happy states lead to rather mindless behavior. Happy people are not as evaluative of other people's actions as angry people are. Moreover, assessing the conditions that led to goal success does not appear to be as frequent as when failure occurs.

These findings may hold for the initial period immediately following goal success. However, success also requires maintenance activities. When subjects realize that an effort has to be made to maintain valued goals, then an analysis of the conditions that led to goal success should be of central importance. If goal-related activities have not been successful, the initial focus of attention should be on attempts to understand and control the conditions that might lead to goal success. If, however, repeated attempts at goal attainment end in failure, the typical reaction might be one of assessing the consequences of failure rather than focusing on conditions that led to failure. What we are suggesting is that the degree of uncertainty associated with goal maintenance might regulate the type of thinking carried out subsequent to an emotional reaction rather than the valence of the expressed emotion.

Furthermore, different negative emotions such as sadness, anger, and fear have very different effects on subsequent thinking and reasoning activities. Although each of these emotions is defined as negative, each carries with it a different plan of action (Stein & Jewett, 1986; Stein & Levine, 1987). Anger and fear are both active emotions in that plans are oriented toward goal reinstatement or maintenance. However, the two are different. Anger tends to orient people toward an assessment of the conditions that would result in a reinstatement of the goal. This desire often leads people to assess the conditions that actually caused goal failure so that any obstacle can be removed. Thus, thinking about angry situations tends to promote backward thinking.

Fear, on the other hand, is oriented toward maintaining valued goal states (Stein & Jewett, 1986). Specifically, self-preservation, either psychological or physical, is at stake. Thus attention is focused primarily on methods to ensure self-preservation. Often, this desire leads to a plan of removing the self from the threatening situation. Therefore, the conditions that led to the threatening situation are not assessed. Rather, plans for preventing harm are central. Given that the focus of attention is different for fear and anger, we are curious as to how each of these emotions would affect subsequent thinking on tasks unrelated to the experience of the emotion. Moreover, we would ask how the immediacy of formulating a plan of action in each emotion state would affect subsequent thinking and reasoning.

And finally, the intensity of the emotional reaction should be an important predictor of thinking and reasoning. Intensity, as it is currently defined (Mandler, 1975, 1984), is most often associated with the importance of the goal at stake. However, the amount of effort that needs to be expended in carrying out goal activities, as well as the necessity to act quickly, may also be pertinent in assessments of intensity. The important point, however, is that the intensity of an emotional reaction restricts the amount of attention that can be given to subsequent thinking activities. As Rachman (1978) has noted, the intensity of a fear response precludes processing any extraneous information to a great extent. Rather, attention becomes narrowed to specific dimensions of the situation related to expected impending harm.

REFERENCES

Averill, J. R. (1979). Anger. In H. E. Howe & R. A. Dienstbier (Eds.), *Nebraska Symposium on Motivation: Human Emotions* (Vol. 26, pp. 1–80). Lincoln: University of Nebraska Press.

Berkowitz, L., & Heimer, K. (1989). Aversive events and negative priming in the formation of feelings. In L. Berkowitz (Ed.), *Advances in experimental social psychology.* New York: Academic Press.

Bower, G., & Cohen, P. R. (1982). Emotional influences in memory and thinking: Data and theory. In M. S. Clark & S. T. Fiske (Eds.), *Affect and Cognition: 17th Annual Carnegie Symposium on Cognition.* Hillsdale, NJ: Lawrence Erlbaum Associates.

Burns, G. (1988). Gracie: A love story. New York: Putnam.

Ekman, P. (1977). Biological and cultural contribution to body and facial movements. In J. Blocking (Ed.), *Anthropology of the body.* London: Academic Press.

Emde, R. (1980). Levels of meaning in infant development. In W. A. Collins (Ed.), *Minnesota Symposium on Child Psychology* (Vol. 13). Hillsdale, NJ: Lawrence Erlbaum Associates.

Fernald, A. (1984). The perceptual and affective salience of mothers' speech to infants. In L. Feagans, C. Garvey, & R. Golinkoff (Eds.), with M. T. Greenberg, C. Harding, & J. Bohannon, *The origins and growth of communication.* Norwood, NJ: Ablex.

Folkman, S., and Lazarus, R. S. (in press). Coping and emotion. In N. L. Stein, B. Leventhal, & T. Trabasso (Eds.), *Psychological and biological approaches to emotion.* Hillsdale, N.J.: Lawrence Erlbaum Associates.

Gallistel, C. R. (1985). Motivation, intention, and emotion: Goal-directed behavior from a cognitive neuroethological perspective. In M. Frese & J. Sabini (Eds.), *Goal-directed behavior: The concept of action in psychology.* Hillsdale, NJ: Lawrence Erlbaum Associates.

Isen, A. (1984). Toward understanding the role of affect in cognition. In R. Wyer & T. Srull (Eds.), *Handbook of social cognition* (Vol. 3, pp. 179–236) Hillsdale, NJ: Lawrence Erlbaum Associates.

Isen, A. (1987). Toward understanding the role of affective cognition. In R. S. Wyer & T. S. Srull (Eds.), *Handbook of social cognition* (Vol. 3). Hillsdale, NJ: Lawrence Erlbaum Associates.

Johnson, E. J., & Tversky, A. (1983). Affect, generalization, and the perception of risk. *Journal of Personality and Social Psychology, 45,* 20–31.

Lazarus, R. S., & Folkman, S. (1984). *Stress, appraisal, and coping.* New York: Springer.

Lutz, C. (1985a). Ethnopsychology compared to what? Explaining behavior and consciousness among the Ifaluk. In G. M. White & J. Kirkpatrick (Eds.), *Person, self, and experience: Exploring pacific ethnopsychologies.* Berkeley: University of California Press.

Lutz, C. (1985b). Cultural patterns and individual differences in the child's emotion meaning system. In M. Lewis & C. Saarni (Eds.), *The socialization of affect* (pp. 161–186). New York: Plenum Press.

Mandler, G. (1975). *Mind and emotion.* New York: Wiley.

Mandler, G. (1982). The structure of value: Accounting for taste. In M. S. Clark & S. T. Fiske (Eds.), *Affect and cognition: 17th Annual Carnegie Symposium on Cognition.* Hillsdale, NJ: Lawrence Erlbaum Associates.

Mandler, G. (1984). *Mind and body: Psychology of emotion and stress.* New York: Norton.

Mandler, J. (1988). How to build a baby: On the development of an accessible representation system. *Cognitive Development, 3,* 113–136.

Piaget, J. (1981). *Intelligence and affectivity.* Palo Alto, CA: Annual Reviews.

Rachman, S. J. (1978). *Fear and courage.* San Francisco: W. H. Freeman.

Roseman, I. J. (1979). *Cognitive aspects of emotion and emotional behavior.* Paper presented at the American Psychological Association Meetings, New York.

Roseman, I. J. (1984). Cognitive determinants of emotions: A structural theory. In P. Shaver (Ed.), *Review of personality and social psychology: Emotions, relationships, and health* (Vol. 5, pp. 11–36). Beverly Hills: Sage.

Scherer, K. R. (1984). On the nature and function of emotion: A component process approach. In K. R. Scherer & P. Ekman (Eds.), *Approaches to emotion.* Hillsdale, NJ: Lawrence Erlbaum Associates.

Schwarz, N. (1988, August). *Happy but mindless.* Paper presented at the Symposium: Affect and Cognition, 24th International Congress of Psychology, Sydney, Australia.

Sroufe, A. (1979). Socioemotional development. In J. Osofsky (Ed.), *The handbook of infant development.* New York: Wiley.

Stein, N. L. (1988). The development of storytelling skill. In M. B. Franklin & S. Barten (Eds.), *Child language: A book of readings.* New York: Cambridge University Press.

Stein, N. L., & Jewett, J. (1986). A conceptual analysis of the meaning of negative emotions: Implications for a theory of development. In C. E. Izard & P. Read (Eds.), *Measurement of emotion in infants and children* (Vol. 2, pp. 238–267). New York: Cambridge University Press.

Stein, N. L., & Levine, L. J. (1987). Thinking about feelings: The development and organization of emotional knowledge. In R. E. Snow & M. Farr (Eds.), *Aptitude, learning, and instruction: Cognition, conation and affect* (Vol. 3, pp. 165–198). Hillsdale, NJ: Lawrence Erlbaum Associates.

Stein, N. L., & Levine, L. J. (1989). The causal organization of emotional knowledge: A developmental study. *Cognition and Emotion,* Special Issue on the Development of Emotion.

Stein, N. L., & Trabasso, T. (1989). Children's understanding of changing emotion states. In
C. Saarni & P. L. Harris (Eds.), *Children's understanding of emotion.* New York: Cambridge
University Press.

Tavris, C. (1982). Anger: The misunderstood emotion. New York: Simon & Shuster.

Weiner, B. (1985). An attributional theory of achievement motivation and emotion. *Psychological
Review, 92* (4), 548–573.

Worden, J. W. (1982). *Grief counseling and grief therapy.* New York: Springer.

Zajonc, R. (1980). Feeling and thinking: Preferences need no inferences. *American Psychologist,
35,* 151–175.

4

The Influence of Positive and Negative Affect on Cognitive Organization: Some Implications for Development

Alice M. Isen
Cornell University

The purpose of this chapter is to consider the impact that feelings can have on cognitive structure and organization, and to examine some of the implications of these effects for the development of affect, cognition, and social behavior. In particular, the chapter focuses on two points: first, the asymmetry between happiness and sadness in effects on memory and the implications of this asymmetry for matters of cognitive structure related to affect; and second, the influence of positive affect on creative problem solving, remote associations, and integration of diverse material—what might be called cognitive flexibility—and the implications of this kind of process for cognitive and affective structure.

This volume addresses the integration of psychological and biological approaches to the study of emotional development. I have chosen to discuss the topics just described because they raise interesting questions about the development of affect and the impact of affective experience on subsequent emotional, cognitive, and social development. At the same time, they seem to be somewhat puzzling points, not well explained by current cognitive models, that might benefit from an integration of psychological and biological approaches to understanding emotion.

In conjunction with each topic, then, it is of interest to consider two questions about affect, looking in two directions, about origins and about likely effects: (1) What kinds of processes might underlie and *give rise* to the effects of feelings that are being discussed; and (2) what do these effects suggest the influence of affective experiences on *subsequent* affective and cognitive development might be?

The first topic addressed is the asymmetry in the influence of happiness and sadness on memory. A growing body of research indicates that positive affect facilitates retrieval of positive material in memory (e.g., Isen, Shalker, Clark, & Karp, 1978; Laird, Wagener, Halal, & Szegda, 1982; Nasby & Yando, 1982; Natale & Hantas, 1982; Riskind, 1983; Teasdale & Fogarty, 1979; Teasdale & Russell, 1983; Teasdale, Taylor, & Fogarty, 1980; see Isen, 1984, for more complete review and discussion of the affect-memory findings). However, most of the studies that report such effects, and that attempt simultaneously to investigate the influence of comparable sadness on recall of negative material, report a nonsymmetrical effect of sadness and happiness (e.g., Isen et al., 1978; Nasby & Yando, 1982; Natale & Hantas, 1982; Riskind, 1983; Teasdale & Fogarty, 1979; Teasdale et al., 1980; see Isen, 1984, for a more complete review of these findings); that is, sadness either fails to facilitate the recall of negative material, or it is less effective as a retrieval cue than positive feelings.

These kinds of comparisons are inherently difficult to make because it is hard to be sure that equivalent amounts of negative and positive affect are induced. For example, it might be argued that more positive than negative affect was induced in the studies described, and that this is the reason that positive feelings were effective but negative were not. This could occur in either of two ways: It might be that the positive-affect induction was more intense or more effective than the negative-affect induction. Or it is possible that positive- and negative-affect inductions desagned to be equally intense and effective nonetheless produced different degrees of affect and that, for this reason, a Greater degree of positive than negative affect was present.

However, such interpretations based on methodological considerations would not seem to dispel the issue of the asymmetry between positive and negative affect in their effects on memory, because of the growing number of studies reporting asymmetrical findings. In many studies, attempts have been made to induce comparable affective states of opposite sign; that is, most studies that attempt to investigate effects of happiness and sadness use parallel procedures—for example, success versus failure on the same task, reading of positive statements versus reading of negative statements such as are contained in the Velten (1968) mood induction procedure, or association to positive words versus negative words. In many cases, pretests indicate that the induction materials and response stimuli are equivalent in affective extremity or in the degree of affect that they generate (e.g., Isen, Johnson, Mertz, & Robinson, 1985). Often, however, these comparable procedures fail to induce equivalent amounts of affect (e.g., Isen et al., 1985). If procedures designed to induce comparable affects consistently fail to do so, perhaps there is more than just a methodological reason for the difference. Moreover, this body of literature indicates that sometimes even when comparable degrees of affect are induced, at least as indicated by questionnaires assessing self-ratings of affect (manipulation checks), the effects of happiness and sadness on cognitive processes may still not be equivalent.

Thus, the growing body of literature indicating asymmetry between happiness and sadness may reflect genuine differences between these kinds of states, and it may be worth investigating the situation in greater detail.

It has been suggested that this asymmetry may reflect a difference in the way in which negative versus positive material is organized in memory or is accessed from memory (Isen, 1985). That is, negative and positive material in mind may be structured differently, in, for example, internal consistency or interrelatedness with other material; and/or these classes of material may differ in the amount of each that is available in memory, in total. More specifically, the negative structures may be smaller, more specific, and less well interconnected with other material. Thus, a particular affect such as sadness may not be an effective retrieval cue for the whole class of material that might be considered negative but rather may cue only a very limited set of material that is specifically related to sadness. In contrast, positive material may be more extensive and well interconnected, so that any given positive feeling state more readily cues a wide variety of positive material. This suggestion would be compatible with the observed asymmetry between negative and positive affect in ability to cue material of generally like valence.

Another possible interpretation of the asymmetry noted is that it may reflect differences in peoples' strategies for coping with, or enjoying, their affective states. Thus, it may be that people who are feeling happy try to think about affect-compatible material, in part because that will allow them to maintain their positive states, but that, in contrast, those who are feeling sad are motivated to think about affect-incompatible material because they want to change their feelings. This suggestion, too, would be compatible with the asymmetry that has been observed, but it would suggest that one should expect difficulty in finding sadness to cue material even if the material is specific to the affect state. These ideas are discussed at greater length elsewhere (Isen, 1985, 1987).

It should be noted that the distinction between structure and process is not a clear one, and that these two possibilities are not mutually exclusive. Use of certain strategies or processes can contribute to the creation of certain kinds of structures; and the existence of certain kinds of structures can promote the use of processes and strategies that are especially compatible with those structures. Thus, these two interpretations may both be valid.

Moreover, the very term *structure* may be misleading, because it suggests a firm, unchanging edifice. It may be possible, instead, to view what we think of as structure, in process terms—as ways of relating ideas, sometimes involving plans or blueprints for action. Thus, cognition would consist of processes and relationships, but the relationships would be seen as changeable, better described as "relationships for a given purpose, under a given set of conditions"; and cognitive organization could be seen as flexible and changing, depending on circumstances, context, goals of the person, and so forth. This suggestion is compatible with the contextualist position in cognitive psychology, rather than with more associationistic models of cognition, which holds that cognition is dependent on a person's interpretation of stimuli—the meaning of the stimulus to the person—which in turn depends on aspects of the entire context in which the stimulus is experienced (e.g., Bartlett, 1932; Bransford, 1979; Jenkins, 1974). Recent research in cognitive psychology suggests, compatibly with this view, that cognitive structure or organization (relationships among sets of material) can change in response to other factors in the situation (e.g., Isen & Daubman, 1984; Medin, 1983; Murphy & Medin, 1985; Roth & Shoben, 1983), and this, then, implies that the distinction between structure and process may not be a firm one.

Although the cognitive and strategic interpretations may not be completely independent, as noted before, still they may have some different implications. For example, if the asymmetry between positive and negative affect is due to differences in the structure of the material cued (elaborated and well-interconnected vs. specific and isolated), then structuring studies so that more specific material is presented to subjects might result in negative affect successfully cueing the negative material in these studies. However, if the failure of negative affect to cue negative material is due to a motivational factor such as a desire to improve feelings, then making the to-be-recalled stimuli more similar to the source of the negative affect should not facilitate the recall process and, in fact, might even make cueing less likely, as the person fights harder to avoid thinking about the negative-affect-relevant (and possibly negative-affect-inducing) material.

The idea that negative and positive affective material may be organized differently has led recently to studies intended to see whether it is possible to identify sets of negative material that might be cued by various negative affective states, in particular sadness and anger (Stephens & Isen, 1986). The idea underlying this work is that negative material may be represented in a less extensive, less elaborated, less well-interconnected structure than positive. If this is the case, then the ability of the negative state to cue the material might be dependent on there being a more exact relationship between the affective state and the material to be recalled than is true in the case of positive affect, or than is true in the existing studies of sadness as a retrieval cue. Thus, although sadness has not tended to be an effective retrieval cue generally in the existing studies, it may be that sadness will be found to cue negative material that is more specifically structured to be precisely related to that state.

Results of the studies on this topic are still preliminary, because procedures and materials are still being refined; however, the preliminary results may be of interest: In one study anger has been found to facilitate recall of specifically anger-related words, but so far sadness has not been effective. One possibility is that sadness may be related to self-concept, and that the negative material to be cued may need to relate to self-concept in order to be cued by sadness. This would be compatible with some theories of affect that suggest that self-concept plays a central role in affect (e.g., Lewis & Michaelson, 1983). Thus, we have not yet found sadness to facilitate recall of material in memory, but more refinement of materials is needed, and in addition there are still some theoretically sensible alternative possibilities to be tried. These preliminary results are somewhat promising, however, because of the success with anger. Perhaps sadness is different from other negative affects in this regard, but it is too soon to tell. Hopefully, there will be more to report on these matters soon.

In any case, independent of whether sadness ever serves as a retrieval cue for any material, and what eventually has to be done in order to observe it, if it does, the implications of these preliminary findings for the cognitive representation of affect are interesting. They suggest that negative affect may be relatively narrowly and specifically organized or represented in memory. And the individual negative affects (e.g., anger, sadness) may be differentiated still further in this way.

The effects observed with positive affect, on the other hand, are in marked contrast to those observed with negative affect. Good feelings appear to cue readily a wide range of positive material. For a long time it has been known that positive material is broad ranging and extensive relative to other kinds of material. Studies of word association, for example, over several decades have shown that people give more association to positive *words* than to other words, and that the pool of associates to positive words is larger (e.g., see Cramer, 1968, for a review of this literature). More recently it has also been shown that a positive affective *state* also increases the diversity of word associations, to neutral words (Isen et al., 1985). Thus, there is reason to believe that positive affect, in contrast with negative, has a large and well-interconnected structure or set of material associated with it.

In addition, it now appears that positive affect may also cue other themes as well as specifically "positive" material. A recent study has obtained results suggesting that positive affect cues *social* material even if that material is neutral in affective tone (Isen, Herren, & Geva, 1986). This study found that persons in whom positive affect had been induced (by a gift of a small bag of candy) showed better recall for neutral social adjectives (as identified by Rosenberg and Sedlack's (1972) multidimensional scaling of trait adjectives) than of other neutral adjectives, and that they recalled them better than did a control group. This suggests that social material is part of the schema or network or image that is cued by positive affect. This is not to say that this material—social material—is positive. The words used in this study were words that had been judged to be neutral, according to Anderson's (1968) ratings of the likeability of trait words, and equivalent in affective tone with the nonsocial words used. (For example, the social words included words such as "bashful," "social," "passive," and "naive"; the nonsocial words included "normal," "precise," "persistent," and "changeable.") For some other reason, not positive affective tone, neutral social words appear related to positive affect (that is, they are primed and rendered accessible by a positive affective state). If this result holds up, it may suggest that certain themes are intimately related to affect (at least positive affect), and this may have important implications regarding the development of affect.

The result in this particular case may be attributable to the social nature of the way in which affect was induced (a gift); and therefore it would seem important to investigate whether positive affect induced by means of a nonsocial method would also cue social material. Nonetheless, this study highlights the possibility that cognitive domains not specifically affective in content may be, or may become, part of the positive-affect schema, either generally or under specified conditions that may frequently occur in everyday life.

These points—that negative affect seems to be specifically organized cognitively, whereas positive affect appears to be more globally organized—raise a more basic theoretical issue regarding how affective material is structured in the mind, and perhaps—even more fundamentally—about cognitive structure in general. But it might be helpful to defer consideration of these fundamental questions until later in the chapter, so that we can relate them also to questions raised by the findings regarding cognitive flexibility, which is the topic discussed next.

The second point to be considered is the fact that positive affect tends to facilitate creativity, remote associations, perception of relatedness among cognitions, and other indications of integration and cognitive flexibility (Isen, 1987; Isen, Daubman, & Nowicki, 1987; Isen et al., 1985). As noted earlier, there is evidence that positive material is more extensive, far ranging, and well interconnected than other material (e.g., Cramer, 1968). Recent studies also suggest that positive affect may result in more flexible thinking and a more integrated organization of cognitive material (neutral cognitive material), as well. This effect has been demonstrated using tasks involving categorization, word association, similarity and difference judgment, and creative problem solving.

For example, persons in whom positive affect has been induced tended significantly to categorize a wider range of neutral stimuli together, as reflected by either of two measures, a rating task or a sorting task (Isen & Daubman, 1984). The rating task was fashioned after that used by Eleanor Rosch (1975) to study prototypicality. In this task people were asked to rate on a scale from 1 to 10 the degree to which they felt an item was a member of a category. Results showed that those in whom positive affect had been induced rated nontypical exemplars (that is, words like "camel," "feet" and "elevator" in the category "Vehicle") more as members of the category than did subjects in a control group. Similarly, in the sorting task, people in whom positive affect had been induced sorted the stimuli into larger groupings than did control subjects, when asked to sort the materials into groups of items that could go together. This was true for three different types of stimuli: colors, animal names, and trait words. In a more recent study, it has also been found that, if given multiple trials and asked how many different ways the items can be organized, positive-affect subjects, in contrast with controls, sort stimuli (in this case, self-stimuli) into more *different* groupings (Isen, 1987); that is, they identify more different dimensions along which to sort the stimuli, and they combine the items in more different ways.

Thus, it seems that people are more cognitively flexible and more able to see dimensions and see potential relations among stimuli with they feel happy than at other times.

Evidence supportive of this suggestion also comes from studies of word association and creative problem solving. A recent series of studies shows, for example, that persons who are happy give more unusual and more diverse first associates to neutral stimulus words than do people in control conditions (Isen et al., 1985). For example, when given the stimulus word, "house," people in positive-affect conditions (induced in any of four ways: being offered refreshments, being asked to give associates to positive words, being shows 5 minutes of a comedy film, or being given a small bag of candy as a gift) tended significantly more than control subjects to respond with related but uncommon words such as "residence" or "apartment," rather than with the most common associate listed in the corpus of norms (Palermo & Jenkins, 1964), "home." For another example, to "carpet" they tended to give responses such as "plush," "living room," and "texture" instead of the most common associate, "rug." These examples are intended to illustrate that the unusual responding of persons in the positive-affect conditions was not an artifact of their giving unrelated positive words (that is, responding only to their positive feelings), but rather that, as a group, their associations to the target words were more far ranging and their thoughts more flexible. The fact that their responses were more *diverse* than those of control subjects also suggests that this interpretation is appropriate, because the diversity measure indicates the variety of responses within each group, independent of any standard norms for the word associations typical of a given word. This means that, within the positive-affect group, to a greater extent than within the control group, subjects responded with more *different* associates to a given word.

This suggestion that people who are happy are more flexible in the way they see relations among things and organize cognitive material is also supported by the results of studies showing that people in whom positive affect has been induced are more innovative and more effective in solving problems requiring creativity (e.g., Isen et al., 1988). Most current conceptualizations of "creativity" view it as involving the bringing together of diverse material in a useful, new way, or the combining of different "frames of reference" (e.g., Koestler, 1964; Mednick, 1962). The studies mentioned indicate that persons in whom positive affect has been induced, by receipt of a small bag of candy, by watching 5 minutes of a comedy film, or by reading and focusing on statements reflective of feeling good, are better able to solve tasks usually considered to require creativity, in this case Duncker's (1945) candle task and the Mednicks' (M. T. Mednick, S. A. Mednick, & E. V. Mednick, 1964) Remote Associates Test.

The "candle task" is the one used by Karl Duncker (1945) in his demonstrations of what he called *functional fixedness*. It is usually considered to require innovation or a creative solution. In this task the subject is presented with a box of tacks, a candle, and a book of matches and is asked to attach the candle to the wall (a cork board) in such a way that it can be lighted and will burn without dripping wax on the table or floor beneath (and without setting fire to the wall and building, of course). This problem can be solved in the box containing the tacks is emptied, tacked to the wall, and used as a platform for the candle, like a candleholder.

Our studies indicated, as observed previously, that the normal rate of solution of this task is very low (about 15%), but that positive affect induced by means of a comedy film (5 minutes of "bloopers") could facilitate performance on it. Another treatment that aided performance on this task was presenting the materials for the task in a display that disrupted one's usual way of thinking about the box (as a holder of tacks). This display, similar to that used by Adamson (1952), had the items arrayed with the box emptied of tacks and the tacks in a pile next to it.

A second study suggested that arousal alone did not produce the same facilitative effect on solution of this problem. It is hard to know exactly how to represent "arousal," but one way that is sometimes used is physical exercise (e.g., Zillmann, 1979). Thus, this study included a condition in which subjects exercised (2 minutes of the step exercise—stepping up and down on a cinderblock, which on average raises heartrate by more than 50%). Also included was a negative affect condition, which might also be thought of as "arousal," from another perspective. (Negative affect was induced by viewing a shocking 5-minute segment of "Night and Fog," a French documentary of the Nazi death camps.) Rates of solution in these two conditions were not significantly different from that of the control condition (and were significantly different from that of the comedy-film condition).

The second task that was used to examine the influence of positive affect on creative problem solving or cognitive flexibility was based on the Mednicks' (1964) Remote Associates Test. This test was designed as an individual-difference measure of creativity, in accord with Mednick's (1962) theory that creativity involves the combination of elements that are remotely associated. As noted previously, this view of creativity is compatible with others generally adopted in the literature.

This test presents subjects with three words and a blank line, and they are asked to provide, in the blank, a word that relates to each of the three words given in the item. An example of a Remote Associates Test item is

MOWER   ATOMIC   FOREIGN   (POWER)

Results of three studies using Remote Associates Test items of moderate difficulty indicated that positive affect can improve people's performance on this second measure of creativity or cognitive flexibility. Affect induced by viewing 5 minutes of the comedy film, by receipt of a gift of a small bad of candy (10 wrapped hard candies in a sandwich bag decorated with cartoon figures and tied with a colorful piece of yarn), or by reading statements designed to reflect happy feelings in college students, facilitated performance on this task.

One of the studies included an "arousal" condition in which, as before, subjects had been asked to exercise (the step test) for 2 minutes; but the results indicated that this condition did not facilitate performance on the task (Isen et al., 1987). Another of the studies included negative-affect inductions of anger and anxiety induced by reading statements reflective of those states in college students, and of tension induced by music. None of these conditions influenced performance on the Remote Associates Test, but again the candy induction facilitated performance, as did the positive-statements condition. Most recently, preliminary results of another study suggest that negative affect induced by focusing on negative self-statements may *impair* performance on this task, although (compatibly with the findings of previous studies inducing negative affect) a condition in which negative affect was induced by having participants read statements reflective of tension did not differ from the control group.

These studies, then, indicate that positive affect promotes cognitive flexibility. Because they included some examination of the effects of arousal and negative affect and indicated that these treatments did not have the same effect as positive feelings, they also suggest that there is something specific to good feelings that promotes this ability to think creatively or flexibly.

Although detailed discussion of the contrast between positive affect and arousal is beyond the scope of this chapter, this matter may merit some consideration (see Isen, 1984; Isen & Daubman, 1984; Isen et al., 1987; Isen & Hastorf, 1982; and Isen et al., 1985, for fuller discussion of this and related issues). Some readers may take issue with the neutral arousal condition as unconvincing, or unrepresentative of what is meant by "arousal" (perhaps something more like "anxiety"), and may think of the negative film used in the study as depressing rather than arousing (assuming those two states to be opposite or incompatible, despite the existence of phenomena such as "agitated depression" in the clinical literature). Therefore, it may seem to those people that "arousal" has not been studied in this work. I have referred to the negative film as arousing (or representing a more typical idea of arousal than the exercise manipulation) because it is upsetting and seems to involve anxiety, disgust, and related affects that are usually thought of as agitating or arousing. The film clip is certainly shocking and horrifying. In addition, in more recent studies, as noted earlier, we have also included other negative-affect inductions that might also be considered to represent arousal (e.g., anxiety statements, anger statements, tension music). None of these has resulted in improved performance on the Remote Associates Test.

Nonetheless, this discussion highlights the problem of trying to deal with the concept of arousal, because it is difficult to be sure exactly what arousal is, how it can be induced, and how it can be measured. Indeed, although some theorists have called for doing away with the concept of emotion in favor of arousal (e.g., Duffy, 1934, 1941), others suggest that "arousal" is too global a concept to be useful (e.g., Lacey, 1967, 1975; Lacey, Kagan, Lacey, & Moss, 1963). Several researchers point to the need for more precision in the use of the term, citing, for example, the need to distinguish between visceral and cortical arousal (e.g., Martindale, 1981; Sokolov, 1963). Scientists working on the topic point out that measures often presumed indicative of arousal, such as heart rate and electrodermal response, do not always correlate highly with one another, and that the significance of changes in such measures is not immediately apparent because they can be associated with a diverse range of psychological phenomena or responses (e.g., Lacey, 1967; Lacey et al., 1963). Moreover, if "arousal" is to be included in studies of cognitive functioning, researchers will have to develop not only reliable and valid ways of defining and measuring it, but also more precise measures than are typically employed. This is because the available literature suggests rather complex relationships between arousal and behavior, such as the inverted U-shaped function between arousal (e.g., anxiety) and performance (e.g., Berlyne, 1971; Yerkes & Dodson, 1908). This means, in that example, that both high and low levels of arousal are associated with impaired performance, and only the optimal, intermediate level of arousal is thought to facilitate performance. Thus, it will be necessary to measure arousal rather precisely, to have some way of determining not just relatively higher or lower arousal, but whether the optimal point is achieved or passed.

Moreover, in any discussion of the issue of arousal, the matter of the relationship between task complexity or novelty and optimal level of arousal must be considered. Studies from differing perspectives suggest that arousal should facilitate performance of routine or familiar or simple tasks but should impair performance on tasks requiring innovation or novel responding or solution of complex tasks (see, for example, Martindale, 1981; Matlin & Zajonc, 1968; and Zajonc, 1965 for discussion of the relationship between arousal and performance on novel vs. routine tasks; and Isen, 1984; Isen & Daubman, 1984; and Isen et al., 1985 for discussion of this matter specifically applied to the relationship between affect and performance on creative tasks). When all of the issues and available data are taken into consideration, it does not appear that the results of positive-affect inductions can be attributed simply to arousal (see especially Isen & Daubman, 1984; Isen et al., 1985 for discussion). Positive affect appears to facilitate novel responding and flexible cognitive organization in a way that other kinds of so-called "arousal" do not.

Indeed, it is not even clear that positive affect is arousing (its effects on task performance do not fit any simple model of arousal's impact on performance), although intuitively, of course, it seems arousing to us, based on our subjective feeling of energy when happy. It might be argued, however, that positive affect is relaxing or defocusing of attention rather than arousing or focusing of attention. That negative affect may serve to focus attention more specifically on certain material has been suggested by studies of, for example, cue utilization under conditions of high drive or arousal (e.g., Bruner, Matter, & Papanek, 1955), which indicate that the range of attention is more limited under those conditions.

Perhaps the concepts of focused versus defocused attention may be more helpful than "arousal" in understanding the impact of affective states on task performance (e.g., Isen, 1987; Martindale, 1981). In any case, it seems likely that happy feelings will need to be differentiated from other feelings in predicting effects on cognitive processes and behavior.

Finally, regarding the influence of good feelings on cognitive organization, three studies indicate that positive affect also influences young children's creative play, realization of relations among stimuli, and categorization processes. This suggests that affective experiences may thus play a very important role in the way children organize thoughts and come to see the world (Nevin, Isen, & Winer, 1988; Roelle, Winer, & Isen, 1986; Williams & Isen, 1988). In one study, nursery-schoolaged (average age 43 months, range 36–51 months) children who had been given five colorful paper "stickers" as a gift differed from controls in their ways of playing with a set of nesting cups (Williams & Isen, 1988). First, they correctly nested significantly more of the cups, indicating a greater ability to see the relations among a larger set of stimuli. Children in the control group averaged 1.48 cups nested, whereas those in the positive-affect condition averaged 2.63 cups nested. In addition, children in the positive-affect condition were significantly more likely than those in the control condition to turn the cups over and stack them (making a tower), thus indicating a difference between conditions in likelihood of basing play on a second dimension of the stimulus items.

Two additional studies indicated that positive affect can influence children's categorization processes. In one, positive affect was found to facilitate performance on Piaget's (Inhelder & Piaget, 1964) class-inclusion problem, in second- and third-grade children, mean ages 95 to 106 months, respectively (Nevin et al., 1988). This task is usually thought to involve the ability to deal with classes additively, to see the part–whole relationship between hierarchically related classes, or to hold in mind and work with two different hierarchical levels of classes simultaneously (Inhelder & Piaget, 1964). It has been suggested that these processes require multiple comparisons of classes and involve flexibility of thought (Nevin et al., 1988). Thus, it may be that these processes are facilitated in this study because positive affect promotes the tendency to see more potential relations among stimuli and concepts and to make multiple comparisons among them.

In this study, as in the previous one described (the nesting-cups experiment), it might be noted that positive affect and the processes it fosters resulted in an increase in children's ability to perform at a developmentally advanced level. This may be because positive affect promotes the development or use of more advanced skills or ways of approaching materials (such as complexity and flexibility in approach). However, because the developmental advances observed in these cases may be transitional or emerging ones (that is, ones on the verge of appearing), it may be that the effect occurs because positive affect increases the likelihood of less dominant responses appearing (e.g., Isen et al., 1985); that is, the flexibility promoted by positive affect may foster the emergence of transitional processes by increasing the likelihood of these incipient but still weak responses. Still, the mechanism would likely involve some process like flexibility and multiple comparison. But the effect might be limited to concepts and skills in transition. This remains to be investigated. However, because we observed the effect in both second-grade and third-grade children in the class-inclusion problem study, it may not be quite so limited. In any case, these results indicate an influence of positive affect on children's categorization processes.

Third, a pilot study also suggested another kind of influence of positive affect on children's categorization processes (Roelle et al., 1986). In this study, first-grade children were given 24 stimuli to sort. They were shown two boxes and told to put the items that were alike together and in the boxes, so that each box would contain items that were alike in one way. The set of stimuli contained three possible dimensions (to the adult eye): color, shape, and affect/face; that is, they were blue or white, squares or triangles, and contained on them either just a line or a line and two dots arranged to look like a smiling face.

In this study, on the first sort, children in whom positive affect had been induced by receipt of two colorful, paper "stickers" differed from control subjects in two ways: First, they were significantly more likely to sort the stimuli according to the affect/face dimension on their first round of sorting (10 of 12 positive-affect children, in contrast with 5 of 12 control subjects, did this). This difference is significant by a Fisher Exact Test ($p < .05$). Thus, it may be possible to say that affect may figure more prominently in the thinking processes of children who are happy—affect may be a more useful and salient dimension for a person, including a young child, who is feeling happy than it is for someone in a more neutral state. For young children this may also represent a developmental advance or acceleration, because they use a functional dimension rather than color on their first opportunity to sort.

Second, the children in whom positive affect had been induced produced significantly more "atypical" sorts. In these instances, the children divided the objects that they had placed within one box into two subcategories. For example, they often divided the smiling faces that they had placed in one box into white and blue piles within the box. These results suggest not only that affect may sensitize children to the affective dimension in stimuli, but they are also consistent with the suggestion that positive affect promotes cognitive flexibility—awareness of multiple categories or dimensions. It certainly shows that the children do not *lose* the other dimensions when they see the affective one. That the children created a way to express their view of the materials, even though it resulted in nontypical sorting, is also consistent with past research suggesting the possibility of more independence or freedom in the behavior of persons in whom positive feelings have been induced (see Isen, 1987, for discussion of these ideas).

These findings suggest that positive affect may sensitize people to affective and/or social aspects of situations. This may turn out to be related to the finding reported earlier, that positive affect serves as a cue for social material in adult subjects; but, as noted, more work needs to be done on that preliminary result, and clearly the effects described here also need to be replicated and extended.

In summary of the work investigating the influence of positive affect on apparent cognitive organization, then, these findings all suggest that positive affect is associated with flexibility in cognitive organization and with broader or more interrelated cognitive structures, reflected in the ability to make unusual or remote associations, to reason about relations among stimuli and classes of stimuli, and to see potential relations among ideas. They also suggest that positive affect is a salient dimension of experience by which thoughts are organized, and a salient dimension of cognition.

What implications do these two phenomena, the asymmetry of happiness and sadness in cognitive effects and the influence of positive affect on cognitive organization and integration, have for emotional development? As mentioned earlier, they may not only be influenced by the development of cognitive and emotional processes, but they may subsequently themselves influence cognitive and emotional development.

Focusing first on origins, these results make us wonder about the underlying structures and processes that produce them. The increased cognitive flexibility observed as a function of positive affect may result from the increased accessibility that positive affect affords to positive material (because positive material is known to be diverse and extensive). However, like the findings discussed earlier regarding the asymmetry between positive and negative affect, these results raise a number of questions relating to fundamental cognitive and neurological processes possibly underling them.

What kinds of processes might underlie and give rise to these effects of feelings on cognitive structure? What kind of fundamental *cognitive* process would allow for positive feelings to enhance retrieval of positive material, and what produces the apparent asymmetry between happiness and sadness in effects on memory? What is it about positive affect, and about cognitive structure or process, that results in positive affect influencing word associations and creativity? Do these data support the idea that cognition is best understood as a network of propositions or other elements? Do they suggest any new ways of thinking about thought or feeling? Do these data suggest that *affect* is organized as, or within, an associative network? Or do they suggest that the organization of affect (and related concepts such as self) might be different? Might it be that, at least for certain kinds of material, but perhaps more generally, people learn something more global rather than (or in *addition* to) elements organized into hierarchically or otherwise-arranged networks?

In fact, it has been suggested that associative-network models have difficulty accounting for some of these data, as well as some of the other findings regarding the influence of affect on cognition (Isen, 1984, 1987; Isen et al., 1978). For example, as originally formulated, the network-and-spreading-activation model of the way in which affect influences cognition (Bower, 1981) does not predict the observed asymmetry between happiness and sadness in effect on memory. (Neither, in fact, does it predict any retrieval effect of feelings; rather the prediction derived from that model is of a state-dependent-learning effect based on induced affect. As noted elsewhere, these expectations seem not to be substantiated by the majority of the accumulating data. See Isen, 1984, 1987, for discussion of these issues.)

Likewise, with respect to the data showing an effect of positive feelings on cognitive organization and integration, the network model does not appear to anticipate these findings, nor to account for them completely even post hoc. For example, the model does not predict effects on unusualness of responding or creativity. After the fact, it might explain the increase in unusual word associations under conditions of positive affect by postulating the activation of additional associative domains represented by the affective state. Thus, more unusual word associations might occur to people who are feeling happy because, for them, two associative domains (that of the stimulus word and that of the positive affect state) are activated and together determine the associate. This associate might thus be unusual according to standard norms because presumably the norms are obtained under test conditions that involve the activation of only one domain, that of the stimulus word. This interpretation is not completely successful, however, because it would not account for the interaction that was observed between affect and word type: It was only for neutral words, but not for positive or negative words, that positive affect resulted in more unusual associates (Isen et al., 1985). (The associative-network view might account for the failure to observe more unusual associates among positive-affect subjects when the stimulus words were positive, because the positive domain might be seen as already having been cued by the positive stimulus words themselves—no new domain would be activated by the presence of positive affect. But the absence of the unusual-associate effect of positive mood with negative words is more difficult to understand from an associative-network perspective.)

Here I would like to suggest that perhaps neurological studies might shed light on questions about the origins of positive affect's influence on cognitive flexibility and of the asymmetry between negative and positive affect. Thus, we might ask what, in the neurobiology of the organism, suggests that cognitive flexibility should be possible? Perhaps more to the point, what, neurologically, are the conditions under which cognitive flexibility is likely to occur; and can this information suggest something about why positive affect increases cognitive flexibility? These are questions that are now beginning to be pursued by researchers working at the interface between affect and neurological processes (see, for example, Davidson, 1984; Tucker, 1981; and the several chapters in this volume that address related questions). This line of inquiry seems to hold promise for increasing our understanding of all these phenomena and the processes that contribute to them.

Turning now to the issue of the effects or implications of the two types of findings presented, what do these findings suggest might be the influence of affective experiences on *subsequent* affective and cognitive development? What impact will the broader organization that gives rise to creativity and remote association have on subsequent thinking and behavior? Are different patterns of thought and behavior likely to result from the kinds of cognitive structures or styles accompanying positive versus negative affect?

In this context, it may be possible to bring together the two topics addressed in this chapter, the influence of positive affect on creativity and integration, and the asymmetry between positive and negative affect in cognitive structure or ability to cue affect-compatible material. These sets of data suggest that there might be important influences of affective experience on subsequent affective and cognitive development.

First, one set indicates that positive affect tends to lead to a broad, flexible cognitive organization and ability to integrate diverse material. Extrapolating from these data to questions of cognitive, affective, and social development, one wonders whether experience with such ways of organizing cognitive material might, as a person grows up, lead to this kind of flexibility, not only on a temporary basis, but relatively characteristically; that is, experience with positive affect might, through development of cognitive patterns and habits, help to promote the kinds of cognitive structures or patterns of intercommunication of ideas that relatively regularly, then, lead to flexibility and creativity. One must be cautious with this idea, because the data showing that positive affect can promote creativity suggest that creativity can be fostered in everyone. Thus, it tends to deemphasize the individual-difference approach to creativity. Still, it is possible to recognize differences among people on cognitive-style variables such as are discussed here (Mischel, 1968); and it is reasonable to propose that cognitive patterns such as flexibility versus rigidity may develop over the years, in part out of experiences that tend to promote or impair ways of structuring thought that are conducive to creativity and integration. If so, it is interesting to think about the role that affective experience may play in the development of such a flexible, integrated, creative cognitive style.

Negative affect, then, might also lead to characteristic ways of organizing or structuring material. But, in contrast with positive feelings, which lead to a broad organization and integration of diverse material, negative affect may lead to more narrow, specific structures and/or processes. As noted earlier, there is some evidence suggesting that negative affect can restrict the range of attention and reduce cue utilization (Bruner et al., 1956; Easterbrook, 1959). Thus, given these considerations, the difficulty in observing sadness to facilitate recall of negative material and the preliminary data suggesting that negative affect may tend to focus attention more specifically on particularly related material, it may be that negative affective experiences as one develops will lead to tighter, more segregated or compartmentalized, inflexible cognitive processing, as a cognitive style.

Thus, although it is possible to speak of an asymmetry between negative and positive affect (in ability to cue affectively relevant material in memory), it may be that in a larger sense—in the sense of the kinds of cognitive organization they tend to foster—the two kinds of states are symmetrical, or at least countervaling, in the sense of producing opposite effects. Other things equal, positive affect appears to promote defocused attention, flexibility in cognitive organization, and integration of seemingly diverse material; whereas negative affect may focus attention more specifically and may narrow the range of cue utilization and integration of material. Many questions remain regarding this suggestion, only one of which is whether all negative affects are alike in this way, or whether some will be more likely than others to produce such cognitive patterns.

These considerations also point to the value in conceptualizing the area in terms of affects and the thoughts cued by those feelings, rather than in terms of global "arousal" alone as had been suggested by some theorists (e.g., Duffy, 1934, 1941). Because negative and positive arousal, or even more specifically, particular feeling states, may have different effects on attentional focus, it seems advantageous to think of them in terms of those attentional effects, rather than as representing more general arousal. Even further, research over the past 20 years indicates that the influence of affect on behavior will depend on what thoughts the affect cues—on what the feelings make the person think about and expect in the situation (e.g., Batson, Coke, Chard, Smith, & Taliaferro, 1979; Batson, Duncan, Ackerman, Buckley, & Birch, 1981; Berkowitz, 1972; Isen, 1970, 1984, 1987; Isen & Levin, 1972). Thus, to know the effects of feelings in particular situations, it will be necessary to know some details of the meaning of the situation to the person. This again suggests the value of conceptualizing the affective states more specifically rather than less so, as arousal, for example.

Many of the points raised in this chapter are suggestions for future investigation. We know that induced positive affect can lead to the kinds of cognitive processing associated with flexible thinking, and that induced negative affect can sometimes lead to a more focused kind of processing that may be related to narrow thinking or rigidity. But we need more information about negative affect's influence on creativity and other integrative tasks. Perhaps there are some types of tasks or situations in which negative affect may facilitate creativity or innovative problem solution. Likewise, we have little information about the long-term effects of affective experiences on cognitive structures and habits. Thus, studies designed to examine the possibly different representations, or cognitive structures, associated with different affect states may also prove very useful. All of this will require research in order to move these suggestions out of the realm of speculation.

Finally, it is of interest to consider the kinds of affect inductions that might be especially likely to promote, in daily life, the kinds of effects that we have been discussing. In much of the research described here affect has been induced by means of small gifts, pleasant surprises, and humor. Some studies have also employed success and failure as ways of inducing affect, and these experiments have found that this manipulation produces effects like those described. The kinds of affect inductions used in this body of research have been validated in a number of ways (see, for example, Isen, 1984, for discussion of this matter); and many are quite naturalistic and realistic, such as having subjects who do not know that they are subjects in an experiment find money in the coin return of a public telephone (e.g., Isen & Levin, 1972) or receive a useful free sample (e.g., Isen et al., 1978). But such events cannot always be arranged in various life situations. Also, there is the possibility that if techniques such as gifts or parties are arranged frequently, they will come to be expected and lose the ability to induce positive affect. Thus, on a long-term basis, positive affect may need to be induced by something timeless like feelings of worth and competence. Moreover, given that in some of the studies, techniques such as success and failure have been found to produce similar kinds of effects, and that a preliminary study mentioned earlier did find a deleterious effect of negative self-thoughts, and a positive effect of favorable self-thoughts, on problem-solving performance, it is not completely inappropriate (although it is something of an extrapolation) to suggest that a good technique of affect induction to use in daily life may be that of conveying respect to people, enabling them to feel good about themselves. Feeling good about oneself may be a very important source of positive affect that promotes cognitive flexibility and openness to ideas, and conveying esteem to people may promote such positive self-feelings. This needs to be investigated further, but it seems a promising possibility. As teachers, parents, and co-workers, we have many occasions on which we can help people to feel respected and valued, and thus we may be able to help them perform at their best. When we do so, however, we will need to keep in mind the full range of effects that may result (see Izen, 1987, for discussion).

In closing, this and related work suggests that positive affect has a substantial impact on cognitive processes and behavior. Traditionally, there has been more study of negative affect—anxiety, frustration, or depression—than of positive in psychology. However, recently there has been growing recognition of the importance of positive affect in various domains. Positive feelings seem capable of bringing out our better nature socially (Isen, 1987) and our creativity in thinking and problem solving. Thus, for the developing child perhaps, and indeed for all of us, positive feelings are an important potential source of interpersonal cooperativeness (e.g., Carnevale & Isen, 1986) and personal strength, growth, and development that should not be ignored.

ACKNOWLEDGMENT

This work was supported by Research Grant BNS 8406352 from the National Science Foundation.

REFERENCES

Adamson, R. E. (1952). Functional fixedness as related to problem solving. *Journal of Experimental Psychology, 44,* 288–291.

Anderson, N. H. (1968). Likeableness ratings of 555 personality trait words. *Journal of Personality and Social Psychology, 9,* 272–279.

Bartlett, F. (1932). *Remembering: A study in experimental and social psychology.* New York: Cambridge University.

Batson, C. D., Coke, J. S., Chard, F., Smith, D., & Taliaferro, A. (1979). Generality of the "glow of goodwill": Effects of mood on helping and information acquisition. *Social Psychology Quarterly, 42,* 176–179.

Batson, C. D., Duncan, D. B., Ackerman, P., Buckley, T., & Birch, K. (1981). Is empathic emotion a source of altruistic motivation? *Journal of Personality and Social Psychology, 40,* 290–302.

Berkowitz, L. (1972). Social norms, feelings, and others factors affecting helping and altruism. In L. Berkowitz (Ed.), *Advances in experimental social psychology* (Vol. 6, pp. 63–108). New York: Academic Press.

Berlyne, D. E. (1971). *Aesthetics and psychobiology.* NY: Appleton Century Crofts.

Bower, G. H. (1981). Mood and memory. *American Psychologist, 36,* 129–148.

Bransford, J. D. (1979). *Human cognition.* Belmont, CA: Wadsworth.

Bruner, J. S., Matter, J., & Papanek, M. L. (1955). Breadth of learning as a function of drive-level and maintenance. *Psychological Review, 62,* 1–10.

Carnevale, P. J. D., & Isen, A. M. (1986). The influence of positive affect and visual access on the discovery of integrative solutions in bilateral negotiation. *Organizational Behavior and Human Decision Processes* (formerly *Organizational Behavior and Human Performance*), *37,* 1–13.

Cramer, P. (1968). *Word association.* New York: Academic Press.

Davidson, R. J. (1984). Affect, cognition, and hemispheric specialization. In C. E. Izard, J. Kagan, & R. B. Zajonc (Eds.), *Emotions, cognition, and behavior.* New York: Cambridge University Press.

Duffy, E. (1934). Emotion: An example of the need for reorientation in psychology. *Psychological Review, 41,* 184–198.

Duffy, E. (1941). An explanation of "emotional" phenomena without the use of the concept of "emotion." *Journal of General Psychology, 25,* 282–293.

Duncker, K. (1945). On problem-solving. *Psychological Monographs, 58,* Whole No. 5.

Easterbrook, J. A. (1959). The effect of emotion on cue utilization and the organization of behavior. *Psychological Review, 66,* 183–201.

Inhelder, B., & Piaget, J. (1964). *The early growth of logic in the child.* New York: Harper & Row.

Isen, A. M. (1970). Success, failure, attention and reactions to others: The warm glow of success. *Journal of Personality and Social Psychology, 15,* 294–301.

Isen, A. M. (1984). Toward understanding the role of affect in cognition. In R. Wyer & T. Srull (Eds.), *Handbook of social cognition* (pp. 179–236). Hillsdale, NJ: Lawrence Erlbaum Associates.

Isen, A. M. (1985). The asymmetry of happiness and sadness in effects on memory in normal college students. *Journal of Experimental Psychology: General, 114,* 388–391.

Isen, A. M. (1987). Positive affect, cognitive processes, and social behavior. In L. Berkowitz (Ed.), *Advances in experimental social psychology* (pp. 203–253). New York: Academic Press.

Isen, A. M., & Blundo, R. (1988). *Self-concept and creativity.* Manuscript, University of Maryland.

Isen, A. M., & Daubman, K. A. (1984). The influence of affect on categorization. *Journal of Personality and Social Psychology, 47,* 1206–1217.

Isen, A. M., Daubman, K. A., & Nowicki, G. P. (1987). Positive affect facilitates creative problem solving. *Journal of Personality and Social Psychology, 52,* 1122–1131.

Isen, A. M., & Hastorf, A. H. (1982). Some perspectives on cognitive social psychology. In A. H. Hastorf & A. M. Isen (Eds.), *Cognitive Social Psychology.* New York: Elsevier.

Isen, A. M., Herren, L. T., & Geva, N. (1986). *The influence of positive affect on the recall of social information.* Poster presented at the annual meeting of the American Psychological Association, Washington, DC.

Isen, A. M., Johnson, M. M. S., Mertz, E., & Robinson, G. F. (1985). The influence of positive affect on the unusualness of word associations. *Journal of Personality and Social Psychology, 48* (6), 1413–1426.

Isen, A. M., & Levin, P. F. (1972). The effect of feeling good on helping: Cookies and kindness. *Journal of Personality and Social Psychology, 21,* 384–388.

Isen, A. M., Shalker, T., Clark, M., & Karp, L. (1978). Affect, accessibility of material in memory and behavior: A cognitive loop? *Journal of Personality and Social Psychology, 36,* 1–12.

Jenkins, J. J. (1974). Remember that old theory of memory? Well, forget it! *American Psychologist, 29,* 785–795.

Koestler, A. (1964). *The act of creation.* New York: Macmillan.

Lacey, J. I. (1967). Somatic response patterning and stress: Some revisions of activation theory. In M. H. appley & R. Trumbul (Eds.), *Psychological stress: Issues in research.* New York: Appleton–Century–Crofts.

Lacey, J. I. (1975). Psychophysiology of the autonomic nervous system. In J. R. Nazarrow (Ed.), *Master lectures on physiological psychology.* Washington, DC: American Psychological Association.

Lacey, J. I., Kagan, J., Lacey, B., & Moss, H. A. (1963). The visceral level: Situational determinants and behavioral correlates of autonomic response patterns. In P. H.Knapp (Ed.), *Expressions of the emotions in man.* New York: International Universities Press.

Laird, J. D., Wagener, J. J., Halal, M., & Szegda, M. (1982). Remembering what you feel: The effects of emotion on memory. *Journal of Personality & Social Psychology, 42,* 646–657.

Lewis, M., & Michaelson, L. (1983). *Children's emotions and mood: Developmental theory and measurement.* New York: Plenum.

Martindale, C. (1981). *Cognition and consciousness.* Homewood, IL: Dorsey.

Matlin, M. W., & Zajonc, R. B. (1968). Social facilitation of word associations. *Journal of Personality and Social Psychology, 10,* 455–460.

Medin, D. L. (1983). Structural principles in categorization. In T. J. Tighe and B. E. Shepp (Eds.), *Perception, cognition and development: Interactional analyses* (pp. 203–230). Hillsdale, NJ: Lawrence Erlbaum Associates.

Mednick, M. T., Mednick, S. A., & Mednick, E. V. (1964). Incubation of creative performance and specific associative priming. *Journal of Abnormal and Social Psychology, 69,* 220–232.

Mednick, S. A. (1962). The associative basis of the creative process. *Psychological Review, 69,* 220–232.

Mischel, W. (1968). *Personality and assessment.* New York: Wiley.

Murphy, G. L., & Medin, D. L. (1985). The role of theories in conceptual coherence. *Psychological Review, 92,* 289–316.

Nasby, W., & Yando, R. (1982). Selective encoding and retrieval of affectively valent information. *Journal of Personality and Social Psychology, 43,* 1244–1255.

Natale, M., & Hantas, M. (1982). Effects of temporary mood states on memory about the self. *Journal of Personality and Social Psychology, 42,* 927–934.

Nevin, P., Isen, A. M., & Winer, G. A. (1988). *The influence of positive affect on classification responses in children.* Manuscript.

Palermo, D. S., & Jenkins, J. J. (1964). *Word association norms: Grade school through college.* Minneapolis: University of Minnesota Press.

Riskind, J. H. (1983). Nonverbal expressions and the accessibility of life experience memories: A congruence hypothesis. *Social Cognition, 2,* 62–86.

Roelle, D., Winer, G., & Isen, A. M. (April, 1986). *The influence of positive affect on children's classification.* Paper presented at the biennial meeting of the Midwestern Society for Life-span Development, Chicago.

Rosch, E. (1975). Cognitive representations of semantic categories. *Journal of Experimental Psychology: General, 104,* 192–233.

Rosenberg, S., & Sedlack, A. (1972). A structural representation of implicit personality theory. In L. Berkowitz (Ed.), *Advances in experimental social psychology, 6.* New York: Academic Press.

Roth, E. M., & Shoben, E. J. (1983). The effect of content on the structure of categories. *Cognitive Psychology, 15,* 346–378.

Sokolov, E. N. (1963). *Perception and the conditioned reflex.* Oxford: Pergamon.

Stephens, L., & Isen, A. M. (1986). *Attempts to find conditions under which sadness cues negative material.* Symposium paper presented at the annual meeting of the American Psychological Association, Washington, DC.

Teasdale, J. D., & Fogarty, S. J. (1979). Differential effects of induced mood on retrieval of pleasant and unpleasant events from episodic memory. *Journal of Abnormal Psychology, 88,* 248–257.

Teasdale, J. D., & Russell, M. L. (1983). Differential effects of induced mood on the recall of positive, negative and neutral words. *British Journal of Clinical Psychology, 22,* 163–171.

Teasdale, J. D., Taylor, R., & Fogarty, S. J. (1980). Effects of induced elation–depression on the accessibility of memories of happy and unhappy experiences. *Behavior Research and Therapy, 18,* 339–346.

Tucker, D. M. (1981). Lateral brain function, emotion, and conceptualization. *Psychological Bulletin, 89,* 19–46.

Velten, E. (1968). A laboratory task for induction of mood states. *Behavior Research and Therapy, 6,* 473–482.

Williams, K., & Isen, A. M. (1988). *The influence of positive affect on young children's play with nesting cubes.* Manuscript, University of Maryland.

Yerkes, R. M., & Dodson, J. D. (1908). The relationship of strength of stimulus to rapidity of habit formation. *Journal of Comparative and Neurological Psychology, 18,* 459–482.

Zajonc, R. B. (1965). Social facilitation. *Science, 149,* 269–274.

Zillmann, D. (1979). *Hostility and aggression.* Hillsdale, NJ: Lawrence Erlbaum Associates.

II BIOLOGICAL PERSPECTIVES TO EMOTION

5

Neuropsychological Studies of Emotional Changes Induced by Right and Left Hemispheric Lesions

Kenneth M. Heilman
Dawn Bowers
Department of Neurology and Center for Neuropsychological
Studies, College of Medicine, University of Florida, and Veterans
Administration Medical Center, Gainesville, FL

INTRODUCTION

The major assumption underlying neuropsychology is that behavior and experiential states are physically mediated by the brain. It follows that emotional behavior and affect are also physically mediated by the brain, and that pertubations of the brain may affect emotional experience (affect) and emotional behavior.

There are many ways to study how the brain may mediate emotions including electrophysiological (e.g., evoked potentials), physiological imaging (e.g., positron emission tomography), and pharmacological; however, in this chapter we review what has been learned by studying patients who have naturally occurring brain ablations secondary to neurological diseases. Based on these observations we attempt to build a model of how the brain may mediate emotion. This model, like all current neuropsychological models, is crude and most likely incorrect; however, we hope such a model will have heuristic value.

In this chapter we discuss emotional changes resulting from lesions in either hemisphere. These changes may result from interference with specific neocortical emotional functions or with cognitive processes necessary for the evaluation of stimuli that should excite emotions. These changes may also interfere with the expression of emotions or may even interfere with subjective feelings (affect). In addition to discussing how right or left hemispheric dysfunction may influence the evaluation and production of emotions and feelings, we also discuss the implications of these observations on a model of how the brain may mediate emotions and affect.

CLINICAL OBSERVATIONS

Right Hemisphere Dysfunction

Babinski (1914), Hecaen and associates (1951), and Denny-Brown and associates (1952) noted that patients with right hemisphere lesions were often inappropriately indifferent or even euphoric. Gainotti's (1972) study of 160 patients supported these earlier clinical observations. Terzian (1964) and Rossi and Rodadini (1967) studied the emotional reactions of patients recovering from barbiturate-induced hemispheric anesthesia (Wada test) and observed that right carotid injections were associated with a euphoric manic response. Whereas Gainotti (1972) thought the indifference reaction was associated with denial of illness (anosognosia), recent research has offered alternative explanations.

Left Hemisphere Dysfunction

In contrast to the flattened emotional response associated with right hemisphere damage, Goldstein (1948) noted that many patients with left hemisphere lesions and aphasia were depressed. He called this agitated depression the *catastrophic reaction*. Gainotti (1972) confirmed Goldstein's observations and suggested that this depression was a normal response to a serious disease. Terzian (1964) and Rossi and Rodadini (1967) observed that barbiturate injections into the left carotid artery (Wada test) could induce a depression.

Benson (1979) observed that this catastrophic reaction is most frequently associated with frontal lobe damage. Robinson and his co-workers' (1984) studies have supported Benson's observations. Although it is apparent from these clinical observations that the cerebral hemispheres play a critical role in emotional behavior, the clinical evaluations mentioned before do not in and of themselves tell us the nature of these patients' defects.

LeDoux (1986) has proposed that emotions contain at least three major elements: evaluation, expression, and conscious feelings. We discuss how each of these major elements may be affected by hemispheric dysfunction.

EVALUATION—PERCEPTUAL AND COGNITIVE DEFECTS

Right Hemisphere Dysfunction

Auditory Nonverbal Processes. Patients with right hemisphere lesions might have a defect in the comprehension of emotional stimuli or in the expression of emotion, or both. Speech may simultaneously carry propositional and emotional messages. The propositional content is conveyed by a complex code requiring semantic and phonemic decoding and encoding. Prosody, which includes pitch, tempo, and rhythm, may also convey linguistic content, (e.g., declarative vs. interrogative sentences). Prosody, however, is more important in conveying emotional content (Paul, 1909; Monrad-Krohn, 1947).

In most individuals the left hemisphere is clearly superior to the right when decoding the propositional content of speech. A little more than a decade ago we attempted to learn if the right hemisphere was more adept than the left in decoding the emotional components of speech. In two studies (Heilman, Scholes, & Watson, 1975b; Tucker, Watson, & Heilman, 1977) sentences with propositionally neutral content were read in four different emotional intonations (happy, sad, angry, and indifferent) to patients with right hemisphere infarctions and to aphasic patients with left hemisphere infarctions. The patients were asked to identify the emotional tone of the speaker. We found that patients with right hemisphere lesions performed worse on this task than those with left hemisphere lesions, suggesting that the right hemisphere is more involved in processing the emotional intonations of speech than is the left hemisphere.

Similar findings were reported by Ross (1981). In contrast, Schlanger and colleagues (1976) failed to find any differences between right hemisphere-damaged and left hemisphere-damaged patients in their comprehension of emotional prosody, although both groups performed more poorly than normal controls. However, only 3 of the 20 right hemisphere patients in the Schlanger et al. study had lesions involving temporoparietal areas.

Subsequent research has indicated that not only do right hemisphere-damaged patients have difficulty comprehending emotional prosody; they are also impaired in their comprehension of nonemotional prosody. Weintraub and colleagues (1981) reported that, relative to normal controls, right hemisphere-damaged patients had difficulty determining whether speech-filtered sentences were statements, commands, or questions. Based on these findings, they suggested that a generalized prosodic disturbance might underlie the poor performance of right hemisphere-damaged patients on emotional prosody tasks. However, a left hemisphere-damaged group was not tested in this study. Recently, we (Heilman, Bowers, Speedie, & Coslett, 1984) compared right hemisphere-damaged and left hemisphere-damaged patients for their comprehension of emotional (happy, sad, angry) or nonemotional prosody (questions, commands, statements). We found that both the right hemisphere-damaged and the left hemisphere-damaged groups were equally impaired on the nonemotional prosody task, relative to normal controls. However, on the emotional prosody task, the right hemisphere-damaged patients performed significantly worse than the left hemisphere-damaged patients. These results suggest that, whereas both hemispheres may be important in comprehending propositional prosody, the right hemisphere plays a dominant role in comprehending emotional intonations.

The nature of the defect underlying the impaired ability of patients with right hemisphere disease to identify emotional intonations in speech, however, was not entirely clear. It may be related to a cognitive defect whereby these patients fail to denote and classify emotional stimuli, or it could also be induced by an inability to discriminate or recognize the difference between various emotional intonations. We (Tucker et al., 1977) therefore studied patients with right hemisphere disease to learn if they could discriminate between emotional intonations without having to classify or denote these intonations. Right and left hemisphere-damaged patients listened to identical pairs of sentences spoken in either the same or different emotional tones. These subjects did not have to identify the emotional intonation but had to tell whether the emotional intonations sounded the same or different. Right hemisphere-damaged subjects performed more poorly on this task than did left hemisphere-damaged controls. These findings suggest that the perceptual discrimination between emotionally intoned stimuli was impaired in the patients with right hemisphere damage.

In addition to discrimination and classification defects, another basis for the poor performance of right hemisphere-damaged patients on emotional prosody tasks is that these patients are "distracted" by the proposition semantic message of affectively intoned sentences. Both in normal conversation and in various experimental tasks, emotional prosody is often superimposed on propositional speech. Findings from recent studies of hemispheric asymmetries of attention in normal adults suggest that each hemisphere is more disrupted by stimuli it normally processes. Heilman, Bowers, Rasbury, and Ray, (1977) found that the discrimination of tonal sequences was more disrupted by simultaneous speech distractors (running conversation) when both types of stimuli were monaurally presented to the right ear than to the left ear. The opposite ear asymmetry was found when the tonal patterns were paired with music distractors. These results suggest that the left hemisphere is more disrupted by speech distractors (i.e., running conversation), and the right hemisphere is more disrupted by music distractors.

In those patients with right hemisphere damage, it is possible that the "intact" left hemisphere can comprehend emotional prosody, but it is distracted by the propositional semantic message. To test this hypothesis, we gave right and left hemisphere-damaged groups an emotional prosody task in which we varied the degree of "conflict" between the emotional message conveyed by the prosody and that conveyed by the semantic content (Bowers, Bauer, Speedie, & Heilman, 1987). We reasoned that if right hemisphere-damaged patients were "distracted" by the semantic content, then their comprehension of emotional prosody should be worse when the semantic content and prosody are strongly conflicting (i.e., "all the puppies are dead" said in a happy tone of voice) than when they are less conflicting (i.e., "all the puppies are dead" said in neutral tone of voice). Our results supported this hypothesis. The performance of the right hemisphere-damaged group was more disrupted when the semantic and prosodic emotional messages were highly conflicting than when they were less conflicting. In contrast, the left hemisphere-damaged group was unaffected by increasing the discrepancy between the two messages. These results suggest that at least part of the defect in comprehending emotional prosody by right hemisphere-damaged patients is related to a "distraction" defect, whereby they are "pulled" to the propositional-semantic content of emotionally intoned sentences. However, this distraction defect cannot entirely account for their poor performance, in that right hemisphere-damaged patients remained impaired in identifying emotional prosody even when the semantic content is rendered completely unintelligible by speech filtering (Bowers et al., 1987).

Taken together, these findings suggest that right hemisphere-damaged patients have both a processing defect and a distraction defect that contribute to their poor performance on emotional prosody tasks. The coexistence of both defects might emerge when a right hemisphere lesion induces defective processing/miscategorization of emotional prosody due to disruption of right hemisphere prosodic processors. Defective processing of emotional prosody might in turn render the right hemisphere-damaged patients more susceptible to the distracting effects of semantic stimuli.

Auditory Verbal Processes.   Although the comprehension of emotional prosody appears to be mediated by the right hemisphere, emotion can also be expressed and comprehended using verbal-proposition speech. Unfortunately, however, no studies have been performed that fully assessed right hemisphere-damaged patients' ability to comprehend emotion communicated through propositional speech. However, several investigators have reported that right hemisphere-damaged patients have difficulty comprehending the affective-emotional content of stories that are carried not only by specific emotional words, but also by the overall meaning conveyed by the propositional sentences (Gardner, Brownell, Wapner, & Michelon, 1983). Gardner and colleagues (1983) reported that right hemisphere-damaged patients had problems relating a sentence to its larger context, understanding its emotional connotation, and drawing inferences from it. Additional studies have found that right hemisphere-damaged patients have little difficulty understanding emotionality in simple propositional sentences, provided that the targeted emotions are explicitly stated (e.g., "the party was festive and gay"; Bowers et al., 1987), but have more difficulty with such tasks when emotionality is not explicitly stated and inferences are required (Wapner et al., 1981).

Visual Nonverbal Processes.   Emotional communication depends not only on comprehending auditory stimuli but also on perceiving and comprehending visual stimuli such as facial expressions, gestures, and scenes. Whereas Gardner and colleagues (1975) found that patients with left hemisphere disease performed better on cartoons without captions than with captions, patients with right and left hemisphere disease were equally impaired in selecting the most humorous of a group of cartoons. We gave a series of facial emotional tests to patients with left or right hemisphere lesions and to controls without brain disease (DeKosky, Heilman, Bowers, & Valenstein, 1980). Both the right and left hemisphere-damaged patients had difficulty naming and selecting emotional faces. However there was a trend for patients with right hemisphere disease to perform more poorly on these tests than patients with left hemisphere disease. Left hemisphere-damaged subjects may have been impaired because these tests were in part verbal. Using a nonverbal test we found that patients with right hemisphere disease were more impaired in making same–different discriminations between emotional faces than were left hemisphere-damaged subjects.

To determine if a visuospatial defect may be responsible for the emotional face discrimination defect, we covaried for neutral facial discrimination (a nonemotional visuospatial task) and found that differences between the two groups disappeared. Whereas findings appear to suggest a perceptual-discrimination deficit underlies right hemisphere-damaged patient's emotional judgment deficits, two observations call this interpretation into question. First, retrospective review of the DeKosky et al. (1980) data revealed that a small subgroup of the right hemisphere-damaged patients performed normally on the neutral visuoperceptual task but were nevertheless impaired on the affective facial tasks. This observation suggests that visuoperceptual deficits do not account for impaired affective processing in all right hemisphere-damaged patients.

Second, the study by DeKosky et al. (1980) included emotional face tasks that right hemisphere-damaged patients may have performed by using strategies that did not require knowledge of the emotionality depicted on faces. For example, on DeKosky et al.'s (1980) emotional discrimination subtest, two pictures of the same actor were presented. Sometimes the actors displayed the same emotions, and sometimes they displayed different emotions. The patients were asked to judge whether the emotional expressions conveyed by the actors were the same or different. Because this judgment was made across two pictures of the same actor, the task could have been accurately performed without regard to emotion by simply deciding whether the two face stimuli had the same physiognomic configuration; that is, patients could have performed this "emotional discrimination" task by doing nonaffective "template matching" in which differences in the physical properties of the faces were noted (e.g., upturned mouth versus downturned mouth), without any necessary reference to the emotional meaning of the faces per se. This is what might be referred to as a "perceptual" rather than an "associative" judgment task. To circumvent the use of pure template matching in an affective discrimination task, two different actors would have to be presented, sometimes displaying the same emotion and sometimes displaying different emotions. In this way, affective judgments would have to take place in an "associative" context (i.e., across two faces with inherently different visuoperceptual/physiognomic properties). Recently, we tested controls and patients with right or left hemisphere damage on a series of seven "perceptual" and "associative" affective facial tasks (Bowers, Bauer, Coslett, & Heilman, 1985). We found that the right hemisphere-damaged group performed significantly worse than left hemisphere-damaged controls across all facial tasks. Even when the patient groups were statistically equated on a measure of visuoperceptual ability, the right hemisphere-damaged group remained impaired on three of the emotional face tasks and not on the others. These three tasks included naming, selecting, and discriminating emotional expressions across two different actors. We proposed that the critical factor distinguishing these tasks from those that did not give rise to hemispheric asymmetries of emotional processing was related to the task demand of "categorizing" facial emotions. These findings suggest that the defect shown by right hemisphere-damaged patients on facial affect tasks cannot be solely attributed to defects in visuoperceptual processing, and that the right hemisphere superiority for processing facial affect exists above and beyond its superiority for processing facial identity. Furthermore, the salient role of the right hemisphere in processing emotional faces may be that it contains schemata or prototypes for facial expressions or at least the hardware for activating these representations that would enable one to categorize facial expressions (Bowers & Heilman, 1984). Other investigators, such as Cicone, Wapner, & Gardner, (1980), also presented emotional faces to patients with right or left hemisphere damage and also found that right hemisphere-damaged patients were impaired in recognizing emotional faces. Based on these studies, we believe that the right hemisphere is important in perceiving both faces and facial expressions. These processes may be either interdependent (i.e., one must perceive faces before perceiving the emotions expressed by the face) or they may be independent.

In addition to emotional faces, several studies have tested the ability of unilateral brain damaged patients to comprehend the emotions conveyed by various pictorial scenes. DeKoksy et al. (1980) found that when compared to nonbrain-damaged controls and left hemisphere-damaged patients, right hemisphere-damaged subjects had difficulty in interpreting the emotion associated with the scene. Similar findings have been reported by Cicone et al. (1980).

Visual Verbal.   No one has closely examined the emotional response of right hemisphere-damaged patients to written emotional stories.

Left Hemisphere Dysfunction

Auditory Verbal and Nonverbal Processes.   Patients with word deafness or Wernicke's, global, transcortical sensory, or mixed transcortical aphasia may be unable to comprehend propositional speech. Therefore, when the development of an emotional state is dependent on propositional language, patients with language comprehension deficits would not be able to develop the appropriate emotional state. Patients with Broca's and conduction aphasia have no difficulty identifying the emotion conveyed by simple declarative sentences that are neutrally intoned. However, they are distracted by the emotional prosody when the emotional prosody message differs from that conveyed by the propositional content (Bowers et al. 1987).

Although left hemisphere-damaged patients may have impaired comprehension of propositional speech, many of these patients can comprehend emotional intonations. In addition, their comprehension of propositional speech may be aided by intonations if the two messages are not in conflict (Coslett, Brasher, & Heilman, 1984; Heilman et al., 1975a, 1975b).

Visual Verbal and Nonverbal Processes.   Emotional messages may be conveyed by written words. Patients with left hemisphere dysfunction may be alexic and, in those cases where alexia interferes with comprehension, left hemisphere-damaged patients may be unable to comprehend emotions expressed in writing. However, Landis and associates (1982) visually presented emotional and nonemotional words to aphasic patients with left hemisphere lesions. Their task was to read the words. Unlike speech, which can be affectively intoned, the written word carries no prosody. Nevertheless, Landis and co-workers found that emotional words were read better than nonemotional words. Thus emotionality appeared to improve the reading performance of alexic subjects.

When left hemisphere-damaged patients were asked to name an emotional face or point to an emotional face, the performance, although not as poor as that of right hemisphere-damaged patients, was worse than that of nonbrain damaged controls. Berent (1977) noted that left hemisphere dysfunction induced a defect in naming faces and posited that verbal mediation and verbal labeling might underlie the naming defect. Berent's hypothesis is supported by the observation that patients with left hemisphere lesions asked to match faces (a test of visuospatial skills) performed no differently than nonbrain damaged controls (Bowers et al., 1985; DeKosky et al., 1980).

In regard to emotional scenes, right hemisphere-damaged subjects had more difficulty naming emotional scenes than did left hemisphere-damaged controls (DeKosky et al., 1980).

EXPRESSIVE DEFICITS

Right Hemisphere Dysfunction

Verbal Expression.   To determine whether patients with right hemisphere disease can express emotionally intoned speech (Tucker et al., 1977), we asked right hemisphere-damaged subjects and controls to say semantically neutral sentences (e.g., "The boy went to the store.") using a happy, sad, angry, or indifferent tone of voice. These left hemisphere-damaged patients were severely impaired. They spoke in a flat monotone and often verbally denoted the target affect by using emotional words. Ross and Mesulam (1979) described two patients with right anterior cerebral lesions who could not express emotionally intoned speech but who could comprehend emotional speech. Ross (1981) described patients who could not comprehend affective intonation but who could repeat affectively intoned speech.

Facial Expression.   Buck and Duffy (1980) studied right and left hemisphere-damaged patients' emotional facial expressions when they were viewing slides of familiar people, unpleasant scenes, and unusual pictures. Buck and Duffy (1980) showed that right hemisphere-damaged patients were less facially expressive than left hemisphere-damaged patients.

Left Hemisphere Dysfunction

Verbal Expression.   Aphasic patients may have difficulty expressing emotions as a spoken or written propositional message. In regard to emotional intonations, Hughlings Jackson (1932) observed that even nonfluent aphasics could imbue their simple utterances with emotional content by using affective intonation. Some nonfluent aphasics when frustrated may fluently use expletives. Jackson thought the right hemisphere may be mediating emotional expression.

Speedie, Coslett and Heilman (1984) studied several patients with transcortical aphasia from cerebral infarctions in a watershed distribution. These patients were able to repeat sentences almost flawlessly. However, when they were asked to repeat sentences that were intoned with emotional prosody, they repeated the words but the intonation remained flat. These watershed infarctions spared the left hemisphere perisylvian areas critical for the production of propositional speech but disconnected these speech areas from other portions of the brain. Speedie, Coslett and Heilman's (1984) study suggested that the mixing of propositional speech with emotional prosody takes place in the cerebral hemispheres and that these watershed lesions may have disconnected the right hemisphere, which is important in the expression of prosody, from the left hemisphere, which is important in the production of propositional speech.

Written Expression.   Roeltgen, Sevush, and Heilman (1983) demonstrated that aphasic agraphic patients were able to write emotional words better than unemotional words.

CHANGES IN THE AUTONOMIC NERVOUS SYSTEM

It has been well established that changes in the autonomic nervous system may accompany emotions.

Right Hemisphere Dysfunction

To determine whether patients with right hemisphere lesions had normal autonomic responsitivity to uncomfortable stimuli, we (Heilman et al., 1978) stimulated the normal side of patients with right or left hemisphere disease and simultaneously recorded galvanic skin responses. The galvanic skin response is a measure of peripheral sympathic activity. We found that patients with right hemisphere disease and emotional indifference had smaller galvanic skin responses than aphasic and non-brain damaged controls. Trexler and Schmidt (1981) and Morrow and co-workers (1981) also found that patients with right hemisphere disease had reduced galvanic skin responses. Recently, Yokoyama et al. (1987) measured heart rate changes to preparatory stimuli and demonstrated that patients with right hemisphere damage were less responsive than controls.

Left Hemisphere Dysfunction

In measuring the galvanic skin response to uncomfortable stimuli, we found not only that patients with right hemisphere lesions were hypoaroused (Heilman, Schwartz, & Watson, 1978), but also that patients with left hemisphere disease had a greater arousal response than normal controls. Trexler and Schmidt (1981) have reported similar findings. When measuring heart rate, Yokoyama et al. (1987) found that left hemisphere-damaged patients had, when compared with normal controls, an increased cardiac response.

FEELINGS (AFFECT) ASSOCIATED WITH LEFT AND RIGHT HEMISPHERE DYSFUNCTION

Many patients with right hemisphere disease who have the indifference reaction may not appear depressed because they have anosognosia and do not recognize that they are disabled; that is, they have no reason to be depressed. In the clinic, however, we see patients who do not explicitly deny illness, in that they recognize that they have had a stroke, are in the hospital, and have a left hemiparesis, but nevertheless appear unconcerned (anosodiaphoria) (Critchley, 1953). Although a portion of this flattening and unconcern may be induced by a loss of ability to express affective intonations in speech or to use affective facial expressions, even when one uses propositional speech to assess affect, these patients still convey a lack of concern about their illness. Gasparrini, Satz, Heilman, and Coolidge (1978) administered the Minnesota Multiphasic Inventory (MMPI) to patients with unilateral hemisphere lesions. The right and left hemisphere-damaged patients were matched for severity of cognitive (e.g., IQ) and motor defects (e.g., motor tapping). The MMPI is widely used to determine affect but does not require that the subject intone their voice or make facial expressions. Patients with left hemisphere damage showed an elevation on the depression scale but patients with right hemisphere disease did not. These results suggest that the differences in emotional reactions of patients after right versus left hemisphere disease cannot be attributed entirely to either difference in the severity of their defects or to difficulties in perceiving or expressing affective stimuli.

PATHOPHYSIOLOGY UNDERLYING
THE INDIFFERENCE REACTION ASSOCIATED
WITH RIGHT HEMISPHERE DYSFUNCTION

The pathophysiological basis for the emotional flattening associated with right hemisphere dysfunction may be related to perceptual cognitive deficits; that is, patients with right hemisphere lesions may not be able to interpret emotional stimuli, and therefore they may be incapable of developing the appropriate feelings. Although peripheral sympathetic activity was measured in patients with right hemisphere dysfunction, measures of peripheral sympathetic activity often correlate with central measures of arousal. In addition, in an unpublished study we found that there was EEG evidence for hypoarousal (see Heilman, 1979). Cannon (1927) proposed that whereas cortical activation induces the conscious emotional state, the visceral changes that occur serve adaptive purposes. Because the thalamus can be stimulated by either peripheral sensory input or central (visceral) impulses, Cannon considered the thalamus an important central structure in the mediation of emotion.

Subsequently, Berger (1933) reported that the electroencephlographic activity decreased in amplitude and increased in frequency during behavioral arousal (i.e., desynchronization). EEG desynchronization occurs during emotional states (Lindsley, 1970). Moruzzi and Magoun (1949) noted that animals stimulated in the nonspecific thalamic nuclei or in the mesencephalic reticular formation show behavioral indices of arousal and electroencephalographic desynchronization. Electrical stimulation of specific cortical areas, such as portions of the frontal or temporoparietal cortex, appears to activate the mesencephalic reticular formation (French, Hernandez-Peon, & Livingston, 1955) and elicit an arousal response (Segundo, Naguet, & Buser, 1955). Portions of the limbic system have connections with the cortex and also have input into the reticular formation. The limbic system, therefore, also appears to play a role in arousal (Heilman & Valenstein, 1972; Watson et al., 1973).

In 1924 Maranon (Fehr & Stern, 1970) studied the relationship between arousal and emotion by administering sympathomimetic drugs to normal subjects. After drug administration most of his subjects reported feeling "no emotions"; however, many reported they experienced "as if" feelings. Maranon asked his subject to recall an emotional event. When this memory was not strong enough to produce an emotion in the normal state, emotion was felt if there was a concomitant pharmacological arousal. Schachter (1970) also found pharmacological arousal alone did not produce emotional states. However, stressful situations produced less emotion when the subjects were not pharmacologically aroused than when they were.

These pharmacological studies suggest that the experiencing of emotion requires the appropriate cognitive state and arousal. Brain arousal is mediated by the brainstem reticular formation, nonspecific thalamic nuclei, and certain regions of the neocortex (Heilman, 1979). The visceral changes associated with emotions are mediated by the hypothalamus, and the hypothalamus is strongly influenced by portions of the limbic system, especially by the basolateral limbic circuit, which in turn receives considerable input from the neocortex. Emotions, therefore, depend on varied anatomic structures in a distributed system that includes the cortex for producing the appropriate cognitive set, the mesencephalic and thalamic activating systems for producing arousal, and the limbic system for activating the mesencephalic and thalamic activating centers and for controlling the hypothalamus, which regulates the endocrine and autonomic systems.

Because patients with right hemisphere disease have difficulty comprehending emotionally intoned speech, faces, and scenes, they may not be able to develop an appropriate cognitive state. These patients are also inadequately aroused, and this combination of cognitive and arousal defects may underlie the emotional flattening associated with right hemisphere dysfunction.

PATHOPHYSIOLOGY UNDERLYING AFFECTIVE CHANGES ASSOCIATED WITH LEFT HEMISPHERE DYSFUNCTION

Tucker (1981) proposed that normally the right hemisphere is more involved in processing negative emotions and the left hemisphere processes positive emotions. Catastrophic reactions, therefore, may result from left hemisphere damage because of the consequent predominance of right hemisphere "negative" emotion. Tucker's postulate (that each hemisphere processes different aspects of emotion), however, has not been consistently substantiated (Ley & Bryden, 1979).

We used the galvanic skin response to measure arousal in patients with hemispheric lesions and found not only were patients with right hemisphere lesions hypoaroused (Heilman, Schwartz, & Watson, 1978), but also that patients with left hemisphere disease had a greater arousal response than non-brain damaged controls. Trexler and Schmidt (1981) replicated these findings, and Yokoyama (1987) also found an increased cardiac responsivity to stimuli. Because left hemisphere-damaged patients are disabled and do not have anosognosia, they have a cognitive state compatible with depression. This cognitive state together with hyperarousal may be inducing their catastrophic reaction.

The mechanism underlying the heightened arousal seen with left hemisphere damage is not known. However, one possibility is that the left hemisphere has inhibitory control over other areas responsible for activating the arousal systems. The left hemisphere may directly control the limbic or reticular systems. With damage to the left hemisphere, these systems are disinhibited. Alternatively, the left hemisphere may exert inhibitory control over the right hemisphere. With left hemisphere lesions the right hemisphere, which mediates arousal by controlling the limbic and reticular systems, is disinhibited and arousal is heightened. If the left hemisphere does provide the right hemisphere with inhibitory control and this control is mediated by the corpus callosum or the anterior commissure, then section of the commissures would be expected to increase arousal. Although we have seen one patient who had a transection of their corpus callosum and claimed to be more emotional and anxious after surgery, this hypothesis has yet to be formally tested. One of the problems in testing this hypothesis, however, would be that during surgery the medial frontal structures, such as the cingulate gyrus, may be damaged. In addition, many of the callosally sectioned patients are epileptic and are on medications. Both of these factors may influence the results of any formal evaluation of this hypothesis.

NEUROPSYCHOLOGICAL MODELS OF EMOTION

The purpose of this discussion is not to perform an extensive critique of theories and models of emotion. These can be found in some excellent reviews (Buck, 1986). In this discussion we wish to develop a neuropsychological model of affect. Prior to discussing this model, however, we need to briefly discuss the three classical theories: James–Lang's feedback theory, the Maranon–Schacter self-attribution theory, and Cannon's thalamic central theory.

According to James, "the bodily changes follow directly the perception of the exciting fact and that our feelings of the same changes as they occur is the emotion." "We feel sorry because we cry." James also felt that facial expression was not important, but the changes induced by the autonomic nervous system were important. Although the observation that different emotions may produce different psychophysiological changes appears to support the feedback hypothesis, the observation that patients with high cervical cord transections are able to feel emotions is inconsistent with this theory. However, there are bodily changes that may be detected with a cord transection (e.g., changes in blood composition), and structures such as facial muscles may still play a role (Tomkins, 1982).

What seems to be the fatal flaw in the feedback hypothesis is that drugs such as epinephrine, when administered to subjects, affect structures that are innervated by the autonomic nervous system but do not induce specific emotions. This discrepancy led Maranon and Schacter to develop the self-attribution theory. According to this theory, it is bodily arousal combined with a cognitive state that induces the conscious feeling of an emotion. Either of these alone is insufficient for the conscious feeling of emotion. Unlike the James–Lang theory, cognition precedes arousal and the feeling of emotion (affect).

Our observations in brain damaged subjects are consistent with the self-attribution theory. It appears that the right hemisphere is critical not only for emotional–perceptual–cognitive processes but also for the control of arousal.

One of the major problems with the cognitive-arousal or self-attribution theory is the observation that patients with partial complex seizures emanating from limbic structures may experience emotions such as fear, even in the absence of a cognitive state. Similarly, it has been demonstrated that electrical stimulation of portions of the limbic system can also produce emotions.

The observation that an emotion can be elicited by either a seizure or brain stimulation suggests that emotions are mediated by central nervous system activity. This of course does not preclude the postulate that feedback plays an important role in the experience of emotion. It also does not preclude the possibility that certain emotions (fear and anger) are mediated differently than other emotions (sadness and happiness).

Based on these observations, we suspect that both limbic and reticular activity, as well as peripheral feedback, are monitored by a portion of the brain that is responsible for recognizing affective feelings. Because there are neurologically impaired patients who have mask-like faces but have emotional feeling (affect) and other patients who portray emotional faces but who are not feeling the emotions they portray, we suspect that the portions of the brain that control motor output are independent from the system that is responsible for developing the affective percept. What is not clear is whether or not the interpretation of emotional stimuli (that precedes the development of affect) is an independent system or if it is the same system that interprets autonomic feedback. In order to determine the neural basis of emotion more work needs to be performed.

REFERENCES

Babinski, J. (1914). Contribution a l'etude des troubles mentaux dans l'hemisplegie organique cerebrale (anosognosie). *Revue Neurologique, 27,* 845–848.

Benson, D. F. (1979). Psychiatric aspects of aphasia. In D. F. Benson (Ed.), *Aphasia, alexia and agraphia.* New York: Churchill Livingstone.

Berent, S. (1977). Functional asymmetry of the human brain in the recognition of faces. *Neuropsychologia, 15,* 829–831.

Berger, H. (1933). Uber das electroenkephalogram des menschen. *Archiv fur Psychiatrie und Nervenkrankheiten, 99,* 555–574.

Bowers, D., Bauer, R., Coslett, B., & Heilman, K. M. (1985). Processing of faces by patients with unilateral hemisphere lesions. *Brain and Cognition, 4,* 258–272.

Bowers, D., Coslett, H. B., Bauer, R. M., Speedie, L. J., & Heilman, K. M. (1987). Comprehension of emotional prosody following unilateral hemispheric lesions: Processing defect vs. distraction defect. *Neuropsychologia, 25,* 317–328.

Bowers, D., & Heilman, K. M. (1984). Dissociation between processing of affective and nonaffective faces: A case study. *Journal of Clinical Neuropsychology, 6,* 367–379.

Buck, R. (1986). The psychology of emotion. In J. E. LeDoux & W. Hirst (Eds.), *Mind and brain.* New York: Cambridge University Press.

Buck, R., & Duffy, R. J. (1980). Nonverbal communication of affect in brain damaged patients. *Cortex, 16,* 351–362.

Cannon, W. B. (1927). The James–Lange theory of emotion: A critical examination and alternative theory. *American Journal of Psychology, 39,* 106–124.

Cicone, M., Wapner, W., & Gardner, H. (1980). Sensitivity to emotional expressions and situation in organic patients. *Cortex, 16,* 145–158.

Coslett, H. B., Brasher, H. R., & Heilman, K. M. (1984). Pure word deafness after bilateral primary auditory cortex infarcts. *Neurology, 34,* 347–352.

Critchley, M. (1953). *The parietal lobes.* London: E. Arnold.

DeKosky, S., Heilman, K. M., Bowers, D., & Valenstein, E. (1980). Recognition and discrimination of emotional faces and pictures. *Brain and Language, 9,* 206–214.

Denny-Brown, D., Meyer, J. S., & Horenstein, S. (1952). The significance of perceptual rivalry resulting from parietal lesions. *Brain, 75,* 434–471.

Fehr, F. S., & Stern, J. A. (1970). Peripheral psychological variables and emotion: The James–Lange theory revisited. *Psychological Bulletin, 74,* 411–424.

French, J. E., Hernandez-Peon, R., & Livingston, R. (1955). Projections from the cortex to cephalic brainstem (reticular formation) in monkeys. *Brain, 18,* 74–95.

Gainotti, G. (1972). Emotional behavior and hemispheric side of lesion. *Cortex, 8,* 41–55.

Gardner, H., Brownell, H., Wapner, W., & Michelon, P. (1983). Missing the point: The role of the right hemisphere in the processing of complex linguistic materials. In E. Perecman (Ed.), *Cognition processing in the right hemisphere.* New York: Academic Press.

Gardner, H., Ling, P. K., Flam, I., & Silverman, J. (1975). Comprehension and appreciation of humorous material following brain damage. *Brain, 98,* 399–412.

Gasparrini, W. G., Satz, P., Heilman, K. M., & Coolidge, F. L. (1978). Hemispheric asymmetries of affective processing as determined by the Minnesota multiphasic personality inventory. *Journal of Neurology, Neurosurgery and Psychiatry, 41,* 470–473.

Goldstein, K. (1948). *Language and language disturbances.* New York: Grune & Stratton.

Hecaen, H., Ajuriaguerra, J., & de Massonet, J. (1951). Les troubles visuoconstructifs par lesion parieto–occipitale droit. *Encephale, 40,* 122–179.

Heilman, K. M. (1979). Neglect and related syndromes. In K. M. Heilman & E. Valenstein (Eds.) *Clinical neuropsychology.* New York: Oxford University Press.

Heilman, K. M., Bowers, D., Rasbury, W., & Ray, R. (1977). Ear asymmetries on a selective attention task. *Brain Language, 4,* 390–395.

Heilman, K. M., Bowers, D., Speedie, L., & Coslett, B. (1984). Comprehension of affective and nonaffective speech. *Neurology, 34,* 917–921.

Heilman, K. M., Gold, M. S., & Tucker, D. M. (1975a). Improvement in aphasics' comprehension by use of novel stimuli. *Transactions of the American Neurological Association 100,* 201–202.

Heilman, K. M., Scholes, R., & Watson, R. T. (1975b). Auditory affective agnosia: Disturbed comprehension of affective speech. *Journal of Neurology, Neurosurgery, and Psychiatry, 38,* 69–72.

Heilman, K. M., Schwartz, H., & Watson, R. T. (1978). Hypoarousal in patients with the neglect syndrome and emotional indifference. *Neurology, 28,* 229–232.

Heilman, K. M., & Valenstein, E. (1972). Frontal lobe neglect. *Neurology* (Minneapolis), *22*, 660–664.

Hughlings Jackson, J. (1932). In J. Taylor (Ed.), *Selected writings of John Hughlings Jackson.* London: Hodder & Stoughton.

Landis, T., Graves, R., & Goodglass, H. (1982). Aphasic reading and writing: Possible evidence for right hemisphere participation. *Cortex, 18,* 105–112.

LeDoux, J. E. (1986). The neurobiology of emotion. In J. E. LeDoux & W. Hirst (Eds.), *Mind and brain.* New York: Cambridge University Press.

Ley, R., & Bryden, M. (1979). Hemispheric differences in recognizing faces and emotions. *Brain and Language, 1,* 127–138.

Lindsley, D. (1970). The role of nonspecific reticulo-thalamo-cortical systems in emotion. In P. Black (Ed.), *Physiological Correlates of Emotion.* New York: Academic Press.

Monrad-Krohn, G. (1947). The prosodic quality of speech and its disorders. *Acta Psychologica Scandanavia, 22,* 225–265.

Morrow, L., Vrtunski, P. B., Kim, Y., & Boller, F. (1981). Arousal responses to emotional stimuli and laterality of lesions. *Neuropsychologia, 19,* 65–72.

Moruzzi, G., & Magoun, H. W. (1949). Brainstem reticular formation and activation of the EEG. *EEG Clinical Neurophysiology, 1,* 455–475.

Paul, H. (1909). *Principien der Sprachgeschichte* (4th ed.). Niemeyer.

Robinson, R. G., Kubos, K. L., Starr, L. B., Rao, K., & Price, T. R. (1984). Mood disorders in stroke patients. *Brain, 107,* 81–93.

Roeltgen, D. P., Sevush, S., & Heilman, K. M. (1983). Phonological agraphia: Writing by the lexical semantic route. *Neurology, 33,* 755–765.

Ross, E. D. (1981). The aprosodias: Functional-anatomic organization of the affective components of language in the right hemisphere. *Annals of Neurology, 38,* 561–589.

Ross, E. D., & Mesulam, M. M. (1979). Dominant language functions of the right hemisphere? Prosody and emotional gesturing. *Archives of Neurology, 36,* 144–148.

Rossi, G. S., & Rodadini, G. (1967). Experimental analysis of cerebral dominance in man. In C. Millikan & F. L. Darley (Eds.), *Brain mechanisms underlying speech and language.* New York: Grune & Stratton.

Schachter, S. (1970). The interaction of cognitive and physiological determinants of emotional state. In Berkowitz (ed.), *Advances in experimental social psychology* (Vol. 1). New York: Academic Press.

Schlanger, B. B., Schlanger, P., & Gerstmann, L. J. (1976). The perception of emotionally toned sentences by right-hemisphere damaged and aphasic subjects. *Brain and Language, 3,* 396–403.

Segundo, J. P., Naguet, R., & Buser, P. (1955). Effects of cortical stimulation on electrocortical activity in monkeys. *Journal of Neurology, Neurosurgery and Psychiatry, 18,* 236–245.

Speedie, L., Coslett, H. B., & Heilman, K. M. (1984). Repetition of affective prosody in mixed transcortical aphasia. *Archives of Neurology, 41,* 268–270.

Terzian, H. (1964). Behavioral and EEG effects of intracarotid sodium amytal injections. *Acta Neurochirurgica* (Vienna), *12,* 230–240.

Tompkins, S. (1982). Affect theory. In P. Ekman (Ed.), *Emotions of the human face.* Cambridge University.

Trexler, L. E., & Schmidt, N. D. (1981). *Autonomic arousal associated with complex affective stimuli in lateralized brain injury.* Paper presented before International Neuropsychological Society, Bergen, Norway.

Tucker, D. M. (1981). Lateral brain function, emotion, and conceptualization. *Psychological Bulletin, 89,* 19–46.

Tucker, D. M., Watson, R. T., & Heilman, K. M. (1977). Affective discrimination and evocation in patients with right parietal disease. *Neurology, 17,* 947–950.

Wapner, W., Harby, S., and Gardner, H. (1981). The role of the right hemisphere in the apprehension of complex linguistic stimuli. *Brain and Cognition 14*, 15–33.

Watson, R. T., Heilman, K. M., Cauthen, J. C., and King, F. A. (1973). Neglect after cingulectomy. *Neurology 23*, 1003–1007.

Weintraub, S., Mesulam, M. M., and Kramer, L. (1981). Disturbances in prosody. *Archives of Neurology 38*, 742–744.

Yokoyama, K., Jennings, R., Ackles, P., Hood, P., & Boller, F. (1987). Lack of heart rate changes during an attention demanding task after right hemisphere lesions. *Neurology, 37*, 624–630.

6 Neocortical Substrates of Emotional Behavior

Bryan Kolb
Laughlin Taylor
University of Lethbridge

INTRODUCTION

Virtually all the activities of central nervous system activity contribute to an individual's emotional behavior. Any changes in these activities can therefore affect how an individual expresses behavior or perceives the behavior of others. Nevertheless, the scientific study of the physiological basis of emotional behavior lags far behind the study of cognitive functions, in large part due to the difficulties in defining, recording, and evaluating this behavior. The goal of this chapter is to comment on these difficulties by summarizing the contribution of recent neuropsychological evidence to the understanding of the role of the neocortex in emotional behavior.

Interest in the biology of emotions dates back to Darwin's work, *The Expression of the Emotions in Man and Animals,* published in 1872. In this book Darwin attempted to explain the origin and development of the principal expressive behaviors in humans and other animals. Darwin believed that human emotional expression could only be understood in the context of the expressions of other animals for, he suggested, our emotional behavior is determined by our evolution. Although Darwin's book was a best seller, its influence was short-lived and temporarily forgotten. Psychologists began to speculate about emotions by the turn of the century, but with little knowledge about the neural bases of emotional behavior. By the 1930s many studies began to examine the relationship between autonomic, endocrine and neurohumoral factors, and inferred emotional states, with particular emphasis on measuring indices like heart rate, blood pressure, and skin temperature (for reviews, see Brady, 1960; Dunbar,

1954). Systematic studies of the role of the central nervous system in emotion were slower in developing. There had been occasional observations on the emotional behavior of laboratory animals with cortical injury in the late 1800s (Brown & Schafer, 1888; Goltz, 1892) and with midbrain and diencephalic injury in the early 1900s (Bard, 1928; Woodworth & Sherrington, 1904), but it was not until 1939 that work became focused. In that year Kluver and Bucy described dramatic changes in the emotional behavior of monkeys with bilateral removal of the temporal lobes, including the amygdala. About the same time, Papez proposed a theory that the hypothalamus, cingulate cortex, hippocampal formation, and their interconnections represent the anatomical basis of emotions. McLean later elaborated on this theory and resurrected the name limbic lobe or limbic system to describe Papez' hypothetical circuit (McLean, 1949).

There is little doubt that Papez' proposal (1937) had a significant impact and led to extensive study on the limbic system and behavior, especially emotional behavior. Unfortunately it had the effect of directing attention away from the role of the neocortex in affective behavior. Therefore, until very recently, most of the data on the role of the cortex has come from clinical observations, rather than from systematic laboratory study, in spite of the prevalence in the 1940s of frontal leucotomy and related procedures that had become a major method of treating people with abnormal emotional behavior. Among these clinical observations two stand out. First, damage to the frontal lobes is reliably associated with changes in emotional behavior. Perhaps the most publicized example of personality change following frontal lobe damage is that of Phineas Gage, first reported by Harlow in 1868. Gage suffered a large lesion to his frontal lobes when an iron bar passed through the front of his head. After the accident his personality was changed radically, although at the same time his "intellectual faculties" seemed to be left more or less intact. The second observation is that there is an apparent asymmetry in the effect of large unilateral lesions of the cerebral hemispheres. The best known descriptions of their asymmetry are those of Goldstein (1948), who suggested that left hemisphere lesions produce "catastrophic" reactions characterized by fearfulness and depression, whereas right hemisphere lesions produce "indifference" and sometimes "euphoria." To our knowledge no formal studies of cortical lesions and emotional behavior in either laboratory animals or human patients supplemented these observations until the 1960s, and then only a handful of studies were published before the mid-1970s. Fortunately, there has been much experimental activity in the last decade, and it is now possible to identify some important features of neocortical involvement in emotional behavior. Before turning to these data, however, we consider some methodological problems that plague studies of emotional behavior.

APPROACHES TO THE STUDY
OF EMOTIONAL BEHAVIOR

The fundamental problem one encounters is in deciding what emotional behavior is and how to study it objectively. It is nearly impossible to agree on a simple definition of emotional behavior, but most theories of emotional behavior agree that the concept of emotion includes three principal components. First, there are physiological components that include central and autonomic system activity and the resulting changes in visceral activity, as well as neurohormonal activity. Second, there are distinctive behaviors. Examples would be facial expression or tone of voice. Third, there are inferred processes often referred to as subjective or experiential states. These are often referred to by labels such as fear, love, or anger. The way one approaches the study of emotional behavior will be influenced to a large extent by the emphasis one places on each of these components. For example, social or cognitive psychologists are more likely to concern themselves with the subjective component, whereas more biologically oriented psychologists would place more emphasis on physiological processes, with little concern to subjective states. As neuropsychologists, our bias is toward the latter approach.

Having chosen the orientation of study, we are still confronted with the problem of how to study the behavior. Historically, there have been two principal ways of studying biological bases of behavior. The first, which is often called the psychological approach, places emphasis on questions of ontogenetic development, environmental constraints and influence, and physiological mechanisms. The second, often referred to as the ethological approach, emphasizes questions of immediate causation, the function of behaviors, and evolutionary development. It is apparent that the nature of research questions will vary according to the methodology of behavioral analysis. Thus, two investigators interested in facial expression might film people surreptitiously and then carefully analyze the film. One investigator might look for stimuli that release smiling behavior and consider the effect that smiling has on other people. These studies could lead to inferences about the immediate causation and function of smiling. Another investigator might analyze the same film by studying the symmetry in the facial musculature of individuals during smiling and reach inferences about the role of the cerebral hemispheres in controlling smiling. The point is that both investigators are interested in emotional behavior but, because of the differences in orientation, the methodology and conclusions are rather different. It is important here to recognize that both concerns are legitimate, a point that has not always been conceded (Lehrman, 1970).

The emphasis that our studies have taken is both comparative and physiological. It is comparative in that (a) it includes work with several mammalian species, and (b) it compares the behavior of normal adult humans to children, as well as to those with neurological or psychiatric disorders. The work is physiological in that we are concerned with the cortical mechanisms underlying emotional behavior.

CORTICAL MECHANISMS OF EMOTIONAL BEHAVIOR: EVIDENCE FROM NONHUMAN SPECIES

Because our main concern here is with humans, we are brief, giving examples of the types of changes most commonly observed in rodents, carnivores, and nonhuman primates with cortical lesions. The definition of what emotional behavior might be in nontalking subjects is problematic so that we use a broad definition to include all those behaviors made in response to conspecifics.

Rodents

The rodent cortex is smaller in volume and simpler in anatomy than the primate, but there is evidence of a special role of the frontal cortex in social behavior. Thus, in our studies of the affect of cortical or limbic lesions on social behavior in rats and hamsters, we observed that frontal but not posterior association cortex lesions change the manner in which the animals respond to one another (Kolb, 1974; Kolb & Nonneman, 1974; Shipley & Kolb, 1977). In particular, rats with orbital lesions show sharp reductions in the amount of social interaction with conspecifics. Thus, unlike normal rats who tend to huddle together in a strange environment, rats with orbital lesions sit alone and fail to initiate social contact. When they do interact, they are unusually submissive and do not respond normally to social cues such as social grooming. In fact, social grooming often results in fights in these animals. Further, rats with orbital frontal lesions appear overly defensive, often standing up in a "boxing" posture when interacting with intact animals. Recently, it has been suggested that the right hemisphere might have a special role in the social behavior of rats (e.g., Denenberg, Hofmann, Rosen, & Yutzey, 1984), so we compared the effect of left versus right hemidecortication on tests of social behavior that had proven sensitive to frontal damage; but although the lesions changed social behavior, we could find no evidence for any asymmetry in the behavioral effect of the lesions (Kolb, MacIntosh, Sutherland, & Whishaw, 1984).

Carnivores

Like rats with frontal cortex lesions, cats with similar lesions do not interact normally with conspecifics (Nonneman & Kolb, 1974; Warren, 1964; Warren, Warren, & Akert, 1972). For example, when placed in a large familiar room with a strange cat, normal cats show considerable interest in the stranger, often leading to a fight. In contrast, cats with frontal lesions are submissive and evade the stranger. Similarly, when confronted with a silhouette of a cat, normal cats approach the model and are piloerected. Cats with frontal lesions do not approach the model, although they are piloerected. Finally, when normal cats encounter species-typical odors (such as urine), they engage in a stereotyped behavioral pattern known as "flehmen" (Kolb & Nonneman, 1975). Cats with frontal lesions fail to show the flehmen response, although they do sniff the odor. Lesions elsewhere in the cortex do not produce similar changes.

Nonhuman Primates

The first report of a change in emotional behavior in a primate with a frontal lesion was probably Jacobsen's (1935) report on two chimpanzees that had large frontal lesions. One of the chimps, who had been quite outgoing preoperatively, was apparently docile postoperatively. This result was described in the context of delayed response-learning performance, but it led to the development of prefrontal lobotomy. Remarkably, there was little formal study of social behavior in monkeys with frontal lesions until the 1960s. During the past 20 years studies have been conducted on several species of Old and New World monkeys with frontal, anterior temporal, anterior cingulate, posterior cingulate, or visual association cortex damage. Taken together, the results show six consistent changes in emotional behavior, which are summarized in Table 6.1.

First, there is overwhelming consensus that there is a reduction in social interaction following frontal lesions, especially orbital frontal lesions. Thus, following orbital frontal lesions monkeys become socially withdrawn and fail even to re-establish close preoperative relationships with family members. The

TABLE 6.1
Summary of Changes in Social Behavior of Monkeys with
Frontal Cortical Lesions

Symptoms	Reference
1. Reduced social interaction	Franzen & Myers, 1973
	Deets et al., 1970
	Raleigh et al., 1979
	Raleigh & Steklis, 1981
	Bowden et al., 1971
	Myers & Swett, 1970
	Myers, Swett, & Miller, 1973
2. Inappropriate social interaction	Brody & Rosvold, 1952
	Deets et al., 1970
	Butter & Snyder, 1972
3. Altered social preference	Suomi et al., 1970
4. Reduced vocalization	Aitken, 1981
	Myers, 1972
	Franzen & Myers, 1973
5. Reduced facial expression and/or body gestures	Myers, 1972
	Franzen & Myers, 1973
6. Loss of social dominance	Snyder, 1970

animals sit alone, seldom if ever social groom or contact other monkeys, and in a free-ranging natural environment become solitary, leaving the troop all together. Anterior temporal lesions produce a milder version of this syndrome, as producing a reduction in social grooming and social interaction with conspecifics. Lesions elsewhere in the cortex have no obvious effect.

Second, there is a loss of social dominance following orbital frontal lesions: Monkeys that were previously dominant in a group do not maintain their dominance postoperatively, although the fall may take weeks to occur.

Third, monkeys with orbital frontal lesions show inappropriate social interaction. For example, frontal females may challenge and threaten unfamiliar male monkeys, whereas normal females typically exhibit gestures of submission in response to dominance gestures displayed by unfamiliar males. Frontal operates may also approach any animal without hesitation, irrespective of the latter animal's social dominance. This behavior frequently results in retaliatory aggression from the dominant intact animals. Similarly, when approached by dominant animals, frontal monkeys may simply ignore them or run away, rather than perform normal submissive gestures such as allowing mounting.

Fourth, monkeys with large frontal lesions show a change in social preference. When normal monkeys are released into a large enclosure that has conspecifics behind a glass barrier, they will generally sit next to an animal that is only visible through the glass. Whereas normal animals prefer to sit beside intact monkeys of the opposite sex, frontal monkeys prefer frontal monkeys of the opposite sex. Curiously, control animals prefer to sit with frontal monkeys of the same sex, presumably because they are less threatening. Frontal monkeys show no preference between intact and frontal monkeys of their own sex.

Fifth, frontal and anterior temporal operates largely lose the use of their facial expressions, posturings, and gesturings in social situations, the effects being larger after frontal than temporal lesions. Thus, monkeys with frontal lesions show a drastic drop in the frequency and variability of facial expressions and are described as being "poker-faced." The one exception to this is in the frequency of submissive or agitated expressions such as the "grimace" expression. This loss of facial expression is not simply a result of muscle control of the face, because the animals do produce expressions. They just fail to produce them often. Lesions of the cingulate or visual association cortex seem to have no effect.

Sixth, lesions of the frontal or anterior cingulate cortex reduce spontaneous social vocalizations. Indeed, following anterior cingulate lesions rhesus monkeys effectively make no normal vocalizations at all. Curiously, the nonvocal social behavior of these animals is normal.

Summary

Rodents, carnivores, and nonhuman primates all show a very similar change in social behavior after lesions of the orbital frontal cortex: They become less socially responsive and fail to respond normally to species-typical stimuli. The details of the changes vary from species to species, and the changes are more dramatic in monkeys than in cats and in cats than in rats. Nonetheless, the cross-species consistency of this result suggests that the orbital frontal cortex has an important function in emotional behavior across mammals. In addition, in monkeys there appears to be a role for the anterior temporal cortex, a zone that may not have a clear homologue in nonprimate species.

The changes in social behavior in monkeys with frontal lesions are especially intriguing for they suggest that similar changes might be found in humans with frontal-lobe injuries. In particular, because monkeys fail to make appropriate vocal and gestural behaviors and fail to respond normally to those made by conspecifics, one might predict that humans would show similar abnormalities. We see next that this is indeed the case.

CORTICAL MECHANISMS OF EMOTIONAL BEHAVIOR: EVIDENCE FROM NEUROLOGICAL PATIENTS

When we began in 1975 to study emotional behavior in patients with focal cortical lesions, there were almost no studies in the literature to guide us. Since that time there have been numerous studies of patients with lateralized lesions (i.e., right versus left hemisphere) that have looked at many aspects of emotional behavior. Several excellent recent reviews have summarized these studies, so we do not intend to review them extensively here (Borod & Koff, 1984; Campbell, 1982; Davidson, 1984; Heilman, Bowers, & Valenstein, 1985; Kinsbourne & Bemporad, 1984). The important general conclusion from these studies is that there is some asymmetry in the control of emotional behavior in the human brain; that is, lesions of the left hemisphere tend to produce different effects than equivalent lesions of the right hemisphere. Still, little is known, however, on the effects of focal cortical lesions that would be analogous to the results from studies of nonhumans. It is these data that are central to the question of localization of cortical control of emotional behavior, so we therefore focus on this question.

Problems

Virtually all the studies of neocortical mechanisms of emotional behavior in both human and laboratory animal subjects involve the lesion technique. There are several problems in the study of humans that complicate comparisons between human studies as well as with studies of nonhumans and are thus worth reviewing briefly before considering the data. First, nearly all studies of nonhumans have used bilateral lesions of a cortical region. In contrast, most studies of humans are of subjects with only unilateral lesions. This difference is not trivial, especially because it has been shown that bilateral frontal lesions in humans often produce deficits not observed following unilateral lesions of either hemisphere (Benton,

1968). A related problem is that lesions in humans seldom correspond to anatomically defined areas, whereas in laboratory subjects they normally do. Second, although there is evidence of lateralization of cortical functions in nonhumans, there is little doubt that the degree of lateralization is greater in humans. Thus, direct comparisons to nonhuman subjects with unilateral lesions are not entirely satisfactory. Third, several factors including handedness, environmental effects, and sex are likely to complicate the results in humans. Handedness appears to have no systematic relationship to functional asymmetry in nonhumans, and environment is more difficult to control in studies of human patients. Fourth, the etiology of different patient groups may influence the results. Thus, studies are commonly done of stroke patients, epileptic patients, tumor patients, and patients with elective surgery for nonlife-threatening disorders. Lesions in the different populations are not equivalent. Stroke patients have lesions that conform to vascular boundaries rather than functional boundaries. Epileptic patients may have a clear focal abnormality, but the epileptic discharges may disrupt regions far removed from the focus. Tumor patients vary depending on treatment (surgery, radiation) and malignancy. Elective surgery patients often have congenital disorders or at least disorders acquired at an early age, conditions that are likely to affect cerebral growth. Elective surgery patients with disorders acquired later in life may be the closest analogue of the studies in nonhuman subjects, but even these patients do not have normal preoperative brains, a condition quite unlike the laboratory animals.

Effects of Focal Lesions

The changes in affect seen in patients with left or right hemisphere lesions can be inferred by an observer from a number of factors. First, the production of behavior can be changed. Mood is inferred largely by facial expression and other nonvocal gestures, such as posture, tone of voice, frequency of talking, and presence or absence of "humor," so changes in these behaviors would be expected to change the "mood" of a subject. On the other hand, emotional behavior might appear abnormal not only because a person is unable to produce the appropriate behavior, but also because a person misinterprets the social or emotional signals coming from others. Thus, it is sensible to look at the effects of lesions on each of these behaviors. Our discussion centers on our own work with patients with unilateral frontal, temporal, or parietal cortex removals for the relief of intractable epilepsy, or the removal of indolent tumors or cysts. The patients all had Full-Scale Wechsler IQ ratings in the range of 80–146, and none of the patients were aphasic at the time of testing. There were no sex differences. Our criteria for inclusion in the experiments has been strict. Lesions must be restricted to the frontal, temporal, or parietal cortex, speech must be exclusively in the left hemisphere, and there must be no evidence of persisting epileptic foci elsewhere in the brain following surgery. The reader will appreciate that the research has therefore gone slowly, and the sample sizes for some experiments we report are sometimes as small as five for the left frontal and parietal lobe groups.

Production of Emotional Behavior

Over the past decade we have devised a series of measures of the production of facial expressions and facial movements, which we have taken as measures of emotional behavior. Our measures range from observations of spontaneous expressions, to the ability to copy expressions, and to make discrete facial movements. The principal result is that frontal lobe patients have several abnormalities of facial expression.

Spontaneous Facial Expression. The facial expression of patients was scored surreptitiously using a time-sampling procedure either before and during a preoperative sodium Amytal procedure or during the administration of routine neuropsychological tests. The results showed patients with frontal lobe lesions exhibit far less spontaneous facial expression than patients with posterior lesions (see Fig. 6.1). Patients with unilateral excisions of the Rolandic sensorimotor cortex representing the face did not show a reduction in the number or range of spontaneous facial expressions, in spite of a transient unilateral facial weakness. It is significant that although frontal lobe lesions reduced the frequency of facial expressions, they had no effect on their diversity. Thus, it was the spontaneity of the expressions that was reduced, not the ability to produce them. Analysis of the frequency of different expressions and movements (e.g., brow up, open-mouth smile, blink, etc.) showed that, although frontal lobe patients occasionally smiled, this expression was markedly reduced relative to all other expressions.

The reduced spontaneous facial expressions of frontal lobe patients can be contrasted with their spontaneous talking. Thus, the number of spontaneous interruptions with irrelevant comments during the performance of various tests was counted. Patients with left frontal lobe removals made almost no comments; patients with right frontal lobe lesions made an excessive number of comments (see Fig. 6.2). These data thus show a clear dissociation between the two hemispheres. Curiously, when asked to write words beginning with a particular letter (such as "s"), neither frontal lobe group was normal, a result found repeatedly by others (e.g., Milner, 1964).

The changes in facial expression and spontaneous speech in frontal lobe patients clearly influence the impression of their emotional state. In particular, the lack of facial or verbal expression in left frontal lobe patients often leads to the conclusion that they are depressed or "pseudodepressed" (e.g., Benson & Blumer, 1975). Similarly, the excessive banter of right frontal lobe patients, in addition to their flippant attitude, has led to a description of "pseudopsychopathic (e.g., Benson & Blumer, 1975).

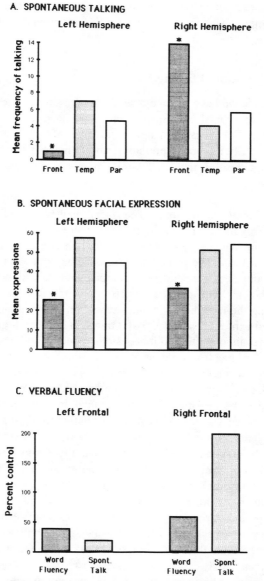

FIG. 6.1. Relative frequencies of spontaneous talking (A), facial expressions (B), and comparison of spontaneous talking to verbal fluency (C). (After Kolb & Taylor, 1981.)

Copying Facial Movements.   Although our frontal lobe patients showed no obvious facial weakness, the absence of facial expression led us to ask if these patients could control their facial musculature normally. To test this, in collaboration with Dr. Brenda Milner, we asked the patients to copy a series of individual

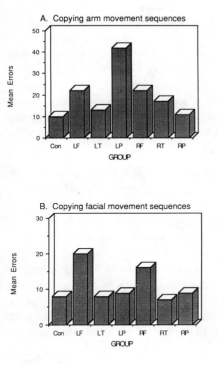

FIG. 6.2. Copying of facial movement sequences (A) and arm movements (B). (After Kolb & Milner, 1981.)

facial movements (e.g., raising the brows, sticking out the tongue) and then asked them to copy a series of three of these movements in sequence (Kolb & Milner, 1981). None of the patients, including those with sensorimotor face area lesions, had any difficulty in copying the individual movements. Both left and right frontal lobe groups were impaired, however, at copying the movement sequences (see Fig. 6.2). To determine if the difficulty in copying the movement sequences was specific to facial movement sequences, we also had the patients copy arm and hand movement sequences. Although frontal lesions produced a small deficit, those patients with left parietal lesions were particularly poor on this test, even though they were normal on the facial movement copying. One unexpected finding with this test was that when we studied a small sample of callosal patients, they too were very bad at copying the arm movements (Milner & Kolb, 1985). More surprisingly, however, they were worse at the face movement sequence copying test than were the frontal lobe patients. Because the patients with left or right sensorimotor face area removals were normal at these tests it appears that only one face area is required to perform the task. The callosal patients had both face areas and both frontal lobes intact, but they were disconnected, so in principle one would not have predicted a large deficit. Perhaps the frontal lobes tried to move the face independently, resulting in the deficit?

Copying Facial Expression.   To determine if our patients could produce facial expressions when asked, we presented a series of photographs of real (i.e., not posed) expressions taken from old copies of *Life* magazine, as well as line drawings of similar photographs in which the expressions were emphasized. Analysis of video tapes using a scoring system devised by Ekman (Ekman & Friesen, 1975) showed that all patient groups were less expressive than control subjects when producing these facial expressions, but the left frontal lobe patients were significantly less expressive than the other patient groups (Fig. 6.3).

Producing Facial Expression.   Because our patients could clearly produce expressions, we asked if they could produce them in ambiguous situations. Thus, a series of cartoons of real-life situations were produced, and we asked subjects to produce a facial expression that would be appropriate to the situation (see Fig. 6.3). Once again although all of the patient groups were less expressive than controls, the left and right frontal lobe patients produced relatively little expression. This observation leads us to suspect that the production of facial expression in normal social interaction involves multiple processes including: (a) the ability to move the face, (b) the production of expressions, and (c) the ability to understand the situation. Right frontal lobe and temporal lobe patients seem to be normal in the first two processes and not in the third. Left frontal lobe patients

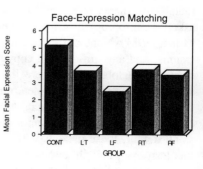

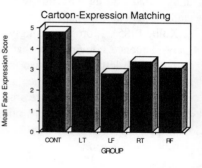

FIG. 6.3. Summary of facial expressions made to photographs of faces (top) and to cartoon situations (bottom).

seem to have difficulty with all three processes. This conclusion accords well with previous evidence of visual and auditory perceptual deficits in patients with temporal lobe lesions (for a review see Kolb & Wishaw, 1989).

Related Observations.   We have emphasized changes in facial expression but the production of emotion obviously is inferred from many other behaviors. Gainotti (1969, 1972) was the first to record systematically the "emotional reactions" of patients with unilateral lesions. He noted that patients with left hemisphere lesions were far more likely to produce "catastrophic" reactions during routine neuropsychological evaluation than were patients with right hemisphere lesions. These catastrophic reactions included bursts of tears, refusals to cooperate, swearing, and "anxiety reactions." In contrast, right hemisphere lesions were more likely to produce "indifference" behavior including such things as joke telling and lack of concern about the performance on the tests. Whereas these observations seem to confirm general clinical impressions, it is unclear just what they imply.

A number of groups have tried to localize some of these symptoms in patients with more restricted lesions. For example, several different questionnaires have been given to temporal lobe epileptics, with and without temporal lobe removals (e.g., Bear & Fedio, 1977; Fedio & Martin, 1983; Strauss, Risser, & Jones, 1983). Overall, there is a tendency for left temporal lobe patients to rate themselves more harshly and to be generally more negative, whereas right temporal lobe patients tend to be more obsessional and less depressive. Although these results suggest an asymmetry, there is considerable variance in the data as individual patients often show the reverse pattern. Further, one tends to be more impressed by the presence of a "temporal lobe personality" than an asymmetry; that is, temporal lobe patients are very different from frontal lobe patients. Indeed, recent studies of stroke patients by Robinson and his colleagues (e.g., Lipsey et al., 1983; Robinson, Kubos, Starr, Rao, & Price, 1984) shows that the intrahemispheric lesion location is a better predictor of mood change than is the side of the lesion. Thus, in their studies the severity of depression correlated with left anterior and right posterior damage, whereas right anterior damage was associated with either cheerfulness or apathy (cf. Sinyor, Jacquews, Kaloupek, Becker, Goldenberg, & Coopersmith, 1986). These results seem to be in accord with our observations in excision patients.

Social Interaction.   Emotional behavior is most commonly produced in a social context, with other people, and as we saw earlier in rats, cats, and monkeys, frontal lesions produce changes in conspecific interaction. To study this in human subjects, Deutsch, Kling, & Steklis (1979) videotaped frontal lobe patients and normal controls in a number of "free-field" settings. The overall result was that patients with unilateral frontal lobe lesions of either hemisphere responded differently, the main difference being one of less social interaction with other people and a strong tendency to be physically distant from others. This result is strikingly similar to that observed in monkeys with frontal lobe lesions (see earlier).

Perception of Emotional Stimuli

For humans the most potent emotional stimuli that we respond to in others are visual and auditory. In particular, we are very responsive to facial expression and body posture visually, and to tone of voice aurally. To examine the ability of patients to perceive such stimuli, we devised a series of tests in parallel with those described before.

Recognition of Faces. We began by looking at the patients' ability to recognize faces. Our colleague, Dr. Benda Milner, had been using the Closure Faces Test of Mooney (1956), which is illustrated in Fig. 6.4, to study face recognition in patients. This test consists of a series of incomplete representations of faces, in which the highlights and shadows are exaggerated but the contour is poorly defined. The subjects' task is to discover the face and state the sex and approximate age of the person depicted. Milner (1980) found that patients with right temporal or parietal lesions performed poorly on this test, suggesting that they were poor at recognizing faces, regardless of the expression. To pursue this possibility we borrowed a test devised by Wolff (1933) and subsequently used by many others (see Fig. 6.4). The test entails splitting full-face photographs (and their mirror-images) down the middle, then rejoining the corresponding halves to make two symmetrical composite photographs, one created from the left side of the face, the other from the right. Thus, in Fig. 6.4, we see the normal face on top and the two composite faces below. The task is to indicate which of the composite pictures resembles the real face more closely. Normal right-handed subjects show a significant bias (about 70%) in favor of the right side of the normal face. In contrast, patients with either right temporal or right parietal lesions respond ideosyncratically to each photograph, presenting no overall bias in favor of either side of the face (Fig. 6.5), a result suggesting that these patients process faces differently than normal subjects, or those patients with lesions elsewhere.

Matching Facial Expressions. To study patients' ability to appreciate different facial expressions, we did a series of experiments in which subjects were to match different photographs of faces on the basis of emotion inferred from the facial expression, or from verbal captions given to the photographs. In one test patients were given a set of six key photographs representing Ekman's distinct classes of facial expressions including happy, sad, angry, surprise, afraid, and disgust (e.g., Ekman, Friesen, & Ellsworth, 1972). They were then shown a series of photographs from *Life* magazine and asked to choose one of the six key

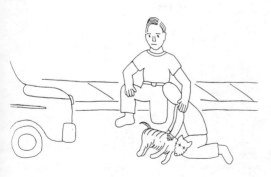

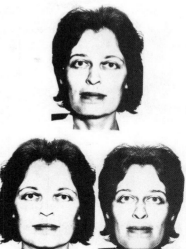

FIG. 6.4. Examples of the cartoon situations (A), composite faces (B), and Mooney's facial closure (C).

faces that best matched each of the *Life* faces. Patients with right hemisphere lesions were very poor at matching facial expressions, a result consistent with the inferred role of the right hemisphere in the processing of faces. A surprising finding, however, is that lesions in the right hemisphere had no focal effect, as both anterior and posterior lesions had an equivalent effect.

Matching Expressions to Situations. In this test we asked our subjects to take the six key faces and choose the one most appropriate for the cartoon situations we used earlier (Fig. 6.2). The patients with either frontal or temporal lesions were impaired but the deficit was significantly larger in the frontal lobe patients. Patients with left parietal lesions performed as well as control subjects, which indicates that the task is not simply a nonspecific measure of cortical

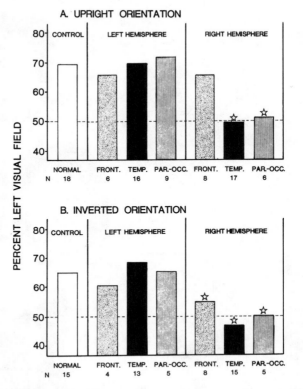

FIG. 6.5. Percentage of left visual field choices in the composite figures test when the pictures were presented in the normal upright orientation (A) and inverted to an upside-down orientation (B). (After Kolb et al., 1983.)

injury. The larger impairments of both the left and right frontal lobe patients is concordant with the results of the facial expression production experiments as both left and right frontal lobe patients appear to have the largest deficits in choosing or making facial expressions appropriate to an imaginary situation. This result is similar to that observed in nonhuman primates with frontal or temporal lobe lesions: the changes in social behavior are always large after frontal lobe lesions.

Because it has been suggested that the two hemispheres might be differentially involved in particular emotions (e.g., left for happy, right for sad), we analyzed the individual photographs to determine if the errors were related to type of emotion. They were not, implying that in our tests, at least, there is no compelling reason to think the two hemispheres participate in different emotions, a conclusion reached previously by others (e.g., Strauss, 1983).

Verbal Descriptors of Emotion in Faces.   Our face-matching tests were intentionally constructed to try to avoid a confound between verbal and nonverbal descriptions of emotional state. There is evidence, however, that left hemisphere lesions might impair the ability to comprehend propositional affect (Brownell, Michel, Powelson, & Gardner, 1983; Gardner, Ling, Flamm, & Silverman, 1975). We therefore devised three tests in which verbal labels were used. In the first, subjects were shown a series of photographs of faces from *Life* magazine and were asked to choose one of six verbal descriptors (happy, sad, angry, surprised, disgusted, afraid) that best described the feeling that the person in the photograph was experiencing. These verbal labels described the key photographs used in the face tests. Next, the subjects were read a series of sentences describing the events surrounding the people in the photographs (e.g., This man is at a funeral.). Again, they were to choose the verbal descriptor of emotional state. Finally, the subjects were again given the six key photographs from the faces test and asked to match them with the verbal label.

Our results surprised us. First, we found that when subjects were read the sentence and asked to match it with the verbal label, the patients with left hemisphere lesions made significantly more errors than those with right hemisphere lesions (see Fig. 6.6). Second, when verbal and visual components of the test were confounded, all patients did poorly relative to controls, who made virtually no errors. This latter result suggests that the two hemispheres play a complementary role in emotional behaviors, a distinction that is quite compatible with the complementary hemispheric specialization for cognitive behaviors. As we found for the face tests, there was no evidence of differential participation of the two hemispheres in particular emotions in the verbal tests.

Related Observations.   Our results suggest that damage to the right hemisphere is associated with deficits in appreciating faces and facial expression, a conclusion that is consistent with studies of stroke patients with larger lesions (e.g., Bowers et al., 1985; Cicone et al., 1980; DeKosky et al., 1980). Three points arise, however. First, it appears that the right temporal lobe is especially important in perceiving facial expression, as patients with right temporal lobe lesions are impaired at all face tests we have administered. Second, both left and right frontal lobe patients are impaired at perceiving facial expression. Third, patients with left temporal lobe lesions are also impaired at some aspects of facial perception, namely when they must match an expression to a situation. These three observations suggest that although there is undoubtedly some left/right asymmetry in the neural mechanisms involved in the interpretation of emotion in faces, both frontal and temporal lobes play a role. It is likely that a similar conclusion is true of the interpretation of tone of voice as well. Several studies have shown that right hemisphere lesions impair the perception of tone of voice (e.g., Heilman, Scholes, & Watson, 1975; Tompkins & Mateer, 1985), and we have found that when asked to match one of the key photographs to the mood

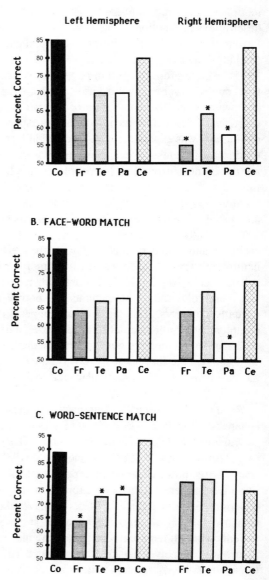

FIG. 6.6. Summary of the tests of face-face matching (A) and word-sentence matching (B). (After Kolb & Taylor, 1981.)

heard in a sentence, both left and right temporal lobe groups are impaired severely. Indeed, patients with right temporal lobe lesions scored only marginally above chance. Again, there is likely some asymmetry, the right hemisphere being dominant in this ability, but both temporal lobes appear to be necessary to interpret tone of voice accurately.

Conclusions

The results of our experiments lead us to several conclusions. First, the frontal lobes play a special role in the control of the face, and especially in the production of spontaneous facial expression. Significantly, frontal lobe patients are able to produce expressions when appropriate; they simply do not. This is important for it may reflect a general deficit of frontal lobe patients in generating spontaneous behavior of which facial expression is only an example. Second, the temporal lobes play a special role in the perception of emotion, be it in facial expression or in tone of voice. This role is consistent with the general role of the temporal lobes in processing complex sensory information. Furthermore, the deficit in appreciation of emotion in others probably leads to a deficit in producing emotional expression appropriately. Third, there is a complementary specialization of the two hemispheres in emotional behavior, the left hemisphere being more involved in verbal components and the right in nonverbal components. It follows that the cortical control of emotional behavior cannot be localized to either the left or the right hemisphere, as both play a role. Fourth, the role of cortical site (i.e., frontal, temporal) is at least as important as that of cortical side (i.e., left, right) in the control of emotional behavior. Indeed, in many ways the differences between the effects of frontal and temporal lobe lesions are greater than the differences between the left and right frontal or temporal lobes. Comparisons of frontal, temporal, and parietal lobe contributions is difficult, however, as naturally occurring lesions seldom respect the anatomical boundaries. Finally, we note that the effects of frontal lobe lesions on social behaviors of human subjects are conceptually similar to those observed in nonhuman subjects. In particular, frontal lobe lesions reduce the emotional spontaneity and social interaction in all mammals that have been studied.

CORTICAL MECHANISMS OF EMOTIONAL BEHAVIOR; EVIDENCE FROM PSYCHIATRIC PATIENTS

People with psychiatric disorders are often found to have difficult social relationships and sometimes become socially isolated. Clinical descriptions of schizophrenia in particular typically refer to disturbances of affective communication. The nature of the affective difficulty in disorders like schizophrenia is poorly understood, however, because most studies have employed rating scales, few of which are free of theoretical preconceptualizations.

Recent neurological studies of schizophrenics have shown abnormalities in cortical activity as measured by PET scans and blood flow studies. These results are particularly germaine to the current discussion because it is the frontal lobes and medial temporal areas that are consistently found to have abnormal activity in these studies. We therefore wondered how schizophrenic patients might compare to our neurological population. One immediate problem we had to concern ourselves with was medication, because poor performance on given tests could be due to the medication rather than to a deficit in cortical processing per se. At the same time we had an opportunity to study a population of people suffering from Gilles de la Tourette's disease. Little is known of the etiology of this disorder, but it is characterized by involuntary facial and body tics, in addition to involuntary vocalizations. No treatment is particularly effective but most patients are prescribed either haloperidol or clonidine. The Tourette's Syndrome patients therefore provide a good control for our schizophrenic group, who are on similar drugs, and in addition the changes in facial movements make them an interesting comparison to the frontal lobe patients.

To provide a direct comparison with our neurological patients, it was necessary first to do a complete neuropsychological evaluation on these subjects (Kolb & Whishaw, 1983; Sutherland et al., 1982). To summarize briefly, these data show that the schizophrenic patients (mean age 28 yr, mean total hospitalization of less than 6 mo) were impaired at all tests sensitive to frontal and temporal lobe excision but performed normally on tests sensitive to parietal lobe excision (Kolb & Whishaw, 1983). In contrast, Tourette's Syndrome patients showed a more focal pattern of results, so their deficits were largely restricted to certain tests performed poorly by right temporal lobe patients.

Production of Emotion

The Tourette Syndrome patients were indistinguishable from the control subjects on tests requiring the production of emotional expression, whereas the schizophrenic subjects were poor at all measures.

Spontaneous Expressions.   Like frontal lobe patients, the schizophrenic subjects produced fewer spontaneous expressions than control subjects (Pitman, Kolb, Orr, & Singh, 1987). Curiously, when the data for subjects classified as paranoid or nonparanoid were separated, there was a clear difference: The paranoid subjects produced less expression than the nonparanoid subjects. When the spontaneous talking was analyzed, the data showed that the schizophrenics did less talking than normal, and so in this respect resembled the left frontal lobe subjects. Again, there was a paranoid–nonparanoid difference within the schizophrenic group with the paranoid subjects being the more talkative (Fig. 6.7). Finally, like the frontal lobe patients, schizophrenic patients had a reduced verbal fluency on formal testing.

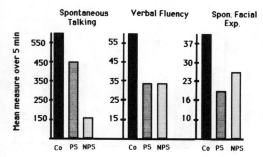

FIG. 6.7. Spontaneous talking, verbal fluency, and spontaneous facial expression in control (C), paranoid schizophrenic (PS), and nonparanoid schizophrenic (NPS). (Data after Pitman et al., 1987, and Kolb & Whishaw, 1983.)

Movement Copying.   When asked to copy sequences of arm or face movements, the Tourette Syndrome subjects performed normally, but once again the schizophrenics did poorly, especially on the face movements. In fact, the schizophrenic subjects made more than twice as many errors as the frontal lobe subjects on the copying of the facial movement sequences, even though essentially no errors were made in copying the individual movements.

Interpretation of Emotion

Recognition of Faces.   Both the schizophrenic and Tourette Syndrome groups performed normally on the Mooney closure test, and both responded at chance on the composite faces test. Thus, it appears that both groups recognize faces but do not necessarily process faces normally. This result differs from the right temporal lobe patients who performed both tests poorly, and the frontal lobe patients who did not differ from normal control subjects on either test.

Matching Facial Expressions and Situations.   Both the schizophrenic and Tourette's Syndrome subjects performed within normal limits on the facial expression-matching test. When asked to use context to predict the appropriate expression, the Tourette Syndrome subjects still performed normally, but the schizophrenic subjects were significantly poorer than controls. Thus, like left temporal lobe patients, schizophrenics were able to match facial expressions in different people but were impaired at using context to determine the expression appropriate to an emotional situation.

Verbal Matching.   The schizophrenic patients performed poorly on the tests requiring the matching of verbal labels to emotional expression, whereas the Tourette Syndrome subjects were normal once again (see Fig. 6.8).

Conclusions

Our comparison of schizophrenic and Tourette Syndrome patients leads to several conclusions. First, we believe that the drug effects in the schizophrenic subjects are not directly responsible for the poor performance on the tests because the

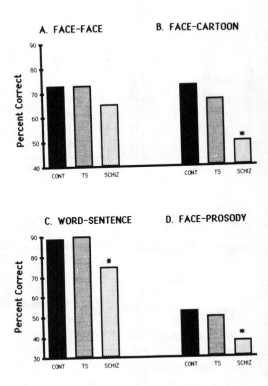

FIG. 6.8. Summary of the performance of control (cont), Tourette's Syndrome (TS), and schizophrenic (schiz) subjects on four tests: Face–face matching, face–cartoon matching, word–sentence matching, and face–prosody matching. The TS group never differed from controls, whereas the schizophrenic was significantly poorer than both other groups on the latter three tests. (Kolb, Buday, & Wilson, 1989.)

Tourette Syndrome patients on similar medication performed normally on nearly all the tests. Second, the difficulty of the schizophrenic subjects in perceiving the meaning of facial expressions in context, combined with their low spontaneous facial and verbal expression, is consistent with the clinical impression of a deficit in affective communication in these subjects. Third, the performance of the schizophrenic patients is poor on all the tests that *either* our frontal or temporal lobe patients perform poorly on, a result that is consistent with neurological data suggesting that neither the frontal nor temporal lobes are functioning normally in schizophrenics. Also note that the pattern of deficits on the perceptual tests is more similar to that of left than right temporal lobe patients, a result that is consistent with claims of left temporal dysfunction in schizophrenia (e.g., Flor-Henry, 1979). However, the expressive disorder seen in schizophrenic patients is not found in temporal lobe patients. Finally, the generally normal performance of patients with Tourette's Syndrome implies that their problem is not largely cortical, a conclusion already reached by others.

DEVELOPMENTAL CHANGES IN EMOTIONAL
EXPRESSION IN CHILDREN

There are significant challenges to the study of the development of the neural basis of behavior in children. When the child is born the complete complement of neurons are present, but many neural elements are very immature such as dendritic fields, synaptic contacts, and connections. The development of these elements continues for up to 16–18 years, and the development is uneven across the cortex. Thus, the primary sensory areas mature relatively quickly, whereas the frontal lobes continue to change until about 16 years of age. In principle, it is logical to correlate the emergence of behaviors and the maturation of particular cortical areas and to infer a relationship, but like all correlations this is not without problems. For example, a child may have difficulty with a verbal test because the speech areas are slow to develop or because he has an impoverished environment and has acquired only a limited vocabulary. Furthermore, just because a child does well on a test does not mean that the child's brain is solving the problem in the same manner as the adult brain. Indeed, there are examples of tests in which children do well, only to do more poorly the following year, followed later by improvement again. Thus, in their studies of facial recognition in children, Carey, Diamond, and Woods (1980) found that children improved in performance between ages 6 and 10, declined until age 14, and then attained adult levels by age 16. This result can be taken to imply that the younger children were solving the problem in a different manner than the older children and adults and were presumably using different cortical tissue. In sum, although there are clear limitations to the inferences that can be made about the development of specific brain regions, much can be learned using this type of approach. In particular, we consider the performance of children on the perceptual tests as well as on some tests of frontal and temporal lobe function.

Changes in Neuropsychological Test Performance

Over the last decade several colleagues (Roger Barnsley, Brenda Kosaka, Ian Whishaw, Barbara Wilson) have collaborated with us to look at changes in the performance of children on tests of dichotic listening, word fluency, nonverbal memory, drawing, digit span, and the face perception tests.

Cognitive Tests. The data, which are illustrated in Fig. 6.10, show two important results. Fist, the developmental changes vary markedly from test to test. Thus, report of dichotically presented words improves until 16–18 years, although the right ear bias asymptotes at 5 years, digit span reaches adult level about 11 years of age, word fluency continues to improve until about 18 years of age, and recall of a complex geometric figure (Rey-Osterrith) reaches asymptotes at about 12 (Fig. 6.9). Second, performance of children is often no better than

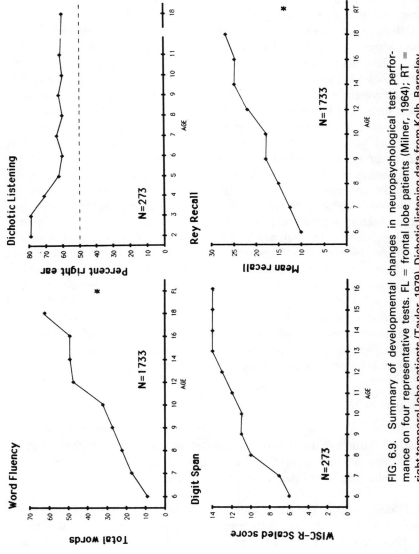

FIG. 6.9. Summary of developmental changes in neuropsychological test performance on four representative tests. FL = frontal lobe patients (Milner, 1964); RT = right temporal lobe patients (Taylor, 1979). Dichotic listening data from Kolb, Barnsley, and Kosaka (unpublished, 1977). Word fluency and Rey recall from Whishaw and Kolb (unpublished, 1982).

adults with a cortical excision. For example, the recall of the Rey figure by children up to about age 8 is not reliably different from that of adults with a right temporal lobectomy (Fig. 6.10).

Face Perception Tests.   Like the cognitive tests, there are clear developmental changes in the performance on these tests, changes that vary markedly from test to test. It appears that the ability to locate faces in the closure test improves for a long time even though the processing of faces, as inferred from the composite faces test, is adult-like early. As one might expect, the ability to match facial expressions is mature well before the ability to choose an expression appropriate for a situation.

The development of adult performance on both the cognitive and face perception tasks certainly reflects more than just the development of cortical tissue. In particular, it probably indicates an interaction of experience and cortical development. Significantly, however, the differential developmental rates at different ages show that the tests are probably measuring different abilities and, by inference, different cortical areas. The frontal and temporal cortices are the last to develop, and it is tempting to speculate that the late development of the face cartoon-matching ability reflects the slow development of the temporal cortex. At any rate, it is reasonable to predict from our results that emotional behavior in children will continue to develop until mid to late adolescence.

CONCLUSIONS

The goal of this chapter has been to examine the role of the neocortex in the control of emotion. We have shown that damage to the frontal and temporal regions of all mammalian species seems to lead to unambiguous changes in social/affective behavior that are strikingly similar across species. Further, psychiatric disorders that are believed to result from frontal and/or temporal lobe dysfunction produce changes in social/affective behavior that are similar to those observed in neurological patients with frontal or temporal lobe injury. The development of the neural bases of emotional behavior is difficult to study, for normal social interaction surely requires the development of both the requisite neural circuits as well as the learning of sociocultural rules. Nonetheless, it is interesting to note that the frontal and temporal lobes are the last regions to become fully mature in humans, and this anatomical development correlates with certain developmental changes in social and affective behavior in children. We believe the data from our experiments point to a conclusion that the cortex has an important, and vastly underestimated, role in emotional behavior. Most studies of humans to date have emphasized the complementary specialization of the two cerebral hemispheres in the control of emotional behavior, and we too have seen evidence of this in our work. We believe, however, that other factors are as important to

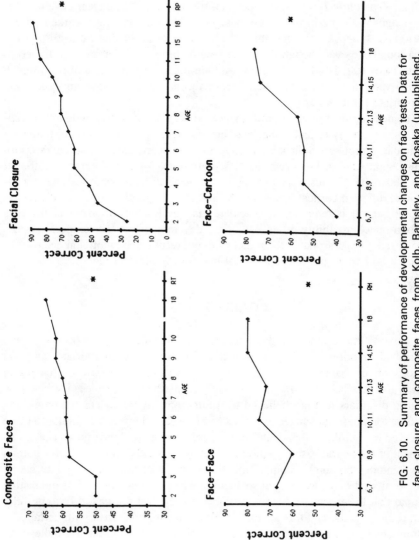

FIG. 6.10. Summary of performance of developmental changes on face tests. Data for face closure and composite faces from Kolb, Barnsley, and Kosaka (unpublished, 1977). Data for face–face match and face–cartoon match from Kolb and Wilson (unpublished, 1985).

our understanding the role of the cortex in emotional behavior. For example, we have found that the differences between frontal and temporal lobe contributions to emotional behavior are probably larger than those between the hemispheres. Similarly, other biological factors such as handedness and sex, which are known to influence cortical organization, will have to be considered in the future as will the role of experience, which has been shown to alter cerebral organization in laboratory animals. The task will be formidable, but we will not have a complete understanding of the nature of human emotion until we can better understand the requisite neural hardware that allows the expression of our emotional life.

REFERENCES

Aitken, P. G. (1981). Cortical control of conditioned and spontaneous vocal behavior in rhesus monkeys. *Brain and Language, 14,* 171–184.

Bard, P. (1928). A diencephalic mechanism for the expression of rage with special reference to the sympathetic nervous system. *American Journal of Physiology, 84,* 490–515.

Bear, D. M., & Fedio, P. (1977). Quantitative analysis of interictal behavior in temporal lobe epilepsy. *Archives of Neurology, 34,* 454–467.

Benson, F., & Blumer, D. (1975). (Eds.), *Psychiatric aspects of neurologic disease.* New York: Grune & Stratton.

Benton, A. L. (1968). Differential effects of frontal lobe disease. *Neuropsychologia, 6,* 53–60.

Borod, J. C., & Koff, E. (1984). Asymmetries in affective facial expression: behavior and anatomy. In N. A. Fox & R. J. Davidson, (Eds.), *The psychobiology of affective development* (pp. 293–324). Hillsdale, NJ: Lawrence Erlbaum Associates.

Bowden, D. J. M., Goldman, P. S., Rosvold, H. E., & Greenstreet, R. L. (1971). *Experimental Brain Research, 12,* 265–274.

Bowers, D., Bauer, R. M., Coslett, H. B., & Heilman, K. M. (1985). Processing of faces by patients with unilateral hemisphere lesions. *Brain and Cognition, 4,* 258–272.

Brady, J. V. (1960). Emotional behavior. *Handbook of Physiology,* (Vol. III, pp. 1529–1552). New York: American Physiological Society.

Brody, E. B., & Rosvold, H. E. (1952). Influence of prefrontal lobotomy on social interaction in a monkey group. *Psychosomatic Medicine, 14,* 405–415.

Brown, S., & Schafer, E. A. (1888). An investigation into the functions of the occipital and temporal lobe of the monkey's brain. Philosophical *Transactions of the Royal Society, (part B), 179,* 303–327.

Brownell, H. H., Michel, D., Powelson, J., & Gardner, H. (1983). Surprise but not coherence: sensitivity to verbal humor in right-hemisphere patients. *Brain and Language, 18,* 20–27.

Butter, C. M., & Snyder, J. D. R. (1972). Alterations in aversive and aggressive behaviors following orbital frontal lesions in rhesus monkeys. *Acta Neurobiologiae Experimentalis, 32,* 525–565.

Campbell, R. (1982). The lateralisation of emotion: A critical review. *International Journal of Psychology, 17,* 211–229.

Carey, S., Diamond, R., & Woods, B. (1980). The development of face recognition—a maturational problem? *Developmental Psychology, 16,* 257–269.

Cicone, M., Wapner, J. W., & Gardner, H. (1980). Sensitivity to emotional expressions and situations in organic patients. *Cortex, 16,* 145–158.

Davidson, R. J. (1984). Affect, cognition, and hemispheric specialization. In C. E. Izard, J. Kagan, & R. Zajonc (Eds.), *Emotions, cognition, and behavior.* New York: Cambridge University Press.

Deets, A. C., Harlow, H. F., Singh, S. D., & Blomquist, A. J. (1970). Effects of bilateral lesions on the frontal granular cortex of the social behavior of rhesus monkeys. *Journal of Comparative and Physiological Psychology, 72,* 452–461.

De Kosky, S. T., Heilman, K. M., Bowers, D., & Valenstein, E. (1980). Recognition and discrimination of emotional faces and pictures. *Brain and Language, 9,* 206–214.

Denenberg, V. H., Hofmann, M. J., Rosen, G. D., Yutzey, D. A. (1984). Cerebral asymmetry and behavioral laterality: Some psychobiological considerations. In N. A. Fox & R. J. Davidson (Eds.), *The psychobiology of affective development* (pp. 77–118). Hillsdale, NJ: Lawrence Erlbaum Associates.

Deutsch, R. D., Kling, A., & Steklis, H. D. (1979). Influence of frontal lobe lesions on behavioral interactions in man. *Research Communications in Psychology, Psychiatry and Behavior, 4,* 415–431.

Dunbar, H. F. (1954). *Emotions and bodily changes* (4th ed.). New York: Columbia.

Ekman, P., & Friesen, W. V. (1975). *Unmasking the face.* Englewood Cliffs, NJ: Prentice-Hall.

Ekman, P., Friesen, W. V., & Ellsworth, P. (1972). *Emotion in the human face.* Elmsford, NY: Pergamon.

Fedio, P., & Martin, A. (1983). Ideative-emotive behavioral characteristics of patients following left or right temporal lobectomy. *Epilepsia, 24,* S117–S130.

Flor-Henry, P. (1979). Schizophrenic-like reactions and affective psychoses associated with temporal lobe epilepsy. *American Journal of Psychiatry, 126,* 400–403.

Franzen, E. A., & Myers, R. E. (1973). Neural control of social behavior: prefrontal and anterior temporal cortex. *Neuropsychologia, 11,* 141–157.

Gainotti, G. (1969). Reactions catastrophiques et manifestations d'indifference au cours des atteintes cerebrales. *Neuropsychologia, 7,* 195–204.

Gainotti, G. (1972). Emotional behavior and hemispheric side of lesion. *Cortex, 8,* 41–55.

Gardner, H., Ling, P. K., Flamm, L., & Silverman, J. (1975). Comprehension and appreciation of humorous material following brain damage. *Brain, 98,* 399–412.

Goldstein, K. (1948). *Language and language disturbances.* New York: Grune & Stratton.

Goltz, J. F. (1960). On the functions of the hemispheres. In G. von Bonin (Ed.), *The cerebral cortex.* Springfield, IL: Charles C. Thomas.

Harlow, J. (1868). Recovery from the passage of an iron bar through the head. *Publication of the Mass. Medical Society,* Boston, 2, 327–346.

Heilman, K. M., Scholes, R., & Watson, J. T. (1975). Auditory affective agnosia: Disturbed comprehension of affective speech. *Journal of Neurology, Neurosurgery, and Psychiatry, 38,* 69–72.

Jacobsen, C. F. (1935). Functions of the frontal association area in primates. *Archives of Neurology and Psychiatry, 33,* 558–569.

Kinsbourne, M., & Bemporad, B. (1984). Lateralization of emotion: A model and the evidence. In N. A. Fox & R. J. Davidson (Eds.), *The psychobiology of affective development* (pp. 259–292). Hillsdale, NJ: Lawrence Erlbaum Associates.

Kluver, H., & Bucy, P. C. (1939). Preliminary analysis of the temporal lobes in monkeys. *Archives of Neurology and Psychiatry, 42,* 979–1000.

Kolb, B. (1974). Social behavior of rats with chronic prefrontal lesions. *Journal of Comparative and Physiological Psychology, 87,* 466–474.

Kolb, B., Barnsley, R., & Kosaka, B. (1977). *Development of laterality in dichotic listening scores in children.* Unpublished research.

Kolb, B., Buday, M., & Wilson, B. (1989). *Perception of faces and facial expression by schizophrenic and Gilles de la Tourette's patients.* Manuscript in preparation.

Kolb, B., MacKinstosh, A., Whishaw, I. Q., and Sutherland, R. J. (1984). Evidence for anatomical but not functional asymmetry in the hemidecorticate rat. *Behavioral Neuroscience, 98,* 44–58.

Kolb, B., & Milner, B. (1981). Observations on spontaneous facial expression after focal cerebreal excisions and after intracarotid injection of sodium amytal. *Neuropsychologia, 19,* 505–514.

Kolb, B., Milner, B., & Taylor, L. (1983). Perception of faces by patients with localized cortical excisions. *Canadian Journal of Psychology, 37*, 8–18.

Kolb, B., & Taylor, L. (1981). Affective behavior in patients with localized cortical excisions: Role of lesion site and side. *Science, 214*, 89–91.

Kolb, B., & Nonneman, A. J. (1974). Frontolimbic lesions and social behavior in the rat. *Physiology and Behavior, 13*, 637–643.

Kolb, B., & Nonneman, A. J. (1975). The development of social responsiveness in kittens. *Animal Behavior, 23*, 368–374.

Kolb, B., & Whishaw, I. Q. (1983). Performance of schizophrenic patients on tests sensitive to left or right frontal, temporal, or parietal function in neurological patients. *Journal of Nervous and Mental Disease, 171*, 435–443.

Kolb, B., & Whishaw, I. Q. (1989). *Fundamentals of human neuropsychology* (3rd ed.). New York: W. H. Freeman.

Lehrman, D. S. (1970). Semantic and conceptual issues in the nature-nuture problem. In L. R. Aronson, E. Tobach, D. S. Lehrman, & J. S. Rosenblatt (Eds.), *Development and evolution of behavior* (pp. 17–52). San Francisco: W. H. Freeman.

Lipsey, J. R., Robinson, R. G., Pearlson, G. D., Rao, K., & Price, T. R. (1983). Mood disorders in stroke patients: Importance of location of lesion. *Brain, 107*, 81–93.

McLean, P. (1949). Psychosomatic disease and the "visceral brain" and their bearing on the Papez theory of emotion. *Psychosomatic Medicine, 11*, 338–353.

Milner, B. (1964). Some effects of frontal lobectomy in man. In J. M. Warren & K. Akert (Eds.) *The frontal granular cortex and behavior* (pp. 313–334). New York: McGraw-Hill.

Milner, B. (1980). Complementary functional specializations of the human cerebral hemispheres. *Pontificiae Academiae Scientiarulm Scripta Varia, 45*, 601–625.

Milner, B., & Kolb, B. (1985). Performance of complex arm movements and facial-movement sequences after cerebral commissurotomy. *Neuropsychologia, 23*, 791–799.

Mooney, C. J. M. (1956). Closure with negative after-images under flickering light. *Canadian Journal of Psychology, 10*, 191–199.

Myers, R. E. (1972). Role of prefrontal and anterior temporal cortex in social behavior and affect in monkeys. *Acta Neurobiologiae Experimentalis, 32*, 567–579.

Myers, R. E., & Sweet, C. (1970). Social behavior deficits of free-ranging monkeys after anterior-temporal cortex removal: A preliminary report. *Brain Research, 18*, 551–556.

Myers, R. E., Swett, C., & Miller, M. (1973). Loss of social group affinities following prefrontal lesions in free-ranging macaques. *Brain Research, 64*, 257–269.

Nonneman, A. J., & Kolb, B. (1974). Lesions of hippocampus or prefrontal cortex alter species-typical behaviors in the cat. *Behavioral Biology, 12*, 41–54.

Papez, J. W. (1937). A proposed mechanism of emotion. *Archives of Neurology and Psychiatry, 38*, 725–744.

Pitman, R. K., Kolb, B., Orr, S. P., & Singh, M. M. (1987). Ethological study of facial behavior in nonparanoid and paranoid schizophrenic patients. *American Journal of Psychiatry, 144*, 99–102.

Raleigh, M. J., & Steklis, H. D. (1981). Effects of orbitofrontal and temporal neocortical lesions on the affiliative behavior of vervet monkeys (Cercopithecus aethiops sabaeus). *Experimental Neurology, 73*, 378–389.

Raleigh, M. J., Steklis, H. D., Ervin, F. R., Kling, A. S., & McGuire, M. T. (1979). The effects of orbitofrontal lesions on the aggressive behavior of vervet monkeys (Cercopithecus aethiops sabaeus). *Experimental Neurology, 66*, 158–168.

Robinson, R. G., Kubos, K. L., Starr, L. B., Rao, K. & Price, T. R. (1984). Mood disorders in stroke patients: Importance of location of lesion. *Brain, 107*, 81–93.

Shipley, J. E., & Kolb, B. (1977). Neural correlates of species-typical behavior in the Syrian Golden hamster. *Journal of Comparative and Physiological Psychology, 91*, 1056–1073.

Sinyor, D., Jacquews, P., Kaloupek, D. G., Becker, R., Goldenberg, M., & Coopersmith, H. (1986). Poststroke depression and lesion location: An attempted replication. *Brain, 109,* 537–546.

Snyder, D. R. (1970). Fall from social dominance folloywing orebitral freontal ablation in monkeys. *Proceedings of the 78th Annual Convention of the American Psychological Association* (pp. 235–236).

Strauss, E. (1983). Cerebral representation of emotion. In P. Blanck, R. Buck, & S. Rosenthal (Eds.), *Nonverbal communication in the clinical context.* State College: Penn State Press.

Strauss, E., Risser, A., & Jones, M. (1982). Fear responses in patients with epilepsy. *Archives of Neurology, 39,* 626–630.

Suomi, S. J., Harlow, H. F., & Lewis, J. K. (1970). Effect of bilateral frontal lobectomy on social preferences of rhesus monkeys. *Journal of Comparative and Physiological Psychology, 70,* 448–453.

Taylor, L. B. (1979). Psychological assessment of neurosurgical patients. In T. Rasmussen & R. Marino (Eds.), *Functional neurosurgery.* New York: Raven Press.

Tompkins, C. A., & Mateer, C. A. (1985). Right hemisphere appreciation of prosodic and linguistic indications of implicit attitude. *Brain and Language, 24,* 185–203.

Warren, J. M. (1964). The behavior of carnivores and primates with lesions in the prefrontal cortex. In J. M. Warren & K. Akert (Eds.), *The frontal granular cortex and behavior* (pp. 168–191). New York: McGraw-Hill.

Warren, J. M., Warren, H. B., & Akert, K. (1972). The behavior of chronic cats with lesions in the frontal association cortex. *Acta Neurobiologiae Experimentalis, 32,* 345–392.

Whishaw, I. Q., & Kolb, B. (1982). *Developmental changes in neuropsychological test performance.* Unpublished research.

Wolff, W. (1933). The experimental study of forms of expression. *Character and Personality, 2,* 168–176.

Woodworth, R. S., & Sherrington, C. S. (1904). A pseudoaffective reflex and its spinal path. *Journal of Physiology, 31,* 234–243.

7 Arousal and Activation Systems and Primitive Adaptive Controls on Cognitive Priming

Don M. Tucker
Kathryn Vannatta
Johannes Rothlind
University of Oregon

Certain things may be expected from a biological approach to emotion. It may be expected to deal with elementary, primitive things, like visceral stirrings or animalistic urges. It may also be expected to review facts and observational evidence rather than theorize about mental processes. The account of emotion we provide in this chapter should be satisfying to such expectations on the first count. We propose that the primitive substrates of mammalian motivational and emotional systems are integral to the human psychological functions. Our account may not meet the second expectation. Although there are observed facts on neural arousal systems that serve as a foundation for our approach, these facts do not speak for themselves. To proceed from concepts of neural control mechanisms to address issues of attentional and emotional control requires substantial theorizing. We take this theorizing as an important component of a neuropsychological approach to emotion, and as the work of this chapter. Our contention is that by developing concepts required to fit the neurophysiological evidence we may find novel ways of thinking about human motivation and emotion.

ACTIVATION AND AROUSAL THEORY

Interpreting Hemispheric Specialization for Emotion

In modern psychological models of emotion (Mandler, 1985; Schacter & Singer, 1962), the construction of emotional experience often seems to occur through verbal, propositional cognition. Neuropsychologists have recently become intrigued with the nonverbal cognitive operations of the right hemisphere that

145

support many aspects of emotional communication (Borod, Koff, & Buck, 1986; Tucker, 1981). The evidence is strong that understanding emotion in facial expressions or in tone of voice requires an intact right hemisphere (Tucker, Watson, & Heilman, 1976), and several findings suggest that greater reliance on right hemisphere processing is characteristic of normal emotional communication (Safer, 1981; Safer & Leventhal, 1977). Greater intensity of facial expressions on the left side of the face may suggest right hemisphere facilitation of emotional expression (Sackeim, Gur, & Saucy, 1978). However, this asymmetry could also reflect greater inhibition of emotion by the left hemisphere (Buck & Duffy, 1980; Dopson, Beckwith, Tucker, & Bullard-Bates, 1985). If we can assume that the cognitive processes in emotional communication are indicative of those that are integral to emotional experience, these findings suggest that verbal cognition may not be the most direct form of cognitive elaboration of emotion. Rather, the analogical and syncretic processing skills of the right hemisphere may provide important ways of monitoring and conceptualizing emotional experience (Buck, 1985; Tucker, 1981).

Another line of evidence suggests that the left and right hemispheres both contribute to the person's emotional orientation, but in opposite ways. The important initial finding was that lesions to the left hemisphere often produce a depressive–catastrophic reaction, which may not be surprising; yet lesions to the right hemisphere may produce inappropriate optimism and indifference to misfortune (Gainotti, 1972). Observations of emotional effects after recovery from unilateral hemisphere sedation (Terzian, 1964) showed similar results. These findings have led many investigators to conclude that the left hemisphere normally contributes a positive emotional orientation, and the right hemisphere a negative one. This position has been argued most convincingly by Sackeim, Greenberg, Weiman, Gur, Hungerbuhler, and Geschwind (1982). In addition to the unilateral lesion evidence, Sackeim et al. reviewed reports of emotional effects following other neurologic disorders to support their position. Laughing during an epileptic seizure is most common with a left hemisphere focus, suggesting an exaggeration of left hemisphere function in this positive emotion.

Although the contralateral release interpretation of the unilateral lesion evidence has been influential, one of us (Tucker, 1981) has argued for an opposite interpretation. An important neurological principle is that a cortical lesion may disinhibit subcortical processes (Jackson, 1897/1958). Hemispheric lesions have been observed to exaggerate aspects of the hemisphere's apparent contribution to perceptual organization (Hall, Hall, & Lavoie, 1968). Thus a depressive–catastrophic response following a left hemisphere lesion could represent a disinhibition of the left hemisphere's negative affect rather than a release of that of the right. The emotional reactions in the unilateral sedation studies only occurred after the EEG of the sedated hemisphere had returned to an activated state; this does not fit with the contralateral release interpretation. And with respect to laughing during left-sided seizures, it is not clear that a seizure would necessarily result in an integrated action such as laughing more than it would disrupt the cortical inhibition of subcortical affect, as in pseudobulbar palsy.

Furthermore, human emotion is difficult to categorize on a unidimensional positive–negative axis. Tucker (1981) suggested that the basic dimensions of human emotion should influence the form taken by various forms of psychopathology; yet we do not find a simple positive or negative dimension of emotion in psychiatric disorders. To formulate a model that would account for the changes in hemispheric function found in psychopathology (Flor-Henry, 1976; Gur, 1978) as well as the unilateral lesion effects and the right hemisphere's role in emotional communication, Tucker proposed that the underlying emotional dimension important to the right hemisphere's level of activity and function is mood, varying from depression to elation. Thus mood level seems to preferentially modulate the right hemisphere's affective processing and syncretic conceptualization. The person's general hedonic tone—along the depression–elation dimension—is thus paralleled by variations in right hemisphere function. This formulation is consistent with Levy's (1982) theoretical analysis of cortical–subcortical interactions in emotional control. However, the left hemisphere is not without its motivational characteristics. Tucker (1981) reviewed evidence that the left hemisphere's level of activity and cognitive functioning may be related to anxiety, both in normals and in psychopathological groups.

Much of the difficulty in resolving the controversies over which hemisphere tends toward which emotion may occur because a hemisphere is too gross a unit of analysis. Recent systematic observations on unilateral lesions have shown that the anterior/posterior locus of the lesion has a major bearing on the patient's emotional state (Robinson, Kubos, Rao, & Price, 1984). The catastrophic response seems to follow only frontal left hemisphere lesions, and the inappropriate cheerfulness follows only frontal right hemisphere lesions. Because frontal lesions often produce disinhibition, Tucker (1986) interprets the Robinson et al. data as consistent with an ipsilateral hemispheric disinhibition model. Anterior/posterior interactions have also proven important to the asymmetric frontal EEG changes in normal emotional states (Davidson, 1984; Tucker, Stenslie, Roth, & Shearer, 1981). Because the frontal lobe itself has a major functional differentiation between dorsolateral and orbital regions, it is clear that any real understanding of emotional processes in the brain will require a more fine-grained analysis. Johanson, Risberg, Silfverskiöld, and Smith (in press), for example, found a left frontal increase in blood flow in anxiety-disorder patients that was further localized to orbital frontal cortex.

Regardless of the exact mechanisms of the emotional release in the lesion studies, the literature on brain lateralization provides two different perspectives on cognition-emotion interactions. It suggests that each hemisphere's cognition may play a unique role elaborating and regulating emotion—a top-down view.

But it also suggests that the two hemispheres' levels of functioning may be dependent on different kinds of emotional arousal—formulated by Tucker (1981) as mood and anxiety. This latter perspective is a bottom-up view, wherein elementary emotional and motivational mechanisms differentially regulate hemispheric cognition. Regardless of which hemisphere does which emotion, it is clear that the changes in hemispheric function that occur with lesions or unilateral sedation are not simply emotional but include dramatic changes in cognitive appraisal. In the emotional response while recovering from left hemisphere sedation, for example, the patient doesn't simply cry but engages in catastrophic evaluations of his current and future life circumstances (Terzian, 1964). This suggests that the emotional mechanisms of the two hemispheres may play markedly different roles in regulating the cognitive appraisal processes of normal cognition.

Neural Control Systems

In an effort to understand the nature of neural arousal mechanisms, and how these might be involved in asymmetric brain activity in emotional states, Tucker and Williamson (1984) reviewed the literature on the neurophysiological and neurochemical mechanisms through which the brain self-regulates its level of activity. These mechanisms are complex and manifold, involving multiple inhibitory as well as excitatory influences, and involving an intricate interplay between primitive adaptive mechanisms and more recently evolved cortical systems. An important conclusion to be drawn from the evidence on the functional characteristics of these neural regulatory systems is that there is no mechanism that alters the brain's activity in a simple quantitative fashion. Rather, there are multiple systems, each of which qualitatively modulates neural operations as it regulates the quantity of ongoing activity.

This principle is illustrated by the effects of the two primary systems for augmenting brain function: the noradrenergic and dopaminergic pathways. The dopaminergic pathways, integral to the activation or motor readiness system, increase motoric function when stimulated by drugs, and when they are lesioned motor initiation is disrupted. Yet there is not a simple 1 : 1 increment in motor activity with each increment in dopaminergic modulation. Rather, each increase in dopamine function seems to restrict the animal's range of behavior and intensify the repetition of a limited class of behaviors, until actions become routinized and stereotyped (Iversen, 1977). Observations of behavior of amphetamine addicts suggest this dopaminergic sterotypy occurs in humans as well (Ellinwood, 1967).

To characterize the qualitative form of neural control indicated by these behavioral changes, Tucker and Williamson (1984) proposed that the activation system applies a *redundancy bias* to ongoing neural operations, increasing the constancy in information processing required for sequential motor control. Citing evidence that the dopaminergic and cholinergic substrates of the activation system are particularly important to the left hemisphere, they speculated that the cybernetics of this tonic activation system may be integral to the left hemisphere's cognitive skills. The restriction of the scope of working memory by this redundancy bias would allow a focusing of attention that would facilitate the left hemisphere's perceptual analysis. In addition, by restricting the rate of change in the contents of working memory, a redundancy bias would cause any change that does occur to be highly determined; this may be integral to the left hemisphere's skill in sequential control of cognitive as well as motor operations.

An opposite form of control is applied by the noradrenergic pathways that form a primary neurophysiologic substrate of the arousal system. These pathways support perceptual orienting processes, consistent with Pribram and McGuinness' (1975) model of a phasic arousal system. Furthermore, they seem to be particularly important to habituation processes (Mason & Iversen, 1975). Tucker and Williamson (1984) speculated that the phasic arousal system applies a *habituation bias* to information-processing operations. By so doing it leads the brain to respond only to novel events. In an ongoing process of perception, a cybernetic bias selecting novelty would result in many unique events being brought into working memory. In contrast to a redundancy bias, which constricts the contents of working memory to a few elements that are thoroughly represented, a habituation bias saturates working memory with many unique data, producing an expansive though shallow representation of the environmental context. Given evidence that noradrenergic pathways are right lateralized (Robinson, 1979), it may be that the cybernetics of habituation serve as the underlying attentional mechanism for the right hemisphere's holistic and global cognitive skills.

In searching for a way of understanding lateralized emotional processes, Tucker and Williamson (1984) thus proposed a theoretical framework for attentional control that may explain a major features of hemispheric specialization for cognition. The particularly interesting feature of the activation and arousal systems is that they are at the same time attentional control systems and emotional and motivational control systems. As the brain regulates its attentional scope— from focused to expansive—it does so with primitive mechanisms that are fundamentally adaptive, and affective. Focusing may require a certain degree of anxiety. An expansive attention may be intrinsic to elation.

By describing these systems as "adaptive" we mean that they are directly linked to biological requirements for survival and reproduction. They are not necessarily adaptive in the sense of invariably generating successful cognition and behavior. The fact that we humans have avoided extinction thus far is a certain kind of evidence of successful adaptation. Yet many features of distorted attention and cognition in psychopathology may be explained by excessive operation of these control systems (Tucker & Williamson, 1984).

Self-regulation of Brain Activity and Hedonic State

There have been a number of suggestions that brain activity level and hedonic tone are linked. One concept in theories of individual differences in temperament is that people differ in their characteristic arousal level, and that they regulate their level of sensation to achieve an optimal hedonic tone. The extravert's external attentional orientation is thought to reflect a low brain arousal level and need for excitement; the introvert's internal orientation reflects a greater sensitivity to overstimulation that stems from a characteristically high level of brain of arousal (Eysenck, 1967). Tucker and Williamson (1984) proposed that these characteristic attentional orientations reflect not high or low levels of a unidimensional brain arousal mechanism, but rather two qualitatively different neural control modes: a greater influence of the tonic activation system in the introvert's self-regulation, and greater reliance on the phasic arousal system for the extravert. Given the hypothesized lateralization of these systems, this formulation is consistent with Levy's (1982) discussion of the introvert as more influenced by left hemisphere cognition, and the extravert as more influenced by right hemisphere cognition.

In his research on factors determining the hedonic value of stimuli, Berlyne (1971) described psychophysical (intensity, rate of change), collative (novelty–familiarity, complexity–simplicity, and clarity–ambiguity), and ecological/motivational dimensions along which stimuli can vary. Consistent with Wundt's classic inverted U curve relating pleasantness to stimulus intensity, Berlyne found that increases on any one of these dimensions initially produces increases in the hedonic value of the stimulus. However, beyond a certain point on the dimension, further increases in what Berlyne termed *arousal potential* lead to decreases in positive hedonic valence, and eventually to the experience of discomfort and displeasure. In reviewing the neurophysiologic evidence for separate mechanisms regulating approach and avoidance behavior, Berlyne (1971) proposed that there are two functions underlying the Wundt curve: an approach function determining the up-slope, and an avoidance function that is engaged at higher stimulus intensities to antagonize or inhibit the reward mechanism.

The differentiation of self-regulation of brain activity into two factors rather than a single dimension may be consistent with what is known about the relation of hedonic appraisal to stimulus intensity. More specifically, we propose that the qualitative controls of the phasic arousal and tonic activation systems seem to have evolved from elementary mechanisms of neural habituation and sensitization, respectively. These mechanisms are differentially engaged by stimuli of varying intensities. At low intensities, increases in intensity are experienced as pleasurable; this seems to reflect a greater influence of the habituation bias, selecting for greater intensity to overcome the habituation. At high intensities, a different mechanism appears to become engaged; the sensitization associated with the redundancy bias of the tonic activation system appears to decrement hedonic tone with increasing intensity.

An important feature of this way of thinking about a two-factor hedonic-intensity function is that these control systems may alter the shape of the he-donic-intensity function as a function of the person's current motivational and emotional state. Thus with low phasic arousal and high tonic activation a person would sensitize even to moderate intensities. With lower tonic activation and high phasic arousal, there would be less aversiveness at high intensity, and a bias toward more positive hedonic tone with increasing intensity. The manic habitu-ates to a given intensity quickly and craves more. For the anxious person, even mild stimulation can grate on the nerves.

Neurotransmitter Mechanisms and Affective Control of Appraisal

The modulation of the hedonic-intensity function by the individual's current level of activation and arousal can also be seen in the way catecholaminergic agonists change the person's appraisal of the hedonic value of external stimuli. The initial euphoriant effect of a stimulant such as amphetamine or cocaine seems to be largely due to enhanced norepinephrine transmission (Cooper, Bloom, & Roth, 1974; Kokkinidis & Anisman, 1980), consistent with the notion that elation is linked to exaggerated function of the phasic arousal system. In the euphoric state, there is both a positive bias in evaluating perception and an increased need for excitement. The euphoria is not without its influence on cognitive processes; many cocaine abusers report that their increased self-confidence while high is a major factor in their continued use of the drug.

It seems to be an unavoidable fact of neurochemistry is that euphoria is short-lived. With amphetamines, the "crash" or depression following the euphoria is accompanied by a decrease in norepinephrine metabolites in the urine (Schild-kraut, 1965). With continued use of increasing doses of amphetamine in an attempt to maintain the increasingly elusive euphoria, the addict chronically augments dopaminergic function (Kokkinidis & Anisman, 1980), leading not only to motor stereotypies (Ellinwood, 1977), but to a chronic hypervigilance. The hypervigilance accompanying dopaminergic activation is consistent with the notion that more complex forms of adaptive attentional control have emerged from the motor readiness system which at a primitive level supports the fight–flight response. There are direct effects of this primitive hypervigilance on cog-nitive appraisal. Even normal individuals gain amphetamine in high doses over a period of time begin to show paranoid ideation that is difficult to discriminate from frank psychopathology (Ellinwood, 1967).

The effects of drug-induced changes in these neural regulatory mechanisms are important because they show the bottom-up nature of primitive adaptive controls: An artificial neurophysiologic change produces a coordinated change in attentional scope, hedonic tone, and responsivity to external stimuli. We can also consider how more naturalistic variations in the functioning of these systems, from genetic endowment or environmental conditioning, could create relatively permanent alterations in the person's hedonic response to events of daily life. The impulsivity and social disinhibition of the hypomanic or psychopathic personality is associated with sensation seeking. The social anhedonia of a schizophrenic figures importantly in the person's adaptive decline.

A THEORY OF PRIMITIVE ADAPTIVE PRIMING

So far, our bottom-up model of emotion as influencing cognition has suggested that neural control processes are related to attentional structure: the expansive versus constricted scope of attention; the novelty versus constancy in the contents of working memory. In this section we consider the possibility that the activation and arousal systems are also involved in primitive adaptive priming—the priming of specific cognitive contents according to elementary adaptive needs. We propose that the activation system specifically primes access to threatening material, and the arousal system primes access to the representation of pleasures. To be sure, the controls provided by these mechanisms are primitive, and cognitive constructions must provide substantial top-down control as well. But higher cognitive appraisal processes may operate in part by modulating the level of function of the activation and arousal systems. This may result in a continuity between elementary neural control mechanisms and the underlying dimensions of adaptive cognitive priming.

Emotional Controls of Limbic Memory

The question of how cognitive and emotional processes interact has been approached from several perspectives. Traditional cognitive approaches have proposed that cognitive attributions determine emotion (Mandler, 1985; Schacter & Singer, 1962). In these accounts, emotion is considered to be a vague, visceral affair, which provides only nonspecific clues to the cognitive apparatus. A greater role for emotional processes influencing cognition comes from the assumption that emotion is a cue in memory like any other perceptual or cognitive cue (Bower, 1981). Thus an emotional state could serve to facilitate access to a memory of an event if the state were present during the encoding of the event.

The assumption that emotions occupy the representational mechanisms like any other cognitive contents may be a heuristic one. Our understanding of emotion should improve as the methods of cognitive psychology are applied to understanding emotions and their interactions with cognitive representations. However, from a neuropsychological perspective, considering the importance of limbic and brainstem mechanisms to emotional processes, it seems difficult to equate emotions with cognitive representational mechanisms. Furthermore, as Isen (1984) has pointed out, some of the evidence on how emotion influences cognition is not consistent with the assumption that emotions function through cognitive representational networks.

If an emotion operates like a cognitive cue, then when an emotion is elicited there should be a facilitation that spreads to semantically related cognitive elements. Johnson and Tversky (1983) had subjects read a story about a death from a particular cause, such as homicide, then predicted that estimates of the risk of similar causes of death, such as other violent crimes, would be increased, due to the effect of spreading activation through the semantic network primed by the story. What they observed was increased estimates of risk for many of the negative events they examined, not just violent crimes. This suggests that emotion does not operate through spreading activation but operates on the cognitive representational network as a *parallel* control process, altering access to all cognitive elements relevant to that emotion.

The anatomy of the memory apparatus may itself suggest a parallel adaptive control of representational processes. The current neuropsychological evidence on memory (see Squires, 1986) suggests that long-term memory is carried out by the cortical structures responsible for the initial perceptual and cognitive processing of the information. However, another essential component is an intact limbic system; with bilateral hippocampal and amygdala damage a patient may be unable to form useable memories. Thus the cognitive representational process in the normal brain appears to involve not only cortical handling of the information, but an essential contribution from limbic structures. Traditionally, these structures were not implicated in higher cognitive processes but in more primitive motivational and emotional functions.

Papez (1937) first described a neural circuit proceeding from the mammilary bodies through the anterior thalamus to cingulate cortex, into hippocampus then back to mammilary bodies through the fornix. Particularly through cingulate cortex, Papez believed this circuit was integral to the higher elaboration of emotional processes eminating from more primitive subcortical structures. In current research on cortical attentional systems, cells of cingulate cortex of monkeys have been shown to respond to the presence of a stimulus only if that stimulus has adaptive significance for the organism (Mesulam, 1981). Thus the primitive limbic cortex appears to perform an adaptive or hedonic monitoring function to direct attentional processing. In addition, the lesion evidence with both monkeys and humans shows that the circuit described by Papez is essential for memory (Squire, 1986).

A second limbic structure, the amygdala, is also essential to memory (Squire, 1986) but may form a separate functional division of the limbic system, because it is not as closely interconnected with the Papez circuit as the structures just outlined (Isaacson, 1974). The emotional functions of the amygdala have been characterized by many experiments. Complete removal decreases aggressiveness in a variety of species. In addition to strong interconnections to orbital frontal cortex, the amygdala exerts substantial control over hypothalamic functions, including autonomic activity. Some findings suggest there may be a functional differentiation of regions within the amygdala between defensive and aggressive behavior (Isaacson, 1974).

The recognition of the role of limbic structures in memory provides an exciting opportunity for cognitive neuropsychology. In order for perceptual data to be retained in cortical storage in an accessible form, they must first be processed in some fashion by limbic structures. The unique electrophysiological features of limbic structures—the low threshold for seizure activity in the amygdala and the long-term potentiation of neural activity in the hippocampus—may suggest neurophysiological mechanisms for working memory. Most importantly for present purposes, the fact that the control of memory occurs in structures with such elementary motivational and emotional functions should cause us to ponder whether primitive adaptive controls may not be integral to all memory operations.

Drawing on Mishkin's (1972) research delineating the two cortical visual pathways targeting hippocampus and amygdala, Bear (1983) has proposed that hemispheric specialization for emotion may be understood in terms of differential hemispheric interrelations with these two routes into the limbic system. The right hemisphere, with its spatial abilities, may draw on the dorsal, spatial-orienting pathway that targets hippocampus. This pathway is particularly important to integrating peripheral visual information. The right hemisphere may thus be specialized for integration of attention with emotion, what Bear calls *emotional surveillance.*

Bear (1983) proposes that the left hemisphere may draw on the more ventral pathway that is important for foveal vision and for the process of object recognition in visual memory. Bear suggests that in the emotional domain this pathway supports emotional learning and response organization. In addition to lateral specialization for these different cortical-limbic pathways, Bear questions whether the right hemisphere may have more of its cognitive operations directed by the limbic system than the left. The left hemisphere, on the other hand, may perform its unique cognitive functions by relying more on transcortical interconnections.

Tucker and Williamson (1984) took a different approach to explaining hemispheric specialization for emotion, emphasizing asymmetric function of elementary activation and arousal processes. Yet the central formulations of activation and arousal theory dealt with how these elementary mechanisms alter the nature of working memory. In addition to the bottom-up controls on activation and arousal from the brainstem dopaminergic and noradrenergic pathways, a complete model of controls on working memory would require concepts of the limbic mechanisms that seem to modulate the functioning of these more elementary controls. Is the amygdala's circuitry more important to the redundancy bias of the tonic dopaminergic activation system? The amygdala does seem to be a major target of the mesolimbic dopamine pathways, implicated in emotional aspects of dopaminergic control (Bunney & Aghajanian, 1977). Similarly, is the cingulate cortex of the Papez circuit integral to the hedonic responsiveness of the phasic arousal system? Researchers have remarked on the particularly dense nor-adrenergic innervation of cingluate cortex (Descarries & Lapierre, 1973).

The primary characterization of attentional control in the Tucker and Williamson (1984) model was in terms of changes in attentional structure—a focal versus an expansive scope of attention produced by a preponderance of tonic activation versus phasic arousal. An alignment of these controls with the ventral versus dorsal pathways, respectively, would seem consistent with the functional specialization of the ventral pathway for foveal perception, and of the dorsal pathway for more peripheral vision (Bear, 1983; Mishkin, 1972).

Although an integration of the evidence on attentional processes mediated by neurotransmitter-specific activation and arousal systems with the evidence on memory processes mediated by limbic structures is beyond the scope of this chapter, we can at least superficially consider the interesting possibilities for emotion theory. Does the evidence on the importance of the amygdala to defensive and aggressive behavior (Isaacson, 1974) suggest a relation to this limbic structure to the fight–flight functions that Tucker and Williamson (1984) emphasized for the tonic motor readiness system? Does the evidence on the hedonic monitoring function of cingulate cortex (Mesulam, 1981) provide a clue as to the integration of the phasic arousal system with higher evaluative processes?

The Notion of Primitive Adaptive Priming

We suggest that these parallels are meaningful, and that they might be understood in the following way. The control of access to memory by limbic structure is closely directed by motivational and emotional processes. The limbic structures serve as gatekeepers of the mind, determining which events in perceptual experience gain access to maintenance in working memory—and thus storage in long-term representation. Most importantly, this determination occurs as a function of the perceived adaptive significance of the events. The limbic structures have as their primary tools two kinds of regulatory influence on working memory—the redundancy or constancy bias of the tonic activation system and the habituation or novelty bias of the phasic arousal system. The affective qualities of these elementary control processes are integral to their roles in adaptive memory control. The anxiety or hostility associated with high tonic activation occurs simultaneously with the attentional focusing of this control system. The elation concomitant with high levels of phasic arousal may be inherent to an expansive attention (Tucker & Williamson, 1984).

In addition, recognizing how pervasive the limbic control of cognitive function seems to be, we propose that the content as well as structure of attention and memory will be controlled through the limbic modulation of the activation and arousal mechanisms. The tonic activation system will be engaged most strongly under threatening conditions. Not only does it apply a redundancy bias to current attention and working memory: As it lays down current memory traces it tags them with the potential to elicit an affective/attentional state appropriate to threat avoidance (i.e., hostility and anxiety). On later occasions, the engagement of this anxiety/hostility state is sufficient to "prime" all threat-related representations— in parallel and through a separate mechanism from the semantic associations to the current perceptual features of experience.

Similarly, we propose that the phasic arousal system—with its affective quality of depression–elation—is integral to the organism's monitoring of the hedonic value of ongoing perception and memory. Thus, an object is encoded in memory not only for its sensory qualities, but for the degree of elation it engenders. This operates as another adaptive control on memory access. Becoming elated at a later point in time facilitates access to the object, and accessing the object in memory augments elation.

With the typical parsimony of evolutionary selection, as more complex brains evolved they seem to have reworked the most elementary control mechanisms to serve more complex needs. The coding of cognitive representations for their perceived adaptive significance seems to be accomplished by linking these representations to the system that would be engaged if the adaptive significance were to be acted out. Thus the representation of a threatening event is tagged with a link to the anxiety or tonic activation system. When that event is recalled, it calls up a certain degree of anxiety: This automatically places the brain in an affective/attentional state that is appropriate to that representation. This is an efficient mechanism. There is no need to evaluate the representation, assign some degree of significance to it, then decide the appropriate motivational or emotional state and enter into it: The recall itself automatically engages the associated state of motivational readiness.

The simplest scenario is probably that the adaptive tagging of a stored event occurs as a function of the individual's current affective state at the time of encoding. Few events would be tagged with links to only one system; most would be linked to some degree to both the anxiety and elation control mechanisms. These links would then work both ways: They would facilitate access to the event when the organism was in a similar state of anxiety and elation, and when the event were accessed through perceptual or semantic channels it would automatically engender anxiety and elation (or relaxation and depression) in proportion to the memory's "loadings" on those dimensions.

In this model, access to information in memory is thus regulated through at least two channels: through the sensory qualities of the representation encoded at the cortical level and through the perceived adaptive significance of the representation that is tied to one of the affective/attentional controls at the limbic and brainstem levels.

As a theory of emotion-cognition interface, this model extends the Tucker and Williamson (1984) formulation to propose a specificity of the content of adaptive cognitive priming. Greater hostility/anxiety primes access to threatening memories. Relaxation decreases this priming. Greater elation primes access to pleasurable memories. Depression decreases this priming.

This model makes some predictions that are similar to Bower's (1981) theory that an emotional state is associated with other elements in memory and can serve as a retrieval cue. However, it makes several more specific predictions. First, it proposes that emotions are not equivalent in their potential for association with other memory elements: There is rather a specificity of the primary affective controls on memory—the anxiety and elation of the tonic activation and phasic arousal systems. Second, it proposes that the adaptive controls do not operate through semantic network associations like representational features of memory elements, but rather they operate through parallel access channels, such as observed by Johnson and Tversky (1983). Third, it proposes that memory access is regulated by neural control systems that have qualitatively distinct attentional control features. As it primes access to threat representations (MacLeod et al., 1986), anxiety automatically focuses attention and routinizes cognitive processing. As it primes access to pleasures, elation introduces an inherent expansiveness to attention and a bias toward novelty in cognitive processing.

Affective Priming and the Dimensionality of Emotion

The dimensions of relaxation–anxiety and depression–elation that we propose are integral to the limbic control of memory may be the primary dimensions of normal emotion. Tellegen (1985) reviewed factor analytic studies of emotion self-report scales. The two most common higher order factors reported in the literature are a pleasantness–unpleasantness factor and an intensity of emotion factor. Tellegen argues that these factors are dependent on what is essentially an arbitrary rotation decision; an equally valid rotation characterizes the dimensionality of emotion as comprised of a negative affect factor (varying from serene or relaxed to anxious and hostile) and a positive affect factor (varying from sluggish to elated). The specificity of these dimensions in relation to clinical disorders was shown by the finding that depressed patients were characterized more by low positive affect than by high negative affect (Tellegen, 1985).

Could it be that the statistical dimensionality of the ratings of emotion words reflects the underlying dimensionality of primitive adaptive controls on memory access? Tellegen's positive and negative affect factors seem to show the latent structure of the subjects' cognitive characterization of their own affective states. We propose that this structure reflects limbic mechanisms of adaptive priming emergent from the tonic activation (anxiety) and phasic arousal (elation) systems.

This hypothesis of a relation between primary dimensions of emotion and neural activation and arousal systems may be supported by other factor analytic work. Thayer (1978), in developing a scale for subjects to use in self-reporting their level of physiological activation, found that two factors emerged. One varied from "sleepy, tired, and drowsy" to "lively, full of pep, and energetic." The second factor varied from "at rest, quiescent, calm," to "jittery, fearful, clutched up." Thayer's factors seem to parallel Tellegen's. This parallel may suggest that the neural mechanisms through which the brain self-regulates its level of activity—and perhaps memory operations—are isomorphic with primitive but subjectively meaningful dimensions of emotional experience.

There is a substantial literature showing that emotional states influence cognition and memory. Some of this research may be consistent with the dimensionality we propose. Isen (1984) reviews several studies showing that inducing a positive mood in subjects, such as by giving them an unexpected gift or providing them with a success experience, facilitates the subjects' memory access to positively valenced information. In social psychology studies, the evidence on effects of a negative mood is not as consistent; Isen suggests this may be due to contamination of the mood effect of self-regulatory mood-enhancement strategies that subjects use when they encounter a negative mood.

With depressed persons, however, there is evidence of facilitated access to negative information. Lloyd and Lishman (1975), for example, found that the degree of depression in depressed psychiatric patients was correlated with faster retrieval of negative past experiences and slower retrieval of positive ones. The importance of current emotional state to this effect in patients as well as normals has been shown by Lewinsohn, Steinmetz, Larson, and Franklin (1981). They followed up a large community sample and found that negative cognition was observed only during a currently depressed state, not before or after.

These findings suggest that cognitive processes are dynamically regulated by the individual's current mood level, apparently toward some adaptive end. The person's mood state appears to change as a function of the perceived success or failure of current coping efforts, and as it does it primes memory access for similarly valenced events. This would be consistent with our view of depression–elation as an adaptive control mechanism, acting on encoding as well as retrieval, such that memories associated with success or failure are tagged with the appropriate hedonic access code.

Isen (1984) points out the close relation of arousal to hedonic tone, and to the difficulty of separating the two. In biological psychiatry, the conventional view of depression holds that the variations in mood for the depressed person arise from variations in norepinephrine, a major neurochemical pathway for the phasic arousal system. Does the phasic arousal system simultaneously alter the hedonic controls on memory access as it elevates subjective mood level?

Another indication that affective influences on cognition occur through specific channels may have been provided in a study by Nasby and Yando (1982; reviewed by Isen, 1984). Children in a happy mood showed facilitated access to positive information. But a sad mood did not facilitate access to negative information; rather it impaired access to the positive information. Similarly, when Teasdale and Fogarty (1979) examined the effects of an induced depressed mood on normal subjects' speed of recall of positive and negative memories, they found the depressed mood slowed the recall of positive events but did not change the recall of negative events. Both of these findings would be consistent with a model that proposes that variations along the depression–elation dimension specifically regulate the degree of positive hedonic priming.

Primitive Priming and the Structure of Memory Access

Perhaps the most specific prediction from the present model, and the greatest divergence from more top-down, cognitively based theories of emotion and cognition, is the notion that specific modes of structuring attention will be integral to primitive controls on access to threats and pleasures. The extension of activation and arousal theory to describe adaptive priming effects predicts that the structural alterations of attention by these neural control systems will be intrinsic to their cognitive priming effects. When anxiety is a major factor in regulating memory access, the brain is in a specific attentional mode. The redundancy bias of the activation system causes constancy in the contents of working memory. This creates a temporal continuity in attention, an effect that is important when a threat is present. The generation of the anxiety prime facilitates access to other threatening events (which are also tagged with anxiety). However, because of its structural characteristics, anxiety and its redundancy bias will also apply a general constriction of the access to long-term memory.

Cognitive studies have shown that access to long-term memory is facilitated by placing an event or a semantically related event in working memory. As the redundancy bias of the tonic activation system restricts the range of unique information held in working memory, it thereby restricts the range of access to long-term storage as well. When primed for threats, memory as well as attention is focused. This is an appropriate state when the adaptive concern is preparation for active, motivated coping. When anxiety is excessive, however, we find not only routinized motor behavior but obsessions, suggesting pathological redundancy in memory access.

A well-documented effect of anxiety on perceptual functioning is impaired access to peripheral cues (Easterbrook, 1957). Does this suggest a dominance of the ventral visual memory system with its specialization for foveal data? A traditional finding in experimental psychology has been that anxiety impairs memory for remote associates, but not high-probability associates, on word association tasks (Bruner, Matter, & Papanek, 1955; Spence, 1958). Is this the redundancy bias inherent to the threat-priming system?

Opposite structural effects are created by the cybernetics of the phasic arousal system, and these may interact with its control of hedonic priming. As the degree of elation increases, there is a facilitation of access to pleasurable events. The habituation bias, and the resultant novelty selection bias, of the phasic arousal system also expand attention, spreading the capacity of working memory over many unique data. Because each element in working memory primes access to semantically related elements in long-term memory, this attentional mode facilitates access to a broader range of memory than does tonic activation. However, this is a correspondingly less definite and stable access. In contrast to the continuity of working memory over time created by the redundancy bias of activation, the fluidity of memory when modulated by phasic arousal causes cognition to be less deliberate and focused, and, because of its limited temporal span, perhaps less conscious. The manic's attention is drawn by so many exciting possibilities that it may not support rational continuity.

When manics are given lithium to stabilize mood, some patients complain that their creativity suffers (Schou, 1979). A survey of creative artists found they showed not only an overinclusive conceptual style similar to that of manics, but a surprisingly high history of affective disorder (Andreason & Powers, 1979). Recently, Shaw, Mann, Stokes, and Manevitz, (1986) found that when lithium was discontinued in a double blind design, manics gave more remote associations to a word association task—a common index of creativity—and when lithium was resumed the remoteness of their associations declined. Although the central effects of lithium are complex, administration to normals has been shown to produce EEG slowing in the right hemisphere specifically (Flor-Henry, 1979). When norepinephrine pathways are stimulated with drugs such as cocaine (Cooper, Bloom, & Roth, 1974), the result is not only an expansive attention but the subjective experience of elation. Pearlson and Robinson (1981) found that lesions of right but not left frontal lobe in rats decreased norepinephrine bilaterally. Assays of norepinephrine in human thalamus show it is higher on the right in the majority of regions (Oke, Keller, Mefford, & Adams, 1978). Taken together, these findings may be consistent with the notion that variation on the right-lateralized depression–elation dimension modulates the structure as well as the content of memory access.

Isen (1984) describes findings that an experimentally manipulated positive mood state in normals can change both the content of memory facilitation and structural features of cognition. On a problem-solving task, subjects in whom positive affect had been induced were more likely to use an intuitive heuristic rather than a more effortful logical strategy. Was this a shift from a more focused and sequential activation-based approach toward the expansive and holistic attentional mode of the phasic arousal system? In other experiments, Isen and her associates found that a positive mood resulted in more flexible and novel problem solving on a test of creativity, and in more remote associates in a word association task. Drawing from her psychological studies of positive affect, Isen (this volume) has formulated a model of affect and cognition that is quite similar to the notions we have derived from a neuropsychological framework. She proposes that the structural change in memory access that occurs with positive affect—the increased range of access—interacts with the facilitation of positive content to allow the person experiencing positive affect the opportunity for integrating positive information across a variety of experiential domains.

It is important to emphasize that the facilitation of remote associates in an elated mood is directly opposite to the modulation of memory high anxiety, which restricts responses to only the most highly probable associates (Spence, 1958). Two ways of incrementing "arousal" thus have opposite influences on the structure of memory, one tight, the other loose. This cannot be accounted for by unidimensional notions of arousal and performance, but it is consistent with the qualitative control effects of the tonic activation and phasic arousal systems.

ATTRIBUTIONS WITHIN A PRIMITIVELY PRIMED SEMANTIC MATRIX

If there is adaptive priming that operates in parallel to cognitive representational networks, then the cognitive attributions that are important to higher order handling of emotion would operate within a matrix that is powerfully conditioned by the individual's current adaptive state. The person who has just encountered success—if he or she experiences elation—will be reasoning out the attributions for this success within a cognitive matrix that is hedonically primed. Would this not lead to a higher probability of pleasurable attributions?

Another example of bottom-up control is paranoia. The traditional clinical interpretation for the mechanism of paranoia—projected hostility—seems a rather strained causal explanation. It might be simpler to propose that the mechanisms are within the paranoid's own cognitive-affective interactions. By engaging the vigilant attention of the motor readiness system, the paranoid's anxiety/hostility primes threatening material. Hostility in particular seems to have a remarkable ability to fixate attention on a threatening object. As this adaptive priming becomes chronic, it conditions the representational network that frames the context for ongoing cognitive attributions. If the person's ability to draw objective inferences is not the best, there may be a cascading of mistaken attributions for the pervasive appearance of threat.

The influence of adaptive priming on cognitive operations may have a dimensionality that is common to all people, but it also must reflect the cumulative effects of the individual's previous emotional influences on memory. Thus most of us suffer the slings and arrows of fortune, and a given day's disappointment makes us pessimistic for a time. But the same disappointment for a depressive may unleash a chronic and catastrophic pessimism. This could occur because the disappointment triggers a stronger elation decrement—due to experiential or genetic factors—or it could be an equivalent phasic elation decrement that operates on a cognitive network that is conditioned by experience to be strongly influenced in this direction by this hedonic access mechanism.

To go beyond the most simple examples of adaptive priming thus requires consideration of top-down as well as bottom-up interactions, whereby the person carries out cognitive operations that are effective not only in dealing with current environmental demands, but in regulating access to the threats and pleasures of memory. No doubt, the strategies that are worked out to achieve some balance in these cognitive-affective interactions must be as varied as individual people. However, if there is an inherent dimensionality in attentional control and adaptive priming, we might expect to see this reflected in more complex coping strategies as well.

The interaction of cognitive and emotional processes in adaptation have been considered in the cognitive model of stress and coping developed by Lazarus and Folkman (1984). This model goes beyond a cognitive account of the genesis of an emotional reaction by considering how stress, appraisal, and coping processes influence one another and change over time. Although theoretically this approach recognizes the bidirectional influence of emotion and cognition, the research it has generated has been largely focused on delineating the influence of cognitive appraisal and coping on emotion. By comparison, there is a scarcity of research reported on the alteration of appraisal and coping processes by emotional states and reactions.

We suggest that there might be a specificity in how coping efforts are influenced by the activation and arousal systems and their effects on adaptive cognitive priming. Perhaps the most obvious application of this model would be in emotion-focused coping. If the primary dimensions of emotion are depression–elation and relaxation–anxiety, then a person's efforts to self-regulate emotion with emotion-focused coping should reflect this dimensionality. Are there certain strategies people use to maintain elation that would differ from those used to avoid anxiety? Do some people respond to life events with greater self-regulation along the depression–elation dimension than the anxiety dimension?

Although emotions are certainly important outcomes of coping efforts, the implication of our formulation that is unusual in psychological theories of emotion is that they are more than outcomes—they are causal influences operating to control attention and cognition. In traditional views, emotions seem to have been seen as end products of mental processes—they influence coping because we like them or not and because we do things to create them or not. In our view, the primary dimensions of emotional activation and arousal are actual mechanisms of cognitive control—as they are elicited they exert specific regulatory influences on attention and memory. This would suggest that self-regulation of these emotional dimensions may be integral to problem-focused coping as well.

Thus just as the interaction between emotion and attention becomes quite strong when considering the cognitive control effects of the activation and arousal systems, our formulation of emotional influences on memory suggests new ways of thinking about the interaction between emotion-focused and problem-focused coping. To achieve optimal cognitive and attentional functioning, one may need to self-regulate the appropriate affective state.

Imagine a situation in which the individual's emotional response may be primarily characterized by anxiety. If such a response is normatively generated by an appraisal of the situation as involving high stakes, great difficulty, and ambiguous circumstances during the anticipation of an event (Folkman & Lazarus, 1985; Lazarus & Folkman, 1984), it seems reasonable to assert that an emotional response with the shared characteristic of focused, vigilant attention might indeed be adaptive; that is, an optimal level of threat or anxiety may facilitate processing information and problem solving associated with adaptation. At extremely high levels of anxiety, the individual may become hypervigilant and inflexible, and thus ineffective. In contrast, at low levels of anxiety, attention may be inadequate to maintain focused concentration on the situation at hand.

Another kind of self-regulation of problem solving may occur through positioning oneself on the depression–elation dimension. Adequate elation may be necessary to prime cognitive appraisals of possible successful outcomes—and in turn appraisals of ongoing progress may be important to maintenance of an appropriate level of elation. In everyday affairs, maintaining coping efforts may require adequate elation. Yet within the general framework of affective self-regulation, depression—a lower level on this dimension—may be as adaptively necessary as elation. Depression would decrement the appraisal of positive outcomes under conditions in which current perceptions indicate lack of progress or likelihood of failure. It is perhaps easiest to see how the inability to self-regulate out of a depressive state would lead to psychopathology. But it may also occur that the capacity for depression to be elicited by failure, and for it to operate on one's semantic matrix, may also be essential for effective self-regulation.

CONCLUSION

We have emphasized a bottom-up view of the neuropsychology of emotion-cognition interactions because this seems to be the neglected perspective in current theories of emotion. Perhaps an emphasis on cognitive factors as determining emotion is inherent to psychological theories. When explanations of emotion are offered in psychological terms, it may not be surprising that emotions begin and end in cognitive representations.

The perspectives gained from considering the organization of the brain, however, include bottom-up as well as top-down influences. The primitive structures of reptilian brains are still to be found in gross outline within the deeper recesses of the human brain. And the operations of primitive brains are inherently wired to adaptive functions, survival and reproduction. The emergence of more complex brains has involved much top-down control—inhibition of primitive regions. But it has also involved the incorporation of the functions of these primitive structures within higher systems. Without the activation and arousal systems of the protoreptilian brainstem, we could not achieve the attentional control required for tenacious reasoning, or for an expansive imagination. Without the controls of our protomammalian limbic system, we could not access memories to provide the experiential context for current emotions. And at each level, emotional and motivational processes exert specific controls on the cognitive representational system. The biological view shows that emotions are not just epiphenomenal, subjective products of the mental apparatus. They are indeed the engines of the mind.

REFERENCES

Andreasen, N. J. C., & Canter, A. (1974). The creative writer: Psychiatric symptoms and family history. *Comprehensive Psychiatry, 15,* 123–131.

Bear, D. M. (1983). Hemispheric specialization and the neurology of emotion. *Archives of Neurology, 40,* 195–202.

Berlyne, D. E. (1971). *Aesthetics and psychobiology.* New York: Appleton-Century-Crofts.

Borod, J. C., Koff, E., & Buck, R. (1986). The neuropsychology of facial expression: Data from normal and brain- damaged adults. In P. Blanck, R. Buck, & R. Rosenthal (Eds.), *Nonverbal communication in the clinical context.* University Park: Penn State Press.

Bower, G. H. (1981). Mood and memory. *American Psychologist, 36,* 129–148.

Bruner, J. S., Matter, J., & Papanek, M. L. (1955). Breadth of learning as a function of drive-level and mechanization. *Psychological Review, 62,* 1–10.

Buck, R. (1985). Prime theory: An integrated view of motivation and emotion. *Psychological Review, 92,* 389–413.

Buck, R., & Duffy, J. (1980). Nonverbal communication of affect in brain-damaged patients. *Cortex, 16,* 351–362.

Bunney, B. S., & Aghajanian, G. K. (1977). Electrophysical studies of dopamine-innervated cells in the frontal cortex. *Advances in Biochemical Psychopharmacology, 16,* 65–70.

Cooper, J. R., Bloom, F. E., & Roth, R. H. (1974). *The biochemical basis of neuropharmacology.* New York: Oxford University Press.

Davidson, R. J. (1984). Affect, cognition and hemispheric specialization. In C. E. Izard, J. Kagan, & R. Zajonc (Eds.), *Emotion, cognition and behavior.* New York: Cambridge University Press.

Descarries, L., & Lapierre, Y. (1973). Norepinephrine and axon terminals in the cerebral cortex of the rat. *Brain Research, 51,* 141–160.

Dopson, W. G., Beckwith, B. E., Tucker, D. M., & Bullard-Bates, P. C. (1985). Asymmetry of facial expression in spontaneous emotion. *Cortex, 20,* 243–251.

Easterbrook, J. A. (1959). The effect of emotion on cue utilization and the organization of behavior. *Psychological Review, 66,* 183–201.

Ellinwood, E. H. (1967). Amphetamine psychosis: I. Description of the individuals and process. *Journal of Nervous and Mental Disease, 144,* 273–283.

Eysenck, H. J. (1967). *The biological basis of personality.* Springfield: Thomas.

Flor-Henry, P. (1976). Lateralized temporal-limbic dysfunction and psychopathology. *Annals of the New York Academy of Science, 280,* 777–797.

Flor-Henry, P. (1979). On certain aspects of the localization of cerebral systems regulating and determining emotion. *Biological Psychiatry, 14,* 677–698.

Folkman, S., & Lazarus, R. S. (1985). If it changes it must be a process: Study of emotion and coping during three stages of a college examination. *Journal of Personality and Social Psychology, 48,* 150–170.

Gainotti, G. (1972). Emotional behavior and hemispheric side of the lesion. *Cortex, 8,* 41–55.

Gur, R. E. (1978). Left hemisphere overactivation in schizophrenia. *Journal of Abnormal Psychology, 87,* 226–238.

Hall, M. M., Hall, G. C., & Lavoie, P. (1968). Ideation in patients with unilateral or bilateral midline brain lesions. *Journal of Abnormal Psychology, 73*, 526–531.

Isaacson, R. L. (1974). *The limbic system.* New York: Plenum Press.

Isen, A. (1984). Toward understanding the role of affect in cognition. In R. S. Wyer, Jr. & T. K. Srull (Eds.), *Handbook of social cognition* (Vol. 3). Hillsdale, NJ: Lawrence Erlbaum Associates.

Iversen, S. D. (1977). Brain dopamine systems and behavior. In L. L. Iversen, S. D. Iversen, & S. H. Snyder (Eds.), *Handbook of psychopharmacology, Vol. 8: Drugs, neurotransmitters and behavior* (pp. 333–384). New York: Plenum Press.

Jackson, J. H. (1897). In Taylor, J. (Ed.), *Selected writings of John Hughlings Jackson.* New York: Basic Books, 1958.

Johanson, A. M., Risberg, J., Silversklold, P., & Smith, G. (in press). Regional changes of cerebral blood flow during increased anxiety in patients with anxiety neurosis. In U. Hentschel, G. Smith, & J. G. Draguns (Eds.), *The roots of perception.* Amsterdam: North-Holland.

Johnson, E. J., & Tversky, A. T. (1983). Affect, generalization and the perception of risk. *Journal of Personality and Social Psychology, 45*, 20–31.

Kokkinidis, L., & Anisman, H. (1980). Amphetamine models of paranoid schizophrenia: An overview and elaboration of animal experimentation. *Psychological Bulletin, 88*, 551–578.

Lazarus, R. S., & Folkman, S. (1984). *Stress, appraisal and coping.* New York: Springer.

Levy, J. (1982). Individual difference in cerebral hemisphere asymmetry: Theoretical issues and experimental considerations. In J. Hellidge (Ed.), *Cerebral hemisphere asymmetry: Method, theory and application.* New York: Praeger Scientific Publishers.

Lewinsohn, P. M., Steinmetz, J. L., Larson, D. W., & Franklin, J. (1981). Depression-related cognitions: Antecedent or Consequence? *Journal of Abnormal Psychology, 90*, 213–219.

Lloyd, G. G., & Lishman, W. A. (1975). Effect of depression on the speed of recall of pleasant and unpleasant experiences. *Psychological Medicine, 5*, 173–180.

MacLeod, C., Mathews, A., & Tata, P. (1986). Attentional bias in emotional disorders. *Journal of Abnormal Psychology, 95*, 15–20.

Mandler, G. (1985). *Mind and body: Psychology of emotion and stress.* New York: W. W. Norton.

Mason, S. T., & Iversen, S. D. (1977). Learning in the absence of forebrain noradrenaline. *Nature, 258*, 422–424.

Mesulam, M. M. (1981). A cortical network for directed attention and unilateral neglect. *Annals of Neurology, 10*, 309–325.

Mishkin, M. (1972). Cortical visual areas and their interaction. In A. G. Karczman, J. C. Eccles (Eds.), *The brain and human behavior.* Berlin: Springer-Verlag.

Nasby, W., and Yando, R. (1982). Selective encoding and retrieval of affectively valent information. *Journal of Personality and Social Psychology, 43*, 1244–1255.

Oke, A., Keller, R., Mefford, I., and Adams, R. V. (1978). Lateralization of norepinephrine in human thalamus. *Science, 200*, 1141–1143.

Papez, J. W. (1937). A proposed mechanism of emotion. *Archives of Neurology and Psychiatry, 38*, 725–744.

Pearlson, G. D., & Robinson, R. G. (1981). Suction lesions of the frontal cerebral cortex in the rat induce asymmetrical behavioral and catecholaminergic responses. *Brain Research, 218*, 233–242.

Pribram, K. H., & McGuinness, D. (1975). Arousal, activation, and effort in the control of attention. *Psychological Review, 82:2*, 116–149.

Robinson, R. G. (1979). Differential behavioral and biochemical effects of right and left hemispheric cerebral infarction in the rat. *Science, 205*, 707–710.

Robinson, R. G., Kubos, K. L., Rao, K., & Price, T. R. (1984). Mood disorders in stroke patients: Importance of location of lesion. *Brain, 107*, 81–93.

Sackeim, H. A., Greenberg, M. S., Weiman, A. L., Gur, R. C., Hungerbuhler, J. P., & Geschwind, N. (1982). Hemispheric asymmetry in the expression of positive and negative emotions: Neurologic evidence. *Archives of Neurology, 39*, 210–218.

166   TUCKER, VANNATTA, ROTHLIND

Sackeim, H. A., Gur, R. C., & Saucy, M. C. (1978). Emotions are expressed more intensely on the left side of the face. *Science, 202,* 434–436.

Safer, M. A. (1981). Sex and hemisphere differences in access to codes for processing emotional expressions and faces. *Journal of Experimental Psychology: General, 110,* 86–100.

Safer, M. A., & Leventhal, H. (1977). Ear differences in evaluating emotional tone of voice and verbal content. *Journal of Experimental Psychology: Human Perception and Performance, 3,* 75–82.

Schacter, F., & Singer, J. E. (1962). Cognitive social and physiological determinants of emotional states. *Psychological Review, 69,* 379–399.

Schildkraut, J. (1965). The catecholamine hypothesis of affective disorders: A review of supporting evidence. *American Journal of Psychiatry, 122,* 509–522.

Schou, M. (1979). Artistic productivity and lithium prophylaxis in manic-depressive illness. *British Journal of Psychiatry, 135,* 97–103.

Shaw, E. D., Mann, J. J., Stokes, P. E., & Manevitz, Z. A. (1986). Effects of lithium carbonate on associative productivity and idiosyncracy in bipolar outpatients. *American Journal of Psychiatry, 143,* 1166–1169.

Spence, K. W. (1958). A theory of emotionally based drive (D) and its relation to performance in simple learning situations. *American Psychologist, 13,* 131–141.

Squire, L. R. (1986). Mechanisms of memory. *Science, 232,* 1612–1619.

Teasdale, J. D., & Fogarty, S. J. (1979). Differential effect of induced mood on retrieval of pleasant and unpleasant events from episodic memory. *Journal of Abnormal Psychology, 88,* 248–257.

Tellegen, A. (1985). Structures of mood and personality and their relevance to assessing anxiety, with an emphasis on self-report. In A. H. Tuma & J. D. Maser (Eds.), *Anxiety and the anxiety disorders.* Hillsdale, NJ: Lawrence Erlbaum Associates.

Terzian, H. (1964). Behavioral and EEG effects of intracarotid sodium amytal injection. *Acta Neurochirgia, 12,* 230–239.

Thayer, R. E. (1978). Toward a psychological theory of multidimensional activation (arousal). *Motivation and Emotion, 2,* 1–34.

Tucker, Daniel M., Watson, R. G., & Heilman, K. M. (1976). Affective discrimination and evocation in patients with right parietal disease. *Neurology, 26,* 354.

Tucker, Don M. (1981). Lateral brain function, emotion, and conceptualization. *Psychological Bulletin, 89,* 19–46.

Tucker, D. M. (1986). Neural control of emotional communication. In P. Blanck, R. Buck, & R. Rosenthal (Eds.), *Nonverbal communication in the clinical context.* Cambridge, England: Cambridge University Press.

Tucker, D. M., Stenslie, C. E., Roth, R. S., & Shearer, S. (1981). Right frontal lobe activation and right hemisphere performance decrement during a depressed mood. *Archives of General Psychiatry, 38,* 169–174.

Tucker, D. M., & Williamson, P. A. (1984). Asymmetric neural control systems in human self-regulation. *Psychological Review, 91,* 185–215.

8

The Neuropsychology of Emotion: Developmental Patterns and Implications for Psychopathology

Wendy Heller
University of Chicago

INTRODUCTION

The investigative approaches to the study of human emotion have emphasized both cognitive (Lazarus, 1982, 1984) and biological factors (Kelley & Stinus, 1984). Despite the insights produced by these studies, there have been few attempts to integrate the cognitive and biological aspects of emotional function. In most of the influential theories of emotion, physiological correlates of emotional experience are acknowledged to be crucial (James, 1890; Mandler, 1984; Schacter & Singer, 1962), but these formulations have focused on functions of the autonomic nervous system, ignoring higher order control mechanisms in the brain. Biological models of emotion, on the other hand, have concentrated primarily on neurological mechanisms and have failed to translate these processes into a coherent theory of emotional behavior (Panksepp, 1985; Swerdlow & Koob, 1987).

Recent research in neuropsychology, a field specifically interested in the link between behavior and brain organization, brings a new and integrative perspective to the study of human emotion. Research on brain-damaged, split-brain, and normal subjects, carried out over the past 30 years, has contributed a great deal to our understanding of the way the cerebral cortex is organized for speech, language, and visuospatial abilities. It is now well established that the left hemisphere is specialized to comprehend language and to control speech production (e.g. Levy & Trevarthen, 1976; Sperry, Gazzaniga, & Bogen, 1969; Zaidel, 1977), whereas the right hemisphere is specialized to comprehend the relationships between objects in space and the meaning of complex non-linguistic patterns (e.g. Kimura & Durnford, 1974; Leehey, Carey, Diamond, & Cahn, 1978; Rudel, Denckla, & Hirsch, 1977). More recently, evidence has accumulated to show that the cerebral hemispheres are as different in their affective responses as they are in their cognitive specializations (Flor-Henry, 1979; Tucker, 1981; Wexler, 1980). These findings have made it possible to delineate, for the first time, the role of the cortex in affective regulation among both normal individuals and in clinical populations. This topic has been the subject of a number of recent reviews (Coffey, 1987; Davidson, 1984; Leventhal & Tomarken, 1986; Otto, Yeo, & Dougher, 1987; Silberman & Weingartner, 1986; Tucker, 1988; Tucker & Williamson, 1984).

The findings, unfortunately, are not unambiguous, and as many hypotheses have been put forth as there are theorists. In this chapter, I will suggest that it is possible to integrate many of the seemingly contradictory viewpoints that have been offered. As an attempt at integration, the purpose of this chapter is not to provide an exhaustive review; indeed, the literature cited will be selective, with the express goal of constructing a conceptual skeleton within which to organize a mass of often conflicting data. Other frameworks, perhaps, could be devised; this one is offered as a preliminary exercise in blending the findings from some of the various paradigms that have been applied to the study of emotion. Within this framework, the neuropsychological findings from children will then be reviewed, and the implications for the development of both normal and aberrant emotional functioning will be discussed.

To set the stage, several critical issues must first be clarified. These include a) the extent to which the ability to interpret emotional information can be equated with the experience of emotion, or mood (also see Davidson, 1988a), b) the relative importance in emotional functioning of hemispheric specialization versus the dynamic interaction of the hemispheres (also see Davidson, 1988b), and c) differences in emotional functions between anterior and posterior regions of the brain (also see Davidson, 1988b, and Tucker, 1988).

THE EVALUATION OF EMOTION VERSUS
THE EXPERIENCE OF EMOTION

One major topic of contention has been the extent to which the right hemisphere is uniquely involved in emotional functions. Some authors conclude that the right hemisphere is solely responsible for cortical mediation of emotion (e.g. Coffey, 1987; Flor-Henry, 1979; Levy, Heller, Banich, & Burton, 1983a; Ley & Bryden, 1982), while others assert that each hemisphere is specialized to process different types of emotion (e.g. Davidson, 1984; Sackeim, Greenberg, Weiman, Gur, Hungerbuhler, & Geschwind, 1982).

The evidence to support right hemisphere dominance in emotional function is primarily derived from studies investigating the cognitive processing of emotional information in brain-damaged and normal subjects, whereas most of the evidence supporting differential hemispheric involvement in emotional function derives from studies investigating the lateralization of mood states. Therefore, the first issue that must be clarified is the extent to which the ability to evaluate emotional information is equivalent to the experience of emotion.

The ability to *evaluate* emotional information in all modalities, including facial expression, tone of voice, gesture, and interpretation of emotional scenes, is disrupted by damage to the temporo-parietal regions of the right hemisphere, but not the left (Cicone, Wapner & Gardner, 1980; DeKosky, Heilman, Bowers & Valenstein, 1980; Etcoff, 1984a & b; Heilman, Bowers, Speedie, & Coslett, 1984; Heilman, Scholes & Watson, 1975; Hughes, Chan, & Su, 1983; Kolb & Taylor, 1981; Tucker, Watson & Heilman, 1977; Wapner, Hamby & Gardner, 1981). In addition, normal subjects show a right-hemisphere superiority for discriminating emotional information conveyed through facial expression and tone of voice (Buchtel, Campari, DeRisio, & Rota, 1978; Heller & Levy, 1981; Ladavas, Umilta & Ricci-Bitti, 1980; Ley & Bryden, 1982; Pizzamiglio, Zoccolotti, Mammucari, & Cesaroni, 1983; Safer & Leventhal, 1977; Strauss & Moscovitch, 1981).

In contrast, when mood is assessed, the left hemisphere has been found to be more active during positive (cheerful or euphoric) mood states, whereas the right hemisphere is more active during negative (depressed or sad) mood states (e.g. Davidson, 1984, and see later sections of this chapter for further review). After damage to the left hemisphere, moreover, patients characteristically display a depressive reaction, whereas after damage to the right hemisphere, patients tend to be inappropriately cheerful and indifferent to the magnitude of their impairment (e.g. Gainotti, 1972; Starkstein & Robinson, 1988).

As long as mood is considered indistinguishable from the ability to interpret emotional information, these findings will remain contradictory. However, there is no compelling reason to assume, as is commonly done, that because a hemisphere is associated with a particular mood state, that hemisphere is specialized to process information corresponding to that emotion. Although some authors have suggested that the experience of emotion is necessarily dependent upon a cognitive representation of that emotion (Lazarus, 1982), evidence from brain-damaged as well as depressed patients supports the assertion that "feeling" an emotion can be dissociated from "knowing" about an emotion (Etcoff, 1986; Ross, Harney, deLacoste-Utamsing & Purdy, 1981; Zajonc, 1980). Just as speech output may be localized to one region of the left hemisphere (Broca's area) and speech comprehension localized to another (Wernicke's area), the neuropsychological system involved in feeling can be similarly independent of the system governing the interpretation of that feeling. In brief, the right hemisphere may well be specialized for the interpretation of emotion, without implying that it is similarly specialized for the regulation of mood. This is not to claim that the evaluation of emotion does not influence the experience of emotion; however, the neuropsychological mechanisms underlying the two processes need not be the same.

HEMISPHERIC SPECIALIZATION VERSUS HEMISPHERIC ACTIVATION

The second issue that requires clarification is the relationship between hemispheric specialization, or differential hemispheric competence, and hemispheric activation. The assumption is often made that when a hemisphere is more active during a particular task, it is specialized for that task. However, such an assumption is not always justified. The dynamic aspects of brain activity may operate partially, if not entirely, independently of more static aspects of specialized processing (see Gur & Reivich, 1980; Davidson, 1988b). Although activation of particular brain regions is certainly related to specialized processing, there is by no means a one-to-one correspondence between specialization and activation. This has been demonstrated in research with split-brain patients, in whom the hemisphere least suited for a task has been shown, nonetheless, to dominate performance of that task (Levy & Trevarthen, 1976). Similarly, normal subjects who display the typical left hemisphere superiority for linguistic material and right hemispheric superiority for nonverbal material, nevertheless show, in some cases, greater activity for the less specialized hemisphere. In fact, there appears to be a characteristic tendency to engage one hemisphere preferentially, regardless of the task (Davidson, Taylor, & Saron, 1979; Furst, 1976; Glass & Butler, 1977; Gur & Reivich, 1980; Levine, Banich, & Koch-Weser, 1984, 1988; Levy, Heller, Banich & Burton, 1983a). For example, right-handers with a characteristic tendency toward higher right hemisphere activation will show a greater right hemisphere response to a spatial task, as expected. They may also, however, show a greater right than left hemisphere response to a linguistic task, because the characteristic tendency toward right hemisphere activation may not be offset by task-specific left hemisphere activation.

These observations are made to underscore the point that left hemisphere activation during positive mood states, and right hemisphere activation during negative mood states, need not imply that the left hemisphere is specialized to process positive information, or that the right hemisphere is specialized to process negative information. Hemispheric competence for interpreting and evaluating emotional information may be relatively independent of hemispheric activity during different mood states.

ANTERIOR VERSUS POSTERIOR REGIONS
OF THE BRAIN

In discussing cortical regulation of emotion, finally, it becomes necessary to distinguish not only between the hemispheres, but also between the functions of the anterior and posterior regions of the brain, which appear to play important, but very different, roles in emotional function (Tucker, 1988). Studies that investigate the interpretation of emotional information typically implicate parietal or temporal regions of the right hemisphere (e.g. Etcoff, 1984a and b), whereas studies that investigate mood typically implicate frontal regions of both hemispheres (e.g. Davidson, 1984; Starkstein & Robinson, 1988). As discussed above, although the evaluation of emotion and the experience of mood may not be entirely independent of each other, they may well depend primarily upon different regions of the brain. Given these considerations, it is clear that a full understanding of the neuropsychology of emotion will entail an understanding of the mechanics of the interaction between frontal and posterior regions.

THE NEUROPSYCHOLOGICAL BASES OF EMOTIONAL
EVALUATION, VALENCE, AND AROUSAL

Theories of emotion have frequently discriminated between a cognitive component involving the appraisal, or evaluation of emotion (Lazarus, 1982; 1984), an arousal component, generally viewed in terms of autonomic activity (Cannon, 1929; James, 1890; Hunt, Cole, & Reis, 1958; Mandler, 1984; Ruckmick, 1936; Schachter, 1959; Schachter & Singer, 1962) and a feeling or experiential component (Mandler, 1984; Zajonc, 1980; 1984). The latter two components appear to correspond broadly to the two factors that emerge in multi-dimensional scaling and factor-analytic studies, which measure the criteria used by both children and adults to judge emotional expressions, words, and experiences (Rusell & Bullock, 1985; Watson & Tellegen, 1985; Mayer & Gaschke, 1988). It will be proposed in this chapter that distinct brain regions are involved in these different aspects of emotion, and that these regions interact in particular ways to produce emotional experience. Specifically, the cognitive evaluation or appraisal of emotional information is assumed to depend primarily on the functions of the right hemisphere, the parietal-temporal regions in particular, as suggested by the studies reviewed earlier. The two-dimensional structure of emotion is postulated to involve relative levels of activity between the right and left hemispheres of the brain. The neuropsychological bases of the two-dimensional structure of emotion is the issue to which we now turn our attention.

171

When a neuropsychological interpretation was first applied to the dimensional structure of emotion (Heller, 1986), it was suggested that the critical dimensions were degree of arousal (high versus low) and valence (pleasure versus displeasure). This conclusion was supported by research from a variety of sources (see Dittman, 1972), including multidimensional-scaling studies of perceived similarity between emotions expressed in the face or voice and between the meaning of emotional words (Cliff & Young, 1968; Russell, 1978; 1980; Russell & Bullock, 1985) and factor-analytic studies of self-reports of emotion (Russell, 1979; 1980; Russell & Steiger, 1982), all suggesting that Valence and Arousal were the major dimensions underlying the way adults and children interpret emotions (Russell & Bullock, 1986). Furthermore, the same two dimensions emerged in other languages and cultures (Russell, 1983). These studies were taken to support a model that locates "feeling states in a circular order around the perimeter of a two-dimensional space, the axes of which are pleasure-displeasure and arousal-sleepiness" (Russell & Bullock, 1986).

More recently, other dimensional schemes have been validated, using the rotated factors of Positive Affect and Negative Affect (Tellegen, 1985; Watson & Tellegen, 1985). As discussed by Mayer and Gaschke (1988), both sets of dimensions appear to be valid ways of representing emotional experience, and there is no evidence at the present time to indicate that one has more applicability than the other. These authors suggest that choice of dimension set be based on the population studied and the question being asked. It is interesting to note, however, that when mood adjectives from the Brief Mood Introspection Scale were subjected to a principle factor analysis, the unrotated dimensions (Pleasant, Arousal) accounted for slightly more of the variance (44.6%) compared to the rotated dimensions (Positive, Negative) (37.4%). These results could, of course, reflect the bias of the particular adjectives chosen for the scale. In any case, the dimensions of Valence (pleasant/unpleasant), and Arousal (high/low) continue to be highly consistent and reliable structures in the organization of emotion. Moreover, they appear to relate rather readily to specific functions of certain regions of the brain.

In particular, the parietal region of the right hemisphere appears to play a special role in the mediation of both cortical and autonomic arousal, whereas the frontal regions appear to play a special role in emotional valence. High activation of the right parietal region, relative to the left, appears to be associated with increased cerebral and autonomic arousal; low activation of the right parietal region is associated with decreased cerebral and autonomic arousal. In contrast, high activation of the left frontal lobe relative to the right appears to be associated with biases in mood valence towards the positive pole, and low activation of the left frontal lobe relative to the right is associated with biases in mood valence towards the negative pole.

These observations led to the proposal (Heller, 1986) that feeling states are associated with the relative pattern of activation of these regions of the brain, which together comprise two systems subserving the two dimensions of valence and arousal. Position along each axis is determined by the relative degree of activation—as measured by EEG and blood flow, or as inferred by measures of autonomic, behavioral, or cognitive activity—of the underlying neurological systems that mediate each dimension. Overall mood, then, is a function of the level of activation of the frontal lobes relative to each other and to the parietal lobes.

Thus, it was proposed that when mood is happy, right parietal activity is high relative to left parietal activity, but right frontal activity is lower than left frontal activity; when mood is depressed, right parietal activity is low relative to left parietal activity, and right frontal activity is higher than left frontal activity; when mood is meditative or calm, right parietal activity is low relative to left parietal activity, and right frontal activity is lower than left frontal activity; and finally, when mood is anxious or fearful, right parietal activity is high relative to left parietal activity, and right frontal activity is higher than left frontal activity (see Fig. 8.1).

Note that for happy and depressed moods, it is predicted that there should be a trend toward a reciprocal relation between activation of the parietal and the frontal areas. When mood is happy, left frontal should be higher than right frontal activity, and right parietal activity should be relatively high. In depression, the pattern should be reversed: right frontal activity should be higher than left frontal

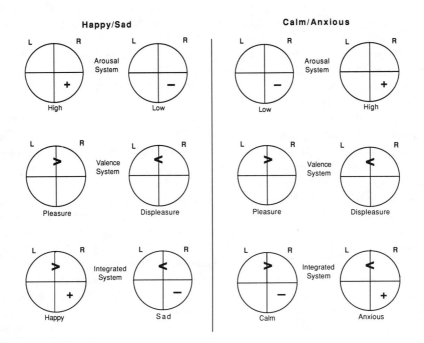

FIG. 8.1.   Model of regional cerebral interactions.

activity, and right parietal activity should be relatively low. For mood states associated with fear or anxiety, the reciprocal relation between anterior and posterior areas should no longer appear: rather, right frontal should be higher than left frontal activity, and right parietal activity should be relatively high. Conversely, for calm, peaceful, or meditative states, left frontal should be higher than right frontal activity, and right parietal activity should be relatively low. In the following sections of the chapter, evidence will be reviewed that bears on these relationships.

AROUSAL FUNCTIONS AND THE RIGHT PARIETAL REGION

Data from brain-damaged and normal subjects strongly suggest that right parietal regions are critical for the regulation of cerebral and autonomic arousal (see Heilman & Van Den Abell, 1980; Heilman, Watson, & Valenstein, 1985; Mesulam, 1981; Reivich, Gur, & Alavi, 1983; Tucker & Williamson, 1984). Brain-damaged patients with damage to this region, in contrast to patients with damage to corresponding areas of the left hemisphere, show a variety of abnormalities in autonomic and cerebral arousal functions. Although reaction times to respond to a stimulus are generally slower after all cortical lesions, right parietal lesions produce the greatest slowing (Benton, 1986; DeRenzi & Faglioni, 1965; Howes & Boller, 1975). On galvanic skin response, a measure of autonomic arousal, patients with right parietal damage show markedly decreased responses relative to left-brain damaged patients and normal controls (Heilman, Schwartz, & Watson, 1978; Morrow, Vrtunski, Kim, & Boller, 1981; Myslobodsky & Horesh, 1978; Valenstein & Heilman, 1984). In addition, unilateral neglect (the failure under normal circumstances to direct attention to the side of space opposite the lesion) is most common and severe after damage to the parietal region of the right hemisphere (Damasio, Damasio, & Chui, 1980; Heilman, 1979). Patients with right compared to left parietal lesions also show deficits in attention to stimuli on both sides of space, as indexed by performance on letter and shape cancellation tasks (Caplan, 1985; Weintraub & Mesulam, 1987).

The right hemisphere has also been shown to be differentially involved in both autonomic and attentional functions in non-brain-damaged subjects. When normal subjects were asked to tap in synchrony with their heart beat, they performed better with the left than with the right hand (Davidson, Horowitz, Schwartz, & Goodman, 1981). In addition, subjects who appear to be characterized by relatively greater reliance on the right hemisphere were better at detecting the link between a series of stimuli and their own heart rate (Hantas, Katkin, & Reed, 1984; Montgomery & Jones, 1984).

In another paradigm, when normal subjects were asked to respond to a central stimulus by pushing a button as fast as they could, warning signals presented in the left visual field and hence to the right hemisphere, enhanced subsequent reaction time for both left and right hands compared to warning signals to the left hemisphere (Heilman & Van Den Abell, 1979). In the same subjects, EEG desychronization (which is associated with increased attention) occurred to the same extent over the right hemisphere for both right and left visual field stimuli, but for the left hemisphere occurred most for right visual field stimuli. Similarly, on a left-hemisphere task (identification of lateralized nonsense syllables), Levy, Wagner, Luh, Heller, & Levine (1989) found that trials projected to the right hemisphere enhanced performance on subsequent trials to both hemispheres, compared to trials projected to the left hemisphere.

Suggesting a direct link between the observed autonomic responses, activity of the right hemisphere, and attentional processing, the greatest amplitude of auditory evoked potentials is over the right hemisphere during low heart rate (Walker & Sandman, 1979), which in turn is associated with increased attention to the environment (see Lacey & Lacey, 1970). These results are consistent with the findings reviewed above suggesting that a right-hemisphere mechanism is differentially involved in allocating cerebral arousal across the hemispheres as well as in mediating autonomic responses.

Further support for a special role of the right hemisphere in mediating arousal can be seen in the pharmacological literature as reviewed by Tucker & Williamson (1984). They suggested that cerebral arousal is mediated by norepinephrine (NE), which appears to be differentially associated with the functions of the right hemisphere. Compared to dopaminergic innervation, which is highly specific and localized primarily to frontal cortex (Saledate & Orrego, 1977; Emson & Lindvall, 1979), NE, as would suit an arousal system, is diffusely distributed throughout the neocortex, limbic system, and thalamus (Kostowski, 1980). Single-unit recordings in the pontine locus coeruleus, from whence NE pathways originate, reveal that activity in this region covaries directly with the level of alertness in the waking state of unanesthetized squirrel monkeys (Aston-Jones & Bloom, 1981). This activity is not simply a non-specific arousal, but rather facilitates the animal's response to novel input from the environment (see Tucker & Williamson, 1984).

Although NE is widespread, there is evidence that right hemisphere pathways are critical to overall function. Ligation of the middle cerebral artery on the right, but not left, decreased NE levels ipsilaterally in rats (Robinson, 1979). Furthermore, lesions in the right-frontal lobe, but not in the left-frontal lobe, decreased levels of NE bilaterally in the cortex and in the locus coeruleus as well (Pearlson & Robinson, 1981). In the thalamus, higher levels of NE have been observed on the right in both rats (Oke, Lewis, & Adams, 1980) and people, particularly in somatosensory areas (Oke, Keller, Mefford, & Adams, 1978).

In multi-dimensional scaling studies, sadness is typically associated with lower levels of arousal. Thus, we would expect depression to be associated with reduced activity of the right parietal region, and that such underactivation should be reflected in both behavioral and neurological measures. Indeed, the pattern has not escaped comment (see Otto et al., 1987, in particular; also Jaeger, Borod, & Peselow, 1987), and quite a bit of evidence can be marshalled from a variety of sources.

First, the deficits in activity and attention after right parietal brain damage are remarkably similar to those seen in depressed patients (Albus, Engel, Muller, Zander, & Ackenheil, 1983; Bruno, Myers, & Glassman, 1983; Myslobodsky & Horesh, 1978; Reiss, Peterson, Eron, & Reiss, 1977; Ward, Doerr, & Storrie, 1983). Furthermore, studies that have measured brain activation in depressed patients have found reduced activity in posterior regions of the right hemisphere. In clinically-depressed adults, EEG activation was reduced in right-parietal regions (Flor-Henry, 1979), and method actors, when adopting a state of depression, showed reduced posterior right hemisphere EEG activation (Tucker & Dawson, 1984). In addition, EEG and PET studies have found diminished cerebral activation over both hemispheres in depressed patients (Baxter, Phelps, Maziotta, Schwartz, Gerner, Selin, & Sumida, 1985; Post, DeLisi, Holcomb, Uhde, Cohen, & Buchsbaum, 1987; Schaffer, Davidson, & Saron, 1983). These data are consistent with the hypothesis that low right parietal arousal in depression would be associated with a general reduction in overall cerebral (as well as autonomic) arousal.

Uytdenhoef, Portelange, Jacquy, Charles, Linkowski, & Mendlewicz (1983) found reduced blood flow to posterior regions of the right hemisphere for patients with major depressive disorder. A study investigating glucose utilization in the temporal lobes of affectively ill adults using positron emission tomography (PET) also found a significant reduction in right temporal lobe glucose utilization (Post et al., 1987). Since these studies did not specifically investigate activity over the parietal lobes, these results can of course only be viewed as suggestive.

Research measuring right- and left-hemisphere cognitive functions also supports the inference that posterior regions of the right hemisphere are underactivated when affect is negative. The conclusions are based on evidence that when performance is dependent upon a particular brain region, activation of that region and performance are positively correlated (see Gur & Reivich, 1980; Levy et al., 1983a). Specifically, clinically-depressed adults are selectively impaired on tasks that are sensitive to right-posterior function (Flor-Henry, 1976; Goldstein, Filskov, Weaver, & Ives, 1977; Fromm & Schopflocher, 1984) and their performance improves with successful treatment of the depression (Kronfol, Hamsher, Digre, & Waziri, 1978).

Using a dichotic listening paradigm, in which either consonant-vowel syllables, consonant-vowel-consonant nonsense syllables, or complex tones were presented to each ear, Bruder, Quitkin, Stewart, Martin, Voglmaier, and Harrison (1989) found that depressed subjects showed left ear (right hemisphere) deficits for all types of stimuli. Since processing of auditory stimuli is likely to depend upon posterior regions of the brain, these results are consistent with underactivation of right parietal regions. Similarly, bipolar, but not unipolar patients, failed to show a right-hemisphere advantage on a dot enumeration task, although control subjects did (Bruder et al., 1989). These results are also consistent with right posterior underactivation, although only for the bipolar patients. In a related case report, when dichotic stimuli were presented to a 42-year-old man with a bipolar disorder (Sackeim, Decina, Epstein, Bruder, & Malitz,

1983), the results suggested relatively low right parietal activity during a depressive episode, and relatively high right parietal activity during a hypomanic episode.

Another piece of evidence for reduced right parietal activity was recently reported by Jaeger, Borod, & Peselow (1987), who found that depressed patients showed a reduced hemispatial bias toward the left on a free-vision task of chimeric face perception devised by Levy, Heller, Banich, & Burton (1983b). Levy et al. argued that the face task reflects the effects of hemispheric activity as well as specialization, and a number of studies have found the degree of leftward hemispatial bias on the face task to correlate with the degree of lateralization on tasks likely to involve right parietal lobe functions, such as visual discrimination of complex patterns (Levine, Banich, & Koch-Weser, 1984, 1988; Levy et al., 1983a). Smaller biases toward the left half of space in depressed patients, therefore, may reflect a reduction in right parietal activity. Furthermore, if the variability among individual bias scores is due, at least in part, to differences in degree of activation (as suggested by Levy et al., 1983a), one would predict that variability among bias scores would be reduced for depressed patients, which is exactly as reported by Jaeger et al. (1987).

To date, results of research with normal subjects have been consistent with the findings from psychiatric populations. Impaired reaction time to lateralized visual stimuli was observed in normal subjects who were simply asked to feel sad, but only the right-hemisphere was affected (Ladavas, Nicoletti, Umilta & Rizzolatti, 1984). These results were confirmed in subsequent study (Banich, Stolar, Heller, & Goldman, 1990) using a more complex conceptual task and a more formal mood induction procedure. Subjects induced into a depressed mood showed a selective increase in reaction time on a digit-matching task for right- but not left-hemisphere trials compared to subjects induced into a neutral mood. Furthermore, the induction procedures increased sadness and decreased happiness for subjects in the depressed but not the neutral mood condition. Since subjects were blind to the hypothesis that depressed mood would interfere with right-hemisphere function, the findings are unlikely to be due to demand characteristics of the situation.

Few studies have measured the effects of positive mood on cognitive functioning from a neuropsychological perspective, but Isen, Means, Patrick, and Nowicki (1982) provide some interesting data in this regard. They found that positive affect was associated with an increased tendency to use intuitive rather than analytic-logical strategies for problem solving. As suggested by Leventhal and Tomarken (1986), these problem solving strategies, along with a tendency to generate more inclusive categories when rating low-prototype exemplars (Isen & Daubman, 1984), may reflect increased right parietal activation.

In summary, converging evidence from a variety of sources gives credence to the proposal that not only do parietal regions of the right hemisphere play a special role in cerebral and autonomic arousal, but that these regions are underactive in depressed mood states. The evidence that parietal regions of the right hemisphere may be particularly involved in arousal and attentional responses seems compatible with the fact that the same area is important in the perception of spatial relationships, response to novel stimuli, and the capacity to evaluate emotional signals (which can be viewed as one of many important sources of information about the environment). It appears quite sensible that the region most efficient in processing such information would have, as a result, privileged access to other systems that initiate adaptive responses.

MOOD VALENCE AND THE FRONTAL LOBES

Observations of brain-damaged patients have provided abundant evidence that relative activation of the right hemisphere versus the left hemisphere is critical for mood valence. In 1972, Gainotti systematically confirmed numerous case studies that reported that right-brain-damaged patients frequently display an inappropriately cheerful or euphoric mood state (the "indifference/euphoria reaction"), whereas left-brain-damaged patients, in contrast, often show a pronounced dysphoric mood state (the "catastrophic" reaction).

Similar emotional responses have been described in patients undergoing the WADA test. Injections of sodium amytal that deactivate the left hemisphere are associated with the "catastrophic" reaction, whereas amytal injections that deactivate the right hemisphere are associated with the "indifference/euphoria" reaction (Alema, Rosadini, & Rossi, 1961; Lee, Loring, Meador, & Flanigin, 1987; Perria, Rosadini, Rossi, 1961; Rossi & Rosadini, 1967; Terzian, 1964).

More recently, it has been demonstrated that frontal lobe function in particular is associated with these differential emotional responses. In a series of reports, 60% of patients with left frontal lobe lesions had the symptom cluster of major affective disorder by DSM III criteria, and severity of the disorder correlated significantly with proximity of the lesion to the frontal lobe (Lipsey, Robinson, Pearlson, Rao, & Price, 1983; Robinson, Kubos, Starr, Rao, & Price, 1984; Robinson & Szetela, 1981). In patients with right-brain damage, frontal lobe lesions were associated with indifferent or euphoric behavior. Again, depression scores correlated significantly with distance of the lesion from the frontal lobes, but in the opposite direction from the patients with left brain damage.

In support of these findings, mood changes in clinically-depressed subjects are associated with variations in activation of the frontal lobes. During a resting, eyes-closed condition, depressed subjects showed increased activity in right relative to left frontal regions (Schaffer, Davidson, & Saron, 1983). Non-depressed subjects showed the opposite pattern. Similarly, increased activity in right frontal regions relative to the left is correlated with increased severity of depression (Perris, 1975; Perris & Monakhov, 1979; Perris, Monakhov, Von

Knorring, Botskarev, & Nikiforov, 1978). This pattern tends to disappear as the clinical status of the patient improves (Perris, 1975).

Conjugate lateral eye movements, mediated largely by the frontal eye fields (Brodal, 1981), tend to be directed toward the side of space opposite the more active hemisphere. These are more left-biased in depressed patients in response to analytic or neutral questions than in controls (Myslobodsky and Horesh, 1978), again consistent with a relative increase in activation of right frontal regions.

Electroconvulsive therapy (ECT), commonly used to treat depression in patients who have not responded to medication, appears to affect mood differently during the immediate post-ictal period compared to later periods. Decina, Sackeim, Prohovnik, Portnoy, & Malitz (1985) found that ECT to the left hemisphere produces a euphoric state in the immediate post-ictal period, while ECT to the right hemisphere resulted in a dysphoric state. They interpreted these results to reflect temporary heightened metabolic activity of the treated hemisphere, a view that is compatible with evidence for increased right frontal activity in depression.

In the long run, ECT is thought to exert its therapeutic effects by suppressing neural activity (Davidson, 1984; Decina et al., 1985). If so, the observed results are again consistent. ECT to the right hemisphere is more effective than ECT to the left hemisphere in alleviating depression (Flor-Henry, 1979; Cohen, Penick, & Tarter, 1974; Deglin & Nikolaenko, 1975). In addition, as would be expected if depression is associated with low activation of the left relative to the right frontal lobe, ECT to the left hemisphere is reported to exacerbate the symptoms of depression, producing dysphoria and anxiety (Cohen, Penick, & Tarter, 1974; Deglin & Nikolaenko, 1975; Decina et al., 1985).

Interestingly, epileptic patients with foci in the left temporal lobe were reported to describe themselves in negative terms compared to epileptic patients with foci in the right temporal lobe (Bear & Fedio, 1977). These positive/negative self-descriptions appear to be part of an epileptic personality that develops gradually, and which is most likely an interictal phenomenon related to suppression of excitation in the neural tissue proximal to the focus (Engel, 1984). Conceivably, reduced activation of the temporal regions is carried over to the frontal regions as well. Although speculative, one might test such a possibility by examining whether the relation between positive or negative self-descriptions and asymmetry of foci becomes stronger with proximity of the focus to the frontal lobes.

Investigations of normal, non-brain-damaged, non-depressed adults have also provided evidence for differential hemispheric activation during happy versus sad moods. For example, positive affect was associated with high left relative to right frontal lobe activation and negative affect was associated with high right relative to left frontal lobe activation in EEG recordings from subjects watching emotionally salient television shows (Davidson, Schwartz, Saron, Bennett & Goleman, 1979).

A variety of studies investigating judgments of emotional stimuli by normal subjects have been remarkably consistent in finding that judgments of the left hemisphere are positive relative to those of the right hemisphere. These studies generally have in common that they require subjects to view and to rate or judge emotional stimuli. For example, when emotionally arousing films with either a positive or negative theme were presented to one or the other hemisphere (by restricting input to one visual field using contact lenses), subjects rated the films seen initially by the right hemisphere as more "horrific" and unpleasant (Dimond & Farrington, 1977; Dimond, Farrington, & Johnson, 1976). Furthermore, recordings of heart-rate revealed greater responses to the unpleasant films when they were presented to the right hemisphere, and greater responses to the pleasant films when they were presented to the left hemisphere. Similarly, subjects who rated unilaterally-presented emotional and neutral faces on the degree to which the faces *evoked emotions in themselves* reported more happiness in response to both happy and sad faces when they were presented to the left hemisphere, and more sadness to happy and sad faces when they were presented to the right hemisphere (Davidson, 1984).

Because many researchers have regarded the task of judging emotional quality as equivalent to the task of analyzing emotional information, many of these findings have been interpreted to indicate that the left hemisphere is specialized to process positive emotional information and the right to process negative emotional information. In view of the evidence that the right is superior to the left hemisphere in all aspects of emotional interpretation, however, and of the fact that the positive bias emerges for the left hemisphere regardless of stimulus content, this seems an unlikely interpretation.

The findings that the same emotional material is judged as more positive by the left hemisphere than by the right hemisphere have been better explained by positing that the task or measure is actually producing, inducing or somehow resonating with an emotional state in the subject, such that the ratings reflect asymmetric activation of the frontal lobes (Davidson, 1984). Since the stimuli are generally of a complex visual nature and hence would be expected to elicit higher right parietal activation relative to left, one must suppose that the final output is based on frontal lobe as opposed to parietal lobe activation, even though parietal lobe activation was posited to underlie the patterns observed for other cognitive tasks, such as the visuo-spatial tasks used to test depressed subjects (Flor-Henry, 1976; Goldstein, Filskov, Weaver, & Ives, 1977), and the visual task used by Ladavas et al. (1984). Indeed, it seems reasonable that tasks which require a judgment might involve the frontal regions during later stages of processing more than tasks which emphasize accuracy of discrimination or performance. In support of this interpretation, Davidson (1984) found no hemifield differences when subjects were asked to discriminate the degree of emotion expressed by the face, as opposed to judging their own emotional response to the face. These results strongly suggest that the asymmetries were elicited by the mood-inducing instructions.

A similar conclusion was reached in another study where subjects were asked to judge whether unilaterally-presented chimeric faces (one half-face happy, and one half-face sad), were more positive or negative (Natale, Gur, & Gur, 1983). In this case, a positive bias was displayed by the left hemisphere, and there was no bias for the right hemisphere. Although the paradigm might not be expected to elicit mood, it is possible that subjects generated an emotional response to help cue their ratings, since the stimuli presumably expressed both happiness and sadness equally and hence were inherently unbiased along the positive/negative dimension.

RECIPROCAL RELATIONS BETWEEN FRONTAL AND PARIETAL REGIONS DURING DEPRESSED AND NONDEPRESSED STATES

Unfortunately, few studies have directly compared parietal and frontal activity in the same subjects under different mood conditions. In the majority of studies that investigated electrocortical asymmetries, parietal activation did not distinguish between positive and negative moods (Davidson, 1984). Yet behavioral decrements have been observed for tasks that are likely to involve at least some degree of right parietal function when mood was negative. It may be that since the parietal lobes are specialized for rather specific cognitive functions, variations in cognitive performance may be more sensitive indicators of variations in activation than electrocortical recordings. Possibly, mood-related levels of activity have to be relatively extreme to overcome task-induced activity.

For example, positive affect in normal subjects was associated with high left relative to right frontal lobe activation and negative affect was associated with high right relative to left frontal lobe activation in EEG recordings from subjects watching emotionally salient television scenes (Davidson et al., 1979), but parietal asymmetries did not distinguish between moods. However, as would be expected for a visual task, the right parietal region was active relative to the left. In this case, the visual-processing-induced activation may have masked more subtle variations associated with the different mood states.

In another study with normal university students, hypnotically-induced depression was associated with high electrocortical activation of right frontal areas, accompanied by a deficit in quality of imagery, but not in arithmetic performance (Tucker, Stenslie, Roth, & Shearer, 1981). Furthermore, students who described themselves as characteristically depressed showed higher right than left frontal lobe EEG activation and also reported poor imagery (Tucker et al., 1981). Even though the deficit in imagery is likely to be linked to reduced activation of the right posterior regions, recordings from central, parietal, and occipital leads did not manifest asymmetries as a function of mood.

However, the results of studies that have investigated perceptual asymmetries, cognitive performance, and personality characteristics are consistent with the existence of a reciprocal relationship between activation in frontal and posterior regions. These studies have found that enhanced performance and greater left visual field asymmetries on visuospatial tasks (which suggests greater right-parietal activation) are associated with positive self-evaluations, extraversion, and an optimistic bias in rating performance (Charman, 1979; Frumpkin, Ripley, & Cox, 1979; Levy, Heller, Banich, & Burton, 1983a). In contrast, enhanced performance and increased right visual field advantages on verbal tasks (which suggests greater left-parietal activation) are associated with negative self-descriptions, introversion, and pessimistic biases in rating performance. Similarly, Swenson & Tucker (1983) found that subjects who described themselves as more intuitive and non-verbal (considered by the authors to be a right-hemisphere cognitive style) were more likely to describe themselves in positive terms, while subjects who considered themselves to be analytic and verbal (a left-hemisphere cognitive style) were more likely to describe themselves in negative terms. The aspects of "cognitive style" measured in these studies are likely to be associated with functions of the parietal regions, and the reported personality characteristics correspond to the emotional tone predicted if asymmetries of frontal and posterior activation are reciprocal.

In summary, it is a task for future research to specify the conditions under which a reciprocal pattern of activation between frontal and posterior regions emerges or can be measured. While the evidence is favorable, it is by no means conclusive. Studies in which patterns of activation over both anterior and posterior regions are compared to performance on a variety of cognitive tasks in the same depressed patients or non-depressed subjects would be useful in this regard. Furthermore, if levels of activity related to mood effects must be relatively extreme to be expressed over the parietal region, it might be expected that such a pattern would be most likely to emerge in more severely depressed individuals.

NONRECIPROCAL RELATIONS BETWEEN FRONTAL AND PARIETAL REGIONS FOR ANXIOUS AND FEARFUL STATES

A number of studies have investigated neurological and neuropsychological functioning in anxious subjects. A study that investigated neuropsychological functioning in patients with panic attack (Yeudall, Schopflocher, Sussman, Barabash, Warneke, Gill, Otto, Howarth, & Termansen, 1983) yielded data that are highly consistent with the prediction that left hemisphere activation over both anterior and posterior regions is low relative to right hemisphere activation in such patients. Panic attack patients who met DSM III criteria were compared to normal subjects on an extensive battery of neuropsychological tests and for latency of brainstem evoked potentials to auditory stimuli. Compared to controls, panic attack patients were impaired on a variety of tasks sensitive to left hemisphere function (e.g. Wepman-Jones Aphasia, Speech Perception, Oral Word Fluency, Written Word Fluency, Williams' Verbal Learning, WAIS Verbal IQ). In addition, on measures of evoked potentials, they found lateralized dysfunction from brainstem to midbrain levels, with 62.5% of the patients showing greater left than right compromise of caudal brainstem functioning, and 81.3% showing greater left than right compromise of rostral functioning.

Tucker, Antes, Stenslie, & Barnhardt (1978) investigated hemispheric functioning during anxious states in normal subjects. Extremely anxious normal subjects showed deficits in performance on right-visual-field (left hemisphere) trials, manifesting a right hemisphere advantage for both a spatial as well as a verbal task. In contrast, medium and low anxious subjects showed a normal left hemisphere advantage for the verbal task, and a right hemisphere advantage for the spatial task. These results can clearly be interpreted as consistent with the hypothesis that relative to right, left hemisphere activation is deficient during anxious moods. However, Tucker et al. interpreted their results to indicate a relatively high level of left hemisphere activation, arguing that the visual field asymmetries were accompanied by decreased left eye movements, increased non-lateral gazes, and a relative increase in loudness judgements for an auditory stimulus presented to the right ear as compared to the left ear. Although further research is clearly in order, several questions can be leveled at their interpretation. It may be that rather than having specific left-hemisphere overactivation, the traits observed by Tucker et al. could be explained by the fact that these subjects were likely to be hypervigilant and apprehensive (DSM III-R, 1987), particularly in a face-to-face situation where they were being questioned by an examiner. For example, the decrease in leftward eye movements was accompanied by an increase in non-lateral gazes, or stares, which might reflect the hypervigilant state of the subject. Although trait anxiety was correlated with fewer left eye movements and with more nonlateral trials, the authors did not report the correlation between left eye movements and nonlateral trials. Conceivably, the relationship between trait anxiety and left eye movements was mediated entirely by the increase in nonlateral trials. Finally, no independent evidence was cited to support the notion that an increase in perception of loudness is related to increased hemispheric activation.

Several studies have investigated regional cerebral blood flow in patients with anxiety disorders or in relatively anxious normal subjects. Reiman, Raichle, Butler, Herscovitch, & Robins (1984) measured regional cerebral blood flow in patients with panic disorder in the absence of a panic attack. Seven out of 10 patients with panic disorder showed greater right than left blood flow, blood volume, and metabolic rate for oxygen in a region of the parahippocampal gyrus. Six out of 6 normal control subjects did not demonstrate such an asymmetry. Similarly, Reivich, Gur, and Alavi (1983) divided subjects into high and low anxiety groups on the basis of an anxiety questionnaire and compared blood flow for the two hemispheres. They found that the high anxiety group had significantly higher rates of blood flow for the right compared to the left hemisphere than the low anxiety group.

Thus far, the results reviewed are consistent with the proposal that left hemisphere activation would be low relative to right, over *both* frontal and parietal regions. It should be noted, however, that two recent studies measuring cerebral blood flow in normal but anxious subjects (Gur, Gur, Skolnick, Resnick, Silver, Chawluk, Muenz, Obrist, & Reivich, 1988; Reiman, Fusselman, Fox, & Raichle, 1989) did not detect asymmetries of blood flow. However, in the Gur et al. study, the task employed was a verbal analogies task; possibly, the higher left hemisphere activity induced by this task masked the effects of anxiety. Reiman et al. (1989) found significant bilateral increases in temporal regions of both hemispheres; these results are interesting in view of the suggestion made earlier that increased right parietal arousal would lead to increases in bilateral cortical arousal. Whether such a mechanisms is in fact operating is a question for future research. Another issue that should clearly be addressed in future research is the degree to which subjects are anxious, and whether the anxiety is trait-related or state-related. The two studies that found relatively higher blood flow in right hemisphere regions may have been examining subjects who were more anxious, and hence more likely to show differential hemispheric effects.

THE ROLE OF THE HEMISPHERES
IN MEDIATING VALENCE

In and of themselves, the data reviewed above do not particularly suggest that the valence dimension is more dependent on one hemisphere than the other, nor do they cast light on the mechanisms by which the balance of activation between the hemispheres is maintained. However, there are data to suggest that each hemisphere plays a crucial, but possibly very different role, in the determination of mood valence. The findings raise the possibility that, contrary to many current theories (e.g. Coffey, 1987; Otto, Yeo, & Dougher, 1987) the left hemisphere may be critically involved in mood, particularly in maintenance of positive mood.

In patients with bilateral lesions (Lipsey, Robinson, Pearlson, Rao, & Price, 1983), patients with left anterior lesions were significantly more depressed than patients without left anterior lesions, and depressive symptoms correlated exclusively with the degree to which the lesion involved the left frontal lobe. The patients' mood was unrelated to the location of a lesion in right hemisphere. The indifference/euphoria reaction was not observed in patients with right anterior lesions when left anterior lesions were present, nor did right anterior lesions ameliorate to any degree the magnitude of depression when left anterior lesions were present. Since measures of cognitive or physiological impairment were uncorrelated with magnitude of depression, it is unlikely that these factors contributed significantly to the patients' mood.

Additional evidence that the system regulating emotional valence may be asymmetric is suggested by reports that outbursts of emotion during epileptic seizures are predominantly episodes of laughing (gelastic epilepsy or epileptic laughter). Crying is quite rare (Sackeim, Greenberg, Weiman, Gur, Hungerbuhler, & Geschwind, 1982). Furthermore, epileptic laughter is associated with foci in the left hemisphere. In a review of cases reported in the literature (Sackeim et al., 1982), twice as many children and adults with lateralized foci and epileptic laughter had foci on the left than on the right. Similar conclusions are reached by Myslobodsky (1983), who reports, in addition, that epileptic outbursts of laughter are accompanied by gyratory or adversive symptoms directed toward the right side, including eye deviation, head turning, turning of an arm, or both arms and a shoulder, or turning movement continuing into a complete rotation.

The fact that epileptic laughter is not uncommon and occurs predominantly in the presence of left hemisphere foci, whereas epileptic crying is very rare, suggests that the system regulating normal mood function is not organized symmetrically. Although one might argue that laughing and crying behaviors may not necessarily characterize the opposite ends of the positive/negative dimension to the same degree (i.e. laughing may be less associated with genuine emotion, or serve more of a communicative function), in conjunction with the data on brain-damaged patients, the findings suggest that the left hemisphere may be more hard-wired for positive emotion than the right is hard-wired for negative emotion. The evidence that positive mood is associated with such hard-wired programs for motoric expression is compatible with other evidence for left hemisphere specialization for motor programming (Tucker & Williamson, 1984).

Additional evidence that the left hemisphere has a special role in the regulation of positive mood states can be marshalled from studies investigating neural substrates of affect (Tucker & Williamson, 1984; Tucker, 1988). In particular, a number of studies suggest that dopamine, which appears to be related to central reward mechanisms that mediate positive affect, is asymmetrically represented in the left hemisphere of the human brain. Asymmetric distributions of dopamine receptors have been located particularly in areas receiving massive projections from regions associated with affective behavior, including the frontal lobes.

Studies that have examined neurochemical asymmetries in rat brains have established that dopaminergic asymmetries are associated with behavioral asymmetries, particularly in orienting behavior. Rats with lesions in the striatum (caudate nucleus) and/or nigrostriatal pathways containing dopamine rotate in circles towards the side of the lesion (see Glick & Shapiro, 1985 for review). Normal rats, when administered drugs that enhance dopaminergic function (amphetamine, apomorphine, L-dopa, scopoloamine), also rotate at a higher rate than normal, and the direction of rotation is consistently contralateral to the side of the brain with higher dopamine levels. Generally, the asymmetry in concentration of striatal dopamine is about 15%, and increases to about 25% with high doses of d-amphetamine (Glick & Shapiro, 1985). Rats also show paw preferences in lever pressing and side preferences in a t-maze that correlate with amphetamine-induced rotation, and dopamine concentration has been shown to be higher in the striatum contralateral to the lateral preference (Glick & Shapiro, 1985).

Although extrapolations of these findings to people remains somewhat speculative, some evidence indicates similar lateralization of dopaminergic function. Neuroleptic drugs, used in the treatment of schizophrenia, interfere with dopaminergic transmission, often causing dyskinesia as a side effect. These dyskinesic symptoms have been reported to occur more frequently and are more pronounced on the right side of the body (Waziri, 1980) which suggests a selective interference with left hemisphere function. More direct evidence of neurochemical asymmetries in human subjects has been provided by Glick, Ross, & Hough (1982) who reanalyzed data from Rosser, Garrett, & Iversen (1980) on concentrations of several neurotransmitters in the left and right sides of nine structures in normal post-mortem human brains. Absolute asymmetry of striatal dopamine was found to be 30.7%, approximately twice that found in the rat. Furthermore, levels of dopamine were significantly higher in the left globus pallidus than in the right globus pallidus. Thus, levels are higher on the side contralateral to hand preference (which can be assumed to be the right for the majority of these subjects, although hand dominance data was not available). Although the left-right asymmetry was significant only for dopamine concentration in the globus pallidus, left-right asymmetries were significantly positively correlated in all striatal regions measured (globus pallidus, caudate, and putamen), and left-right asymmetries were in the same direction 73% of the time.

The striatum receives a massive topographical projection from frontal and temporal areas associated with limbic function (Kelley & Stinus, 1984). The striatum, including the nucleus accumbens (a subregion of the striatum) receives input relevant to affect from numerous other parts of the limbic system as well, including massive projections from the amygdala (Kelley, Domesick, & Nauta, 1982), ventral tegmental area, thalamic nuclei, and hippocampus (Kelley & Domesick, 1982). The striatum-accumbens complex has two major motor output routes, one of which is to the globus pallidus, where dopamine has been shown to be asymmetrically represented on the left.

The association of dopaminergic transmission with positive affect is indicated by a variety of studies. Amphetamine, which induces increased locomotor activity and exploratory behavior in animals and mood elevation in humans, acts both to increase release and prevent re-uptake of dopamine. The locomotor response in animals has been shown to be mediated by dopaminergic transmission in the nucleus accumbens and other regions of the striatum (see Kelley & Stinus, 1984, for review of these studies). Furthermore, animal studies of self-administration of amphetamine and cocaine indicate that dopamine mediates the reinforcing properties of these drugs, since various methods of blocking or decreasing central dopamine reduce or abolish responding (Davis & Smith, 1973; De Wit & Wise, 1978; Risner & Jones, 1976; Roberts, Corcoran, & Fibiger, 1977; Wilson & Schuster, 1972, 1974; Yokel & Wise, 1976). Other studies have demonstrated that the reward value of conditioned stimuli is reduced by decreasing dopaminergic activity (Robbins & Everitt, 1982) and enhanced by increasing dopaminergic activity (Beninger & Phillips, 1980; Royall & Klemm, 1981). On the basis of the studies reviewed above, Kelley & Stinus (1984) suggest the following: ". . . it is likely that the release of dopamine enhances positive aspects of such sensory events (and) potentiates the rewarding aspects of stimuli, perhaps by increasing the inherent pleasure of acoustic, visual, or internal sensations. Such a state of positive affect would be closely associated with approach behavior, reflected in increased locomotion and exploratory tendencies." It is of interest to note here that in patients with panic attack, those most likely to be agoraphobic were also those with the largest degree of left hemisphere abnormality (Yeudall et al., 1977). These data are also relevant to suggestions by Fox & Davidson (1984) that the association of frontal asymmetries with variations in affect reflect more primitive approach-avoidance patterns.

In summary, the evidence suggests that dopamine is crucial in mediating positive affect, that it may be asymmetrically represented in the left hemisphere, and that dopaminergic neurons project primarily to frontal areas. It has been suggested (Silberman & Weingartner, 1986) that a model of "interactive inhibition between a right negatively biased and left positively biased hemisphere" is most compatible with the available data. This suggestion is certainly supported here. However, if such a system were equally balanced between the hemispheres one would have predicted that bilateral lesions should have ameliorated depressed mood in patients with left frontal lobe damage. In view of this and other evidence, it seems likely that although the right hemisphere may play a crucial inhibitory role in normal mood modulation (Silberman & Weingartner, 1986), the neural substate that permits the experience of positive emotion may be located in the frontal regions of the left hemisphere. Furthermore, the mechanisms that mediate right hemisphere activity may be different from the mechanisms mediating left hemisphere activity.

NEUROPSYCHOLOGICAL BASES OF EMOTION
IN CHILDREN

Just as it is of value to explicate the lines of convergence in research on emotion in adults, an examination of the linkage between the neuropsychological bases of emotion and the accumulated knowledge about emotional behavior in children may provide important insights into the validity and applicability of the hypotheses that have been developed. For example, should the relationships postulated in this chapter hold true, certain predictions can be made regarding the manner in which functions are organized in the developing brain. The following sections of this chapter, therefore, will review the findings of studies of brain organization in children and examine the extent to which they conform to the general framework that has been constructed in the foregoing discussion.

Since an awareness of the mechanisms upon which a particular function is dependent can illuminate sources of vulnerability and breakdown, an understanding of developmental patterns in emotion can also yield special insights into the mechanisms underlying abnormal emotional functioning. Accordingly, the final section of this chapter will discuss the implications of these patterns for our understanding of pathological emotional function.

HEMISPHERIC ASYMMETRIES IN THE EVALUATION OF EMOTION IN CHILDREN

Indeed, certain aspects of brain organization for emotion in children appear to be quite similar to those in adults. The few studies that have investigated the evaluation of emotional information in children using traditional methods of lateralized presentation of stimuli indicate that five to 14-year-olds show a right-hemisphere advantage for discriminating emotional faces (Saxby & Bryden, 1985), emotional tone of voice (Saxby & Bryden, 1984), and emotional non-speech sounds such as laughing and crying (Knox & Kimura, 1973). They also show a bias, similar to adults, to perceive emotional chimeric faces as happier when the smile is in the left visual field (Heller, 1986; Levine & Levy, 1986).

Additional evidence for right hemisphere specialization for emotion in children can be obtained from a growing body of research investigating social and emotional functioning in children with evidence for right-hemisphere dysfunction (Rourke, 1987; 1988; Rourke, Young, & Leenaars, 1989; Tranel, Hall, Olson, & Tranel, 1987; Voeller, 1986; Weintraub & Mesulam, 1987). These studies have described a syndrome, often referred to as a nonverbal learning disability, in which a difficulty in interpreting emotional and social information is a central feature. These children are also described as having little insight into their own emotional functioning, and are said to be deficient in their ability to express emotion. Although other aspects of the syndrome could in part account for their problems in the social domain (e.g. difficulties in modulating attention, problems processing complex, nonverbal information) it seems likely that central impairments in comprehending and evaluating emotional information are present. Furthermore, according to Rourke (1988), these difficulties are likely to appear at very early ages, and may be detectable in infancy. The clinical data therefore are consistent with early right-hemisphere specialization for the evaluation of emotional information.

HEMISPHERIC ASYMMETRY FOR VALENCE IN CHILDREN

The role of the hemispheres in emotional valence in children has also been investigated and, according to a series of studies by Fox and Davidson, patterns of lateralization for mood states in infants appear to be similar to those of adults. They measured EEG asymmetries in infants during happy and sad mood states, induced by a variety of elicitors, including the approach of the infant's mother versus a stranger, the administration of a pleasant taste versus an aversive one, and videotaped presentation of a happy versus a sad person (Davidson & Fox, 1982; Fox & Davidson, 1986, 1987, 1988). Regardless of the means by which a positive mood was elicited, it was consistently accompanied by greater left frontal activation relative to right. Similarly, negative moods were associated with greater right frontal activation relative to left. These patterns, moreover, appear to reflect characteristic biases toward relatively greater activation of one hemisphere compared to the other; infants who cried in response to maternal separation showed greater right-hemisphere activation during baseline EEG recordings than infants who did not cry (Davidson & Fox, 1989).

Additional evidence that the neurological organization of valence in children is similar to adults was obtained in a study investigating the emotional content in the drawings of school-age children (Heller, 1986, 1987). Several reasons led to the choice of drawings as an index to the lateralization of emotion. First, the drawings of normal children are typically rich in affective content and depict emotions that are readily recognized by adults (Gardner, 1980). Furthermore, drawings are sensitive to frontal lobe function, as demonstrated by patients with damage to the frontal lobes, who show both qualitative and quantitative deficits compared to patients with damage to other regions of the brain (Jones-Gotman & Milner, 1978; Kimura & Faust, 1985).

Since frontal lobe function is important in the production of both drawings and mood, there remains only to find some way of reliably relating the two. The key is in the fact that asymmetric activity of the hemispheres produces an attentional bias to the side of space opposite the more aroused hemisphere. Asymmetric arousal of the hemispheres affects attentional biases under free-viewing conditions not only in brain-damaged patients, as discussed earlier, but also in normal subjects. For example, when a verbal task is given, activating the left hemisphere, subjects find words on the right side of space more salient (Levy & Kueck, 1985), exhibit contralateral eye movements toward the right (Gur & Gur, 1977), and show more motoric behavior with the right hand (Kimura, 1973). In contrast, nonverbal tasks elicit biases towards the left side of space (Gur & Gur,

1977; Levy et al., 1983b). Along these lines, Borod, Vingiano, and Cytryn (1988, 1989) found that subjects made more eye movements toward the left side of space when imagining emotional scenes, and Koff, Borod, and White (1983) found that visual images of imagined emotional scenes were located more often on the left side of space.

Furthermore, at least under some circumstances, different mood states appear to be associated with different patterns of attention towards the two sides of space relative to body midline. As discussed earlier, clinically-depressed subjects showed more leftward eye movements in response to neutral questions (Myslobodsky & Horesh, 1978). Similarly, non-depressed subjects directed more eye movements to the left in response to emotionally-negative questions and more eye movements to the right in response to emotionally-positive questions (Ahern & Schwartz, 1979; Schwartz, Ahern, Davidson, & Pusar, cited in Davidson, 1984). [Earlier studies had found more leftward eye movements in response to both positive and negative emotional questions (Schwartz, Davidson, & Maer, 1975; Tucker, Roth, Arneson, & Buckingham, 1977) but were criticized by Davidson (1984) for employing question sets of more negative than positive questions].

Given these observations, it was hypothesized that opposite patterns of frontal lobe activation for sad versus happy moods might be reflected in the child's use of space on the paper when depicting feelings in drawings. In particular, emotional content in sad pictures should be displaced towards the left side of the page, due to asymmetrically higher right hemisphere activation. In contrast, emotional content in happy pictures should be displaced towards the right side of the page, due to asymmetrically higher left hemisphere activation. Children were therefore requested to draw pictures of something that made them feel either happy or sad. As a control condition, all children were asked to draw a picture of anything they wished, before drawing either of the emotional pictures. Since a review of the literature on children's drawings suggested that human figures tend to be the emotional focus, it was decided to compare the placement of the figure(s) in the different drawings.

The children were tested in the classroom either during a period scheduled by the classroom teacher (University of Chicago Laboratory Schools) or during art class at the Park Forest schools. All children were first observed by an examiner while signing his or her name on a line, both to confirm self-reported handedness and to document hand posture. Handedness was classified according to the hand used for writing, and only right-handed children were included in the analyses reported below.

Unlined, white paper was then distributed to all the children, and the following instructions were given. First, the children were asked to draw anything they wished. They were then asked to draw "a picture of something that makes you feel happy" and a "picture of something that makes you feel sad". (Note that they were *not* asked to draw a "happy picture", or a "sad picture".) Half the children drew the sad picture first and half drew the happy picture first. Children were allowed their choice of crayons, pencils, or felt-tip markers for the drawings.

Since the question of interest concerned placement of emotional content, figures were distinguished according to whether or not they were expressing an emotion or representative of one. Two judges independently scored the location of the figures in the pictures. These scores were then reviewed by a third judge, and if they did not agree, the judges were asked to rescore the figure(s). Failure to agree was due to scoring error in the majority of cases.

The location of the figure was scored in each drawing using an x,y coordinate grid of clear plastic, with 0 as the midpoint on both the x and y axes. Drawings were placed under the grid and centered, and each figure was given a score locating its midpoint on the x axis. The score reflected the proportionate distance of the figure to either the left or right of center. A negative score on the x axis indicated that the horizontal midpoint was to the left of zero, and a positive score indicated that the horizontal midpoint was the right of zero. A score of −.10, for example, indicated that the figure was located 10% of the distance from the midline to the left side of the page.

The children were also administered a free-vision task of chimeric face perception which correlates with tasks that are likely to reflect activity of the parietal lobes (Levine, Banich, & Koch-Weser, 1988; Levy, Heller, Banich, & Burton, 1983b). An additional 146 children in Grades 2 through 6 were asked to draw a person [from the Draw-A-Person Test (Koppitz, 1968)].

As predicted, children placed the important content in sad drawings significantly to the left of the important content in "happy" and "anything" drawings (see Fig. 8.2). Not surprisingly, the emotional quality of the pictures that the children drew of "anything" turned out to be as "happy", in the opinion of 12 judges, as the pictures drawn of "something that makes you feel happy". The results of the study are thus consistent with the hypothesis that relatively higher activation of the right frontal region during negative mood states would bias attention toward the left half of space for sad drawings, whereas relatively higher activation of the left frontal region during positive mood states would bias attention towards the right half of space for happy drawings. Furthermore, the interpretation that lateralized placement of emotional content in children's draw-

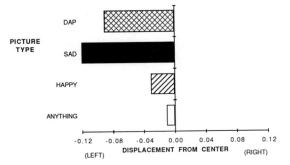

FIG. 8.2.   Figure placement in emotional pictures.

ings reflects activation of the frontal regions was supported, since scores on the face perception task, which were assumed to reflect activity of the parietal region, were uncorrelated with the placement of emotional content in the drawings.

It can be seen in Fig. 8.2 that under all conditions the average figure placement was slightly biased toward the left side of the page. In fact, the figures in the non-emotional Draw-A-Person task were significantly displaced towards the left side of the page (Heller, 1989). Normal children and adults showed a similar small but significant leftward bias on a line bisection task (Bradshaw, Nettleton, Wilson, & Bradshaw, 1987). A likely explanation for these results is that nonverbal visuospatial tasks, such as drawing or line bisecting, engage the right hemisphere, hence biasing attention towards the left half of space. This mild leftward bias was reflected in the placement of the non-emotional figure from the Draw-A-Person Test, which was intermediate between the happy and sad figures. The differences in lateral placement of happy versus sad figures, presumably reflecting differential frontal lobe activation for emotion, appear to be superimposed rather neatly upon the intermediate placement of the non-emotional figure.

HEMISPHERIC ASYMMETRY FOR AROUSAL IN CHILDREN

It is currently unknown whether, as is the case in adults, the right hemisphere plays a differentially important role in attentional and arousal functions during development. In 1985, Kolb and Wishaw stated that they were "unaware of any reports of visual neglect following early lesions to the right hemisphere". However, there have been several recent case reports of hemi-neglect in unilaterally brain damaged children. Johnston and Shapiro (1986) described a case of a boy with persistent rightward neglect following a congenital left hemisphere lesion, and Ferro, Martins, and Tavora (1984) described 3 children with transient leftward neglect following right brain damage acquired before the age of 6. Ferro et al. (1984) suggest that contralateral neglect in these children resembles that of adults, but that it clears rapidly and completely. Finally, Heller and Levine (1988) reported clear evidence of neglect as indexed by picture placement on the Draw-A-Person Test in a large group of right-brain-damaged children compared to left-brain-damaged children and non-brain-damaged, age-matched controls. These results suggest that, although the effects may not be as prominent, parietal regions of the right hemisphere are differently involved in arousal and attentional functions, even at very early ages.

If so, the question arises as to whether sad mood in children would be reflected in reduced activation of the right parietal region, as appears to be the case in depressed adults. Several studies can be brought to bear on this issue. In an investigation of depressed children (Brumback, Staton, & Wilson, 1980; Staton, Wilson, & Brumback, 1981), tasks dependent upon cognitive functions of the right hemisphere were found to be impaired, a pattern which reversed with treatment. These results appear to be similar to those of adult depressed patients, who also did more poorly on tasks specialized to the right hemisphere.

To investigate further whether depressed mood would be associated with deficits in attention and performance for the right hemisphere (Heller, 1986), happy and sad moods were induced on subsequent days in a group of 48 children, who were then given a lateralized tachistoscopic task (Levine, Banich, & Koch-Weser, 1984) that appears to be sensitive to right parietal functions in adults. The primary method of mood induction was a reminiscence procedure, where children were encouraged to dwell on an emotional event of their own choosing (from Moore, Underwood, & Rosenham, 1973). Analysis of self-reported mood indicated that the mood induction technique was effective.

The tachistoscopic test was a test of chair recognition, chosen because individual right-handers' laterality scores on this test have been found to predict the extent to which the subjects show a right hemisphere superiority on a task of face recognition, assumed to be mediated in large part by the right parietal region. The fact that performance on the test was unlateralized for the group as a whole can be taken to suggest that the task is sensitive to individual differences in characteristic right parietal activation or arousal. Thus, it was hypothesized that the task might also be sensitive to small variations in parietal arousal induced by mood.

The results were consistent with the prediction that right parietal activation would be reduced in sad moods relative to happy moods, but only among children older than 10. During happy moods, older children recognized significantly more chairs in both visual fields than during sad moods. For the younger children, in contrast, the ability to attend to both sides of space was not affected differently by happy versus sad moods. Since activation of the right parietal region has been shown to mediate attention to both sides of space in brain-damaged (e.g. Caplan, 1985) and normal subjects (e.g. Heilman & Van Den Abell, 1979), these findings suggest that in older children, but perhaps not in younger children, depressed mood is associated with a relative reduction in right parietal activity, with concomitant effects on overall cerebral arousal and attentional efficiency.

DEVELOPMENTAL CHANGES
IN THE NEUROPSYCHOLOGICAL ORGANIZATION
OF EMOTION

The results described above suggest that maturation of neural systems may be particularly important in the degree to which the organization of emotion resembles that of adults. Although the basic neuropsychological substrates for emotion appear to be similar, some recent evidence suggests that there may be important differences between children and adults.

Best and Queen (1989) reported that infants are judged by adults to express more emotion on the right side of the face, contrary to a variety of reports that adults express more emotion on the left side of the face (Borod, Koff, & Caron, 1983; Campbell, 1978; Heller & Levy, 1981; Sackeim & Gur, 1978). Greater right-side expressivity was found for both positive (smiling) and negative (crying) emotional states. Best and Queen suggest that their data reflect an increase in right hemisphere maturation, causing greater inhibition of right subcortical systems that mediate contralateral facial expressivity. Their results have been replicated by Rothbart, Taylor, & Tucker (1989) and were previously supported by Weber (1983), suggesting that the phenomenon is robust.

These findings bear certain similarities to those of a recent study investigating judgments of emotional intensity in school-aged children (Heller, 1986, 1988). As reviewed earlier, emotional judgments are typically more positively biased for stimuli presented to the left hemisphere compared to stimuli presented to the right hemisphere (e.g. Davidson, 1984). To investigate lateralization of emotional judgments in children, two groups of 24 children each, one averaging about 9 years old and the other averaging about 12 years old, were shown scenes in which positive, negative or neutral emotional content was projected tachistoscopically to either the left or the right hemisphere. The scenes were illustrations reproduced in color from children's books, chosen on the basis of judges' ratings of emotional content. The emotional content of the slide was primarily expressed by the facial expression and posture of the figure. The size of the figure and the distance from midline were equal in all the slides. Each slide had one and only one human figure in it, either on the left or right. Each scene was mirror-imaged and presented twice, once with the figure in the left visual field (right hemisphere) and once with the figure in the right visual field (left hemisphere). The children were asked to rate the scenes as to how happy or sad the picture made them feel (*not* whether the pictures were happy or sad). Ratings were made by making a mark on a vertically-oriented visual analog scale.

For older children, the left hemisphere was more positive than the right, regardless of the emotional content of the scene, a pattern entirely consistent with that seen in normal adults (e.g. Davidson, 1984). For the younger children, however, the pattern was different. The left hemisphere was more responsive to the actual emotional content of the scene than was the right hemisphere. "Happy" stimuli presented to the left hemisphere caused children to feel happier than when the same stimuli were presented to the right hemisphere. Similarly, "sad" stimuli presented to the left hemisphere caused children to feel sadder than when they were presented to the right hemisphere.

It seems highly unlikely that these results reflect superior cognitive discrimination for the left hemisphere in younger children; this conclusion would lead one to claim that the left hemisphere was better than the right at discriminating emotions. This explanation would conflict with compelling evidence that, even in children, it is the right hemisphere that is specialized for the task of processing visual-emotional information (Levine & Levy, 1986; Saxby & Bryden, 1985). Rather, it seems more likely that emotional judgments reflect relatively non-cognitive, emotional reactions that are dependent on frontal lobe patterns of activity (as suggested by Davidson for adults, 1984). Furthermore, the findings of the tachistoscopic study suggest that reactivity to an emotional stimulus is greater for the left than for the right hemisphere in younger, but not in older children.

Best and Queen's (1989) suggestion that the greater right-face expressivity in infants is due to increased right hemisphere inhibition of subcortical reflexive activity has interesting implications with regard to the findings from the school-age children in Heller's (1986, 1988) study. Assuming that the right hemisphere is specialized for the production of facial expression, Best and Queen argue against the idea that greater right-face expressivity could be due to greater left hemisphere activation during facial expression in infants. They point out that there is little evidence for reversals of hemispheric specialization during development (Levine, 1985; Witelson, 1985), which would have to be postulated if one were to suggest that control of facial expression switches from the left to the right hemisphere sometime during development. However, some questions can be raised about the assumption that all expressions are more intense on the left side of the face in adults. When studies have specifically compared negative to positive emotional expressions, negative expressions are consistently expressed more intensely on the left side of the face, whereas positive expressions tend to be random (see Borod, Koff, & Caron, 1983). Thus, in line with the distinction made earlier in this chapter, there is some doubt as to whether facial expression is mediated solely by *specialized* processes of the right hemisphere. Conceivably, asymmetric facial expression is mediated, at least in part, by levels of *activation* in the frontal lobes that vary as a function of mood. In fact, as Best and Queen point out, the frontal cortex is the substrate of voluntary control of facial expressions (Rinn, 1984). From this perspective, greater expressivity of the right face is indeed a reflection of left hemisphere activity, and the question becomes one of understanding the neural mechanisms that influence and modulate that activity. These observations are, in fact, compatible with Best and Queen's interpretation of their data; furthermore, as these authors point out, they underscore the importance of intra- and interhemispheric connections in the mediation of emotional expression and experience.

As suggested by Best and Queen, if regulation of emotion is based on as dynamic and finely-tuned a modulatory system as is being proposed here, adult patterns should be highly dependent on efficient neural communication pathways. Maturation of these pathways is one of the ongoing developmental processes of childhood. Complete myelinization of the corpus callosum, for example, the pathway that mediates interaction between the hemispheres, does not occur until around puberty (see Spreen, Tupper, Risser, Tuokko, & Edgell, 1984). A number of studies have described what might be compared to a "disconnection syndrome" in young children, in which transfer of sensory and motor information from one hemisphere to the other was deficient (Galin, Johnstone, Nakell, & Herron, 1979; O'Leary, 1980). Indeed, as late as the third decade of life, intra-hemispheric communication pathways within the pre-frontal cortex, as well as pathways leaving this region, continue to myelinate (Yakovlev & Lecours, 1967). Thus, it would not be surprising to find a distinct developmental process in the regulation of emotional functions, whereby neurological substrates that are present at birth become increasingly integrated with age.

One possibility suggested by the data reviewed above is that in the normal mature brain the right hemisphere may play an important role in modulating the affective reactivity of the left hemisphere (also see Silberman & Weingartner, 1986). When the corpus callosum and other communication pathways are immature, the right hemisphere may not be able to exert inhibitory control over the left hemisphere, which results in increased affective reactivity. With maturation of the corpus callosum, the right hemisphere's inhibitory capacity becomes increasingly capable of exerting itself. The evolution of this neurobehavioral sequence would account for the truism that younger children are less able to modulate their affective expression than are older children or adults.

To investigate the possibility that communication pathways in the younger children were less mature in the study described above (Heller, 1986, 1988) left hemisphere ratings were compared to right hemisphere ratings for the same pictures. If interhemispheric functioning is in fact more integrated in older children, it might be expected that judgments of a stimulus by one hemisphere would be more highly correlated with judgments of the same stimulus by the other hemisphere. Confirming this expectation, the average correlation for the older children as significantly higher than that for the younger children.

That the left hemisphere appears more emotionally reactive in younger children is consistent with other interesting data suggesting that the neural substrate underlying mood valence also may be more dependent upon the left hemisphere in adults, as reviewed in earlier sections of this chapter. In patients with bilateral brain damage, symptoms of depression correlate exclusively with proximity of the lesion to the left frontal lobe. A lesion in the right hemisphere, associated with euphoria when occurring unilaterally, does not ameliorate the depression to any degree when left frontal lesions are present (Lipsey et al., 1983). In addition, outbursts of laughing associated with unilateral epilepsy occur most often with left hemisphere foci and are more common than crying (Sackeim et al., 1982).

As in adults, uncontrollable laughing in children with epilepsy is much more common than crying, and outbursts occur much more frequently in children with left-sided temporal lobe foci than right-sided foci. In children, however, these symptoms are also seen in the presence of bilateral foci (Weber & Sackeim, 1984). If right hemisphere activation plays a critical role in maintaining the equilibrium of the system, then bilateral foci in adults may be associated with more balanced levels of activation between the hemispheres. This would inhibit the abnormal expression of emotion. In children, however, neural connections are not mature, and right hemisphere activation might not be as involved in the overall maintenance of a balanced system. Although bilateral foci might normalize the balance of activation in a child's brain, this would have little effect on the left hemisphere, since the right hemisphere is less capable of exerting an inhibitory influence via interhemispheric pathways. In the absence of right-hemisphere input, therefore, outbursts of laughing, presumably mediated by left-hemisphere mechanisms, would still occur. These data also suggest that activity of the left hemisphere, even with increased lability, still biases emotional valence more towards the positive pole.

If right hemisphere inhibition, mediated by interhemispheric pathways, modulates the positive emotionality associated with left hemisphere activity, it follows that younger children, in general, might report more happiness than older children. In fact, they do (Heller, 1986). When asked to rate how they feel, younger children rate themselves as significantly more happy than older children. As noted by Silberman and Weingartner (1986), other observations are also consistent with the hypothesis that the balance of activation between the hemispheres plays some role in inhibiting the expression of positive emotion. Adult subjects who presumably have reduced lateral dominance, such as ambidextrous subjects (Rossi & Rosadini, 1967), patients with bilateral lesions (Alema, Rosadini, & Rossi, 1961), and subjects with bilateral speech representation (Hommes & Panhuysen, 1971), tend to show euphoric rather than depressive responses after amytal injection in the WADA test.

IMPLICATIONS FOR PSYCHOPATHOLOGY

The findings with children support the hypothesis that neuropsychological regulation of emotion involves a dynamic interaction between a number of cortical regions. They also suggest that normal emotional functioning is dependent not only upon the integrity of the regions involved but also upon the ability of these regions to communicate with each other. When developmental or pathological factors, such as lesions or developmental disturbances of connective pathways, interfere with this communication, the balance of activation of the entire system could be disrupted. Along these lines, abnormalities in neurochemical transmission, which mediates cerebral arousal, could have far-reaching effects on mood, depending on the regions affected. As an example, a number of researchers have suggested that there may be atypical functioning of the corpus callosum in schizophrenia (Dimond, Scammell, Pryce, Huws, & Grey, 1980; Green, 1978). Conceivably, a disruption in this pathway could be the mechanism underlying at least some of the abnormal emotional symptoms of schizophrenia.

Similarly, it appears that depression in older children and adults is associated, at least in part, with underactivation of the left frontal lobe relative to the right. This pattern of activity could be generated in a variety of ways. In some cases, it appears that the left hemisphere is intrinsically underactive, due to a lesion

(Robinson et al., 1981). In other cases, it appears that the right hemisphere is intrinsically overactive, as in clinically-depressed adults, where EEG activation for the right is greater than for the left hemisphere (Davidson et al., 1979). Possibly, the important factor lies more in the relative levels, as opposed to absolute levels, of activity.

If the balance of activation across the hemispheres is important in depression, it may be possible to explain why younger children are more resistant to depression, and why diagnoses of depression increase around the age of puberty (Cantor, 1983). Around puberty, the corpus callosum and other neural pathways become mature. One possible scenario is that in younger children, overactivation of the right hemisphere does not result in a concomitant inhibition of the left hemisphere, since callosal pathways are immature. As a result, depressed mood is less likely to be experienced.

Currently, it is not known how anterior/posterior pathways influence the overall balance of activation in the brain. Although evidence has been reviewed that in older children and adults right parietal activation is associated with mood changes, it is not known how activity in this region influences the dynamic balance of the entire system or how the relationship between parietal and frontal areas is mediated. Perhaps variations in right parietal activation have specific effects upon the relationships among other structures in the system, with concomitant correlates in emotional behavior. These matters, however, are subjects for future research.

CONCLUSION AND QUESTIONS
FOR FUTURE RESEARCH

Current research in neuropsychology suggests that it may be possible to differentiate specific patterns of cerebral arousal that characterize different emotional states. In this chapter, I have proposed that emotional states are associated with the activity of two neurological systems. One, localized in the frontal lobes, is involved in determining emotional valence along a dimension of pleasure/displeasure. The other, localized in the parietal lobe and particularly in the right hemisphere, is involved in determining the level of overall cerebral and autonomic arousal. Emotional states can be characterized by the relative activation of these two neurological systems, which correspond to the psychological dimensions that people use to describe emotions, as revealed by multidimensional scaling studies.

When the neuropsychological mechanisms of emotion are conceived in this manner, a number of issues become moot. As discussed by Leventhal and Tomarken (1986), such a perspective diminishes the attractiveness of arguments that require the pairing of a cognitive label with an autonomic state to produce an emotional experience. Unique patterns of neural activity could be produced in any number of ways, any and all of which could result in a genuine and unique emotional experience. Under some circumstances, cognitions would be capable of inducing an emotional experience, regardless of prior arousal level; under other circumstances, the reverse could be true. Factors that interfere with or influence the activity of particular regions, such as abnormalities in neurotransmitter systems or alterations in metabolism or blood flow, could also induce emotional experiences. Depending on the mechanisms involved and the effect on mood, the results could be viewed as pathological (as in major depression) or beneficial (as in the effects of exercise, which one might speculate are due to increased activation of right parietal regions through a "bottom-up" influence of increased autonomic arousal).

The fact that it has been difficult to associate specific patterns of autonomic activity with specific emotional states can also be interpreted within this framework, particularly from the perspective that individual people vary in the sensitivity and responsivity of different bodily systems (Lacey & Lacey, 1970). A characteristic tendency to emphasize different autonomic systems, such as heart rate, gastric motility, or blood pressure, in association with emotion has been suggested to begin as early as infancy. These channels of expression, unique as they are to each individual, may have similar relationships to relative patterns of neural activity. Whether they in fact do is a question for further research.

Although I do not wish to claim that more cognitive aspects of specialized processing may not be important in the regulation of emotional states, there is evidence at least to suggest that right-hemisphere specialization for processing emotional information may be independent of the neuropsychological processes underlying mood, since Etcoff (1986) found no correlation between the degree of impairment in perceiving emotions and the extent to which mood was disrupted in brain-damaged individuals. However, the relationship may be a qualitative one, as opposed to a quantitative one that can be measured simply by degree of severity. Certainly, the contribution of cognition to emotional experience must be far more complex than the ability simply to evaluate emotional information; at least in adults, emotional experience involves an historical and developmental framework of cognitive organization that has evolved through a dynamic interplay between actual events and one's responses to those events. Although these are issues that will have to be addressed in future research, it nonetheless seems possible to discern a pattern of regional cerebral activation in neuropsychological studies of mood that can account for a large body of diverse data without invoking differential hemispheric competence for cognitive processing of those emotions.

Given this remarkable diversity and complexity of human emotion, the formulation described in this chapter is certainly a simplification, and it raises as many questions as it answers. For example, if there are two cortical systems associated with mood states, what are the relations between them? To what extent is each involved in different emotional states, and to what degree are they independent? What are the mechanisms by which the balance of activation is maintained? Furthermore, in attempting to discern a broad pattern, this review has blurred distinctions between occipital, temporal, and parietal areas, frequently subsuming them under the heading "posterior". Examination of the validity of these conceptualizations will certainly focus, in part, on a more finely tuned analysis of specific cortical areas in relation to emotion. Another issue involves the well-established importance in emotional function of the limbic system (Kelley & Stinus, 1984; MacLean, 1969; Papez, 1937; also see Starkstein, Robinson, & Price, 1987). How does the limbic system interact with the cortex to modulate emotion? Neurochemical transmission between limbic and cortical structures that affects arousal and activation of various brain structures may be a crucial link in the cortical/subcortical interaction (Starkstein & Robinson, 1988; Starkstein, Robinson, & Price, 1987; Tucker & Williamson, 1984). The specifics of these interactions remains a challenge for future research.

Finally, the brain regions involved in emotion are clearly engaged in a dynamic interaction which requires sophisticated neural communication and coordination. Thus, in children or other individuals where neural communication is immature or has been disrupted, predictions can be made as to ways in which emotional function may be different or disregulated. Furthermore, investigation of different subgroups of patients with affective disorders may help to clarify the neurological mechanisms underlying their symptom profiles. Certain disparities between the neuropsychological performance of unipolar versus bipolar patients, for example, suggest that different patterns of brain activity may underlie the differences in symptomatology manifested by these two types of patients.

Although the answers to these questions await further study, both basic and clinical science will benefit from the interdisciplinary efforts that are currently being undertaken. In this sense, the status of the field can be compared to neuropsychological development: a more mature understanding of emotion will undoubtably emerge from the growing collaboration between various fields of inquiry.

ACKNOWLEDGMENTS

Some of the research described in this chapter was conducted as part of the requirements for a doctoral dissertation that was submitted to the University of Chicago, December, 1986. I gratefully acknowledge support from an NIMH Training Grant to the Committee on Biopsychology, an NIMH National Research Service Award, and a grant from the Spencer Foundation to Jerre Levy. I thank Marie T. Banich, Joan C. Borod, Zanvel Klein, Bennett L. Leventhal, and Don M. Tucker for extremely helpful comments on earlier drafts of this chapter. The thoughtful comments of four anonymous reviewers regarding a related paper were also much appreciated. I am indebted to Edwin H. Cook, Robert A. Butler,

Richard J. Davidson, Susan C. Levine, Jerre Levy, and John Metz for encouragement, support, and for sharing their ideas in many invaluable discussions. Marie Ifollo, art coordinator and teacher, Park Forest, IL, was an inspiration to me, and she and the teachers and staff at the University of Chicago Laboratory School generously donated their time and their students' artwork. I am also obliged to the Laboratory School library staff for allowing me unlimited access to their collection. Finally, I thank all the independent study students who participated in various phases of the research.

REFERENCES

Ahern, G. L. & Schwartz, G. E. (1979). Differential lateralization for positive versus negative emotion. *Neuropsychologia, 17,* 693–698.

Albus, M., Engel, R. R., Muller, F., Zander, K. J., & Ackenheil, M. (1983). Experimental stress situations and the state of autonomic arousal in schizophrenic and depressed patients. *International Pharmacopsychiatry, 17,* 129–135.

Alema, G., Rosadini, G., & Rossi, G. F. (1961). Psychic reactions associated with intracarotid amytal injections and relation to brain damage. *Excerpta Medica, 37,* 154–155.

Aston-Jones, G., & Bloom, F. E. (1981). Norepinephrine containing locus coeruleus neurons in behaving rats exhibit pronounced responses to non-noxious environmental stimuli. *Journal of Neuroscience, 1,* 887–900.

Banich, M. T., Stolar, N., Heller, W., & Goldman, R. B. (1990). Deficits in right-hemisphere processing. *Journal of Clinical and Experimental Neuropsychology, 12.*

Baxter, L. R., Phelps, M. E., Maziotta, J. C., Schwartz, J. C., Gerner, R. H., Selin, G. E., & Sumida, R. M. (1985). Cerebral metabolic rates for glucose in mood disorders. *Archives of General Psychiatry, 42,* 441–447.

Bear, D. N., & Fedio, P. (1977). Quantitative analysis of interictal behavior in temporal lobe epilepsy. *Archives of Neurology, 34,* 454–467.

Beninger, R. J., & Phillips, A. G. (1980). The effect of pimozide on the establishment of conditioned reinforcement. *Psychopharmacology, 68,* 147–153.

Benton, A. (1986). Reaction time in brain disease: Some reflections. *Cortex, 22,* 129–140.

Best, C. T., & Queen, H. F. (1989). Baby, it's in your smile: Right hemiface bias in infant emotional expressions. *Developmental Psychology, 25,* 264–276.

Borod, J. C., Koff, E., & Caron, H. S. (1983). Right hemispheric specialization for the expression and appreciation of emotion: A focus on the face. In E. Perecman (Ed.), *Cognitive processing in the right hemisphere.* New York: Academic Press.

Borod, J. C., Vingiano, W., & Cytryn, F. (1988). The effects of emotion and ocular dominance on lateral eye movement. *Neuropsychologia, 26,* 213–220.

Borod, J. C., Vingiano, W., & Cytryn, F. (1989). Neuropsychological factors associated with perceptual biases for emotional chimeric faces. *International Journal of Neuroscience, 45,* 101–110.

Bradshaw, J. L., Nettleton, N. C., Wilson, L. E., & Bradshaw, C. S. (1987). Line bisection by left-handed preschoolers: A phenomenon of symmetrical neglect. *Brain and Cognition, 6,* 377–386.

Brodal, A. (1981). *Neurological anatomy in relation to clinical medicine. Third edition.* New York: Oxford University Press.

Bruder, G. E., Quitkin, F. M., Stewart, J. W., Martin, C., Voglmaier, M. M., & Harrison, W. M. (1989). Cerebral laterality and depression: Differences in perceptual asymmetry among diagnostic subtypes. *Journal of Abnormal Psychology, 98,* 177–186.

Brumback, R. A., Staton, R. D., & Wilson, H. (1980). Neuropsychological study of children during and after remission of endogenous depressive episodes. *Perceptual and Motor Skills, 50,* 1163–1167.

Bruno, R. L., Myers, S. J., & Glassman, A. H. (1983). A correlational study of cardiovascular autonomic functioning and unipolar depression. *Biological Psychiatry, 18,* 227–235.

Buchtel, H., Campari, F., DeRisio, C., & Rota, R. (1978). Hemispheric differences in discriminative reaction time to facial expressions. *Italian Journal of Psychology, 5,* 159–169.

Campbell, R. (1978). Asymmetries in interpreting and expressing a posed facial expression. *Cortex, 19,* 327–342.

Cannon, W. B. (1929). *Bodily changes in pain, hunger, fear, and rage: An account of recent researches into the function of emotional excitement.* New York: Appleton-Century-Crofts.

Cantor, P. (1983). Depression and suicide in children. In C. E. Walker & M. C. Roberts (Eds.), *Handbook of clinical child psychology.* New York: Wiley.

Caplan, B. (1985). Stimulus effects in unilateral neglect. *Cortex, 21,* 69–80.

Carey, S., & Diamond, R. (1977). From piecemeal to configurational representation of faces. *Science, 195,* 312–314.

Charman, D. K. (1979). Do different personalities have different hemispheric asymmetries? A brief communique of an initial experiment. *Cortex, 15,* 655–657.

Cicone, M., Wapner, W., & Gardner, H. (1980). Sensitivity to emotional expressions and situations in organic patients. *Cortex, 16,* 145–158.

Cliff, N., & Young, F. W. (1968). On the relation between unidimensional judgments and multidimensional scaling. *Organizational Behavior and Human Performance, 3,* 269–285.

Coffey, C. E. (1987). Cerebral laterality and emotion: The neurology of depression. *Comprehensive Psychiatry, 28,* 197–219.

Cohen, B. D., Penick, S. B., & Tarter, R. E. (1974). Antidepressant effects of unilateral electric convulsive shock therapy. *Archives of General Psychiatry, 31,* 673–675.

Damasio, A. R., Damasio, M., & Chui, H. C. (1980). Neglect following damage to frontal lobe or basal ganglia. *Neuropsychologia, 18,* 123–132.

Davidson, R. J. (1984). Affect, cognition, and hemispheric specialization. In C. E. Izard, J. Kagan, & R. Zajonc (Eds.), *Emotion, cognition, and behavior.* New York: Cambridge University Press.

Davidson, R. J. (1988a). Cerebral asymmetry, affective style, and psychopathology. In M. Kinsbourne (Ed.), *Cerebral hemisphere function in depression.* Washington, DC: American Psychiatric Press.

Davidson, R. J. (1988b). EEG measures of cerebral asymmetry: conceptual and methodological issues. *International Journal of Neuroscience, 39,* 71–89.

Davidson, R. J., & Fox, N.A. (1982). Asymmetrical brain activity discriminates between positive and negative affective stimuli in ten month old infants. *Science, 218,* 1235–1237.

Davidson, R. J., & Fox, N. A. (1989). Frontal brain asymmetry predicts infants' response to maternal separation. *Journal of Abnormal Psychology, 98,* 127–131.

Davidson, R. J., Horowitz, M. E., Schwartz, G. E., & Goodman, D. M. (1981). Lateral differences in the latency between finger tapping and the heartbeat. *Psychophysiology, 18,* 36–41.

Davidson, R. J., Schwartz, G. E., Saron, C., Bennett, J., & Goleman, D. J. (1979). Frontal versus parietal EEG asymmetry during positive and negative affect. *Psychophysiology, 16,* 202–203.

Davidson, R. J., Taylor, N., & Saron, C. (1979). Hemisphericity and styles of information processing: Individual differences in EEG asymmetry and their relationship to cognitive performance. *Psychophysiology, 16,* 197.

Davis, W. M., & Smith, S. C. (1973). Blocking effect of alpha-methyl tyrosine on amphetamine based reinforcement. *Journal of Pharmacy and Pharmacology, 25,* 174–177.

Decina, P., Sackeim, H. A., Prohovnik, I., Portnoy, S., & Malitz, S. (1985). Case report of lateralized affective states immediately after ECT. *American Journal of Psychiatry, 142,* 129–131.

Deglin, V. L., & Nikolaenko, N. N. (1975). Role of the dominant hemisphere in the regulation of emotional states. *Human Physiology, 1,* 394–402.

DeKosky, S. T., Heilman, G. E., Bowers, D., & Valenstein, E. (1980). Recognition and discrimination of emotional faces and pictures. *Brain and Language, 9,* 206–214.

DeRenzi, E., & Faglioni, P. (1965). The comparative efficiency of intelligence and vigilance detecting hemisphere damage. *Cortex, 1,* 410–433.

DeWit, H., & Wise, R. A. (1978). Blockage of cocaine reinforcement in rats with the dopamine receptor blocker pimozide, but not with the noradrenergic blockers phentolamine and phenoxybenzamine. *Canadian Journal of Psychology, 31,* 195–203.

Dimond, S., & Farrington, L. (1977). Emotional response to films shown to the right or left hemisphere of the brain measured by heart rate. *Acta Psychologica, 41,* 255–260.

Dimond, S., Farrington, L., & Johnson, P. (1976). Differing emotional response from right and left hemispheres. *Nature, 261,* 690–692.

Dimond, S. J., Scammell, R., Pryce, I., Huws, D., & Gray, C. (1980). Some failures of intermanual and cross-lateral transfer in chronic schizophrenia. *Journal of Abnormal Psychology, 89,* 505–509.

Dittman, A. T. (1972). *Interpersonal messages of emotion.* New York: Springer.

Emson, P. C., & Lindvall, O. (1979). Distribution of putative neurotransmitters in the cortex. *Neuroscience, 4,* 1–30.

Engel, J. (1984). The use of positron emission tomographic scanning in epilepsy. *Annals of Neurology, 15,* 180–191.

Etcoff, N. L. (1984a). Perceptual and conceptual organization of facial emotions: Hemispheric differences. *Brain and Cognition, 3,* 385–412.

Etcoff, N. L. (1984b). Selective attention to facial identity and facial emotion. *Neuropsychologica, 22,* 281–295.

Etcoff, N. L. (1986). The neuropsychology of emotional expression. In G. Goldstein, & R. E. Tarter (Eds.), *Advances in clinical neuropsychology* (Vol. 3). New York: Plenum.

Ferro, J. M., Martins, I. P., & Tavora, L. (1984). Neglect in children. *Annals of Neurology, 15,* 281–284.

Flor-Henry, P. (1976). Lateralized temporal lymbic dysfunction and psychopathology. *Annals of the New York Academy of Sciences, 280,* 777–795.

Flor-Henry, P. (1979). On certain aspects of the localization of the cerebral systems regulating and determining emotion. *Biological Psychiatry, 14,* 677–698.

Fox, N. A., & Davidson, R. J. (1984). Hemispheric substrates for affect: A developmental model. In N. A. Fox & R. J. Davidson (Eds.), *The psychobiology of affective development.* Hillsdale, NJ: Erlbaum.

Fox, N. A., & Davidson, R. J. (1986). Taste-elicited changes in facial signs of emotion and the asymmetry of brain electrical activity in newborn infants. *Neuropsychologia, 24,* 417–422.

Fox, N. A., & Davidson, R. J. (1987). Electroencephalogram asymmetry in response to the approach of a stranger and maternal separation in 10-month-old infants. *Developmental Psychology, 23,* 233–240.

Fox, N. A., & Davidson, R. J. (1988). Patterns of brain electrical activity during facial signs of emotion in 10-month-old infants. *Developmental Psychology, 24,* 230–236.

Fromm, D., & Schopflocher, D. (1984). Neuropsychological test performance in depressed patients before and after drug therapy. *Biological Psychiatry, 19,* 55–71.

Frumpkin, L. R., Ripley, H. S., & Cox, G. B. (1979). A dichotic index of laterality that scores linguistic errors. *Cortex, 15,* 687–691.

Furst, C. J. (1976). EEG alpha asymmetry and visuospatial performance. *Nature, 260,* 254–255.

Gainotti, G. (1972). Emotional behavior and hemisphere side of lesion. *Cortex, 8,* 41–55.

Galin, D., Johnstone, J., Nakell, L., & Herron, J. (1979). Development of crossed and uncrossed tactile localization on fingers. *Science, 204,* 1330–1332.

Gardner, H. (1980). *Artful scribbles: The significance of children's drawings*. New York: Basic Books.

Glass, A., & Butler, S. R. (1977). Alpha EEG asymmetry and speed of left hemisphere thinking. *Neuroscience Letters, 4,* 231–235.

Glick, S. D., Ross, D. A., & Hough, L. B. (1982). Lateral asymmetry of neurotransmitters in human brain. *Brain Research, 234,* 53–63.

Glick, S. D., & Shapiro, R. M. (1985). Functional and neurochemical mechanisms of cerebral lateralization in rats. In S. D. Glick (Ed.), *Cerebral lateralization in non-human species* (pp. 157–183). New York: Academic Press.

Goldstein, S. G., Filskov, S., Weaver, L. A., & Ives, J. O. (1977). Neuropsychological effects of electroconvulsive therapy. *Journal of Clinical Psychology, 33,* 798–806.

Green, P. (1978). Defective interhemispheric transfer in schizophrenia. *Journal of Abnormal Psychology, 87,* 472–480.

Gur, R. E., & Gur, R. C. (1977). Correlates of conjugate lateral eye movements in man. In S. Harnad, R. W. Doty, L. Goldstein, J. Jaynes, & G. Krauthamer (Eds.), *Lateralization in the nervous system*. New York: Academic Press.

Gur, R. C., Gur, R. E., Skolnick, B. E., Resnick, S. M., Silver, F. L., Chawluk, J., Muenz, L., Obrist, W. D., & Reivich, M. (1988). Effects of task difficulty on regional cerebral blood flow; Relationships with anxiety and performance. *Psychophysiology, 25,* 392–399.

Gur, R. C., & Reivich, M. (1980). Cognitive task effects on hemispheric blood flow in humans: Evidence for individual differences in hemispheric activation. *Brain and Language, 9,* 78–92.

Gustafson, L., Johanson, M., Risberg, J., & Silfverskiold, P. (1981). Regional cerebral blood flow in organic dementias, affective disorders and confusional states. In C. Perris, G. Struwe, & B. Jansson (Eds.), *Biological psychiatry 1981: Proceedings of the 111th world congress of biological psychiatry* (pp. 276–279). New York: Elsevier/North Holland.

Hantas, M. N., Katkin, E. S., & Reed, S. D. (1984). Cerebral lateralization and heartbeat discrimination. *Psychophysiology, 21,* 274–278.

Heilman, K. M. (1979). Neglect and related disorders. In K. M. Heilman & E. Valenstein (Eds.), *Clinical neuropsychology*. New York: Oxford University Press.

Heilman, K. M., Bowers, D., Speedie, L., & Coslett, H. B. (1984). Comprehension of affective and nonaffective prosody. *Neurology, 34,* 917–930.

Heilman, K. M., Scholes, R., & Watson, R. T. (1975). Auditory affective agnosia: Disturbed comprehension of affective speech. *Journal of Neurology, Neurosurgery, and Psychiatry, 38,* 69–72.

Heilman, K. M., Schwartz, H. D., & Watson, R. T. (1978). Hypoarousal in patients with the neglect syndrome and emotional indifference. *Neurology, 28,* 229–232.

Heilman, K. M., & Van Den Abell, T. (1979). Right hemispheric dominance for mediating cerebral activation. *Neuropsychologia, 17,* 315–321.

Heilman, K. M., & Van Den Abell, T. (1980). Right hemisphere dominance for attention: The mechanism underlying hemispheric asymmetry of inattention. *Neurology, 30,* 327–330.

Heilman, K. M., Watson, R. T., & Valenstein, E. (1985). Neglect and related disorders. In K. M. Heilman & E. Valenstein (Eds.), *Clinical neuropsychology, second edition* (pp. 243–295). New York: Oxford University Press.

Heller, W. (1986). *Cerebral organization of emotional function in children*. Unpublished dissertation, University of Chicago, Chicago.

Heller, W. (1987). Lateralization of emotional content in children's drawings. *Scientific Proceedings of the Annual Meeting of the American Academy of Child and Adolescent Psychiatry, 3,* 63.

Heller, W. (1988). Asymmetry of emotional judgments in children. *Journal of Clinical and Experimental Neuropsychology, 10,* 36.

Heller, W. (1989). Hemi-spatial biases in right- and left-handed children on the Draw-a-Person Test. *Journal of Clinical and Experimental Neuropsychology, 11*, 83.

Heller, W., & Levine, S. C. (1989). Unilateral neglect after early brain damage. *Journal of Clinical and Experimental Neuropsychology, 11*, 79.

Heller, W., & Levy, J. (1981). Perception and expression of emotion in right-handers and left-handers. *Neuropsychologia, 19*, 263–272.

Hommes, O. R., & Panhuysen, L. H. H. M. (1971). Depression and cerebral dominance: A study of bilateral intracarotid amytal in eleven depressed patients. *Psychiatria, Neurologia, Neurochirurgia, 74*, 259–270.

Howes, D., & Boller, F. (1975). Simple reaction times: Evidence for focal impairment from lesions of the right hemisphere. *Brain, 98*, 317–332.

Hughes, C. P., Chan, J. L., & Su, M. S. (1983). Aprosodia in chinese patients with right cerebral hemisphere lesions. *Archives of Neurology, 40*, 732–736.

Hunt, J. McV., Cole, M. W., & Reis, E. E. (1958). Situational cues distinguishing anger, fear, and sorrow. *Archives of Neurology, 40*, 732–736.

Isen, A. N., & Dabman, K. A. (1984). The influence of positive affect on decision making strategy. *Social Cognition, 2*, 18–31.

Isen, A. M., Means, B., Patrick, R., & Nowicki, G. (1982). Some factors influencing decision-making strategy and risk taking. In M. S. Clark & S. J. Fiske (Eds.), *Affect and Cognition.* Hillsdale, NJ: Lawrence Erlbaum Associates.

Jaeger, J., Borod, J. C., & Peselow, E. (1987). Depressed patients have atypical hemispace biases in the perception of emotional chimeric faces. *Journal of Abnormal Psychology, 96*(4), 321–324.

James, W. (1890). *The principles of psychology.* New York: Holt.

Johnston, C. W., & Shapiro, E. (1986). Hemi-inattention resulting from left hemisphere brain damage during infancy. *Cortex, 22*, 279–287.

Jones-Gotman, M., & Milner, B. (1978). Design fluency: The invention of nonsense drawings after focal cortical lesions. *Neuropsychologia, 6*, 53–60.

Kelley, A. E., & Domesick, V. B. (1982). The distribution of the projection from hippocampal formation to nucleus accumbens in the rat: An anterograde- and retrograde-horseradish peroxidase study. *Neuroscience, 7*, 2321–2335.

Kelley, A. E., Domesick, V. B., & Nauta, W. J. H. (1982). The amygdalostriatal projection in the rat: An anatomical study by anterograde and retrograde tracing methods. *Neuroscience, 7*, 615–630.

Kelley, A. E., & Stinus, L. (1984). Neuroanatomical and neurochemical substrates of affective behavior. In N. A. Fox & R. J. Davidson (Eds.), *The psychobiology of affective development.* Hillsdale, NJ: Lawrence Erlbaum Associates.

Kimura, D. (1973). Manual activity during speaking–I. Right handers. *Neuropsychologia, 11*, 45–50.

Kimura, D., & Durnford, M. (1974). Normal studies on the function of the right hemisphere in vision. In S. Dimond & G. Beaumont (Eds.), *Hemisphere function in the human brain.* New York: Halsted Press.

Kimura, D., & Faust, R. (1985). Spontaneous drawing in an unselected sample of patients with unilateral cerebral damage. *Research Bulletin #624*, Department of Psychology, The University of Western Ontario, London, Canada.

Knox, C., & Kimura, D. (1973). Cerebral processing of non-verbal sounds in boys and girls. *Neuropsychologia, 8*, 227–237.

Koff, E., Borod, J. C., & White, B. (1983). A left hemispace bias for visualizing emotional situations. *Neuropsychologia, 21*, 273–275.

Kolb, B., & Taylor, L. (1981). Affective behavior in patients with localized cortical excisions: Role of lesion and site and side. *Science, 214*, 89–90.

Kolb, B., & Whishaw, I. Q. (1985). *Fundamentals of Human Neuropsychology.* New York: Freeman.

Koppitz, E. M. (1968). *Psychological evaluation of children's Human Figure Drawings.* New York: Grune & Stratton.

Kostowski, W. (1980). Noradrenergic interactions among central neurotransmitters. In W. B. Essran (Ed.), *Neurotransmitters, receptors, and drug action.* New York: SP Medical and Scientific Books.

Kronfol, Z., Hamsher, K. deS., Digre, K., & Waziri, R. (1978). Depression and hemisphere functions: Changes associated with unilateral ECT. *British Journal of Psychiatry, 132,* 560–567.

Lacey, J. I., & Lacey, B. C. (1970). Some autonomic-central nervous system interrelationships. In P. Black (Ed.), *Physiological correlates of emotion.* New York: Academic Press.

Ladavas, E., Nicoletti, R., Umilta, C., & Rizzolati, G. (1984). Right hemisphere interference during negative affect: A reaction time study. *Neuropsychologia, 22,* 479–485.

Ladavas, E., Umilta, C., & Ricci-Bitti, P. E. (1980). Evidence for sex differences in right hemisphere dominance for emotions. *Neuropsychologia, 18,* 361–367.

Lazarus, R. S. (1982). Thoughts on the relations between emotion and cognition. *American Psychologist, 37,* 1019–1024.

Lazarus, R. S. (1984). On the primacy of cognition. *American Psychologist, 39,* 124–129.

Lee, G. P., Loring, D. W., Meador, K. J., & Flanigin, H. F. (1987). Emotional reactions and behavioral complications following intracarotid sodium amytal injection. *Journal of Clinical and Experimental Neuropsychology, 10,* 83.

Leehey, S., Carey, S., Diamond, R., & Cahn, A. (1978). Upright and inverted faces: The right hemisphere knows the difference. *Cortex, 14,* 411–419.

Leventhal, H., & Tomarken, A. J. (1986). Emotion: Today's problems. *Annual Review of Psychology, 37,* 565–610.

Levine S. C. (1985). Developmental changes in right hemisphere involvement in face recognition. In C. T. Best (Ed.), *Hemispheric function and collaboration in the child.* New York: Academic Press.

Levine S. C., Banich, M. T., & Koch-Weser, M. (1984). Variations in patterns of lateral asymmetry among dextrals. *Brain and Cognition, 3,* 317–334.

Levine, S. C., Banich, M. T., & Koch-Weser, M. (1988). Face recognition: A general or specific right hemisphere capacity? *Brain and Cognition, 8,* 303–325.

Levine S. C., & Levy, J. (1986). Perceptual asymmetry for chimeric faces across the life span. *Brain and Cognition, 5,* 291–306.

Levy, J., Heller, W., Banich, M. T., & Burton, L. A. (1983a). Are variations among right-handed individuals in perceptual asymmetries caused by characteristic arousal differences between hemispheres? *Journal of Experimental Psychology: Human Perception and Performance, 9,* 329–359.

Levy, J., Heller, W., Banich, M. T., & Burton, L. A. (1983b). Asymmetry of perception in free viewing of chimeric faces. *Brain and Cognition, 2,* 404–419.

Levy, J., & Kueck, L. (1986). A right-hemispatial advantage on a verbal free-vision task. *Brain and Language, 27,* 24–37.

Levy, J., & Trevarthen, C. (1976). Metacontrol of hemispheric function in human split-brain patients. *Journal of Experimental Psychology: Human Perception and Performance, 2,* 299–312.

Levy, J., Wagner, N., & Luh, K. (in press). Laterality and response accuracy for the previous visual field: Effects on syllable identification. *Neuropsychologia.*

Ley, R. G., & Bryden, M. P. (1982). Hemispheric differences in processing emotions and faces. *Brain and Language, 7,* 127–138.

Lipsey, J. R., Robinson, R. G., Pearlson, G. D., Rao, K., & Price, T. R. (1983). Mood change following bilateral hemisphere brain injury. *British Journal of Psychiatry, 143,* 266–273.

MacLean, P. D. (1969). *A triune concept of brain and behavior.* University of Toronto Press: Toronto.

Mandler, G. (1984). *Mind and body: Psychology of emotion and stress.* New York: Norton.

Mayer, J. D., & Gaschke, Y. N. (1988). The experience and meta-experience of mood. *Journal of Personality and Social Psychology, 55,* 102–111.

Mesulam, M. M. (1981). A cortical network for directed attention and unilateral neglect. *Annals of Neurology, 10,* 309–325.

Montgomery, W. A., & Jones, G. E. (1984). Laterality, emotionality, and heartbeat perception. *Psychophysiology, 21,* 459–65.

Moore, B. S., Underwood, B., & Rosenham, D. L. (1973). Affect and altruism. *Developmental Psychology, 8,* 99–104.

Morrow, L., Vrtunski, P. B., Kim, Y., & Boller, F. (1981). Arousal responses to emotional stimuli and laterality of lesions. *Neuropsychologia, 19,* 65–71.

Myslobodsky, M. S. (1983). Epileptic laughter. In Myslobodsky, M. S. (Ed.), *Hemisyndromes: Psychobiology, Neurology, Psychiatry.* New York: Academic Press.

Myslobodsky, M. S., & Horesh, N. (1978). Bilateral electrodermal activity in depressive patients. *Biological Psychiatry, 6,* 111–120.

Natale, M., Gur, R. E., & Gur, R. C. (1983). Hemispheric asymmetries in processing emotional expressions. *Neuropsychologia, 21,* 555–567.

O'Leary, D. (1980). A developmental study of interhemispheric transfer in children aged five to ten. *Child Development, 51,* 743–750.

Oke, A., Keller, R., Mefford, I., & Adams, R. (1978). Lateralization of norepinephrine in human thalamus. *Science, 200,* 1411–1413.

Oke, A., Lewis, R., & Adams, R. N. (1980). Hemispheric asymmetry of norepinephrine distribution in rat thalamus. *Brain Research, 188,* 269–272.

Otto, M. W., Yeo, R. A., & Dougher, M. J. (1987). Right hemisphere involvement in depression: Toward a neuropsychological theory of negative affective experiences. *Biological Psychiatry, 22,* 1201–1215.

Panksepp, J. (1985). Toward a general psychobiological theory of emotions. *Behavioral and Brain Sciences, 5,* 407–467.

Papez, J. W. (1937). A proposed mechanism of emotion. *Archives of Neurological Psychiatry, 38,* 725–743.

Pearlson, G. D., & Robinson, R. G. (1981). Suction lesions of the frontal cortex in the rat induce asymmetrical behavior and catecholaminergic responses. *Brain Research, 218,* 233–242.

Perria, P., Rosadini, G., & Rossi, G. F. (1961). Determination of side cerebral dominance with Amobarbital. *Archives of Neurology, 4,* 175–181.

Perris, C. (1975). EEG techniques in the measurement of the severity of depressive syndromes. *Neuropsychobiology, 1,* 16–25.

Perris, C., & Monakhov, K. (1979). Depressive symptomotology and systemic structural analysis of the EEG. In J. Gruzelier & P. Flor-Henry (Eds.), *Hemisphere asymmetries of function in psychopathology.* Amsterdam/New York/Oxford: Elsevier/North-Holland.

Perris, C., Monakhov, K., Von Knorring, L., Botskarev, V., & Nikiforov, A. (1978). Systemic structural analysis of the electroencephalogram of depressed patients: General principles and preliminary results of an international collaborative study. *Neuropsychobiology, 4,* 207–228.

Pizzamiglio, L., Zoccolotti, P., Mammucari, A., & Cesaroni, R. (1983). The independence of face identity and facial expression recognition mechanisms: Relation to sex and cognitive style. *Brain and Cognition, 2,* 176–188.

Post, R. M., DeLisi, L. E., Holcomb, H. H., Uhde, T. W., Cohen, R., & Buchsbaum, M. (1987). Glucose utilization in the temporal cortex of affectively ill patients: Positron emission tomography. *Biological Psychiatry, 22,* 545–553.

Reiman, E. M., Fusselman, M. J., Fox, P. T., & Raichle, M. E. (1989). Neuroanatomical correlates of anticipatory anxiety. *Science, 243,* 1071–1074.

Reiman, E. M., Raichle, M. E., Butler, F. K., Herscovitch, P., & Robins, E. (1984). A focal brain abnormality in panic disorder, a severe form of anxiety. *Nature, 310,* 683–685.

Reiss, S., Peterson, R. A., Eron, L. D., & Reiss, M. M. (1977). *Abnormality: Experimental and clinical approaches.* New York: MacMillan.

Reivich, M., Gur, R., & Alavi, A. (1983). Positron emission tomographic studies of sensory stimuli, cognitive processes and anxiety. *Human Neurobiology, 2,* 25–33.

Rinn, W. E. (1984). The neuropsychology of facial expression: A review of the neurological and psychological mechanisms for producing facial expressions. *Psychological Bulletin, 95,* 52–77.

Risner, M. E., & Jones, B. E. (1976). Role of noradrenergic and dopaminergic processes in amphetamine self-administration. *Pharmacology, Biochemistry, and Behavior, 5,* 477–482.

Robbins, T. W., & Everitt, B. J. (1982). Functional studies of central catecholamines. *International Review of Neurobiology.* New York: Academic Press.

Roberts, D. C. S., Corcoran, M. E., & Fibiger, H. C. (1977). On the role of ascending catecholaminergic systems in intravenus self-administration of cocaine. *Pharmacology, Biochemistry, and Behavior, 6,* 615–620.

Robinson, R. G. (1979). Differential behavior and biochemical effects of right and left hemisphere cerebral infarction: Evidence for cerebral lateralization in the rat. *Science, 205,* 707–710.

Robinson, R. G., Kubos, K. L., Starr, L. B., Rao, K., & Price, T. R. (1984). Mood disorders in stroke patients: Importance of location of lesion. *Brain, 107,* 81–93.

Robinson, R. G., & Szetela, B. (1981). Mood change following left hemisphere brain injury. *Annals of Neurology, 9,* 447–453.

Ross, E. D., Harney, J. H., deLacoste-Utamsing, C., & Purdy, P. D. (1981). How the brain integrates affective and propositional language into a unified behavioral function. *Archives of Neurology, 38,* 745–748.

Rosser, M., Garrett, N., & Iversen, L. (1980). No evidence for lateral asymmetry of neurotransmitters in post-mortem human brain. *Journal of Neurochemistry, 35,* 743–745.

Rossi, G. F., & Rosadini, G. R. (1967). Experimental analysis of cerebral dominance in man. In D. H. Millikan & F. L. Darley (Eds.), *Brain mechanisms underlying speech and language.* New York: Grune & Stratton.

Rothbart, M. K., Taylor, S. B., & Tucker, D. M. (in press). Right-sided facial asymmetry in infant emotional expression. *Neuropsychologia.*

Rourke, B. P. (1987). Syndrome of nonverbal learning disabilities: The final common pathway of white-matter disease/dysfunction? *The Clinical Neuropsychologist, 1,* 209–234.

Rourke, B. P. (1988). The syndrome of nonverbal learning disabilities: Developmental manifestations in neurological disease, disorder, and dysfunction. *The Clinical Neuropsychologist, 2,* 293–330.

Rourke, B. P., Young, G. C., & Leenaars, A. A. (in press). A childhood learning disability that predisposes those affected to adolescent and adult depression and suicide risk. *Journal of Learning Disabilities.*

Royall, D. R., & Klemm, W. R. (1981). Dopaminergic mediation of reward: evidence gained using a natural reinforcer in a behavioral contrast paradigm. *Neuroscience Letters, 21,* 223–229.

Ruckmick, C. A. (1936). *The psychology of feeling and emotion.* New York: McGraw-Hill.

Rudel, R., Denckla, M., & Hirsch, S. (1977). The development of left-hand superiority for discriminating Braille configurations. *Neurology, 27,* 160–164.

Russell, J. A. (1978). Evidence of convergent validity on the dimensions of affect. *Journal of Personality and Social Psychology, 36,* 1152–1168.

Russell, J. A. (1979). Affective space is bipolar. *Journal of Personality and Social Psychology, 37,* 345–356.

Russell, J. A. (1980). A circumplex model of affect. *Journal of Personality and Social Psychology, 39,* 1161–1178.

Russell, J. A. (1983). Pancultural aspects of human conceptual organization of emotion. *Journal of Personality and Social Psychology, 45,* 1281–1288.

Russell, J. A., & Bullock, M. (1985). Multidimensional scaling of emotional facial expressions: Similarity from preschoolers to adults. *Journal of Personality and Social Psychology, 48,* 1290–1298.

Russell, J. A., & Bullock, M. (1986). On the dimensions preschoolers use to interpret facial expressions of emotions. *Developmental Psychology, 22,* 97–102.

Russell, J. A., & Steiger, J. H. (1982). The structure in persons' implicit taxonomy of emotions. *Journal of Research in Personality, 16,* 447–469.

Sackeim, H. A., Decina, P., Epstein, D., Bruder, G. E., & Malitz, S. (1983). Possible reversed affective lateralization in a case of bipolar disorder. *American Journal of Psychiatry, 140,* 1191–1193.

Sackeim, H. A., Greenberg, M. S., Weiman, A. L., Gur, R. C., Hungerbuhler, J. P., & Geschwind, N. (1982). Hemispheric asymmetry in the expression of positive and negative emotions: Neurological evidence. *Archives of Neurology, 39,* 210–218.

Sackeim, H. A., & Gur, R. C. (1978). Lateral asymmetry in intensity of emotional expression. *Neuropsychologia, 16,* 473–481.

Safer, M. A., & Leventhal, H. (1977). Ear differences in evaluating emotional tones of voice and verbal content. *Journal of Experimental Psychology: Human Perception and Performance, 3,* 75–82.

Saledate, M. C., & Orrego, F. (1977). Electrically induced release of 3H dopamine from slices obtained from different rat brain cortex regions. *Brain Research, 130,* 483–494.

Saxby, L., & Bryden, M. P. (1984). Left-ear superiority in children for processing auditory material. *Developmental Psychology, 20,* 72–80.

Saxby, L., & Bryden, M. P. (1985). Left-visual-field advantage in children for processing visual emotional stimuli. *Developmental Psychology, 21,* 253–261.

Schachter, S. (1959). *The psychology of affiliation.* California: Stanford University Press.

Schachter, S., & Singer, J. E. (1962). Cognitive, social, and physiological determinants of emotional state. *Psychological Review, 69,* 379–399.

Schaffer, C. E., Davidson, R. J., & Saron, C. (1983). Frontal and parietal EEG asymmetry in depressed and non-depressed subjects. *Biological Psychiatry, 18,* 753–762.

Schwartz, G. E., Davidson, R. J., & Maer, F. (1975). Right hemisphere lateralization for emotion in the human brain: Interactions with cognition. *Science, 19,* 286–288.

Silberman, E. K., & Weingartner, H. (1986). Hemispheric lateralization of functions related to emotion. *Brain and Cognition, 5,* 322–353.

Sperry, R. W., Gazzaniga, M. S., & Bogen, J. E. (1969). Interhemispheric relationships: The neocortical commissures; syndromes of hemispheric disconnection. In P. J. Vinken & G. W. Brayn (Eds.), *Handbook of clinical neurology,* (Vol. IV). Amsterdam: North Holland.

Spreen, O., Tupper, D., Risser, A., Tuokko, H., & Edgell, D. (1984). *Human developmental neuropsychology.* New York: Oxford University Press.

Starkstein, S. E., & Robinson, R. G. (1988). Lateralized emotional response following stroke. In M. Kinsbourne (Ed.), *Cerebral hemisphere function in depression.* Washington, D.C.: American Psychiatric Press.

Starkstein, S. E., Robinson, R. G., & Price, T. R. (1987). Comparison of cortical and subcortical lesions in the production of poststroke mood disorders. *Brain, 110,* 1045–1059.

Staton, R. D., Wilson, H., & Brumback, R. A. (1981). Cognitive improvement associated with tricyclic antidepressant treatment of childhood major depressive illness. *Perceptual & Motor Skills, 53,* 219–234.

Strauss, E., & Moscovitch, M. (1981). Perception of facial expressions. *Brain and Language, 13,* 308–332.

Swenson, R. A., & Tucker, D. M. (1983). Lateralized cognitive style and self-description. *International Journal of Neuroscience, 21,* 91-100.

Swerdlow, N. R., & Koob, G. F. (1987). Dopamine, schizophrenia, mania, and depression: Toward a unified hypothesis of cortico-striato-pallido-thalamic function. *Behavioral and Brain Sciences, 10,* 197-245.

Tellegen, A. (1985). Structures of mood and personality and their relevance to assessing anxiety with an emphasis on self-report. In A. H. Tuma, & J. D. Maser (Eds.), *Anxiety and the anxiety disorders.* Hillsdale, NJ: Lawrence Erlbaum Associates.

Terzian, H. (1964). Behavioral and EEG effects of intracarotid sodium amytal injections. *Acta Neurochirurgica, 12,* 230-240.

Tranel, D., Hall, Olson, S., & Tranel, N. N. (1987). Evidence for a right-hemisphere development learning disability. *Developmental Neuropsychology, 3,* 113-127.

Tucker, D. M. (1981). Lateral brain function, emotion and conceptualization. *Psychological Bulletin, 89,* 19-46.

Tucker, D. M. (1988). Neuropsychological mechanisms of affective self-regulation. In M. Kinsbourne (Ed.), *Cerebral hemisphere function in depression.* Washington, DC: American Psychiatric Press.

Tucker, D. M., Antes, J. R., Stenslie, C. E., & Barnhardt, T. M. (1978). Anxiety and lateral cerebral function. *Journal of Abnormal Psychology, 87,* 380-383.

Tucker, D. M., & Dawson, S. L. (1984). Asymmetric EEG power and coherence as method actors generated emotions. *Biological Psychology, 19,* 63-75.

Tucker, D. M., Roth, R. S., Arneson, B. A., & Buckingham, V. (1977). Right-hemisphere activation during stress. *Neuropsychologia, 15,* 697-700.

Tucker, D. M., Stenslie, C. E., Roth, R. S., & Shearer, S. L. (1981). Right frontal lobe activation and right hemisphere performance decrement during a depressed mood. *Archives of General Psychiatry, 38,* 169-174.

Tucker, D. M., Watson, R. T., & Heilman, K. M. (1977). Discrimination and evocation of affectively intoned speech in patients with right parietal disease. *Neurology, 27,* 947-950.

Tucker, D. M., & Williamson, P. A. (1984). Asymmetric neural control in human self-regulation. *Psychological Review, 91,* 185-215.

Uytdenhoef, P. Portelange, P., Jacquy, J., Charles, G., Linkowski, P., & Mendlewicz, J. (1983). Regional cerebral blood flow and lateralized hemispheric dysfunction in depression. *British Journal of Psychiatry, 143,* 128-132.

Valenstein, E., & Heilman, K. M. (1984). Emotional disorders resulting from lesions of the central nervous system. In K. M. Heilman & E. Valenstein (Eds.), *Clinical neuropsychology.* New York: Oxford University Press.

Voeller, K. K. S. (1986). Right-hemisphere deficit syndrome in children. *American Journal of Psychiatry, 143,* 1004-1009.

Walker, B. B., & Sandman, C. A. (1970). Human visual evoked responses are related to heart rate. *Journal of Comparative and Physiological Psychology, 93*(4), 717-729.

Wapner, W., Hamby, S., & Gardner, H. (1981). The role of the right hemisphere in the apprehension of complex linguistic materials. *Brain and Language, 14,* 15-33.

Ward, N. G., Doerr, H. O., & Storrie, M. C. (1983). Skin conductance: A potentially sensitive test for depression. *Psychiatry Research, 10,* 295-302.

Watson, D., & Tellegen, A. (1985). Toward a consensual structure of mood. *Psychological Bulletin, 98,* 219-235.

Waziri, R. (1980). Lateralization of neuroleptic-induced dyskinesia indicates pharmacological asymmetry in the brain. *Psychopharmacology, 68,* 51-53.

Weber, S. L. (1983). *Facial asymmetry in the expression of emotion in infants.* Unpublished doctoral dissertation, New York University, New York.

Weber, S. L., & Sackeim, H. A. (1984). The development of functional brain asymmetry in the regulation of emotion. In N. A. Fox & R. J. Davidson (Eds.), *The psychobiology of affective development*. Hillsdale, NJ: Lawrence Erlbaum Associates.

Weintraub, S., & Mesulam, M. (1987). Right cerebral dominance in spacial attention: Further evidence based on ipsilateral neglect. *Archives of Neurology, 44,* 621–625.

Wexler, B. (1980). Cerebral laterality and psychiatry: A review of the literature. *American Journal of Psychiatry, 136,* 279–291.

Wilson, M. C., & Schuster, C. R. (1972). The effects of chlorpromazine on psychomotor stimulant self-administration in the rhesus monkey. *Psychopharmacologia, 26,* 115–126.

Wilson, M. C., & Schuster, C. R. (1974). Aminergic influences on intravenous cocaine self-administration by rhesus monkeys. *Pharmacology, Biochemistry, and Behavior, 1,* 563–571.

Witelson, S. F. (1985). Hemispheric specialization from birth: Mark II. In C. T. Best (Ed.), *Hemispheric function and collaboration in the child* (pp. 33–85). New York: Academic Press.

Yakovlev, P., & Lecours, A. R. (1967). The myelogenetic cycles of regional maturation of the brain. In A. Minkowski (Ed.), *Regional development of the brain in early life*. Oxford: Blackwell.

Yeudall, L. T., Schopflocher, D., Sussman, P. S., Barabash, W., Warneke, L. B., Gill, D., Otto, W., Howarth, B., & Termansen, P. E. (1983). Panic attack syndrome with and without agoraphobia: Neuropsychological and evoked potential correlates. In P. Flor-Henry & J. Gruzelier (Eds.), *Laterality and psychopathology*. New York: Elsevier.

Yokel, R. A., & Wise, R. A. (1976). Attenuation of intravenous reinforcement by central dopamine blockade in rats. *Psychopharmacology, 48,* 311–318.

Zaidel, E. (1977). Unilateral auditory language comprehension on the Token Test following cerebral commissurotomy and hemispherectomy. *Neuropsychologia, 15,* 1–18.

Zajonc, R. B. (1980). Feeling and thinking: Preferences need no inferences. *American Psychologist, 35,* 151–175.

Zajonc, R. B. (1984). On the primacy of affect. *American Psychologist, 39,* 117–123.

III DEVELOPMENTAL PERSPECTIVES ON EMOTION

9 Developments in Expression: Affect and Speech

Lois Bloom
Teachers College, Columbia University

ABSTRACT

Affect and speech are two modes of expression for making known to others the contents of our feelings, beliefs, and desires. Whereas affect expression is available from the beginning of life, language has to be learned. Two questions concerning the developmental relation between these two modes of expression guided the research that is discussed in this chapter. The first began with the observation that many aspects of affect expression are already in place before language development begins and asked whether the expression of affect facilitates the emergence of speech in the second year of life. The second asked how affect and speech are integrated developmentally so that infants say words at the same time that they express positive or negative emotion. Four studies are reviewed here from a longitudinal investigation of the development of a group of 12 infants from 9 to about 30 months of age. In the first study, individual differences in the infants' age of language achievements were correlated with individual differences among them in the frequency of nonneutral affect expression and time spent in neutral affect expression. More time in neutral expression and less frequent emotional expression were associated with earlier language achievements. In the second study, different developmental trends in affect expression from 9 to 21 months were found for infants who also differed in their profiles of language development. In the third study, we looked at the words that the children said and the valence and intensity of affect that was expressed at the same time. And in the last study reviewed here, the kinds of meanings that could be attributed to the children's linguistic and emotional expressions are described (a) at the beginning of the single-word period when expression was predominantly affective, and (b) at the end of the period when the children were saying words as often as they expressed emotion. The results of these several studies are discussed in terms of the cognition required for emotional expression and language learning in early language development.

215

An expression is an embodiment; something internal to the individual is made manifest and put in a public space (Taylor, 1985). Speech is a mode of expression that we, as adults, take for granted. But we have other modes of expression, and affect is one of them. Affect as a system of emotional expression is already in place when infants begin the transition to language. The research discussed in this chapter was concerned with how emotional expression relates to expression with speech as children acquire words in the second year. Whereas we already know a great deal about how language develops, we know little about its relation to emotional expression in this period of transition from infancy to language.

Our theoretical perspective on this transition departs from the commonly held view that language is acquired by children as a tool for designating objects and events, and influencing the actions of other persons. Tool use should not be central to a theory of language development any more than it is to a theory of emotions. We have proposed, instead, that children learn the forms of speech for expressing the contents of conscious states of mind and for interpreting the speech of others so as to attribute contents of mind to them (Bloom & Beckwith, 1988). Expression is central to the theory. All of the functions of language, including its instrumental and designative functions, depend on the fact that what one has in mind determines what is said and what is understood of what others say. Speech can function to influence other persons and get things done in the world only because language makes one's desires and beliefs, purposes and goals, known to others. Expression, then, makes the functions of language possible and is not, itself, just one of language's functions. This perspective on the centrality of expression has allowed us to inquire into the relation between affect and speech, the two modes of expression available to the young child, and the developments that allow such expression to occur.

The studies we have carried out concern two issues: (a) whether the expression of emotion, which is already in place, facilitates the emergence of speech, and (b) how the young infant, who is just starting to learn language, integrates speech with affect for saying words and expressing emotion together.

The first issue, whether emotional expression facilitates the emergence of speech, is relevant to the theory that language development builds on emotional expression in the second year of life. This idea is implied if not explicit in contemporary accounts of the communication of affect between infants and their caregivers in the first year (e.g., Dore, 1983; Trevarthen, 1979). The idea is not new; it has its origins in the classic phylogenetic theories of language. In one of the most influential of these, Condillac, in the 18th century, proposed that the conventional signs of speech originated when the involuntary vocal gestures that express "the passions of joy, fear, or of grief" were deliberately repeated, in the absence of their reflexive eliciting conditions, for the benefit of others (cited in

Aarsleff, 1976, p. 10). However, in the results of the studies reported here, we see that the emergence of speech did not build upon the infants' emotional expression.

The second issue, how infants coordinate speech and affective expression for saying words with emotion, is relevant to both linguistic and emotional development. Expression begins in earliest infancy with *affect,* and much of the form and content of communication between infants and their caregivers is affective in the first year of life (e.g., Emde, Gaensbauer, & Harmon, 1976; Stechler & Carpenter, 1967; Stern, 1977). Children do not learn the words of the emotions lexicon (e.g., "happy," "mad," "scared") for actually naming feelings until the third year (Bretherton & Beeghly, 1982; Bretherton, McNew, & Beeghly-Smith, 1981; Ridgeway, Waters, & Kuczaj, 1985). However, the studies discussed in this chapter concern the period, in the second year, when *words* (but not emotion words) begin to emerge for expressing the contents of mental states. This is the period that intervenes between communication with affect expression before speech in early infancy, and acquisition of the names for emotions and feelings in the third year. We have asked how the two systems of expression, speech and affect, are integrated during this time so that infants come to express their feelings together with contents of what those feelings are about.

The first of the four studies described in this chapter (and reported in full in Bloom & Capatides, 1987) tested the hypothesis that emotional expression facilitates the emergence of speech. Certain measures of infants' affect expression were correlated with the ages at which they reached several achievements in language learning: first words, a vocabulary spurt, and multiword speech. Because the infants reached these language achievements at different ages, the result of this first study was an account of individual differences among them in the relation between affect expression and age of language achievement.

The second study was concerned with developmental function in affect expression with the children equated for age, at 9, 13, 17, and 21 months (reported in full in Bloom, Beckwith, & Capatides, 1988). However, because of the stable individual differences among the infants in the relation between affect expression and age of language achievements, we also examined the developmental functions for two subgroups of infants who were early and later word learners. The result is an account of how the expression of affect and the emergence of words covaried developmentally in these children's early word learning.

The third study was concerned with how the two systems, emotional expression and speech, come together (reported in Bloom & Beckwith, 1989). The question we asked was how infants, who have been expressing emotion virtually since birth, express emotion when they are also saying words in the second year of life. This study, then, looked at the words that the children said and the valence and intensity of the affect that was expressed at the same time.

The last study discussed in this chapter was concerned with the kinds of meanings that could be attributed to these infants' expressions (reported in full in Bloom, Beckwith, Capatides, & Hafitz, 1988). The attributions we made concerned the contents of desires and beliefs that were expressed by speech and emotional expression. The attributions were compared for the two forms of expression at the beginning of the single-word period when expression was predominantly affective, and toward the end of the period when the children were saying words as often as they expressed affect.

We were unaware of any explicit theoretical or empirical claims that might have led us to expect that expressions of the discrete emotions (e.g., anger, joy, sadness) would relate in any interesting ways to language development. For this reason, the coding scheme for affect that we devised used gradient information: (a) *valence* (positive, negative, neutral, mixed, and equivocal affect tone), and (b) *intensity* (three degrees indicating the fullness of an expression). Cues from facial expression, vocalization, and body posture were used to code affect continuously in the stream of activity as each child and mother played with groups of toys in a playroom. The result was a continuous record of changes in expressed affect and the duration of each affect expression. Thus, these studies concern the developments that occurred in expressed affect and speech in a single, essentially constant situation, beginning at 9 months of age.

THE RESEARCH PROJECT

Our subjects were 12 infants, 6 girls and 6 boys. All were firstborn, from different ethnic and economic backgrounds, and their mothers were not employed outside the home at the time the study began. They came from homes in the New York metropolitan area and were contacted through letters to pediatricians and social service agencies, and notices posted in laundromats, community centers, apartment house lobbies, banks, and the like. Each infant and mother visited our laboratory playroom once each month, from about 8 months to about 30 months of age. Each session lasted 1 hour. The children were also visited at home every month until they were 15 months old, and then every 3 months thereafter. Tests of comprehension and sensorimotor development were presented in the home visits. The mothers also kept diaries of the words their infants both said and understood in the monthly intervals between playroom visits. The playroom sessions provided the primary data for the studies discussed here.

The playroom was furnished with a child-size table and chairs, a 3-foot plastic slide with a crawl-through tunnel between the steps and the incline, and a changing table. A group of toys was on the floor when the mother and infant entered the room. One of two investigators brought in additional groups of toys on schedule at 8-minute intervals and brought in a snack (cookies with juice for the baby and coffee or tea for the mother) after the first half hour. All the children were presented with the same groups of toys in the same sequence. The toys were selected to balance possible girl–boy interest (e.g., doll, truck) and manipulative-enactment play (e.g., nesting blocks, miniature cutlery). (See Lifter & Bloom, 1989, for description of these toys.)

The observations were stereo-videorecorded (SLO-383 Sony 1/2 inch Beta). The camera was mounted on a 3-foot high movable tripod in the playroom, and the second investigator maneuvered the camera so that the infant was in view all the time. Each child and mother interacted with only one pair of investigators, both in the playroom and on the home visits, and the investigators and children were matched for ethnicity. Because the infants and mothers were visited at home before the data collection began and then saw the investigators twice a month, they knew the investigators well and gave every indication that they were relaxed and comfortable in the playroom sessions.

At the time of recording, a time-code generator (FOR-A SMPTE) imposed a discrete auditory signal on the second sound track for each frame of the tape. This allowed the data to be manipulated to within 1/30th of a second (each second of videotape containing 30 frames) at the time of data processing. The videotape deck was interfaced at playback with a SMPTE time-code reader and an Apple II plus computer for data coding and transcription. Each transcription entry included the times of onset and offset of the expression. The time code allowed separate passes through the data (for example, affect expression coded in one pass and transcribed speech in a second pass) to be merged, preserving the temporal relations between them, for integrated analyses.

Transcription of Speech

Two speech transcription passes were made through the data to assure reliability. The first was a transcription of the children's words (and all other nonword vocalizations) and was originally written out by hand, with nonspeech vocalizations and questionable words transcribed phonetically. A second transcriber then entered the speech and vocalizations into the computer, with times of onset and offset, using the original transcription while reviewing the video record. Differences between transcribers in identifying words were resolved by having both review the tape together; when agreement could not be reached, the vocalization was discounted as speech and not included in the analyses.

Three reference points were used to define the period of *transition* to language. The first was the month when each child reached the criterion for "first words" (FW): the first use of at least one conventional word, said at least 2 times. That month was the reference point for the beginning of the transition into language. The second measure of these infants' language development was the age at which the children reached a "vocabulary spurt" (VS). This was a sharp increase in the slope of cumulative word acquisition from 1 month to the next. The VS was operationalized for the purpose of this study as the first increase of at least 12 new words (utterance types) after the child had already acquired at least 20 different words. Any conventional words were counted for determining the FW and VS achievements, including interjections and parts of routines, but imitations of mothers' speech and self-repetitions were not. These two developments—beginning to say words and a sharp increase in the number of words— have long been considered major developments defining the transition to language in the single-word period (e.g., Bloom, 1973; Corrigan, 1983; Dromi, 1982; Gopnik & Meltzoff, 1987; McCarthy, 1954; Nelson, 1973; Stern & Stern, 1907).

The third language achievement was the transition to multiword speech (MW). The criterion for the transition to multiwords was a mean length of utterance of 1.5 words, discounting imitations, self-repetitions, bound morphemes, "yeah" and "no," and the articles "a" and "the." The mean ages of these three language achievements (FW, VS, MW) were 13 ; 2, 19 ; 2, and 24 ; 1 (months; weeks), respectively.

Coding Affect Expression

A coding scheme was devised to capture the gradient properties of emotional expression—valence and intensity—and discrete emotions were not labeled. (Precedence for this procedure can be found, for example, in the studies by Adamson & Bakeman, 1982, 1985; Ricciuti & Poresky, 1972; and Stechler & Carpenter, 1967. See, also, the discussion in Bullock and Russell, 1986.)

Every change in expressed affect in the stream of the child's activities was recorded with time of onset, in the first half hour of the observations at FW and VS, and at 9, 13, 17, and 21 months. The coding yielded a continuous record of (a) changes in expressed affect and (b) the duration of affect expressions from one shift in expression to another. A shift in affect expression was defined as any observable change in either valence or intensity in the infant's emotional expression, which included changes in facial expression, body tension and posture, and affective vocalizations (whining, laughing, and the like). Because affect was coded continuously in the stream of the child's activity, the onset time of any emotional expression was also the offset time of the previous expression.

These affect expressions were coded for their *valence*, whether neutral, negative, positive, mixed, or equivocal tone. A neutral expression was defined by the face being in a resting or baseline position, as described by Ekman and Friesen (1975), and without body tension or affective vocalization. Mixed affect was an expression that included elements of both positive and negative valence. Equivocal affect was not positive, negative, nor neutral, as happened with expressions of surprise or excitement. Nonneutral affect expressions were also coded for *intensity* with three levels of intensity indicating the fullness of a display. Thus, the coding scheme for capturing the gradient properties of expressed affect included three levels of intensity: 1, 2, 3, and five qualities of valence: neutral, negative, positive, mixed, and equivocal. Photographs of examples of these affect expressions can be found in Bloom, Beckwith, Capatides, and Hafitz (1988). (See Schlosberg, 1954, for discussion of the "pleasantness—unpleasantness" and intensity dimensions of emotion; and Stern, Barnett, & Spieker, 1983, for discussion of gradient and categorical information in the emotional signal.)[1]

Ambiguous episodes (the occurrence of a momentary vocalization or facial movement that could not be assigned to one of the aforementioned categories) were also coded with time of onset. These were least frequent at 17 months (M = 14.9) and most frequent at 21 months (M = 19.3); they were not included in the data analyses. In addition, the infant was sometimes moving away from the camera, or the infant's face was not visible for affect coding with no cues from body tension or affective vocalization. These intervals of "backturn" were also coded for onset so that coding affect in the stream of the child's activity was not interrupted. The average amount of time spent in backturn and ambiguous episodes at 9, 13, 17, and 21 months was 4.3, 5.7, 4.7, and 5.9 minutes, respectively. All the remaining minutes of the half hour were coded for valence and intensity of affect expression. (The coding scheme used in this study is available from the authors; see Bloom, Beckwith, & Capatides, 1988, for description of reliability procedures.)

The time code enabled the separate passes for transcribing speech and coding affect to be merged by computer, so that the temporal relations between speech and affect expression were preserved. Accuracy in determining onset and offset times, after training, was high. The mean discrepancy was 2 video frames (1/15 second) for speech onset time, and 5 video frames (1/6 second) for speech offset. The mean discrepancy in recording affect onset time was an average of 16 video frames, or approximately 1/2 second. (The somewhat lesser accuracy in finding onset time of an affect expression was due to the fact that several kinds of cues were used to code affect, e.g., facial expression and body tension).

The processed data were transferred to an IBM-XT computer for analyses. The coded data were reduced using a program that (a) counted all speech and affect expressions (including any change in valence or intensity of expression); (b) counted the number of video frames for the duration of each expression; and

---

[1]This study was concerned only with the perceived expression of affect through facial movement, body posture and tension, and affective vocalization (which included whining, laughing, and the like). We are aware of the considerable literature (summarized in Buck, 1984) which has documented an inverse relation between such overt signs of expressivity as these, and the possible internal experience of emotion as revealed through psychophysiological measures. Thus, infants expressing neutral affect may well have been experiencing emotionally toned affect in these moments. In addition, neutral expressions could have included other affect features that might be captured with a finer grained analysis than was employed in the studies discussed here. The relevance of other, possibly covert manifestations of affect to language learning and the further exploration of the features of neutral affect expressions are issues for further research.

(c) calculated the mean duration and total time spent in speech and in the nine categories of affect expression: three degrees of positive valence; three degrees of negative valence; neutral, mixed, and equivocal valence; and in backturn and ambiguous cases.

Measures of Affect and Speech Expression

The following studies used two different kinds of variables: one was the unit of an *expression* and the other was the measure of *time*. An expression was a discrete event with an onset and an offset—either in speech or affect—that could be counted, so that we can talk about numbers of words and numbers of affect expressions. The frequency of emotional expression included any change in nonneutral valence (positive, negative, mixed, or equivocal) or intensity of expression. Because frequency of neutral expression was the complement of emotional expression, it was not a separate measure.

Time—speech time and affect time—was the duration of an expression. Time was measured by counting the number of video frames (with 30 video frames per second) from the onset to the offset of speech, and from the onset of an affect expression to the onset of the next expression). One measure of time that was used in the following studies was a summary measure: out of the total amount of observation time (30 minutes less backturns and ambiguous cases), the percentage that was spent (a) speaking, (b) expressing neutral affect, (c) expressing emotional affect (positive, negative, mixed, or equivocal valence), or (d) both speaking and expressing affect.

For all the studies reported here, different persons were responsible for coding affect and transcribing speech, and all were naive to the units of analysis and hypotheses that were tested in each of the studies.

THE INFLUENCE OF AFFECT ON LEARNING WORDS

One of the most frequently cited facts of child language is that children differ widely in onset and rate of language development. For the children whom we have studied, differences in age of language achievement were associated with differences among them in the quality of expressed affect (Bloom & Capatides, 1987).

The first hypothesis tested in this study built upon the temporal precedence of affect for communication, and the theoretical assumptions in both the phylogenetic and ontogenetic literature that the origins of language could be found in affective communication. Given the temporal precedence of affect for communication, the expression of emotion might be expected to facilitate learning words. Accordingly, the first hypothesis we tested was the Emotionality Hypothesis: that the frequency with which infants display positive and negative emotion would predict (a) early emergence of words and (b) frequency of expression with words.

The second, alternative hypothesis built upon the theoretical assumptions that guided the research project, and the fact that learning words and expressing emotion have different cognitive requirements. Words are arbitrary linguistic units and they have to be learned. The mental representations that underlie linguistic actions of expression and interpretation are constructed from aspects of knowledge recalled from memory and the data available in perception (Bloom & Beckwith, 1988). Language emerges in the child's endeavor to recall and recognize words that express these mental contents, and this endeavor entails cognitive effort. Underlying an expression of emotion is an *evaluative* stance—one in which the individual evaluates the situation in relation to existing contents of a mental state (e.g., Arnold, 1960; Sroufe, 1984; Wozniak, 1986). The cognitive component of an emotion is often the evaluation of the situation in relation to some goal (e.g., Campos, Barret, Lamb, Goldsmith, & Stenberg, 1983; Oatley & Johnson-Laird, 1987; Stein & Levine, 1986). The evaluative stance underlying emotions and emotional expression could preempt the resources needed for learning words, and vice versa. Learning words would be more likely to occur in a reflective stance with neutral affect expression than when emotions are being expressed. Accordingly, the alternative hypothesis that we tested was the Reflectivity Hypothesis: that the time spent in neutral affect expression would be associated with early achievements in learning words.

In the first analysis, to test the Emotionality hypothesis, frequency of emotional expression at FW and VS was correlated with the ages of the three language achievements (FW, VS, and MW). These correlations (in Table 9.1) were all in the positive direction and all but one were statistically significant. The more frequently the infants expressed emotions, the older they were at the time of the language achievements. In addition, when frequency of emotional expression

TABLE 9.1
Correlation of Frequency of Emotional Expression
with Age at Language Achievements

Frequency of Expression	Age		
	FW	VS	MW
FW	.658	.593	(.476)
VS	.662	.684	.668
N = 12			

Note: Pearson *r*, all are significant, *p* < .05, except value in parentheses.

was correlated with the numbers of words (both utterance tokens and types) at FW and VS, none of the correlations was significant. Thus, high emotionality was associated with later age of language achievements and did not predict either the number of words that the children learned (types) or their frequency of speech (tokens). We concluded therefore that the frequency with which infants express emotions does not facilitate early word learning.

In the second analysis, to test the Reflectivity hypothesis, the percentage of total time that the infants spent in neutral affect expression (which was the percentage of all the frames coded, excluding backturns and ambiguous cases) was correlated with the ages of the language achievements FW, VS, and MW. All the correlations in Table 9.2 between time in neutral affect expression and age of language achievement were in the negative direction and (except for those enclosed in parentheses) statistically significant. This means that the more time these infants spent in neutral affect expression at FW and VS, the younger they were at the time of FW and VS. Moreover, the time they spent in neutral affect expression at VS predicted early age at MW. For the infants in this study, then, more time spent in neutral affect expression was associated with early language achievements, confirming the reflectivity hypothesis.

However, we had to consider the possibility that these findings could have been related to developments in affect expression in this period of time. A developmental increase in the frequency of emotional expression could be expected to have a corresponding decrease in neutral expression. If the frequency of emotional expression increased in the second year, more frequent expression of emotion may be inadvertently associated with later age of language achievement, and more time spent in neutral expression associated with earlier age of language achievement.

TABLE 9.2
Correlation and Time Spent in Neutral Affect
Expression with Age at Language Achievements

Time in Neutral Expression	Age		
	FW	VS	MW
FW	−.697	−.578	(−.538)
VS	(−.522)	−.828	−.711
N = 12			

Note: Pearson r, all are significant, p < .05, except values in parentheses.

DEVELOPMENTS IN THE EXPRESSION OF AFFECT

The data just presented demonstrated individual differences among the infants across the variables of affect expression and age of language achievement. Such correlational analyses of an individual child relative to other children across different variables are, however, only part of the picture. Correlational analyses do not describe the *process* of development or developmental changes over time within a particular variable such as, in this case, affect expression. Both analyses of individual differences (the previous study) and developmental change (this next study) are necessary for understanding development (McCall, 1986). This is so because individuals within a group may keep their relative ranks across two variables, even though the group may still vary across age, or the mean difference between two naturally occurring subgroups may vary. Such variance would indicate dynamic developmental process, even though the performance of each child relative to the others did not change. The next study (reported in Bloom, Beckwith, & Capatides, 1988) concerned developments over time in the infants' affect expression, in order to explore the relation between developmental function and the individual differences already observed. For this purpose, affect expression was coded with the infants equated for age, at 9, 13, 17, and 21 months.

We already knew that the infants differed from one another, with some expressing emotion more frequently than others, and that these differences among them were stable in relation to age of language achievements. We expected, therefore, that they might differ in developmental function as well. If one suspects that children might show different developmental trends, then the mean of the group as a whole is not the most representative statistic with which to describe developmental function. Because we wanted to look at changes in emotional expression across age in the period in which the children began to learn language, and we knew that emotional expression was highly related to age of language achievement, we had to consider the possibility of different developmental functions for different groups of children. For this reason, we examined separate developmental functions for the means of two subgroups: early and later language learners. We did this because we hypothesized that not only was age of language achievement related to emotional expression at a given point in time, but differences in age of language achievement would predict different courses of development.

The infants were divided into two subgroups of early and later word learners based on age of the first language achievement, FW. The mean age of FW was 408 days (range = 305–510 days); 6 infants below the mean and 6 infants above the mean formed the two groups of early word learners (EWL) and later word learners (LWL), respectively. Splitting the group in half this way was the most stringent test because of the likelihood of overlap between groups. The mean ages of the three language achievements (FW, VS, MW) are presented in

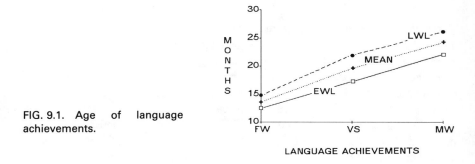

FIG. 9.1. Age of language achievements.

LANGUAGE ACHIEVEMENTS

Fig. 9.1 for the two groups of infants.[2] The middle line in the figure is the mean for the total group ($n = 12$). Thus, the study of the infants' affect expression at 9, 13, 17, and 21 months began before they said their first words and extended through the single-word period for all of them, and through the transition to multiword speech for some of them.

Later language achievement for the infants in this study did not mean that their language was delayed or otherwise deviant, and none were considered at risk for language problems in this period. As can be seen in Fig. 9.1, the ages at which the later word learners achieved the milestones FW, VS, and MW were within normal limits (Bloom & Lahey, 1978), and the two groups of infants progressed at similar rates.

Several measures of affect expression were examined in this study, but only frequency of emotional expressions and the percentage of total time spent in neutral affect expression are presented here. To determine change, the data were tested with a 2 (EWL/LWL) by 4 (9, 13, 17, 21 months) repeated measures analysis of variance and paired comparisons t-tests. The frequency of emotional expression (including positive, negative, mixed, and equivocal affect) did, indeed, increase significantly over time for the group of infants as a whole, $N = 12$, $F(1,30) = 4.464$, $p = .01$.

However, when the two groups were tested separately, the developmental change in frequency of expression was significant only for the LWL, $n = 6$, $F(3,15) = 5.018$, $p = .013$, and not for the EWL ($p = .37$). These developmental trends in frequency of emotional expression are presented in Fig. 9.2, with one graph for all nonneutral expressions (including positive, negative, mixed, and

---

[2]Although the number of subjects in this study is obviously too small for comparisons of ethnic and gender group differences, we can report that of the non-White children in our sample, 3 were above and 1 below the mean age of FW and 2 were above and 2 below the mean age at both VS and MW. With respect to gender differences, 5 males were above and 1 below the mean age at FW, and 4 above and 2 below the mean age at both VS and MW.

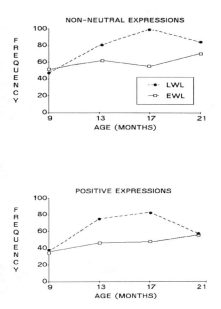

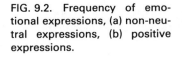

FIG. 9.2. Frequency of emotional expressions, (a) non-neutral expressions, (b) positive expressions.

equivocal) (Fig. 9.2a), and one graph for positive (Fig. 9.2b) expressions alone. The two groups of infants, early and later word learners, were clearly different in their profiles of emotional development.

The valence of most of the infants' expressions of emotional affect was positive, 79% on average, and later word learners expressed positive affect more often than the early word learners at 13 months, $t(1) = 2.512$, $p = .031$, and again at 17 months, $t(1) = 2.987$, $p = .014$. Although the later word learners increased in positive expression significantly between 9 and 17 months, $t(5) = 3.598$, $p = .016$, they *decreased* in positive expression between 17 and 21 months, $t(5) = -3.018$, $p = .029$. This was the period that encompassed the development from FW to VS for the LWL; their mean age at VS was 22 months.

Corresponding to the difference between the groups in frequency of emotional expression, the early word learners did not change in the relative amount of time they spent in neutral affect expression (see Fig. 9.3). The apparent decrease between 9 and 17 months in percentage of time in neutral expression by the later word learners was not significant, $F(2,10) = 2.611$, $p = .122$. However, the two groups were different at 17 months, $t(1) = 2.253$, $p = .048$.

We concluded from these results that the chronological developments in these infants' affect expression covaried with their language acquisition. The two groups of infants were not different at 9 months. Those infants who began to say words relatively early (EWL, mean age at FW = 12;3) showed little change in frequency of emotional expression. In contrast, the infants who did not begin to say words between 9 and 13 months of age increased in frequency of emotional

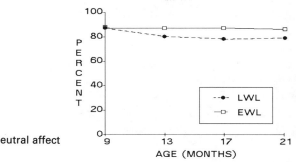

FIG. 9.3.   Time in neutral affect
expression.

expression instead. Thus, all the infants increased in their expressivity. However, one group of infants increased in expression by learning to say words relatively early, whereas the other group increased in their frequency of emotional expression and did not also learn to say words at the same time. Those infants who began to say words relatively early did not change in the amount of time they spent in neutral affect expression, nor in the frequency with which they expressed emotion—throughout the single-word period and into the transition to multiword speech. In contrast, those infants who were later in their language achievements increased in emotional expression in the period before they began to say words and decreased in frequency of expression in the interval between their FW and VS achievements. The result was an interaction between the developmental trends in these infants' affect expression and their language learning, such that differences in learning words covaried with different developmental trends in affect expression.

In the first set of results reported before (from Bloom & Capatides, 1987), early word learning was correlated with a greater amount of time spent in neutral affect and later word learning was correlated with more frequent emotional expression. Those results, then, were not an artifact of developmental trends in affect expression, with early word learning associated with neutral affect because neutral affect decreased with age, and later language learning associated with emotional expression because emotional expression increased with age. On the contrary, the developmental function of emotional expression did increase, but only for the later word learners, and in the period before they began to say words. Time spent in neutral affect did not change for the early word learners.

Early achievements in language were associated with more time in neutral affect expression and less frequent expression of emotion. We have interpreted this result in terms of the different cognitive requirements for learning words and expressing emotion: Neutral affect would allow the reflective stance that is required for learning words, whereas the evaluative stance underlying emotional expressions may compete for these cognitive resources. And, indeed, the later word learners decreased significantly in frequency of positive expression at 21 months, which was close to the mean age (22 months) of their vocabulary spurt. Although the two groups of infants were significantly different in neutral affect expression at 17 months, they were no longer different at 21 months.

We proposed (Bloom & Capatides, 1987) that time in neutral affect expression has its antecedents in the "quiet alert states" during which neonates and young infants attend to visual and auditory stimuli (e.g., Brazleton, 1979; Wolfe, 1965). These quiet alert states are generally considered to be the moments during which infants are perceiving and learning from objects and events in their environments (e.g., Lamb & Campos, 1982; Olson & Sherman, 1983). Just as quiet alert states support the cognitive activity of the younger infant, neutral affect supports the cognition required for early language learning in the second year. In addition, the neutral affect expression coded in this study included expression of the emotions category of "interest" (C. Malatesta, personal communication), and interest, as an emotion, has been considered important for processes of attention and cognition (Izard, 1986; Piaget, 1954/1981).

TALKING WITH FEELING

In the studies reviewed so far, we were concerned with the relation between affect *expression* and language *learning*. We now turn to the first of two studies that were concerned with affect and speech as modes of expression for making the contents of feelings, beliefs, and desires known to others. We know that infants are already successful in communicating before speech begins, and that much of the form and the content of that communication is affective in nature. We also know that the words that name the emotions are not represented in children's early vocabularies (Beckwith, 1989; Bretherton & Beeghly, 1982; Bretherton, McNew, & Beeghly-Smith, 1981; Ridgeway, Waters, & Kuczaj, 1985) so that infants cannot use words to tell us what their feelings are. The question we asked (in Bloom & Beckwith, 1989) was: How are affect expression and speech integrated with one another when speech begins, before infants are able to say the words that name their emotions?

On the one hand, if neutral affect expression supports the reflective stance required for learning words and for recalling words to express mental contents, then words and emotional expression should not occur together when words begin to appear. On the other hand, we also know that words and sentences are spoken with emotional expression to convey emotional meaning by adults (e.g., Davitz, 1964, 1969) and preschool children (e.g., Camras, 1985). Thus, we might expect development in the ability to say words with emotional valence. The hypothesis tested in this study, the Integration hypothesis, was that early words would occur primarily with neutral affect, but speech and emotional expression would come to overlap with one another toward the end of the single-word period.

Another group of hypotheses concerned the factors that might contribute to the integration of speech and emotional expression. We know from the studies of Stein and her colleagues (1986) that more cognitive work occurs with expression of negative affect than with positive affect. The evaluative activity underlying negative emotion often results in a plan, for example, to remove an obstacle to a goal, as in the case of anger, or to generate a new goal, as in the case of sadness. For this reason, one might expect that expressing negative emotion would be most likely to interfere with the reflective stance required for recalling a word for the expression of mental contents. In contrast, expressing positive emotion should not be expected to interfere with saying words given that the positive evaluation of a situation relative to a goal need not entail new cognitive activity (Rothbart, 1973). Accordingly, the third hypothesis tested was the Facilitating Affect hypothesis: that when speech and emotional expression are integrated, the emotion would be a *positive* one most often, and expressed with lesser rather than heightened intensity.

The ability to say words while expressing emotion should also be influenced by the actual words themselves. Accordingly, we proposed a Facilitating Words hypothesis: that the words said together with emotional expression would be (a) those words that the children knew best, that is, their most frequent words and the words that they learned earliest, and (b) those words that possibly carry inherently affective meaning, such words as, for example, "no" and "Mama."

In sum, the hypotheses tested in this study were (a) words would be said most often with neutral valence; (b) the convergence of speech with positive and negative emotional expression would increase developmentally; (c) when infants say words at the same time they express emotion, that emotion would be low intensity and have positive valence more often than negative valence; and (d) the words that children say when they also express emotional meaning would be their most frequent words, the words they learned earliest, and words with inherently affective connotation.

Two different measures were used to determine the overlap of speech and emotional expression. The first was a *frequency* measure: the number of times that a word was said at the same time as an affect expression. Affect coded with positive and negative valence and the highest level of intensity took precedence over neutral valence for assigning the affect value that was in place at the time of speech. For example, if a neutral expression occurred before speech onset but then an instance of $+1$ affect occurred either (a) during speech (between speech onset and speech offset), or (b) within a 10 frame window after speech offset, that word was considered to have occurred with $+1$ affect. The use of the 10 frame window after speech offset was the control for the margin of error in coding times of speech offset and affect onset.

The results of this first analysis are presented in Fig. 9.4 for both FW and VS. Here we have the frequency of words spoken with the different values of affect valence and intensity, presented as a percentage of the number of words spoken by all the children ($N = 12$). The distribution in Fig. 9.4 makes clear that these

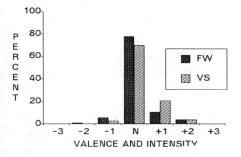

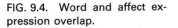

FIG. 9.4. Word and affect expression overlap.

children said most of their words when they were also expressing neutral affect. When they did speak and express emotion at the same time, that emotion was positive more often, and more likely to be level one ($+1$ or -1) intensity. Thus, these children were not inclined to be speaking when they were also expressing emotion and did not speak when they were expressing emotion with heightened intensity ($+3$ or -3).

Although the children said most of their words with neutral valence, they were also expressing neutral affect most of the time (84% of the time, on average). Thus, one could argue that speech with neutral valence was conditioned by the amount of time that was spent in neutral affect. For this reason, a second measure of overlapping *time* was also used.

For the analysis of overlapping speech time and emotion time, the number of video frames (with 30 frames per second) was counted for time spent (a) speaking, (b) expressing emotion, and (c) in speech and emotion together. Time in speech and emotion together (overlapping speech time/emotion time), at FW and VS, is presented in Fig. 9.5 as the percentage of all the frames of transcribed speech. The dashed lines in the figure represent how much overlapping speech time and emotion time was expected. This was based on the percentage of all the frames coded for affect that were coded with emotional valence (emotion time). The children were expressing emotion less than 20% of the time at both FW and VS. AT FW, the amount of speech time/emotion time overlap was independent

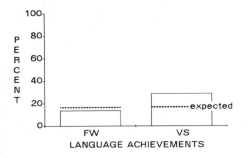

FIG. 9.5. Time in speech with emotion. *Note.* The bar represents the percentage of transcribed speech that occurred with overlapping emotional expression. The expected value is the percentage of time coded for affect expression that was coded as emotional expression.

of the amount of emotion time, Chi-square $= 1.78$, $p = .182$. In contrast, at VS, speech was expressed with emotion more than expected, given the time spent in expressing emotion, Chi-square $= 1578.48$, $p < .001$. Comparing FW and VS, speech time/emotion time overlap increased between the two language achievements, Chi-square $= 271.63$, $p < .001$, confirming the Integration hypothesis.

In sum, when these infants began to say words, the two systems of expression, speech and emotion, were statistically independent. The children said most of their words when they were also expressing neutral affect. However, by the time they reached the vocabulary spurt, the two systems had converged. The remaining analyses concerned those factors that contributed to this integration.

When the infants did speak and express emotion at the same time, the expression was more likely to be level one ($+1$ or -1) intensity. At VS, more words were said with level 1 intensity and fewer words with levels 2 and 3 than was expected, given the frequency of emotional expression at the different intensity levels, Chi-square $= 13.26$, $p < .001$. The same comparison was not significant at FW, $p > .50$. Thus, the children were not inclined to be speaking at VS when they were expressing emotion with heightened intensity ($+2,3$ or $-2,3$).

The words that these infants said with emotional expression were said with positive valence primarily. This result is presented in Fig. 9.6 as the percentage of all the frames of overlapping speech time/emotion time that were coded as positive valence. The expected values were the percentage of positive valence of all the frames coded for positive and negative valence. At VS, time spent in speech with positive affect expression was greater than was predicted by the time spent in positive affect expression overall, and time spent in speech with negative affect expression was less than was predicted by the time spent in negative affect expression overall, Chi square $= 81.06$, $p < .001$. Thus, the Facilitating Affect hypothesis was confirmed; if these infants expressed emotion and speech together, the emotion they expressed was more likely to be positive than negative.

Finally, what were the words that these infants said when they were also expressing emotion? The words that they said with emotion were either among the most frequent words that they said or among their earliest learned words

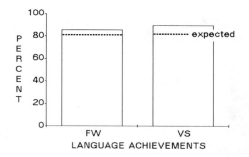

FIG. 9.6.   Time in positive emotional expression in speech time/emotion time overlap. *Note.* The bar represents the percentage of overlapping speech and emotion with positive emotional expression. The expected value is the percentage of time coded for emotional expression that was coded as positive expression.

(words reported in the mothers' diaries before FW, or words that were observed in the interval between FW and VS). Either frequency, priority, or *both* predicted which words were said with emotional valence for all the infants except one. This means that when the infants said words at the same time that they also expressed emotion, the words they said were the words that they presumably knew best: words they said most frequently and/or words they had learned to say at an earlier time.

Included as words in the speech transcription were those words that have traditionally been thought to be most likely to carry emotional tone (i.e., the interjections such as "oh" and "uhoh"; Sapir, 1921). However, these interjections were not more likely than other words to occur with emotional expression. Of all the words that were said with emotional valence, most were said by only one child and usually only one time. However, a small group of words were said with emotion by at least four of the children and these are listed in Table 9.3.

Several of the words in Table 9.3 are among those that one might expect to have inherent emotional meaning for infants. These were (a) salient relational words for infants ("no" and "more"); (b) words typically associated with well-known routines ("Hi," and "whee" when rolling the ball, using the slide, and the like); and (c) person words ("Mama" and its variants, and "baby"). Both "Mama" and "baby" were also said of the small rubber family and farm animal figures.

Thus, emotional expression and expression through speech were integrated in the period of single-word development as these children came to be able to say words with emotional valence. However, several cognitive constraints influenced their saying words with emotional valence. The words that were said with emotional valence were said with positive emotion primarily, were the words that the children knew best, and were often person words and parts of well-known play and relational routines.

TABLE 9.3
The Most Frequent Words with Emotional Valence

First Words			Vocabulary Spurt		
Word	Children	Proportion	Word	Children	Proportion
Hi	6	.53	Hi	5	.90
Mama	5	.60	Mama	6	.43
No	3	.36	No	3	.50
			Baby	8	.41
			Whee	5	.79
			More	4	.19

Note: Words said with emotional valence by at least 4 children (except "no").

None of the words were the names of the emotions themselves. The infants were not telling their mothers what they were feeling with words like "happy" or "mad" but, instead, were learning to express what their feelings were about. These were words that named the causes and circumstances that contributed to their emotional experiences and expression. Reports in the literature of the "early" use of emotion words by English speaking children have generally relied on mothers' reports of whether such words occur at all, through the use of checklists. The youngest children in these studies have generally not been less than 20 months old (e.g., Bretherton et al., 1986). Similarly, the mothers of the children whom we studied used emotion words very infrequently when talking in the moments that surrounded their children's emotional expression. Instead, they talked about the situations that were the causes, consequences, and circumstances of their children's emotional expressions (Capatides, 1989) and similar data have been reported by Dunn, Bretherton, & Munn (1987).

EXPRESSION OF MEANING THROUGH AFFECT AND WORDS

Both emotional expressions and speech afford attributions of the contents of an expressor's beliefs and desires. We were able to make such attributions for the speech and emotional expressions of the infants whom we studied. We then used the contents of the attributions of these states of mind as an heuristic for comparing the meanings that the children expressed with affect and with words (reported in Bloom, Beckwith, Capatides, & Hafitz, 1988). (This study was not concerned with the contents of neutral expressions; the affect expressions described next were expressions with positive, negative, mixed, or equivocal valence.)

Two levels of attribution are relevant to the findings discussed here. The first, more global level was whether a "belief" or a "desire" was the infant's psychological attitude toward the mentally present objects and events expressed by affect or words. This first distinction, then, was whether the infant believed the event in mind to be the case or desired the event to be the case (leaving aside, for the present, the fact that desires entail beliefs; see Bloom & Beckwith, 1988, for discussion of this point).

A belief represents reality as it is from the child's point of view; that is, a belief matches the world as the infant sees or imagines it to be. A desire is an intention, with or without a plan, to make a change in the world; that is, a desire matches the way the infant considers that the world ought to be (see Searle, 1983, for this differentiation). For example, we attributed a belief to the infant if the infant was considering an object or action without trying to influence or change the events in the context. We attributed a desire to the infant if the infant appeared to be thinking about doing an action, obtaining an object, or fulfilling some other kind of goal.

The second level of attribution was more molecular and concerned the contents of the beliefs and desires that the infants had in mind. These contents were considered to be the meanings that were expressed in speech and affect displays. The contents of mental states were coded as propositions, with three predicates *be* (static state), *do* (dynamic state), and *go* (change of place). The arguments of these predicates were persons, objects, and actions and, most often, these were the persons, objects, and actions in the playroom that figured in the child's activity.

The coding scheme, its theoretical rationale, and the results of its application are presented more fully in Bloom, Beckwith, Capatides, and Hafitz (1988). Here I report only the results of attributions of beliefs and desires, with contents that included the infant and the mother, for the infants' speech and affect expressions. For this analysis we were interested in what the infants had in mind when saying words or expressing affect: whether the infants had a goal to change the world (an expression of desire) or expressed a belief in the way the world was (to them), and whether their desires or beliefs concerned themselves or other persons. Because of the essentially exploratory nature of this analysis and the lack of independence between speech and affect expressions (given that some words were said with emotional valence so that two attributions were made for the same expression), we have treated these data only descriptively. The results are comparisons between the two reference points, first words (FW) and vocabulary spurt (VS), for relative frequency of desires and beliefs, and how often these mental contents included representation of the mother or the child.

As was expected at FW, emotional expressions were far more frequent than words. As can be seen in Fig. 9.7, at VS, words were eight times more frequent than they had been at FW. This was neither surprising nor interesting because an increase in numbers of words was the criterion for the vocabulary spurt. However, although words and propositions attributed to words increased, the frequency of emotional expressions and propositions attributed to emotional expressions remained essentially the same from FW to VS. This means that the frequency of emotional expression (and number of propositions attributed to emotional ex-

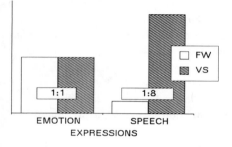

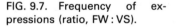

FIG. 9.7.   Frequency   of   expressions (ratio, FW : VS).

pressions) did not change *between the two language achievements* for the group of 12 infants as a whole. Language, then, does not replace affect expression with development. We return to this finding of stability in affect expression between language achievements in the discussion that follows.

Desires were expressed more frequently than beliefs, with both emotional expression and speech. At FW, the ratio of desires to beliefs attributed to emotional expression was 2 to 1, but the ratio for word attributions was less, 1.3 to 1. At the time of VS, the ratio of desires to beliefs was essentially 2 to 1 for both emotion and word attributions. Thus, these infants expressed desires more often than beliefs. However, words at FW tended to express beliefs somewhat more often than did their emotional expressions at the same time, or their word and emotional expressions at a later time. This means that early words (at FW) articulated what the infant saw or imagined the world to be relatively more often than did later words (at VS) or emotional expression at either time.

The desires that the infants expressed at both FW and VS were, overall for both speech and affect together, desires concerning themselves primarily, rather than their mothers, as actors (5.4 to 1 at FW and 4.4 to 1 at VS). They expressed what they wanted to do or were doing to change the world more often than they expressed what they wanted their mothers to do. The ratio for affect expressions was somewhat higher than for words: the ratio for affect expressions of desires directed toward the self rather than mother was almost 6 to 1 at FW and 4.4 to 1 at VS. The ratio for words at both FW and VS was 4 to 1. Thus, the children in this study expressed desires concerning their own actions in regard to their own purposes and goals primarily, through both words and emotional expressions. They did not acquire words as tools for influencing the actions of other persons.

Corresponding to the increase in the number of words compared to the number of emotional expressions between FW and VS, words also expressed more of each category of mental contents at VS, with one exception. The only category of attributed propositions that continued to be expressed with affect more than with speech at VS (56% of the time), was beliefs that included another person (the mother most often). For example, the mother smiled and her infant smiled back; or the child watched the mother rolling the truck down the slide and said "down." Desires, in contrast, whether they concerned the mother or the infant were expressed more often with words. Thus, although words came to assume most of the responsibility for expressing beliefs and desires at the vocabulary spurt, these infants continued to express beliefs that included other persons and their actions more often through expressions of affect.

DISCUSSION

Affect and language are two modes of expression available to the young language-learning child. Their forms are fundamentally different (e.g., Sapir, 1921), and their developmental histories differ as well. Some forms of affect are available from birth (Izard, Huebner, Risser, McGinnes, & Dougherty, 1980), and, at least in infancy, an affect display is virtually a symptom of the emotion that it expresses. The units of language, in contrast, are conventional and arbitrary and they have to be learned. They are independent of internal states and external conditions (Chomsky, 1966).

The studies discussed in this chapter are a beginning effort to understand the developmental relation between these two systems of expression. Infants, in their second year, acquire words and begin to learn rules for sentences, and one aspect of these studies concerned the relation between this language *learning* and affect expression. For the infants in this study, expression of emotion did not facilitate early language learning. Rather, early language learning—both words and simple sentences—was associated with more time in neutral affect. The second aspect of these studies concerned the developmental relation between *expression* in speech and in affect. When speech first appeared, these infants said most of their words with neutral affect expression. Thereafter, development in the single-word period consisted of two things. First, and obviously, the children learned more words. But, in addition, they also learned to say words with emotional valence so that affect expression and speech were integrated by the end of the period. However, the affect expressed with words was positive affect, and more often than expected, given the amount of positive affect expressed overall. Whereas emotional expression had not facilitated early word learning, positive emotional expression contributed to the infants saying words with emotional valence.

Several factors come together in explaining these results and how it is that the two systems of expression, with their different developmental histories, are integrated developmentally. One such factor may be differences in caregivers' socialization practices. Mothers have been shown to discourage the frequency of their infants' emotional expressions in the context of their socialization of affect in early infancy (Malatesta & Haviland, 1982), and such practices might have influenced the early word learners in this study. Thus, less frequent emotional expression can be associated with learning words, without sacrifice to intersubjectivity. Other potentially explanatory factors include temperament, cognition, and neuropsychological function, and each of these are discussed in turn.

The Role of Temperament

Emotionality—the valence, frequency, and intensity of affect expression—is a function of temperament (e.g., Buss & Plomin, 1986; Goldsmith & Campos, 1982; and Rothbart, 1986). Positive and negative emotionality are considered the predominant forces in the structure of mood and personality (e.g., Tellegen, 1984). The infants whom we studied differed in their profiles of emotionality, and these differences covaried with differences in their language learning. In another study that explored the role of temperament in this interaction between emotionality and language learning, patterns of stability in affect expression were examined for the group of 12 infants together and for the two groups of early and later word learners separately (Bloom & Wikstrom, 1987). For the 12 infants as a whole, Pearson product-moment correlations were significant for frequency of affect expression only between 13 and 17 months. This was the period between first words and a vocabulary spurt for the early word learners and the period that encompassed the later word learners beginning to say their first words.

However, when stability of affect expression over time was examined for the two groups of infants separately, the early word learners were highly stable in this period of time. For example, the early word learners were highly stable in time spent in positive affect (see Table 9.4). In contrast, the later word learners, who spent more time in positive affect and expressed positive affect more frequently than the early word learners in the same period, were not as stable over time. The only correlation that was significant for the LWLs was between 17 and 21 months.

We have explored two ways of explaining this result. On the one hand, infants who are less labile in their emotional expression, spend more time in neutral affect expression, and are stable in their emotionality profile may be infants who are predisposed to learn language earlier. That is, such a temperament profile may facilitate the processes necessary for early language learning. We have argued that time in neutral affect expression allows the reflective stance required for early word learning. For the child who is not temperamentally predisposed to such prevalent neutral affect expression, expression through displays of emotion would be more common.

On the other hand, recall that the two groups of early and later word learners were not different at 9 months of age on the measures of affect we used. The subsequent ages studied, 13, 17, and 21 months, turned out to coincide fairly closely with the ages of language achievements for the early word learners but not for the later word learners (in Fig. 9.1 earlier), which may have accounted for their different patterns of stability. That is, learning to say words may have, itself, a stabilizing influence on expression of affect. In fact, frequency of emotional expression was stable between language achievements, i.e., between First Words and Vocabulary Spurt, when the children differed widely in age, as re-

TABLE 9.4
Early Word Learners: Stability of Percentage of Time
in Positive Expressions (Pearson *r*)

	9 Months	13 Months	17 Months
13 Months	.904	—	—
17 Months	.853	.808	—
21 Months	.689	.599	.618
n = 6			

Note: Pearson *r*, all are significant, $p < .05$.

ported earlier. Given that affective communication is in place from early infancy, learning language entails a shift in attentional resources. Change in one domain (i.e., language) may require stability in another (i.e., emotionality) and thereby influence the individual's temperament profile. Clearly, further research will be needed for deciding between these alternative explanations and the direction of influence between developments in personality and language (Dunn, 1986).

Cognition and Affect Expression

One result in these studies was the developmental interaction between affect expression and the cognition required for language learning. Early achievements in language were associated with time in neutral affect expression and less frequent expression of emotion. A second result was that saying words with emotional valence was a development that occurred with certain cognitive constraints. The infants whom we studied were most likely to express emotion in their speech when the emotional valence was positive and the words they said were well known to them. We have already seen how these results may be relevant to individual differences attributable to underlying temperament. However, the results are relevant as well to developmental process and the fact that speech and expressing emotion differ in their underlying cognitive requirements.

If the infant is evaluating a situation and responding emotionally to it, then the infant would be less able to attend to and assimilate words that are heard at the same time. The evaluative stance underlying emotion, together with the expression of affect, would compete with the reflective stance required for learning words. And, indeed, although the two groups of infants were significantly different in neutral affect expression at 17 months, they were no longer different at 21 months, the age that coincided with the mean age of the vocabulary spurt for the later word learners.

In addition, affect would compete for the attentional resources required for *saying* early words, before the organization of speech becomes automatic. Thus, the infants in this study said their early words with neutral affect expression because neutral affect would allow the reflective stance that is required for recalling a word for the expression of desires and beliefs. The evaluative stance accompanying an emotion, along with its affective expression, would preempt these attentional resources. In addition, however, saying words for the children in this study also had a reciprocal effect on the expression of emotion. The results of a lag sequential analysis (Bloom & Beckwith, 1989) revealed a substantial dip below the baseline rate of emotional expression in the seconds previous to saying a word. As the organization and recall of speech become automatic, the two forms of expression can withstand the competition for the young child's cognitive resources, allowing the two forms of expression to converge. This is precisely what happened in the present study by the time of the vocabulary spurt, when saying words and expressing emotion were integrated.

However, this integration of speech and affect expression at VS was constrained both affectively and cognitively. When words were said with emotional valence, that valence was most often positive. Positive emotion occurs when an evaluation of the situation reveals that "existing schemas" are not challenged (Rothbart, 1973) and entails less cognitive activity than negative emotion. The negative emotions, like anger, fear, or sadness, in contrast, entail the cognitive activity associated with evaluating an obstacle to a goal, plans for removing the obstacle, or substituting new goals (Oatley & Johnson-Laird, 1987; Stein & Jewett, 1986; Stein & Levine, 1986). In addition, the words that these infants said with emotional valence were also the words that they knew best: the words they used most frequently and/or the words they had known for the longest time. These were the words that were presumably most readily accessible for recall from memory.

The developmental history of the ability to say words with emotional affect was just beginning in this period of time. We can expect these infants will experience the cultural and social norms that guide such expression through their continued interactions with others. The development of emotional understanding continues throughout the school years (e.g., Bullock & Russell, 1986; Dimitrovsky, 1964), influenced by social and linguistic development as well as by cognitive development (Ochs & Schieffelin, 1989).

Neuropsychological Considerations

A substantial literature exists that documents the effects of brain lesions on the integration of speech and affect expression for adult communication. For example, Kolb (this volume), has described the various dissociations between speech and affect that accompany cortical lesions that are located at different points along the posterior/anterior axis of the brain. Certain lesions result in speech that is fluent but without emotional prosody (affectively 'flat' speech rather than the neutral affect we have described). Other lesions produce patients who are highly expressive emotionally but lacking in speech. The fact that the two systems of expression can become dissociated as a consequence of pathology in adulthood is support for the proposal that the integration of speech and affect is a developmental phenomenon in infancy.

Connections between developmental and clinical findings are necessarily speculative at the present time. However, clinical research has revealed an asymmetry between the two hemispheres of the brain for speech and emotion, and an asymmetry for cerebral function may be particularly informative for understanding the developmental results that we have reported. Speech depends on left hemisphere function whereas the right hemisphere controls nonverbal aspects of communication, and emotional expression in particular. The contribution of the brain's right hemisphere to emotional expression and interpretation has been well documented for both facial displays and vocal intonation (see, for example, Buck, 1984, Davidson, 1984; and Tucker, 1986, for reviews).

The fact that language is specialized in the left hemisphere means that affect and speech are organized separately in the brain. This could mean that the coordination between them waits on certain aspects of neurological maturation. In fact, Tucker (1986) has already suggested the possibility "that early in life integration between the hemispheres is minimal and that hemispheric parallelism is the normal state of affairs. Lateralized contributions to communication thus may develop before the child has the capacity to coordinate them" (p. 273). This speculation finds support in the findings presented here. We expect that the competition we have described between affect and speech, for both language learning and expression, might have a neurological basis underlying the cognitive explanation we have offered. (See Bloom and Beckwith, 1989, for a fuller discussion of this point.)

CONCLUSION

Before words appeared, the infants whom we studied were already able to express their feelings affectively, through their body posture, facial expression, and the emotional valence of their prespeech vocalizations. Two versions of the transition in infancy from early communicating with affect to the emergence of language have attributed different functions to affect expression before and after speech appears. In one version, affect is described as the "content" of communication in infancy, but affect becomes the "context" of communication when speech appears (Bullowa, 1979). In another version, affect is the "topic" of communication in infancy, but once speech begins, words name the topic whereas affect functions as the "comment" on that topic (Adamson & Bakeman, 1985). Both these views imply that the function of emotional expression changes in this period of time. However, the function of affect expression does not change. Children express how they feel about their beliefs and desires through affect expression *both* before speech and once speech appears. Words do not replace affect. Rather, children continue to express feelings about mental contents while words are learned to express what those contents are.

The view of language that has dominated contemporary efforts to explain language development is the instrumental view: Language designates objects and events in the world—to describe, to characterize, to get things done. But in these functions and in all the functions of language, expression is central. An expression reveals, discloses, makes manifest something of the individual in the sense of putting that something in "a public space" (Taylor, 1985). Very young infants do not have language but they do have the capacity to express, to make manifest, to put something in the public space that includes themselves and other persons, and they do so through displays of affect. Expression through affect does not give way to expression through language, as these studies make clear. Emotional expression continues to develop along with language to allow individuals to participate in the public spaces of society in subtle and profound ways throughout life.

What drives the child to learn language is that language not only expresses, it also articulates (to paraphrase Taylor), and this is what the forms of affect cannot do. Children learn language in order to express and make explicit the contents of their beliefs and desires. The infants whom we have studied continued to express their feelings affectively, but their capacity for expression was considerably enhanced by the power to use words for articulating the contents of their thoughts and feelings.

ACKNOWLEDGMENTS

My collaborators on the research that I discuss in this chapter were Richard Beckwith, Joanne Bitetti Capatides, and Jeremie Hafitz; they coauthored the original research reports to which I refer and their ideas as well as their words are prevalent throughout this presentation. In addition, Karin Lifter and Matthew Rispoli made valuable contributions to the research project within which these studies were carried out. Kathleen Bloom contributed to both the data analyses and their interpretation in important ways; I thank her also for her helpful comments on an earlier draft. Financial support for the project was generously provided by The National Science Foundation and The Spencer Foundation.

REFERENCES

Aarsleff, H. (1976). An outline of language-origins theory since the Renaissance. In S. Harnad, H. Steklis, & J. Lancaster (Eds.), *Origins and evolution of language and speech* (Vol. 280, pp. 4–13). New York: Annals of The New York Academy of Sciences.

Adamson, L., & Bakeman R. (1982). Affectivity and reference: Concepts, methods, and techniques in the study of communication development of 6- to 18-month-old infants. In T. Field & A. Fogel (Eds.), *Emotion and early interaction* (pp. 213–236). Hillsdale, NJ: Lawrence Erlbaum Associates.

Adamson, L., & Bakeman, R. (1985). Affect and attention: Infants observed with mothers and peers. *Child Development, 56*, 582–593.

Arnold, M. (1960). *Emotion and personality, Psychological aspects* (Vol. 1). New York: Columbia University.

Beckwith, R. (1989). The language of emotion, the emotions, and nominalist bootstrapping. In C. Moore & D. Frye (Eds.), *Children's theories of minds*. Hillsdale, NJ: Lawrence Erlbaum Associates.

Bloom, L. (1973). *One word at a time: The use of single word utterances before syntax.* The Hague: Mouton.

Bloom, L., & Beckwith, R. (1988). *Intentionality and language development.* Unpublished manuscript.

Bloom, L., & Beckwith, R. (1989). Talking with feeling: Integrating affective and linguistic expression in early language development. *Cognition and Emotion.*

Bloom, L., Beckwith, R., & Capatides, J. (1988). Developments in the expression of affect. *Infant Behavior and Development, 11*, 169–186.

Bloom, L., Beckwith, R., Capatides, J., & Hafitz, J. (1988). Expression through affect and words in the transition from infancy to language. In P. Baltes, D. Featherman, & R. Lerner (Eds.), *Life-span development and behavior* (Vol. 8, pp. 99–127). Hillsdale, NJ: Lawrence Erlbaum Associates.

Bloom, L., & Capatides, J. (1987). Expression of affect and the emergence of language. *Child Development, 58*, 1513–1522.

Bloom, L., & Lahey, M. (1978). *Language development and language disorders.* New York: Wiley.

Bloom, L., & Wikstrom, P. (1987, July). *The role of temperament in language development.* Paper presented at the meeting of the International Congress for the Study of Child Language, Lund, Sweden.

Brazelton, T. (1979). Evidence of communication in neonatal behavioral assessment. In M. Bullowa (Ed.), *Before speech: The Beginning of interpersonal communication* (pp. 79–88). Cambridge: Cambridge University Press.

Bretherton, I., & Beeghly, M. (1982). Talking about internal states: The acquisition of an explicit theory of mind. *Developmental Psychology, 18*, 906–921.

Bretherton, I., Fritz, J., Zahn-Wexler, C., & Ridgeway, C. (1986). Learning to talk about emotions: A functionalist perspective. *Child Development, 57*, 529–548.

Bretherton, I., McNew, S., & Beeghly-Smith, M. (1981). Early person knowledge as expressed in gestural and verbal communication: When do infants acquire a "theory of mind?" In M. Lamb & L. Sherrod (Eds.), *Infant social cognition* (pp. 333–373). Hillsdale, NJ: Lawrence Erlbaum Associates.

Buck, R. (1984). *The communication of emotion.* New York: Guilford.

Bullock, M. & Russell, J. (1986). Concepts of emotion in developmental psychology. In C. Izard & P. Read (Eds.), *Measuring emotions in infants and children* (Vol. 2, pp. 203–237). Cambridge: Cambridge University Press.

Bullowa, M. (1979). Introduction: Prelinguistic communication: A field for scientific research. In M. Bullowa (Ed.), *Before speech: The beginning of interpersonal communication* (pp. 1–62). Cambridge: Cambridge University Press.

Buss, A., & Plomin, R. (1986). The EAS approach to temperament. In R. Plomin, & J. Dunn (Eds.), *The study of temperament: Changes, continuities and challenges* (pp. 67–79). Hillsdale, NJ: Erlbaum.

Campos, J., Barret, K., Lamb, M., Goldsmith, H., & Stenberg, C. (1983). Socioemotional development. In M. Haith & J. Campos (Eds.), P. Mussen (Series Ed.), *Handbook of child psychology* (Vol. II, pp. 783–915). New York: Wiley.

Camras, L. (1985). Socialization of affect communication. In M. Lewis & C. Saarni (Eds.), *The socialization of the emotions* (pp. 141–160). New York: Plenum Press.

Capatides, J. (1989). *Mothers' socialization of their children's affect expression.* Doctoral dissertation. Columbia University.

Chomsky, N. (1966). *Cartesian linguistics: A chapter in the history of rationalist thought.* New York: Harper & Row.

Corrigan, R. (1983). The development of representational skills. In K. Fischer (Ed.), *Levels and transitions in children's development. New directions for child development.* San Francisco: Jossey-Bass.

Davidson, R. (1984). Hemispheric asymmetry and emotion. In K. Scherer & P. Ekman (Eds.), *Approaches to emotion.* Hillsdale, NJ: Lawrence Erlbaum Associates.

Davitz, J. (1964). *The communication of emotional meaning.* New York: McGraw–Hill.

Davitz, J. (1969). *The language of emotion.* New York: Academic Press.

Dimitrovsky, L. (1964). The ability to identify the emotional meaning of vocal expressions at successive age levels. In J. Davitz (Ed.), *The language of emotion.* New York: Academic Press.

Dore, J. (1983). Feeling, form, and intention in the baby's transition to language. In R. Golinkoff (Ed.), *The transition from prelinguistic to linguistic communication* (pp. 167–190). Hillsdale, NJ: Lawrence Erlbaum Associates.

Dromi, E. (1982). *In pursuit of meaningful words: A case study analysis of early lexical development*. Unpublished doctoral dissertation, University of Kansas, Lawrence.

Dunn, J. (1986). Commentary: Issues for future research. In R. Plomin & J. Dunn (Eds.), *The study of temperament: Changes, continuities and challenges* (pp. 163–171). Hillsdale, NJ: Lawrence Erlbaum Associates.

Dunne, J., Bretherton, I., & Munn, P. (1987). Conversations about feeling states between mothers and their young children. *Developmental Psychology, 23,* 132–139.

Ekman, P., & Friesen, W. (1975). *Unmasking the face: A guide to recognizing emotions from facial cues*. Palo Alto, CA: Consulting Psychologists Press.

Emde, R., Gaensbauer, T., & Harmon, R. (1976). *Emotional expression in infancy*. New York: International Universities Press.

Goldsmith, H., & Campos, J. (1982). Toward a theory of infant temperament. In R. Emde & R. Harmon (Eds.), *The development of attachment and affiliative systems* (pp. 161–193). New York: Plenum Press.

Gopnik, A., & Meltzoff, A. (1987). The development of categorization in the second year and its relation to other cognitive and linguistic developments. *Child Development, 58,* 1523–1531.

Izard, C. (1986). Approaches to developmental research on emotion-cognition relationships. In D. Bearison & H. Zimiles (Ed.), *Thought and emotion: Developmental perspectives* (pp. 21–37). Hillsdale, NJ: Lawrence Erlbaum Associates.

Izard, C., Huebner, R., Risser, D., McGinnes, G., & Dougherty, L. (1980). The young infant's ability to produce distinct emotion expressions. *Developmental Psychology, 16,* 132–140.

Lamb, M., & Campos, J. (1982). *Development in infancy*. New York: Random House.

Lifter, K., & Bloom, L. (1989). Object play and the emergence of language. *Infant Behavior and Development*.

Malatesta, C., & Haviland, J. (1982). Learning display rules: The socialization of emotion expressions in infancy. *Child Development, 53,* 991–1003.

McCall, R. (1986). Issues of stability and continuity in temperament research. In R. Plomin & J. Dunn (Eds.), *The study of temperament: Changes, continuities, and challenges* (pp. 13–25). Hillsdale, NJ: Lawrence Erlbaum Associates.

McCarthy, D. (1954). Language development in children. In L. Carmichael (Ed.), *Manual of child psychology* (pp. 492–630). New York: Wiley.

Nelson, K. (1973). Structure and strategy in learning to talk. *Monographs of the Society for Research in Child Development, 38* (1–2, Serial No. 149).

Oatley, K., & Johnson-Laird, P. (1987). Towards a cognitive theory of emotions. *Cognition and Emotion, 1,* 29–50.

Ochs, E., & Schieffelin, B. (1989). Language has a heart. *Text, 9,* 7–25.

Olson, G., & Sherman, T. (1983). Attention, learning, and memory in infants. In M. Haith & J. Campos (Eds.), *Infancy and developmental psychobiology*. In P. Mussen (Ed.), *Handbook of child psychology* (Vol. II, pp. 1001–1080). New York: Wiley.

Piaget, J. (1981). *Intelligence and affectivity: Their relationship during child development* (T. Brown & C. Kaegi, Trans.). Palo Alto, CA: Annual Reviews (Original work published 1954).

Ricciuti, H., & Poresky, R. (1972). Emotional behavior and development in the first year of life: An analysis of arousal, approach–withdrawal, and affective responses. In A. Pick (Ed.), *Minnesota Symposium on Child Psychology* (Vol. 6, pp. 69–96). Minneapolis: University of Minnesota Press.

Ridgeway, D., Waters, E., & Kuczaj, S. (1985). Acquisition of emotion-descriptive language: Receptive and productive vocabulary norms for ages 18 months to 6 years. *Developmental Psychology, 21,* 901–908.

Rothbart, M. (1973). Laughter in young children. *Psychological Bulletin, 80,* 247–256.

Rothbart, M. (1986). Longitudinal observation of infant temperament. *Developmental Psychology, 22,* 356–365.

Sapir, E. (1921). *Language.* New York: Harcourt, Brace.

Schlosberg, H. (1954). Three dimensions of emotion. *Psychological Review, 61,* 81–88.

Searle, J. (1983). *Intentionality: An essay in the philosophy of mind.* Cambridge: Cambridge University Press.

Sroufe, A. (1984). The organization of emotional development. In K. Scherer & P. Ekman (Eds.), *Approaches to emotion* (pp. 109–128). Hillsdale, NJ: Lawrence Erlbaum Associates.

Stechler, G., & Carpenter, G. (1967). A viewpoint on early affective development. In J. Hellmuth (Ed.), *Exceptional infant: The normal infant* (Vol. 1, pp. 164–189). Seattle, WA: Special Child Publications.

Stein, N., & Jewett, J. (1986). A conceptual analysis of the meaning of negative emotions: Implications for a theory of development. In C. Izard & P. Read (Eds.), *Measuring emotions in infants and children* (Vol. 2, pp. 238–267). Cambridge: Cambridge University Press.

Stein, N., & Levine, L. (1986). Thinking about feelings: The development and origins of emotional knowledge. In R. Snow & M. Farr (Eds.), *Aptitude, learning, and instruction* (Vol. 3, *Cognition, conation, and affect,* pp. 165–197). Hillsdale, NJ: Lawrence Erlbaum Associates.

Stern, D. (1977). *The first relationship.* Cambridge, MA: Harvard University Press.

Stern, D., Barnett, R., & Spieker, S. (1983). Early transmission of affect: Some research issues. In J. Call, E. Galenson, & R. Tyson (Eds.), *Frontiers of infant psychiatry* (pp. 74–84). New York: Basic Books.

Stern, W., & Stern, C. (1907). *Die Kindersprache* [Childspeech]. Leipzig: Barth.

Taylor, C. (1985). *Human agency and language, philosophical papers* (Vol. 1). Cambridge: Cambridge University Press.

Tellegen, A. (1984). Structure of mood and personality and their relevance to assessing anxiety, with an emphasis on self-report. In A. Tuma & J. Maser (Eds.), *Anxiety and the anxiety disorders* (pp. 681–706). Hillsdale, NJ: Lawrence Erlbaum Associates.

Trevarthen, C. (1979). Communication and cooperation in early infancy: A description of primary intersubjectivity. In. M. Bullowa (Ed.), *Before speech: The beginning of interpersonal communication* (pp. 321–347). Cambridge: Cambridge University Press.

Tucker, D. (1986). Neural control of emotional communication. In Blanck, R. Buck, & R. Rosenthal (Eds.), *Nonverbal communication in the clinical context.* University Park: Pennsylvania State University Press.

Wolfe, P. (1965). The development of attention in young infants. *Annals of the New York Academy of Sciences* (Vol. 118, pp. 815–830). New York: The New York Academy of Sciences.

Wozniak, R. (1986). Notes toward a co-constructive theory of emotion-cognition relationships. In D. Bearison & H. Zimiles (Eds.), *Thought and emotion: Developmental perspectives* (pp. 39–64). Hillsdale, NJ: Lawrence Erlbaum Associates.

10 The Development of Anger Expressions in Infancy

Craig R. Stenberg
Duke University

Joseph J. Campos
University of California, Berkeley

THE IMPORTANCE OF ANGER

Anger has long been regarded as a basic element of affective life, a fundamental or primary human emotion. It is crucial for human survival, having important internal regulatory and social communicative functions. Physiologically, it prepares the body to initiate and sustain high levels of focused and directed activity. Psychologically, it is linked to self-protective and aggressive action tendencies. As a form of social communication, anger conveys distinct messages to others, forcasting predictable consequences, and eliciting affective and behavioral responses in others (e.g., Camras, 1977; Frijda, 1986; Izard, 1977). Defects in the ability to modulate or express anger may have serious consequences for an individual's physical or psychological well-being. Societies seek in various ways to control, channel, and even proscribe certain angry actions, because intense anger can damage a person's judgment and foster behaviors resulting in injuries to self, others, or property. It can damage interpersonal relationships if inappropriately displayed or suppressed (Holmes & Horan, 1976; Holt, 1970). Further, it has been implicated as a contributing factor in numerous diseases and psychopathological disorders (e.g., Alexander & Flagg, 1965; Kutash, 1965; Rado, 1959; Wolman, 1965).

The study of anger, then, is of both scholarly interest and practical importance. Surprisingly, especially given recent speculation that it may be innate (Ekman, 1972; Izard, 1971; Tomkins, 1962), little scientific research exists on its ontogenesis. In 1931, Florence Goodenough began her monograph, *Anger in young children,* with this observation: "Despite the theoretical importance of

247

anger in the emotional make-up of the individual, very few quantitative studies on the subject have appeared in the psychological literature." A half century later, her comment remains apt. Whereas the study of fear, smiling, laughter, surprise, distress, and even sadness has been widespread in infancy, the study of anger has not. When it has been studied, it has been in the context of investigating other socioemotional processes, such as hunger (Marquis, 1943; Sears & Sears, 1940), attachment (Shiller, Izard, & Hembree, 1986), and pain (Izard, Huebner, Risser, McGinnes, & Dougherty, 1980), or as a test of Watson's theory of emotions (Dennis, 1940).

Why has anger been so neglected in infancy? We believe there are two major factors that have led researchers to conclude that the study of anger in infancy is not promising. One is the conclusion drawn that Watson was in error in claiming that there are both specific elicitors and specific response patterns unique to anger in the infant. A second is the absence of an agreed-upon behavioral metric that reflects the state of anger with some degree of specificity.

The Controversy Surrounding Watson's Theory of Innate Emotions

The claim that newborns show anger to the frustration of restraint of movement is one of the most bitterly contested issues in the early study of emotional development in infancy. The behaviorist John B. Watson, while testing eye coordination in neonates, serendipitously observed that when the newborns' heads were immobilized they frequently reacted negatively. In 1917, he and Clifford Morgan hypothesized that "rage," or what we are calling anger, is an innate, instinctual response to restraint of movement. They employed numerous techniques to restrain very young infants, including pressing the arms to the sides, holding the legs tightly together, holding the infant's head between pieces of cotton or between the experimenter's hands, and holding the nose to obstruct breathing. They (Watson & Morgan, 1917) described rage as follows:

> If the face or head is held, crying results, quickly followed by screaming. The body stiffens, and fairly well-coordinated slashing or striking movements of the hands and arms result; the feet and legs are drawn up and down; the breath is held until the child's face is flushed. In older children the slashing movements of the arms and legs are better coordinated and appear as kicking, slapping, pushing, etc. These reactions continue until the irritating situation is relieved, and sometimes do not cease then. Almost any child can be thrown into a rage if its arms are held tightly to its sides. (p. 170)

Clear and specific as Watson's observations were, follow-up studies (with the exception of a report in German by Stirnimann, 1940) disputed Watson's claims that specific anger elicitors produce a discrete anger response pattern. Sherman (1927a), for instance, reported that restraint of body movement and delay in feeding did not elicit a universal response, and that informed judges (nurses, medical students, psychology students) classified newborns' responses to restraint and other emotion elicitors at about chance levels. Similarly, both Pratt, Nelson, and Sun (1930) and Taylor (1934) reported that a variety of restraint conditions, such as holding the infant's arms firmly against the body, and holding the infant's nose, produced no patterned anger response.

Dennis (1940), in an influential review of research on restraint and anger, also cast serious doubt on the link between restraint and anger in the young infant. He reported a series of experiments undertaken with a set of dizygotic twins. When the infants were about 2 months old, they were subjected to a series of stimulations for 18 days. Each day, the stimuli they were given included holding the head between the experimenter's hands so that it could not be moved, and pressing the nose of the subject with the experimenter's forefinger. Dennis also subjected these infants to strong taste stimuli, including a saturated salt solution, a very bitter quinine solution, and diluted citric acid.

Dennis claimed that the responses observed to restraint were indistinguishable from the responses to strong taste stimuli. On the basis of these data, he argued that many strong and persistent stimuli will cause the same kind of infant reaction, and thus that Watson was wrong in contending that restraint causes rage. He (Dennis, 1940) concluded that: "the infant reacts with crying and restlessness to any form of intense and enduring stimulation, of which rough restraint may be one form. Restraint of movement achieved without the use of intense stimulation does not cause negative reactions in the newborn" (p. 126).

Taken as a group, then, the studies by Sherman, Pratt et al., Taylor, and Dennis discredited both Watson's theory of instinctual rage, and his observations that young infants react with a patterned anger expression in response to restraint. However, each of these studies is beset with serious conceptual and methodological problems. First of all, in spite of statements to the contrary by the authors, each study found some evidence that infants react negatively when restrained. The eliciting circumstances posited by Watson may thus be more successful elicitors of negative emotionality, and possibly even anger, than has been widely assumed.

Secondly, the responses of young infants to restraint have never been studied systematically or developmentally. Although Dennis mentioned that rage is a phenomenon that begins to be observed only in older children, and although he studied the reactions of much older (11-month-old) infants in response to having a rattle taken away, or to restraint of the arms during dressing, he left unclear at what age anger reactions can be expectably observed in older infants. At one point in his writings, he seems to suggest that rage should emerge toward the end of the first year of life, and yet he cites anecdotes of anger behaviors in children who are 2 months of age.

Thirdly, discrete patterning of emotional expressions in response to anger elicitors in infancy—especially facial expressions—has not been convincingly disproven. Some of the studies did not assess facial patterning at all. Others used techniques that permitted only limited observation of facial behavior and may have distorted facial responses because of the pressure applied to the head and nose. Our reading of the literature thus suggests that contrary to widespread impression restraint may be an effective elicitor of negative affect in early infancy, and that specific patterned anger expressions in response to restraint very well may have been missed in the early studies.

The Lack of a Metric for the Study of the Development of Anger Expression

There is no single response indicator for the expression of anger, as the smile is for joy, or the cry is for distress. Although historically many theoreticians have proposed that anger is expressed by patterns of reactions, particularly in the face (Darwin, 1872, 1877; Duchenne, 1876; Hall, 1899; Stirnimann, 1940), their claims have met with widespread skepticism. This attitude was largely produced by the frequently cited work of Sherman (1927a, 1927b) and Landis (1929), which purportedly found no evidence for discrete anger facial or behavioral responses in children and adults. Sherman, whose work was cited earlier in connection with the refutation of Watson's theory of emotion, reported that when judges were allowed to see only the facial and behavioral responses of newborns to restraint and other elicitors, they were not able to classify the resulting emotion above chance levels. However, when observers saw both the stimuli and the responses, the judges agreed highly significantly with one another about the infant's state. At best, many psychologists concluded that only rudimentary hedonic tone differences (e.g., positive vs. negative affect) could be detected reliably from observations of facial or other behaviors alone. The judgments of specific emotional states such as anger, fear, or sadness were produced by knowledge of the instigating circumstances.

Recently, a line of research has sharply challenged the widespread conviction that behavioral expressions provide no information about discrete emotions such as anger. The work of Tomkins (1962, 1963), Izard (1971, 1972, 1977), and Ekman (1972, 1973; Ekman, Friesen, & Ellsworth, 1972; Ekman & Oster, 1979) has provided compelling empirical support for the claim that anger expressions can be recognized through differences in facial patterning even in the absence of contextual information.

Two patterns of facial expression have been proposed as communicating anger to judges (Ekman & Friesen, 1975). The two patterns involve lowering and drawing together of the eyebrows, narrowing and squinting of the eyelids, and elevation of the cheeks. The two patterns differ, however, insofar as in one the mouth is open, squarish, and angular, whereas in the other the lips are pressed together tightly.

A number of theorists have proposed adaptive functions for the features of angry faces (Darwin, 1872; Ekman, 1973; Frijda, 1986; Izard, 1977; Spencer, 1890). The lowering of the eyebrows, for instance, may serve to enhance visual acuity by shielding the eyes from direct sunlight. The tensing and narrowing of the eyelids may accompany visual concentration and further serves to shield the eyes from the sun and protect them somewhat from other environmental intrusions such as wind, dust, and moderately sized objects. The flaring of the nostrils may facilitate the rapid, intense intake of oxygen, and also provides a measure of protection against external blocking of the air passage. The open mouth may facilitate the uncovering of the canine teeth when preparing for battle. The closed-mouth display, by contrast, may be a socially acquired expression that emerges as the angry person learns to conceal or disguise the baretoothed expression. This concealment may serve either of two goals: To control the outward manifestation of anger altogether, or to gain advantage over an adversary through the element of surprise. The closed-mouth display may also be a product of less intense anger arousal.

Distinctive facial expressions have also been identified for a number of discrete emotions in addition to anger: disgust, sadness, surprise, fear, and happiness (Ekman, 1973; Izard, 1977). Most recently, contempt has been added to this list (Ekman & Friesen, 1986). The fact that these patterns have proven to be cross-culturally recognizable (Ekman, Sorenson, & Friesen, 1969; Izard, 1971) and can be distinguished from each other has had several important consequences. First, facial scoring techniques have been created and refined that identify these emotional expressions and permit the discrimination of anger patterns from patterns expressive of other emotions. Second, the study of facial expressions of infants has become an important means of investigating discrete emotional response patterns, and of testing the hypothesis that facial expression patterns for emotions such as anger are innate, and by implication, present in the young infant.

The Importance of Studying Facial Expression of Emotion in Infancy

Researchers studying emotion expressions in adults have noted that the presumptive universal expression patterns are sometimes altered by social conventions (Ekman, 1980; Izard, 1977). In particular, some evidence exists that cultural attitudes may influence the expression of anger in its universally recognized forms (Heider, 1974). The study of naturally occurring emotions is also confounded by the capacity of persons to abort facial expressions, to express them in the absence of accompanying feeling state (faking), or to alter them by masking (i.e., by substituting other movements).

These human capabilities have lent great significance to the study of emotional expression in infancy. Unlike older individuals, infants are less influenced by social display rules governing affective expressions. Also, young infants probably do not possess the cognitive abilities required for them intentionally to modify their facial responses or to react to eliciting situations with as potentially complex an array of responses as older children or adults. The deliberate disguise of an emotion, for instance, requires the capacity for deferred imitation, which may not develop until the second year of life (Meltzoff, 1988; Piaget, 1951). The study of emotional reactions in infancy, then, facilitates the investigation of the constitutive elements of emotional response largely unconfounded by the factors found in adults. It also provides corroborating evidence for the universality and genetic origins of emotion patterning.

Research on infant facial behaviors has convincingly demonstrated that infants are capable of responding with facial movements that are patterned in emotionally meaningful ways even in the neonatal period, and that at least some of these configurations cannot be interpreted merely as a result of random facial posturing (Oster & Ekman, 1979). Infants have also been shown to exhibit discrete facial patterning in response to specific eliciting circumstances producing fear, happiness, surprise, and other emotions (Hiatt, Campos, & Emde, 1979; Izard et al., 1980).

Recently, studies of facial patterning in infants have demonstrated anger expression in older infants. Stenberg, Campos, and Emde (1983) devised a task— pulling an object out of an infant's mouth—and used a revision of the Facial Affect Scoring Technique (Ekman & Friesen, 1975) to assess the presence of patterned facial movements related to anger. The results of this study revealed that anger facial expressions are well developed by 7 months of age. Anger facial patterning was detected reliably in the absence of contextual information about eliciting circumstances, and by coders whose task was not to judge the presence of an affective state in the infant, but to score facial movement changes in individual regions of the face. However, the study left unanswered questions about the ontogenesis of anger expressions, how anger social signals are targeted, or how facial and vocal expressions are related to one another.

These issues led to the research that is described in this chapter. The study was an attempt to trace the development of facial expressions of anger in the first 7 months of life. The research permitted us to address a number of issues currently unanswered by the existing literature. Among these issues are the following: When does the capacity for angry reactions to an eliciting situation emerge? Do infant facial expressions resemble patterns recognized as anger in adults, and if so, when does this patterning originate? Further, how do these responses change with developmental transformations? Perhaps even more importantly, when do the infant's anger expressions come to serve selective signaling functions? In particular, when do infants' anger reactions become targeted to the sources of frustration in the environment, and to significant social figures (Blurton-Jones, 1972; Brannigan & Humphries, 1969, 1972; Darwin, 1872)?

The Selection of a Paradigm to Elicit Anger in Young Infants

Because the biscuit task used by Stenberg, Campos, and Emde (1983) cannot be used with younger infants, a series of pilot investigations prior to this study tested experimental manipulations that could be used to study the expression of anger over a broad age range. The experimental manipulations needed to meet a number of criteria, as follows:

1. The task must be selected from a class of events commonly identified as anger elicitors.

2. It must produce negative affective reactions which appear to researchers and caregivers to be anger.

3. It should be mild enough not to elicit immediate, intense crying.

4. It must not add substantially to the frustration or discomfort that a child experiences on any given day.

5. It should be similar to events that occur frequently in the child's naturalistic environment.

6. It must be usable with infants ranging widely in age.

7. It must permit the study of the use of anger expressions as a social signal.

8. It must facilitate the facial, physiological, and vocalic measurement of emotional expression, as well as the assessment of instrumental behaviors consequent to or concomitant with the measures of expression.

Initially, a survey was conducted of a group of mothers whose infants ranged in age from 1 to 18 months. Based on these interviews a number of anger-producing tasks that were modeled after real-life events were devised. From that group, several tasks were selected that appeared to meet many of the criteria. The tasks piloted included (a) removing from the infant's mouth a bottle filled with various substances (e.g., formula, glucose water, or juice), (b) removing pacifiers from babies' mouths, (c) taking away various toys from the hands or mouth, (d) wiping infants' faces with a damp cloth, and (e) gently holding the infants' forearms to the sides of the body.

Although, as mentioned earlier, restraint had been discredited by influential reports that claimed that it probably did not even produce negative reactions, we observed in the conduct of the previous anger study that many infants displayed negative reactions when their mothers held their arms and/or legs to dress them in outerwear as they were preparing to leave the lab. Also, mothers in our initial survey reported observing anger sometimes while holding the infant's arms and legs to dress them, clip their nails, or change their diapers. To our surprise, this mild restraint-of-movement task was reported to elicit anger and distress reactions more frequently than the others.

As an experimental variable, the restraint condition also has several desirable features compared to the other alternatives. Unlike withdrawal tasks that often must be repeated in order for them to register on a substantial percentage of the sample, restraint is a continuous event devoid of stops and starts. Compared with the washcloth condition or restraint techniques that hold the head or nose, gentle holding of the forearms does not interfere with the recording of the infant's facial movements. A related problem also exists in bottle, pacifier, or other tasks that withdraw objects from the infant's mouth. Many infants anticipate the return of the object and appear to configure their mouths in ways that may make it difficult to judge the affective significance of movements of the musculature in that region.

Because it involves the frustration of such a rudimentary human competency—involuntary and voluntary arm movement—restraint is a task that is well suited for use with both young and old infants. An additional advantage is that the task is suitable for the study of affective expressions in a social context. When the forearms are held, the infant can still turn his or her head and body substantially. By placing persons with different roles vis-a-vis the task (e.g., frustrator/nonfrustrator) and different relationships to the child (e.g., caretaker/stranger) near him or her, it is possible to study whether the infant responds differentially to the different persons in the environment. It had appeared to us in conducting the earlier study of anger facial expression patterning (Stenberg et al., 1983) that anger expressions were not only being emitted but also targeted: When a stranger withdrew a teething biscuit, infants tended to rise up in their high chairs and to turn to the mother, seated behind them, as if to express their dissatisfaction. Moreover, when the mother did not oblige, the infants seemed to express their anger more intensely. For these reasons, then, the restraint task was chosen for use in this study.

The Choice of Ages for Investigation of the Development of Anger

One-, 4-, and 7-month-old infants were chosen for study because these ages permit the examination of various theoretical predictions and observations about the ontogenesis of anger as a social signal. The 1-month age group permitted a test of Watson's contention that restraint produces neonatal anger. Although an even younger group would have been desirable, logistical considerations precluded testing at ages less than 1 month. In addition, 1-month-olds are likely to be free of the effects of perinatal medication, and more prone to spend longer periods in quiet, alert states.

The 4-month-old group provided a test of the predictions of Darwin (1877), Bridges (1932), and Izard (1977), that anger expression is not present in neonates but emerges in the third or fourth month of life. Bridges maintained that anger was distinguishable from generalized distress at this age by the presence of facial flushing, protest shouts of short duration, and crying with few tears. Distress, by contrast, was manifested by prolonged crying and marked shedding of tears. Four months is also an age when infants have developed a rudimentary sense of means/ends relation (Piaget, 1951). This cognitive achievement may make the restraint task more clearly thwarting for the infant and may also enable him/her to selectively manifest the frustration.

The 7-month-old group permitted an examination of the influences of more elaborated understandings of means/ends relations on the expressions of anger. For instance, the infants' richer appreciations of the mother as a nurturing figure, and possibly a person who can intervene and halt frustrations, can possibly result in even more directed anger displays. Testing 7-month-olds also permitted validation of the conclusions drawn from our previous research (Stenberg et al., 1983).

One theorist, Sroufe (1979), predicted distinctively different patterns of behavior at each of the age points chosen for study. He proposed that neonates display primitive distress reactions to restraint, whereas 3- or 4-month-olds show signs of "primitive rage." Sroufe describes this rage as a global nondirected expression growing out of prolonged distress or interruption of specific ongoing activities. Finally, he predicts that 7-month-olds should exhibit anger instrumentally to objects and people. In his view anger emerges out of physical discomfort as a result of the infant's increasing capacity to understand the causes of frustration. Although this study attempted no direct assessment of cognitive abilities, our data are relevant to Sroufe's predictions of major shifts in affective expression at these three age points.

Hypotheses of the Study

One major hypothesis of this study was that infants at all ages would exhibit more negative facial reactions following the frustration than preceding it, but that the nature of these reactions would vary as a function of age. The expressions of 1-month-olds were predicted not to be coherent or well organized across facial regions. Instead, they were expected to show reactions in individual facial movement components (such as bringing the eyebrows together), but not in all facial movements that collectively constitute the anger facial expression pattern. This prediction was based on the observation that, although reports of negative reactions to restraint are common, even previous investigators sympathetic to the notion that the capacity to express anger is innate (e.g., Darwin, 1872, 1875; Marquis, 1943; Sears & Sears, 1940; Watson, 1930) reported only diffuse facial patterns in neonates. In contrast, previous research (Stenberg et al., 1983) and the pilot work leading to this study suggested that 7-month-olds and possibly 4-month-olds do indeed manifest discrete anger facial patterning.

Another hypothesis of the study dealt with whether there would be differences among the infants in the directedness of their responses as a function of age. The negative reactions of 1-month-old infants were expected to be undirected, whereas 4- and 7-month-olds were expected to display more socially meaningful patterns. In particular, the following patterns were anticipated: (a) facial and vocal reactions of 1-month-olds would be shown indiscriminately in relation to the frustrating event or persons near the child (perhaps because of the very limited understanding of external circumstances or persons by young infants); (b) 4-

month-olds' reactions would begin to be directed toward the frustrating event (perhaps because of their emerging though rudimentary understanding of means-ends relations); (c) 7-month-olds would show behaviors directed toward the proximal eliciting event (the restraint and the restraining person) and maybe even toward their mothers (perhaps because of increased capacities to understand the frustrating event, to distinguish the frustrator from the frustration, and to appreciate their mothers more as a special source of protection and comfort).

Finally, the relations between restraint of arm movement and several other variables was assessed. These variables included facial flushing, vocalizations, and the presence of tears. On the basis of previous research (Stenberg et al., 1983), flushing was expected to accompany anger expressions. Anger facial patterning was also expected to be observable in the absence of a crying state, and not merely to accompany crying. The presence and absence of tears was therefore measured to determine whether tears accompany anger facial expressions.

Experimental Procedures

We tested 48 infants, divided into groups of 1-, 4- and 7-month-olds, with 16 infants (8 male, 8 female) in each group. Four additional infants were brought to the lab but provided no data.

After an initial warm-up period, the infant was brought into the experimental room and seated comfortably in a reclining infant seat (or, in the case of some 7-month-olds, a high chair set at the same angle as the reclining chair). The mother and a female experimenter (experimenter A) were positioned in chairs 3 feet away and 90° toward either side in the periphery of the child's visual field. A second female experimenter (experimenter B) was seated 3 feet in front of the infant and slightly to the right.

After the baseline recordings were completed, experimenter B slowly reached out and gently grasped the infant's forearms at the wrists. She moved the infant's arms until they were extended inward toward the infant's sides and approximately 6 inches in front of the torso. She held the forearms until an emotionally negative response was observed. To minimize the intensity and duration of negative emotional reactions, the infant was held no longer than 3 minutes; the experiment was immediately terminated and the infant comforted by the mother and experimenters if the subject showed signs of intense distress.

The baby's facial and bodily expressions were recorded continuously throughout the experiment using two color video cameras equipped with zoom lenses. One camera was focused close up on the face. The other was further back to include the whole body. The cameras were hidden behind a one-way mirror so they would not distract the children. An audio recorder and two directional microphones were used to record all vocalizations. In addition, two independent raters (Experimenters A and B) recorded whether the infant showed visible signs of facial flushing.

We measured a number of responses of the infants to the restraint task, including: (a) facial expression components; (b) the direction of the infant's face relative to the position of the mother, stranger, frustrator, hands, and other objects; (c) vocalic expressions; (d) latencies from onset of restraint to first negative facial response, and from first negative facial expression to first cry; (e) facial flushing; and (f) lacrimation.

Facial Expression Scoring. We chose to score facial movements (i.e., component responses such as elevation of the eyelids, upturning of the corners of the lips, etc.) rather than global judgments of emotion, primarily because Hiatt et al. (1979) reported much greater evidence of patterning of emotional expressions using careful component (i.e., facial movement) measurement than global perceptual ratings of the presence/absence of an affective state.

Of the several component measurement techniques available, we chose Izard's Maximally Discriminative Facial Movement Coding System (MAX) (Izard, 1979) to record facial responses. MAX is the only facial component system currently available specifically designed for studying infant emotional expressions. In addition, MAX's 27 distinct facial movements may be organized to form patterns that specify *random* facial posturing, *blends* of emotions, or *discrete emotions* including anger–rage, interest–excitement, enjoyment–joy, surprise–startle, sadness–dejection, fear–terror, or discomfort–pain (see Table 10.1 for listing of verbal descriptions of each facial component, and Table 10.2 for the listing of affectively meaningful combinations; the predicted anger components and combinations are italicized in Table 10.1). Third, MAX identifies 27 distinct components of facial movements. The pattern identified for discrete emotions is derived from theoretical predictions concerning which facial configurations specify each emotion and empirical research confirming that these configurations or templates are cross-culturally recognized as discrete emotion expressions. The system thus permits detection of a cross-culturally validated "anger template" but does not predispose a scorer to identify more anger-related movements than other configurations.

The facial expression scorers were trained to use MAX with instructional materials supplied by Izard, including a comprehensive manual, a video description of MAX, and practice materials precoded by Izard. These materials were supplemented by video recordings of infants responding to a variety of eliciting situations already scored by experienced scorers at the Infant Laboratory. Scorers were considered trained when their reliability with both the tape and other scorers exceeded .70. Reliability was calculated as the proportion of agreements divided by agreements plus disagreements. The scorers were kept naive about the purpose of the study.

Selection of Facial Expression Scoring Segments. We decided not to score all the facial movements manifested by the infants in the course of the experiment. Facial component scoring is so labor intensive that the cost of scoring the entire episode was prohibitive. Instead, two facial expression scorers, experi-

TABLE 10.1
Max Codes
Maximally Discriminative Facial Movements

Brows, (B) (Forehead, F; Nasal Root, N)	Eyes/Nose/Cheeks	Mouth/Lips
20. *B*: Raised in arched or normal shape. (F: Long transverse furrows or thickening; *N*: Narrowed.)	30. Enlarged, roundish appearance of eye region due to tissue between upper lid and brow being stretched (upper eye furrow may be visible); upper eyelids not raised	50. Opened, roundish or oval
21. *B*: One brow raised higher than other (other one may be slightly lowered).		51. Opened, relaxed
		52. Corners pulled back and slightly up (open or closed)
22. *B*: Raised; drawn together, straight or normal shape. (*F*: Short transverse furrows or thickening in mid-region; *N*: Narrowed.)	31. Eye fissure widened, upper lid raised (white shows more than normal)	53. Opened, tense, corners retracted straight back
	33. Narrowed or squinted (by action of eye sphincters or brow depressors)	*54. Angular, squarish (open)*
23. *B*: Inner corners raised; shape under inner corner. (*F*: Bulge or furrows in center above brow corners; *N*: Narrowed.)	36. Gaze downward, askance	56. Corners drawn downward–outward (open or closed); *chin* may push up center of lower lip
	37. Eye fissure scrouged, tightly closed	
	38. Cheeks raised	59A.(=51/66). Opened relaxed; tongue forward (beyond gum line), may be moving
24. *B*: Drawn together, but neither raised nor lowered. (Vertical furrows or bulge between brows.)	39. Gaze cast downward, head tilted back	
	42. Nasal bridge furrowed (or shows lumpy ridge running diagonally upward from nasolabial fold). (42 need not be coded separately; it can be used as an additional cue in coding 54 and 59B)	59B.(=54/66). Opened, angular, upper lip pulled up; tongue forward (beyond gum line), may be moving
25. B: Lowered and drawn together. (F: Vertical furrows or bulge between brows; N: broadened, bulged.)		61. Upper lip raised on one side
		63. Lower lip lowered (may be slightly forward)
		64. Lower lip (or both lips) rolled inward (not illustrated and not observed in our video records of infants)

O = No observable movement (e.g., smooth forehead, brows in resting position, eyes normally open, mouth closed, relaxed), or return to baseline, or noncoded movement (e.g., blinking, chewing).

NS = Noncorable. Movement is suspected, but not clear enough to code.

OBS = Obscured—Area to be coded is out of view for at least 1 sec.

65. Lips pursed

66. Tongue forward (beyond gum line), may be moving

TABLE 10.2
Formulas Used to Identify Discrete Emotions and the Infant
Pain Expression

Interest: IE
Any one or more of the following movement units (A):

A

20	30	51	65
24	33	59A	66
25	38		

if the following movements (B) are *not* presented simultaneously:

B

21	31	50	61
22	37	52	63
23		53	64
		54	
		56	
		59B	

IE Blends: Movements that can participate in IE blends
24   33,38   51,59A   65,66
33,38 must not be concomitant with 25 or 37
Enjoyment-Joy: EJ
38 + 52
Surprise-Astonishment: SA
20 + 30 + 50
Sadness-Dejection: SD
23 + 33,38 + 56
Anger: AR
25 + (33,38) + 54
Disgust: DR
25 + 33,38 + 59B + 63
Contempt: CS
21 + 61 + 39
Fear: FT
22 + 31 + 53
Shame: SH
36 + 64 + 75 (head lowered)
Discomfort-Pain: DP
25 + 37 + 54
Awake or asleep, no coded movements
NC + NC + NC (awake) or (sleep)
0 + 0 + 0 (awake) or (sleep)
Sleep with coded movements present
Coded movements + sleep (sleep)

---

enced in facial expression research but naive to the purposes of the study, pre-
viewed the close-up tapes (which revealed no information about eliciting conditions), in order to judge the presence/absence of affectively positive, neutral, or
negative expressions (the latter category lumped together sadness–dejection,
disgust, contempt, fear, shame, discomfort–pain, anger, and undifferentiated
negative emotionality).

On the basis of these scorers' decisions, three 3-second segments were selected for each subject. The first segment was taken randomly from the prestimu-
lus period. It provided a *baseline* of the infant's facial movements in the absence
of a frustrating event. The second segment encompassed the *first intense or peak
(but not necessarily angry) expression* following the first negative facial reaction.
It comprised the infant's initial intense negative reaction of any kind to restraint.
The third segment was composed of the *last intense affect expression observed by
the judges prior to the termination of restraint*. It sampled the infant's reactions
to prolonged restraint.

By examining the presence or absence of the predicted anger movements
within each of these three periods, as well as the presence or absence of other,
unpredicted, components, we were able to assess whether the task elicited angry
facial patterns, and whether they occurred more frequently than other, unpredicted, templates. We were also able to assess whether anger facial movements
were observed more frequently than other facial movements.

Face Positioning Scoring.   Two different scorers, also naive to the purposes
of the experiment and the presence of multiple adult figures in the room, categorized the directions toward which the infant positioned his or her face during
the entire experiment. These measurements were used to assess whether distinct
face positioning patterns accompanied facial affect displays. The figures were
positioned in the room in such a manner as to facilitate distinguishing to whom
(or what) the infant's face was turned.

We identified five primary targets for the face: to the far right, to the far left,
to the frustrator, to the hands, and to miscellaneous environmental targets (described in subsequent places as *O* for "other"). Because the mother and a
stranger were positioned (in counterbalanced fashion) at the far right and left,
these categories yielded face positioning time toward each respective human
target. Because the frustrator sat slightly to one side of the infant, it was possible
to separate face positioning toward the frustrator's face from positioning toward
the frustrator's or infant's *hands*. "Other" included head positionings such as
near left and right, upwards and straight ahead, far upwards toward the ceiling,
and downwards away from any other target.

By comparing the proportion of time the infants positioned their faces toward
each target across the three periods, it was possible to assess whether the infant's
face positioning patterns changed as a function of the onset of negative facial
affect.

Infant Vocalic Expressions.   Two scorers also naive to the purposes of the experiment judged the presence of (a) positive or neutral, (b) negative, and (c) crying vocalics during each of four periods: (1) Prerestraint; (2) nonfacially negative during restraint; (3) facially negative during restraint; and (4) postrestraint. Positive and neutral vocalizations were described as laughs, coos, or squeals, which in the scorer's judgment seemed to convey happiness, delight, surprise, or which could not be confidently specified by the other categories. Negative vocalizations were characterized as short utterances (e.g., grunts, groans, or yells), which the scorer felt were hedonically negative and which had discrete beginnings and ends separated by periods of silence not attributable to factors such as gasping for air. Crying was described as negative sounds persisting over time and often having a rhythmical, repetitive quality. Before scoring the data from experimental subjects, the scorers practiced assessing vocalic expressions with infants who had been subjected to a variety of eliciting situations including a peek-a-boo game, visual cliff placement, a biscuit withdrawal task, and a Strange Situation paradigm. From the vocalic scores we calculated the proportion of subjects emitting each of these vocalizations during the four periods distinguished before.

Reliability Data.   Reliability between scorers was consistently high for all analyses. For the facial expression component judgments, reliabilities were calculated as the proportion of agreements divided by agreements plus disagreements. When the raters determined that no targeted facial movement had occurred, this decision was tallied as one agreement. The percentage of agreement on segments selected randomly was 82%.

Tabulations of amount of time infants turned toward the mother, stranger, frustrator, their hands, or miscellaneous were also made quite reliably. Product-moment correlations between two independent calculations of the number of seconds the infant turned to each target ranged from .88 to .97 with a mean of .94. The scorers agreed perfectly on the direction of first head turns following restraint and first negative facial affect.

Two independent ratings of the number of seconds from the onset of restraint until first negative affective expression and the onset of facial flushing were compared using a Pearson product-moment correlation, r_{1st} negative affect $= .97$; $r_{flush} = .91$. Ratings of time from 1st negative facial affect to 1st cry were also quite accurate, $r = .95$.

THE FACIAL EXPRESSION OF ANGER TO RESTRAINT

There were three principal questions addressed by this research. Does restraint elicit the facial expression of anger and at what age is it manifest? Is anger directed at social targets? And, what is the relation of flushing, shedding of tears, and vocalizations to restraint and anger?

Does Restraint Elicit the Facial Pattern of Anger?

The first set of analyses performed to answer this question involved nominal data and addressed two major questions: (1) At any given age, how many subjects showed *all four* facial expression components (i.e., the "template") presumed indicative of anger, without also displaying movements associated with facially similar nonanger affective states (disgust, pain/discomfort)? (2) Of those subjects who showed the anger template, how many gave no evidence of an *additional* component or components indicative of *any other negative emotion* (e.g., fear, sadness) besides anger?

We called the former analysis the *semidiscrete template* analysis to convey the sense that movements indicative of anger were detected, but that they could be accompanied by movements indicative of certain other negative emotions (like fear or sadness). The second analysis was called the *specific anger template* analysis to convey the notion that of all possible negative emotions observable, only anger was seen, and then only in its full manifestation across the four components.

The former analysis was important, because both pain/discomfort and disgust templates share three of the four facial movements of the anger template and deviate from it primarily if component 37 (eye fissure scrouged and eyes tightly closed—a pain/discomfort component) or 59b (mouth open and angular with the tongue protruding out beyond the gum line—a disgust component) is present. It thus ruled out the possibility that anger scores might have been spuriously inflated by the presence of emotions designated by very similar facial movement combinations.

The second analysis was even more stringent. It eliminated the blending of anger scores with *all other facial affects*. The results obtained with the second analysis, then, cannot be simply a function of heightened but nondiscrete facial activity. The data relevant to these analyses are presented in Tables 10.3 and 10.4.

The results of both analyses provide the same clear conclusion: The anger templates were shown only by 4- and by 7-month-olds, and then only following restraint. There was no evidence for response patterning in accordance with the anger template for any subject in any prestimulation period at any age. Nor was there evidence in either type of analysis that the anger response pattern was elicited by the restraint task in 1-month-olds, although the 1-month-olds did show considerable undifferentiated negative expression.

The effects of Age and Scoring Epoch were highly significant by Chi Square and Cochran Q-tests presented in Tables 10.3 and 10.4. Specifically, χ^2 tests contrasting the three ages within each of the two poststimulation periods showed that at 4 and 7 months significantly greater numbers of subjects showed the anger template than at 1 month. Moreover, pairwise Cochran Q-tests (Siegel, 1956)

TABLE 10.3
Number of Subjects at Each Age Displaying the
"Semidiscrete Template"

Age	Prestimulation	Immediate Poststimulation	Prolonged Poststimulation
1	0	1	1
4	0	8	9
		$Q = 8, p < .01$	
		$Q = 9, p < .01$	
7	0	10	9
		$Q = 10, p < .01$	
		$Q = 9, p < .01$	
	$X^2imm = 14.5, p < .001$	$X^2pro = 14.5, p < .001$	

Note: Only significant pairwise comparisons are shown.

showed that at both 4 and 7 months there was a significant increase from base levels in the number of subjects showing the anger template both immediately following restraint, and during the prolongation of restraint.

Although only the anger template was observed at significantly greater than the chance frequency of 1 : 10 (there being 10 possible templates in MAX), only occasionally were other nonpredicted templates manifested, and then only by a few infants. For instance, the only template observed in more than two infants at any given age in the immediate poststimulation period was pain/distress. Fear and disgust were never observed in the full manifestation required for this type of template analysis. In summary, then, restraint elicited the pain/distress facial

TABLE 10.4
Number of Subjects at Each Age Displaying the
"Discrete Anger Template"

Age	Prestimulation	Immediate Poststimulation	Prolonged Poststimulation
1	0	0	0
4	0	5	4
		$Q = 5, p < .05$	
		$Q = 4, p < .05$	
7	0	6	6
		$Q = 6, p < .05$	
		$Q = 6, p < .02$	
	$X^2imm = 11, p < .001$	$X^2pro = 10, p < .002$	

Note: Only significant pairwise comparisons are shown.

pattern in some 1-month-olds but anger in no baby that age. However, by 4 months of age, restraint elicited the anger template in a substantial number of subjects.

Parametric Component Analyses.   A more specific test of the presence of emotional expression patterning is provided by a type of profile analysis that includes the contribution of all 27 MAX components scorable in the infant's face. By calculating the proportion of components predicted to be elicited by the restraint task (i.e., the anger components), one can determine whether the predicted components occur significantly more often than do the components belonging to the expression of other emotions; that is, by pooling the data into two mean scores—the proportion of *predicted* components that were actually observed, and the proportion of *unpredicted* components that were observed for each subject—one can then analyze the separate and interactive effects of Age, Sex, and Scoring Epoch in an Analysis of Variance.

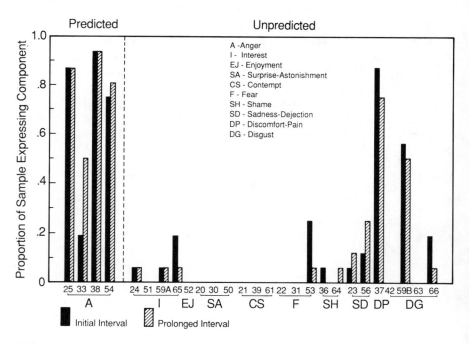

FIG. 10.1.   The proportion of one-month-old subjects in the sample showing each of the MAX facial movement components during the initial negative response interval, and after prolonged restraint. A = anger; I = interest; EJ = joy; SA = surprise/atonishment; CS = Contempt; F = fear; SH = shame; SD = sadness/distress; DP = distress/pain; DG = Disgust.

The proportion of subjects showing each of the components during the imme-diate stimulation period is presented in Fig. 10.1 for the 1-month-olds, Fig. 10.2 for the 4-month-olds, and Fig. 10.3 for the 7-month-olds. Within each figure, the components are organized into emotion clusters, with anger components set off from the facial movements theoretically linked to other emotions. Facial move-ments during the pre-restraint period were few, and did not cluster systematically.

These graphs demonstrate a dramatic shift in components from those associ-ated with neutral or positive emotional expressions during the prerestraint period, to movements indicative of negative reactions following the restraint. Across all subjects and all ages, the pattern of changes in expression is as follows: Prior to restraint, only .08% of all possible anger components were observed. Following the onset of restraint, 73% of possible anger components were observed, and just prior to the termination of restraint, subjects displayed 90% of the predicted components was displayed. By contrast, 11% of all possible nonpredicted com-ponents were observed during the immediate poststimulation period, and 9% after the prolonged poststimulation period.

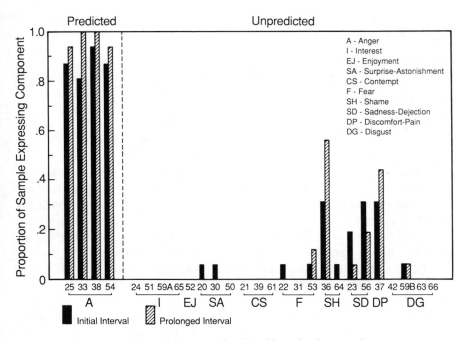

FIG. 10.2. The proportion of four-month-old subjects in the sample showing each of the MAX facial movement components during the initial negative response interval, and after prolonged restraint. A = anger; I = interest; EJ = joy; SA = surprise/astonishment; CS = Contempt; F = fear; SH = shame; SD = sadness/distress; DP = dis-tress/pain; DG = Disgust.

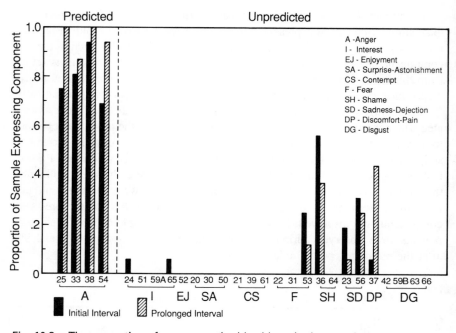

Fig. 10.3.   The proportion of seven-month-old subjects in the sample showing each of the MAX facial movement components during the initial negative response interval, and after prolonged restraint. A = anger; I = interest; EJ = joy; SA = surprise/astonishment; CS = Contempt; F = fear; SH = shame; SD = sadness/distress; DP = distress/pain; DG = Disgust.

A repeated measures analysis of variance was used to compare statistically the occurrence of anger movements before and after the onset of restraint. Sex and Age were between-subjects variables, and Epochs (Pre, Immediate, Prolonged) was the within-subjects variable. The scores entered into this analysis were corrected for the a posteriori probability that anger movements were observed only by chance. The correction involved three steps: (1) determining the observed number of facial expression movements (predicted plus unpredicted) for each subject during each epoch, (2) multiplying this number by the a priori probability that any of these movements would be classified as an anger movement (i.e., 4/27), and (3) subtracting this product from the sum total of all observed anger movements for that subject (a number that could range from 0 to 4). Consequently, the figure that was entered into the ANOVA for each subject was the observed number of anger movements corrected for chance expectations.

The ANOVA revealed separate highly significant main effects of Age, and Epochs, as well as a Sex by Age interaction (which reflected a tendency for girls to display more anger components than boys at 4 months, and boys more than girls at 7 months). The Epochs effect, F (2,84) = 283.67, p < .0001, was followed by Newman-Keuls posthoc analyses, which revealed that all the pre-restraint epoch means were significantly lower than the immediate and prolonged postrestraint epochs. More anger movements were observed in the prolonged as compared to the immediate postrestraint epoch, but the trend did not prove significant.

The Age main effect, F (1,42) = 6.27, p < .002, revealed significantly more anger components present in 4- and 7-month-olds than in 1-month-old infants when followed up by Newman-Keuls posthoc tests. Infants did not show significantly different anger reactions prior to the onset of the task but 1-month-olds displayed fewer anger movements than older infants during the postrestraint epochs, especially epoch three.

In sum, 1-month-olds showed higher proportions of components indicative of several negative emotional expressions, but no specific patterning of facial expression of anger. The 4- and 7-month-olds showed a clear patterning of facial components of anger, suggesting that at least some infants demonstrated the expression of anger without features of other emotions.

Is the Anger Expression Directed at Social Targets?

The next set of analyses was designed to determine whether the infants' emotional expressions were differentially directed toward the mother, stranger, frustrator, the point of the frustration itself (i.e., the restraining hands), or other possibilities (like the floor, ceiling, walls), cumulatively labeled *miscellaneous*. Two sets of analyses were run. In one, the direction of first head orientation was measured at the onset of restraint; in the other, the direction of head turning was measured after the onset of the first negative facial expression (which was predominantly indiscriminate distress for 1-month-olds, and anger for 4- and 7-month-olds).

The results of the analyses using the first head turn data are presented in Tables 10.5 and 10.6, which reveal substantial differences in direction of initial head turn as a function of age and target at the onset of restraint.

TABLE 10.5
Number of Subjects Whose Initial Head Turn Was in the Direction of
a Particular Target at Onset of Restraint

Age	Mother	Stranger	Frustrator	Hands	Miscellaneous
1	4	4	2	0	6
4	0	1	6	9	0
7	1	0	8	7	0

TABLE 10.6
Number of Subjects Whose Initial Head Turn Was in the Direction of
a Particular Target After Onset of First Facial Negative Expression

Age	Mother	Stranger	Frustrator	Hands	Miscellaneous
1	0	2	1	0	11
4	4	0	6	6	0
7	14	1	1	0	0

The 1-month-olds tended to orient their heads with equal frequencies to the possible targets, except for absence of orientation toward the hands. Four- and 7-month-olds tended to direct their head movements more specifically to the frustrator and to the hands during the initial postrestraint period. A z test comparing proportion of subjects revealed that significantly more older infants faced either their hands or the frustrator than did 1-month-olds, $z = 2.46$, $p < .01$. One-month-old infants looked more toward miscellaneous room areas than did the older babies, $z = 3.77$, $p < .001$.

Table 10.6 presents the direction of head movement after the onset of negative facial expression. Inspection of the table reveals three noteworthy trends: (1) Significantly more 4-month-olds than 1-month-olds looked to the mother, $z = 2.14$, $p < .04$, and in turn, significantly more 4-month-olds looked to the mother than 7-month-olds, $z = 3.56$, $p < .001$; (2) Significantly more 4-month-olds directed their head movements toward the frustration (either the frustrator or the hands) than either 1-month-olds, $z = 3.96$, $p < .001$, or 7-month-olds, $z = 3.96$, $p < .001$; (3) most 1-month-olds tended to orient toward miscellaneous targets. An analysis assessing the proportion of time the infants spent looking at the various targets yielded a very similar pattern of results.

In summary, then, our analyses revealed that 1-month-olds did not discriminatively face any person or the point of frustration during any period. Four-month-olds were positioned selectively toward the frustrator and their hands at the onset of restraint, while primarily facing the frustrator just prior to the end of the restraint period. Seven-month-olds behaved similarly to 4-month-olds during the beginning of restraint. Once they showed facial negativity, however, their behavior differed from the other two age groups in being directed predominantly toward their mothers. Coincidentally, it should be noted that the high incidence of MAX component 36 (see Figures 10.2 and 10.3) resulted from the older infants' tendency to look askance toward persons, or down toward the frustrating hands.

Is Facial Flushing or Tear Shedding Specifically Related to Restraint?

Facial Flushing.   Flushing was observed in 92% of the subjects. All the flushing occurred following restraint. There were also considerable individual differences in latency to flush. An examination of whether flushing occurred before or after the infants' first negative facial expression revealed a substantial difference between 1-month-olds and the older children. More 1-month-olds flushed *before* the first negative facial reaction than after (pre: 50%; post: 31%; not shown: 19%). Four- and 7-month-olds exhibited the opposite pattern (pre: 9%; post: 88%; not shown: 3%), flushing significantly more *after* first negative affect than before, z post first negative affect versus chance $= 4.30, p < .0001$.

Thus, flushing in 1-month-olds was unrelated to the first expression of negative facial affect. Four- and 7-month-olds overwhelmingly manifested flushing subsequent to the facial display of anger.

Tears.   The infants displayed very little shedding of tears throughout the experiment. Only one child produced tears (a 4-month-old girl). This reaction followed the onset of intense crying.

Do Negative Vocalizations Follow Restraint or Negative Facial Expressions?

For 4- and 7-month-olds the onset of negative vocalizations followed the onset of restraint but preceded the onset of negative facial expressions. Many more older infants reacted vocalically negatively in period 2 (nonfacially negative during restraint) than period 1 (prerestraint), $z = 4.90, p < .0001$. The results for both period 3 (facially negative during restraint) and 4 (postrestraint) were also significantly different from period 1, $z$periods 1 versus 3 $= 5.10, p < .0001$; $z$periods 1 versus 4 $= 3.87, p < .001$. The proportion of 1-month-olds expressing negative vocalizations did not change between periods 1 and 2, $z = 1.06, p = $ ns. A significantly higher percentage of 4- and 7-month-olds, then, began vocalizing negatively in period 2 compared with 1-month-olds, $z = 3.03, p < .003$. The only period in which more 1-month-olds vocalized negatively than in period 1 was in period 3, $z = 2.06, p < .05$.

To examine the expression of negative vocalization more carefully, the number of 4- and 7-month-olds whose initial negative vocalization was directed at each of the five targets during period 2 was tabulated. This analysis was limited to period 2. One-month-olds were excluded in this tabulation because they did not significantly alter their pattern of negative vocalic expression from period 1 to period 2, unlike the older infants. The results are presented in Table 10.7.

TABLE 10.7
Number of Subjects Directing Their First Negative Vocalization to
Specific Targets Within the Immediate Postrestraint Interval

Age	Mother	Stranger	Frustrator	Hands	Miscellaneous
4	0	2	1	9	0
7	7	0	5	0	0

Notice in the table that more 4-month-olds exhibited their first negative vocalization when positioned toward their hands than did 7-month-olds, $z = 3.54$, $p < .001$. More 7-month-olds expressed their first negative vocalization toward their mother than did the 4-month-olds, $z = 2.99$, $p < .003$. Four- and 7-month-olds did not differ significantly from each other on any other targets. Looking at these results in a slightly different manner, 7-month-olds expressed their first negative vocalization exclusively in the direction of persons, $\chi^2 = 12$, $p < .001$. More 4-month-olds expressed their first negative vocalization to the site of the frustration (hands) than they did to the figures in the room, although not significantly more, $\chi^2 = 3$, $p < .10$. The same overall pattern of results was observed when the first negative vocalizations of the infants were tabulated irrespective of period of onset. The vocalic expressions of 7-month-olds, then, were decidedly person specific; those of four-month-olds were task specific. One-month-olds were indiscriminate. Not only were 1-month-olds' first negative vocalizations not discriminatively expressed in period 2, but even when they were first observed these infants were facing the miscellaneous target areas as often as persons or hands (7 vs. 7), $\chi^2 = 0$, $p = $ ns.

Is Crying Related to Restraint, Anger Facial Expressions, Flushing, or Shedding of Tears?

The presence of crying did not account for the anger facial behaviors reported previously. During the initial postrestraint facial expression scoring segment among 4- and 7-month-olds, there were 18 subjects who showed the "semi-discrete template," and 10 who showed the "discrete anger template" (see Table 10.3). Only 2 of the 18 subjects cried while manifesting the "semidiscrete template," and only 1 of 10 babies cried while showing the "discrete anger template."

Nor did the data conform to the hypothesis that the infants were posturing their faces in the predicted manner in anticipation of crying (i.e., a precry face). The expression of anger was not more prevalent in crying versus noncrying children. During the prolonged facial scoring epoch, when more than half the subjects were crying, the presence of crying was not significantly related to the expression of either type of template.

CONCLUSIONS

This study lends strong support to the claim that the capacity to express anger through coordinated facial patterning emerges before 4 months of age. In addition, it reveals that by at least 4 months anger facial displays may function as discrete social signals. These signals are at first directed proximally to the immediate source of frustration, but by 7 months they become expressed directly to social objects such as the mother. Furthermore, it provides evidence that these facial expressions are not the result of crying, and it indicates that several measures other than facial expression may be useful in discriminating anger reactions.

Facial Expression Patterning

The finding that both 4- and 7-month-olds clearly displayed anger facial patterning has several important implications. First, it corroborates the conclusions drawn by Stenberg, Campos, and Emde (1983). Among the most important of them are the following. The anger response pattern identified in previous work with actor-posed anger faces (e.g., Ekman, 1972; Izard, 1971) generalizes to context-appropriate laboratory-induced anger states in infants. Also, anger facial expressions can be assessed reliably, even without contextual information about eliciting circumstances. Furthermore, both studies provide support for the claims of Tomkins (1962, 1963), Ekman (1972; Ekman et al., 1972), and Izard (1971, 1972, 1977), that facial expressions specify discrete emotional states. In both studies the response components specific to anger were observed, rather than a composite of components belonging to several negative emotional states such as fear, disgust, or distress.

The similarity of facial patterning in the two studies is particularly noteworthy because the present study used a different eliciting task and a recently devised facial expression scoring system. The previous observations, then, are not task specific, and they are confirmed with a facial scoring system designed specifically for infants that was unavailable during the former investigation. Also, the current study demonstrated that anger facial patterns are evident even when the data are examined from a number of perspectives and cannot be interpreted merely as the by-product of emotionally undifferentiated crying.

These results are thus consistent with and extend the work of Hiatt et al. (1979). Some evidence of facial patterning in infants exists not only for happiness and surprise, but for the hedonically negative emotion of anger as well.

A second major implication of the facial expression finding is that the capacity to express anger in discrete form may not exist in neonates but emerges before 4 months of age. Neonates displayed a mixture of negative components including many anger movements, but no convincing indication of coherent, well-organized patterning. In sharp contrast, 4- and 7-month-olds exhibited full-faced configurations recognizable as anger. This outcome is more consistent with the views of Darwin (1872), Bridges (1932), and Izard (1977) than with the positions of other theorists, some of whom have argued that anger should be seen in the neonate (Watson, 1930), whereas others have predicted that anger should be seen only after considerable socialization (Averill, 1979). The former three writers have propounded theories that specify that the expression of anger develops between the third and fourth month of life.

Interestingly, these data may also provide empirical support for a common interpretation of the widely cited Sherman experiment, which failed to find discrete anger facial patterning in neonates as well. Many reviewers (Ekman, 1973; Goodenough, 1931; Honkavaara, 1961; Murphy, Murphy, & Newcomb, 1937) have suggested that Sherman may not have detected differences in facial patterning to different elicitors because the capacity to express different negative affects develops after the age when Sherman tested his subjects.

Of course, neither Sherman's experiment nor the present one rules out the possibility of neonatal anger. For instance, restraint might have had less effect on 1-month-olds than on older infants and thus produced no clear anger patterning. Another elicitor might be found that would evoke an unambiguous neonatal anger response.

Also, some 1-month-olds may have reacted angrily but not displayed it facially in the same way as the older infants. Consequently, there is a need for further research within the period from birth to 4 months to provide a more convincing test of theories of the differentiation of emotional states, and to study more carefully the emergence of facial movement regularities in early infant negative responsivity. Such research may require a large number of subjects and the utilization of multiple eliciting circumstances (including both anger and nonanger negative elicitors) as well as facial scoring techniques that facilitate the study of facial patterns in addition to theory-specified templates (e.g., Ekman & Friesen's 1982 Facial Action Coding System). Especially if done longitudinally, such research would permit the detection of movement regularities resulting from different classes of environmental events. It could also specify the role these action patterns play in the ontogenesis of discrete anger expressions. As an added advantage, such a study would also provide much-needed information about the ontogenesis of other negative emotions and their discriminability from each other in young infants.

Pending the execution of this work, several observations based on these data may be made in defense of the position that the facial response pattern of anger develops between 1 and 4 months. First, the possibility that the restraint task had a reduced stimulus value for the younger infants does not seem likely. Regardless of age, infants, with but two exceptions, reacted negatively. Also, younger and older infants took the same amount of time on the average initially to react negatively and to become more intensely upset (as indexed by crying). Because all the infants' initial reactions were sampled at the point of the first intense negative facial display, the observed age effect probably reflects a difference in the capacity to configure the face in the cross-culturally recognizable manner and/or to react angrily.

Second, whereas pilot work for this study did not include a comprehensive list of negative elicitors, it sampled a broad range of frustrating events. None of them appeared to produce more anger-like responses in neonates than restraint. Although this observation does not preclude the existence of some viable elicitor or isolated cases of coherent neonatal anger faces, it makes the prospect of finding well-developed full-face patterning less likely.

Last, the possibility that an infant might actually experience anger but express it differently than older children or adults introduces a thorny definitional issue. What is anger, after all? Is it a distinct internal sensation or feeling? Any response produced by a certain class of elicitors? A discrete behavioral response pattern? An appraisal or an evaluation of events in the world that may result in a discrete behavioral pattern and/or certain action consequences? Is it the reaction to frustration of progress toward a goal? Or some other definition? Clearly, these issues cannot be resolved on purely empirical grounds and raise philosophical questions far beyond the scope of this chapter, but several remarks may be in order.

For research purposes, the operational definition of anger guiding this investigation has taken the conservative approach of studying the occurrence of discrete and recognizable anger facial configurations in an appropriate context—a context in which an action is impeded from attaining its usual end. Consequently, the conclusions that may be drawn are limited to *expression* and not to inner experience. This approach was taken because it avoids the difficult, if not impossible, problem of determining what precisely an infant is feeling, whereas at the same time looking for specific patterns linked to anger in older children, adults, and even animals. Theorists who posit neonatal anger usually do so on the basis of the observation that infants act negatively in circumstances that would probably give rise to protests and anger were the infant an adult. Not only are these definitions dangerously adultomorphic, they tend to be behaviorally unspecific and overly inclusive. Dollard, Doob, Miller, Mowrer, and Sears (1939), for example, define anger as any observed response to frustration, and frustration as any condition resulting from the blocking of a goal. This definition permitted Sears and Sears (1940), Marquis (1943), and others to conclude that anger exists in neonates because they cry and exhibit general body movements in response to blocking the intake of food. Watson (1930) and Stirnimann (1940) similarly infer anger from generalized negative displays to restraint.

On the basis of these criteria, this study has also demonstrated neonatal anger, because negative reactions were produced by a frustrating event. By defining anger in terms of contextual factors without specifying response outcomes, these definitions countenance a wide array of behaviors that may be observed as frequently in other contexts. This line of reasoning quickly leads to the position (Kagan, 1978; Skinner, 1974) that emotion words such as anger are useless descriptors and should be abandoned in favor of a new language demarking classes of eliciting events. This extreme position does not seem defensible in the face of mounting evidence for both the universality of emotional expression (Ekman et al., 1972) and the roles played by these expressions in the internal and social regulation of behavior (Campos, Barrett, Lamb, Goldsmith, & Stenberg, 1983).

Theorists who posit that anger emerges later in development than 4 months require that for a "true emotion" to exist the person expressing it must also be self-conscious or reflectively aware of the context and/or internal feeling state. Lewis and Brooks-Gunn (1979), for example, have argued that the infant cannot be in a state of anger until near the end of the first year of life, because until this point the infant does not possess the cognitive capacities required for knowing that a feeling state belongs to the self. On the basis of this criterion, the present study provides no evidence of the existence of an anger experience in younger infants, and therefore, no information about the expressive features accompanying an anger state.

However, this type of definition may be too restrictive, requiring unnecessary cognitive accompaniments. Not only does it ignore the possibility that affective expressions may serve social signals before they become organized parts of conscious human experience; it appears to rule out observations of emotional behavior in lower animals as truly emotional (because, except for the great apes, these animals do not possess the required higher order cognitive processes). Also, these definitions at least implicitly advance a premise that has long plagued empirical emotion research, namely, that the final arbiter of whether an emotion has been generated is the person experiencing it.

Although self-consciousness of an emotional reaction is often valuable and an accurate index of the meaning of an emotional expression or state, it is by no means unquestionably veridical. Not all emotional experience is necessarily conscious (e.g., traumatic neurosis), nor are persons' judgments about their own emotional reactions always accurate. Sometimes, for example, a person may become aware of being angry only after someone else points out convincing evidence from the person's expressions or actions.

A further problem with this definition is that it embodies a widespread prejudice in favor of the preeminence in development of cognition over emotion. The relation between the two has by no means been compellingly or definitively delineated empirically.

In any case, whether the results of the present experiment are interpreted as evidence for the existence of anger in neonates or in 4-month and older infants or are regarded as no indication that a true anger state was evoked, there is substantial support for the conclusion that facial expressions of 4- and 7-month-olds fit the cross-culturally recognized anger pattern. Although responses of 1-month-olds contain many anger-like movements, their similarity to the full-faced adult template is far more ambiguous.

A third implication of the facial expression results is that the open-mouth form of the anger face may be the earliest version ontogenetically. In fact, only one infant in the sample (a 7-month-old) displayed a coherent closed-mouth expression. This outcome is consistent with the speculations of many theorists that the open-mouth anger face may be the more primitive of the two, both ontogenetically and phylogenetically (Darwin, 1972; Izard, 1979). Research with older infants would probably be helpful in studying the onset of the closed-mouth face and may provide useful information about its relationship to variables such as intensity of feeling and masking.

Directionality of Emotional Expressions

When examined in light of the facial expression findings, the signal-targeting (i.e., the head positioning) data provide strong support for the claim that the capacity to express anger in a socially meaningful manner emerges between 1 and 4 months and is further refined by 7 months. One-month-olds' emotionally indistinct but decidedly negative reactions were not directed toward any socially meaningful target, whereas both 4- and 7-month-olds displayed their predominantly angry reactions selectively. Although the emotional content remained the same for the 4- and 7-month-olds, the face positioning pattern changed dramatically. Four-month-olds' facial expressions were clearly event oriented. These infants attended to the frustrating situation immediately following the restraint, expressed their negative reactions toward it, and continued focusing on the frustrator following its termination. From a functional standpoint, their behavior left little doubt about what was troubling them. The change in their vocalic and facial expressions made their reactions known to anyone who could see or hear them. The change in their looking patterns identified the source of frustration.

However, although their behavior was socially significant in that it served as a signal to the persons present, it does not demonstrate that the infants were actually directing the signals toward those persons. Both their vocalic and facial expressions were emitted as much toward the site of the frustration as to the humans capable of receiving them. The directionality may have resulted because 4-month-olds looked toward the site of frustration to determine the source of restraint and then expressed anger toward the frustration (which coincidentally was produced by a person). By 7 months, however, there is little doubt that the expression had become more socially targeted. These infants sized up the frustration in the same manner as the 4-month-olds (by looking both at the frustrator and the site of the frustration), but their facial expressions were preponderantly addressed to humans. Their first negative facial and vocalic expressions were still more selective. They went overwhelmingly toward persons.

This observation strongly supports the conclusion that, by at least 7 months, infants exhibit rudimentary facial and vocalic social communication. The first negative facial expressions were the most specifically directed. Functionally, this finding makes sense because facial expressions must be directed more toward the receiver's face than vocalics in order to be detected by a particular person. These expressions were definitely mother specific. Because this pattern was observed only after the onset of facial negativity, these results do not merely reflect a general preference of 7-month-olds for their mothers. Probably they demonstrate the infant's awareness that mother was the only person present who had helped him/her in the past. Perhaps they conveyed more than the infant's anger at the frustration. They may have indicated anger with mother because she had not met the infant's expectation that she would intervene quickly and halt the frustration.

In any case, they served as a signal that was not only emotionally discrete and socially directed but was selectively emitted in such a fashion that it functioned to elicit or encourage a response from social figures, especially the caretaker.

The two 7-month-olds who did not react toward mother in the initial negative facial expression interval were both in extended day care. The mother of one of them remarked spontaneously prior to the experiment that the female experimenter looked very much like her child's babysitter. During period 3, this child turned first and primarily to that experimenter, who was playing the role of stranger. She was the only child to exhibit this pattern. The other infant behaved somewhat like the 4-month-olds. He looked first and predominantly to the frustrator. His reactions were somewhat more sophisticated than many 4-month-olds, however, because his expressions were directed more toward faces than the hands. The former pattern is consistent with the view that 7-month face positioning is focused on the most likely source of help. The latter suggests a possible developmental progression from (a) event-specific expression patterns, to (b) person-directed signaling, to (c) person-specific signaling.

After the restraint was terminated, the tendency of the 4-month-olds to face the frustrator and for 7-month-olds to prefer the mother may indicate more than a progression in signaling skill. It may evidence a shift in the infant's capacity to utilize mother as a soothing or comforting resource. Immediately following the restraint, all the adults in the room, and especially the mothers, began comforting the infants. The 4-month-olds, for the most part, did not respond to these initiatives. Instead, they continued to focus their attention on the frustrator and express negative reactions.

This pattern continued even when the mothers were touching or holding their infants, and as they began to calm down. The change in state did not appear closely related to the soothing efforts. Once calm, many 4-month-old infants appeared to be wary when the frustrator approached them and spontaneously displayed renewed negative reactions toward her. The infants did not react in that manner to the mother or several strangers similarly approaching the infants after the frustration. Although no systematic assessments were made, several of the 4-month-olds reacted intensely negatively when extraneous circumstances resulted in the frustrator leaving the room for more than a half hour and then reentered and approached the infant. In another, the infant appeared to strike out at the frustrator— a behavior that may have been accidentally connected with her approach, but which because of its apparent instrumental appropriateness startled the observers present. In general, 4-month-olds seemed hard to console and inattentive to the efforts of their mothers or others to soothe them. Seven-month-olds, in contrast, focused primarily on their mothers throughout the same interval. Although some looked away initially (as if to ignore or reject her), they continued to turn back toward her until they were primarily attending to her ministrations.

This face positioning behavior made it appear that the mother's actions played a crucial and effective part in fostering the infant's transition from a negative reaction to a calm state—certainly more so than did the actions of the female experimenters. Once calm the frustrator was usually able to approach the infant and initiate playful interaction.

Flushing and Anger

The flushing analyses provide suggestive but not conclusive evidence that this autonomically mediated response may be an index of the arousal of strong anger. For both 4- and 7-month-olds, flushing predominantly followed the onset of anger, yet preceded crying. Although flushing was also observed in 1-month-olds, it did not occur at the same point in the reaction sequence. It was not linked either to the onset of negative facial expressions or crying. And, it was observed more quickly following restraint than in older infants. Perhaps in the young infants it was associated with early efforts to overcome the restraint by straining against the resistance. In the older infants the processes regulating flushing were probably better developed and more closely tied to affective reactions. Whether flushing is more prevalent or intense during anger responses than during other negative states cannot be determined from this investigation.

These findings point to the desirability of assessing in future studies how flushing is related to negative emotions and physical exertion. Because flushing results from peripheral vasodilation, it may prove useful in discriminating at least some negative emotions from fear, which has been described as involving peripheral vasoconstriction antithetical to this dilation (Duffy, 1962).

Tears and Anger

The failure to detect the presence of tears in this study is consistent with Bridges' (1932) prediction that, once the infant is capable of an anger response, the absence of lacrimation distinguishes anger reactions from global distress. From a theoretical perspective the notion that tears are not likely to be associated with anger (unless anger is masked or blended with other emotions) seems defensible, because tearing would seem to impair the visual acuity necessary for effective defensive or aggressive action. However, because tears were not observed in 1-month-olds or during crying episodes at any age, its absence is probably attributable to other factors as well, such as the incapacity of very young infants to shed tears. As with flushing, the study of tearing in response to different classes of elicitors may also be profitable, then, for determining its value in discriminating among negative affective states.

Vocalics

The vocalic analyses established that the task produced decidedly negative reactions independently corroborating the facial expression results. Further, negative vocalization preceded the onset of negative facial expressions indicating that the infants' negative reactions were first conveyed through a nonfacial channel. Four- and 7-month-olds clearly used vocalizations in a more context-appropriate manner than 1-month-olds. Whereas vocalizations of 1-month-olds can be interpreted only as a transition from a hedonically ambiguous state to intense negativity, 4- and 7-month vocalics demonstrated a progression from initially positive to negative to more intensely negative (crying). The finding that negative vocalics of short duration precede and accompany angry facial expressions in 4- and 7-month-olds is consistent with Bridges' hypothesis that this vocalic phenomenon accompanies anger and distinguishes it from more affectively ambiguous distress. However, further research is needed to determine if certain vocalizations are recognizable as angry, and discriminable from other negative vocalizations. Such research might be a first step toward a much-needed metric for assessing the capacity of the voice to communicate discrete affects in infancy.

Suggestions for Future Research

In addition to the avenues for further research just described, the restraint paradigm creates the possibility for many additional investigations. One line of study should focus on the effects that the presence of different social figures has on the infant's reactions (e.g., as a function of age and sex). A variety of permutations might produce interesting differences in latency to respond, the affective content of the reaction, its intensity, its duration, the directionality of expression, or other measures. For example, if caretakers were to assume the role of frustrator this might produce more emotional ambiguity for an infant, than if the frustrator were a stranger (perhaps resulting in more sadness or distress in the mother compared with the stranger condition).

The relative influences of the roles taken during the experiment versus roles maintained in real life on infant reactions during the frustration might be measured by placing figures with different relationships to the child (e.g., mother, father, sibling, extended family member, family friend, babysitter, or stranger) in the experimental roles in different combinations. For instance, the salience of "mother" versus "potential helper" may be assessed by placing mother in both the roles of frustrator (with stranger as bystanders) and bystander (with strangers as frustrator and an additional bystander), while determining if the infant consequently exhibits different patterns of directionality of expressions.

Another line of study should explore the effects of different reactions by the social figures to the situation. For example, when infants are able to recognize and interpret emotional expression in the face, voice, or gestures, they may react differently to restraint when it is performed with hedonically positive, soothing

278

messages than when it is performed with fearful or hostile signals. In the former instance, they may respond at least for awhile as Dennis has observed (1940)—as if restraint were a game—whereas in the latter instance, they might react very quickly negatively. This kind of approach may facilitate both the study of the development of the capacity of infants to recognize discrete emotions, and to use affective information to regulate their behavior. Because a number of permutations are possible (e.g., varying the nature of the affective signal [in one modality such as the face, in several, or as a comprehensive gestalt or mixed messages either from one sender or different messages for various participants] or in the social properties of the sender, e.g., mother vs. stranger), substantial information might be gathered about the infant's understanding and utilization of affective signals.

Further, the paradigm can be used to investigate the consequences of making the reactions of social figures contingent on specific infant behaviors. These responses might not only be contingent emotional reactions (e.g., smiling at the infant when he/she looks puzzled). They might include, for example, releasing the infant subsequent to the first negative vocalization or the first negative facial expression or the first cry or some other expressions that may mark a progression in intensity (e.g., annoyed to angry) or state (e.g., angry to intense global distress). These variations might result in different outcomes as a function of age, drive state, or point in the sequence that the contingent action took place. The reaction may result in different latencies to return to a calm state, different patterns of soothing (e.g., when a prolonged restraint is terminated the infant may at first express anger for the mother and then become calmed by her soothing efforts versus when restraint is brief the infant may be able to calm him/herself without mother's intervention); it may lead to differences in subsequent reactions to figures occupying various roles (e.g., more negative reaction to the approach of the frustrator post frustration when restraint is prolonged vs. short and more positive reactions to bystanders in both instances), or it may lead to differences in mood (e.g., as measured by the propensity to react negatively to subsequent irritation, Zillman & Bryant, 1974). This kind of investigation could enrich our knowledge about infant emotional states and their impact on infant behaviors. It could also be useful in the analysis of affective interaction sequences between infants and others.

One further line of study could examine the relation of temperament and cognitive variables to several of the phenomena observed during this research. Temperament variables may well account for the substantial individual differences in latencies to react discovered in this study. Because latencies to display emotional reactions as indicated by facial expression or crying did not seem to vary by age, there may be some observable consistencies in these parameters measurable longitudinally. Cognitive variables may play a role in the infant's emerging understanding of the nature of frustration and of social figures. Further research is needed to specify what cognitive achievements may be prerequisites for the observed behaviors.

ACKNOWLEDGMENTS

The research described in this chapter was supported by NIMH grants MH-22356 and MH-22566, as well as by a grant from the Developmental Psychobiology Research Group Endowment Fund of the University of Colorado Health Sciences Center.

REFERENCES

Alexander, F., & Flagg, G. W. (1965). The psychosomatic approach. In B. B. Wolman (Ed.), *Handbook of clinical psychology*. New York: McGraw-Hill.

Averill, J. R. (1979). Anger. In R. Dienstbier (Ed.), *Nebraska Symposium on Motivation* (Vol. 26, pp. 1–80). Lincoln: University of Nebraska Press.

Blurton-Jones, N. (1972). *Ethological studies of child behavior*. Cambridge: Cambridge University Press.

Brannigan, C., & Humphries, D. (1969). I see what you mean. *New Scientist*, 406–408.

Brannigan, C., & Humphries, D. (1972). Human non-verbal behavior, a means of communication. In N. Blurton-Jones (Ed.), *Ethological studies of child behavior* (pp. 37–64). Cambridge: Cambridge University Press.

Bridges, K. (1932). Emotional development in early infancy. *Child Development, 3*, 324–334.

Campos, J. J., Barrett, K. C., Lamb, M. E., Goldsmith, H. H., & Stenberg, C. (1983). Socioemotional development. In M. Haith & J. Campos (Eds.), *Infancy and developmental psychobiology* (Vol. 2). P. Mussen (Series Ed.), *Handbook of child psychology*. New York: Wiley.

Camras, L. (1977). Facial expressions used by children in a conflict situation. *Child Development, 48*, 1431–1435.

Darwin, C. R. (1872). *The expression of emotions in man and animals*. London: John Murray.

Darwin, C. R. (1877). A biographical sketch of an infant. *Mind, 2*, 286–294.

Dennis, W. (1940). Infant reactions to restraint. *Transactions of the New York Academy of Science, 2*, 202–217.

Dollard, J., Doob, L. W., Miller, N. E., Mowrer, O. H., & Sears, R. R. (1939). *Frustration and aggression*. New Haven: Yale University Press.

Duchenne, G. B. (1876). *Mecanisme de la physionomic humaine ou analyse electro-physiologique de l'expression des passion*. Paris: J. B. Balliere.

Duffy, E. (1962). *Activation and behavior*. New York: Wiley.

Ekman, P. (1972). Universals and cultural differences in facial expressions of emotion. In J. K. Cole (Ed.), *Nebraska Symposium on Motivation* (Vol. 19, pp. 207–283). Lincoln: University of Nebraska Press.

Ekman, P. (1973). Cross-cultural studies of facial expression. In P. Ekman (Ed.), *Darwin and facial expression* (pp. 169–222). New York: Academic Press.

Ekman, P. (1980). Biological and cultural contributions to body and facial movement in the expression of emotions. In A. Rorty (Ed.), *Explaining emotions* (pp. 73–102). Berkeley: University of California.

Ekman, P., & Friesen, W. (1975). *Unmasking the face*. Englewood Cliffs, NJ: Prentice-Hall.

Ekman, P., & Friesen, W. V. (1982). Measuring facial movement with the Facial Action Coding System. In P. Ekman (Ed.), *Emotion in the human face* (pp. 178–211). New York: Cambridge University Press.

Ekman, P., & Friesen, W. V. (1986). A new pan-cultural facial expression of emotion. *Motivation and Emotion, 10*, 159–168.

Ekman, P., Friesen, W., & Ellsworth, P. (1972). *Emotion in the human face*. New York: Pergamon Press.

Ekman, P., & Oster, H. (1979). Facial expressions of emotion. *Annual Review of Psychology, 30,* 527–554.

Ekman, P., Sorenson, E., & Friesen, W. (1969). Pan-cultural elements in facial displays of emotion. *Science, 164,* 86–88.

Frijda, N. (1986). *The emotions.* New York: Cambridge University Press.

Goodenough, F. L. (1931). *Anger in young children.* Minneapolis: University of Minnesota Press.

Hall, G. S. (1899). A study of anger. *American Journal of Psychology, 10,* 516–591.

Heider, K. (1974). *Affect display rules in the Dani.* Paper presented at American Anthropological Association meetings, New Orleans.

Hiatt, S., Campos, J. J., & Emde, R. N. (1979). Facial patterning and infant emotional expression: Happiness, surprise, and fear. *Child Development, 50,* 1020–1035.

Holmes, D. P., & Horan, J. J. (1976). Anger induction in assertion training. *Journal of Counseling Psychology, 23,* 108–111.

Holt, R. R. (1970). On the interpersonal and intrapersonal consequences of expressing or not expressing anger. *Journal of Consulting and Clinical Psychology, 35,* 8–12.

Honkavaara, S. (1961). The psychology of expression. *British Journal of Psychology Monograph Supplements, 32,* 1–96.

Izard, C. E. (1971). *The face of emotion.* New York: Appleton-Century-Crofts.

Izard, C. E. (1972). *Patterns of emotions: A new analysis of anxiety and depression.* New York: Academic Press.

Izard, C. E. (1977). *Human emotions.* New York: Plenum Press.

Izard, C. (1979). *MAX training manual.* Unpublished manuscript, University of Delaware.

Izard, C. E., Huebner, R., Risser, D., McGinnes, G., & Dougherty, L. (1980). The young infant's ability to produce discrete emotion expressions. *Developmental Psychology, 16,* 132–140.

Kagan, J. (1978). On emotion and its development: A working paper. In M. Lewis & L. Rosenblum (Eds.), *The development of affect* (pp. 11–42). New York: Plenum Press.

Kutash, S. B. (1965). Psychoneuroses. In B. B. Wolman (Ed.), *Handbook of clinical psychology.* New York: McGraw-Hill.

Landis, E. (1929). The interpretation of facial expression in emotion. *Journal of General Psychology, 2,* 59–72.

Lewis, M., & Brooks-Gunn, J. (1979). *Social cognition and the acquisition of self.* New York: Plenum Press.

Marquis, D. P. (1943). A study of frustration in newborn infants. *Journal of Experimental Psychology, 32,* 123–138.

Meltzoff, A. (1988). Infant imitation and memory: Nine-month-olds in immediate and deferred tests. *Child Development, 59,* 217–225.

Murphy, G., Murphy, L., & Newcomb, T. (1937). *Experimental social psychology.* New York: Harper.

Piaget, J. (1951). *Play, dreams, and imitation in childhood.* New York: Norton.

Pratt, K. C., Nelson, A. K., & Sun, K. H. (1930). *The behavior of the newborn infant.* Columbus: Ohio State University Press.

Rado, S. (1959). Obsessive behavior, so-called obsessive–compulsive neurosis. In S. Arieti (Ed.), *American handbook of psychiatry.* New York: Basic Books.

Sears, R., & Sears, P. (1940). Minor studies of aggression: Strength of frustration-reaction as a function of strength of drive. *Journal of Psychology, 9,* 297–300.

Sherman, M. (1927a). The differentiation of emotional responses in infants. I: Judgments of emotional responses from motion picture views and from actual observation. *Journal of Comparative Psychology, 7,* 265–284.

Sherman, M. (1927b). The differentiation of emotional responses in infants. II: The ability of observers to judge the emotional characteristics of the crying of infants and of the voice of the adult. *Journal of Comparative Psychology, 7,* 265–284.

Shiller, V., Izard, & Hembree, E. (1986). Patterns of emotion expression during separation in the Strange-Situation procedure. *Developmental Psychology, 22,* 378–382.

Siegel, S. (1956). *Non-parametric statistics for the behavioral sciences.* New York: McGraw Hill.

Skinner, B. (1974). *About behaviorism.* New York: Knopf.

Spencer, H. (1890). *Principles of psychology.* New York: D. Appleton.

Sroufe, L. A. (1979). Socioemotional development. In J. Osofsky (Ed.), *Handbook of infant development.* New York: Wiley.

Stenberg, C. R., Campos, J. J., & Emde, R. N. (1983). The facial expression of anger in seven-month-old infants. *Child Development, 54,* 178–184.

Stirnimann, F. (1940). *Psychologie des neugebornen kindes.* Munich: Kindler Verlag.

Taylor, J. H. (1934). Emotional responses in infants. *Ohio State University Contributions in Psychology: Studies in Infant Behavior, 12,* 69–93.

Tomkins, S. (1962). *Affect, imagery, consciousness (Vol. 1). The positive affects.* New York: Plenum Press.

Tomkins, S. (1963). *Affect, imagery, consciousness (Vol. 2). The negative affects.* New York: Plenum Press.

Watson, J. (1930). *Behaviorism.* New York: Norton.

Watson, J., & Morgan, C. (1917). Emotional reactions and psychological experimentation. *American Journal of Psychology, 28,* 163–174.

Wolman, B. (1965). Schizophrenia and related disorders. In B. Wolman (Ed.), *Handbook of clinical psychology.* New York: McGraw-Hill.

Zillman, D., & Bryant, J. (1974). The effect of residual excitation on the emotional response to provocation and delayed aggressive behavior. *Journal of Personality and Social Psychology, 30,* 782–791.

11

Emerging Notions of Persons

Janellen Huttenlocher
University of Chicago

Patricia Smiley
University of Illinois

INTRODUCTION

In the past few years we have done a series of studies of early conceptual development. Much of the work has been concerned with the emergence of person categories. These conceptual categories are different from many other categories in that they encompass two distinct types of instances. First, they include instances involving other people as observed entities. As observed, persons are material bodies that display various facial expressions, that are sources of movement and change, and so on. Second, they include instances involving the self as subject of experience. As subjects, people have internal states—emotions, perceptions, memories, and intentions to act. The various concepts that apply to persons each encompass instances involving others as observed and self as subject. This chapter is concerned with the emergence of notions of persons in early childhood, and with the emergence of emotion categories as one type of person category.

In studying the development of notions of persons, we have used children's word meanings as evidence. The data on word meanings have been drawn from spontaneous speech. Most of our evidence has been based on the acquisition of words for intentional actions and words for persons. Children use these words frequently, and they are rich sources of information about the emergence of person categories. In contrast, words for emotions are rare in child speech and provide much less information about conceptual development. At the end of the chapter, we consider the evidence from language concerning the emergence of emotion categories, including the results of a comprehension study and the sparse evidence from the spontaneous use of emotion words. The evidence shows that emotion words appear at the same time as other words for persons, suggesting that emotion concepts may be one of a group of concepts related to persons that emerge all at once.

Based on our studies of word meanings, the overall picture of conceptual development is the following. For the first 8 to 10 months of speech, most of children's words are names of small inanimate objects such as *ball,* and *bottle.* Children also use words for people (notably *mommy, daddy,* and names of siblings or friends) and words for movement such as *up* and *out.* During this period, children use no words for self, and they use almost no verbs. We believe that in this period—until shortly before 2 years—children's names for people do not encode persons as subjects of experience and their words for movement do not encode intentional actions. As children approach 2 years, they begin to use words for themselves (personal pronouns and their own names), as well as words for intentional actions (like *get* and *give*) and inner state words (notably *want*), in relation to their own actions and desires. These usages provide evidence that the child has developed an explicit notion of a self with inner states, but not a notion of others as possessors of inner states. As children approach 2½ years, they begin to describe other people as subjects of experience, using words like *get, give,* and *want* in relation to others. At this time, we believe the child's word use provides evidence of having acquired the critical elements of the adult notion of person.

Words as Evidence about Conceptual Development

Certain issues must be considered in using the words children produce as evidence about their conceptual development. The first issue concerns the use of children's utterances as the basis for inferences concerning their word meanings. It is difficult to infer children's meanings from their single-word utterances, and even from early multiword speech, because utterance function is not explicitly marked linguistically. Thus the child says only "ball," not "I see the ball," "I want the ball," or "Where is the ball?" For this reason, when utterances are used in situations where no category member is present, or when they are used for only a restricted range of situations, a problem arises. It may be, as many earlier investigators have argued, that such overgeneral or undergeneral uses provide evidence that the child's categories are immature (e.g., Piaget, 1962). Alternatively, however, it is possible that words are used to perform functions other than naming present category instances; that is, utterances may be used in the absence of category instances (apparently overgenerally) because they are requests or comments. Further, utterances may be used only in circumscribed situations (i.e., undergenerally) because those are the only situations in which children have communicative purposes involving those words. This latter issue arises for the words predicated of persons because children initially use these words in sentences only for themselves and not for others. Before inferring that children initially fail to categorize other people as subjects of experience, one must establish that they do not simply lack the motive to describe other people's actions.

The other issue that must be considered is the extent to which children's words provide evidence about their conceptual development. Correct use of a word indicates possession of the concept the word encodes. However, it does not necessarily indicate when the concept was first acquired. To learn a word, children must not only be able to form the concept; they also must have heard that word used. Further, the word must be presented so its sound pattern can be isolated from the stream of incoming speech, and in contexts that permit the assignment of a meaning to it. Hence, in using the acquisition of words to assess conceptual development, parent usage must be taken into account. A couple of specific examples show that *either* conceptual development *or* parent usage might explain patterns of child word usage.

First, consider the case where a child's meaning differs from the adult meaning for a word. There are two possible explanations. The child might be unable to form the adult concept. Alternatively, the child may have heard the word used for a biased sample of instances. For example, if parents name mainly the child's actions, not the actions of others, that could explain why the child initially fails to apply verbs to observed actions.

Second, consider the case where a child acquires two different words in a particular order. Again, there are two possible explanations. The two concepts may differ in complexity. Alternatively, the amount of exposure to the two words may have differed. Similarly, if two words are acquired at the same time, this may be because the two concepts are of equal complexity. Alternatively, their conceptual complexity might vary, but the simpler word may have been presented less frequently than the more complex one. Thus, for example, object words may be acquired earlier than action words either because parents name objects more frequently than actions or because they are conceptually simpler. In short, if we are to use the acquisition of word meanings to assess conceptual development, it is important to consider data on parent word use as well. Next we present the results of two studies of person words (for actions and people) and a study of parent use of those words. We also present the results of a study of emotion words and of parent use of those words.

Person Words as Evidence about Person Categories

In treating utterances containing person words, such as words for actions and inner states, as evidence about notions of persons, uses referring to experiences of the child her or himself have a more straightforward interpretation than those referring to experiences of other people. If a child uses a word in relation to his or her own action or experience, it is likely that the word encodes an intention or other inner state. However, inferences about the inner states of other people are based on observable cues. If children use emotion words or intentional action words for others, one cannot be certain whether the words encode inferred inner states of other people or observable cues such as facial expression or bodily movement. In fact, different cues might be used in applying emotion words to self and other—a feeling state for self and a facial expression or bodily stance for others. Of course, even adults may use different cues in applying emotion words to self and other. Nevertheless, when adults use person words, they probably intend to describe inner states of others, whereas young children may not. Thus, when children use internal state words productively both for the self and other, it is likely, but not certain, that the child infers that others experience feelings similar to those of the self.

Children's Use of Person Words

In our first study (Huttenlocher, Smiley, & Charney, 1983) we examined the acquisition of verbs for intentional action. We obtained data on the production of verbs by 14 children, aged 23 to 28 months. These children produced verbs for their own actions and in requests for others to do things for them. Uses to describe other people's actions were so rare that it was not clear that they were used productively for such instances. At first glance, requests may appear to encode acts by others, because in making requests, children ask people to act in their behalf. But requests encode the child's intentions, not other people's intentional acts independent of the child. Thus, it seemed to us that, initially, children encode their own intentions and do not encode the intentional actions of others.

Before concluding that children do not encode other people's intentional actions, however, it is important to determine whether the observed restriction in production might reflect utterance function rather than word meaning; that is, children might be able to encode other people's actions but lack a motive to do so. To address this issue we tested comprehension of these verbs. We made a set of brief movies of contrasting actions, for example, *get* versus *push*. In one film loop, a boy was shown reaching to a table and getting a toy car, and in the other, the same boy was shown next to the table pushing the car on the floor. After labeling both actions, we asked children to point to one of them. Many children up to 3 years were unable to select the correct films for the same verbs that all the children in the production study had used for themselves by 2 years. These results strongly suggest that verb meanings initially do not extend to other people's intentional actions.

The question arises as to why actions, which have similar observable behavioral components whether the actor is the self or another person, are applied first to the self. For example, the highly frequent verbs like *get*, *give*, and *put* encode visible changes in the locations of objects. But, as we found, these actions are categorized much later when observed in others. In forming categories of actions, one *could* draw on similarities in the appearance of instances in which changes in object location are brought about. However, in these actions, the change in the state of affairs may not be perceptually salient. What may be more salient about such transfers is the desire for an object and the intention to obtain it. Thus, for actions of these kinds, children may first note these intentions in the self and categorize other people's behavior only when they begin to infer their intentions. There are other actions, however, that have more constant perceptual features—for example, sitting down, jumping, etc. We wondered whether words for these acts might also encode intentions (or just observable movement patterns) and if so, whether they encode intentions either in the self or others before 2 years.

In considering the earliest words for behavior, we turn to the data from our second study (Huttenlocher & Smiley, 1989). This was a longitudinal study of 10 children who were followed from the time of their earliest words (at about 13 months) until their mean length of utterance was 2.5 (at about 2½ years). For a 5-hour period each month, all child utterances were transcribed together with the contexts to which the child's attention was directed. We looked for words, not necessarily verbs, which encoded people's behavior—perhaps behavior with more constant perceptual features—and which might also encode intentionality for self and other—perhaps even earlier for others than for the self.

We found a set of words for movement and change that were used as early as 16 months, namely, the words *up*, *down*, *off*, and *out*, and the verbs *open* and *sit*. These words were used for behavior of the self and others as well as for changes occurring in inanimates; that is, there is a class of events in which the self and others are involved that *can* be categorized quite early, apparently on the basis of observable cues. But these early words are unlike the words that are acquired later on in an important respect. Words like *get* or *give* can be posited only of creatures with intentions, whereas *up* can legitimately be said of any moving body. Neither adults nor children ever say of bottles or apples that they get or give anything. Therefore, we argued that this group of words does not encode intentional action at all; they are just words for events. Further, our longitudinal data showed that words that *are* posited only of the behavior of animates (*get* and *give*, etc.) did not emerge until 20 to 24 months. And, when they emerged, they were applied initially only to movement and change produced by the child.

Consider now the emergence of words for people. Again the data are from our longitudinal study (Huttenlocher, Smiley, & Prohaska, 1989). Words for people, notably *mommy* and *daddy*, are among the child's earliest words. Let us consider what aspects of the notion of person are encoded in the early uses of these words. There is evidence to suggest that people are not categorized as just another type of inanimate object. First, person names, notably *mommy*, are frequently used in requests. Object names and event words are used in requests too, but much less frequently. Further, words for objects are used to request the named objects and words for events are used to request the named event, whereas person names are *not* generally used to request persons themselves. Rather they are used to request objects or events the person can procure or produce. This suggests that people are categorized as creatures who can act in the child's behalf. Second, person names are used in calls. This is perhaps the strongest evidence that persons are not categorized as inanimate. Calls are restricted to person words; that is, children often call "Mommy" to get her to come, but they never call "apple."

Although people are categorized differently from inanimates, there is no reason to argue that, at the time when these uses appear, people are categorized as having inner states. First, words for intentional acts of others clearly are not present at 14 to 20 months. Second, 14- to 20-month-olds do not use any words for inner states, even for themselves. Third, and this is perhaps the strongest evidence, young children do not use any words to denote the self. If, as is reasonable to suppose, notions of persons as subjects of experience, with inner states, derive from one's own experience as subject, it is unlikely that children categorize others as creatures with inner states when they have not yet conceptualized themselves in this way. One might expect children to encode others as subjects either at the same time as or after they begin to encode themselves as subjects.

Words for self (i.e., personal pronouns and the child's name) emerge in children's speech shortly before 2 years, about 8 months after the beginning of speech. The late emergence of the personal pronouns *I* and *me* relative to certain other kinds of words may be because pronouns are deictic terms and not because an explicit notion of self is lacking. Pronouns are words whose reference shifts with the speaker and hence are more linguistically complex than other early terms. The child's own name, however, has a fixed reference to a particular object, namely, the child. Despite this difference in linguistic complexity, we have found that children start to use their own names at the same age as they start to use personal pronouns, that is, at 20 to 24 months.

In short, words for self and intentional action words used for the self both appear across the same brief age range. These data strongly suggest that an explicit notion of self with intentional states emerges at just before 2 years. Words for other people appear early, but they seem to encode others *only* as capable of movement. Words for intentional actions of others emerge much later, at around 2½ years.

Parent Use of Words for Action and for the Child

Before drawing any firm conclusions about conceptual development based on child speech data alone, we examine our data on parent word use. First, consider the age of emergence of the concept of a self with internal states. Because this notion appears to emerge only at around 2 years, the question is whether parents use intentional action words and words for the child less frequently or saliently than words the child acquires earlier. In our third study we examined parent speech to children (Huttenlocher, Haight, Bryk, Seltzer, & Lyons, in press). We followed 11 mother–child pairs longitudinally from 14 to 26 months. We found that the frequency with which parents use words has a great effect on when the words are acquired. The Huttenlocher et al. corpus also shows that words acquired early, notably words for objects and for events, are used frequently and appear either alone or in last position in adult sentences. However, words for intentional action, which are acquired late, were also very frequent, in fact, even more frequent than object names and words for events, but they were rarely used alone or in last position. They tended to be transitive verbs like *get* or *put* that occur in the middle of sentences, as in "I'm getting your cereal." Thus, it is possible that children have difficulty isolating intentional action words from the stream of incoming speech. One could argue that the reason object and event words are acquired earlier than words for intentional action is that their sound patterns are easier to extract from the speech stream, not that the conceptual categories they encode are more easily formed.

Consider next parent use of words for self, all of which are acquired late. *Me* occurs in salient last position in parent utterances, but it is infrequent. In contrast, *I* is never used alone or in last position. Thus, in addition to the problem of shifting reference, the sound pattern of this word may be less accessible than for words acquired earlier. However, such arguments cannot explain why children acquire their own names late and at the same time as personal pronouns. The child's name is not only *very* frequent in parent speech, but the sound pattern is easily accessible; it is frequently used alone or in last position. It is also used in the clearest possible manner with respect to its referent: in calling the child, offering things to the child, etc. Thus, parent usage cannot explain why children start to use their own names late. These data on child use of pronouns and names and on parent use of names suggest that, until just before 2 years, children may lack an explicit notion of themselves not only as subjects of experience, but even as material objects or as sources of movement or change.

This may seem a radical position because it is informally thought that children respond to their own names much earlier than 20 months even though they do not produce them. There is, to our knowledge, no systematic data on this issue. Even if children did look up or come when they heard their names, that would still not be convincing evidence that the child had an idea of self. Children, like animals, might respond differentially to a particular sound pattern. If children produced a word spontaneously across a range of communicative situations rather than just responded to it as an incoming stimulus, this would constitute much more convincing evidence that the word sound encoded a concept.

Consider now the data on parent use of intentional action verbs in relation to the actions of other people. We found that intentional action words are used for self at around 2 years but are only applied to others at around 2½ years. If adults used these words only for child action, then this later use for others might reflect the focus of parent attention rather than the child's difficulty in conceptualizing others' intentions. Our data show that when children are still under 2 years, parents use intentional action words slightly more frequently for child action, but 40% of uses are for parent action. Whereas child usage is biased in favor of child action, the degree of bias in parent usage seems insufficient to explain the complete restriction to self in child usage. Further, for certain verbs like *get*, there are more uses for parent action than for child action. Even so, *get*, like the other verbs, encodes only the child's own action, not observed action, for several months. Thus, these data strengthen our conclusion that at 2 years children conceptualize the self but not others as intentional actors.

Emergence of Emotion Words

Finally, we turn to parent usage of emotion words and to our comprehension study of these words. If the notion of a self with inner states emerges between 20 and 24 months, children should also use words for emotions themselves at this time. However, words for emotions are very infrequent in parent speech. Only 1 inner state word is used frequently by mothers, namely, *want*. For the 11 mothers we followed, it was used an average of 70 times per mother in a period of 5 hours, about the same frequency as action verbs such as *get* and *put*. In these 5-hour samples, we found only 3 other words for internal states that were used even once by more than 3 of the 11 mothers—*tired, hungry,* and *happy*. Taking all inner state words together (30 types, excepting *want*), there were a total of only 9 uses per mother in the 5-hour observations. Because frequency of usage is important in the acquisition of words, one might expect that even if the child could form categories of emotional states of self before 2 years of age, they still might not acquire those words.

Indeed, much of the literature on the development of emotion words suggests that they *do* emerge considerably later than 2 years. These studies test the comprehension of emotion terms, using as stimuli photographs or line drawings of faces or situations or verbal descriptions of situations. The studies test the application of emotion words to others, not to the self. Indeed, in comprehension studies it would be difficult to test for meaning in relation to self. One cannot instruct the child to enter into a particular emotional state in order to show that he understands the word for that state.

Several comprehension studies using facial expressions as stimuli show that the basic terms acquired over the course of 1 to 3 years, beginning at age 4. *Happy* is acquired first, followed by *mad* and *scared,* and finally, *sad* (e.g., Felleman, Barden, Carlson, Rosenberg, & Masters, 1983; Izard, 1971; Reichenbach & Masters, 1983). However, in a study where faces were presented with short verbal descriptions of events, 4-year-olds were found to comprehend words for all the basic emotions (Camras & Allison, 1985). In more recent studies, Bullock and Russell (1985, 1986) found that even when the most perceptually confusable faces are pitted against one another and presented without context, 3-year-olds can differentiate *mad* and *scared* and 4-year-olds, *sad,* from other expressions.

Studies using drawings or descriptions of situations likely to evoke certain emotional reactions show that emotion terms are acquired between 3 and 5 to 7 years, again with *happy* first (Borke, 1973; Eisenberg-Berg & Lennon, 1980; Reichenbach & Masters, 1983). Comprehension of *scared* and *sad* is reported in 4- to 8-year-olds (Borke, 1971; Eisenberg-Berg & Lennon, 1980; Gnepp, 1983; Reichenbach & Masters, 1983; Stein & Jewett, 1985); and *mad,* in children over 5 (Borke, 1971, 1973; Reichenbach & Masters, 1983; Stein & Jewett, 1985). Finally, a few studies have contrasted application of words to faces versus situations and find either no difference in difficulty (Gnepp, 1983) or a difference favoring situations (Barden, Zilko, Duncan, & Masters, 1980).

We studied comprehension of five emotion words (*happy, sad, mad, surprised,* and *scared*). We showed children aged 2½ to 5 years movies of faces that changed from neutral to full emotional expressions and of situations that might evoke particular emotions, where facial expressions could not be seen. Our short color movies involved real people, objects, and locations. In these movie tasks, each of the five words was paired with every other word. We also tested comprehension of two emotion words (*mad* and *scared*) using line drawings to study the effect of the realism of the stimuli. These also were displayed with contrasting emotional expressions and situations (in four-item displays). Our criterion for comprehension was 100% correct identification—4 of 4 movie pairs or 2 of 2 drawing displays—so that a child would not reach criterion for a particular word by chance.

First, we found an effect of the realism of the stimuli. For the same subjects, it was much easier for them to apply the words *mad* and *scared* to real moving faces and events than to static pictures. Second, we found that emotion words were more easily applied to faces than to situations. As shown in Table 11.1, children chose the correct faces significantly more often than they selected correct situations.

Third, the order of acquisition was different for faces and situations. Tables 11.2 and 11.3 show the number of children in each age group who comprehended each emotion word. As shown in Table 11.2, at 2½ to 3 years, the majority of children (two-thirds or more) understood *happy* for faces; at 3 to 3½ years, the majority of children (two-thirds or more) understood the words *happy, mad,* and *scared* for faces, and by 3½ to 4 years, the majority understood all five words for faces. In contrast, as shown in Table 11.3, only by 3½ to 4 years did a majority comprehend one word for situations, and this word was *scared*. By 4 to 4½ years, a majority also understood *happy* and *mad*. Even at 5 years, few children correctly applied *sad* to situations. (These data are presented more fully in Smiley and Huttenlocher, 1989.)

Given that a variety of intentional action words apply to other people by about 2½ years, but only one emotion word, this represents quite a lag. In trying to understand these results, note that even in our comprehension study where we used movies of real people and situations the children were exposed to only a subset of the stimuli available in the real world; that is, we showed faces isolated

TABLE 11.1
Means and Standard Deviations of Emotion
Words Correct for Movies of Faces and Situations

Age	Faces		Situations	
	Mean	Standard Deviation	Mean	Standard Deviation
2;6–2;11[a]	2.7[b]	1.8	.4	.6
3;0–3;5	3.2	1.2	1.7	1.4
3;6–3;11	4.1	1.0	2.1	1.2
4;0–4;5	4.6	.8	2.9	1.2
4;6–4;11	4.5	.9	2.9[c]	1.5

[a]n = 15 for each age group.
[b]Maximum score is 5.
[c]Scores are significantly higher for faces than for situations
($p < .0001$, repeated measures ANOVA).

from situations, and situations involving people whose faces were turned away. When observing a naturally occurring event, the child sees both of these cues at once and also hears the speech and voice quality and sees the subsequent action of the person experiencing the emotion. Thus, the children were essentially presented with degraded stimuli. In addition, at least for situations, although we (and other investigators) tried to present situations that the child would see as emotion producing, we may have failed. Thus, one might expect that emotion words applied to other people might be acquired earlier than appears to be the case from experimental comprehension studies.

In fact, there is some evidence suggesting that occasional uses of emotion words appear in spontaneous speech before 2 years, at least for the self. Our longitudinal data reveal very few uses of inner state words other than *want* by children, just as by their parents. However, a few of the 21 children in our two

TABLE 11.2
Percentage of Children in Each Age Group Comprehending
Emotion Words for Faces

Age	Emotion Word				
	Happy	Sad	Mad	Surprised	Scared
2;6–2;11[a]	.80[b]	.33	.60	.53	.47
3;0–3;5	.73	.47	.80[b]	.53	.67[b]
3;6–3;11	.87	.80[b]	.93	.73[b]	.73
4;0–4;5	1.00	1.00	.87	.87	.87
4;6–4;11	.93	.80	.93	.87	.93

[a]n = 15 for each age group.
[b]67% or more of children this age and older comprehended this word.

TABLE 11.3
Percentage of Children in Each Age Group Comprehending
Emotion Words for Situations

	Emotion Word				
Age	Happy	Sad	Mad	Surprised	Scared
2;6–2;11[a]	.00	.00	.13	.13	.13
3;0–3;5	.20	.27	.40	.47	.33
3;6–3;11	.47	.13	.40	.40	.67[b]
4;0–4;5	.67[b]	.20	.67[b]	.40	.93
4;6–4;11	.67	.27	.47	.60	.87

[a]n = 15 for each age group.
[b]67% or more of children this age and older comprehended this word (except for *mad*).

longitudinal studies produced emotion words for themselves. The children were 22- to 26-months-old when they first used them, and the words included *happy, mad, sad,* and *afraid.* Some of the uses are quite convincing. For example, one child who kicked sand at another child was reprimanded by his mother, and he then said, "I'm mad." Another child was inside a closed cardboard box, started to cry, and said, "I afraid."

We heard only one utterance in which an emotion word was used for another person. This child said, "My Mommy's sad," as she watched her mother crying during a telephone call to a good friend who was moving out of town. In this case, *sad* could be a word that encodes only the observable experience of crying. However, because this child also used *sad* for herself a few months earlier, it *could* be an inference about mother's inner state. Other investigators, using parent reports, also have found some uses of emotion words for self and other in this age range (Bretherton & Beeghly, 1982). Finally, we have some evidence for the understanding of emotion words by 2-year-olds from a pilot study for our larger comprehension study. We showed the facial expression movies to eight children aged 24 to 28 months, and six of them understood from 1 to 3 of the 5 emotion words. As noted before, these young children may be categorizing only facial expressions and not internal states. However, because there are some uses for self in production, children *may* be making inferences about others' emotional states at the time when they are beginning to make inferences about others' intentional states. In short, there is not yet enough information about the categorization of emotional experiences for others, but the uses in production for self provide powerful evidence for the categorization of the child's own internal states. They are especially convincing because our observations are of spontaneous applications to novel events that were not collected via retrospective reports.

Assuming that such uses in production genuinely encode emotional states, at least in the child, categorization of these states clearly becomes possible at the same time as categorization of other inner states in the child. Because at least some children use emotion words for others by 2½ years or earlier, this *may* indicate that categorization of these states in others also becomes possible no later than categorization of intentions and desires in other persons. The findings that words referring to self—names and pronouns, and intentional action and emotion words used for self—all emerge at a similar age, and that person predicates apply to others at a similar age, suggest that the ability to form an adult-like category of person emerges in two steps during this age period. However, an alternative scenario is suggested by the infrequency of parent uses of emotion words; that is, it is possible that concepts of emotions in self and other develop even earlier than other person categories, but that word meanings are not established until a sufficient number of instances have been heard by the child. As with any other word, the age of acquisition of a word meaning only sets an upper limit on the age of development of the concept.

It would not, after all, be surprising if the categorization of emotional states emerged early relative to other person categories. In the self, these states may be more accessible or less complex cognitively than intentions to carry out particular types of actions. In others, the observable cues to at least some emotional states may be more easily perceptible to an observer than are the movements and changes involved in goal-directed actions. Or, the content of emotional experiences in others might even be experienced by the child through a process not properly called inferential. These alternative possibilities about the emergence of emotion categories cannot be evaluated from the empirical evidence presently available from language use. But exploring them would certainly be important to a more complete understanding of the child's developing notion of person.

REFERENCES

Barden, R., Zilko, F., Duncan, S., & Masters, J. (1980). Children's consensual knowledge about the experiential determinants of emotion. *Journal of Personality and Social Psychology, 39*, 968–976.

Borke, H. (1971). Interpersonal perception of young children: Egocentrism or empathy? *Developmental Psychology, 5*, 263–269.

Borke, H. (1973). The development of empathy in Chinese and American children between three and six years of age. *Developmental Psychology, 9*, 102–109.

Bretherton, I., & Beeghly, M. (1982). Talking about internal states: The acquisition of an explicit theory of mind. *Developmental Psychology, 18*, 906–921.

Bullock, M., & Russell, J. (1985). Further evidence on preschoolers' interpretation of facial expressions. *International Journal of Behavioral Development, 8*, 15–38.

Bullock, M., & Russell, J. (1986). Concepts of emotion in developmental psychology. In C. E. Izard & P. B. Read (Eds.), *Measuring emotions in infants and children* (Vol. II). Cambridge: Cambridge University Press.

Camras, L., & Allison, K. (1985). Children's understanding of emotional facial expressions and verbal labels. *Journal of Nonverbal Behavior, 9,* 84–94.

Eisenberg-Berg, N., & Lennon, R. (1980). Altruism and the assessment of empathy in the preschool years. *Child Development, 5,* 552–557.

Felleman, E., Barden, R., Carlson, C., Rosenberg, L., & Masters, J. (1983). Children's and adults' recognition of spontaneous and posed emotional expressions in young children. *Developmental Psychology, 19,* 405–413.

Gnepp, J. (1983). Children's social sensitivity: Inferring emotion from conflicting cues. *Developmental Psychology, 35,* 805–814.

Huttenlocher, J., Haight, W., A. Bryk, M. Seltzer, & T. Lyons. (in press). Early vocabulary growth: Relation to language input and gender. *Developmental Psychology.*

Huttenlocher, J., & Smiley, P. (1989). *Breaking into language: The emergence of words for events.* Unpublished manuscript.

Huttenlocher, J., Smiley, P., and Charney, R. (1983). Emergence of action categories in the child: Evidence from verb meanings. *Psychological Review, 90,* 72–93.

Huttenlocher, J., Smiley, P., & Prohaska, V. (1989). *Origins of the category of person: Evidence from speech.* Unpublished manuscript.

Izard, C. (1971). *The face of emotion.* New York: Appleton-Century-Croft.

Piaget, J. (1962). *Play, dreams, and imitation in childhood.* New York: Norton.

Reichenbach, L., & Masters, J. (1983). Children's use of expressive and contextual cues in judgments of emotion. *Child Development, 54,* 993–1004.

Smiley, P., & Huttenlocher, J. (1989). Young children's acquisition of emotion concepts. In C. Saarni & P. Harris (Eds.), *Children's understanding of emotion.* New York: Cambridge University Press.

Stein, N., & Jewett, J. (1985, April). *A conceptual analysis of the meaning of anger, fear, and sadness.* Paper presented at the Biennial Meeting of the Society for Research in Child Development, Toronto.

12

Anger in Young Children

Marian Radke-Yarrow
Grazyna Kochanska
National Institute of Mental Health
Bethesda, Maryland 20892

INTRODUCTION

Despite the extraordinary presence of emotions in the lives of children, and despite our usual confidence in identifying children's emotions in social interaction, research-based knowledge of children's emotions is limited. Uncertainties about the construct of emotion and difficulties in measuring emotions have dampened efforts in empirical research. In particular, developmental researchers have been slow to give children's moods and emotions the benefit of the kinds of efforts that have given theory and substance to research on other aspects of child behavior and development. The empiricists of the 1930s, Katherine Bridges (1932), Florence Goodenough (1931), Arthur Jersild and Frances Holmes (1935), Mary Cover Jones (1924) provide us still with our classic studies of children's emotions.

Moreover, the concepts and issues relating to emotional development have not been clearly laid out. What do we expect with development in childhood? Is it changing elicitors and changing forms of expression, or more self-understanding of emotions, or more control of emotions? Do we expect to determine norms or stages in emotional development? How important is cognition in the development of children's emotions? Are social behaviors and social relationships the ultimate targets for study as they "carry" different affective meaning; that is, do emotions refine concepts of social behavior such as aggression, inhibition, assertiveness, and the like? The anger, fear, or pleasure with which anyone of these behaviors is carried out modifies the meaning of the behaviors. Does investigation of emotions in child development also involve a concern about how emotions organize the child's behavior in the course of development?

As we know, children's emotions have been little studied for four decades. In the 1980s children's emotions have again become a respectable topic of study, and a very active area. As researchers have become interested in this domain, conceptual issues and development of methods of assessing emotions have been prominent considerations (e.g., Campos, Barrett, Lamb, Goldsmith, & Stenberg, 1983). Empirical studies of affective processes in children, except for the infant period, have lagged.

Our interest in this chapter is in emotions in the period following infancy from 1½ to 5 years. When children are changing profoundly—physically, motorically, cognitively, linguistically, socially—what is happening in emotions? In this chapter, we are exploring how young children are experiencing, expressing, and regulating emotion. We have chosen to examine these issues in one emotion, anger in young children. Although anger or oppositional behavior is a major presenting problem in clinics and other treatment services for children and can be a serious signal of risk for continuing problems, it is not always indicative of pathological disturbance. The children we have studied are "ordinary" children; they have not been selected as problem children. We are in a position then to observe what is "normal": how anger is elicited in children, how it is expressed, and how it is socialized.

In addressing these issues, we are not reporting a study of anger; we are instead drawing on a series of studies that are part of a continuing program of research on children's affective behavior and development. The studies differ in research objectives, kinds and ages of child participants, and methodological approaches, but all concern anger in young children.

The Concept of Anger

Anger is familiar in the literature of child development—as rage in the infant, temper tantrums in the preschooler, in the repertoire of responses to frustration or "hurt" at all ages, a component of temperament, and as oppositional disorder and conduct disorders in older children. Yet, anger is difficult to define or describe. It involves physiological activation, muscle tension, cognitive processing, subjective experience, and overt behaviors. It has distinguishable expressive features—in facial expression and tone of cry and voice. Verbal content, too, can define the anger. Its specific overt behaviors are of many varieties; it may be undirected kicking, stomping and the like; it can also be expressed in aggressive behavior or in subtle forms of destructive, harassing behavior. Anger may be transient; it may also be a chronic form of coping with stress. Despite these many facets and impurities in conceptualization and description, anger in young children is recognizable. This comfortable familiarity does not, however, override the conceptual and measurement issues. How one thinks about emotions or what one thinks emotions are influences how one proceeds to investigate them.

Hinde (1972) discusses the phenomena of emotions in traditional terms. He distinguishes emotional input (the independent variables of study), intervening state (of subjective experience or energizing state), and emotional output (dependent variables of expression and behavior), but, in doing so, he quickly destroys the simple neatness of these distinctions. He emphasizes that none can be defined independently of the other. Thus, emotional input cannot be considered independent of emotional "state," and "state" and emotion expression are similarly influencing each other in a complex way. These interdependencies are especially important in investigating development and in investigating emotions in real-life circumstances. Thus, in considering the interaction of cognitive and affective factors, one would anticipate that the effect of emotional input or experience on children of different ages would be different. Also, one might expect that young children with different affective relationships with their mothers would respond differently to emotional stimuli and regulate their own emotions in a different way. Children's expressive emotional behavior would likewise be dependent on their immediate as well as their more enduring emotional states.

Research Issues

Keeping in mind these issues of interdependency, we have approached emotional development in young children through four lines of questions. The first concerns the effects on children of experiences of anger, not anger in themselves but in their social environments. How do young children respond to this class of stimuli? The second set of questions concerns normative developmental characteristics in young children. Third is the issue of the socialization of anger, which involves how others, especially mothers, respond to the child's anger. And fourth is the issue of origins of anger in young children.

The Sources of Data

We are drawing on data sets obtained in investigations represented by three basic paradigms. A brief description at this point of each data source allows us later in the chapter to move among the studies and to integrate the information that they offer relating to the questions we are examining. In one paradigm we have used a naturalistic approach. Natural events of emotion in the daily experience of young children were systematically recorded, along with the children's reactions to these events. The children were 1- to 2½-year-olds ($n = 60$); a sample of whom was followed-up at 7 years ($n = 22$) (Cummings, Zahn-Waxler, & Radke-Yarrow, 1981; Radke-Yarrow, Zahn-Waxler, Cummings, Strope, & Sebris, 1981). The early study by Goodenough (1931) provided a model for the approach we developed (Yarrow & Waxler, 1977). We trained the mothers of these young children to serve as research assistants. They were trained for a very specific observing purpose and in a specific observing method. They reported daily on incidents in which emotion was manifested in someone other than the child, and for which the child was either a witness or the cause of the emotions. Usually the events involved family members or peers. In typical incidents a mother and father are fighting (quarreling), a sibling is crying and hitting at the dog because it has knocked over her dishes, or a peer is scolding and frowning because our child has grabbed her doll. Reactions by our child to the other's emotion were recorded. Standard, simulated emotion incidents were inserted into the natural stream of behavior. Mother and a research staff person carried out the simulations (e.g., simulating a hurt and feeling pain, or getting into an angry exchange on the telephone). A specified reporting format was followed by mothers for dictating their observations into a tape recorder, close in time to the incidents. Reporting was done over a period of months. The details of the method, the reliability of the reports, and the findings are in published reports (Radke-Yarrow, Zahn-Waxler, C., Cummings, E. M., Strope, B., & Sebris, L., 1981; Zahn-Waxler & Radke-Yarrow, 1982). For our present purposes, we are interested only in reported incidents of anger and in the child's reactions to anger.

In a second set of studies an experimental approach was used. The purpose of these studies was to examine the role that anger in the environment plays in regulating the child's behavior. Again, the literature of the 1930s supplied the source of our research approach. The creation of experimental "climates" by Lewin, Lippitt, and White (1939) (in that instance, autocratic and democratic climates) provided a model for the creation of emotional "climates." In these studies (Cummings, Iannotti, & Zahn-Waxler, 1985), an emotional background of anger was controlled. The experimental procedure was as follows: pairs of 2-year-olds who knew each other ($n = 90$) were observed in a play session in a suite of rooms with an adjoining kitchenette. The mothers were present, but they were asked to remain relatively uninvolved. During the session, two unfamiliar staff members entered to wash the dishes. Their verbal interactions followed a sequence that began with friendly conversation and affect, developed into an intense verbal quarrel, and returned to a reconciliation. The staff members were never unfriendly to the mothers or children and their argument was confined to their disagreement over their share of the dish-washing task. Sessions were videotaped. The children's reactions before, during, and after the manipulations were compared. A control group had no affect variation, only the neutral interaction of the staff members. After 1 month, one child of each pair returned with a new peer friend, and similar procedures were repeated. Measures of cumulative effects and a replication in the new peer sample were thereby obtained.

The third research approach utilizes extensive observations of children with their parents, in research settings that combine naturalistic and experimental methods, and also clinical assessments. The children ($n = 252$) were selected on the basis of their parents' psychiatric status (either no history of psychiatric disorder or a diagnosis of bipolar or major depression; Radke-Yarrow, 1989). The children, two siblings from each family, are 2 to 3 years and 5 to 8 years of age. Children and mothers were observed (videotaped) in an informal, home-like research apartment over a series of half-days. Time and physical environment were scripted to conform to our conceptualization of rearing. Routines and events that are likely in the ordinary day (lunch, watching TV, reading a story, etc.), and less usual occurrences (a stranger's visit, a "doctor's" examination) were structured into a smooth sequence of activities. Assessments were made of mothers' and children's moods and emotions. This was done by dividing behavior into 1-minute intervals and coding for each interval the emotion(s) expressed. (For details of procedures, see Radke-Yarrow, Kuczynski, Belmont, Stilwell, Nottelmann, & Welsh, 1986.) This procedure provided profiles of emotions during 2½-hour sessions on three separate half-days. Mothers' handling of children's emotions was also observed. A psychiatric assessment of each child provided an independent appraisal of the child's emotional functioning.

From this varied set of studies, we attempt to organize data on the development of children's anger, in terms of the issues we have identified.

The Effects of Anger in the Environment of the Young Child

The discipline has long made use of the novel stimulus as a way of learning about the child's capabilities and dispositions. By presenting the infant with a dangling toy, or placing a cloth to its face, or introducing a stranger, we have learned a great deal from infants' attending, the coming and going of their smiles, their signs of fear and anger; we have learned about infants' capacities and vulnerabilities. The manifestation of emotion, too, is a novel stimulus to the observing infant or toddler. It cannot, however, be presented at will like a dangling toy. The methodological and ethical limitations are obvious. With the alternative approach (that has been described), which keeps the emotion stimulus intact, many naturally occurring emotions present themselves to the child. The mothers' recordings, over months of time, supply a developmental record of how the child works with these complex stimuli, how the meaning of the stimuli appears to change, and how exposure to anger has different effects on the child's behavior. These records allow us to observe the developmental time of appearance of various responses to events defined as anger by overt characteristics of yelling, hitting, facial expressions, gestures, etc., in contexts that are congruent with this interpretation. The changes in responses, by the same children, over time provide clues to developmental course. (We cannot from mothers' records draw conclusions regarding frequencies; Radke-Yarrow & Zahn-Waxler, 1984).

When 1-year-olds are confronted with events of anger, they respond with troubled attention—reported by their mothers as frowns, concerned looks, staring, sometimes whimpering. Anger rarely brings smiles or laughter. Responses, however, are not distinguishable from responses to other observed emotion events—signs of pain, sad crying, loud laughter. Over the next few months mothers report that as part of their concerned attention the children look to mother, an act of social referencing that has been noted in infants (Klinnert, Campos, Soce, Emde, & Svejda, 1983) in situations that appear uncertain.

Beginning at 16 to 18 months, and characteristic of their responses to the end of our observations at 2 to 2½ years, children's aroused attention is mobilized into flight or fight patterns of behavior in many instances. Some children withdraw by covering their ears, clutching a blanket and slipping out of the room, or "freezing." Other children take a stand, demanding that the fight stop ("Stop it, Stop it." "Shut up, Mommy"), or bodily protecting a sibling from an angry mother.

There are three especially interesting types of responses that provide information regarding which aspects of the other persons' anger are registered by the child and what is comprehended or experienced by the child. They are imitative responses, self-referential comments or gestures, and verbal statements that identify the cues to which the child is attending when observing anger. Fighting or quarreling between parents is particularly revealing in this regard.

Children in the first half of the second year attempt to reproduce different facets of the parents' behavior. They try to imitate parents' facial expressions, their sounds, words, or exclamations including their rhythm and intonation (e.g., a preverbal child imitates his mother's angry phone conversation with loud, rapid babbling). In imitative matching, the children sometimes seem uncertain about the stimulus. This is less the case when children's matching includes expression of the feelings as well as the form involved in the observed event of anger.

Children's self-referential behavior indicates an affective consequence for them. The event is threatening, and they take the battered role themselves (though not in an imitative fashion). An example of self-reference occurs in a child's observation of a quarrel between father and mother, leading to mother's tears, and whereupon the child cries and asks for comfort. How important to this response is the fact that the fighting was between the child's parents we cannot say.

Older children in the toddler-age group are sometimes explicit about the cues they are reading for anger: "Don't talk so loud and fast Daddy." "Stop yelling Mommy, shut up."

Toddlers also respond with anger to the anger in another person. We see this by examples. In a parents' quarrel, the child scowls and hits her father as she pushes him away saying, "No, Daddy, no," and then kisses her mother. Stopping the stimulus seems the objective that is uppermost in the minds of many children. Sometimes their approach is subtle, as the child who hovers around her quarreling parents repeating "Hi Daddy, hi Mommy." Sometimes the child simply states a firm, "Stop it." At the extreme, the child becomes caretaker of the parents: "You have to get over that yelling trouble you have."

Clearly, by 2 to 2½ years, children, with few exceptions, are acting as if they have classified quite divergent events into one meaningful cluster and that their own state has been changed by the impact of anger from the environment. They appear to have knowledge of a likely sequence or script in the incidents of anger (as indicated by the child who shields her sibling from her mother's angry scolding). They experience the anger as unpleasant, as evidenced in their telling responses.

These naturalistic findings were tested experimentally in the laboratory procedures of background anger, described earlier. The children exposed to anger responded with reactions that were very like those reported by the mothers. Distress was reflected in body posture and movements (e.g., going to mother, "freezing") and sometimes in voice and face. Distress during the anger was expressed by more than 40% of the children. In the control group without exposure, behaviors of distress occurred in 10% of the children. Part of the sample returned for a similar procedure a month later. The effects were increased with this repeated exposure to anger. Also, increases in interpeer aggression took place after the anger incidents, again showing the cumulative effect of repeated exposure. Girls showed more distress than boys *during* the anger ($p < .05$); boys showed more aggression than girls *after* the exposure ($p < .05$).

A further replication of the naturalistic and experimental results was obtained in a clinical study (Zahn-Waxler, McKnew, Cummings, Davenport, & Radke-Yarrow, 1984), in which seven 2-year-olds, the offspring of severely affectively ill parents (one of the parents was a manic–depressive, the other parent had a major depression or other affective disturbance), were obser ved in the laboratory paradigm. The effects of background anger on these children and children of a normal comparison group were similar to the earlier study. One difference appeared between the clinical and the normal group when exposed to the anger. The children of the depressed parents showed more signs of emotionality during the adults' angry interactions ($p < .01$). This is of special interest because it can be assumed that the families from which these children come are chaotic environments of greatly dysregulated emotions, including anger. We can, therefore, interpret the laboratory quarrel as an event for the child that is embedded in a family background of emotional dysregulation. The child's elevated response in the laboratory probably reflects sensitization stemming from the unpleasant affects to which he or she has been exposed in the home.

Another indication of the early link between anger in the family and anger in the child is found in our observations of mothers' and children's interactions in our laboratory apartment. Frequency of anger expressed by mothers in the research apartment is significantly correlated with the frequency of anger displayed by their children ($r = +.47$). There is also a significant correlation between levels of siblings' anger ($r = +.43$). Although associations cannot disentangle influences, they reflect a synchrony of angry affect that describes family interactions.

In summary, these experimental and naturalistic studies converge in finding that, in the first 2 years, environmental stimuli of anger influence children's behavior—by modifying their emotional states and their emotion-related social interactions. The patterned and chronic nature of the affective environment of the family has been shown to have a significant impact on its members (Wallerstein & Kelley, 1981).

Children's Expression of Anger

When Goodenough in 1931 undertook a kind of census of children's anger, she chose the tantrum as an unambiguous index. This study has remained a major source of information about anger in normal children and the preschool years. Hundreds of hours of mothers' observing were required to accumulate frequencies of this kind of out-of-control, dysregulated behavior. But anger occurs in most children in many forms and intensities, as momentary or prolonged dysregulation. Our objective here is to examine the role that anger plays in the day-to-day behavior of children, and some of the modifiers of this behavior. For this purpose, we have drawn on observations of mothers and their toddler-age children interacting in situations representative of day-to-day family routines and demands. To describe anger we have used the percentage of the total (400 to 500) minutes of interaction in which the emotion occurred. Anger or irritability appears, on average, in 7% of the minutes. There is, however, considerable variability, with some children displaying this affect in almost a third of all minutes, others, in none. The amount of anger displayed by the individual toddler shows moderate consistency across days ($r = +.56$). These data suggest that a characteristic affective approach to experience is apparent in many children by 2 to 3 years of age. Although gender differences are small by the index of frequency of anger or irritability (girls 6% and boys 9%), in the psychiatric evaluations of these children, angry oppositional behavior is more likely in the boys than in the girls (Cytryn, McKnew, & Sherman, 1989).

The Socialization of Anger

It was possible to follow the fate of each of the child's displays of anger. What do mothers do when children express anger? To determine how mothers handle children's anger, mothers' responses to each naturally-occurring episode of child anger in the apartment were coded (Kochanska, 1987). Within the toddler age range (2 to 3½ years), age and gender influence how mothers react. The older the child, the less likely is the child's anger to result in the mother's affection and support ($r = -.42$), $p < .005$, the less likely is the mother to inquire about the reasons for the child's anger ($r = -.34$), $p <. 05$, and the more likely is anger to be met by mother's telling the child that anger was not called for ($r = +.38$), $p < .01$. With increasing age, children are increasingly commanded to stop expressing anger ($r = +.33$), $p < .05$. It is increasingly clearly defined as inappropriate.

But within these age trends, the fate of boys' and girls' anger differs. Mothers "give in" to the child's anger by providing gratification desired by the child more often for boys than for girls (27% and 14%, $p < .05$). Well and depressed mothers do not approach boys and girls anger regulation in the same way. The anger of toddler boys mobilizes well mothers' attentive concern. Rarely is boys' anger ignored. Although they tell their sons that displays of anger are not called for, mothers are "soft" on little boys, and the displays result in boys' getting what they want. Well mothers react quite differently to their daughters. They tend to show little attentive concern to toddler-girls' anger. They ignore the anger if it is not compelling or they simply demand that the anger stop. Girls' anger infrequently leads to their getting what they want. Little attention and little reward for girls are quite in contrast to the supportive pattern for boys that would seem not to discourage their anger displays.

These findings are consistent with the work of Haviland, Malatesta, & Lelivica (1984) with college students' responses to the emotional expressions of infants. When the same infants were labeled boys and girls for different respondents, many more interpretations of fear and anger were given for the infants labeled "boy," and more frequent ratings of joy were given the same infants labeled "girl." These labelings follow the gender stereotypes of emotions—the patterns that the well mothers are pursuing. Our speculative projections for the developmental course of anger regulation in children of well mothers would be that, as socialization proceeds, anger of boys and girls would become more "contained." Girls would continue to be subject to both the developmental pressures and the sex-typed measures to contain anger. Boys would be subject to the developmental pressures but would feel freer in expression of anger—both sexes fitting mothers' and society's expectations.

The socialization practices by depressed mothers partly reverses the gender pattern found with the well mothers. It is daughters' anger that brings depressed mothers' attentive involvement and also affection. Their boys more often get reactions that do not involve mothers emotionally. However, boys and girls are similarly frequently given what they want in response to their anger (22% boys, 17% girls).

For speculative interpretations concerning what is happening in depressed mother—child dyads, we have drawn on a larger set of data. We found that depressed mothers are more apprehensive and more critical concerning their children's affective characteristics than are well mothers (Kochanska, Radke-Yarrow, Kuczynski, & Friedman, 1987). Depressed mothers' apprehensive and critical attitudes about their daughters, coupled with their attentive and affectionate responses when confronted with their daughters' anger would seem to create a difficult situation for the little girls, who may feel anxious and guilty about their anger.

Boys of depressed mothers achieve gratification as a result of their displays of anger often enough to make it effective reinforcement. They are not much drawn into the concern and affect of their depressed mothers. The speculation that boys and girls of depressed mothers will express their affective difficulties differently is supported by our earlier findings (Zahn-Waxler, Cummings, McKnew, &

Radke-Yarrow, 1984): When children of depressed mothers showed difficulty in regulating their emotions after exposure to natural and simulated incidents of anger, boys were dysregulated in aggressive behaviors, and girls, in manifestations of distress.

Angry Mothers and Children

Thus far we have described anger but not angry mothers or angry children. From these group analyses, we cannot determine children's individual experiences of anger, their perceptions of themselves and their family, or the influence of anger in their adaptive or maladaptive behaviors. We cannot make predictions of individual developmental trajectories. To move a bit closer to the individual child, we have turned to children who, by one or more criteria, are extremes regarding the total anger in their lives, either as input from others or as their own expressed anger.

We chose eight families in which the mothers ranked highest on anger. Assuming that mothers' behavior in the laboratory reflects their emotions and conduct at home, their children have been exposed to prolonged and greater than usual maternal anger. We wondered how these children's views of themselves and of their families might be influenced. The 5- to 8-year-olds were given a series of pictures involving interpersonal conflict or distress within family or among peers (Zahn-Waxler, Kochanska, Krupnik, & Mayfield, in press) and asked to describe what was going on, assuming that their images of their own families might be imposed on the pictured families.

The descriptions from these eight children were compared to the descriptions given by children coming from the other less angry and nonangry families. The target children displayed, twice as often as the other children, the themes of anger and aggression against the story "mother," often blaming her for her distress (respectively, 25% and 10%). Some children portrayed a malicious story child ("the little girl wanted the mother to cry"). When presented with pictures depicting a conflict between peers, or a crying baby with an older child bent toward the crib, these children produced violent and extreme explanations more frequently than did the comparison children (25% and 16%). Some of their responses were quite hostile: "He pinched the baby in the face"; "Made him cry," "Hit"; "Was messing with the baby." Satisfaction in a distressed or victimized person's suffering was sometimes present ("Called him dummy"; "Made a fool out of him"; "Baby starts crying and he starts laughing").

The story mother figure tended to be pictured as hostile, punitive, prohibiting, and power asserting by the children of the angry mothers (63% as compared to 38% in children of nonangry mothers). When asked to describe the disciplinary techniques of the story mother, they tended to use expressions such as: "She will punish him"; "Spank him"; "She is going to beat the brother." Interestingly, the themes of feeling "sorry" and uneasy when confronting a person in distress were less common among the children of angry mothers than among other children (12% compared to 41%), as were the themes of apology and reparation (37% and 65%). This preliminary qualitative analysis suggests rather strongly that a relationship with an angry mother has consequences not only for heightened anger expression in the child but also for symbolic processes and for how the environment is interpreted.

Data on these children from psychiatric interviews back up the findings from their responses to the pictures. In the interview, all the children but one described their families with bitterness and anger. Parents are described only in negative terms. They describe themselves as feeling best when away from home or wanting to run away. Self-destructive and depressive thoughts were present in eight of the children (e.g., feels she deserves to be punished, feels she is mean too much, feels hopeless, thinks about dying). At the same time, these children also present some strands of good self-images; they have attributes they are proud of, yet all view themselves as "showing temper," being a "troublemaker," and fighting. Although based on a very small sample, the association between mothers' frequent anger and the trilogy of problems in their children—high anger, distressing self-conceptions and feelings, and negative images of their families—leaves little doubt about the pathology in their relationships in the family.

Our second approach to individual analyses was to select the toddlers who themselves were at the extreme of high frequencies of expressed anger. Thirteen children, 9 boys and 4 girls, were identified as extremely angry children. Their profile duplicates the picture of mothers and children when the criterion for extreme anger was anger in the mothers. With three notable exceptions, the mothers of these children are high or relatively high in anger. These extremely angry children come from families of well and depressed mothers. On psychiatric evaluations based on a play interview and observations of child with mother, eight (62%) of these children were rated by the psychiatrists as moderate to high in risk for the development of pathology. (Such a rating occurred in 22% of the total sample.) Of this group of angry toddlers, eight families have thus far been brought back 3 years later for follow-up assessments. On psychiatric evaluations at 5 to 6 years, six of the children had clusters of symptoms in a variety of problem areas (e.g., overanxious, attentional deficit, impulse control). The extreme anger of the 2- to 3-year-old-child is thus a strong signal of problems not only in current functioning, but also a signal of the potential for subsequent developmental problems.

Concluding Comments

We have focused on anger in the lives of young children—their expression of anger and their responses to anger that is expressed around them and to them. Development, gender, and family contexts have been examined in relation to children's anger. We have explored briefly how anger is organized in child personality, and how cognitive and social processes are involved in the child's experience and expression of anger. The findings document the influence of ambient anger in the child's environment and of parents' anger that is directed to the child. Both influence children's affect, perceptions, and conduct. Both appear to increase children's sensitivity and emotionality in the face of anger. Children's anger seems primed by the synchrony of family members' levels of anger. Children's responding to anger appears early (at less than 2 years of age). In the older children (5 to 8 years of age), we have seen how mothers' anger influences children's views of their families.

Anger is understood not as a quality of children, but rather as an interaction of children with their environments. The cycles and spirals of anger between parents and child that Patterson (1982) has described with older children have earlier beginnings and broader beginnings, as evidenced in the present data.

We know very little about how anger is best socialized, but we do know that parents respond variously to children's anger. We need to know more about how parents' different strategies affect the child's regulation of anger. The data discussed here provide a glimpse of different gender-linked socialization experiences with respect to anger. Our interpretation of the transformation of the overt anger of daughters of depressed mothers into anxious and guilty feelings remains speculative. Detailed individual studies combined with group studies will help to come closer to understanding the processes involved.

A most promising frontier in research on children's anger is the study of how, as in the case of other emotions (Bower, 1981; Isen, Shalker, Clark, & Karp, 1978), anger has selecting and organizing influences on children's cognitive and symbolic processes. Experienced anger may result in attribution of anger to others (Dodge, 1980), as well as facilitating recall of events of angry content, building thereby an early legacy for the young child that could only be a developmental risk.

ACKNOWLEDGMENTS

This research was supported by the National Institute of Mental Health and the John D. and Catherine T. MacArthur Foundation, Network on the Transition from Infancy to Early Childhood, Chicago.

We wish to acknowledge the assistance of Frances Go and Elizabeth Crudo in the preparation of this chapter.

REFERENCES

Bower, G. H. (1981). Mood and memory. *American Psychologist, 36*(2), 129–148.
Bridges, K. M. B. (1932). Emotional development in early infancy. *Child Development, 3,* 324–341.

Campos, J., Barrett, K., Lamb, M., Goldsmith, H., & Stenberg, C. (1983). Socioemotional development. In P. Mussen (Ed.), *Handbook of child psychology,* (pp. 783–916). New York: Wiley.

Cummings, E. M., Iannotti, R. J., & Zahn-Waxler, C. (1985). Influence of conflict between adults on the emotions and aggression of young children. *Developmental Psychology, 21*(3), 495–507.

Cummings, E. M., Zahn-Waxler, C., & Radke-Yarrow, M. (1981). Young children's responses to expressions of anger and affection by others in the family. *Child Development, 52,* 1274–1282.

Cytryn, L., McKnew, D. H., & Sherman, T. (1989). *Psychopathological syndromes in childhood.* Unpublished manuscript.

Dodge, K. A. (1980). Social cognition and children's aggressive behavior. *Child Development, 51,* 162–170.

Goodenough, F. L. (1931). *Anger in young children.* Minneapolis: University of Minnesota Press.

Haviland, J., Malatesta, C., & Lelivica, M. (1984). Emotional communication in early infancy. *Infant Mental Health Journal, 5*(3), 135–147.

Hinde, R. A. (1972). Concepts of emotion. *Symposium on Physiology, Emotion and Psychosomatic Illness,* Ciba Foundation, London (pp. 3–13). Amsterdam: Elsevier.

Isen, A., Shalker, T., Clark, M., & Karp, L. (1978). Affect, accessibility of material in memory, and behavior: A cognitive loop. *Journal of Personality and Social Psychology, 36,* 1–12.

Jersild, A. T., & Holmes, F. B. (1935). Children's fears. *Child Development Monograph No. 20.* New York: Columbia University Press.

Jones, M. C. (1924). The elimination of children's fears. *Journal of Experimental Psychology, 7,* 382–390.

Klinnert, M., Campos, J., Soce, I., Emde, R., & Svejda, M. (1983). Emotions as behavior regulators: Social referencing in infancy. In R. Plutchik & H. Kellerman (Eds.), *Emotions in early development: Vol. 2. The emotions.* New York: Academic Press.

Kochanska, G. (1987). *Socialization of young children's anger by well and depressed mothers.* Paper presented at the Biennial Meeting of the Society for Research in Child Development.

Kochanska, G., Radke-Yarrow, M., Kuczynski, L., & Friedman, S. L. (1987). Normal and affectively ill mothers' beliefs about their children. *American Journal of Orthopsychiatry, 57*(3), 345–350.

Lewin, K., Lippitt, R., & White, R. K. (1939). Patterns of aggressive behavior in experimentally created "social climates." *Journal of Social Psychology, 10,* 271–299.

Patterson, G. R. (1982). *Coercive family process.* Eugene, OR: Castillia Press.

Radke-Yarrow, M. (1989). Family environments of depressed and well parents and their children: Issues of research methods. In G. R. Patterson (Ed.), *Aggression and depression in family interactions* (pp. 169–184). New Jersey: Lawrence Erlbaum Associates, Inc., Publishers.

Radke-Yarrow, M., Kuczynski, L., Belmont, B., Stilwell, J., Nottelmann, E., & Welsh, J. (1986). *Affect in families with normal parents and families with depressed parents.* Unpublished manuscript.

Radke-Yarrow, M., & Zahn-Waxler, C. (1984). Roots, motives, and patterns in children's prosocial behavior. In E. Staub, D. Bar Tal, J. Karylowski, & J. Reykowski (Eds.), *Development and maintenance of prosocial behavior* (pp. 81–100). New York and London, Plenum Press.

Radke-Yarrow, M., Zahn-Waxler, C., Cummings, E. M., Strope, B., & Sebris, L. (1981, April). *Continuities and change in the prosocial and aggressive behavior of young children.* Paper presented at the Biennial Meeting of the Society for Research in Child Development.

Wallerstein, J. S., & Kelley, J. B. (1981). *Surviving the breakup: How children and parents cope with divorce.* New York: Basic Books.

Yarrow, M. R., & Waxler, C. Z. (1977). Emergence and functions of prosocial behaviors in young children. In R. D. Parke & E. M. Hetherington (Eds.), *Child psychology: Contemporary readings.* New York: McGraw-Hill.

Zahn-Waxler, C., Cummings, E. M., McKnew, D. H., & Radke-Yarrow, M. (1984). Altruism, aggression, and social interactions in young children of manic–depressive parents. *Child Development, 55,* 112–122.

Zahn-Waxler, C., Kochanska, G., Krupnick, J., & Mayfield, A. (In press). Children's interpretations of interpersonal distress and conflict. *Developmental Psychology.*

Zahn-Waxler, C., McKnew, D. H., Cummings, E. M., Davenport, Y. B., & Radke-Yarrow, M. (1984). Problem behaviors and peer interactions of young children. *The American Journal of Psychiatry, 141*(2), 236–240.

Zahn-Waxler, C., & Radke-Yarrow, M. (1982). The development of altruism: Alternative research strategies. In N. Eisenberg-Berg (Ed.), *The development of prosocial behavior* (pp. 109–137). New York: Academic Press.

IV COPING AND PSYCHOPATHOLOGY

13 Coping and Emotion

Susan Folkman
University of California, San Francisco

Richard S. Lazarus
University of California, Berkeley

Historically, coping has been viewed as a response to emotion. Our purpose here is to evaluate this idea and offer a broader view based on cognitive and relational principles concerning the emotion process. We explore the ways emotion and coping influence each other in what must ultimately be seen as a dynamic, mutually reciprocal relationship.

TRADITIONAL APPROACHES TO EMOTION AND COPING

The emotion and coping relationship has been discussed in the context of two quite distinct systems of thought: the animal and ego psychology models. In the animal model emotion and coping are viewed from a Darwinian phylogenetic perspective (cf. Miller, 1980; Ursin, 1980), which emphasizes learned behaviors that contribute to survival in the face of life-threatening dangers. In the psychoanalytic ego psychology model, coping is defined as cognitive processes, such as denial, repression, suppression, and intellectualization, as well as problem-solving behaviors that are invoked to reduce anxiety and other distressing emotion states (e.g., Menninger, 1963; Vaillant, 1977). The feature that is common to both the animal and ego psychology models is that coping is viewed as a response to emotion and as having the function of arousal or tension reduction.

Within the animal model emotion, which is treated as drive, activation, or arousal, motivates behavioral responses that enable the animal to protect itself and/or vanquish its enemy. Two forms of emotion are emphasized: fear and anger. Fear motivates the behavioral response of avoidance or escape, and anger motivates confrontation or attack.

Emotion has another important survival-related function that is emphasized by ethologists: It communicates what an animal is feeling and hence allows another animal to know whether, for instance, a potential predator is about to attack. The expressive aspect of emotion can also communicate when it is safe to approach, as in mating rituals, or that help is needed, as when expressions of grief in baby monkeys generate sympathy and help in adult monkeys.

Other theorists have made additional suggestions about the adaptive functions of emotion. For example, based on Freud's (1926/1959) later treatment of anxiety, emotion has been viewed as a way of signaling intrapsychically the need for a protective behavioral or ego-defensive response. Mandler (1975) speaks of the interrupt function of emotion, which can be viewed as a way of rechanneling attention and action from an ongoing activity to a new, intrusive emergency. And Tomkins (1965) speaks of emotion as an amplifier that gives greater urgency to appraisals of threat or harm (or for that matter, challenge) and the adaptive response.

There has long been interest in the ways emotion can impair adaptation by interfering with cognitive functioning, as when anxiety interferes with performance (Krohne & Laux, 1982; Spielberger, 1966, 1972; van der Ploeg, Schwarzer, & Spielberger, 1984). Two mechanisms of interference have been emphasized, a motivational one in which attention is redirected from a task at hand to a more pressing emergency (Easterbrook, 1959; Schönpflug, 1983), and a cognitive one in which anxiety-related thoughts impede functioning because they are irrelevant to or counterproductive for performance (Alpert & Haber, 1960; Child & Waterhouse, 1952, 1953; Sarason, Mandler, & Craighill, 1952; see also Lazarus, 1966, for an analysis).

There are several major differences between the animal and ego psychology models of coping. One is that the animal model focuses exclusively on behavioral responses, whereas the ego psychology model focuses more on thoughts (ego processes). A second difference is that the primary criterion of successful coping in the animal model is survival, whereas the ego psychology model includes criteria concerning the quality of the process, such as its adherence to reality and its flexibility (Haan, 1977; Menninger, 1963) as well as a large range of adaptive outcomes including psychological well-being, somatic health, and social functioning.

Two key difficulties inhere in the traditional animal and ego psychology models of coping and emotion. The first is incompleteness, which results from emphasizing emotional arousal or drive tension as the antecedent of coping. Coping is not merely a response to such tension; it is also strongly influenced by

the appraised significance for well-being of what is happening, which is incorporated in the emotional arousal and affects the quality of the emotion, that is,
whether it is anger, fear, guilt, disappointment, etc. Any model that fails to
specify the nature of the cognitive activity in the emotion process is bound to be
ambiguous and incomplete.

The second difficulty is that the relationship between emotion and coping is
unidirectional and static. Undoubtedly emotion both facilitates and interferes
with coping in the ways that the aforementioned theorists have noted. However,
if what is happening is viewed over time, it will be seen that coping can also
affect the emotional reaction. The effects of coping on emotion have not been
emphasized in theory, nor even taken seriously, yet their importance in adaptational encounters seems to us to be equal to, if not greater than, the effects of
emotion on coping. Therefore, our emphasis here is on the flow from coping to
emotion.

COGNITIVE AND RELATIONAL PRINCIPLES
OF EMOTION AND COPING

In this section we briefly present our definitions of emotion, coping, and cognitive appraisal, which is the centerpiece of our theory, and our process-oriented
approach.

Definitions

Emotion. We have defined emotions as complex, organized psychophysiological reactions consisting of cognitive appraisals, action impulses, and patterned somatic reactions (Lazarus, Averill, & Opton, 1970; Lazarus, Kanner, &
Folkman, 1980). The three components operate as a unit rather than as separate
responses, and the patterning of the components reflects the emotion quality and
intensity. Cognitive appraisal is an integral part of the emotion state. Anger, for
example, usually includes an appraisal of a particular kind of harm or threat, and
happiness includes an appraisal that a particular person–environment condition is
beneficial. We have used the term action impulses rather than action to draw
attention to the idea that the action of emotion can be inhibited as well as
expressed. The mobilization that is often involved in action impulses is an
important feature of the third component, the patterned somatic reaction, which
refers to the physiological response profile that uniquely characterizes each emotion quality. (For a discussion of the debate about generalized arousal or specific
response patterns see Lazarus & Folkman, 1984.)

Coping. Coping consists of cognitive and behavioral efforts to manage specific external and/or internal demands that are appraised as taxing or exceeding
the resources of the person. These cognitive and behavioral efforts are constantly
changing as a function of continuous appraisals and reappraisals of the person–

environment relationship, which is also always changing. Some of the changes in relationship result, in part, from coping processes directed at altering the situation that is causing distress (problem-focused coping) and/or regulating distress (emotion-focused coping), from changes in the person that are a result of feedback about what has happened, and from changes in the environment that are independent of the person.

Note that this definition refers to two functions of coping: problem focused and emotion focused. Among the most striking and consistent findings that we and others have replicated (e.g., Baum, Fleming, & Singer, 1983; Folkman & Lazarus, 1980, 1985; Folkman, Lazarus, Dunkel-Schetter, DeLongis, & Gruen, 1986a; McCrae, 1982) is that people rely on both forms of coping, and their subvarieties, in managing the demands of stressful encounters. A full understanding of coping, therefore, requires that both functions be considered, as well as their subtypes.

Cognitive Appraisal. We speak of two forms of appraisal, primary and secondary. In primary appraisal the person asks "What do I have at stake in this encounter?" The answer to the question contributes to the emotion quality and intensity. For example, if self-esteem is at stake there is a potential for shame or anger as well as worry or fear, whereas if one's physical well-being is at stake, only worry and/or fear are likely to be dominant.

In secondary appraisal the concern of the person is "What can I do? What are my options for coping? And how will the environment respond to my actions?" The answer influences the kinds of coping strategies that will be used to manage the demands of the encounter. For example, problem-focused forms of coping are more likely to be used if the outcome of an encounter is appraised as amenable to change, whereas emotion-focused forms of coping are more likely if the outcome is appraised as unchangeable (Folkman & Lazarus, 1980).

Appraisals of person–environment relationships are influenced by antecedent person characteristics such as pattern of motivation (e.g., values, commitments, and goals), beliefs about oneself and the world, and recognition of personal resources for coping such as financial means, social and problem-solving skills, and health and energy. Individual differences in these variables help explain why an encounter may be appraised as a threat by one person and as neutral or a challenge by another. For example, an entrance exam for medical school will be appraised as more relevant to well-being by a student who is deeply motivated to practice medicine than by a student who is not. And given a high level of motivation, the exam will be appraised as more threatening by students who question their ability than by those who are confident, regardless of the realities. Appraisal processes are also influenced by environmental variables such as the nature of the danger, its imminence, ambiguity and duration, and the existence and quality of social support resources to facilitate coping.

Emotion and Coping as Processes

To understand the relationship between emotion and coping it is essential to view them from the standpoint of process, which refers to the changing character of what the person thinks and does during the unfolding of specific person–environment encounters and across encounters. Structural approaches, in contrast, focus on recurrent cognitive, behavioral, and emotional patterns that express more or less stable features of the person's emotional life. A structural approach allows persons to be described as sad, angry, or cheerful (Ortony & Clore, 1981) and assumes stable coping dispositions such as repression-sensitization (Byrne, 1961), fatalism-flexibility (Wheaton, 1983), or irrational cognitive assumptions that dispose the person to react in a characteristic way from occasion to occasion, as in the case of depression (Beck, 1976; Ellis, 1962; Ellis & Bernard, 1985).

Although it is legitimate and useful to assess stable patterns of emotion and coping, they constitute only a part of the total picture. Clinical observation and empirical research (Epstein, 1980; Folkman & Lazarus, 1980, 1985; Folkman, Lazarus, Gruen, & DeLongis, 1986b; Menaghan, 1982) make clear that emotion and coping are normally characterized by a high degree of variability among and within persons. Given the power of environmental conditions to shape reactions, this variability is functional and should not be a surprise. The evidence further suggests that existing measures of coping dispositions do not predict very well how people actually cope in particular encounters (Cohen & Lazarus, 1973).

Furthermore, coping is a multidimensional process. For example, in a series of recent studies (Folkman & Lazarus, 1985; Folkman et al., 1986a; Folkman, Lazarus, Pimley, & Novacek, 1987) we identified eight kinds of coping using the revised 67-item Ways of Coping, which lists a broad range of cognitive and behavioral strategies that people use to manage the demands of specific stressful encounters. Two kinds are primarily problem focused in that they are directed at altering the troubled person–environment relationship. One of these is confrontive and interpersonal, and the second emphasizes planful problem solving. Six additional kinds of coping are primarily emotion focused in that they are directed at managing distress rather than altering the troubled person–environment relationship. These kinds of coping include distancing, escape–avoidance, accepting responsibility or blame, exercising self-control over the expression of feelings, seeking social support, and positive reappraisal. Factor analyses by other investigators who have used the Ways of Coping (e.g., Braukmann, Filipp, Angleitner, & Olbrich, 1981; Felton, Revenson, & Hinrichsen, 1984; Vitaliano, Russo, Carr, Maiuro, & Becker, 1985) have produced similar patterns.

Our designation of the eight kinds of coping as having primarily a problem-focused or emotion-focused function is provisional. The actual function of a given type of coping can be determined only in the context in which it is used. A strategy that is at first glance problem focused, such as making a plan of action,

FOLKMAN AND LAZARUS

can have an emotion-focused function, as when a person who is anxious about having too much to do realizes that the best way to reduce anxiety is to rank order the tasks and get to work on the first one on the list. Conversely, a strategy that is at first glance emotion focused, such as taking a Valium to reduce anxiety, can be problem focused if the person uses it because he or she knows that, in order to work, the anxiety must be reduced. Sometimes a particular strategy can serve both functions simultaneously as, when in the process of seeking advice, a person receives personal affirmation that reduces anxiety as well as task-related information that helps solve the problem.

COPING AS A MEDIATOR OF EMOTIONAL STATES

We have posited that emotion and coping occur in a dynamic mutually reciprocal relationship. The behavioral flow begins with a transaction appraised as significant for the person's well-being, that is, as harmful, beneficial, threatening, or challenging. The appraisal influences coping, which in turn changes the person–environment relationship, and hence the emotional response. Viewed in this way, coping is a *mediator* of the emotional response. The process is summarized in Fig. 13.1.

Mediator variables are often confused with moderator variables. Moderators are antecedent conditions such as personality traits that interact with other conditions in producing an outcome. An example is the goal hierarchy that the person brings to the transaction. This hierarchy interacts with relevant environmental variables to produce an emotional reaction. A mediating variable, on the other hand, is generated in the encounter, and it changes the original relationship between the antecedent and the outcome variable. Coping, for example, arises during the encounter and transforms the original emotion in some way. The difference between moderator and mediator variables is conceptually and methodologically important and is often misunderstood (cf. Frese, 1986; Stone, 1985; Zedeck, 1971).

The mediating effects of coping on emotion have not been widely investigated. Many clinical interventions, however, are based on the premise that the quality of people's emotional lives can be improved by addressing deficiencies in coping skills. And the burgeoning interest in coping in the fields of behavioral medicine and health psychology is also based on the assumption that coping makes a difference in people's psychological and somatic well-being. Yet despite this apparently widely shared conviction, relatively little research has been devoted to finding out in what ways given forms of coping affect emotional responses. Next we outline some of the possible pathways.

Pathways by Which Coping Affects Emotion

The key question is: How do the various forms of coping alter the person–environment relationship, either actually or phenomenologically, and hence the emotional response? We consider three possibilities, namely, change that is

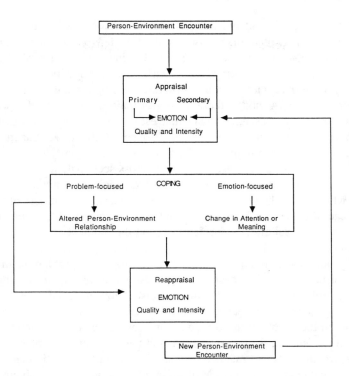

FIG. 13.1. Coping as a mediator of emotion.

brought about by: (a) cognitive activity that influences the deployment of attention, (b) cognitive activity that alters the subjective meaning or significance of
the encounter for well-being, and (c) actions that alter the actual terms of the
person–environment relationship.

1. Deployment of Attention.   This refers to coping activity that diverts attention from the source of distress (avoidant strategies) or directs attention to it
(vigilant strategies).

Coping by avoidance is one of the most common ways people deal with stress.
For example, stress management programs often include jogging, and relaxation.
These are basically techniques for getting away from the source of stress. Vacations and hobbies also fall within this category when their purpose is to get away
from a particular problem, setting, or condition. When such strategies are successful, they neutralize distress emotions, and some strategies such as jogging,
vacations, or hobbies, may have the added benefit of making the person feel
physically better and thereby improve the emotional state. However, avoidant
strategies can also be maladaptive if they draw the person's attention away from a
problem that needs to be addressed.

Another group of avoidant strategies, which we have assessed in our research, seems to be less adaptive than those just described. We have labeled this group *escape-avoidance* on the factored Ways of Coping scale. It describes efforts to escape through wishful thinking (e.g., "wished that the situation would go away or somehow be over with"), eating, drinking, smoking, using drugs or medications, or sleeping. Although these strategies may provide a brief respite from distress, several studies have found that escape-avoidance is associated with symptoms of depression and anxiety (Coyne, Aldwin, & Lazarus, 1981; Folkman et al, 1986b; Vitaliano et al., 1985) and with psychosomatic symptoms (Benner, 1984). Because these studies are cross-sectional, it cannot be determined whether escape-avoidance causes psychological symptoms, or whether people who have such symptoms use escape-avoidance. Regardless of the direction of causality, certain forms of avoidant coping seem less likely than others to produce a beneficial effect, especially beyond the moment.

In contrast to avoidant coping, in which attention is diverted from the problem, vigilant coping strategies direct attention toward the problem in an effort to prevent or control it. The most complete description of vigilant coping is provided by Janis and Mann (1977) in their discussion of decision making under emergency conditions. In our research we assess two forms of coping that focus attention on the problem: information search, which includes strategies such as "I talked to someone to find out more about the situation" and planful problem solving, which includes strategies such as "I made a plan of action and followed it" and "I came up with a couple of different solutions to the problem." These can alter the emotional response in two ways—by leading to plans of action that alter the terms of the person-environment relationship, which ultimately affects the emotional response; and by directly affecting the cognitive appraisals underlying the emotional response.

The mobilization that is involved in vigilance can increase the intensity of emotion. Vigilance that leads to information that things are worse than was previously thought, or that nothing can be done to make things better can also intensify emotion. Finally, vigilance can increase distress in those situations where nothing can be done to alter the outcome of the situation; examples include perseverating with information search beyond the point where anything new is to be learned (cf. Breznitz, 1971; Horowitz, 1976) or with attempts at problem solving when there is no solution (cf. Collins, Baum, & Singer, 1983).

On the other hand, vigilance can reduce distress by increasing understanding and a sense of control (cf. Averill, 1973; Folkman, 1984; Gal & Lazarus, 1975; Rothbaum, Weisz, & Snyder, 1982), even if nothing can be done to alter the outcome. For example, before the advent of antibiotics practitioners of medicine spent a major portion of their time trying to make diagnoses, even though a diagnosis would not mean that anything could be done for the patient. Yet, just having the diagnosis often brought emotional relief to the patient and the patient's family (cf. Thomas, 1983). It may be that an ambiguous state of affairs is often more stressful than knowing even the most negative outcome. Further, the emotional response can change from negative to positive should the information search lead to a plan of action that increases the likelihood of bringing about a favorable outcome.

2. *Changing the Subjective Meaning or Significance of a Person–Environment Transaction.* This type of effect is achieved through cognitive coping activity that ranges from denial-like strategies involving distortion of reality to strategies such as distancing or emphasizing the positive aspects of a situation, which depend on selective attention or interpretation.

We cannot undertake a discussion of the effects of denial on the emotional response here (see Lazarus, 1983; Breznitz, 1983a, 1983b for a discussion of denial in the context of stress). However, we do want to point out that the extent to which denial and denial-like processes alter the quality and intensity of the emotional response depends in part on what is being denied.

Distancing describes efforts to detach oneself, such as "Didn't let it get to me—refused to think about it too much," and "Made light of the situation; refused to get too serious about it." In distancing, the person acknowledges the troubling problem but doesn't want to deal with its emotional significance. Distancing can be used to help people get through extremely stressful situations. For example, nurses in intensive care units use distancing to deal with the unrelenting life-threatening medical crises of their patients without falling apart emotionally (Hay & Oken, 1972). We think of the use of humor in the operating room (e.g., M*A*S*H) as another form of distancing.

Distancing should not interfere with successful problem solving; in fact, as the preceding illustrations suggest, it can actually enable problem solving in situations that are highly stressful. Distancing may also be adaptive in situations where nothing can be done, as when awaiting the outcome of a biopsy. For example, let us say parents are awaiting biopsy results on one of their children. Although there is nothing to do as far as the biopsy is concerned, the parents must tend to their other children's needs too. Successful distancing helps to keep the parents from being totally preoccupied about the biopsy and allows them to function in their parenting and other roles.

Also of interest are those cognitive coping strategies that involve selective attention that not only diminish the negative emotional response but generate positive emotional responses as well. Such strategies include positive comparisons (e.g., Taylor, Wood, & Lichtman, 1983), cognitive restructuring (e.g., Pearlin & Schooler, 1978), comforting cognitions (Mechanic, 1962), and positive reappraisal (Folkman et al., 1986a). These strategies operate by influencing the appraisal process at two different phases of stressful encounters: the anticipatory phase and the outcome phase.

During the anticipatory phase of an encounter, cognitive coping strategies can transform a threat appraisal into a challenge through their effect on secondary appraisal. For example, an upcoming exam in which students have a major stake can be transformed from a threat into a challenge if they consider their coping resources (i.e., ability and time for study) as adequate to the task. It is important to note too that the appraisal of coping resources may itself rest on cognitive coping processes that support what may be an illusion (i.e., the person may be overestimating the available resources). To the extent that the illusion remains intact throughout the preparation period, the student's response is likely to include positive or challenge emotions, such as confidence, hopefulness, and perhaps eagerness, as well as negative emotions such as anxiety.

Another way cognitive coping can transform a threat into a challenge is through focusing on the possibilities for mastery or growth that inhere in a troubled person–environment relationship. Lipowski (1970–1971), for example, speaks of patients who view illness as a challenge, that is "like any other life situation which imposes specific demands and tasks to be mastered and which is accomplished by any means available" (p. 98). There are also numerous anecdotal accounts of cancer patients who transform their appraisal of their fight for life from a threat to a challenge (cf. Moos, 1977).

We have also investigated cognitive coping used to extract positive meaning from harm that has already occurred (Folkman et al, 1986a, 1986b; Folkman & Lazarus, 1988). This form of cognitive coping, which we call positive reappraisal, comes into play at the outcome stage of an encounter. We assess it with items such as "I changed or grew as a person in a good way" and "I came out of the experience better than when I went in." Wortman and her colleagues (e.g., Bulman & Wortman, 1977; Silver & Wortman, 1980) point to the importance of this form of coping in coming to terms with the effects of severe life events. Positive reappraisal can generate benefit emotions such as pride and satisfaction and perhaps reduce harm emotions such as anger and sadness.

The extent to which cognitive coping strategies work depends in part on how much distortion of reality is involved, and whether or not the cognitive construction is likely to be challenged by the environment, as when, for example, an illness that is denied or construed optimistically goes precipitously downhill. A major distortion of reality can be sustained longer if the person is well defended. Presumably such persons are impervious to cues from within themselves or from the environment that contradict the cognitive construction. However, most people are not so well defended that a major distortion of reality can be sustained in the face of continuing evidence to the contrary. Major distortions, such as the denial that a person has died or that one has lost the use of one's legs, are usually temporary and often seen as a stage in bereavement or recovery from a trauma (Horowitz, 1976).

The reduction of distress that is achieved through distancing or denial can be fragile in the face of an unexpected cue from the environment, which can redintegrate the full significance of the encounter. For example, a woman's efforts to put the pending results of a biopsy out of her mind can easily fail if she unexpectedly hears a report about cancer on her car radio, or in passing sees a friend who had a bout with cancer the previous year. Efforts at distancing or denial may also be undermined by cues from within the person in the form of fleeting cognitions or images, or what Horowitz (1976) calls intrusive thoughts. Thus, the effects of cognitive coping processes on the emotional response may only be temporary. If the person reinstitutes the coping strategy after an interruption, the pattern may appear cyclical, such that a period of calm is followed by a period of increased distress.

The palliative effects of strategies that involve selective attention are probably easier to sustain and less likely to be challenged by observers than strategies that involve a distortion of reality, especially if they appear to be boosting morale without interfering with functioning. Indeed, people are often coaxed into using positive reappraisal after a harm has occurred to help them diminish their distress and regain positive morale. People who are laid off from their jobs, for example, are told to look on the event as a challenge, as a chance to change directions, learn new skills, maybe even move to a different part of the country. In such cases, the environment is likely to collaborate with the person in sustaining this kind of cognitive construction.

3. Changing the Actual Terms of the Person–Environment Relationship. This is brought about through what we call problem-focused coping, which involves cognitive problem solving as well as direct action on the environment or on oneself. Our assessment procedures cover two forms of problem-focused coping. One is a confrontive, somewhat aggressive interpersonal form that includes strategies such as "stood my ground and fought for what I wanted" and "tried to get the person responsible to change his or her mind." The second describes rational and planful problem-solving techniques that we mentioned earlier (e.g., "I made a plan of action and followed it" and "I came up with a couple of different solutions to the problem").

Changes in the emotional response depend on a number of factors. One is the extent to which problem-focused forms of coping bring about a desired outcome. An ideal outcome would include a permanent resolution that is satisfactory to the person and to others. However, many real-life stressful encounters do not end quite so neatly. Sometimes resolutions are only partially satisfactory; sometimes there is no resolution at all; and sometimes even if there is a resolution there is little assurance that the situation will not happen again.

A second factor on which the quality of the outcome depends is the person's evaluation of his or her performance. An encounter outcome that is successful by most standards may still be appraised negatively by persons who are not easily satisfied, or who consider the way they conducted themselves or reacted emotionally to be unacceptable.

A third factor concerns the implications of the present encounter for the future. Even a successfully resolved encounter can have threatening implications, as when a student who receives a high grade on an exam experiences threat emotions because of the expectations that the present performance creates for future performances. The varying shades of successful and unsuccessful outcomes and the many dimensions on which outcomes are evaluated mean that the emotional response at the outcome phase of an encounter is likely to be a complex mixture of positive and negative emotions, which is, in fact, what we have found in our research (e.g., Folkman & Lazarus, 1985, 1988).

An important consideration overall in understanding how problem-focused coping alters the person–environment relationship and hence affects the emotional response is the interpersonal aspect of coping. For example, the somewhat aggressive and hostile character of confrontive coping (as we assess it) is likely to generate negative emotions in the person who is being confronted, which in turn can lead to a downward spiral in the person–environment relationship. This pattern has been discussed in the context of depression by Coyne (1976), who pointed out that depressed people interact with others in a way that drives others away.

We found support for this idea in a study in which we compared people who were high and low in depressive symptoms (Folkman & Lazarus, 1986). Those high in symptoms used significantly more confrontive coping and at the same time more self-controlling coping processes (efforts to keep one's feelings to oneself) than those low in symptoms. They also reported more anger and hostility during their encounters. The self-controlling coping may have been used to try to regulate the hostile impulses. Although our data did not provide information as to whether or not the depressed subjects' pattern of coping and emotion caused other people to disapprove or withdraw, the inference is plausible and consistent with theories of depression.

People who engage in rational, planful problem solving, on the other hand, are less likely to communicate hostility than those who use confrontive coping. Instead, their demeanor is likely to be relatively calm and friendly and may even invite others to provide support. This is, in fact, what we observed in a study of the relationship between coping and support received in stressful encounters (Dunkel-Schetter, Folkman, & Lazarus, 1987). Planful problem solving acted as a strong elicitor of all types of support (emotional, tangible, and informational). Confrontive coping, in contrast, elicited primarily information rather than emotional support or tangible assistance.

The interpersonal effects of coping are not limited to problem-focused forms of coping. For example, the reduction of distress that is achieved through coping strategies such as distancing and escape–avoidance can simultaneously reduce the possibility of open communications with a spouse or close other at a time when such communications may be mutually beneficial. This could produce a secondary effect on the interpersonal relationship in that the spouse or close other might feel rejected or unappreciated and respond with sadness, frustration, or resentment.

Although in reviewing the three factors affecting the person–environment relationship noted previously we have emphasized the effects of problem-focused coping on the emotional response, it is important to recognize that the quality of problem-focused coping, and hence its impact on the emotional response, also depends in part on the successful regulation of negative emotions, in effect, on emotion-focused coping. Too much emotional intensity could interfere with the cognitive functioning that is necessary for effective problem-focused coping (cf. Easterbrook, 1959; Heckhausen, 1982; Sarason, 1975). A parent whose child has been injured, for example, knows that distress must be controlled in order to take the steps necessary to get the help the child needs. Also, unregulated emotional intensity might frighten off the person on whom this individual depends for advice or information. Yet there is evidence that a modest degree of intensity has a motivating property that can facilitate problem-focused coping (Yerkes & Dodson, 1908), an idea that emphasizes emotions as antecedents of coping, which we mentioned earlier.

Furthermore, whether negative emotions have a different impact on problem-focused coping than positive emotions have is addressed in a study by Goodhart (1986). Goodhart observed that positive thinking facilitated performance when the thoughts were relevant to the task and when subjects had positive expectations. However, in those situations where one or the other of these conditions was not met, negative thoughts led to better performance than positive thoughts. Because positive thoughts produce positive emotions and negative thoughts negative emotions, Goodhart's study suggests that both types of emotions can facilitate problem-focused coping, depending on the context.

Research Support for the Impact of Coping on Emotion

Previously we have suggested certain ways in which coping can mediate emotions during stressful encounters. Some of our recent research findings (Folkman & Lazarus, 1988) provide empirical support for such a process. We interviewed subjects monthly for 5 months about a recently experienced stressful encounter, asking them to describe the emotions they experienced at the beginning of the stressful encounter and, for those encounters that were concluded at the time of the interview, the emotions they experienced at the end of the encounter. Subjects also described the ways they coped with the demands of the encounter. This information allowed us to ask about the extent to which coping actively mediated the relationship between the emotions subjects reported at the beginning and at the end of each of their encounters.

The sample was composed of 75 married couples with at least one child living at home. The average age of the men was 41.4 years and the average age of the women was 39.6 years. The participants were Caucasian and Protestant or Catholic, and for the most part upper-middle class (mean number of years of education was 15.5 years and the median family income was $45,000).

The measure of emotion used in this study is described elsewhere (Folkman & Lazarus, 1986). Briefly, subjects rated on Likert scales the extent to which they experienced each of a number of emotions at the beginning and end of the stressful encounter. A factor analysis of these emotions suggested four scales:

disgusted/angry; pleased/happy; worried/fearful; and confident/secure. Coping was measured with eight scales derived from factor analyses of the Ways of Coping. These scales, which were mentioned earlier, include confrontive coping, distancing, self-controlling, seeking social support, accepting responsibility, escape–avoidance, planful problem solving, and positive reappraisal.

The extent to which coping mediated the emotional response was evaluated with four hierarchical regression analyses, one for each of the outcome emotion scales. All the concluded encounters were used in the analysis, which meant that each subject had multiple scores. To control for the intercorrelation due to dependent data, the means for each person on each of the variables in the analysis were entered on Step 1. This allowed us to examine the contribution of the remaining variables to the variance around each person's mean. The score on the emotion scale derived from the beginning of the encounter was entered on Step 2, and those on the coping scales were entered on Step 3. In three of the four regression analyses, coping contributed significantly to the variance in outcome emotions over and above that contributed by the emotions at the beginning of the encounter. The exception was the worried/fearful scale. The regression analyses are summarized in Table 13.1.

Because the data were all retrospective, we cannot make definitive causal statements. However, the results suggest that coping is indeed a significant mediator of the emotional response in actual stressful encounters. In the three regression analyses where the mediating effect of coping was significant, the same four coping strategies contributed significantly to the explained variance; planful problem solving and positive reappraisal were significantly and positively associated with the variances of the pleased/happy scale and the confident/secure scale, whereas confrontive coping and distancing were significantly and negatively associated with these scales. The pattern of association was reversed for the angry/disgusted scale: planful problem solving and positive reappraisal were negatively correlated, and distancing and confrontive coping were positively correlated.

It was fascinating to us that one pattern of problem- and emotion-focused coping (planful problem solving and positive reappraisal) contributed to an improved emotional state, whereas a different pattern (confrontive coping and distancing) appeared to make the emotional state worse. The effects of planful problem solving, positive reappraisal, and confrontive coping were consistent with the analysis presented earlier. However, the effects of distancing deviated from our theoretical expectations that it should help reduce distress. Distancing may have positive value as a mediator of emotion only for limited periods and only in certain kinds of encounters, as we noted earlier. To the extent that distancing does not work, not only might it fail to diminish distress, but it might even be associated with increases in distress because of interference with problem solving, as when a woman with a breast lump denies its significance and fails to seek medical attention (Katz, Weiner, Gallagher, & Hellman, 1970;

TABLE 13.1
Coping as Mediator of Emotions: Summary of Regression Analyses

Emotion Scale	R^2	Adj. R^2	R^2 Chg.	$B+$
Worried/Fearful (N = 443)				
Step 1: Scale means	.56	.55		
Step 2: Emotions at beginning				
of encounter	.58	.57	.02***	.18***
Step 3: Coping scales	.60	.58	.01 (ns)	
Disgusted/Angry (N = 444)				
Step 1: Scale means	.44	.43		
Step 2: Emotions at beginning				
of encounter	.49	.48	.04***	.14***
Step 3: Coping scales	.58	.58	.09***	
Distancing				.17***
Planful problem-solving				−.20***
Confrontive coping				.27***
Positive reappraisal				−.24***
Confident/Secure (N = 444)				
Step 1: Scale means	.58	.57		
Step 2: Emotions at beginning				
of encounter	.63	.62	.04***	.24***
Step 3: Coping scales	.68	.66	.05***	
Accept responsibility				−.08*
Confrontive coping				−.08*
Distancing				−.11**
Planful problem-solving				.14***
Positive reappraisal				.19***
Pleased/Happy (N = 442)				
Step 1: Scale means	.46	.45		
Step 2: Emotions at beginning				
of encounter	.52	.51	.06***	.24***
Step 3: Coping scales	.61	.59	.08***	
Confrontive coping				−.22***
Distancing				−.11*
Planful problem-solving				.19***
Positive reappraisal				.25***

+ standardized beta coefficient
*p < .05
**p < .01
***p < .001

Lazarus, 1983). As we have stated elsewhere, it is important to determine the conditions under which distancing (as well as other forms of coping) works or does not work if we are to understand the role of coping in emotion and consider ways of influencing it clinically.

Coping Effectiveness and the Emotional Response

Elsewhere we have pointed out that a key factor in coping effectiveness is whether or not the choice of coping strategy fits the possibilities for coping in an encounter (Folkman, 1984; Lazarus & Folkman, 1984). The major criterion has to do with the extent to which an outcome is within the person's control (cf. Bandura, 1977). If it is, problem-focused forms of coping that are intended to achieve the desired outcome are appropriate, and emotion-focused forms of coping that interfere with problem-focused coping are inappropriate. If, however, the desired outcome is not within the person's control, problem-focused forms of coping are inappropriate, and emotion-focused forms of coping that promote the reduction of distress are appropriate. In our view, coping strategies that have a poor fit with the actual conditions will ultimately have an adverse effect on the emotional response, regardless of any temporary benefits. Thus, problem-solving strategies that are applied to a situation in which no solution is possible are likely to generate frustration and anger, regardless of the quality of problem-solving activity.

The temporal ordering of coping strategies also influences coping effectiveness. For instance, often it is not clear at the outset whether or not an outcome is amenable to change. Clarification may depend on a certain amount of problem-focused coping, such as information search. If avoidant or denial-like processes are called into play prematurely, they can interfere with the information search and thereby prevent a realistic appraisal of the options for coping. In such cases emotional relief in the short run is purchased at the expense of long-run, effective problem-focused coping. On the other hand, as noted earlier, denial-like coping, distancing, and positive reappraisal are likely to be useful when they follow an information search that reveals that an outcome is not amenable to change. (For a full discussion of the costs and benefits of denial and denial-like strategies, see Lazarus, 1983.)

Another interesting feature of coping effectiveness concerns the use of seemingly contradictory coping strategies within the same encounter. We noted one example earlier, namely, the use of self-controlling and confrontive coping within the same encounter. These two forms of coping are moderately correlated (Folkman et al., 1986a). One explanation is that self-control is used along with confrontive coping to moderate the latter's hostile component. Another explanation is that confrontive coping represents a failure of self-control. Although the presence of two forms of coping may at first appear to be contradictory, when they are viewed temporally as efforts to regulate an emotional state while trying to alter the troubled person–environment relationship, their functions appear complementary.

In general, the less effective a given strategy is, the more likely it is that a person will be forced to turn to a different strategy, which is another reason sometimes contradictory forms of coping may be used during the course of a single encounter. If distancing fails, for example, a person might try escape–avoidance. And if escape–avoidance fails, the person might seek social support or use confrontation. This hypothesis receives some support from studies that show that depressed people tend to use more coping strategies, regardless of type, than nondepressed people (e.g., Coyne et al, 1981; Folkman & Lazarus, 1986). The sequence of coping activity in such cases can generate a volatile and complex emotional response.

CONCLUDING COMMENTS

Two principles need to be emphasized. The first is that every encounter, even the most simple, is usually complex and contains multiple facets and implications for well-being that either exist side by side or arise sequentially. This is why there can be more than one emotion in any encounter, and sometimes contradictory ones, as has been seen in younger children who can feel both happy and sad about what has transpired (Harris, 1985; Terwogt, Schene, & Harris, 1985) and in students preparing for exams (Folkman & Lazarus, 1985). To understand the emotion process, therefore, each emotion must be linked analytically to the cognitive appraisal that influences it.

The second principle concerns the temporal and unfolding quality of emotion and coping processes. Social scientists, especially those dealing with disaster, have long recognized that an encounter involving harm or benefit often has three or more stages—anticipation, confrontation, and postconfrontation. Coping in an anticipatory context offers an important opportunity to influence what happens at the point of confrontation by preventing or ameliorating a harm or facilitating a benefit. After confrontation, coping must be aimed at managing the consequences and their implications for the future. Emotions constantly shift throughout this process according to the changing status of the person–environment relationship. It is surprising that to date so little systematic attention has been given to the temporal aspects of the emotion process and to the place of coping within it.

Together, these two principles highlight the complex and dynamic nature of emotions and coping in social encounters and point the way for us to investigate empirically the precise mechanisms through which coping mediates the emotional response. Once their importance in emotion and adaptation is realized, the limitations of static, cross-sectional research designs and theoretical models reminiscent of stimulus–response formulations of the recent past become unacceptable, and systems analyses of the emotion process and research designs that permit intraindividual analysis of the temporal flow of many person and environment variables become mandatory.

REFERENCES

Alpert, R., & Haber, R. N. (1960). Anxiety in academic achievement situations. *Journal of Abnormal & Social Psychology, 61,* 207–215.

Averill, J. R. (1973). Personal control over aversive stimuli and its relationship to stress. *Psychological Bulletin, 80,* 286–303.

Bandura, A. (1977). Self-efficacy: Toward a unifying theory of behavior change. *Psychological Review, 84,* 191–215.

Baum, A., Fleming, R. E., & Singer, J. E. (1983). Coping with technological disaster. *Journal of Social Issues, 39,* 117–138.

Beck, A. T. (1976). *Cognitive therapy and the emotional disorders.* New York: International Universities Press.

Benner, P. (1984). *Stress and satisfaction on the job: Work meanings and coping of mid-career men.* New York: Praeger.

Braukmann, W., Filipp, S-H., Angleitner, A., & Olbrich, E. (1981, September). *Problem-solving and coping with critical life-events—A life-span developmental study.* Paper presented at "First European Meeting on Cognitive-Behavioral Therapy," Kisboa, Portugal.

Breznitz, S. (1971). A study of worrying. *British Journal of Social and Clinical Psychology, 10,* 271–279.

Breznitz, S. (Ed.) (1983a). *The denial of stress.* New York: International Universities Press.

Breznitz, S. (1983b). The seven kinds of denial. In S. Breznitz (Ed.), *The denial of stress.* New York: International Universities Press.

Bulman, R. J., & Wortman, C. B. (1977). Attribution of blame and coping in the "Real World": Severe accident victims react to their lot. *Journal of Personality and Social Psychology, 35,* 351–363.

Byrne, D. (1961). The repression-sensitization scale: Rationale, reliability, and validity. *Journal of Personality, 29,* 334–349.

Child, I. L., & Waterhouse, I. K. (1952). Frustration and the quality of performance: I. A critique of the Barker, Dembo, & Lewin experiment. *Psychological Review, 59,* 351–362.

Child, I. L., & Waterhouse, I. K. (1953). Frustration and the quality of performance: II. A theoretical statement. *Psychological Review, 60,* 127–139.

Cohen, F., & Lazarus, R. S. (1973). Active coping processes, coping dispositions, and recovery from surgery. *Psychosomatic Medicine, 35,* 375–389.

Collins, D. L., Baum, A., & Singer, J. E. (1983). Coping with chronic stress at Three Mile Island: Psychological and biochemical evidence. *Health Psychology, 2,* 149–166.

Coyne, J. C. (1976). Depression and the response of others. *Journal of Abnormal Psychology, 85,* 186–193.

Coyne, J. C., Aldwin, C., & Lazarus, R. S. (1981). Depression and coping in stressful episodes. *Journal of Abnormal Psychology, 90,* 439–447.

Dunkel-Schetter, C., Folkman, S., & Lazarus, R. S. Correlates of social support receipt. *Journal of Personality and Social Psychology, 53,* 71–80.

Easterbrook, J. A. (1959). The effect of emotion on cue utilization and the organization of behavior. *Psychological Review, 66,* 183–201.

Ellis, A. (1962). *Reason and emotion in psychotherapy.* New York: Lyle Stuart.

Ellis, A., & Bernard, M. E. (1985). What is rational-emotive therapy (RET)? In A. Ellis & M. E. Bernard (Eds.), *Clinical applications of rational-emotive therapy* (pp. 1–30). New York: Plenum Press.

Epstein, S. (1980). The stability of behavior: II. Implications for psychological research. *American Psychologist, 35,* 790–806.

Felton, B. J., Revenson, T. A., & Hinrichsen, G. A. (1984). Coping and adjustment in chronically ill adults. *Social Science and Medicine, 18,* 889–898.

Folkman, S. (1984). Personal control and stress and coping processes: A theoretical analysis. *Journal of Personality and Social Psychology, 46,* 839–852.

Folkman S., & Lazarus, R. S. (1980). An analysis of coping in a middle-aged community sample. *Journal of Health and Social Behavior, 21,* 219–239.

Folkman, S., & Lazarus, R. S. (1985). If it changes it must be a process: Study of emotion and coping during three stages of a college examination. *Journal of Personality and Social Psychology, 48,* 150–170.

Folkman, S., & Lazarus, R. S. (1986). Stress processes and depressive symptomatology. *Journal of Abnormal Psychology, 95,* 107–113.

Folkman, S., & Lazarus, R. S. (1988). Coping as a mediator of emotions. *Journal of Personality and Social Psychology, 54,* 466–475.

Folkman, S., & Lazarus, R. S., Dunkel-Schetter, C., DeLongis, A., & Gruen, R. (1986a). The dynamics of a stressful encounter: Cognitive appraisal, coping, and encounter outcomes. *Journal of Personality and Social Psychology, 50,* 992–1003.

Folkman, S., & Lazarus, R. S., Gruen, R., & DeLongis, A. (1986b). Appraisal, coping, health status, and psychological symptoms. *Journal of Personality and Social Psychology, 50,* 571–579.

Folkman, S., & Lazarus, R. S., Pimley, S., & Novacek, J. (1987). Age differences in stress and coping processes. *Psychology and Aging, 2,* 171–184.

Frese, M. (1986). Coping as a moderator and mediator between stress at work and psychosomatic complaints. In M. Appley & R. Trumbull (Eds.), *Dynamics of stress* (pp. 183–206). New York: Plenum.

Freud, S. (1959). Inhibitions, symptoms, and anxiety. *Standard Edition, 20.* London: Hogarth (originally published 1926).

Gal, R., & Lazarus, R. S. (1975). The role of activity in anticipating and confronting stressful situations. *Journal of Human Stress, 1,* 4–20.

Goodhart, D. (1986). The effects of positive and negative thinking on performance in an achievement situation. *Journal of Personality and Social Psychology, 51,* 117–124.

Haan, N. (1977). *Coping and defending: Processes of self-environment organization.* New York: Academic Press.

Harris, P. L. (1985). What children know about the situations that provoke emotion. In M. Lewis & C. Saarni (Eds.), *The socialization of affect* (pp. 161–185). New York: Plenum Press.

Hay, D., & Oken, S. (1972). The psychological stresses of intensive care unit nursing. *Psychosomatic Medicine, 34,* 109–118.

Heckhausen, H. (1982). Task-irrelevant cognitions during an exam: Incidence and effects. In H. W. Krohne & L. Laux (Eds.), *Achievement, stress, and anxiety* (pp. 247–274). Washington, DC: Hemisphere.

Horowitz, M. (1976). *Stress response syndromes.* New York: Jason Aronson.

Janis, I., & Mann, L. (1977). *Decision making.* New York: The Free Press.

Katz, J. J., Weiner, H., Gallagher, T. G., & Hellman, L. (1970). Stress, distress, and ego defenses. *Archives of General Psychiatry, 23,* 131–142.

Krohne, H. W., & Laux, L. (Eds.) (1982). *Achievement, stress, and anxiety.* Washington, DC: Hemisphere.

Lazarus, R. S. (1966). *Psychological stress and the coping process.* New York: McGraw-Hill.

Lazarus, R. S. (1983). The costs and benefits of denial. In S. Breznitz (Ed.), *The denial of stress* (pp. 1–30). New York: International Universities Press.

Lazarus, R. S., Averill, J. R., & Opton, E. M., Jr. (1970). Toward a cognitive theory of emotions. In M. Arnold (Ed.), *Feelings and emotions* (pp. 207–232). New York: Academic Press.

Lazarus, R. S., & Folkman, S. (1984). *Stress, appraisal, and coping.* New York: Springer.

Lazarus, R. S., Kanner, A. D., & Folkman, S. (1980). Emotions: A cognitive-phenomenological analysis. In R. Plutchik & H. Kellerman (Eds.), *Theories of emotion.* New York: Academic Press.

Lipowski, Z. J. (1970–71). Physical illness, the individual and the coping process. *International Journal of Psychiatry in Medicine, 1,* 91–102.

Mandler, G. (1975). *Mind and emotion.* New York: Wiley.

McCrae, R. R. (1982). Age differences in the use of coping mechanisms. *Journal of Gerontology, 37,* 454–560.

Mechanic, D. (1962). *Students under stress: A study in the social psychology of adaptation.* New York: The Free Press. (Reprinted in 1978 by the University of Wisconsin Press.)

Menaghan, E. (1982). Measuring coping effectiveness: A panel analysis of marital problems and efforts. *Journal of Health and Social Behavior, 23,* 220–234.

Menninger, K. (1963). *The vital balance: The life process in mental health and illness.* New York: Viking.

Miller, N. E. (1980). Applications of learning and biofeedback to psychiatry and medicine. In H. I. Kaplan, A. M. Freedman, & B. J. Sadock (Eds.), *Comprehensive textbook of psychiatry, III* (pp. 468–484). Baltimore: Williams & Wilkins.

Moos, R. H. (Ed.) (1977). *Coping with physical illness.* New York: Plenum.

Ortony, A., & Clore, G. L. (1981). Disentangling the affective lexicon. In *Proceedings of the Third Annual Conference of the Cognitive Science Society,* Berkeley, CA.

Pearlin, L. I., & Schooler, C. (1978). The structure of coping. *Journal of Health and Social Behavior, 19,* 2–21.

Rothbaum, F., Weisz, J. R., & Snyder, S. S. (1982). Changing the world and changing the self: A two-process model of perceived control. *Journal of Personality and Social Psychology, 42,* 5–37.

Sarason, I. G. (1975). Test anxiety, attention, and the general problem of anxiety. In C. D. Spielberger & I. G. Sarason (Eds.), *Stress and anxiety* (Vol. 1, pp. 165–187). Washington, DC: Hemisphere.

Sarason, S. B., Mandler, G., & Craighill, P. C. (1952). The effect of differential instructions on anxiety and learning. *Journal of Abnormal and Social Psychology, 47,* 561–565.

Schönpflug, W. (1983). Coping efficiency and situational demands. In G. R. J. Hockey (Ed.), *Stress and fatigue in human performance* (pp. 299–330). New York: Wiley.

Silver, R. L., & Wortman, C. B. (1980). Coping with undesirable life events. In J. Garber & M. E. P. Seligman (Eds.), *Human helplessness: Theory and applications* (pp. 279–340). New York: Academic Press.

Spielberger, C. D. (Ed.) (1966). *Anxiety and behavior.* New York: Academic Press.

Spielberger, C. D. (Ed.) (1972). *Anxiety: Current trends in theory and research* (Vols. 1 & 2). New York: Academic Press.

Stone, A. A. (1985). Assessment of coping efficacy: A comment. *Journal of Behavioral Medicine, 8,* 115–117.

Taylor, S. E., Wood, J. V., & Lichtman, R. R. (1983). It could be worse: Selective evaluation as a response to victimization. In R. Janoff-Bulman & I. H. Frieze (Eds.), *Reactions to victimization. Journal of Social Issues, 39*(2), 19–40.

Terwogt, M. M., Schene, J., & Harris, P. L. (1985, June 23–26). *Self-control of emotional reactions by young children.* Presented at meetings of the International Society for Research on Emotion, Cambridge, MA.

Thomas, L. (1983). *The youngest science.* New York: The Viking Press.

Tomkins, S. S. (1965). Affect and the psychology of knowledge. In S. S. Tomkins & C. E. Izard (Eds.), *Affect, cognition, and personality* (pp. 72–97). New York: Springer.

Ursin, H. (1980). Personality, activation and somatic health. In S. Levine & H. Ursin (Eds.), *Coping and health* (NATO Conference Series III: Human factors). New York: Plenum Press.

Vaillant, G. E. (1977). *Adaptation to life.* Boston: Little, Brown.

van der Ploeg, H. M., Schwarzer, R., & Spielberger, C. D. (1984). *Advances in test anxiety research* (Vol. 3). Hillsdale, NJ: Lawrence Erlbaum Associates.

Vitaliano, P. P., Russo, J., Carr, J. E., Maiuro, R. D., & Becker, J. (1985). The Ways of Coping checklist: Revision and psychometric properties. *Multivariate Behavioral Research, 20,* 3–26.

Wheaton, B. (1983). Stress, personal coping resources, and psychiatric symptoms: An investigation of interactive models. *Journal of Health and Social Behavior, 24,* 208–229.

Yerkes, R. M., & Dodson, J. D. (1908). The relation of strength of stimulus to rapidity of habit-formation. *Journal of Comparative Neurology and Psychology, 18,* 459–482.

Zedeck, S. (1971). Problem with the use of "moderator" variables. *Psychological Bulletin, 76,* 295–310.

14

The Hopelessness Theory of Depression: Current Status and Future Directions

Lyn Y. Abramson
University of Wisconsin-Madison

Lauren B. Alloy
Temple University

Gerald I. Metalsky
University of Texas-Austin

Recently, we (Abramson, Metalsky, & Alloy, 1989) proposed a revision of the 1978 reformulated theory of helplessness and depression (Abramson, Seligman, & Teasdale, 1978) and called it the hopelessness theory of depression. Our motive for proposing the revision was that, although the 1978 reformulation generated a vast amount of empirical work on depression over the past 10 years (see Sweeney, Anderson, & Bailey, 1986, for a meta-analysis of 104 studies) and recently has been evaluated as a model of depression (Barnett & Gotlib, 1988; Brewin, 1985; Coyne & Gotlib, 1983; Peterson & Seligman, 1984), the 1978 article did not explicitly present a clearly articulated theory of depression. Instead, it presented an attributional account of human helplessness and only briefly discussed its implications for depression. Perhaps it is no surprise, then, that much controversy existed about the status of the reformulated theory of depression (e.g., Abramson, Alloy, & Metalsky, 1988a; Abramson, Metalsky, & Alloy, 1988b; Alloy, Abramson, Metalsky, & Hartlage, 1988; Barnett & Gotlib, 1988; Brewin, 1985; Coyne & Gotlib, 1983; Peterson & Seligman, 1984).

In this chapter we present the hopelessness theory of depression. The hopelessness theory posits the existence of an as yet unidentified subtype of depression, *hopelessness depression*. We describe the hypothesized cause, symptoms, course, therapy, and prevention of hopelessness depression as well as its relation to other types of depression and "nondepression." In addition, we discuss how to search for hopelessness depression to see if it exists in nature and conforms to its theoretical description. Finally, because the hopelessness theory is new, the evidence about its validity is not yet in. However, we have conducted a number of studies to test it and will report them. Also, many of the studies conducted to test the reformulated theory as well as other clinical and empirical work on depression are relevant to evaluating the hopelessness theory although few provide a direct test.

PRELIMINARY CONCEPTS

In presenting the hopelessness theory, it is helpful to distinguish among the concepts of *necessary, sufficient,* and *contributory* causes of symptoms. A necessary cause of some set of symptoms is an etiological factor that must be present or have occurred in order for the symptoms to occur. The symptoms can not occur if the etiological factor is absent or has not occurred. However, the symptoms are not required to occur when the necessary cause is present or has occurred. A sufficient cause of some set of symptoms is an etiological factor whose presence or occurrence guarantees the occurrence of the symptoms. An additional feature of a sufficient causal relationship is that if the symptoms do not occur, then the etiological factor can not be present or have occurred. However, the symptoms may occur in the absence of the sufficient cause. A contributory cause of some set of symptoms is an etiological factor that increases the likelihood of the occurrence of the symptoms but is neither necessary nor sufficient for their occurrence.

Causes also may vary in their sequential relationship to the occurrence of symptoms. In an etiological chain or sequence of events culminating in the occurrence of a set of symptoms, proximal causes operate toward the end of the chain, close to the occurrence of symptoms whereas distal causes operate toward the beginning of the chain, distant from the occurrence of symptoms.[1]

STATEMENT OF THE HOPELESSNESS THEORY
OF DEPRESSION

Cause

In contrast to symptom-based approaches to the classification of the depressive disorders (see Kendell, 1968), *cause* figures prominently in the definition of hopelessness depression. Few would disagree that, when possible, classification of psychopathologies by etiology in addition to other factors is more desirable than classification by symptoms alone insofar as the former generally has more

---

[1]For simplicity of exposition, we have presented the proximal-distal distinction in terms of a dichotomy: Proximal versus distal. Strictly speaking, however, it is more appropriate to think in terms of a proximal-distal continuum.

direct implications for cure and prevention than the latter (McLemore & Benjamin, 1979; Skinner, 1981). Overall, the hopelessness theory specifies a chain of distal and proximal contributory causes hypothesized to culminate in a proximal sufficient cause of the symptoms of hopelessness depression.

A proximal sufficient cause of the symptoms of hopelessness depression: Hopelessness. According to the hopelessness theory, a proximal sufficient cause of the symptoms of hopelessness depression is an expectation that highly desired outcomes will not occur or that highly aversive outcomes will occur and that there is nothing one can do to change the likelihood of occurrence of these outcomes.[2] Abramson et al. (1989) viewed this theory as a *hopelessness* theory because the common language term "hopelessness" captures the core elements of the proximal sufficient cause featured in the theory: Negative expectations about the occurrence of highly valued outcomes (a negative outcome expectancy) and expectations of helplessness about changing the likelihood of occurrence of these outcomes (a helplessness expectancy). Throughout this chapter, we use the term hopelessness to refer to this proximal sufficient cause. Abramson et al. used the phrase "generalized hopelessness" when people exhibit the negative outcome/helplessness expectancy about many areas of life. In contrast, "circumscribed pessimism" occurs when people exhibit the negative outcome/helplessness expectancy about only a limited domain. They suggested that cases of generalized hopelessness should produce severe symptoms of hopelessness depression whereas circumscribed pessimism is likely to be associated with fewer and/or less severe symptoms. However, cases in which a person exhibits circumscribed pessimism about extremely important outcomes also may be associated with severe symptoms.

It is useful to compare the hopelessness theory and Seligman's (1975) original helplessness theory with respect to proximal sufficient cause. Seligman's original statement is best characterized as a helplessness theory because it featured the expectation that one cannot control outcomes (regardless of their hedonic valence or likelihood of occurrence) as the proximal sufficient cause. The evolution from a helplessness to a hopelessness theory is consistent with Mandler's (1964, 1972) view that hopelessness, not helplessness, is a cause of the symptoms of depression.

[2]Abramson et al. (1978) cautioned that the problem of "current concerns" (Klinger, 1975) existed in their statement of the proximal sufficient cause of depression featured in the reformulation. They suggested that we feel depressed about the nonoccurrence of highly desired outcomes that we believe we cannot obtain only when they are "on our mind," "in the realm of possibility," "troubling us now," and so on. Although Abramson et al. found Klinger's concept heuristic, they felt it was not sufficiently well defined to be incorporated into the reformulation. We emphasize that the problem of current concerns still remains to be solved.

One hypothesized causal pathway to the symptoms of hopelessness depression. How does a person become hopeless and, in turn, develop the symptoms of hopelessness depression? As can be seen in Fig. 14.1, the hypothesized causal chain begins with the perceived occurrence of *negative life events (or nonoccurrence of positive life events).*[3] In the hopelessness theory, negative events serve as "occasion setters" for people to become hopeless. However, the relationship between life events and depression is imperfect: Not all people become depressed when confronted with negative life events (e.g., Brown & Harris, 1978; Lloyd, 1980a, 1980b). Thus, a key question is when do negative life events lead to depression and when do they not? According to the theory, there are at least three types of inferences people may make which modulate whether or not they become hopeless and, in turn, develop the symptoms of hopelessness depression in the face of negative life events: (1) Inferences about why the event occurred (i.e., inferred cause or causal attribution); (2) Inferences about consequences that might result from the occurrence of the event (i.e., inferred consequences); and (3) Inferences about the self given that the event happened to the person (i.e., inferred characteristics about the self).

Proximal contributory causes: Inferred stable, global causes of particular negative life events and a high degree of importance attached to these events. The kinds of causal inferences people make for negative events and the degree of importance they attach to these events are important factors contributing to whether or not they develop hopelessness and, in turn, the symptoms of hopelessness depression. In brief, relatively generalized hopelessness and, in turn, the symptoms of hopelessness depression, are more likely to occur when negative life events are attributed to stable (i.e., enduring) and global (i.e., likely to affect many outcomes) causes and viewed as important than when they are attributed to unstable, specific causes and viewed as unimportant. For understanding hopelessness depression, we focus on stable, global, as opposed to stable, specific attributions for negative life events because only the former would be expected to contribute to relatively generalized hopelessness. The latter would be expected to contribute to relatively circumscribed pessimism. Whereas the attributional notion was featured in the 1978 statement, the importance concept was only briefly referred to in the 1978 statement and then more fully elaborated by Seligman, Abramson, Semmel, and von Baeyer (1979). Also, in contrast to the 1978 statement, Abramson et al. (1989) deemphasized the internality dimension of causal attributions because it is not hypothesized to contribute directly to hopelessness but instead to lowered self-esteem and dependency, two hypothesized symptoms of hopelessness depression (see below).

---

[3]For the sake of brevity, we will use the phrase "negative life events" to refer to both the occurrence of negative life events *and* the nonoccurrence of positive life events.

Hopelessness Theory of Depression

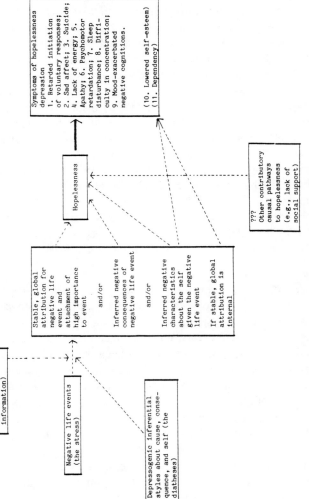

FIG. 14.1.   Causal chain specified in the hopelessness theory of depression. (Arrows with solid lines indicate sufficient causes. Arrows with broken lines indicate contributory causes.)

If causal inferences for negative events do modulate the likelihood of becoming hopeless, then it is important to delineate what influences the kinds of causal inferences people make. Over the past 20 years, social psychologists have conducted studies showing that people's causal attributions for events are, in part, a function of the situational information they confront (Kelly, 1967; McArthur, 1972). People tend to attribute an event to the factor or factors with which it covaries. According to this view, people would be predicted to make internal, stable, and global attributions for an event (e.g., failing a math exam) when they are confronted with situational information suggesting that the event is low in consensus (e.g., others do well on the math exam), high in consistency (e.g., typically failing exams in math), and low in distinctiveness (e.g., typically failing exams in other subjects as well as math; Kelley, 1967; Metalsky & Abramson, 1981). Thus, informational cues make some causal inferences for particular life events more plausible than others and some not plausible at all (see also Hammen & Mayol, 1982). Social psychologists have suggested a number of additional factors that also may guide the causal attribution process, including expectations for success and failure, motivation to protect or enhance one's self-esteem, focus of attention, salience of a potential causal factor, and self-presentational concerns, to name a few. Later we also discuss a more distal factor that also influences the kinds of causal inferences people make.

Proximal contributory causes: Inferred negative consequences of particular negative life events. Hammen and her colleagues (e.g., Gong-Guy & Hammen, 1980; Hammen & Cochran, 1981; Hammen & de Mayo, 1982) have argued that the inferred consequences of negative events, independently of causal inferences for these events, may modulate the likelihood that people will become depressed when confronted with a negative life event. For example, a student may attribute her low scores on the Graduate Record Examination (GRE) to distracting noises in the testing room (an unstable, specific attribution) but infer that a consequence of her poor performance on the GRE is that she never will be admitted to a graduate program in mathematics, her preferred career choice. Abramson et al. (1989) suggested that inferred negative consequences moderate the relationship between negative life events and the symptoms of hopelessness depression by affecting the likelihood of becoming hopeless. Following the same logic as for causal attributions, inferred negative consequences should be particularly likely to lead to hopelessness when the negative consequence is viewed as important, not remediable, unlikely to change, and as affecting many areas of life. When the negative consequence is seen as affecting only a very limited sphere of life, relatively circumscribed pessimism rather than generalized hopelessness should result.

Proximal contributory causes: Inferred negative characteristics about the self given negative life events. In addition to inferred consequences of negative events, inferred characteristics about the self given these events also may modulate the likelihood of formation of hopelessness and, in turn, the symptoms of hopelessness depression. Inferred characteristics about the self refer to the inferences a person draws about his or her own worth, abilities, personality, desirability, etc. from the fact that a particular negative life event occurred. Such a concept appears to be central in Beck's (1967) description of cognitive processes and depression. For example, Beck (1976, pp. 99–100) reported the case of a depressed suicidal woman who previously had had a breach in her relationship with her lover Raymond and said, "I am worthless." When the therapist asked why she believed she was worthless, she replied, "If I don't have love, I am worthless." Again, following the same logic as for causal attributions, inferred negative characteristics about the self should be particularly likely to lead to hopelessness when the person believes that the negative characteristic is not remediable or likely to change and that possession of it will preclude the attainment of important outcomes in many areas of life. When the negative characteristic is seen as precluding the attainment of outcomes in only a very limited sphere of life, relatively circumscribed pessimism rather than generalized hopelessness should result. Inferred characteristics about the self given negative events may not be independent of causal attributions for these events, but it is useful to conceptualize and operationalize them as distinct.

For the occurrence of a given negative life event, the three kinds of inferences (cause, consequence, and self-characteristics) may not be equally important in contributing to whether or not the person becomes hopeless and develops the symptoms of hopelessness depression. For example, a young boy's inferences about the negative consequences of his mother's death, rather than about its cause or immediate implications for his view of himself, may be most important in contributing to whether or not he becomes hopeless. Perhaps events can be classified in terms of which of the three types of inferences will be most important in mediating whether or not the occurrence of the event leads to the development of hopelessness and the symptoms of hopelessness depression.

Distal contributory causes: Cognitive styles. Complementing social psychologists' work on the situational determinants of causal attributions, Abramson et al. (1978) suggested a more distal factor that also may influence the content of people's causal inferences for a particular event: Individual differences in *attributional style* (see also Ickes & Layden, 1978). Some individuals may exhibit a general tendency to attribute negative events to stable, global factors and to view these events as very important (i.e., depressogenic attributional style) whereas other individuals may not.

Individuals who exhibit the hypothesized depressogenic attributional style should be more likely than individuals who do not to attribute any particular negative event to a stable, global cause and view the event as very important, thereby incrementing the likelihood of becoming hopeless and developing the symptoms of hopelessness depression. However, in the presence of positive life events or in the absence of negative life events, people exhibiting the depressogenic attributional style should be no more likely to develop hopelessness, and therefore the symptoms of hopelessness depression, than people not exhibiting this attributional style. This aspect of the theory is conceptualized usefully as a *diathesis–stress component* (Metalsky, Abramson, Seligman, Semmel, & Peterson, 1982). That is, the depressogenic attributional style (the diathesis) is a distal contributory cause of the symptoms of hopelessness depression that operates in the presence, but not in the absence, of negative life events (the stress; see also Alloy, Kayne, Romer, & Crocker, 1989; Metalsky, Halberstadt, & Abramson, 1987).

The logic of the diathesis-stress component implies that a depressogenic attributional style in a particular content domain (e.g., for interpersonal-related events) provides *"specific vulnerability"* (cf. Beck, 1967) to the symptoms of hopelessness depression when an individual is confronted with negative life events in that same content domain (e.g., social rejection). Thus, there must be a match between the content areas of an individual's depressogenic attributional style and the negative life events he or she encounters for the interaction of attributional diathesis and stress to produce symptoms of hopelessness depression (cf. Alloy, Hartlage, & Abramson, 1988; Alloy, Clements, & Kolden, 1985; Anderson & Arnoult, 1985; Anderson, Horowitz, & French, 1983; Hammen, Marks, Mayol, & deMayo, 1985; Alloy et al., 1988; Metalsky et al., 1987).

As with causal inferences, individual differences also may exist in the general tendency to infer negative consequences and negative characteristics about the self given the occurrence of negative life events. It is not known whether or not such cognitive styles are independent of the hypothesized depressogenic attributional style. Abramson et al. (1989) suggested these two additional cognitive styles also are diatheses that operate in the presence, but not in the absence, of negative life events according to the specific vulnerability hypothesis. Abramson et al. referred to these three negative styles as *cognitive diatheses*. Beck's (Weissman & Beck, 1979) concept of dysfunctional attitudes and Ellis' (1977) concept of irrational beliefs appear to overlap, in part, with these cognitive diatheses.

Cognitive styles probably are best conceptualized as continuua with some people exhibiting more negative styles than others. Similarly, it may be more appropriate to speak of a continuum of negativity of life events. The continuum view suggests a *titration* model (cf. Zubin & Spring, 1977) of the diathesis-stress component: The less negative a person's cognitive style, the more negative an event needs to be in order to interact with that style and contribute to the formation of symptoms. Thus, although may cases of hopelessness depression will occur among cognitively vulnerable people when they are confronted with negative events, people who do not exhibit the cognitive diatheses also may develop hopelessness depression when they are confronted with events sufficient to engender hopelessness in many or most people (e.g., a person who is put in a concentration camp and repeatedly told by the guards that the only way to leave the camp is as a corpse). In a related vein, it is likely that major negative life events are not required to initiate the series of inferences hypothesized to culminate in the symptoms of hopelessness depression. Instead, the occurrence of more minor events, chronic stressors or even daily hassles also may trigger the hypothesized depressogenic inferences among cognitively vulnerable people. This discussion underscores the importance of the *causal mediation* component of the hopelessness theory: Each causal factor depicted in Fig. 14.1 contributes to the next causal factor in the proximal direction.

In addition to the cognitive factors described above, interpersonal (e.g., lack of social support; Brown & Harris, 1978), developmental (e.g., death of mother during the child's early years; Brown & Harris, 1978), and even genetic factors also may modulate the likelihood that a person will develop hopelessness and, in turn, the symptoms of hopelessness depression (see Tiger, 1979 for an intriguing discussion of genetic and biological factors in the development of hope and hopelessness).

Symptoms

Hopelessness depression should be characterized by a number of symptoms. Two of these symptoms were described in the 1978 reformulation, and Abramson et al. (1989) retained them in the hopelessness theory: (1) retarded initiation of voluntary responses (motivational symptom); and (2) sad affect (emotional symptom). The motivational symptom derives from the helplessness expectancy component of hopelessness. If a person expects that nothing he or she does matters, why try? The incentive for emitting active instrumental responses decreases (Alloy, 1982; Bolles, 1972). Sadness derives from the negative outcome expectancy component of hopelessness and is a likely consequence of the expectation that the future is bleak. Abramson et al. no longer included the third symptom described in the 1978 reformulation, the cognitive symptom (associative deficit), because work on "depressive realism" (e.g., Alloy & Abramson, 1979, 1988) has not supported it.

Hopelessness depression should be characterized by other symptoms as well. Insofar as Beck and others have demonstrated that hopelessness is a key factor in serious suicide attempts and suicidal ideation, serious suicide attempts and suicidal ideation are likely symptoms of hopelessness depression (Beck, Kovacs, & Weissman, 1975; Kazdin, French, Unis, Esveldt-Dawson, & Sherick, 1983; Minkoff, Bergman, Beck & Beck, 1973; Petrie & Chamberlain, 1983). If lack of energy, apathy, and psychomotor retardation are, in part, concomitants of a severe decrease in the motivation to initiate voluntary responses (see Beck, 1967), then they should be symptoms of hopelessness depression. To the extent that people brood about the highly desired outcomes they feel hopeless to attain, sleep disturbance (e.g., initial insomnia) and difficulty in concentration will be important symptoms of hopelessness depression. Work showing that mood affects cognition (e.g., Bower, 1981) suggests that as individuals suffering from hopelessness depression become increasingly sad, their cognitions will become even more negative.

Although not necessarily symptoms of hopelessness depression, low self-esteem and/or dependency sometimes will accompany the other hypothesized symptoms. Lowered self-esteem will be a symptom of hopelessness depression when the event that triggered the episode was attributed to an internal, stable, global cause as opposed to any type of external cause or to an internal, unstable, specific cause. In contrast to the 1978 reformulation, then, the hopelessness theory postulates that attributing a negative life event to an internal cause does not, by itself, contribute to lowering self-esteem. The revision requiring internal, stable, global attributions for lowered self-esteem is based on a number of studies (e.g., Crocker, Alloy, & Kayne, 1988b; Dweck & Licht, 1980; Janoff-Bulman, 1979) showing that internal attributions per se are not maladaptive and, in some cases, may be very adaptive (e.g., attributing failure to lack of effort leads to increased trying). The link between internal, stable, global attributions for negative life events and lowered self-esteem is based on social psychological work showing that people's self-esteem is influenced by their comparisons with others (e.g., Festinger, 1954; Morse & Gergen, 1970; Rosenberg, 1965; Schachter, 1959; Tesser & Campbell, 1983). If people make internal, stable, global attributions, then they expect that others could attain the outcomes about which they feel hopeless and therefore would feel inadequate compared to others. In addition, lowered self-esteem should occur in cases of hopelessness depression when people have inferred negative characteristics about themselves which they view as important to their general self-concept and not remediable or likely to change. Finally, dependency frequently may co-occur with lowered self-esteem because the conditions that give rise to lowered self-esteem will leave the person feeling inferior to others and thereby increase the likelihood that s/he may become excessively dependent on them (Brewin & Furnham, 1987).

In general, circumscribed pessimism may not be associated with the full syndrome of the symptoms of hopelessness depression. Circumscribed pessimism is likely to produce fewer and/or less severe symptoms than generalized hopelessness, except when the person is pessimistic about an extremely important outcome. Whereas the motivational deficit should occur in cases of circumscribed pessimism, sadness may be less intense or even absent. Similarly, people with circumscribed pessimism should be less likely to commit suicide or exhibit the other hypothesized symptoms of hopelessness depression. Thus, circumscribed pessimism should lead to an identifiable behavioral syndrome, but this syndrome should be characterized primarily by a motivational deficit in the relevant domain.

Course

Insofar as hopelessness is viewed as a proximal sufficient cause of the symptoms of hopelessness depression, the *maintenance* or duration of an episode of hopelessness depression should be influenced by how long this expectation is present. A prediction in the 1978 reformulation that Abramson et al. (in press) retained is that the more stable a person's attribution for a negative life event, the longer the person will be hopeless and, consequently, symptomatic. As a corollary, the maintenance of hopelessness not only should be influenced by the stability of the attribution for the event that "triggered" the given episode but also by the stability of attributions for newly occurring negative life events (see Brown & Harris, 1978; Lloyd, Zisook, Click, & Jaffe, 1981). Maintenance also may be influenced by the consequences the individual infers from the fact that he or she is depressed as well as by the attribution he or she makes for the depression itself. Similarly, maintenance may be influenced by the characteristics the individual infers about himself or herself given that he or she is depressed. More generally, any factor that influences the duration of hopelessness should, in turn, influence the maintenance or chronicity of the symptoms of hopelessness depression. These predictors of the duration of a given episode of hopelessness depression follow directly from the logic of the hopelessness theory. In addition, the possibility exists that once an individual becomes hopeless, some biological or psychological processes are triggered that need to "run their course" and do not dissipate as quickly as hopelessness. Such factors might maintain a hopelessness depression after hopelessness remits.

Needles and Abramson (1989) proposed a model of *recovery* from hopelessness depression that highlights positive events. They suggested that the occurrence of positive events provides the occasion for people suffering from hopelessness depression to become "hopeful" and, in turn, nondepressed. Analogously to the logic of the diathesis-stress component, they suggested that people with a style to attribute positive events to stable, global causes should be particularly likely to become hopeful and, in turn, nondepressed when confronted with a positive event. Thus, positive events and inferences about them (cause, consequence, self-characteristics) may be particularly important in recovery from hopelessness depression.

Given the logic of the hopelessness theory, *relapse* or *recurrence* of hopelessness depression should be predicted by the reappearance of hopelessness because, by definition, a relapse or recurrence is a new onset of hopelessness depression. Thus, the etiological chain hypothesized to culminate in the onset of the symptoms of hopelessness depression also applies directly to the relapse or recurrence of these symptoms. Hence, people with cognitive diatheses will be more likely to have relapses or recurrences of hopelessness depression when confronted with negative life events than people who do not exhibit these diatheses.

Therapy and Prevention

Because the hopelessness theory specifies an etiological chain, each link suggests a point for clinical intervention. A major advantage of using the proximal-distal continuum to order the events that cause hopelessness depression is that it not only suggests points of intervention for reversing current episodes but also suggests points for decreasing vulnerability to hopelessness depression.

Treating current episodes of hopelessness depression.   Any therapeutic strategy that undermines hopelessness and restores hopefulness should be effective in remediating current symptoms of hopelessness depression (see also Hollon & Garber, 1980). Hopelessness could be attacked directly. Alternatively, the proximal causes (e.g., stable, global attributions for particular negative life events) that contribute to a person's current hopelessness could be attacked. Insofar as negative events and situational information supporting depressogenic inferences contribute to the maintenance of hopelessness, therapeutic interventions aimed at modifying the hopelessness-inducing environment should be helpful. Finally, if the person's own behavior is, to some degree, contributing to the depressogenic events and situational information he or she encounters, then personal behavior change would be an important therapeutic goal.

Preventing onset, relapse, and recurrence of hopelessness depression.   According to the hopelessness theory, the three hypothesized cognitive diatheses put people at risk for initial onset, relapse, and recurrence of hopelessness depression. Therefore, modifying cognitive diatheses is an important goal for prevention. Insofar as the cognitive diatheses require negative life events to exert their depressogenic effects, prevention efforts also might be directed toward lessening the stressfulness of events in the environments of cognitively vulnerable people. Finally, "primary prevention" efforts could be aimed at building "nondepressive" cognitive styles and environments.

Relationship of Hopelessness Depression to Other Types of Depression and Psychopathology

Does the concept of hopelessness depression map onto any nosological category of affective disorders currently diagnosed (e.g., dysthymic disorder) or does this concept cut across the various nosological categories of affective or even nonaffective disorders currently diagnosed (cf. Halberstadt, Mukherji, Metalsky, & Abramson, 1989)? Hopelessness depression most likely includes subsets of individuals from various currently diagnosed categories of depression (e.g., major depression, dysthymia, etc.) and may even include some depressed individuals who *a priori* would not be expected to be hopelessness depressives (e.g., some endogenous depressives—see Eaves & Rush, 1984 and Hamilton & Abramson, 1983—note, however, that just because some endogenous depressives in these studies displayed a cognitive diathesis does not necessarily imply that they are suffering from hopelessness depression). Moreover, Alloy, Kelly, Mineka, and Clements (in press), based on empirical and clinical studies of the comorbidity of anxiety and depression, suggested that many hopelessness depressives also may be suffering from anxiety. A subset of individuals who exhibit personality disorders (e.g., borderline personality) may be characterized by extremely negative cognitive diatheses which make them particularly susceptible to hopelessness depression (Rose & Abramson, 1987; Silverman, Silverman, & Eardley, 1984).

A second descriptive psychiatric question is which diagnostic categories of depression, if any, involve fundamentally different etiological processes, and perhaps symptoms and therapy, than those involved in hopelessness depression. Klein's (1974) concept of endogenomorphic depression (see also Costello's, 1972 concept of "reinforcer ineffectiveness depression") which maps closely on to the DSM-III category of major depressive episode, with melancholia, may be fundamentally distinct from the concept of hopelessness depression. The hypothesized core process in endogenomorphic depressions is impairment in the capacity to experience pleasure rather than hopelessness.

A core question concerns the relationship between the concept of hopelessness depression and general depression. Abramson et al. (1989) suggested that the relationship of hopelessness depression to general depression is analogous to the relationship between a subtype of mental retardation (e.g., PKU syndrome, cretinism, etc.) and mental retardation in general. Just as some symptoms of a particular subtype of retardation may be a general feature of retardation (e.g., low IQ), particular hypothesized symptoms of hopelessness depression are considered symptoms of general depression (e.g., sadness). Other hypothesized symptoms of hopelessness depression (e.g., motivational deficit) may only partially overlap with the symptoms of general depression. Finally, still other symptoms of hopelessness depression (e.g., suicide and suicidal ideation) may not overlap at all with the symptoms of general depression. Thus, just as physicians do not define a particular subtype of retardation on the basis of symptoms alone because of potential overlap in some symptoms across subtypes, hopelessness depression is not defined on the basis of symptoms alone. Following the logic of workers in medicine more generally, Abramson et al. defined hopelessness depression in terms of cause, symptoms, course, therapy, and prevention.

SEARCH FOR HOPELESSNESS DEPRESSION:
TOWARD AN EVALUATION
OF THE HOPELESSNESS THEORY

A variety of possible methodological approaches exist for searching for hopelessness depressions and distinguishing them from other types of depression. For example, a symptom-based approach would involve determining if a subgroup of depressives exhibits the symptoms hypothesized to be associated with hopelessness depression (e.g., retarded initiation of voluntary responses, etc.) A symptom-based approach commonly has been utilized by workers in descriptive psychiatry, where categories of depression traditionally have been formed on the basis of symptom similarity. However, we believe a symptom-based approach alone would be unsatisfactory in the context of work on the hopelessness theory. The basic problem is that some or all of the symptoms hypothesized to be characteristic of hopelessness depressions conceivably may be present in other types of depression as well (e.g., endogenomorphic depression; Klein, 1974). In contrast to a purely symptom-based approach, the hopelessness theory of depression points to an additional strategy for searching for hopelessness depressions: a *process-oriented* approach.

Search for Hopelessness Depression: A Research Strategy

The way to search for hopelessness depression is to test the hopelessness theory. A search for hopelessness depression involves at least five components: (1) A test of the etiological chain hypothesized to culminate in the manifest symptoms of hopelessness depression; (2) An examination of the hypothesized manifest symptoms of hopelessness depression; (3) A test of theoretical predictions about the course, remission, relapse, and recurrence of hopelessness depression; (4) A test of theoretical predictions about the cure and prevention of hopelessness depression; and (5) Delineation of the relationship among hopelessness depression, other subtypes of depression, and other types of psychopathology.

A test of the *etiological chain* featured in the hopelessness theory involves an examination of the diathesis-stress and causal mediation components of the theory. An adequate test of the diathesis-stress component involves at least two parts: (1) A demonstration that the *interaction* between the hypothesized cognitive diatheses and negative life events predicts future depressive symptoms, specifically the symptoms of hopelessness depression; and (2) A demonstration that this interaction predicts the *complete constellation of symptoms* hypothesized to constitute the hopelessness subtype of depression as opposed to only a subset of these symptoms or symptoms that constitute other subtypes of depression. "Specific vulnerability" predictions also should be tested.

An adequate test of the *causal mediation* component of the hopelessness theory involves testing these hypothesized probability linkages: (1) Individuals who exhibit the hypothesized cognitive diatheses should be more likely than individuals who do not to make one of the three hypothesized depressogenic inferences (cause, consequence, self). Because depressogenic cognitive styles contribute to, but are neither necessary nor sufficient for, the particular inferences a person makes, this probability linkage should be greater than 0 but less than 1.0; (2) The three hypothesized depressogenic inferences (cause, consequence, self) should increase the likelihood of becoming hopeless. Again, because these inferences are hypothesized to contribute to, but not be necessary or sufficient for, the formation of hopelessness, this probability linkage also should be greater than 0 but less than 1.0; and (3) The occurrence of hopelessness should increase the likelihood of the development of the symptoms of hopelessness depression. Because hopelessness is hypothesized to be a sufficient cause of the symptoms of hopelessness depression, this probability linkage should equal 1.0 in the ideal case of error-free measurements.

A necessary condition for the validity of the hopelessness theory is that the hypothesized manifest *symptoms* of hopelessness depression should be *intercorrelated* with one another (*convergent validity*) and not as highly correlated with other symptoms found both in depression and other psychopathologies (*divergent validity*). Moreover, this hypothesized constellation of symptoms must be correlated with hopelessness. Finally, hopelessness must temporally precede the formation of this symptom constellation.

A basic prediction from the hopelessness theory is that the duration of hopelessness should predict the *course* or *chronicity* of the symptoms of hopelessness depression. The etiological chain hypothesized to culminate in the onset of the symptoms of hopelessness depression also should predict *relapse* and *recurrence* of these symptoms.

Specific predictions follow from the hopelessness theory about the *cure* and *prevention* of hopelessness depression. Reversing hopelessness should result in a remission of a current episode of hopelessness depression. Modifying the three hypothesized cognitive diatheses should decrease vulnerability to future hopelessness depression.

No explicit predictions about the *relationship* of hopelessness depression to other subtypes of depression and other forms of psychopathology can be drawn from the hopelessness theory. However, from a descriptive psychiatry standpoint, it is important to determine if hopelessness depression maps onto any currently diagnosed nosological category of affective disorders (e.g., dysthymic disorder, unipolar major depression, etc.) or, alternatively, cuts across currently diagnosed affective and even nonaffective disorders. This may be accomplished, in part, by following people longitudinally along the etiological pathway explicated in the theory, seeing what results in terms of symptoms, course, prognosis, psychophysiology, family history of psychopathology, and so on, and comparing the results to the corresponding features associated with the current nosological categories of affective disorders and other nonaffective psychopathologies.

In discussing how to search for hopelessness depression, we note the possibility that future work may not corroborate the existence of hopelessness depression as a bona fide *subtype* with characteristic cause, symptoms, course, treatment, and prevention. Instead, the etiological chain featured in the hopelessness theory may be one of many pathways to a final common outcome of depression. In this case, it would be more compelling to speak of a hopelessness cause, as opposed to a hopelessness subtype, of depression.

Empirical Validity of the Hopelessness Theory

Because the hopelessness theory is new, the evidence about its validity is not in. However, we have conducted a number of studies to test it. Also, many of the studies conducted to test the 1978 reformulation, as well as other clinical and empirical work on depression, are relevant to evaluating the hopelessness theory although few provide a direct test. We now report this work.

Etiological chain: Proximal sufficient cause component.   A key prediction of the hopelessness theory is that hopelessness temporally precedes and is a proximal sufficient cause of the symptoms of hopelessness depression. An alternative hypothesis is that hopelessness has no causal status and, instead, is simply another symptom of depression. Relevant to distinguishing between these two views, Rholes, Riskind, and Neville (1985) conducted a longitudinal study and reported that college students' levels of hopelessness at Time 1 predicted their levels of depression five weeks later at Time 2 over and above the predictive capacity of depression at Time 1. Similarly, in their prospective study, Carver and Gaines (1987) demonstrated that, after controlling statistically for earlier levels of depression symptoms, dispositional pessimists were more likely to develop postpartum depression than were optimists. Although these results do not establish that hopelessness actually caused depressive symptoms at a later time, they do support the temporal precedence of hopelessness in predicting change in depressive symptoms (see also Riskind, Rholes, Brannon, & Burdick, 1987, for a demonstration that the interaction of attributional style and negative expectations predict future depression).

In addition to the above longitudinal studies, a number of cross-sectional studies have examined the relationship between hopelessness and depression. A notable feature of these studies is that they tested whether hopelessness is specific to depression or is a more general feature of psychopathology. Abramson, Garber, Edwards, and Seligman (1978) reported that hospitalized unipolar depressives were more hopeless than both hospitalized nondepressed control subjects and nondepressed schizophrenics. Interestingly, the unipolar depressives also were more hopeless than the depressed schizophrenics. Hamilton and Abramson (1983) found that hospitalized episodic unipolar major depressives were more hopeless than a hospitalized nondepressed psychiatric group with mixed diagnoses (e.g., schizophrenia, anxiety disorder, and personality disorders) as well as a nondepressed community control group. Recently, Beck, Riskind, Brown, and Steer (1988) found that psychiatric patients suffering from major depression were more hopeless than patients suffering from generalized anxiety disorder and a group of "mixed" psychiatric patients (diagnoses other than depression or anxiety). Taken together, these studies suggest that hopelessness is specific to depression and not a general feature of psychopathology.

Although the studies examining the association between hopelessness and depression are promising, they do not provide a wholly adequate test of the proximal sufficient cause component of the theory. As we have argued elsewhere (Abramson et al., 1988a, 1988b, 1989; Halberstadt, Andrews, Metalsky, & Abramson, 1984), insofar as hopelessness theory postulates a *subtype* of depression, it is inappropriate to simply lump all depressives together and examine their levels of hopelessness to test the theory. Fortunately, some investigators have begun to examine the relationship between hopelessness and the hypothesized individual symptoms of hopelessness depression and have reported a strong association between hopelessness and suicide attempts and ideation (Beck et al., 1975; Kazdin et al., 1983; Minkoff et al., 1973; Petrie & Chamberlain, 1983).

Etiological chain: Diathesis-stress and causal mediation components. Relevant to these components, a multitude of cross-sectional and longitudinal studies have examined the relationship between attributional style and depression (see Barnett & Gotlib, 1988; Brewin, 1985; Coyne & Gotlib, 1983; Peterson & Seligman, 1984; and Sweeney et al., 1986 for reviews). Overall, these studies have shown that the tendency to make internal, stable, and global attributions for negative events is associated with severity of concurrent and future depressive symptoms in college student, patient, and other samples (see Sweeney et al., 1986 for a meta-analytic review). However, the corroborative findings have not always been strong.

We have argued elsewhere that this research strategy is inappropriate to test the diathesis-stress component (Abramson et al., 1988a, 1988b, 1989; Alloy et al., 1988; Halberstadt et al., 1984). Recently, a number of studies have been conducted that do provide a more powerful test of the diathesis-stress component (and in some cases the causal mediation component) of the hopelessness theory. In a prospective field study, Metalsky et al. (1987) found that college students who showed a style to attribute negative achievement events to stable, global causes experienced a more enduring depressive mood reaction to a low midterm grade than did students who did not exhibit this style. Consistent with the diathesis-stress component, attributional style for negative achievement events was not associated with students' mood reactions in the absence of the low grade. Interestingly, whereas students' more enduring depressive mood reactions were predicted by the interaction between attributional style and midterm grade (consistent with the diathesis stress component), their immediate depressive mood reactions were predicted solely by the outcome on the exam (see also Follette & Jacobson, 1987). The results also provided support for the specific vulnerability hypothesis in that attributional style for negative achievement events, but not for negative interpersonal events, interacted with students' outcomes on the exam (an achievement event) to predict their enduring depressive mood reactions. Finally, consistent with the mediation component of the theory, failure students' attributional styles predicted their particular attributions for their midterm grades which, in turn, completely mediated the relation between attributional style and their enduring depressive mood responses.

With a design similar to Metalsky et al. (1987), Alloy et al. (1989) used causal modelling techniques to test the diathesis-stress and causal mediation components of the hopelessness theory and obtained support for both components. Alloy et al. additionally reported that the interaction between attributional style and midterm grade predicted change in depressive symptoms as well as in transient depressive mood responses. In a longitudinal study, Nolen-Hoeksema, Girgus, and Seligman (1986), asked whether life events and attributional styles interacted to predict school children's future depression. The obtained partial support for the diathesis-stress component of the theory with negative life events interacting with attributional style in some analyses but not in others. Finally, relevant to the causal mediation component, Brown and Siegel (1988) conducted a prospective study of stress and well-being in adolescence and reported that judgments of control over negative events interacted with attributions for them to predict future depression.

Two laboratory studies have examined the diathesis-stress component of the theory. Using a prospective design, Alloy, Peterson, Abramson, and Seligman (1984) found that students who typically attribute negative life events to global causes showed a wider generalization of learned helplessness to new situations when they were exposed to uncontrollable events than did individuals who typically attribute negative life events to more specific causes. Recently, Sacks and Bugental (1987) tested the diathesis-stress component in a laboratory study involving social failure or success (interaction with an unresponsive or responsive confederate). Supporting the diathesis-stress component, attributional style predicted short-term depressive reactions to the stressful social experience as well as the behaviors accompanying such a reaction.

Related to the diathesis-stress component, Clements and Alloy (1988) tested the theory's prediction that depression-prone students should be particularly likely to exhibit the hypothesized depressogenic attributional style. Consistent with prediction, they found that depression-prone students had more negative attributional styles than students who were not depression-prone regardless of current depression level.

Another issue relevant to the diathesis-stress component that has been examined empirically concerns the relationship between attributional style and self-esteem. Consistent with the hopelessness theory, and at odds with the 1978 reformulation, Crocker, Alloy, and Kayne (1988b) found that self-esteem was a function of all three attributional dimensions (internality, stability, and globality) as opposed to just internality. Subjects who made internal, stable, global, as opposed to simply internal, attributions for negative life events exhibited low self-esteem.

Insofar as dysfunctional attitudes overlap, in part, with the cognitive diatheses, studies examining dysfunctional attitudes and negative life events in predicting depression are relevant to evaluating the diathesis-stress component. In this regard, Olinger, Kuiper, & Shaw (1987) administered the Dysfunctional Attitudes Scale (DAS; Weissman & Beck, 1979) and DAS—Contractual Contingencies Scale (DAS—CC; Olinger et al., 1987) to subjects. The DAS–CC was designed to measure the presence or absence of life events that impinge on a person's dysfunctional attitudes. Consistent with the diathesis-stress component, subjects who were cognitively vulnerable (high DAS) and experienced negative events impinging on their vulnerability (high DAS-CC) were more depressed than cognitively vulnerable subjects who did not experience the relevant negative life events (high DAS, low DAS-CC) as well as subjects who were not cognitively vulnerable (low DAS with either high or low DAS-CC scores). Similarly, Wise and Barnes (1986) reported that a normal sample of college students who were cognitively vulnerable (high DAS scores) and exposed to negative life events during the past year were more depressed than students who also were cognitively vulnerable but not exposed to a high rate of negative life events as well as students who were not cognitively vulnerable regardless of life events. In a clinical sample, DAS scores and negative life events scores exerted main effects in predicting depression. A limitation of these two studies is that they employed cross-sectional designs.

Related to the mediation component, some investigators (e.g., Brewin, 1985) have questioned whether people's attributional styles predict their causal attributions for particular negative life events. As we previously indicated, in their tests of the causal mediation component of the theory, Metalsky et al. (1987) and Alloy et al. (1989) found that attributional styles did, in fact, predict particular causal attributions (see also Follette & Jacobson, 1987 for similar results). Moreover, support for the mediation component of the hopelessness theory challenges the alternative hypothesis that some antecedent or correlate of the cognitive diatheses is actually mediating depressive reactions.

A further aspect of the mediation component of the hopelessness theory involves whether people's attributions or attributional styles predict the formation of hopelessness. Consistent with this component, in a laboratory study, Alloy and Ahrens (1987) demonstrated that a depressogenic attributional style contributed to depressives' pessimism in predicting future events. More generally, Weiner's (1985) work has demonstrated that people's causal attributions affect their expectancies about future events.

The hopelessness theory predicts that attributions for life events should be predicted by situational information as well as attributional style. Consistent with this prediction, Haack, Dykman, Metalsky, and Abramson (1989) found that both depressed and nondepressed students' causal attributions were influenced by consensus, consistency, and distinctiveness information. Similarly, Crocker, Alloy, and Kayne (1988a) found that people's perceptions of consensus information mediated their attributional styles (see also Alloy & Ahrens, 1987).

Course. Three studies have tested the course component directly. Consistent with prediction, Needles and Abramson (1989) reported that attributional style for positive outcomes interacted with positive life events to predict recovery from hopelessness. When positive events occurred in their lives, depressed students with a style to attribute positive events to stable, global causes showed a dramatic reduction in hopelessness relative to depressed students who did not exhibit this style. This change in hopelessness was accompanied by a reduction of depressive symptoms. Students who did not experience an increase in positive events, regardless of style, did not show such dramatic reduction of hopelessness.

In a 2-year follow-up, Evans et al. (1989) reported that patients treated cognitively (cognitive therapy alone or in combination with drugs) showed half the rate of relapse of patients treated with drugs alone and then withdrawn from medication. Patients kept on medication also showed reduced relapse. Posttreatment attributional styles evidenced greater change in cognitively treated patients than in patients treated purely pharmacologically and, consistent with prediction, was the only cognitive variable that predicted subsequent relapse when residual depression was partialled out (the other two cognitive diatheses—consequences and self—were not assessed). Further analyses suggested that change in attributional styles mediated the relapse preventive effect of cognitive therapy.

Finally, in a follow-up of psychiatric patients, Rush, Weissenburger, and Eaves (1986) reported that the presence of dysfunctional attitudes (high DAS scores) at remission from depression predicted the presence of depression 6 months later. Although not statistically significant, a similar pattern was found for attributional style. A limitation of this study is the small sample size ($n = 15$).

Three additional studies indirectly tested predictions about course. As predicted, in a longitudinal study, Hamilton and Abramson (1983) found that among a sample of inpatient unipolar, episodic major depressives, dissipation of hopelessness was accompanied by remission of depressive symptoms. Unfortunately, their design did not allow a determination of whether or not dissipation of hopelessness preceded remission of symptoms as required by the theory.

In line with the hopelessness theory, Paykel and Tanner (1976) reported that among recovered depressives, those who relapsed experienced more undesirable events in the preceding 3-month period than those who did not exhibit symptom return (see also Belsher & Costello, 1988). The inferences about cause, consequence, and self these "recovered" depressives made for those negative life events should provide even greater power for predicting relapse.

Lewinsohn, Steinmetz, Larson and Franklin (1981) found that unipolar depressed community volunteers who held negative expectations about the future and perceptions of low control (in our terminology, the two features of hopelessness) at Time 1 were less likely to recover over an 8 month period compared with unipolar depressives who did not exhibit these cognitions, controlling for initial level of depression (see also Eaves & Rush, 1984).

Cure and prevention. A number of studies (e.g., Beck, Hollon, Young, Bedrosian, & Budenz, 1985; Shaw, 1977; Zeiss, Lewinsohn, & Munoz, 1979) have documented the efficacy of cognitive therapy for unipolar depression. The goals of cognitive therapy as currently practiced (cf. Beck, Rush, Shaw, & Emery, 1979) overlap with the goals for treatment and prevention of hopelessness depression. Therefore, empirical work demonstrating the efficacy of cognitive therapy for unipolar depression provides some support for the validity of the hopelessness theory's therapeutic predictions. Future work is needed to examine predictions about treatment of hopelessness depression in particular. In addition, predictions about the prevention of hopelessness depression need to be tested. Finally, the hopelessness theory's novel clinical predictions need to be tested.

Summary and future directions. Based on the above studies, the hopelessness theory appears promising. However, much further research is needed. For example, although powerful tests of the attributional diathesis-stress component have been conducted, no one has examined the cognitive diatheses of inferring negative consequences or characteristics about the self or whether the cognitive style diathesis-stress interaction predicts clinically significant depression. Moreover, it is crucial to determine if this interaction predicts the development of the hypothesized symptoms of hopelessness depression. More generally, an important shortcoming of the prior work is that is has not focussed on the symptoms of hopelessness depression in particular and, instead, simply has examined the symptoms of depression in general. Future work needs to test more fine-grained predictions about the hypothesized symptoms of hopelessness depression. The issue of the stability of the cognitive diatheses has not been resolved satisfactorily. We have only begun, in a preliminary way, to investigate the issues of specific vulnerability and mediational processes. Finally, further tests of the predictions about course, cure, and prevention are needed. We eagerly await this research.

However, difficult methodological issues may arise in the search for hopelessness depression. For example, the hopelessness theory is silent about the time lag between formation of hopelessness and onset of the symptoms of hopelessness depression. If it is very short, then a major challenge will be to develop methods with sufficient temporal resolving power to determine if hopelessness indeed precedes the occurrence of the hypothesized symptoms of hopelessness depression (see Alloy et al., 1988 for proposed methods for testing the hopelessness theory). The results of work to test the hopelessness theory will determine if the concept of hopelessness depression needs to be revised. For example, perhaps the statement of the causal pathway is correct, but it culminates in a different set of symptoms than those currently hypothesized to comprise hopelessness depression. In this case, the symptom, but not the cause, component of the hopelessness theory would need to be modified.

We believe it is important to test the hopelessness theory because increases in understanding depression and nondepression from a cognitive perspective will help build a bridge between clinical and experimental psychology. Although researchers in several areas of psychology (e.g., neuropsychology and visual perception) have utilized the strategy of studying abnormal individuals as a means of developing principles of normal psychological functioning, clinical psychologists rarely have pursued this line of inquiry. Clinical investigators typically conduct research on depression simply to understand this disorder. Such research also can illuminate the functions of pervasive optimistic biases in normal cognition. These biases may be highly robust and have adaptive and/or evolutionary significance (e.g., Abramson & Alloy, 1981; Alloy & Abramson, 1979; Freud, 1917/1957; Greenwald, 1980; Martin, Abramson, & Alloy, 1984; Tiger, 1979).

ACKNOWLEDGMENTS

Preparation of this chapter was supported by a grant from the MacArthur Foundation, a Romnes Fellowship from the University of Wisconsin, and a grant from the University Research Institute at the University of Texas-Austin. We thank Tony Ahrens, Ben Dykman, Dan Romer, Rich Spritz, Carmelo Vasquez, and the members of our research groups for very helpful comments on previous versions of this article.

REFERENCES

Abramson, L. Y., & Alloy, L. B. (1981). Depression, nondepression, and cognitive illusions: A reply to Schwartz. *Journal of Experimental Psychology: General, 110,* 436–447.

Abramson, L. Y., Alloy, L. B., & Metalsky, G. I. (1988a). The cognitive diathesis-stress theories of depression: Toward an adequate evaluation of the theories' validities. In L. B. Alloy (Ed.), *Cognitive processes in depression.* New York: Guilford.

Abramson, L. Y., Garber, J., Edwards, N. B., & Seligman, M. E. P. (1978). Expectancy changes in depression and schizophrenia. *Journal of Abnormal Psychology, 87,* 49–74.

Abramson, L. Y., Metalsky, G. I., & Alloy, L. B. (1989). Hopelessness depression: A theory-based subtype of depression. *Psychological Review, 96,* 358–372.

Abramson, L. Y., Metalsky, G. I., & Alloy, L. B. (1988b). The hopelessness theory of depression: Does the research test the theory? In L. Y. Abramson (Ed.), *Social cognition and clinical psychology: A synthesis.* New York: Guilford.

Abramson, L. Y., Seligman, M. E. P., & Teasdale, J. (1978). Learned helplessness in humans: Critique and reformulation. *Journal of Abnormal Psychology, 87,* 49–74.

Alloy, L. B. (1982). The role of perceptions and attributions for response-outcome noncontingency in learned helplessness: A commentary and discussion. *Journal of Personality, 50,* 443–479.

Alloy, L. B., & Abramson, L. Y. (1979). Judgment of contingency in depressed and nondepressed students: Sadder but wiser? *Journal of Experimental Psychology: General, 108,* 441–485.

Alloy, L. B., & Abramson, L. Y. (1988). Depressive realism: Four theoretical perspectives. In L. B. Alloy (Ed.), *Cognitive processes in depression.* New York: Guilford.

Alloy, L. B., & Ahrens, A. (1987). Depression and pessimism for the future: Biased use of statistically relevant information in predictions for self versus others. *Journal of Personality and Social Psychology, 52,* 366–378.

Alloy, L. B., Clements, C., & Kolden, G. (1985). The cognitive diathesis-stress theories of depression: Therapeutic implications. In S. Reiss & R. Bootzin (Eds.), *Theoretical issues in behavior therapy.* New York: Academic Press.

Alloy, L. B., Hartlage, S., & Abramson, L. Y. (1988). Testing the cognitive diathesis-stress theories of depression: Issues of research design, conceptualization, and assessment. In L. B. Alloy (Ed.), *Cognitive processes in depression.* New York: Guilford.

Alloy, L. B., Kayne, N. T., Romer, D., & Crocker, J. (1989). *Predicting depressive reactions in the classroom: A test of a cognitive diathesis-stress theory of depression with causal modeling techniques.* Manuscript under editorial review.

Alloy, L. B., Kelly, K. A., Mineka, S., & Clements, C. M. (in press). Comorbidity in anxiety and depressive disorders: A helplessness/hopelessness perspective. In J. D. Maser & C. R. Cloninger (Eds.), *Comorbidity in anxiety and mood disorders.* Washington, D.C.: American Psychiatric Press.

Alloy, L. B., Peterson, C., Abramson, L. Y., & Seligman, M. E. P. (1984). Attributional style and the generality of learned helplessness. *Journal of Personality and Social Psychology, 46,* 681–687.

Anderson, C. A., & Arnoult, L. H. (1985). Attributional style and everyday problems in living: Depression, loneliness, and shyness. *Social Cognition, 3,* 16–35.

Anderson, C. A., Horowitz, L. M., & French, R. (1983). Attributional style of lonely and depressed people. *Journal of Personality and Social Psychology, 45,* 127–136.

Barnett, P. A., & Gotlib, I. H. (1988). Psychosocial functioning and depression: Distinguishing among antecedents, concomitants, and consequences. *Psychological Bulletin, 104,* 97–126.

Beck, A. T. (1967). *Depression: Clinical, experimental, and theoretical aspects.* New York: Harper & Row.

Beck, A. T. (1976).*Cognitive therapy and the emotional disorders.* New York: International Universities Press.

Beck, A. T., Hollon, S. D., Young, J. E., Bedrosian, R. C., & Budenz, D. (1985). Treatment of depression with cognitive therapy and amitriptyline. *Archives of General Psychiatry, 42,* 142–148.

Beck, A. T., Kovacs, M., & Weissman, A. (1975). Hopelessness and suicidal behavior: An overview. *Journal of the American Medical Association, 234,* 1146–1149.

Beck, A. T., Riskind, J. H., Brown, G., & Steer, R. A. (1988). Levels of hopelessness in DSM-III disorders: A partial test of content-specificity in depression. *Cognitive Therapy and Research, 12,* 459–469.

Beck, A. T., Rush, A. J., Shaw, B. F., & Emery, G. (1979). *Cognitive therapy of depression.* New York: Guilford.

Belsher, G., & Costello, C. G. (1988). Relapse after recovery from unipolar depression: A critical review. *Psychological Bulletin, 104,* 84–96.

Bolles, R. C. (1972). Reinforcement, expectancy, and learning. *Psychological Review, 79,* 394–409.

Bower, G. H. (1981). Mood and Memory. *American Psychologist, 36,* 129–148.

Brewin, C. R. (1985). Depression and causal attributions: What is their relation? *Psychological Bulletin, 98,* 297–309.

Brewin, C. T., & Furnham, A. (1987). Dependency, self-criticism, and depressive attributional style. *British Journal of Clinical Psychology, 26,* 225–226.

Brown, G. W., & Harris, T. (1978). *Social origins of depression.* New York: The Free Press.

Brown, J. D., & Siegel, J. M. (1988). Attributions for negative life events and depression: The role of perceived control. *Journal of Personality and Social Psychology, 54,* 316–322.

Carver, C. S., & Gaines, J. G. (1987). Optimism, pessimism, and postpartum depression. *Cognitive Therapy and Research, 11,* 449–462.

Clements, C. M., & Alloy, L. B. (1988). *Depression, depression-proneness and self and other evaluation: Perceiving the self when you believe you are another and others when you believe they are the self.* Manuscript in preparation.

Costello, C. G. (1972). Depression: Loss of reinforcers or loss of reinforcer effectiveness? *Behavior Therapy, 3,* 240–247.

Coyne, J. C., & Gotlib, I. H. (1983). The role of cognition in depression: A critical appraisal. *Psychological Bulletin, 94,* 472–505.

Crocker, J., Alloy, L. B., & Kayne, N. T. (1988a). Attributional style, depression, and perceptions of consensus for events. *Journal of Personality and Social Psychology, 54,* 840–846.

Crocker, J., Alloy, L. B., & Kayne, N. T. (1988b). *Depression, self-esteem, and attributional style.* Manuscript under editorial review.

Dweck, C. S., & Licht, B. G. (1980). Learned helplessness and intellectual achievement. In J. Garber and M. E. P. Seligman (Eds.), *Human helplessness: Theory and application.* New York: Academic Press.

Eaves, G., & Rush, A. J. (1984). Cognitive patterns in symptomatic and remitted unipolar major depression. *Journal of Abnormal Psychology, 93,* 31–40.

Ellis, A. (1977). The basic clinical theory of rational-emotive therapy. In A. Ellis & R. Grieger (Eds.), *Handbook of rational-emotive therapy.* New York: Springer.

Evans, M. D., Hollon, S. D., DeRubeis, R. J., Piasecki, J. M., Grove, W. M., Garvey, M. J., & Tuason, V. B. (1989). *Differential relapse following cognitive therapy, pharmacotherapy, and combined cognitive-pharmacotherapy for depression: IV. A 2-year follow-up of the CPT project.* Manuscript submitted for publication.

Festinger, L. A. (1954). A theory of social comparison processes. *Human Relations, 7,* 117–140.

Follette, V. M., & Jacobson, N. S. (1987). Importance of attributions as a predictor of how people cope with failure. *Journal of Personality and Social Psychology, 52,* 1205–1211.

Freud, S. (1917/1957). Mourning and melancholia. In J. Strachey (Ed. and trans.), *Standard edition of the complete psychological works of Sigmund Freud* (Vol. 14). London: Hogarth Press.

Gong-Guy, E., & Hammen, C. (1980). Causal perceptions of stressful life events in depressed and nondepressed clinic outpatients. *Journal of Abnormal Psychology, 89,* 662–669.

Greenwald, A. G. (1980). The totalitarian ego: Fabrication and revision of personal history. *American Psychologist, 35,* 603–618.

Haack, L. J., Dykman, B. M., Metalsky, G. I., & Abramson, L. Y. (1989). *Disambiguating causal dilemmas: Use of causally-relevant information by depressed, depression-prone, and non-depressed subjects.* Manuscript in preparation.

Halberstadt, L. J., Andrews, D., Metalsky, G. I., & Abramson, L. Y. (1984). Helplessness, hopelessness, and depression: A review of progress and future directions. In N. S. Endler & J. Hunt (Eds.), *Personality and behavior disorders.* New York: Wiley.

Halberstadt, L. J., Mukherji, B. R., Metalsky, G. I., Dykman, B. M. & Abramson, L. Y. (1989). *Cognitive styles among college students: Toward an integration of the cognitive theories of depression with cognitive psychology and descriptive psychiatry.* Manuscript under editorial review.

Hamilton, E. W., & Abramson, L. Y. (1983). Cognitive patterns in major depressive disorder: A longitudinal study in a hospital setting. *Journal of Abnormal Psychology, 92,* 173–184.

Hammen, C., & Cochran, S. (1981). Cognitive correlates of life stress and depression in college students. *Journal of Abnormal Psychology, 90,* 23–27.

Hammen, C., & de Mayo, R. (1982). Cognitive correlates of teacher stress and depressive symptoms: Implications for attributional models of depression. *Journal of Abnormal Psychology, 91,* 96–101.

Hammen, C., Marks, T., Mayol., A., & deMayo, R. (1985). Depressive self-schemas, life stress, and vulnerability to depression. *Journal of Abnormal Psychology, 94,* 308–319.

Hammen, C., & Mayol, A. (1982). Depression and cognitive characteristics of stressful life-event types. *Journal of Abnormal Psychology, 91,* 165–174.

Hollon, S. D., & Garber, J. (1980). A cognitive-expectancy theory of therapy for helplessness and depression. In J. Garber & M. E. P. Seligman (Eds.), *Human helplessness: Theory and applications.* New York: Academic Press.

Ickes, W., & Layden, M. A. (1978). Attributional styles. In J. Harvey, W. Ickes, & R. Kidd (Eds.), *New directions in attribution research* (Vol. 2). Hillsdale, NJ: Lawrence Erlbaum Associates.

Janoff-Bulman, R. (1979). Characterological versus behavioral self-blame: Inquiries into depression and rape. *Journal of Personality and Social Psychology, 37,* 1798–1809.

Kazdin, A. E., French, N. H., Unis, A. S., Esveldt-Dawson, K. & Sherick, R. B. (1983). Hopelessness, depression, and suicidal intent among psychiatrically disturbed inpatient children. *Journal of Consulting and Clinical Psychology, 51,* 504–510.

Kelley, H. H. (1967). Attribution theory in social psychology. In D. Levine (Ed.), *Nebraska symposium on motivation* (Volume 15). Lincoln: University of Nebraska Press.

Kendell, R. E. (1968). *The classification of depression illness.* London: Oxford University Press.

Klein, D. F. (1974). Endogenomorphic depression: Conceptual and terminological revision. *Archives of General Psychiatry, 31,* 447–454.

Klerman, G. L. (1978). The evolution of a scientific nosology. In J. C. Shershow (Ed.), *Schizophrenia: Science and practice.* Cambridge, Mass.: Harvard University Press.

Klinger, E. (1975). Consequences of commitment to and disengagement from incentives. *Psychological Review, 82,* 1–25.

Lewinsohn, P. M., Steinmetz, J. L., Larson, D. W., & Franklin, J. (1981). Depression-related cognitions: Antecedent or consequence? *Journal of Abnormal Psychology, 90,* 213–219.

Lloyd, C. (1980a). Life events and depressive disorder reviewed: I. Events as predisposing factors. *Archives of General Psychiatry, 37,* 529–535.

Lloyd, C. (1980b). Life events and depressive disorder reviewed: II. Events as precipitating factors. *Archives of General Psychiatry, 37,* 541–548.

Lloyd, C., Zisook, S., Click, M., Jr., & Jaffe, K. E. (1981). Life events and response to antidepressants. *Journal of Human Stress, 7,* 2–15.

Mandler, G. (1964). The interruption of behavior. In D. Levine (Ed.), *Nebraska Symposium on Motivation* (pp. 163–219). Lincoln: University of Nebraska Press.

Mandler, G. (1972). Helplessness: Theory and research in anxiety. In C. D. Spielberger (Ed.), *Anxiety: Current trends in theory and research* (pp. 359–374). New York: Academic Press.

Martin, D., Abramson, L. Y., & Alloy, L. B. (1984). The illusion of control for self and others in depressed and nondepressed college students. *Journal of Personality and Social Psychology, 46,* 125–136.

McArthur, L. A. (1972). The how and what of why: Some determinants and consequences of causal attributions. *Journal of Personality and Social Psychology, 22,* 171–193.

McLemore, C. W., & Benjamin, L. S. (1979). Whatever happened to interpersonal diagnosis? A psychosocial alternative to DSM III. *American Psychologist, 34,* 17–34.

Metalsky, G. I., & Abramson, L. Y. (1981). Attributional styles: Toward a framework for conceptualization and assessment. In P. C. Kendall & S. D. Hollon (Eds.), *Cognitive-behavioral interventions: Assessment methods.* New York: Academic Press.

Metalsky, G. I., Abramson, L. Y., Seligman, M. E. P., Semmel, A., & Peterson, C. (1982). Attributional styles and life events in the classroom: Vulnerability and invulnerability to depressive mood reactions. *Journal of Personality and Social Psychology, 43,* 612–617.

Metalsky, G. I., Halberstadt, L. J., & Abramson, L. Y. (1987). Vulnerability to depressive mood reactions: Toward a more powerful test of the diathesis-stress and causal mediation components of the reformulated theory of depression. *Journal of Personality and Social Psychology, 52,* 386–393.

Minkoff, K., Bergman, E., Beck, A. T., & Beck, R. (1973). Hopelessness, depression and attempted suicide. *American Journal of Psychiatry, 130,* 455–459.

Morse, S., & Gergen, K. (1970). Social comparison, self-consistency, and the concept of self. *Journal of Personality and Social Psychology, 16,* 148–156.

Needles, D. J., & Abramson, L. Y. (in press). *Positive life events, attributional style, and hopefulness: Testing a model of recovery from depression. Journal of Abnormal Psychology.*

Nolen-Hoeksema, S., Girgus, J. S., & Seligman, M. E. P. (1986). Learned helplessness in children: A longitudinal study of depression, achievement, and explanatory style. *Journal of Personality and Social Psychology, 51,* 435–442.

Olinger, L. J., Kuiper, N. A., & Shaw, B. F. (1987). Dysfunctional attitudes and stressful life events: An interactive model of depression. *Cognitive Therapy and Research, 11*, 25–40.

Paykel, E., & Tanner, J. (1976). Life events, depressive relapse and maintenance treatment. *Psychological Medicine, 6*, 481–485.

Peterson, C., & Seligman, M. E. P. (1984). Causal explanations as a risk factor for depression: Theory and evidence. *Psychological Review, 91*, 347–374.

Petrie, K., & Chamberlain, K. (1983). Hopelessness and social desirability as moderator variables in predicting suicidal behavior. *Journal of Consulting and Clinical Psychology, 51*, 485–487.

Rholes, W. S., Riskind, J. H., & Neville, B. (1985). The relationship of cognitions and hopelessness to depression and anxiety. *Social Cognition, 3*, 36–50.

Riskind, J. H., Rholes, W. S., Brannon, A. M., & Burdick, C. A. (1987). Attributions and expectations: A confluence of vulnerabilities in mild depression in a college student population. *Journal of Personality and Social Psychology, 53*, 349–354.

Rose, D. T., & Abramson, L. Y. (1987). *Negative cognition depression: Preliminary results from a longitudinal study to test the cognitive theories of depression.* Paper presented at the meeting of the American Psychological Association, New York.

Rosenberg, M. (1965). *Society and the adolescent self-image.* New Jersey: Princeton University Press.

Rush, A. J., Weissenburger, J., & Eaves, G. (1986). Do thinking patterns predispose depressive symptoms? *Cognitive Therapy and Research, 10*, 225–236.

Sacks, C. H., & Bugental, D. B. (1987). Attributions as moderators of affective and behavioral responses to social failure. *Journal of Personality and Social Psychology, 53*, 939–947.

Schachter, S. (1959). *The psychology of affiliation.* Stanford, CA: Stanford University Press.

Seligman, M. E. P. (1975). *Helplessness: On depression, development, and death.* San Francisco: Freeman.

Seligman, M. E. P., Abramson, L. Y., Semmel, A., & von Baeyer, C. (1979). Depressive attributional style. *Journal of Abnormal Psychology, 88*, 242–247.

Shaw, B. J. (1977). Comparison of cognitive therapy and behavior therapy in the treatment of depression. *Journal of Consulting and Clinical Psychology, 45*, 543–551.

Silverman, J. S., Silverman, J. A., & Eardley, D. A. (1984). Reply to J. H. Riskind and R. Steer. *Archives of General Psychiatry, 41*, 112.

Skinner, H. A. (1981). Toward the integration of classification theory and methods. *Journal of Abnormal Psychology, 90*, 68–87.

Sweeney, P. D., Anderson, K., & Bailey, S. (1986). Attributional style in depression: A meta-analytic review. *Journal of Personality and Social Psychology, 50*, 974–991.

Tesser, A., & Campbell, J. (1983). Self-definition and self-evaluation maintenance. In J. Suls & A. G. Greenwald (Eds.), *Psychological perspectives on the self* (Vol. 2). Hillsdale, NJ: Lawrence Erlbaum Associates.

Tiger, L. (1979). *Optimism: The biology of hope.* New York: Simon & Schuster.

Weiner, B. (1985). An attributional theory of achievement motivation and emotion. *Psychological Review, 92*, 548–573.

Weissman, A., & Beck, A. T. (1979). *The dysfunctional attitude scale.* Paper presented at the Annual Meeting of the American Psychological Association, New York.

Wise, E. H., & Barnes, D. R. (1986). The relationship among life events, dysfunctional attitudes, and depression. *Cognitive Therapy and Research, 10*, 257–266.

Zeiss, A. M., Lewinsohn, P. M., & Munoz, R. F. (1979). Nonspecific improvement effects in depression using interpersonal skills training, pleasant activity schedules, or cognitive training. *Journal of Consulting and Clinical Psychology, 3*, 427–439.

Zubin, J. E., & Spring, B. (1977). Vulnerability: A new view of schizophrenia. *Journal of Abnormal Psychology, 86*, 103–126.

15

Emotion and Developmental Psychopathology

Dante Cicchetti
University of Rochester and Director, Mt. Hope Family Center
Jennifer White
University of Wisconsin

The study of emotional phenomena has important implications for understanding the development and organization of the processes underlying abnormal ontogenesis. Theoreticians and researchers, trained in a variety of disciplines, have stressed the role that emotions play in the etiology and sequelae of many forms of child and adult psychopathology, including autism (Hobson, 1986; Kanner, 1943), the affective disorders (Beck, 1967; Becker, 1977; Cicchetti & Schneider-Rosen, 1986), and schizophrenia (Arieti, 1955/1974; Bleuler, 1911/1950). Most psychopathological disorders may be characterized either in terms of the intensity and/or the type of affects displayed; moreover, these disorders may be of an expressive and/or of a recognitory nature (Cicchetti & Schneider-Rosen, 1984; Cicchetti & Sroufe, 1978; Hesse & Cicchetti, 1982; Hobson, 1986).

In this chapter, we focus on how the emotions, either alone or in interaction with other ontogenetic domains, play a role in the formation, course, and consequences of developmental psychopathology. We first provide an historical overview of the way in which emotion and emotion-cognition relations have been viewed in mental illness. Next, we examine the nature of the interrelations among the cognitive, emotional, and linguistic domains in several groups of atypical populations. A variety of levels of data drawn from multiple contexts (e.g., the psychiatric clinic, the home, the laboratory), multidomains, and multidisciplines, are presented to illustrate the organization/disorganization of emotional and cognitive/linguistic development in atypical and "high-risk" populations. Illustrations are gathered from studies of three infant and child populations: infants and toddlers with Down syndrome, maltreated infants and children, and the offspring of parents with a manic–depressive disorder.

We likewise illustrate how the study of emotion in clinical populations can elucidate our understanding of several of the fundamental questions underlying the study of normal emotional development. Both in the biological and in the behavioral sciences, major systematizers have underscored the significance of studying deviant development to the formulation of a comprehensive developmental theory (Cicchetti, 1984, in press; A. Freud, 1965; Weiss, 1961; Werner, 1948).

HISTORICAL PERSPECTIVE ON THE MAJOR VIEWS OF THE ROLE OF EMOTION IN MENTAL ILLNESS

The role of emotion in psychopathology has been studied by thinkers and theorists throughout history (Mora & Brand, 1970). For example, writing in the 4th century B.C., Hippocrates viewed madness in relation to the interaction of the four bodily humors—blood, black bile, yellow bile, and phlegm—that resulted from the combination of the four basic qualities in nature—heat, cold, moisture, and dryness. Corresponding temperaments—sanguine, choleric, melancholic, and phlegmatic—were used to classify people's emotional orientation. This conceptualization of madness represented a radical move away from a belief in supernatural causation of mental disorders and a step toward a more medical scientific understanding.

Aristotle, also in the fourth century B.C., was the first person to postulate that the effective treatment of mental illness rested on the release of repressed emotions or passions. The first person to write detailed descriptions of the passions was Cicero. In his *Tusculanae Disputationes,* which was written in the 1st century B.C., Cicero considered "libido" (violent desire) to be the strongest passion. The first to use the term libido in a psychological sense, Cicero believed that excessive perturbation could cause diseases of the soul that resulted from errors in judgment. Contrary to the Stoic dogma of the time that psychological disturbances resulted from defects of reason, the Roman physician, Galen, in the 2nd century A.D., believed that psychological health depended on the proper balance of the rational, irrational, and lustful parts of the soul. Although perhaps most well know for his writings on religious themes, St. Augustine also placed much emphasis on the passions in his work in the 5th century A.D. St. Augustine accepted Cicero's classification of the four main passions as desire, fear, joy, and sorrow and believed, likewise, that these passions could be moderated by reason.

Thomas Aquinas, writing in the 13th century, stressed the body–mind unity and a biological foundation of psychopathology. Aquinas argued that the soul could not become sick; rather he believed that insanity was a somatic disturbance. Aquinas attributed mental disturbance to the deficient use of reason, resulting either from an interference of the passions or a dysfunctioning in the body. The view that the emotions represented an important internal force that, when not regulated by reason, could lead to melancholia through the mediating bodily actions, had begun to gain ground by the 16th century. Against the backdrop of the widespread belief in the role of the supernatural and the occult, Richard Burton, writing in the 17th century, argued in *Anatomy of Melancholy* that emotional factors, such as jealousy, solitude, fear, poverty, unrequited love, and excessive religiosity, played a key role in insanity.

The emphasis on reason and the disdain for irrationality that characterized the 18th century age of enlightenment was reflected in attitudes toward the mentally ill who were regarded as objects of ridicule. The physician Phillippe Pinel, best known for releasing the mentally ill from their chains, stressed the importance of predisposition, in particular concerning the role of the passions to the development of mental illness. According to Pinel, the passions or emotions were considered to be the link between mind and body. Building on Aristotle's belief that a balance of the passions was a prerequisite to good mental health, Pinel's conceptualization of treatment involved the doctor controlling the patients' will with his gaze and placing them in a structured environment. Following Pinel, Jean Etienne Esquirol dominated the early 19th century psychiatric movement and placed strong emphasis on the role of the emotions in the etiology of mental illness.

Kraepelin, writing in the early 20th century, also stressed the role of emotion in the development of schizophrenia and its relationship to the activities of the intellect and volition. Schizophrenia was characterized by a loss of the "inner unity" among emotion, cognition, and the will (Kraepelin, 1919/1971). Noting the schizophrenics' tendency to cry or to laugh without apparent reason, Kraepelin argued that without this underlying organization and integration, emotions did not correspond to ideas. According to this view, emotion and cognition were seen as products of an underlying associational or connective process without which their normal integration was not possible.

Bleuler, also in the early 20th century, placed much emphasis on the role of affectivity in the syptomatology of schizophrenia (1911/1950). Noting that emotional deterioration stands in the forefront of the clinical picture of schizophrenia, Bleuler pointed out that the disappearance of the affects signaled that an "acute curable psychosis" had become "chronic." According to Bleuler, affective indifference characterized schizophrenia. Although in milder cases and in the beginning of the disease there might be an affective oversensitivity, there is a lack of depth to the affect. Bleuler further noted the diagnostic power of the particular type of affect displayed in acute episodes of the disease. He contrasted the deeply felt affective expression of the manic–depressive patient with the superficial, melodramatic, and disunifying aspects of affectivity in the schizophrenic. Unlike the manic–depressive whose emotional lability and thought content are linked together (see also Kraepelin, 1921), the affective mood of the disturbed schizophrenic does not parallel the changing content of thought. Whatever affect is present in the schizophrenic is not, according to Bleuler, in response to thoughts but rather is an abnormal basic state of affectivity. This underlying affective rigidity can invest the expressions of an entire range of moods. For example, Bleuler observed that schizophrenics seem to laugh and cry with the same affective expression.

Bleuler viewed schizophrenia in terms of a breakdown in the relationship between affect and cognition (Bleuler 1911/1950). He attributed the distortions of logic characteristic of schizophrenic thought to the way in which affectively charged associations became substituted for logical operations. Bleuler believed that when logical reasoning weakened the influence of the affects became stronger. As a result, with the disintegration of the association pathways, the affects could connect any material to the split-off complexes of ideas so that any remaining logic served the affective needs.

In his important work on the clinical description of psychopathy, *The Mask of Sanity,* Cleckley (1941/1976) argued that one of the central characteristics of this disorder involved an elimination or an attenuation of affect. Although the expression of emotions appears to be normal in psychopathy, in fact, the psychopath does not really feel the emotions that are being expressed. The psychopath merely pantomimes emotions. Without the ability to feel deeply, the psychopath lacks a sense of value and sound judgment. Cleckley believed that this mimicry of truly felt emotion was paralleled in the cognitive domain. The psychopath appears to have perfectly normal logical thought processes, but basically the psychopath is only imitating these functions superficially. These defects in both emotion and reasoning contribute to the disorder that occurs at deep levels of personality integration and prevents experience from becoming adequately meaningful to the psychopath.

In summary, there has been a long and rich history on the role that emotion-cognition disequilibrium plays in the unfolding of psychopathology. Several themes are present in the earlier views on the role of emotion in psychopathology. One theme suggests a dysregulating, negative role for the emotions. According to this view, psychopathology is conceptualized as the result of unrestrained emotions. A second theme revolves around the regulating role of reason. Reason is conceived as the check by which the emotions can be kept under control. From this viewpoint, psychopathology is understood as resulting from deficits in reason that allow the emotions to become unrestrained in a fashion that is deleterious to the individual. A third, though less frequent, theme, found in the work of Aristotle, is that psychopathology, which results from the imbalance between cognition and emotion, can best be helped by the release of the emotions. A final theme concerns the way in which many of these earlier theorists viewed emotion and reason (cognition) as two very distinct domains.

Even though this work has raised major themes and is of historical, philosophical, and clinical import, until recent times there has been a paucity of experimental inquiry conducted on the nature of the relation between affect and cognition in infant, child and adult clinical populations. Guided by the organizational, developmental psychopathology framework, we next illustrate how research on a variety of clinical conditions in infancy and childhood both enhance our understanding of the organization of development in these populations as well as contribute to our knowledge of normal emotion-cognition relations.

The Organizational Perspective

The organizational approach to development (Cicchetti & Sroufe, 1978; Sroufe, 1979a) is based on a set of regulative principles that can guide research into and theorizing concerning human behavior (Sroufe & Rutter, 1984). These principles are called *regulative* in the sense that they should not be taken as empirical laws that can be seen in research and theory as simple translations of these principles into empirical terms (Werner, 1948). Instead, these principles are to be understood as heuristic tools that can aid in the detection of meaningful patterns in the great variety of data generated in contemporary studies of normal and pathological development (Cicchetti & Schneider-Rosen, 1986; Sroufe & Rutter, 1984).

According to the organizational approach, development may be conceived as a series of qualitative reorganizations among and within biological and behavioral systems, which occur through the processes of differentiation and hierarchical integration. Variables at many levels of analysis determine the character of these reorganizations: genetic, constitutional, neurobiological, biochemical, behavioral, psychological, environmental, and sociological. Furthermore, these variables are viewed as being in dynamic transaction with one another.

The qualitative reorganizations characteristic of development are conceived as proceeding in accordance with the orthogenetic principle (Werner, 1948), which states that the developing organism moves from a relatively diffuse and globally undifferentiated state, by means of differentiation and hierarchical integration, to a state of greater articulation and organized complexity. The orthogenetic principle may be seen as a solution to the problem of the individual's continuous adaptation to the environment and to the question of how integrity of functioning may be maintained via hierarchical integration despite rapid constitutional changes and biobehavioral shifts (Block & Block, 1980; Sroufe, 1979b).

The organizational approach to normal development views it in terms of a series of interlocking social, emotional, and cognitive competencies. When competence occurs at one level, it allows environmental adaptation and prepares the way for future competence (Sroufe & Rutter, 1984). Normal development is marked by the integration of earlier competencies into later modes of functioning. It follows then that early adaptation tends to promote later adaptation and integration.

In contrast, pathological development is perceived as a lack of integration of the social, emotional, and cognitive competencies that underlie adaptation at a particular developmental level (Cicchetti & Schneider-Rosen, 1984; Kaplan, 1966; Sroufe, 1979a). Because early structures often are incorporated into later structures, an early disturbance in functioning may ultimately cause much larger disturbances to appear later on.

The organizational perspective, with its emphasis on the study of developing systems, provides an excellent theoretical framework for conducting research on the interface between emotion and cognition. Contemporary conceptions of the nature of this relation are based on the sequence of emergence of new cognitive or affective qualities or characteristics (Hesse & Cicchetti, 1982). Emotions may be regarded as developing ontogenetically earlier than cognition, thereby providing the context within which cognitive development may occur (*cognitive epiphenomenalism*). The emergence of new emotions may be dependent on cognitive advances that must be made before various emotions may be expressed (*emotional epiphenomenalism*). Emotions may develop along a separate pathway from cognitive advances so that the sequence, rate, and quality of change must be considered distinctly within each domain (*parallelism*). Finally, emotions may emerge in interaction with cognitive advances, thereby suggesting a progression that necessitates a consideration of developmental changes that occur across domains and that exert a reciprocal influence on each other (*interactionism*).

Developmental Psychopathology

The discipline of developmental psychopathology has been built on the idea that a developmental approach could be applied to any unit of behavior or discipline and to all cultures or populations, normal or otherwise atypical (Cicchetti & Pogge-Hesse, 1982; Kaplan, 1966; Werner, 1948). Developmental psychopathology emphasizes the argument put forth by many of the great synthetic thinkers in psychology, that we can learn more about the normal functioning of an organism by studying its pathology and, likewise, more about its pathology by studying its normal condition (see Cicchetti, in press, for a review). To understand more fully the process of maladaptation, consideration must be made of the results of many different scientific domains, including developmental psychology, traditional academic psychology, the clinical sciences of psychiatry and clinical psychology, sociology, epidemiology, and the neurosciences (Cicchetti, 1984). Furthermore, by virtue of its interdisciplinary nature, the field of developmental psychopathology requires that multiple domains of development be studied, including cognitive, socioemotional, linguistic, and biological processes (Cicchetti, 1984; Rutter & Garmezy, 1983).

EMOTION-COGNITION RELATIONS IN INFANTS AND CHILDREN WITH DOWN SYNDROME

The study of children with Down syndrome provides the opportunity to investigate systematically the role of emotion, both alone and in its relation to other developmental domains, in the course of development. Down syndrome provides a particularly valuable case for conducting such an effort for several reasons. For one thing, Down syndrome is etiologically homogeneous. Moreover, because it is detectable at birth, Down syndrome can be charted longitudinally. Furthermore, Down syndrome has a suitable complexity and intactness of phenotypic expression, as well as a frequent enough occurrence, to make possible meaningful developmental analysis (see Cicchetti & Beeghly, in press-a).

Infants with Down syndrome are an atypical population in which the study of the relation between affect and cognition is a particularly worthwhile endeavor. In fact, these retarded infants provide an important test of the relation between emotional and cognitive development. Unlike the case with the rapidly developing normal infant, in whom the simultaneous emergence of behaviors may be viewed as coincidental, the slower advances of children with Down syndrome through the same progression of stages as normal babies allow us to see and to demonstrate true convergences and discontinuities in development. Because of the slower cognitive development of infants with Down syndrome, it is possible to separate the early prototypes of what will later be affective expression from genuine emotional reactions that are dependent on psychological processes (Cicchetti & Sroufe, 1978). Finally, their developmental heterogeneity allows specification of the interdependence of the relation between affect and cognition.

Studies of Positive Affect

The ontogenesis of smiling and laughter in infants with Down syndrome provides a good illustration of the intimate connection that underlies emotional and cognitive development. Previous research with several samples of nonretarded infants between the ages of 4 and 12 months found that changes in laughter were associated with advancing cognitive development (Sroufe & Wunsch, 1972). Whereas infants in the first half year of life laughed mostly in situations that were physically intense or vigorous, increasingly during the second year of life, infants laughed at progressively more subtle and complex social and visual stimulation and were less likely to laugh at simpler stimuli. Based on an organizational understanding of the interdependence of affect and cognition, one would predict that infants with Down syndrome who show atypical cognitive development would also show a parallel lag in their affective development. If affective development is a function of cognitive development, and not merely an epiphenomenon of chronological age, then the sequence of affective stages should occur in the same order as reported by Sroufe and Wunsch (1972), but at a rate corresponding to the degree of cognitive retardation of the child.

In a study conducted with 25 infants with Down syndrome between 4 and 24 months of age, babies were presented with the standard series of 30 laughter items used in studies of normal infants (Cicchetti & Sroufe, 1976, 1978). In addition, cognitive and motor assessments by persons unfamiliar with the infants' performance on the laughter items were conducted. These included the Uzgiris–Hunt (1975) ordinal scales of cognitive development that were administered at 13, 16, 19, 21, and 24 months and the Bayley (1969) Mental and Motor scales, given at 16, 19, and 24 months. The results revealed that, even though infants with Down syndrome showed a later onset of laughter, they laughed at these incongruous stimulus items in the same order as normal infants—initially to intrusive auditory and tactile items, later to the more complex social and visual items. This ordering suggests an interrelation between cognitive and affective development. Furthermore, as is the case with the nonretarded infant, with development it appears that it is the infant with Down syndrome's *effort* in processing the stimulus content or *participation* in the event that produces the tension necessary for smiling and laughter, rather than stimulation per se (Kagan, 1971; Sroufe & Waters, 1976); that is, as schema formation becomes increasingly important in the elicitation of positive affect, it is no longer stimulation per se that produces the affective response but the infant's "effort" in processing of stimulus content. Both infants with Down syndrome and nonretarded infants develop toward an ever more active participation in producing affectively effective stimulation. In this example of the development of smiling and laughter in infants with Down syndrome, the similarity in the ordering of the responsivity to the laughter items to that demonstrated in nonretarded infants suggests that the development of the emotional domain is inextricably interwoven with changes within the cognitive arena.

Moreover, evidence from the results of the cognitive tests strengthens this interactive conceptualization of the relation between affective and cognitive development. It was found that the level of cognitive development as measured by performance on the Uzgiris–Hunt and Bayley scales correlated highly with the level of affective development as measured by the smiling and laughter items.

Studies on the Development of Negative Affect

The organizational perspective assumes a close relation between strong positive and strong negative affect in that they are linked by degree of cognitively produced arousal (Sroufe & Waters, 1976). Because the same event can produce the range of affective reactions, factors beyond information inherent in the event are seen as influencing the direction of and thresholds for affective reactions (Cicchetti & Sroufe, 1976, 1978; Sroufe & Waters, 1976).

Two of the classic paradigms utilized to assess the development of depth perception employed by researchers in perceptual development have been the study of infants' reactions to "looming" objects (Bower, Broughton, & Moore, 1970) and the study of infants' (both prelocomotor and locomotor) responses to the "visual cliff" (Campos, Hiatt, Ramsay, Henderson, & Svejda, 1978; Gibson & Walk, 1960). Cicchetti and Sroufe (1978) found that these experimental procedures have provided valuable information about the relation between the ontogenesis of negative emotions and cognitive development in infants with Down syndrome.

Cicchetti and Sroufe (1978) have compared infants with Down syndrome and nonretarded infants' responses to looming objects at 4, 8, and 12 months and studied infants with Down syndrome's responses at 16 months. Although there were no differences in the amount of crying displayed at 4 months, significantly more normal infants than those with Down syndrome cried at 8 and 12 months. Actually, it was not until 16 months that infants with Down syndrome showed any substantial crying. Moreover, those babies with Down syndrome who cried had significantly higher scores on the Bayley scales of mental and motor development than those who did not. Therefore, those infants with Down syndrome who had high Bayley scales and showed fear and distress reactions early were more differentiated in their cognitive and emotional development.

A close relation between cognitive and emotional development was also found in the study of infants with Down syndrome's reactions to being placed atop the visual cliff. It was found that far fewer infants with Down syndrome than normal infants exhibited fear reactions (for example, crying, heart rate acceleration, behavioral freezing), when placed directly atop the deep side. Just as was found for the looming data, the infants with Down syndrome who manifested negative reactions on the visual cliff were more cognitively mature, with significantly higher scores on the Bayley scales of development than those with Down syndrome who did not show fear.

These studies of infants with Down syndrome suggest that cognitive factors alone are not sufficient to account for the affective behavior of these babies. Analysis of the data indicates that the slower cognitive development of the youngsters with Down syndrome only partially accounts for the reduced incidence of more intense forms of affect expression (for example, laughter and crying). In the laughter studies, even after comparing the infants with Down syndrome with their mental-age-matched normal counterparts, less laughter was found than was the case with the normal infants. Likewise, even when cognitive-developmental level was comparable between infants with Down syndrome and nonretarded infants, normal babies showed more negative reactions to the visual cliff and to looming objects. Fewer infants with Down syndrome were fearful of being placed directly on the deep side of the visual cliff than their cognitive-developmental level would have led us to predict. Even taking developmental level into account, infants with Down syndrome manifested less crying than normal infants (Cicchetti & Sroufe, 1978). We interpret these data to mean that affect and cognition are indeed separate developmental systems, and that both of the epiphenomenalist positions on the relation between cognition and emotion (Hesse & Cicchetti, 1982) are thus refuted in infants with Down syndrome.

Affect-Cognition and Play

Studies examining the play behavior of children with Down syndrome have revealed more about the role of emotional development in Down syndrome. Moreover, they have provided valuable information about the organization of development in children with Down syndrome beyond the sensorimotor period. Researchers have noted that, although emerging cognitive abilities may underlie the structure of children's play, the force behind play is often affective in nature (Cicchetti & Hesse, 1983; Piaget, 1962). Studies of the play of nonretarded children have yielded information about the interrelations among affect, cognition, and symbolic development. Children's enthusiasm and persistence in object play have been found to be significantly correlated with the complexity and maturity of object play in these studies (Bretherton, 1984; Matas, Arend, & Sroufe, 1978). Similar interrelations between cognitive and affective dimensions of object play have been observed in children with Down syndrome (Beeghly & Cicchetti, 1987; Hill & McCune-Nicholich, 1981).

For example, in a longitudinal study of 31 children with Down syndrome, Motti, Cicchetti, and Sroufe (1983) found that both symbolic play maturity and affective play behavior at 3–5 years were significantly correlated with indices of affective and cognitive development assessed during the first and second years of these children's lives, respectively. Marked individual differences existed for these children such that children with a higher level of cognitive development engaged in more mature levels of symbolic and social play, explored toys more actively and thoroughly, were more enthusiastic during play, and exhibited more positive affect than less cognitively advanced children.

In a study conducted by Beeghly and Cicchetti (1987), results of correlational analyses revealed that affective-motivational play style (enthusiasm, persistence, positive affect) was significantly correlated both with level of cognitive development and with symbolic play maturity in children with Down syndrome and in cognitively matched normal children. These findings indicate that affective and cognitive aspects of symbolic development apparent in the play of children with Down syndrome are organized similarly to that of normal children at a comparable level of cognitive development. As was the case with the data on the development of positive and negative affect, these studies support an interactional interpretation on the relation between affect and cognition (Hesse & Cicchetti, 1982).

EMOTION-COGNITION RELATIONS
IN MALTREATED CHILDREN

The empirical study of emotional development in maltreated children is a relatively recent phenomenon (Aber & Cicchetti, 1984; Cicchetti & Carlson, 1989). We believe that the study of maltreated children can make many significant contributions to the understanding of normal emotional development. When there are prominent and pervasive disturbances in the parent–child–environment transaction, such as is the case with child maltreatment, the child is at a greater risk for suffering the negative consequences of the "continuum of caretaking casualty" (Sameroff & Chandler, 1975). Given the negative impact that poor quality parent–child relationships exert on the emotional and cognitive development of normal children (Sroufe, 1979a, 1983), it is likely that maltreated children will manifest even greater disturbances in the organization of their cognitive and emotional systems.

Further evidence for the interdependence of affective and cognitive development comes from a study conducted with maltreated children by Schneider-Rosen and Cicchetti (1984), which demonstrated the importance of the quality of the attachment relationship for the development of visual self-recognition. These investigators hypothesized that the emergence of similar affective and cognitive advances underlie the achievement of these salient developmental tasks, and, therefore, that the finding of a significant relationship between quality of attachment and visual self-recognition would provide evidence for the mutually interacting nature of affective and cognitive development. In a sample of 18 maltreated and 19 matched lower class comparison 19-month-old infants, 41% displayed self-recognition as assessed by the standard mirror-and-rouge paradigm (Lewis & Brooks-Gunn, 1979). When data for the entire sample were analyzed, it was found that those infants who recognized themselves were significantly more likely to be securely attached to their mothers. A separate analysis of the maltreated and comparison group infants revealed a different pattern of results. Of the comparison infants who recognized themselves, 90% were securely attached to their caregivers. In contrast, for those maltreated infants who recognized themselves, there was no significant relationship between this capacity and qualitative differences in the security of attachment (see Schneider-Rosen & Cicchetti, 1984).

An analysis of the infants' affective responses to their rouge-marked noses indicated that maltreated infants possess a differential understanding of this event and tend to be developmentally delayed or impaired in their affective reactions to their mirror images. After observing themselves in the mirror, a significantly greater percentage of the nonmaltreated infants (74%) showed an increase in positive affect following the application of rouge, whereas a greater proportion of the maltreated infants (78%) showed neutral or negative reactions. These results suggest that maltreated toddlers either attempt to mask their feelings or experience themselves in mainly negative ways. In addition, there were no differences between the infants who did and those who did not recognize themselves in age or in level of performance on the object performance subscale of the Uzgiris–Hunt (1975). Thus, these results highlight the importance of affective components in the development of visual self-recognition because cognition was necessary but not sufficient for the emergence of this capacity.

The study of maltreated infants has led researchers to hypothesize about the importance of infants' observations of parents' emotional styles for the development of emotional control (Cicchetti & Schneider-Rosen, 1984). The greater proportion of insecurely attached maltreated infants (Crittenden, 1988; Schneider-Rosen, Braunwald, Carlson, & Cicchetti, 1985) indicates that infants exposed to maltreatment by a primary caregiver may be at greater risk for delays or deviations in their acquisition of emotional control as a result of their caregivers' decreased affective responsiveness and sensitivity. In the normal development literature, Cummings, Zahn-Waxler, and Radke-Yarrow (1981) found that expressions of anger by normal infants' caregivers frequently caused distress in the infants. Repeated exposures to anger between the parents increased the likelihood of a negative emotional reaction by the infants, as well as the active involvement of the infants in their parents' conflict. By approximately 1 year of age, infants not only were aware of angry interactions between persons important to them but also were likely to evidence an emotional reaction to them. These results suggest that infants' sense of security and feelings about the self, as well as their capacity to display certain positive and negative emotional responses, may be affected by either constant strife or harmony in their environment.

Recent work (Goodman & Rosenberg, 1987; Rosenberg, 1987) in the area of emotional maltreatment has demonstrated that children who witness violence in the home (e.g., screaming, repeated beatings, chokings, assaults with weapons, property destruction, suicide and homicide attempts) are highly likely to develop a myriad of emotional and social-cognitive difficulties. For example, children who are exposed to interparental violence may develop problematic coping and interpersonal problem-solving strategies that may interfere with their relationships with family members (e.g., parents, siblings) and peers or with their school performance (Goodman & Rosenberg, 1987). Further research on the role that background anger has on the relation between emotion and cognition in maltreated children is clearly warranted.

Recent studies have implicated the deleterious impact of maltreatment on the development of internal state/emotional language. Although infants can produce and comprehend nonverbal emotional signals by the end of the first year, it is only after mastering verbal internal-state labels that young children can communicate about past or anticipated feelings, goals, intentions, and cognitions. The ability to use internal-state language allows companions to clarify understandings and misinterpretations during ongoing interactions. Earlier research in middle-class samples has shown that internal-state words first emerge during the second year and burgeon during the third (Bretherton & Beeghly, 1982). By 28 months, the majority of children have mastered verbal labels for perception, physiological states, volition and ability; more than half discussed emotion, moral conformity, and obligations, whereas only a few had begun to talk about cognition. In a study conducted by Cicchetti and Beeghly (1987), internal-state language was investigated in maltreated and nonmaltreated toddlers. Maltreated toddlers used proportionally fewer internal-state words, showed less differentiation in attributional focus, and were more context bound in use of internal-state language than their nonmaltreated peers. In contrast, the maltreated and nonmaltreated children did not differ significantly in the categorical content of their internal-state language (e.g., words about perception, volition, etc.) with two exceptions. Nonmaltreated children produced proportionally more utterances about physiological states (hunger, thirst, states of consciousness) and more utterances about negative affect (hate, disgust, anger, bad feelings).

The results of a maternal language interview revealed that, with very few exceptions, the maltreated toddlers produced far fewer internal-state words than did middle-class nonmaltreated youngsters of the same age (see Bretherton & Beeghly, 1982). In contrast, the percentages of nonmaltreated children reported to use different categories of internal-state language were markedly similar to that reported for middle-class children. Similar patterns of results were observed for maltreated childrens' ability to use internal-state words for both self and other; that is, maltreated toddlers lagged greatly behind their nonmaltreated comparisons in the use of internal-state words about the self and other. The lower SES nonmaltreated children were very similar in this capacity to nonmaltreated middle-class youngsters. The tendency for maltreated toddlers to use fewer emotional words may stem from parental disapproval of the expression of affect or of a certain class of affects. In effect, these children may become "overcontrolled" in efforts to meet parental demands. However, the fact that this overcontrolled stance is likely to serve as an adaptive coping strategy for the maltreated child must not be disregarded (cf. Schneider-Rosen et al., 1985).

We believe that these "self-system" difficulties bode poorly for the future adaptation of maltreated children. Bemporad, Smith, Hanson, and Cicchetti (1982) have documented a high incidence of early maltreatment in children with borderline syndromes, viewed by many as a disorder of the "self-system." Moreover, the concurrent relationship between childhood maltreatment and depression, another disorder that is affected by and affects the self-system, has been described by Kazdin, Moser, Colbus, and Bell (1985).

In the area of cognitive control development, the study of maltreated children has also elucidated the interdependence of affective and cognitive development. First formulated by George Klein (1951, 1954; Klein & Schlesinger, 1949), the concept of cognitive controls has been used to explain the way in which individuals coordinate information from the external environment, with the affects, fantasies, and motives from the internal environment, in order to remain in control of the information (Santostefano, 1978). Cognitive controls mediate between the influences of personality and motivation, on the one hand, and cognitions, on the other, and evolve as enduring aspects of the individual's cognitive functioning and adaptive style, while continuing to exert influence over subsequent cognitive experiences (Rieder & Cicchetti, 1989). Rieder and Cicchetti (1989) demonstrated that a history of maltreatment was related to cognitive control development in preschool and early school-age children. Maltreated children were found to be delayed in their cognitive control functioning during the assessment of cognitive controls in a relatively neutral, nonaggressive context. Moreover, maltreated children were found to assimilate aggressive stimuli more readily and with less distortion. Rieder and Cicchetti (1989) argued that the requirements (call for action) of aggressive fantasies of maltreated children pre-scribed a coordination/balance that called for the ready assimilation (sharpening) of aggressive stimuli. In nonmaltreated children, in contrast, the requirements of aggressive fantasies prescribed a coordination/balance between fantasy and stim-uli resulting in avoidance (leveling) of aggressive stimuli. Rieder and Cicchetti (1989) hypothesized that the requirements of a maltreating environment encour-aged the development of a hypervigilance and ready assimilation of aggressive stimuli as an adaptive coping strategy. In addition, Rieder and Cicchetti (1989) noted that the problems in the cognitive-affective balance of maltreated children may lead them to be overly attuned to interpret ambiguous stimuli in the environ-ment as threatening and aggressive. Delays in cognitive control functioning and a readiness to assimilate aggressive stimuli could lead children to experience diffi-culty in their peer interactions (Cicchetti, Lynch, Shonk, & Todd Manly, in press; Mueller & Silverman, 1989). These results point to the importance of environmental factors on the development of the affective-cognitive balance and suggest that there may be negative ramifications for maltreated children's so-cioemotional development.

EMOTIONAL DEVELOPMENT IN THE OFFSPRING
OF PARENTS WITH MANIC–DEPRESSIVE DISORDER

Historically, adults with manic–depressive illness have been characterized as having problems with the regulation of affect. For example, Kraepelin (1921) considered emotional dysregulation to be one of the hallmark symptoms of bipolar disorder. In unipolar depressive disorder, the relation between affect and cognition has been viewed in terms of the circular, positive feedback that can obtain between depressed affect and negative cognitions (Beck, 1967). The study of manic–depressive parents and their offspring provides an important oppor-tunity to examine the roots of affect dysregulation as well as to trace the possible cognitive contributions to the ontogenesis of this disorder. Moreover, the study of the emotional and cognitive development of the offspring of manic–depressive parents can further our understanding of their links with the neurobiological, genetic, and biochemical anomalies characteristic of this disease (Akiskal & McKinney, 1975; Nurnberger & Gershon, 1984; Post & Ballenger, 1984).

Results from the NIMH/Colorado collaborative studies indicate that young children of parents with manic–depressive disorder experience specific difficul-ties in the adaptive regulation of emotion (Gaensbauer, Harmon, Cytryn, & McKnew, 1984; Zahn-Waxler, McKnew, Cummings, Davenport, & Radke-Yar-row, 1984). For example, Gaensbauer et al. (1984) found that, when compared to control children, children of parents with a manic–depressive disorder exhibited more fear in situations in which less fear would be expected (for example, during free play and during reunion with mother after a brief separation at 12 months) and exhibited less fear in situations where more would be expected (for example, during a brief maternal separation at 15 months). These investigators interpreted their findings as indicating that the children of manic–depressive parents appear to prolong the experience and expression of affect (e.g., a slow recovery time from a disruptive emotion). Another interpretation of these findings is that the interjection of fear into the attachment relationship is indicative of the formation of an insecure "disorganized/disoriented" (Type D) attachment with the primary caregiver (Carlson, Cicchetti, Barnett, & Braunwald, 1989; Main & Solomon, in press). Clearly, it is important to further question the way in which these children's cognitive understanding of these situations could impact on their emotional experiencing of them.

Zahn-Waxler, McKnew, and colleagues (1984) noted another important example of the dysregulation of affect in the offspring of manic–depressive parents. When compared to control children, the children of the manic–depressive parents expressed more aggression not toward mother but toward peers, after a brief separation. The pattern of increased anger and aggression toward the mother on reunion after a brief separation is an empirically well-documented and theoretically well-understood characteristic of infants and young toddlers who are insecurely attached to their mothers (Ainsworth, Blehar, Waters, & Wall, 1978; Radke-Yarrow, Cummings, Kuczynski, & Chapman, 1985). Cicchetti and Aber (1986) argue that the expression of anger and aggression toward peers can be analogized to avoidant behavior as a response to reunion; like the avoidant response on reunion with the caregiver that helps children to organize and to maintain some degree of self-control over their potentially disorganizing angry feelings and aggressive behaviors, the expression of aggression against the peer functions as an attempt to maintain proximity without directly seeking or expressing anger at (and risking rejection by) the mother. Cicchetti and Aber (1986) argue that this makes sense based on their clinical observations that the expression of anger between peers usually stimulates parents (including depressed parents) to establish greater physical contact with their children.

Zahn-Waxler, Cummings, McKnew, and Radke-Yarrow (1984) note that during distress simulations offspring of manic–depressive parents are relatively unlikely to seek guidance or reassurance from caregivers or to employ social referencing. Klinnert, Campos, Sorce, Emde, and Svejda (1983) have shown that infants engage in social referencing, a process in which infants look to and are guided by their mothers' emotional expressions in situations of emotional uncertainty. Because the response of the caregiver plays a key role for infants in their emotional learning, infants who do not social reference may be missing out on an important source of learning in affectively arousing situations. However, as Zahn-Waxler, Cummings and their colleagues (1984) argue, if the caregiver is dysfunctional and is providing inappropriate affective cues (as a parent with a major bipolar manic–depressive disorder might be), it may be adaptive for the child not to depend on the adult.

Evidence from several areas of recent research indicates that the developmental changes in cognitive structures and functions impact on the manner in which children experience and express emotions. Cicchetti and Aber (1986) argue that the study of children "at risk" for depression requires a careful investigation of the development of new cognitive competencies and their relation to the development of affect. In particular, they cite the importance of taking into account insights from Kagan's (1981) work on the emergence of self-awareness during the second year of life. Kagan has found evidence that with the growth of certain cognitive capacities during the second year (e.g., speech, memory, relational inference, and symbolic play) also comes the emergence of self-awareness, which he defines as a set of psychological functions on which the ability to meet standards are based.

Kagan notes that 18–24-month-old children show emotional reactions of distress (e.g., clinging, crying, play inhibition, withdrawal) in response to their failure to imitate an adult model performing a series of symbolic acts that are somewhat beyond the children's abilities. Kagan views the affective response of distress primarily as epiphenomenal (Hesse & Cicchetti, 1982), as evidence of a set of two newly acquired cognitive competencies: (a) children's appreciation of adult standards of behavior, and (b) children's negative appraisal of their own ability to meet the adult standards. With the advent of representational thought, children are now assumed to be capable of interpreting the adult behavior of modeling as an obligation for them to imitate adult symbolic behavior. Because children also are able to represent their own abilities to themselves, children recognize their own inability to meet this inferred standard.

The results of this work are particularly relevant to studies of the social and affective development of children at risk for a unipolar or bipolar mood disorder. An appreciation of adult standards and an ability to evaluate one's own competencies to meet standards may be cognitive prerequisites to the capacity to feel shame and pride. Sroufe (1979b) has hypothesized the emergence of the affect of shame at exactly the same point in development as Kagan (1981) infers the onset of self-awareness. In addition, children's confidence in their ability to meet an adult-defined standard appears to have a motivating effect on subsequent efforts to meet adult-defined standards (known as effectance motivation; see Harter 1978). It is important to note that feelings of shame and lack of effectance motivation are central to the phenomenology of adult depressive states. In fact, developmental theorists have recently implicated feelings of shame and lack of efficacy in the development of depression (or vulnerability to depression) in children (Emde, Harmon, & Good, 1986). Other theorists have identified toddlerhood as a critical stage in the development of the self (Cicchetti & Beeghly, in press-b) and one of two stages of childhood (the other being adolescence) of high vulnerability to experiences of shame and shyness (Izard & Schwartz, 1986).

CONCLUSION

Guided by the tenets and principles of the organizational, developmental, psychopathology perspective, we examined the nature of the relation between emotion and cognition in infants and toddlers with Down syndrome, maltreated infants and children, and the offspring of parents with manic–depressive mood disorder. In addition, we discussed the role of emotional factors in the formation, course, and sequelae of these conditions. Quite strikingly, we showed that many of the major themes that emerged in our empirical work have been discussed since the writings of Aristotle. Unfortunately, even today there has been far too little systematic study of the role of emotion, both alone and in combination with other ontogenetic systems, in the etiology, evolution, and consequences of child and adult developmental psychopathology.

A major assumption of the developmental psychopathology perspective is that the study of atypical and/or pathological populations can inform our understanding of normal processes. The research and theoretical work that we have presented nicely illustrates how the study of emotion in abnormal groups of infants and children has contributed to our basic knowledge base on the emotions and on the organization and integration of emotional development with cognition. For example, the studies on the relation between affect and cognition and on the relation between affect and symbolization in infants and toddlers with Down syndrome provide corroborative evidence for an *interactional* interpretation on the relation between affect and cognition, both during the sensorimotor and preoperational period (Cicchetti & Hesse, 1983). Moreover, they refute *epiphenomenalist* viewpoints and buttress the prevailing belief, widely held throughout history, that emotion and cognition are separate developmental domains (cf. Izard & Malatesta, 1987). Likewise, research with maltreated infants and children and with the offspring of manic–depressive parents supports an interactionist view.

As a final example of what atypical populations might reveal about normal emotional development, the work on the relation between cognition and emotion in Down syndrome demonstrates that physiological/biochemical factors play important roles in the emotion-cognition interface. Recall that children with Down syndrome who were mental-age matched with normal children still manifested less positive and negative affect than their cognitive development would suggest. Because a focus on cognitive factors is insufficient to explain these data, individual differences in the strength of external stimulation necessary to produce a given amount of physiological stimulation must be simultaneously considered. Such differential responsiveness to stimuli might have its origins in physiological variables that reflect genotypic variations in the developmental pattern of the human species.

We believe that the arousal difficulties inherent in Down syndrome make it more difficult to energize the affective system in these children. At the physiological level, dopamine-beta-hydroxylase, an enzyme necessary for the conversion of dopamine into norepinephrine, has been found to be abnormally low in the blood of infants and children with Down syndrome (Axelrod, 1974; Weinshilbaum, Thoa, Johnson, Kopin, & Axelrod, 1971). This finding suggests that there are abnormalities in the functioning of their autonomic nervous systems.

An abnormality in catecholamine metabolism in children with Down synhas also been demonstrated by Keele, Richards, Brown, and Marshall (1969). These investigators reported that children with Down syndrome excreted significantly less epinephrine in their urine than did a control group of retarded children without Down syndrome. The finding of Keele and colleagues (1969), as well as the decreased dopamine–beta–hydroxylase levels aforementioned, implicates an immature adrenal system as being a possible explanation. The adrenal system is known to play a very critical role in mobilizing an organism to respond to stress and to respond fearfully. The adrenal medulla in infants with Down syndrome may not be sufficiently mature to support the full arousal of fear to nonpainful stimuli. Perhaps the differing rates and levels of maturation of the neuroendocrinological system, in combination with the slowed rate of cortical development, account, in part, for the muted affect systems of infants and children with Down syndrome (for an elaboration of this thesis, see Cicchetti & Ganiban, in press).

An equally important principle of the developmental psychopathology framework is that the study of pathological populations from a developmental, rather than from a clinical descriptive, approach will elucidate our understanding of disorders in ways that adevelopmental strategies cannot. Again, the results of the research we report substantiate this. For example, until the mid-1970s, the vast majority of the investigations conducted on children with Down syndrome focused on describing their anomalies and deficiencies. Consequently, over and over again it was confirmed that children with Down syndrome were *different* from normal children (Cicchetti & Beeghly, in press-a). From an organizational perspective, however, we have demonstrated that the organization of emotion and cognition is markedly similar between children with Down syndrome and their mental-age-matched counterparts (Cicchetti & Pogge-Hesse, 1982). Moreover, because of the slowed rate of development in these children, we were able to test specific hypotheses extant in the normal literature on the relation between emotion and cognition. In effect, as an "experiment of nature," Down syndrome permits us to observe the ontogenetic process in "slow motion"—albeit through the eyes of a different nervous system.

Furthermore, work with maltreated children enhances our understanding of normal emotional development. The studies reviewed revealed that many of their apparent cognitive problems are best understood with reference to the affective domain. For example, maltreated toddlers possess the cognitive prerequisites for visual self-recognition, yet they show lags in the manifestation of the age-appropriate affective expressions which accompany it. Moreover, their lags in emotional language use, and their hypervigilance with respect to distracting aggressive stimuli during cognitive control assessment, also attest to problems inherent in the emotion-cognition interface. Interestingly, children with Down syndrome, a condition characterized by an extra chromosome, in many ways show healthier development than maltreated children. We believe that these data underscore the importance of the vicissitudes of parenting for contributing to developmental outcome. After all, emotions generally take place in an interpersonal context. When the dyadic-matrix is impaired, as in the case of child maltreatment and manic–depressive disease, it is not surprising to find emotional problems. If investigators of these populations had pursued strictly cognitive research programs, then many of the important phenomena noted herein may have been overlooked and/or misinterpreted.

As for the nature of emotional organization, in children with Down syndrome we see that the differences are largely in intensity and in phenotypic expressiveness. These infants laughed less than mental-age-matched normals and generally showed more muted affect (Hesse & Cicchetti, 1982). Maltreated children and the offspring of manic–depressive parents appear to have genuine emotional problems. For example, maltreated children not only revealed delays and deviances in affect expression but also showed difficulties in the control of affect. Likewise, offspring of manic–depressives manifested problems in the regulation of affect. As such, both maltreated children and the offspring of manic–depressive parents are at great risk for the development of social problems and self-system difficulties. Although all three groups of children show manifest problems either in arousal modulation and/or in the control/regulation of affect, because of different genetic/biochemical diatheses, cognitive and linguistic abilities, and environmental inputs, the pathways to these phenotypically similar outcomes must take different courses (cf. Cicchetti & Schneider-Rosen, 1986).

Despite the great amount of progress that has been made in the area of emotion and developmental psychopathology, much important work lies ahead. As we have seen, the vast majority of research has been conducted with atypical and "high-risk" populations of infants and toddlers. It is essential that this work be extended to a more life-span perspective and include children and adults with DSM-III-R (American Psychiatric Association, 1987) diagnosed mental illnesses. Of course, parallel progress must be made in our understanding of normal emotional development as well as in our knowledge on the relation between emotion and cognition in normal populations during this period of life.

Furthermore, longitudinal studies on the processes underlying the relation between emotion and later developmental outcome are sorely needed in both clinical and normal populations. There are encouraging beginnings in this regard. Knight, Roff, Barrnett, and Moss (1979) have shown that ratings of affectivity and interpersonal competence were better predictors of later outcome in schizophrenics than ratings of thought disorder—the core cognitive symptom of dysfunction in schizophrenia. In a similar vein, researchers have found that family levels of expressed emotions can predict relapse rates among schizophrenic, manic–depressive, and depressed patients (Brown, Birley, & Wing,

1972; Hooley, 1986; Miklowitz, Goldstein, Neuchterlein, Snyder, & Mintz, 1988). Parents and spouses are rated as having either high or low levels of expressed emotion on the basis of scores measuring expressions of criticism, hostility, and overinvolvement toward the patients. Discharged psychiatric patients living at home with relatives with high levels of expressed emotion display significantly higher rates of relapse than patients residing with relatives with low levels. This finding further underscores the importance of the affective environment in the course of psychopathological disturbances. Finally, studies that address the relation between emotion and other ontogenetic systems (e.g., the "self-system" and peer relations), both concurrently and over-time, merit investigations with normal and pathological groups as well.

ACKNOWLEDGEMENTS

The research reported in this chapter was supported by grants from the W. T. Grant Foundation, the John D. and Catherine T. MacArthur Foundation Network on Early Childhood, the March of Dimes Birth Defects Foundation (12–127), the National Center for Child Abuse and Neglect (90-C-1929), the National Institute of Mental Health (R01-MH37960), and the Spencer Foundation to author Cicchetti. We would like to express our thanks to Victoria Gill for typing this manuscript.

REFERENCES

Aber, J. L., & Cicchetti, D. (1984). Socioemotional development in maltreated children: An empirical and theoretical analysis. In H. Fitzgerald, B. Lester, & M. Yogman (Eds.), *Theory and research in behavioral pediatrics,* (Vol. 11). New York: Plenum Press.

Ainsworth, M. D. S., Blehar, M. C., Waters, E. and Wall, S. (1978). *Patterns of attachment: A psychological study of the strange situation.* Hillsdale, NJ: Lawrence Erlbaum Associates.

Akiskal, H. S., & McKinney, W. T., Jr. (1975). Overview of recent research in depression: Integration of ten conceptual models into a comprehensive clinical frame. *Archives of General Psychiatry, 32,* 285–305.

American Psychiatric Association (1987). *Diagnostic and statistical manual of mental disorders* (3rd ed. rev.). Washington, DC, APA.

Arieti, S. (1955/1974). *The interpretation of schizophrenia.* New York: Plenum Press.

Axelrod, J. (1974). Neurotransmitters. *Scientific American, 230,* 58–71.

Bayley, N. (1969). *Bayley scales of infant development.* New York: Psychological Corporation.

Beck, A. T. (1967). *Depression: Causes and treatment.* Philadelphia: University of Pennsylvania Press.

Becker, J. (1977). *Affective disorders.* Morristown, NJ: General Learning Press.

Beeghly, M., & Cicchetti, D. (1987). An organizational approach to symbolic development in children with Down syndrome. In D. Cicchetti & M. Beeghly (Eds.), *Atypical symbolic development.* San Francisco: Jossey–Bass.

Bemporad, J., Smith, H., Hanson, G., & Cicchetti, D. (1982). Borderline syndromes of childhood: Criteria for diagnosis. *American Journal of Psychiatry, 139,* 596–602.

Bleuler, E. (1911/1950). *Dementia praecox or the group of schizophrenias.* New York: International Universities Press.

Block, J. H., & Block, J. (1980). The role of ego control and ego resiliency in the organization of behavior. In W. A. Collins (Eds.), *Minnesota Symposium on Child Psychology* (Vol. 13). Hillsdale, NJ: Lawrence Erlbaum Associates.

Bower, T. G. R., Broughton, J., & Moore, M. K. (1970). Infant responses to approaching objects. *Perception and Psychophysics, 9,* 193–196.

Bretherton, I. (1984). (Ed.). *Symbolic Play: The development of social understanding.* Orlando: Academic Press.

Bretherton, I., & Beeghly, M. (1982). Talking about internal states: The acquisition of an explicit theory of mind. *Developmental Psychology, 18,* 906–921.

Brown, G. W., Birley, J. L. T., & Wing, J. K. (1972). Influence of family life on the course of schizophrenic disorders. A replication. *British Journal of Psychiatry, 121,* 241–258.

Campos, J., Hiatt, S., Ramsay, D., Henderson, C., & Svejda, M. (1978). The emergence of fear on the visual cliff. In M. Lewis & L. Rosenblum (Eds.), *The development of affect.* New York: Plenum Press.

Carlson, V., Cicchetti, D., Barnett, D., & Braunwald, K. (1989). Finding order in disorganization. In D. Cicchetti and V. Carlson (Eds.) *Child maltreatment: Theory and research on the causes and consequences of child abuse and neglect.* New York: Cambridge University Press.

Cicchetti, D. (1984). The emergence of developmental psychopathology. *Child Development, 55,* 1–7.

Cicchetti, D. (in press). An historical perspective on the discipline of developmental psychopathology. In J. Rolf, A. Masten, D. Cicchetti, K. Neuchterlein, & S. Weintraub (Eds.), *Risk and protective factors in the development of psychopathology.* New York/London: Cambridge University Press.

Cicchetti, D., & Aber, J. L. (1986). Early precursors of later depression. In L. Lipsitt & C. Rovee-Collier (Eds.), *Advances in infancy research,* (Vol. 4). Norwood, NJ: Ablex.

Cicchetti, D., & Beeghly, M. (1987). Symbolic development in maltreated children: An organizational perspective. In D. Cicchetti & M. Beeghly (Eds.), *Atypical symbolic development.* San Francisco: Jossey-Bass.

Cicchetti, D., & Beeghly, M. (in press a). *Children with Down syndrome: A developmental perspective.* New York/London: Cambridge University Press.

Cicchetti, D., & Beeghly, M. (In press b) (Eds.), *The self in transition: Infancy to childhood.* Chicago, University of Chicago Press.

Cicchetti, D., & Carlson, V. (Eds.), (1989). *Child maltreatment: Theory and research on the causes and consequences of child abuse and neglect.* New York: Cambridge University Press.

Cicchetti, D., & Ganiban, J. (in press). The organization and coherence of developmental processes in infants and children with Down syndrome. In R. Hodapp, J. Burack, & E. Zigler (Eds.), *Issues in the developmental approach to mental retardation.* New York: Cambridge University Press.

Cicchetti, D., & Hesse, P. (1983). Affect and intellect: Piaget's contributions to the study of infant emotional development. In R. Plutchik & H. Kellerman (Eds.), *Emotion: Theory and research,* (Vol. 2). New York: Academic Press.

Cicchetti, D., Lynch, M., Shonk, S., & Todd Manly, J. (in press). An organizational perspective on peer relations in maltreated children. In R. Parke and G. Ladd (Eds.) *Family-peer relationships: Modes of Linkage.* Hillsdale, NJ: Lawrence Erlbaum Associates.

Cicchetti, D., & Pogge-Hesse, P. (1982). Possible contributions of the study of organically retarded persons to developmental theory. In E. Zigler & D. Balla (Eds.), *Developmental and difference theories of mental retardation.* Hillsdale, NJ: Lawrence Erlbaum Associates.

Cicchetti, D., & Schneider-Rosen, K. (1984). Theoretical and empirical considerations in the investigation of the relationship between affect and cognition in atypical populations of infants: Contributions to the formulation of an integrative theory of development. In C. Izard, J. Kagan, & R. Zajonc (Eds.), *Emotions, cognition, and behavior.* New York: Cambridge University Press.

Cicchetti, D., & Schneider-Rosen, K. (1986). An organizational approach to childhood depression. In M. Rutter, C. Izard, & P. Read (Eds.), *Depression in young people: Clinical and developmental perspectives*. New York: Guilford.

Cicchetti, D., & Sroufe, L. A. (1976). The relationship between affective and cognitive development in Down syndrome infants. *Child Development, 47,* 920–929.

Cicchetti, D., & Sroufe, L. A. (1978). An organizational view of affect: Illustration from the study of Down syndrome infants. In M. Lewis & L. Rosenblum (Eds.), *The development of affect*. New York: Plenum Press.

Cleckley, H. M. (1941/1976). *The mask of sanity.* St. Louis: C. V. Mosby.

Crittenden, P. M. (1988). Relationships at risk. In J. Belsky & T. Nezworski (Eds.), *Clinical implications of attachment theory*. Hillsdale, NJ: Lawrence Erlbaum Associates.

Cummings, E. M., Zahn-Waxler, C., & Radke-Yarrow, M. (1981). Young children's responses to expressions of anger and affection by others in the family. *Child Development, 52,* 1274–1282.

Emde, R. N., Harmon, R. J., & Good, W. V. (1986). The development of depressive feelings: Problems of empathy and a transactional model for research. In M. Rutter, C. Izard, & P. B. Read (Eds.), *Depression in young people: Clinical and developmental perspectives*. New York: Guilford Press.

Freud, A. (1965). *Normality and pathology in childhood: Assessments of development*. New York: International Universities Press.

Gaensbauer, T. J., Harmon, R. J., Cytryn, L., & McKnew, D. H. (1984). Social and affective development in infants with a manic–depressive parent. *American Journal of Psychiatry, 141,* 223–229.

Gibson, E. J., & Walk, R. (1960). The "visual cliff." *Scientific American, 202,* 2–9.

Goodman, G. S., & Rosenberg, M. S. (1987). The child witness to family violence. In D. J. Sonkin (Ed.), *Domestic violence on trial: Psychological and legal dimensions of family violence*. New York: Springer.

Harter, S. (1978). Effectance motivation reconsidered: Toward a developmental model. *Human Development, 21,* 34–64.

Hesse, P., & Cicchetti, D. (1982). Perspectives on an integrated theory of emotional development. In D. Cicchetti & P. Hesse (Eds.), *Emotional development*. San Francisco: Jossey-Bass.

Hill, P., & McCune-Nicholich, L. (1981). Pretend play and patterns of cognition in Down's syndrome children. *Child Development, 52,* 611–617.

Hobson, R. P. (1986). The Autistic child's appraisal of expressions of emotion. *Journal of Child Psychology and Psychiatry, 27,* 321–342.

Hooley, J. M. (1986). Expressed emotion and depression: Interactions between patients and high-versus-low expressed-emotion spouses. *Journal of Abnormal Psychology, 95,* 237–246.

Izard, C., & Malatesta, C. (1987). Perspectives on emotional development I: Differential emotions theory of early emotional development. In J. D. Osofsky (Ed.), *Handbook of infant development*. (Second Edition). New York: Wiley.

Izard, C. & Schwartz, G. (1986). Patterns of emotion in depression. In M. Rutter, C. Izard, & P. Read (Eds.) *Depression in young people: Clinical and developmental perspectives*. New York: Guilford.

Kanner, L. (1943). Autistic disturbances of affective contact. *Nervous Child, 2,* 217–250.

Kagan, J. (1971). *Change and continuity in infancy*. New York: Wiley.

Kagan, J. (1981). *The second year: The emergence of self-awareness*. Cambridge, MA: Harvard University Press.

Kaplan, B. (1966). The study of language in psychiatry: The comparative developmental approach and its application to symbolization and language in psychopathology. In S. Arieti (Ed.), *American Handbook of Psychiatry*, (Vol. I). New York: Basic Books.

Kazdin, A. E., Moser, J. Colbus, D., & Bell, R. (1985). Depressive symptoms among physically abused and psychiatrically disturbed children. *Journal of Abnormal Psychology, 94,* 298–307.

Keele, D., Richards, C., Brown, J., & Marshall, J. (1969). Catecholamine metabolism in Down's syndrome. *American Journal of Mental Deficiency, 74,* 125–129.

Klein, G. S. (1951). The personal world through perception. In R. R. Blake & G. V. Ramsey (Eds.), *Perception: An approach to personality.* New York: Ronald Press.

Klein, G. S. (1954). Need and Regulation. In M. R. Jones (Ed.), *Nebraska Symposium on Motivation,* (Vol. 2). Lincoln: University of Nebraska Press.

Klein, G. S., & Schlesinger, H. J. (1949). Where is the perceiver in perceptual theory? *Journal of Personality, 18,* 32–47.

Klinnert, M. D., Campos, J. J., Sorce, J. F., Emde, R. N., & Svejda, M. (1983). Emotions as behavior regulators: Social referencing in infancy. In R. Plutchik & H. Kellerman (Eds.), *Emotion: Theory, research, and experience* (Vol. II). New York: Academic Press.

Knight, R., Roff, J., Barnett, J., & Moss, J. (1979). Concurrent and predictive validity of thought disorder and affectivity: A 22-year follow-up. *Journal of Abnormal Psychology, 88,* 1–12.

Kraepelin, E. (1921). *Manic–depressive insanity and paranoia.* Edinburgh, Scotland: Livingston.

Kraepelin (1919/1971). *Dementia praecox and paraphrenia.* New York: Kreiger.

Lewis, M., & Brooks-Gunn, J. (1979). *Social cognition and the acquisition of self.* New York: Plenum Press.

Main, M., & Solomon, J. (In press). Procedures for identifying infants as disorganized/disoriented during the Ainsworth Strange Situation. In M. Greenberg, D. Cicchetti, & M. Cummings (Eds.), *Attachment during the preschool years.* Chicago, University of Chicago Press.

Matas, L., Arend, R., & Sroufe, L. A. (1978). Continuity of adaptation in the second year: The relationship between quality of attachment and later competence. *Child Development, 49,* 547–556.

Miklowitz, D., Goldstein, M., Neuchterlein, K., Snyder, K., & Mintz, J. (1988). Family factors and the course of bipolar affective disorder. *Archives of General Psychiatry, 45,* 225–231.

Mora, G., & Brand, J. (Eds.). (1970). *Psychiatry and its history.* Springfield, IL: Charles C. Thomas.

Motti, F., Cicchetti, D., & Sroufe, L. A. (1983). From infant affect expression to symbolic play: The coherence of development in Down's syndrome children. *Child Development, 54,* 1168–1175.

Mueller, N., & Silverman, N. (1989). Peer relations in maltreated children. In D. Cicchetti & V. Carlson (Eds.), *Child maltreatment: Theory and research on the causes and consequences of child abuse and neglect.* New York: Cambridge University Press.

Nurnberger, J. I., & Gershon, E. S. (1984). Genetics of affective disorder. In R. M. Post & J. C. Ballenger (Eds.), *Neurobiology of mood disorders (Vol. 1).* Baltimore: Williams & Wilkins.

Piaget, J. (1962). *Play, dreams, and imitation in children.* New York: Norton.

Post, R. M., & Ballenger, J. C. (Eds.) (1984). *Neurobiology of mood disorders (Vol. 1).* Baltimore: Williams & Wilkins.

Radke-Yarrow, M., Cummings, E. M., Kuczynski, L., & Chapman, M. (1985). Patterns of attachment in two and three year olds in normal families and families with parental depression. *Child Development, 56,* 884–893.

Rieder, C., & Cicchetti, D. (1989). Organizational perspective on cognitive control functioning and cognitive-affective balance in maltreated children. *Developmental Psychology, 25,* 382–393.

Rosenberg, M. S. (1987). New directions for research on the psychological maltreatment of children. *American Psychologist, 42,* 166–171.

Rutter, M., & Garmezy, N. (1983). Developmental psychopathology. In P. Mussen (Ed.), *Handbook of child psychology.* New York: Wiley.

Sameroff, A., & Chandler, M. (1975). Reproductive risk and the continuum of caretaking casualty. In F. D. Horowitz (Ed.), *Review of child development research* (Vol. 4). Chicago: University of Chicago Press.

Santostefano, S. (1978). *A biodevelopmental approach to clinical child psychology: Cognitive controls and cognitive control therapy.* New York: Wiley.

Schneider-Rosen, K., Braunwald, K., Carlson, V., & Cicchetti, D. (1985). Current perspectives in attachment theory: Illustration from the study of maltreated infants. In I. Bretherton & E. Waters (Eds.), Growing points in attachment theory and research *Monographs of the Society for Research in Child Development, 50,* Serial No. 209, 194–210.

Schneider-Rosen, K., & Cicchetti, D. (1984). The relationship between affect and cognition in maltreated infants: Quality of attachment and the development of self-recognition. *Child Development, 55,* 648–658.

Sroufe, L. A. (1979a). The coherence of individual development. *American Psychologist, 34,* 834–841.

Sroufe, L. A. (1979b). Socioemotional development. In J. Osofsky (Eds.), *Handbook of infant development* (First Edition). New York: Wiley.

Sroufe, L. A. (1983). Infant–caregiver attachment and patterns of adaptation in preschool: The roots of maladaptation and competence. In M. Perlmutter (Ed.), *Minnesota Symposium on Child Psychology* (Vol. 16). Hillsdale, NJ: Lawrence Erlbaum Associates.

Sroufe, L. A., & Rutter, M. (1984). The domain of developmental psychopathology. *Child Development, 55,* 17–29.

Sroufe, L. A., & Waters, E. (1976). The ontogenesis of smiling and laughter: A perspective on the organization of development in infancy. *Psychological Review, 83,* 173–189.

Sroufe, L. S., & Wunsch, J. (1972). The development of laughter in the first year of life. *Child Development, 43,* 1326–1344.

Uzgiris, I., & Hunt, J. (1975). *Assessment in infancy.* Urbana: University of Illinois Press.

Weinshilbaum, R., Thoa, N., Johnson, D., Kopin, I., & Axelrod, J. (1971). Proportional release of norepinephrine and dopamine–beta–hydroxylase from sympathetic nerves. *Science, 174,* 1349–1351.

Weiss, P. (1961). Deformities as cues to understanding development of form. *Perspectives in Biology and Medicine, 4,* 133–151.

Werner, H. (1948). *Comparative psychology of mental development.* New York: International Universities Press.

Zahn-Waxler, C., Cummings, E. M., McKnew, D., & Radke-Yarrow, M. (1984). Altruism, aggression, and social interactions in young children with a manic–depressive parent. *Child Development, 55,* 112–122.

Zahn-Waxler, C., McKnew, D. H., Cummings, E. M., Davenport, Y. B., & Radke-Yarrow, M. (1984). Problem behaviors and peer interactions of young children with a manic–depressive parent. *American Journal of Psychiatry, 141*(2), 236–240.

V SYSTEM APPROACHES TO EMOTION

16

Emotions in Relation to Systems of Behavior

James R. Averill
University of Massachusetts, Amherst

The purpose of this chapter is twofold: first, to present a general model for the explanation of emotional behavior, and second to explore some of the implications of that model for the analysis of emotional development. The study of emotion is plagued by terminological confusion. Therefore, I begin by distinguishing emotional syndromes (the primary focus of this analysis) from emotional states and reactions. I then illustrate how the origins and functions of emotional syndromes might be explained by reference to broader systems of behavior, defined in terms of biological, psychological, and social principles of organization. Although no one kind of principle is more "fundamental" than another in an absolute sense, the involvement of social principles of organization means that emotional syndromes are, to a significant degree, social constructions. Hence, the relation of emotional syndromes to social systems is explored in some detail, with special emphasis on the socialization of emotion.

SOME PRELIMINARY DISTINCTIONS

Emotional concepts (e.g., anger, fear, joy, contempt, jealousy, love, grief, and so forth) refer to *syndromes*. The dictionary (*Webster's New World*) defines a syndrome as "a set of characteristics regarded as identifying a type." Like most definitions, this one is ambiguous, especially with regard to the meaning of "type." Syndromes are theoretical entities; they exist "out there," so to speak, but only as abstractions. As such, emotional syndromes must be distinguished from emotional *states*, which are temporary (episodic) dispositions on the part of

385

individuals to respond in a manner representative of one or another emotional syndrome. An emotional *reaction* is the actual (and highly variable) set of responses manifested by an individual when in an emotional state.

To illustrate further the difference between emotional syndromes, states, and reactions, consider an emotion such as anger. As a syndrome, anger consists of the pattern of potential responses to a provocation (e.g., an appraised wrong), and the changes in that pattern over time. When in an angry state, a person is disposed to react in any of a variety of ways consistent with the syndrome. Some of these ways (e.g., physically or verbally attacking the instigator, plotting revenge, talking the incident over with a neutral party, withdrawing from the situation) are more characteristic of anger than are other ways (e.g., becoming extra solicitous toward the instigator). However, no single kind of reaction is a necessary or sufficient condition for the attribution of anger.[1]

Later in the chapter it becomes evident that different kinds of explanations are involved depending on whether an emotional syndrome, state, or reaction is taken as the unit of analysis. This discussion focuses primarily on emotional syndromes.

Three main characteristics of emotional syndromes require further explication. First, a syndrome is a theoretical construct, albeit at a relatively low level of abstraction. A simple physical analogy may help to illustrate this characteristic. The operation of an electrical apparatus can be described by a system of mathematical equations or formulas. Depending on the circumstances, the relevant formulas may be instantiated differently (given different values); the same set of formulas might thus be used to explain (and even guide the construction of) apparatus that, on the surface at least, appear to behave quite differently.

In the preceding analogy, an emotional syndrome is like the system of equations that explains the functioning of the apparatus. (Pursing the analogy further, an emotional state is like the apparatus in an "on" condition, and an emotional reaction is like the actual operation or output of the apparatus.) The analogy has many limitations, of course. Emotional syndromes cannot be represented by mathematical formulas, nor is their instantiation as rigid and invariant as the analogy might suggest. Yet, emotional syndromes do have a form, and they can be described in terms of underlying principles of organization, about which we will have much more to say shortly.

Second, emotional syndromes are polythetic; that is, the syndrome need not be manifested in any one type of response (e.g., a specific kind of cognitive appraisal or pattern of physiological arousal). Stated somewhat differently, emotional syndromes form "fuzzy sets" that lack essences and distinct boundaries (Averill, 1980; Fehr & Russell, 1984). As already noted, some types of responses

---

[1]Throughout this chapter, I draw on anger and related syndromes for examples. The research on which these examples are based has been presented elsewhere (Averill, 1982).

may be more characteristic of an emotion, or of emotion in general, than are other types of responses. Yet, even in the case of highly prototypic (but not essential) responses, what is true of the part (component response) need not be true of the whole syndrome. This "warning" might not seem particularly controversial. However, consider the following observations by Ekman (1984): "Although emotions do vary in duration, . . . I suggest that there may be absolute limits in the total duration of an emotion. Our studies of facial expression suggest that the great majority of expressions of felt emotions last between ½ second and 4 seconds" (p. 332). It is obvious that most emotions—felt or otherwise—endure for more than 4 seconds. In fact, with the possible exception of startle, any episode that lasted only 4 seconds would not be considered emotional at all. (Imagine being angry for 4 seconds, or in love.) Ekman recognizes this, and he proposes the use of the word "mood" to refer to emotional episodes of more standard duration. But such a substitution of terms seems an unnecessary complication, for then we would have to introduce another word for what we now call moods. Moreover, the study of facial expressions is worthwhile in its own right. One need not make the further assumption that what is true of an expressive reaction (e.g., with regard to duration, universality, etc.) is also true of an entire emotional syndrome.

Third, to form a syndrome, the potential responses must be interrelated in a *systematic* way, so that changes in one aspect of the syndrome will lead to changes in other aspects. Put another way, emotional syndromes are *subsystems* of behavior. To explain an emotion is, in a sense, to account for the coherency of the syndrome (in terms of underlying principles of organization), and to trace the origin and functional significance of those principles. The logical features of this kind of explanation are examined next.

THE EXPLANATION OF EMOTIONAL BEHAVIOR

To keep the discussion from becoming overly abstract, it might be helpful to have a concrete example to which we can refer for illustrative purposes. Bill and Joe are good friends. One day, Bill is seen, red in the face, yelling and shaking his fist at Joe. How do we explain this seemingly anomalous behavior?

A first answer to this question might be that Bill is angry at Joe. Becoming red in face, yelling, and shaking one's fist are the kinds of things a person sometimes does when in an angry state, at least in our culture. But whereas this answer rules out a number of other possible explanations for Bill's behavior (e.g., that he is envious of Joe's hard-earned success, or that he is rehearsing for a play), it does not take us very far. Pursuing the issue, we might further ask, Why is Bill angry? A common answer to this question would specify some causal variable (eliciting condition). Perhaps Joe borrowed Bill's car without asking permission, or perhaps Bill was in a nasty mood after breaking up with his girlfriend.

But let us assume that Joe has done nothing out of the ordinary to provoke Bill's wrath; in fact, Bill frequently becomes angry for seemingly innocuous reasons. If we now ask why Bill became angry at Joe, an appropriate answer might take into account Bill's personality structure (capacities and long-term goals). Bill is "hot tempered," even hostile, and he frequently attempts to intimidate others through a display of anger.

I call explanations of this latter type, structural/functional, in order to distinguish them from causal explanations that refer to eliciting conditions. The nature of structural/functional explanations is clarified as our discussion progresses. For the moment, suffice it to say that, in the broadest sense, a structural explanation seeks to uncover the principles that account for ("lie behind") the organization of behavior. However, behavior cannot be organized (structured) *simpliciter;* it must be organized with respect to something. That something helps to specify the function of the behavior. Stated somewhat differently, there cannot be structure without corresponding function, and conversely. The function that a structure serves (or at one time did serve) need not be obvious; and the structures that make a particular function possible are often difficult to identify. Much scientific research is devoted to discovering the function of some presumed structure, or the structure that makes possible some presumed function.

Returning to the example of Bill, the structural/functional explanation we offered for his frequent outbursts of anger appealed to psychological principles of organization (capacities, long-term goals). But we need not stop our inquiry with Bill's anger. How do we account for anger *in general* (i.e., for the syndrome of anger)? This question cannot be answered solely in psychological terms, for emotional syndromes are common to groups of persons. The underlying structure/function of an emotional syndrome must therefore be sought at the biological and/or social levels of analysis, as well as at the psychological.

Systems of Behavior

I now try to indicate more precisely what I mean by the structure/function of an emotional syndrome at biological, social, and psychological levels of analysis. As already indicated, emotional syndromes are (sub)systems of behavior. ("Behavior" is here interpreted very broadly to include thoughts and feelings, as well as overt responses.) As depicted in Fig. 16.1, systems of behavior can be distinguished in terms of levels of organization (the range of behavior included within the boundaries of a system) and principles of organization (the factors that account for the coherence of a system). To these, we add a third consideration, namely, degree of abstractness.

Levels of Organization

Systems are typically organized into hierarchies, such that one system is a component of another, more encompassing system. For example, a cell is part of an organ (the heart, say), the organ is part of a larger (cardiovascular) system,

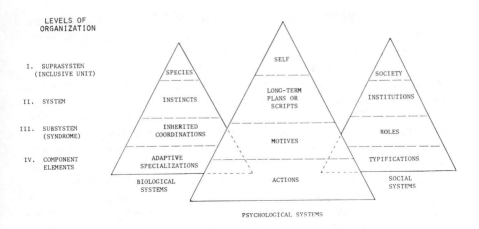

LEVELS OF
ORGANIZATION

I. SUPRASYSTEM
    (INCLUSIVE UNIT)

II. SYSTEM

III. SUBSYSTEM
     (SYNDROME)

IV. COMPONENT
    ELEMENTS

SELF

SPECIES   SOCIETY

INSTINCTS   LONG-TERM   INSTITUTIONS
                   PLANS OR
                   SCRIPTS

INHERITED   ROLES
COORDINATIONS
                   MOTIVES

ADAPTIVE   TYPIFICATIONS
SPECIALIZATIONS

BIOLOGICAL   ACTIONS   SOCIAL
SYSTEMS   SYSTEMS

PSYCHOLOGICAL SYSTEMS

PRINCIPLES OF ORGANIZATION

FIG. 16.1.   Systems of behavior defined in terms of levels and principles (biological, psychological, and social) of organization.

and the latter is part of the entire organism. Any system can thus be a *subsystem*
with respect to a higher order system, and also a *suprasystem* with respect to a
lower order system.

For ease of presentation, I (arbitrarily) limit discussion to four levels of
organization (see Fig. 16.1).

1. The Inclusive Unit.   The *inclusive unit* is the most encompassing (su-
pra)system that can be treated within a given frame of reference (i.e., without
invoking qualitatively different principles of organization). In the case of biological systems, the inclusive unit is the species; in the case of social systems, it is
the society; and in the case of psychological systems, it is the self.

2. Systems (Simpliciter).   *Systems (simpliciter)* are the major subunits that
contribute more or less directly to the survival and enhancement of the inclusive
unit. In the older literature, biological systems of behavior were referred to as
instincts (e.g., aggression, reproduction, and the like; cf. Bowlby, 1982). Analogously broad systems of behavior—labeled institutions in Fig. 16.1—can be
defined in terms of social principles of organization (cf. Giddens, 1979; Luhmann, 1982, Parsons, 1951). Some examples of social systems of behavior (and
their related functions) are the economic system (the production and distribution
of goods), the educational system (the socialization of the young), and the religious system (meaning and value articulation). Psychological systems are represented by cognitive schemata in the form of long-term plans or scripts (cf.

Mandler, 1984). These are more difficult to characterize in general terms than are either biological instincts or social institutions, for psychological systems are more or less idiosyncratic to the individual.

3. Subsystems. *Subsystems* are circumscribed but meaningful patterns of responses. Behavior at this level of organization is often given explicit recognition in ordinary language and may be manifest in conscious experience. Emotional syndromes, for example, are subsystems of behavior, as here conceived. In the biological hierarchy, responses at this level are equivalent to what Dewey (1895) called "teleological coordinations," by which he meant the inherited patterns of behavior that help constitute emotional syndromes. In the social hierarchy, social roles are subsystems of behavior; and hence, from a social perspective, emotions may be defined as social roles (Averill, 1980). In the psychological hierarchy, the term *motive* may be used to refer to subsystems of behavior; psychologically speaking, then, emotions may be regarded as a variety of motives (Buck, 1985).

4. Elements or Component Processes. *Elements or component processes* are the smallest units of analysis with which we are concerned. At the biological level, these are adaptive specializations (e.g., fixed action patterns, unconditioned reflexes); at the social level, typifications (conventionalized responses recognized as a given type, e.g., a handshake as a type of greeting); and at the psychological level, simple actions or instrumental responses. (Parenthetically, it might be noted that component processes, as defined here, are elementary only in a relative sense; they may actually be complex systems in their own right.)

Like the concave and convex sides of an arc, the system hierarchies just described are analytically, not concretely, separable; that is, they are abstractions or ways of analyzing behavior. There could be no social systems if there were no individuals to enter into relationships; nor could there could be psychological systems without biological organisms; and to complete the cycle, human beings could not exist as biological organisms outside of social systems. What differentiates the systems are their principles of organization, not the specific behaviors specified. I explain later exactly what I mean by "principles of organization." First, however, a few words need to be said about the abstractness of the systems.

Degree of Abstractness

As described earlier, emotional syndromes are abstract, theoretical entities (in contrast to emotional states and reactions). Abstractness, however, admits of degrees. Let us return briefly to our earlier example of Bill and his friend Joe. Recall that we explained Bill's aggressive outburst at Joe by reference to his (Bill's) anger. As theoretical explanations go, that is a relatively "low-level" explanation. Some psychologists (e.g., Skinner, 1974) have argued that such explanations are vacuous, because everyday terms such as "anger" are basically summary descriptions of the behavior to be explained. I believe that position is mistaken. As Ryle (1949) pointed out, everyday psychological concepts, including emotional concepts, are more like inference tickets than summary descriptions. Still, it must be admitted that emotional syndromes—as theoretical entities—do not extend far beyond the behavior they help explain.

As conceived of here, emotional syndromes are theoretical but nevertheless relatively concrete (sub)systems of behavior. Concrete systems are close to the behavior they purportedly explain, and they are, in turn, explicable in terms of more abstract (and differentiated) systems. In other words, abstract systems, such as those depicted in Fig. 16.1, "lie behind" more concrete systems (e.g., emotional syndromes) and account for the structural properties of the latter (see Harré, Clarke, & DeCarlo, 1985, for a detailed discussion of this kind of explanation in psychology).

Principles of Organization

For any relatively concrete system or subsystem of behavior, like an emotional syndrome, we can identify three broad classes of principles (biological, psychological, and social) that lend it organization. These principles account for the three abstract system hierarchies depicted in Fig. 16.1.

1. Biological Principles. *Biological principles* are represented by information encoded in genetic material. Except for some very rudimentary component processes (e.g., fixed action patterns and unconditioned reflexes), no concrete system of behavior is organized solely on the basis of biological principles, at least not in higher organisms. Biological principles can nevertheless exert considerable influence on certain patterns of behavior, even among humans. In such cases, it is meaningful to speak of biological systems in the abstract. In conventional terms, such abstract systems are *genotypic.*

2. Social Principles. *Social principles* are rules and resources embodied in symbols and other cultural artifacts. No phenotypic system is a direct and unalloyed expression of sociological principles, although certain religious and political rituals provide good approximations. Socialization is always subject to some biological constraints. Still, we may speak of social systems in the abstract, just as we can speak of biological (genotypic) systems.

3. Psychological Principles. *Psychological principles* are encoded in cognitive schemata or structures of knowledge (Mandler, 1984). Biological principles of organization are the result of biological evolution, and social principles are the result of social evolution. By analogy, it might seem reasonable to conceive of cognitive schemata as acquired during individual development (i.e., through learning). That, in fact, is the way some theorists conceptualize schemata. However, such a conceptualization identifies psychology too closely with learning theory (which, incidentally, is not an unfair characterization of American psychology for much of this century). Psychological systems actually represent an amalgam or product of both genotypic (biological) and sociotypic (social) principles, as these are transformed and elaborated on during the idiosyncratic history of the individual (which would include not only learning in the ordinary sense but also any alterations in functioning due to psychological and physiological trauma, disease, and the like).

The preceding considerations suggest that the distinction between psychological principles, on the one hand, and biological and social principles, on the other, is partly one of origin and partly one of "distance." Psychological principles are closer to the behavior they regulate, whereas biological and social principles are more distal in both an historical and a theoretical sense. (To illustrate this point, psychological systems are depicted in the foreground of Fig. 16.1.) It also follows that the distinction between concrete and abstract systems, described earlier, is less marked in the case of psychological systems; that is, behavior is a more direct and immediate expression of psychological principles than of biological or social principles.

To summarize briefly the discussion thus far, emotional syndromes are relatively low-level (concrete) theoretical entities (subsystems of behavior). By contrast, an emotional state is a disposition on the part of an individual to respond in a manner consistent with the syndrome, and an emotional reaction is the actual manifestation of such a disposition.

Emotional syndromes can be explained in terms of more abstract structures or system hierarchies, defined in terms of biological, social, and psychological principles of organization. These system hierarchies "lie behind" the emotional syndrome, lending it meaning and structure.

Referring to Fig. 16.1, the explanation of emotional syndromes can proceed both horizontally (in terms of principles of organization) and vertically (in terms of levels of organization). With regard to a "horizontal" analysis, some emotional syndromes may be more closely related to one kind of system hierarchy than another (e.g., sudden fright to biological systems, hope to social systems, and hysterical conversion reactions to psychological systems). But most emotional syndromes require all three system hierarchies for their explanation.

With regard to a "vertical" analysis, emotional syndromes are situated at an intermediate level in the system hierarchies. The lowest level in a hierarchy consists of the component processes that help constitute an emotional syndrome. Emotional syndromes, in turn, are components (subsystems) of more encompassing systems of behavior. This means that the explanation of an emotional syndrome can be approached from either a macro or a microlevel. A micro analysis looks downward in the hierarchy and asks the question: What are the constituent parts of a syndrome, and how are those parts organized into a coherent whole? A macroanalysis looks upward in the hierarchy and asks the question: How does an emotional syndrome as a whole contribute or relate to higher order systems of behavior?

As Harré et al. (1985) point out, such a dual (micro and macro) approach to explanation is common in the natural sciences. In physics, for example, the behavior of matter is explained both in terms of its atomic constituents and in terms of cosmological principles concerning the structure of the universe as a whole. In fact, at advanced stages of analysis, the micro and macrolevels are brought together in a unified theory. Similarly, in biology, the theory of evolution is based on the biochemistry of DNA (at the microlevel) and ecology or natural selection (at the macrolevel).

Some Sources of Confusion

With the aforementioned considerations as background, we may now examine what, in my opinion, are some common sources of confusion in the explanation of emotional syndromes.

Hierarchical Versus Heterarchical Interactions.   One source of confusion stems from the tendency to treat biological, psychological, and social systems as forming a hierarchy, and then to assume that systems lower in hierarchy are more basic or fundamental than the others. To illustrate, consider the component processes that constitute the various subsystems depicted in Fig. 16.1. These could be arranged in the following hierarchy:

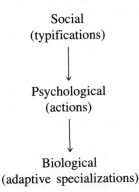

Social
(typifications)

Psychological
(actions)

Biological
(adaptive specializations)

The rationale for the positioning of the components in the above hierarchy might run as follows. People, and infrahuman animals, are born into the world with certain innate potentials. At the simplest level, these innate potentials are manifested as adaptive specializations (e.g., fixed action patterns). However, once a response is emitted, it is either reinforced or not (i.e., it is subject to modification by learning). An additional level of complexity is thus introduced, and we may now speak of more complex actions or instrumental responses. Among humans, actions that are oft repeated are generally of social significance, and hence they are identified as responses of a given type. Language is the main vehicle for such typification. By naming a response, the behavior can be divorced from its immediate context and made part of the social system.

The preceding argument has considerable intuitive appeal, but it can lead to difficulties. By arranging responses in a hierarchy, one is tempted to infer that the social is in some sense "reducible" to the psychological, and the psychological to the biological. By contrast, I have argued earlier that the social differs from the psychological, and psychological from the biological, not in being "higher" or more "complex," but, rather, in terms of principles of organization. If a hierarchical organization is to be constructed, it should be within, not between, behaviors governed by the same principles. Accordingly, adaptive specializations are elementary units in a biological hierarchy; actions are elementary units in a psychological hierarchy; and typifications are elementary units in a social hierarchy (see Fig. 16.1).

The problem of trying to "reduce" one type of system to another is even more evident if we consider the most inclusive unit within each domain—the species in the case of biological systems, the self in the case of psychological systems, and the society in the case of social systems. In what sense, other than in terms of principles of organization, is a species more fundamental or less complex than an individual or a society?

In short, it is less confusing to consider biological, psychological, and social systems as forming a heterarchy rather than a hierarchy. Heterarchical organization occurs when systems interact "on an equal footing," so to speak. Any given emotional syndrome can be explained by relating it to each of the three abstract systems of behavior (biological, social, and psychological), without, however, treating any of the systems as more fundamental or basic than the others, at least not in any absolute sense.

Systems of Behavior and Modes of Response. Another common source of confusion is to identify systems of behavior too closely with particular modes of response or effector mechanisms. For simplicity of discussion, let us recognize three broad modes of response: physiological, behavioral, and cognitive. It is tempting to posit a relationship between physiological responses and biological systems; and to assume that behavioral and cognitive responses fall within the provenance of psychological and/or social systems.[2]

---

[2]For example, Zajonc and Markus (1984) have distinguished between hard representations, which they consider to be innate motor responses, and soft representations, a higher order structuring of events based on socialization and individual learning. Hard representations are further identified with "real" emotion, whereas soft representations supposedly account for the experience of emotion.

Systems of behavior, defined in terms of principles of organization, pertain to the structure and function of a response, not the type of effector mechanism involved (e.g., physiological or cognitive). Biological evolution, for example, influences the way we think and behave, as well as how we react physiologically. Thus, most adaptive specializations (the most elementary components of biological systems) necessarily involve all three modes of response—physiological, behavioral, and cognitive. So, too, do the component processes (actions and typifications) that constitute psychological and social systems.

I emphasize this point because too often the assumption is made that if an emotional syndrome has demonstrable physiological components it is closely related to biological systems. By contrast, the present analysis assumes that the emotions—like other behavioral syndromes—are accompanied by physiological change, but this tells us little about the origins and functions of the response.

Emotional Versus Cognitive Systems.   Still a third source of confusion is to postulate an "emotion system" in opposition to, or independent of, a "cognitive system." A further assumption is often made that the emotion system is hardwired into the nervous system, and hence of biological origin. The cognitive system, by contrast, is supposedly built up through learning and socialization and hence reflects the influence of psychological and social systems.

One basis for this confusion is an ambiguity in the term, *cognition.* In ordinary language, cognition refers to processes associated with the acquisition of factual knowledge, and as such it is often contrasted with motivational and emotional processes, which have to do with wants and desires. In this restricted sense, *cognition* is roughly equivalent to *intellectual.* However, psychologists often use cognition in a much broader sense, namely, to refer to any kind of mental representation. In this broader sense, emotions are as dependent on cognitive structures or schemata as are other kinds of psychological phenomena.

Elsewhere (Averill, in press), I have discussed the features that distinguish emotional ("hot") from intellectual ("cold") cognitions. For example, emotional cognitions relate events to the individual's own well-being; they incorporate information from the body as well as from the environment; and they lead to the interpretation of behavior as a passion (something over which we have little control) rather than as an action (something we do). There are other distinguishing features as well, but we need not go into detail here. Suffice it to say that none of the distinctions necessitate the postulation of fundamental differences in underlying processes, such that is would be appropriate to speak of an "emotion system" separate from a "cognitive system." Stated somewhat differently, the same perceptual, memory, and other psychological mechanisms can subserve emotional functions in one context and intellectual functions in another context.

THE SOCIAL CONSTRUCTION
OF EMOTIONAL SYNDROMES

I now wish to apply the preceding considerations to some issues in emotional development. The term *development* is ambiguous in this context, for it can refer to biological evolution, social history, and/or individual development. Even if our focus is on one of these sources of change (e.g., individual development), assumptions must still be made about the other two. For example, many traditional theories view emotions primarily as the product of biological evolution (e.g., Izard, 1977; McDougall, 1936; Plutchik, 1980). From such a perspective, historical changes in emotional syndromes may be viewed as a process of "civilizing" the coarser or more primitive aspects of human nature; and, analogously, individual development may be seen as a matter of "taming" the emotions (i.e., of achieving self-control, or "emotional maturity").

My own bias is to view emotional syndromes primarily as social constructions. This is not to gainsay the importance of biological or individual development. Social evolution must ultimately work on materials provided by nature; that does not mean, however, that the final product is any less a social construction. And as far as individual development is concerned, each person must incorporate and adapt to his or her own needs that which society provides. There is always some slippage and innovation in the process. Without such individual variation, social evolution would not be possible.

The following discussion is divided into three parts. First, I illustrate briefly some cross-cultural variations in anger-like syndromes. Second, I say a few words about the processes (social evolution) by which such variations arise. Finally, I examine in greater detail the socialization of emotions (i.e., individual development).

Cross-cultural Variations

A social-constructionist view assumes that emotional syndromes vary across cultures—fundamentally, not just superficially. Let us examine this assumption as it relates to anger, which is on nearly everyone's list of "basic" or "primary" emotions. (In the following discussion, I use the term *anger* without quotation marks when referring to the emotional syndrome as it occurs in Western cultures; when referring to anger-like syndromes in other cultures, I will use "anger.")

In the psychological literature, anger is often depicted as an aggressive response, largely disruptive of social relations and occasioned by frustration. By contrast, I have argued that anger is basically a social construction, the function of which is to uphold accepted standards of conduct (e.g., by making the violation of social norms subject to retribution; Averill, 1982). According to this latter formulation, anger is, in a sense, a kind of informal judiciary. I base this contention on four major lines of argument.

396

First, in traditional moral teachings, the failure to become angry at injustice has often been condemned as a "sin." According to this tradition, a presumably righteous person cannot help but become angry at injustice. Only excessive or inappropriate ("unjust") anger is considered wrong. (A contemporary variation on this theme can perhaps be found in assertiveness training.)

Second, within the legal system, anger serves to mitigate a charge for culpable homicide from murder to manslaughter (a "crime of passion"). However, before a jury can attribute anger to a defendant, certain criteria must be met. The primary criterion is the adequacy of provocation, as judged by the so-called "reasonable-man test"; that is, did the provocation violate socially accepted standards of conduct so egregiously that a presumably reasonable member of the community might be roused to violent anger. If so, and the behavior of the defendant was also within certain limits, then the defendant is to an extent "excused" (i.e., voluntary manslaughter is considered a much lesser crime than murder).

Third, in everyday affairs the most common instigation to anger is not frustration per se but some form of misconduct (e.g., negligence or intentional wrongdoing). Moreover, the typical expression of anger seldom involves physical aggression; when aggression does occur, it is primarily symbolic (e.g., verbal); and, more often than not, even symbolic aggression is absent. More significantly, most episodes of anger are constructively motivated; that is, they are intended to correct or prevent recurrence of the "wrong," not to hurt the instigator. Finally, although people generally consider anger as a bad or unpleasant emotion, the typical episode of anger is regarded as more beneficial than harmful.

Fourth, there is considerable cross-cultural variation in anger-like syndromes. It is on this last point that I wish to focus. Specifically, I draw on Rosaldo's (1984) account of "anger" among the Ilongot (a people of the Philippines) to provide a contrast to anger in our own culture.

The Ilongot are extremely aggressive. According to Rosaldo (1984), killing (taking heads) "is probably the occasion for their most intense, most magical, and most focused sense of self" (Rosaldo, 1984, p. 147). The status of the victim is largely irrelevant—a child, a woman, a man, any will do. Nor need there have been any provocation by, or acquaintance with, the victim. It is the act of taking a head that is important, not retribution for some wrong.

In the romantic myth of the noble savage, egalitarianism is generally associated with the absence of aggression. The reality of the Ilongot is different. Ilongot society is relatively egalitarian, and aggression is one of the main ways for a person to assert his equality. "The act of killing does not prove the individual's inner volatility or worth; it is a social fact, permitting equal adult men to engage in the cooperation appropriate to adults" (Rosaldo, 1984, p. 147).

Its association with aggression means that Ilongot "anger" must be tightly controlled whenever it is directed toward members of the in-group (e.g., one's own kin). Otherwise, crucial social relations would be disrupted. And here, another distinction between Western and Ilongot "anger" becomes apparent.

Among Westerners, a rather sharp distinction is made between thoughts and feelings. Returning to our earlier anecdote, Bill thinks that he has been wronged by Joe, and he feels angry. If Bill puts the thought of Joe's wrongdoing out of his mind without forgiveness or other adequate resolution, the angry feeling may persist; and disconnected from its origins, it may continue to fester like a concealed wound, ultimately harming the relationship. That, at least, is a common way of conceiving of anger within our own culture. The Ilongot, by contrast, do not make such a sharp distinction between thought and feeling. Feelings are thoughts that involve the self in an immediate and intimate way. Hence, when a thought is dismissed, the corresponding feeling also "dissolves" or is "forgotten." There is no unconscious realm into which the feeling is submerged and from which it can wreck personal havoc. This feature of Ilongot "anger" is captured by the following anecdote (Rosaldo, 1984) about an Ilongot man who stated that: "Since I couldn't kill my wife, I just decided to forget my anger" (p. 145).

These few observations on the differences between Western and Ilongot "anger" indicate the importance of relating emotional syndromes to social as well as to biological systems. Certain aspects of anger may be universal, due to innate tendencies (e.g., toward aggression) and/or to cultural universals (e.g., the need to uphold social norms). However, the ways these tendencies and needs are organized into specific syndromes is different in different societies.

At this point, an objection might be raised. It is notoriously difficult to draw conclusions about fundamental differences in emotional syndromes from ethnographic accounts. An ethnographer, no matter how astute and objective, cannot report all that is relevant. Selections must be made—some points emphasized, other ignored. The mere fact that Rosaldo used the term, anger, to refer to a particular emotional syndrome among the Ilongot indicates important similarities between that syndrome and anger in our own culture. Are we speaking of variations on a single underlying emotion (*real* anger)? Or are we speaking of two different emotions of sufficient similarity that the same term (anger) can be used, albeit with some imprecision, to refer to both? There is, of course, no definitive answer to this question. However, as examples accumulate from a variety of different cultures, the argument that we are dealing with superficial variations on the same underlying phenomenon becomes less and less tenable. (For additional descriptions of cultural variations in anger-like syndromes and their implications for the presumed universality of anger as a specific emotion, see Averill, 1982, Ch. 3.)

A key corollary of a social-constructionist position is that membership in a society requires more than intellectual knowledge (e.g., of the relevant belief system); it also requires an ability to experience the emotions considered fundamental by the society. Socialization is not simply learning; it is an education of the emotions. But more of that shortly. Let me conclude this brief discussion of cross-cultural variations with an observation by Rosaldo (1984):

I hope this [description of Ilongot 'anger'] suggests the viability of what strikes me as its theoretical counterpart: That affects, whatever their similarities, are no more similar than the societies in which we live; that ways of life and images of the self (the absence in the Ilongot case, of an interior space in which the self might nurture an unconscious rage) decide what our emotions can be like in shaping stories of their likely cause and consequence. Ilongot discourse about anger overlaps with, yet is different from our own. The same can be said about the things Ilongots feel. Or stated otherwise, the life of feeling is an aspect of the social world in which its terms are found. (p. 145)

The Social Evolution of Emotional Syndromes

Let us turn now to a consideration of how emotional syndromes might evolve within a society. The precise mechanisms by which social evolution occurs is a subject of considerable debate (see, for example, Boyd & Richerson, 1985); that debate need not concern us here. The purpose of the following remarks is simply to sketch in broad outline how the three systems of behavior discussed earlier (see Fig. 16.1) interact historically to produce a social world that is a human product and, dialectically, to produce human beings that are social products.

First, we begin with the assumption that, as we ascend the phylogenetic scale, biological systems of behavior have become increasingly relaxed. Genetic constraints on behavior are by no means eliminated; compared with other species, however, human beings are relatively "world open." This means that biological systems must interact with social systems (e.g., by making some responses easier to acquire than others; cf. Lumsden & Wilson, 1983, for a detailed discussion about how this interaction might proceed).

Needless to say, world openness is itself a biological adaptation, one that has allowed the human species to occupy a wide range of environmental niches, from the arctic to the tropics. However, simply because human beings are not "pre-adapted" to a specific environment does not mean that they can survive in an unstructured world. It means, rather, that human beings must impose their own structure on the environment. In a sense, humans must create an environment in which to live. That environment is society.

Once created, the social environment takes on a reality of its own, a reality that can be ignored only at great risk to the individual. Aristotle (*Politics*, I. i. 12, 1959) commented that a man who lives alone is either an animal or a god. To this, Nietzsche (1889/1964) responded that there is a third alternative, namely, in order to live alone a man must be an animal *and* a god. Actually, both Aristotle and Nietzsche were wrong—such a man would be neither an animal nor a god; he would be dead. Social reality is as essential to human survival as is physical reality.

Not surprisingly in view of its importance for survival, social reality is often perceived as independent of human origins. Young children, in particular, tend to regard the world of their parents as overwhelmingly real and unalterable. We never completely outgrow this tendency. Members of all human groups are biased to view their particular social order as "natural" or even "god given." Emotional syndromes are part of the social order. They are a second nature that society provides to help compensate for our relative lack of a first nature (due to the relaxation of biological systems). Needless to say, the social order—no matter how real—does not exist in the same sense as physical reality. It must be created and reconstituted anew with each succeeding generation. During the course of socialization, the human child "takes over" and internalizes the social world into which it is born. It is to this process of socialization that we now turn.

The Socialization of Emotion

The first "emotional" responses of an infant are largely a reflection of biological systems. It could not be otherwise, for at birth there has been little opportunity for socialization to occur. But in what sense are the diffuse and immature responses of an infant a manifestation of emotion? Picture an infant fussing in its crib, screaming and flailing its arms. Is the infant angry? It seems more accurate to say that such fussing is an innate response to discomfort and distress. As the infant matures, cognitive and behavioral associations arise, elementary schemata develop, rules of emotion (social principles) are internalized, and so forth. The experience and expression of emotion changes accordingly. The infant's fussing is not the same thing as the young child's temper tantrum; and the temper tantrum of the child is literally a "far cry" from the anger of an adult on some unwarranted affront. To be sure, there is continuity between the behavior of the infant and the adult, but continuity in emotional development does not imply sameness (Averill, 1984).

The ability to experience anger (or any other emotional syndrome) does not develop all at once. As already discussed, the syndrome of anger includes a wide variety of component processes and more elementary responses (e.g., the evaluation of a situation as right or wrong, verbal and instrumental responses to correct the wrong, biologically and socially determined expressive reactions, and so forth). Each component may be acquired in a semiautonomous fashion (i.e., independent of the others). Hence, the development of an emotional syndrome cannot be understood as proceeding along a straight developmental course. Different components develop at different times and in different contexts; and components that are salient at one stage of development may be eliminated at a subsequent stage, so that little, if anything, remains in common between the initial and final stages.

To illustrate the process of socialization more concretely, I draw on Lutz's (1983) description of emotional development among the Ifaluk, a people of Micronesia. In contrast to the Ilongot, described earlier, the Ifaluk are a gentle people. Outside of childhood, physical aggression is rare. In such a social milieu, one might not expect to find an anger-like syndrome. But just the opposite appears to be the case. As described by Lutz (1983), Ifaluk "anger" (*song*) is central to the maintenance of peaceful relations. A person is expected to experience *song* at the transgression of a cultural norm or taboo. *Song* is most appropriate when experienced by an elder or person of higher rank, who presumably has greater knowledge of norms and moral authority. The person who becomes the target of *song* (i.e., the transgressor) is supposed to experience a complementary emotion, *metagu*. The Ifaluk consider *metagu* to be the primary inhibitor of misbehavior, and it is carefully cultivated in children.

The development of *metagu* among Ifaluk children is encouraged in a variety of ways. The following is a partial list, based on Lutz's (1983) account: (a) From about the first year of age, children are *told* they are *metagu* in fear-provoking situations (e.g., in the presence of strangers or in large groups); (b) children are also told they are *metagu* when they misbehave, so that by 5 years of age, they associate *metagu* with shaming for misdeeds; (c) the child is mocked who doesn't show *metagu* in appropriate contexts; (d) if a child misbehaves, particularly in an aggressive way, he may be told that a ghost may kidnap and eat him, thus inducing *metagu* in an especially dramatic way. (On occasion, this scenario may actually be acted out, with an adult dressed as a ghost.); (e) parents display *song* ("anger") when a child misbehaves, so that the child learns to anticipate *song*, the proper response to which is *metagu*; (f) children are encouraged to express emotions in an adult-like fashion.

Two general principles underlie the preceding techniques. First, responses that occur in one context (e.g., fear of strangers) may be used like scaffolds to support and shape a developing emotion (e.g., *metagu*). Second, language is an important tool in the construction of the final product. Listening is said by the Ifaluk to be the primary way that children acquire adult patterns of behavior, including emotional behavior, hence, the emphasis on *telling* a child how and when it is *metagu*.

Expanding on these two principles, note that the socialization of emotions does not proceed much differently than the acquisition of other complex behaviors. For example, a child learns mathematics through a combination of the rote learning of elementary responses (e.g., the multiplication tables) and an understanding of more general principles (e.g., the "laws" of mathematics). Similarly, emotional socialization proceeds in a piecemeal fashion from the "bottom up" and also in a more holistic fashion from the "top down" (cf. Fig. 16.1). Bateson (1976) provides a good example of the bottom-up approach with respect to the socialization for trance among the Balinese. (A trance is itself only a component of other more complex syndromes, including emotional syndromes.) Bateson begins by breaking socialization into part-processes. One part of the socialization for trance involves the phenomenon of clonus (i.e., the recurrent series of patellar reflexes that occurs endogenously when the leg is held in certain positions). Such biologically based components, when placed in an appropriate social context, are used to reinforce the more general belief among the Balinese that the body can act in a semiautonomous fashion, independent of a person's will. Thus, although clonus is not a component of trance itself, it enters into the socialization for trance (i.e., it is part of the socialization process). Other part-processes include the use of symbols, rituals, and "paradigm experiences" that help make the trance seem a natural and self-explanatory state.

The component responses used in the socialization of emotional syndromes need not involve simple motor responses, as in the example of clonus. Valuative judgments or appraisals are important components of most, if not all, emotional syndromes. For example, anger involves the appraisal of wrongdoing, fear involves the assessment of danger, and so forth. Judgments of these kinds are often acquired in nonemotional contexts and only later incorporated into emotional syndromes.

Of all the components of socialization, those involving language are probably the most crucial for the acquisition of emotional syndromes. I have already mentioned this in connection with the socialization of *metagu* among the Ifaluk, but it is perhaps worth emphasizing again, because some theorists have questioned the significance of ordinary language for the understanding of emotion (e.g., Mandler, 1984). As children learn the proper use of such terms as *anger, fear, love,* and so forth, they are not simply learning to describe or label a preexisting state. Rather, they are learning to make the discriminations, both with respect to situations and to their own behavior, that those terms imply. Stated somewhat differently, the acquisition of emotional concepts requires an understanding of many of the same rules and norms (social principles) that help determine the organization of emotional syndromes.

SUMMARY AND CONCLUSIONS

The first half of this chapter concerned the way emotions might be explained in terms of underlying structures (abstract systems of behavior). To recapitulate briefly, emotional syndromes are subsystems of behavior (i.e., they are intermediate in a hierarchy of behavioral systems). Looking downward in the hierarchy, emotional syndromes can be analyzed into component processes (e.g., expressive reactions, instrumental acts, typified social responses). Looking upward in the hierarchy, emotional syndromes can be related to broader systems of behavior. When dealing with individual persons, the broader systems refer to long-range motives and goals as represented in cognitive schemata; when dealing with emotional syndromes in general (e.g., anger, love, grief), we must extend consideration beyond the individual and relate the emotion to broader biological and social systems of behavior.

The second half of the chapter has presented a few observations on the development of emotional syndromes. Any theoretical account of emotional development on the individual level must begin with assumptions about the origin and function of emotional syndromes on the biological and social levels. A social-constructionist approach assumes that biological systems have become progressively relaxed during the course of human evolution. This does not mean that the influence of biological systems is negligible or that it can be ignored (as is evidenced by the ease of acquisition of some phobic reactions); it does mean, however, that social institutions have become a major vehicle for establishing and maintaining emotional syndromes.

Socialization is the process of emotional education, whereby the individual acquires the norms, rules, and practical skills that help constitute the various emotions. Much emotional socialization occurs in nonemotional contexts; that is, component processes may be acquired piecemeal, only later to be incorporated into a coherent syndrome. Language is an important element in this process. Learning an emotional concept is not a matter of pinning a label on a pre-established internal state; rather, it is one of the means wherewith an emotional syndrome is reconstituted as a coordinate part of the social order and of the individual self.

ACKNOWLEDGMENT

Preparation of this chapter was supported, in part, by a grant (MH40131) from the National Institute of Mental Health.

REFERENCES

Aristotle. (1959). *Politics* (H. Rackham, Trans.). Cambridge, MA: Harvard University Press.

Averill, J. R. (1980). A constructivist view of emotion. In R. Plutchik & H. Kellerman (Eds.), *Emotion: Theory, research and experience: Vol. I. Theories of emotion* (pp. 305–339). New York: Academic Press.

Averill, J. R. (1982). *Anger and aggression: An essay on emotion.* New York: Springer–Verlag.

Averill, J. R. (1984). The acquisition of emotions during adulthood. In C. Z. Malatesta & C. E. Izard (Eds.), *Emotion in adult development* (pp. 23–43). Beverly Hills: Sage.

Averill, J. R. (in press). Emotions on episodic dispositions, cognitive schemas, and transitory social roles: Steps towards an integrated theory of emotion. In D. Ozer, J. M. Healy, & A. J. Stewart (Eds.), *Perspectives in personality.* (Vol. 3) Greenwich, CT: JAI Press.

Bateson, G. (1976). Some components of socialization for trance. In T. Schwartz (Ed.), *Socialization as cultural communication* (pp. 51–63). Berkeley: University of California Press.

Bowlby, J. (1982). *Attachment and loss. Vol. I: Attachment* (2nd ed.). New York: Basic Books.

Boyd, R., & Richerson, P. J. (1985). *Culture and the evolutional process.* Chicago: University of Chicago Press.

Buck, R. (1985). Prime theory: An integrated view of motivation and emotion. *Psychological Review, 92,* 389–413.

Dewey, J. (1895). The theory of emotion. II: The significance of emotions. *Psychological Review, 2,* 13–32.

Ekman, P. (1984). Expression and the nature of emotion. In K. Scherer & P. Ekman (Eds.), *Approaches to emotion* (pp. 319–343). Hillsdale, NJ: Lawrence Erlbaum Associates.

Fehr, B., & Russell, J. A. (1984). Concept of emotion viewed from a prototype perspective. *Journal of Experimental Psychology: General, 113,* 464–486.

Giddens, A. (1979). *Central problems in social theory.* Berkeley: University of California Press.

Harré, R., Clarke, D., & DeCarlo, N. (1985). *Motives and mechanisms.* London: Methuen.

Izard, C. E. (1977). *Human emotions.* New York: Plenum Press.

Luhmann, N. (1982). *The differentiation of society* (S. Holmes, Trans.). New York: Columbia University Press.

Lumsden, C. J., & Wilson, E. O. (1983). *Promethean fire.* Cambridge, MA: Harvard University Press.

Lutz, C. (1983). Parental goals, ethnopsychology, and the development of emotional meaning. *Ethos, 11,* 246–262.

Mandler, G. (1984). *Mind and body: Psychology of emotion and stress.* New York: Norton.

McDougall (1936). *An introduction to social psychology* (23rd ed.). London: Methuen.

Nietzsche, F. (1964). *The twilight of the idols: Maxims and missiles.* (A. M. Ludovici, Trans.). New York: Russell & Russell. (Original work published 1889)

Parsons, T. (1951). *The social system.* New York: Free Press.

Plutchik, R. (1980). *Emotion: A psychoevolutionary synthesis.* New York: Harper & Row.

Rosaldo, M. Z. (1984). Toward an anthropology of self and feelings. In R. A. Schweder & R. A. LeVine (Eds.), *Culture theory: Essays on mind, self, and emotion* (pp. 137–157). Cambridge: Cambridge University Press.

Ryle, G. (1949). *The concept of mind.* London: Hutchinson.

Skinner, B. F. (1974). *About behaviorism.* New York: Alfred A. Knopf.

Zajonc, R. B., & Markus, H. (1984). Affect and cognition: The hard interface. In C. E. Izard, J. Kagan, & R. B. Zajonc (Eds.), *Emotions, cognition, and behavaior* (pp. 73–102). Cambridge: Cambridge University Press.

17 The Biological Significance of Affectivity

Terrance Brown
University of Chicago

> *I have called this principle by which each slight variation, if useful, is preserved, by the term Natural Selection, in order to mark its relation to man's power of selection.*
>
> —Charles Darwin(1964/1859)[1]

> *The biological significance of mind is a necessary condition of scientific psychology.*
> —Lev Vygotsky
> (Zinchenko & Davydov, 1985)

In a thoughtful paper "On the Nature and Function of Emotion," Klaus Scherer (1984) points out that the history of psychology seems to cycle between periods where man is conceived as basically irrational and emotional[2] and periods when he is conceived as an egg-headed creature of reason. Although currently there are indications of a shift away from the rational view inherent in behavioral and cognitivist approaches, renewed interest in emotion, according to Scherer, has so far failed to move us in the direction of more fruitful views of human mental life. One reason for this is that emotion theorists often attempt to deal with individual

---

[1]For historic texts, the original date of publication is given after the date of the edition actually used.

[2]Scherer starts off using the term *emotion* as a rubric for affective phenomena of every type. Later, he distinguishes emotions from affective processes in general as has been done historically for compelling reasons (Fraisse, 1968).

components of affective reactions rather than to treat them within a wholistic framework embracing the full complexity of the affective system. Another reason is that investigators continue to be divided on three important issues: the function of emotion, the definition of emotion, and the role cognition plays in emotional phenomena.

This chapter begins by reviewing the remedies Scherer proposes and then focuses on his rather general functional argument relating to evaluation. Its aim is to provide a foundational analysis and provisional model linking affective evaluation to cognitive activity in specific ways. Finally, it relates the conception that results to recent work in problem solving, decision theory, and philosophy of science in order to demonstrate its import and plausibility.

THE SCHERER MODEL

In contradistinction to interrupt theories, Scherer sees emotion as an important tool for mediating interchanges between organisms and their environments. Viewed from that perspective, emotion's functions appear to be threefold. First, emotion is used to evaluate situations relative to the organism's needs. Second, it is used to prepare physiological and psychological responses. And third, it aids in communicating reactions, states, and intentions to other individuals. With regard to the first two functions, the phylogenetic evolution of emotion allowed organisms to go beyond purely automatic responses by providing on-going evaluation of the salience of stimuli within intentional frameworks and by discriminating adaptive from maladaptive reactions. With regard to the latter, the intentional organization of behavior made possible by emotion becomes evident to others, as do emotional expressions. Taken all together, external manifestations of this kind contribute importantly to social inter-action.

Tentatively, then, Scherer is able to link specific functions to the complex list of emotional components on which he believes modern psychological thought converges. In effect, the function of environmental evaluation results from the "cognitive stimulus processing component" of emotion, the function of system regulation derives from the "neurophysiologic process component," the function of preparing action relates to "motivational components," communicating intentions is linked to the "expressive component," and reflection and monitoring are accomplished by the "subjective component."

Scherer goes on to distinguish affective processes, a generic term for psychological phenomena exhibiting certain general organic and psychological features, from clearly delineated, intensive patterns of affective processes to be called emotions. He believes this distinction can be used to dissolve disagreement about what should properly be termed emotion. Using facet theory, he then sketches out a system for describing affective processes that would allow complex blends of affective components to be identified and the enormous number of affective states to be sorted out. And he ends by presenting a process model of stimulus evaluation that lends itself to theorizing about complex mixtures of emotions. Scherer's definitions, the functions he assigns emotion, his scheme for describing affective processes, and his process model of stimulus evaluation form a natural and coherent approach to the problem of affectivity. At the same time, the evaluative implications of his model lie scattered across psychology like clam shells on a deserted beach, lifeless fragments of related species to be gathered, classified, and integrated into a coherent theory. In what follows, I attempt to make clear what the basis of affective evaluation might be, to indicate how "environmental factors" are evaluated, and to elucidate the way in which affective processes figure in cognitive activities in general. If successful, I believe an analysis of this kind may be able to go beyond Scherer's inventory and attain something approaching an explanation.

THE BIOLOGICAL NECESSITY OF FEELING

Let us begin by recognizing that it is more than coincidental that values and emotions are concepts meaningful only from the point of view of living systems. It makes no sense to speak of a mountain's motives or a river's anger; only intelligent animals have feelings. One must, therefore, establish some biological basis for evaluation. Only then will affective phenomena take on the necessity inherent in explanation.

Simply conceived, living systems establish and maintain their organization by means of compensations.[3] Energy used up in one way or another is restored by eating, sodium diffusion into a cell is counteracted by active transport out, an infant's helplessness is made up for by a mother's caring. If the concerted actions of an organism's subsystems reverse thermodynamic disorganization, the organism lives. In that sense it is "preferred to" or "selected over" or "valued more" than other systems. Thermodynamic "selection," then, forms the bedrock of organic evolution. That it eventually gives rise to systems using "organic" or internal mechanisms of selection does not alter the fact that it lies at the source of Darwin's selective principle (Brooks & Wiley, 1986; Depew & Weber, 1985).

---

[3]Prigogine (1980), Prigogine and Stengers (1984), and Brooks and Wiley (1986) have provided elaborate and somewhat diverse expositions of this idea. Prigogine and Stengers working on non-equilibrial thermodynamic systems demonstrate the possibility of stabilizing dissipative systems far from thermodynamic equilibrium. Such systems have many of the properties of living organisms. Brooks and Wiley interpret the existence of living systems as an instance of their newly formulated entropic theory. Both views are consistent with the global depiction given here.

Such considerations, however, only make clear the way in which material organic systems and some primitive forms of automatic behavior are evaluated. They do not provide any understanding of why an affective evaluative system would be needed. In fact, thermodynamic selection has created an incredible array of organisms where feelings play no part. Dare one suggest, then, that the evaluation inherent in thermodynamic stabilization corresponds functionally to affective evaluation? Do entropic considerations determine what wine we choose for dinner? Is it possible to relate biological selection to Scherer's affective discrimination of adaptive reactions from maladaptive ones?

Certainly such assertions cannot be taken on faith as Scherer seems to do. It is a very long way from thermodynamic processes globally evaluating behavioral responses in terms of an organism's survival to psychological processes estimating a particular response's "survival value" in terms of feeling. Yet, lacking any other basis for human values, compelling theories of affectivity must bridge this gap.

Oddly enough, the first piling on which such a conceptual span might be constructed comes from Piaget, a thinker not noted for his concern with feelings. Piaget's idea that intelligence is an internal, psychological reduplication of organic evolution leads immediately to the need for internal mimicking of thermodynamic selection. Whereas Darwin's theory might, by itself, suffice to explain the development of reflexes or instincts in the form of inborn, automatic patterns of behavior, it cannot account for the acquisition and extinction of the simplest habits and is even more impuissant where intentional phenomena are concerned. This is because habits and all higher levels of behavior are individually selected. Organisms do not have to die to extinguish noxious habits or correct a false idea. Yet thermodynamic selection provides for nothing else. In consequence, theories of habit formation always invoke some internal mechanism of selection and, significantly, this usually takes the form of feeling. That much was clear when Plato (Hubbard & Karnofsky, 1982/4th century B.C.) wrote *Protagoras,* it was evident in Thorndike's "law of effect" (Nuttin, 1968), and it was obvious in Skinner's (1984) "operant conditioning." Even modern cognitivists, although they seldom mention affectivity (Zajonc, 1980) and do not recognize the fact explicitly, have not got round the basic intuition that affective processes determine the "life" and "death," the "selection," of behaviors.[4] But no one knows exactly how.

A provisional answer and, therefore, the second piling on which our biological–psychological bridge is constructed has been developed by George Pugh (1977) in his book, *The Biological Origin of Human Values.* In that work, Pugh

---

[4]See for example John Anderson's (1980, pp. 264–268) discussion of the value subject's place on similarity in his discussion of "Similarity as a Basis for Selecting Operators."

argues from principles of design for the necessity of evaluation in any system capable of making complicated choices. The striking thing about people, according to Pugh, is that they make good decisions about what behaviors will prove adaptive when the knowledge they have available is woefully inadequate, when their computing resources are severely limited, and when the time available is short. Concretely, human beings decide daily where to invest their money, whether to marry and reproduce, what car to buy, or which way to vote. In none of these cases could any amount of computation insure success. Both practically and theoretically, it is impossible to make such choices by developing and exploring every possibility. In fundamental ways, therefore, man is not and cannot be wholly rational in either the logical or praxeological senses of that word.[5] He is, rather, an approximator, a make-doer of remarkable skill who includes within his complex repertoire of decision strategies a middling aptitude for rational deciding that can be applied in fairly simple situations. For the most part, however, values drive the human system, and those values relate to feelings, not to reason. Pugh explains why, even so, this leads to adaptation.[6]

What Pugh does not explain, however, is from whence the knowledge structures needed for a value-driven system stem. We must, then, seek a third and final pillar on which our cognitive–affective bridge can rest. This will be found in Guy Cellérier's integration of Piaget's ideas with American cognitive science and, therefore, Pugh. His synthesis provides provisional solutions to two important problems. The first has to do with the inability of Piaget's "knowledge structures" to explain adapted actions or the affective evaluations that shape them. The second relates to the inability of Pugh's value-driven decision systems to account for how knowledge is acquired.

---

[5]The word rational is ambiguous. Sometimes it is used to imply both possibility and necessity. For example, it is rational to conclude that if one of John's four cats died (and nothing else has changed), he now has three. In this case, there are no other possibilities. At other times, however, rationality implies possibility without necessity. In the instance of a dead battery, using jumper cables to start a car would be possible and in that sense rational; but it is in no way necessary. One might, depending on circumstances, equally well *and with equal rationality* install a new battery or push the car. But even praxeological rationality is not possible in every case. Many human decisions have to do with situations where the rationality of the goal itself may be in question, where ways to reach the goal may be unknown, or where one is uncertain whether an action has led to progress toward the goal. Take, for instance, decisions about foreign aid or child rearing. Can one really know whether providing the Contra's with arms has or will promote the security and well-being of the nation? Can one be sure that teaching Johnny Latin or having him play team sports will produce desired qualities in the man? To understand the complex web of meanings inherent in these different uses, it is necessary to relate success, necessity, and heuristics to one another within the teleonomic framework. How this can be done will be clearer at the end of the chapter than it can be here.

[6]Pugh argues, of course, as has the author elsewhere (Brown & Weiss, 1987), that there are "intellectual values" and that these also are manifest as feelings. My purpose here being to stress the importance of the irrational qua emotional rather than to illuminate the "rationality" of emotion, I have not entered into this troubling proposal. It is discussed later in the chapter.

PIAGET'S CONCEPTION OF INTELLIGENCE

As is well known, Piaget decided while still an adolescent to create a biological explanation of knowledge. In 1936, he laid out the relationships he envisioned between biological and intellectual domains (Table 1; Piaget, 1952/1936). Essentially, he conceived intelligence as a new system of adaptation. Whereas organic evolution proceeds through variation of individuals, thermodynamic selection, and reproductive transmission to succeeding generations, intelligent adaptation proceeds through variation of action schemes, psychological selection, and communicative transmission.[7] With the advent of intelligence, then, a maladapted behavior or idea can be eliminated without sacrificing the organism as a whole. By making it possible for individual psychological structures rather than entire organisms to evolve, the psychological system renders adaptation more rapid and more flexible.

Table 17.1 contains several problems, however, that are not remedied in Piaget's later work. To begin with, although Piaget insists that action is the basis of all knowledge, the table does not make clear how action and knowledge are related. Categories related to action (i.e., goal and means as well as ideal and value) are linked to internal organization; but nowhere in Piaget's own work, then or later, does one find any clear statement of how internal organization results in adapted action. Similarly, space and time, objects and causality are categories used to *understand* the external world, but by themselves they do not *produce adapted action* on it. Even when Piaget (1974) much later takes up the relationship of action to understanding, he does not make clear how action structures are constructed. Nor when, still later, he relates goals and means to equilibrial laws (Piaget, 1985) does he provide an explicit model of how knowledge and action are related. Even in his final paper where he explains that action structures differ from knowledge structures in that they have teleonomic and temporal direction (Inhelder & Piaget, 1979), he only emphasizes the distinction without saying exactly how the two relate. In consequence, Piaget's theory of how knowledge is constructed out of action remains seriously incomplete.

The same is true with regard to values. In *Origins of Intelligence* (1952/1936) where Table 1 appears, Piaget says nothing about the role values play in adapting action. He only includes the idea within the table. When later he identifies values as the diachronic aspect of affectivity and denies the latter a direct role in forming knowledge structures (Piaget, 1981/1953–54), he does not make the procedure-structure distinction (Inhelder & Piaget, 1979), nor does he appreciate the specif-

---

[7]Piaget (1980) strongly criticized neo-Darwinian theories of evolution based on principles of totally random variation and external selection. He believed variation stems from compensatory equilibration of schemes assimilating objects or information to which they are not completely fitted.

TABLE 17.1
Relationships Between Biological and Psychological Adaptation

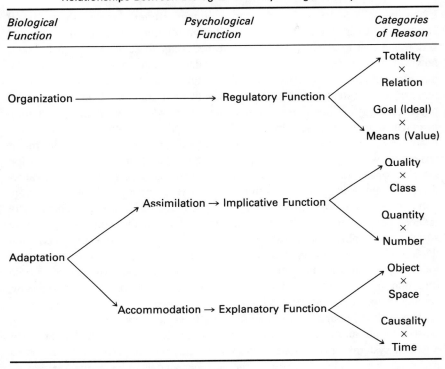

Biological Function	Psychological Function	Categories of Reason

Adapted from Piaget (1952/1936), p. 9.

ic role values play in formulating action. However, he does recognize, at least intuitively, that values play a role in what Cellérier later terms the "pragmatic transformation" (i.e., the construction of action out of knowledge).[8]

What we take from Piaget, then, are the notions that intelligence is a system for evolving adapted action, that knowledge structures differ fundamentally from their procedural counterparts, and that the latter owe their special character, even their very evolution, to teleonomic and temporal asymmetries produced by affective evaluation. What we cannot distill from Piaget's rich ferment is an exact model of the relationships involved or a clear idea of how affective values guide adapted action.

---

[8]For a more complete discussion of these issues, see Brown and Weiss, (1987).

PUGH'S VALUE DRIVEN DECISION SYSTEM

In his book, *The Biological Origin of Human Values,* George Pugh (1977) argues, like Piaget, that the purpose of human intelligence is to evolve adapted action and that knowledge structures are necessary to achieve this goal. Pugh, however, makes the relationship of knowledge to action clearer by elucidating the role evaluation plays. His point of departure is the realization that in designing artificial systems used to decide complicated courses of action, it is, in practice, always impossible to include enough knowledge or enough calculating resources to examine possibilities exhaustively and make optimal solutions. That is not how computer programs operate, and by extension, Pugh concludes that it is not the way people decide complicated questions either. Artificial decision systems, once a certain level of complexity is reached, all converge on the value-driven design. Such systems use limited numbers of operators to generate large numbers of action possibilities from a restricted base of knowledge. This greatly reduces the amount of knowledge that is needed. At the same time, a value structure is employed to assess the utility of action possibilities generated from the knowledge base in order to reduce the number of possibilities to be examined.[9] By avoiding exploration of actions that fail to produce progress in the right direction or, in other words, by pursuing only "good" alternatives, such systems economize on time and calculating resources needed for their operation.

The trick, of course, is to know the bad from the good and, says Pugh, the most difficult of the programmer's tasks is to design the value system. For artificial systems, this is done by trial and error, by comparing the computer's decisions to the values inherent in the designer's goal. Value structures that do not make the machine's decisions converge on the designer's wishes are changed until they do. However, even using this procedure, it is seldom possible in

---

[9]Pugh differs from other cognitive scientists in his explicit recognition of the role evaluation plays and in his equation of evaluation with affective processes. Most mainstream workers in this area invoke heuristics without recognizing that they inscribe a value system or relate to feelings, or they speak of evaluation as if it were a rational, quantitative affair achieved through some exact algorithm where emotion plays no part. For example, the index to Kahneman, Slovic, and Tversky's *Judgment Under Uncertainty: Heuristics and Biases* (1982) contains no references to affectivity, emotion, evaluation, feeling, motivation, or values, although many of the articles are filled with affective terms. Similarly, the index of *Human Problem Solving* (Newell & Simon, 1972) contains no references to affectivity or feeling, whereas emotion, evaluation, motivation, and values are all included either without reference to affectivity or in extremely peripheral ways. For example, emotion is mentioned twice, the first time to label aberrant traces in a cryptarithmetic problem-solving task, the second in a survey of other work in information processing (Abelson's "hot cognitions"); evaluation is referenced many times and is related to heuristic search but is not considered an affective or emotional affair; the several references to motivation are aimed at showing that the problem-solving subject may be considered to be rational; and the few references to value have to do with the values that attributes assume.

412

complex systems to incorporate the designer's value structure in full detail. Almost always "surrogate values" that approximate decisions the designer would make himself must be employed.

With all this in mind, Pugh reasons that, faced with building a decision system that could mimic organic evolution, the genomic system, too, was forced to use a value-driven system and that the values inherent in the system are surrogates for survival value. To have done otherwise (i.e., to have built a machine that could exactly calculate the survival potential of action possibilities) would have required incredible amounts of knowledge and computational machinery. Even nature's resources were outstripped. Consequently, what has evolved are organisms with a set of primary values evaluated against the thermodynamic axiology imposed by biological selection. This means that the hedonic system of the Greeks, at least in its most primitive manifestation, is a system of innate feelings used to approximate survival value. Hedonic feedback either "reinforces" or "extinguishes" activities according to some surrogate heuristic for estimating survival and allows adapted actions to evolve.

Were this the whole story, however, it would not be very interesting. Although it is easy enough to understand the adaptive value of a newborn infant uttering distress cries if it is cold or hungry or ejecting acid solutions from its mouth, it is a long way from such elementary evaluations to a critic's enchantment with a singer, to Dirac's fascination with his equations' beauty, or to a right-to-lifer's disapproval of abortion. Pugh addresses this problem in two ways.

To begin with, says Pugh, even in simple computer systems, the value structures necessary to make reasonable decisions are a good deal more complex than most people realize. Multiple values are often necessary and these must be made to vary temporally in intensity. So the value system with which the human infant starts is much more complex than people suppose and, almost certainly, it includes intellectual and social values as well as values relating to simple physiological needs. From this point of view, it becomes less farfetched to suggest that formal beauty or moral convictions are related to survival.

Secondly, says Pugh, value-driven systems, although they cannot modify their primary value structure, can elaborate secondary values in the form of likes and dislikes, shortcuts, rules of thumb, wise saws and sayings, fashions, esthetic or moral systems, etc., in order to approximate primary values more easily and effectively. Consequently, it is not only possible but it is also to be expected that extremely complicated secondary value systems will evolve through the functioning of the primary system. That being the case, it is less difficult to understand one's feelings faced with Caballé's perfection. From Pugh's perspective, such emotion derives through myriad layers of elaboration from primary values dictating the positive value of others' voices, of symmetries and patterns, of social interaction . . .

It should be noted that the uniqueness of Pugh's interpretation does not lie in his recognition that optimal decision strategies are by and large impossible. Cognitive scientists in general accept that fact. What Pugh adds that is original is explicit recognition that the main heuristic system employed in humans is affective. People do not make most of their decisions by "minimizing distances in problem space," by consciously or unconsciously calculating probabilities, or by employing any other of the host of quasi-rational criteria invoked by modern workers. Not only is it obvious that many of the criteria identified by decision scientists are known to the deciding subject through the medium of feelings, but it is also demonstrable that many of our decisions make no pretense to rationality at all. What modern decision science seems blind to is the fact that feelings are reasons, and in many instances the only ones available. Nor can it see that these "reasons of the heart" have a pragmatic logic of their own.

Whereas Pugh has much more to say about the human value system and how it relates to affectivity, this brief sketch must do. What we take from his account are the ideas that human feelings are the subjective aspect of evaluative activities, that such activities constitute heuristic devices for reducing search spaces in formulating action, that all evaluation derives from a complex system of inborn values surrogate for adaptive value, and that much of mental development has to do with the construction of secondary value systems aimed at making the estimation of primary values simpler when dealing with ever more complicated problems. What we cannot draw from Pugh is any inkling of how the knowledge structures used to generate action possibilities are constructed. For that reason, we turn now to Cellérier.

CELLÉRIER'S EPISTEMIC AND PRAGMATIC TRANSFORMATIONS

Cellérier begins with the assertion that Piaget's genetic psychology and American cognitive science are concerned with the same problem (i.e., how knowledge relates to adapted action). Their apparent opposition, according to Cellérier, stems from the fact that Piaget's structuralism focuses on the "epistemic transformation," or on how knowledge is derived from action, whereas cognitive science focuses on the "pragmatic transformation," or on how knowledge is used to organize action. For Cellérier, both questions are legitimate as is the further question of how to resolve them on the basis of a single model.

To resolve these questions, Cellérier starts from the fact that behavior[10] is organized through cyclic interaction of knowledge and action converging gradually on practical or intellectual success. In interaction of this kind, assimilation to existing knowledge structures produces understanding of the situation requisite to planning action directed toward some goal. Any action undertaken produces a

---

[10]Piaget, of course, objected to the term behavior because of its suggestion of behaviorism, a doctrine he thoroughly rejected. Because his own term, conduct, sounds stilted and carries no specific English meaning, I use behavior to designate all things mental.

new situation that must be assimilated in turn, new understanding or meaning established, a new goal–means structure imposed, and new action implemented. If the aim is simply to succeed in some practical task, the cycle stops when the goal is reached, its product consisting only in an empirical recipe for success. If, on the other hand, the aim is to understand or explain how success has been achieved, interaction must work out alternative solutions and integrate successful and unsuccessful schemes with one another in order to produce an implicative matrix within which the successful scheme is situated. That much is the same for Piaget and Pugh.

Cellérier then argues that the assimilatory frameworks set up to interpret problems and the results of action constitute transitory models, but not just models of the environment as cognitivists suppose. Rather, such frameworks model "adaptive interactions" representable by *production rules* of the form: IF SOME EXTERNAL SITUATION IS DETECTED AND IF SOME MOTIVATIONAL STATE EXISTS, THEN EXECUTE SOME ACTION OR PASS TO A CERTAIN OTHER STATE OR BOTH. That being the case, adaptive interactions can be organized as production systems and are, therefore, programmable. This answers Moore and Newell's (1974) objection that Piaget's explanatory concepts have no substance because they are not "effective procedures." At the same time, it indicates features of existing cognitivist conceptions that must be remedied if one wishes to approach the human situation.

Perhaps the most striking thing about transitory models is that they require three separate kinds of knowledge. Understanding situations in a world of either physical or logicomathematical "objects" requires Piaget's *operatory knowledge;* recognizing motivational states and establishing the value something has within a goal–means framework requires what Cellérier calls *axiological knowledge;* and knowing how to perform some action or pass to some other state requires *pragmatic knowledge.*

A second striking feature of transitory models is that they do not spring from knowledge, however many kinds there are, without the activity of a control system that is itself subject to a value system. Something must coordinate understanding, values, and practical know-how to produce adapted action. Something must formulate intentions, select transformations from among the numerous possibilities made available by knowledge, and assess the effectiveness of actions. Something must make transformations understood and valued as means lead to states or situations understood and valued as goals. This is the function of control.

The importance of transitory models is that their general features may be used to establish correspondences between Piagetian and cognitivist conceptions. With minimal modification, Piaget's "schemes of action" and cognitive science's "procedures" can be brought together under the rubric of pragmatic knowledge. With a bit more difficulty, cognitive science's environmental models can be transformed into Piaget's empirical and pseudoempirical knowledge structures. With substantial imagination, the Piagetian concept of "groupings of qualitative values" and the complex value structure implicit in Newell and Simon's "heuristics" can be subsumed under axiological knowledge. And finally, with a giant leap of creative insight, Newell and Simon's recursive method for analyzing means and ends and Piaget's optimizing equilibration can be interpreted in terms of the "problem of control" posed, respectively, on pragmatic and epistemic axes.

By themselves, however, such correspondences do not lead to an integrated model. With regard to pragmatic knowledge, Piaget vacillates on whether schemes of action constitute procedures or knowledge structures, whereas cognitive science's "effective procedures" have no psychological content (see Cellérier, 1979a, pp. 100–101). With regard to operatory knowledge, cognitive science is largely silent on how its environmental models are constructed, whereas Piaget is not clear as to how empirical and pseudoempirical structures relate to action. Where axiological knowledge is concerned, neither theory appreciates explicitly the role that values play and neither provides a general account of how values are constructed. Finally, although in both cases the control structure consists in task-independent extremalizing mechanisms, it operates on different axes in the two theories. In cognitive science, it acts to minimize the *distance* between starting point and goal; in Piagetian psychology, it acts to maximize both the *invention* of new knowledge structures and the *conservation* of old. Consequently, Cellérier feels forced to create a model of his own.

His basic strategy is to begin with an existing model of the pragmatic transformation and then modify it to include the epistemic transformation. He does this by adding memory, buttressing hierarchical with heterarchical principles of control, and reformulating the notion of procedure. The model he starts with is Newell and Simon's (1972) General Problem Solver (GPS). Briefly, GPS operates on problems where "operators" are used to transform "objects." Various goals are possible and methods relevant to each goal provided. Because problem spaces are relatively complex, heuristic rather than exhaustive methods must be used to seek solutions. Given all that, the control structure of the program is quite simple: The goal inherent in a problem presented to the system is first evaluated to see whether it is worth achieving and whether success seems likely; if that is the case, one of the methods relevant to the goal is selected; if it leads to success, the program stops; if it fails, the loop is repeated, each time selecting another method until all pertinent methods have been exhausted. If necessary, subgoals may be invoked and the aforementioned steps retaken (Newell & Simon, 1972, pp. 416–420).

In Fig. 17.1 the methods employed by the logic-problem version of GPS are provided to the system in the form of a table connecting operators with various differences among objects. Rules prescribing what differences are most important are also furnished. The control structure uses these components to perform means–end analyses by oscillating among goals, the kinds of transformations

----

DIFFERENCES BETWEEN OBJECTS. The differences apply to subexpressions as well as total expressions, and several differences may exist simultaneously for the same expression.

Δt A variable appears in one expression but not in the other. E.g., P v P differs by +t from P v Q, since it needs a Q ; P ⊃ R differs by -t from R, since it needs to lose the P.

Δn A variable occurs different numbers of times in the two expressions. E.g., P • Q differs from (P • Q) ⊃ Q by +n since it needs another Q ; P v P differs from P by -n, since it needs to reduce the number of P's.

Δs There is a difference in the "sign" of the two expressions. E.g., Q versus ~Q , or ~(P v R) versus P v R.

Δc There is a difference in binary connective. E.g., P ⊃ Q versus P v Q.

Δg There is a difference in grouping. E.g., P v (Q v R) versus (P v Q) v R.

Δp There is a position difference in the components of the two expressions. E.g., P ⊃ (Q v R) versus (Q v R) ⊃ P.

OPERATORS.

R1	A v B → B v A	R7	A v (B • C) ↔ (A v B) • (A v C)
	A • B → B • A		A • (B v C) ↔ (A • B) v (A • C)
R2	A ⊃ B → ~B ⊃ ~A	R8	A • B → A
R3	A v A ↔ A		A • B → B
	A • A ↔ A	R9	A → A v X
R4	A v (B v C) ↔ (A v B) v C	R10	A ⎫
	A • (B • C) ↔ (A • B) • C		B ⎬ → A • B
R5	A v B ↔ ~(~A • ~B)	R11	A ⊃ B ⎫ → B
			A ⎭
R6	A ⊃ B ↔ ~A v B	R12	A ⊃ B ⎫ → A ⊃ C
			B ⊃ C ⎭

CONNECTIONS BETWEEN DIFFERENCES AND OPERATORS. +, -, or x in a cell means that the operator in the column of the cell affects the difference in the row of the cell. + in the first row means +t, - means -t, etc.

	R1	R2	R3	R4	R5	R6	R7	R8	R9	R10	R11	R12
Δt								-	+	+	-	x
Δn		x					x	-	+	+	-	x
Δs	x				x	x						
Δc					x	x	x					
Δg				x			x					
Δp	x	x										

CRITERIA OF PROGRESS. All differences in subexpressions are less important than differnces in expressions. For a pair of expressions the differences are ranked: +t, -t, +n, -n, Δs, Δc, Δg, Δp, from most important to least. E.g., Δs is the more important in comparing ~(P v Q) with R ⊃ Q, while Δc is the more important in comparing ~P v Q with P ⊃ Q.

FIG. 17.1. Adapted from Newell and Simon (HUMAN PROBLEM SOLVING, © 1972, pp. 419, 431).

needed, and operators that perform those transformations. For example, instructed to change L1: R · (~P ⊃ Q) into L0: (Q ∨ P) · R, GPS produces the trace shown in Fig. 17.2. Because no operator can directly transform the first expression into the second, a subgoal must be introduced. Because differences between expressions are more important than differences between subexpressions

Given L1: R • (~P ⊃ Q)
Given L0: (Q ∨ P) • R

Step 1: Goal 1: Transform L1 into L0
Step 2:   Goal 2: Reduce Δp between L1 and L0
Step 3:   Goal 3: Apply R1 to L1
Step 4:   Goal 4: Transform L1 into condition (R1)
Step 5:   Produce L2: (~P ⊃ Q) • R

Step 6:   Goal 5: Transform L2 into L0
Step 7:   Goal 6: Reduce Δc between left (L2) and left (L0)
Step 8:   Goal 7: Apply R5 to left (L2)
Step 9:   Goal 8: Transform left (L2) into condition (R5)
Step 10:   Goal 9: Reduce Δc between left (L2) and condition (R5)
Step 11:   Rejected: No easier than Goal 6

Step 12:   Goal 10: Apply R6 to left (L2)
Step 13:   Goal 11: Transform left (L2) into condition (R6)
Step 14:   Produce L3: (P ∨ Q) • R

Step 15:   Goal 12: Transform L3 into L0
Step 16:   Goal 13: Reduce Δp between left (L3) and left (L0)
Step 17:   Goal 14: Apply R1 to left (L3)
Step 18:   Goal 15: Transform left (L3) into condition (R1)
Step 19:   Produce L4: (Q ∨ P) • R

Step 20:   Goal 16: Transform L4 into L0
Step 21:   Identical, QED

FIG. 17.2. Adapted from Newell and Simon (HUMAN PROBLEM SOLVING, © 1972, p. 420).

(See *Criteria of Progress* in Fig. 17.1), they are worked on first. The only difference at this level has to do with the positions of the variables. These must be changed if the two expressions are to become identical. The program will try, therefore, to put the variables L1 into the same position as they are in L0. As it happens, operator R1 affects position, so it is chosen. By proceeding in this way, the program arrives at a solution.

There is however, a glaring difference between GPS and human beings. This is that, like Athena, GPS sprang fully armed from the head of Zeus; the knowledge it possesses is the knowledge it will have forever. Not only does it not improve its understanding of new problems or augment the values inscribed in its heuristics, but it does not even expand its repertoire of procedures. Once a problem has been solved, it forgets what it has done and begins all over. Given the same problem two times running, it always starts from scratch. Cellérier is forced, therefore, to add a memory.

This memory linked to GPS's control structure that invents adapted action schemes from previous knowledge accounts for the pragmatic transformation. Procedures worked out by the control system are retained so that the next time the situation is encountered the system knows exactly what to do. But this elucidates neither the epistemic nor the axiologic transformation. It does not indicate how the general features of procedures in which gravity plays a part are woven into an explanatory structure applicable to all objects having mass. It does not explain how procedures for counting cows, rocks, or kumquats are generalized to counting any objects whatsoever. It does not enlighten us with respect to how interactions with certain pompous people come to make all such people tiresome. Nor does it suggest how experience with many chess games comes to make control of the center of the board desirable. Cellérier deals with the first two situations in the following manner.

In Piagetian psychology, to understand on operatory levels is to be able to reconstruct a casual effect or formal result using explicit, consciously conceptualized operations composed in such a way that they generate *necessarily* the effect or result to be explained. To succeed in understanding involves, therefore, the same control structure as does the pragmatic transformation, but acting on a different logical level. Cellérier (1979a) stated: "It is no longer a matter of tracing a single path through problem space . . . but of constructing a thought geometry of paths by generating the set of all paths possible" (p. 99). Operatory knowledge, then, derives from accommodating an action scheme to conditions imposed by an "external" environment of possibilities and at the same time meeting conditions "internal" to the goal of reconstituting the practical procedure. In the process, actions must be chosen in terms of what is possible within the world of schemes as well as what is necessary to effect the reconstruction. Thus, inventing and remembering internal action schemes unfolding in a space of possibility constitutes the epistemic transformation.

Although highly abstract and difficult to study,[11] this conception provides a preliminary understanding of how operatory knowledge is invented and conserved. It does not, however, shed any light on how evaluative knowledge is constructed, and, in fact, that issue is only partially considered by Cellérier.

What he does say is that axiological knowledge is used both to establish the "pertinence" of pragmatic and operatory knowledge, and to determine the value of transformations vis-a-vis some goal. This means that as a situation is interpreted by assimilation into operatory structures, the various elements identified are evaluated and motivations or goals determined. Once this teleonomic structure is set up, axiological knowledge is then used to evaluate means relative to the goal. Cellérier (1979a) describes how all this transpires in a complicated way:

> The axiological dimension is introduced by the definition of a directed difference between the possible values of a given parameter. Over the multidimensional adaptive surface representing the problem space, i.e., the set of possible situations that may be generated by combining operators, the vector of differences or "dis-

---

[11]Certain aspects have, however, been extensively investigated by the Genevan School in their work on abstraction (Piaget, 1977), generalization (Piaget, 1978), and the construction of possibilities (Piaget, 1987).

tance" between two situations, α and β, is used to construct an evaluative function the optimum of which corresponds to a null distance (α = β). To reduce this distance is both to reach a situation evaluated as better from the axiological point of view and to approach the goal within the teleonomic framework associated with it . . . Certain characteristics of the vector, e.g., its axis, its direction, its intensity, etc., are used to preselect activity. Only operators acting along the proper axis and in the right direction are chosen. Finally, the components of the vector, the different parameters, are ordered according to their importance which introduces a hierarchy into the system's different value scales. . . . This "constituted structure" is furnished prefabricated to the cycle coordinating goals and means which is invariant and independent of the various contents presented to it. Thus, the cycle accepts the definition of a problem in the general invariant form: "transform the initial situation into the terminal situation" which takes on the status of goal. The solution has the general form of a composition or ordered sequence of operators the argument of the first of which is the situation α and the value of the second of which is the situation β. (p. 96)[12]

If we return to Fig. 17.1 and 2 for some concrete help in understanding Cellérier on this issue, we note that, with reference to GPS, the directed difference of which he speaks is embedded in the *Criteria of Progress* central to the program. These criteria establish direction first by focusing on logical differences between expressions rather than, say, variations in typeface. Second, they rank order the logical differences considered relevant by the program in terms of which should be worked on first, which second, etc. Finally, they allow the results produced by operators to be evaluated in terms of whether the difference is diminished or disappears or whether an even more difficult difference is produced.

As an example, consider steps 6 through 10 in Fig. 17.2. In attempting to transform L2 (i.e., [~P ⊃ Q] · R) into L0 (i.e., [Q ∨ P] · R), the program sets up the subgoal of reducing the differences in the binary connectives "⊃" and "∨" in the left-hand terms of both expressions. It chooses to do this—it is most interested in doing this—at this time because the *Criteria of Progress* (Fig. 17.1) prescribe that differences in binary connectives (Δc) are more important than differences in position (Δp). From that point of view, the thing to work on first is the difference chosen rather than the difference in variable position between the two expressions or the difference in sign of variable P (a lower level component). Having decided all this, operator R5 (i.e., A ∨ B ↔ ~[~A · ~B]) is selected using the table of connectives because it is the first rule that operates on the difference targeted. However, because the conditions for applying that operator are not met, it is necessary to transform L2 so that the operator may be used (step 9). This would require that the "⊃" in L2 be transformed into either "∨" or "·."

---

[12]Author's translation.

To do this, however, is just as difficult as doing steps 6 and 7, so R5 is rejected and the program goes on to R6.

Whereas all this is helpful in understanding how evaluation takes place in Cellérier's revamped system, it does not elucidate how axiological knowledge is constructed. As Cellérier points out, the value structure written into the *Table of Connectives* and *Criteria of Progress* was worked out by Newell and Simon, not by the program itself; and the program has no power to change it. Nor are the values inherent in the system of control subject to construction. In fact, Cellérier specifically characterizes this cycle as invariant and content independent. From beginning to end, it values activity of a single kind: set up a goal–means framework for transforming α into β. Although "reduce" and "apply" goals may be invoked to achieve this end, no other activity has any value to it. And finally, the values in the knowledge base and in the control structure were matched a priori by the programmers. Consider, for example, what significance the *Criteria of Progress* or the *Table of Connectives* would have in a program whose content-independent "motivation" was to rewrite formulae in Greek. Obviously, they would be irrelevant.

We must, therefore, look once again to memory to explain the axiological transformation. To begin operating, a system of the type envisioned by Cellérier must have available a list of operators linked to specific features of a problem space along with some heuristic evaluative rules. Such knowledge plus a control structure with built-in "motivations" allows the system to invent new procedures and, thus, makes the growth of knowledge possible. In such a system, new values are created by the decisions of the system. For example, in Fig. 17.2, Steps 5–10, R5 is bad, R6 is good under the goal–means framework of that specific problem. Insofar as the procedure is remembered, this axiology is preserved because it is embedded in the list of operators devised to solve the problem. Such values are, however, specific to the goal–means framework and are derivatives of a general value structure. The construction of such values does not affect the general evaluative structure, and it is not clear whether or in what way Cellérier thinks that structure might evolve. Perhaps new evaluative principles are abstracted from the values inscribed in remembered schemes by some process akin to Piaget's "intellectualization of feelings," but that is only a conjecture. Because Cellérier's model cannot be taken further, a synthesis with Pugh's must be attempted if we are to understand more fully how axiological knowledge is constructed.

PUTTING CELLÉRIER AND PUGH TOGETHER

As we saw earlier, Pugh considers affectivity to be a surrogate, heuristic apparatus used to work out solutions in the problem space of psychological adaptation. Affective phenomena, observable at birth both in the baby's preference system and in his or her emotional expressions, are manifestations of a complex set of innate values that has been selected phylogenetically for the consistency of the choices it determines with the choices that biological selective mechanisms would make were behaviors genomically determined. Pugh is careful to make the point that this "given" value structure is not based on physiological need alone but includes, alongside "selfish" values of that kind, values based on social and intellectual needs. Although this primary value structure cannot be changed by the functioning of the system, it can be used as a reference for evolving secondary value structures. Evaluative criteria set up by the functioning of the system should then, insofar as they are successful, approximate primary values in one way or another.

Cellérier, of course, does not speak of affectivity at all, except to mention "needs" in one place or another. Nor does he explicitly connect axiological knowledge or values with the diachronic aspect of affectivity as did Piaget (1981). For him, values are embedded in the structure of pragmatic and operatory knowledge and in the immutable axiology of the system of control. Although he agrees with Pugh that the psychological system must start with an evaluation system provided by the genome and with a modicum of organically selected knowledge, he does not explicitly invoke the idea of secondary values. Moreover, Cellérier differs from Pugh in his almost exclusive focus on the values operative in rational deciding.

It seems clear from all this that Pugh needs Cellérier in order to incorporate knowledge construction into his model and that Cellérier needs Pugh in order to extend his notion of evaluation to goals, to give it a more thoroughgoing affective interpretation, and to account for axiological constructions. One way to go about effecting such a synthesis is to seek correspondences between the functional components Pugh considers fundamental to any value-driven system and the components Cellérier includes in his model. According to Pugh (1977, p. 54), all value-driven decision systems must have the following elements:

1. A data collection procedure to supply information needed to define the environment as it affects action alternatives.

2. A model of relationships in the environment that defines action alternatives and their consequences.

3. A procedure for exploring available action alternatives and estimating their consequences.

4. A method for assigning values to the estimated consequences.

5. A decision mechanism for selecting the alternatives that show the best value.

6. Procedures for creation, improvement, and refinement of the model (optional).

It is clear from this list that the first five components relate to Cellérier's pragmatic transformation and that the last corresponds to his epistemic transformation. Proceeding one by one, the *first component* on Pugh's list can be seen to conform to what Piaget and Cellérier would call perception. Obviously, this notion would have to be extended to include "perception" of information internal to the system (the "*refléchissement*" in Piaget's (1977) reflective abstraction). Without that, there would be no way to collect information about the internal environment of schemes, making abstraction and generalization, the central mechanisms for constructing operatory knowledge, impossible. Neither Cellérier nor Pugh deals successfully with this issue.

Pugh's *second component,* an environmental model typical of cognitivist conceptions generally, fuses Cellérier's pragmatic and operatory knowledge and is ambiguous about their interactive character. To bring Pugh's models into line with Cellérier's, it would be necessary to specify that all models are interactional, to distinguish pragmatic from operatory knowledge, and to include pseudoempirical knowledge (i.e., knowledge of logicomathematical environments) alongside the empirical knowledge inherent in Pugh's environmental model. Axiological knowledge could then be considered part of Pugh's fourth and fifth components, and Cellérier's requirements would all be met.

Pugh's procedure for exploring action alternatives (i.e., the *third component* on the list) corresponds to the search methods included in Cellérier's structure of control. In either case, it is problematic because in both theories search is conceived relative to intentions, whereas a considerable part of the behavior for which they must account (i.e., instincts and habits) is not intentional. Cellérier (1979b, p. 113) is cognizant of this problem and attempts to handle it by distinguishing unintentional actions ("intrarule transfers of control") in the form of hereditary procedures (instincts) and acquired associations (habits) from intentionally structured actions ("interrule transfers of control") and then using "needs," his only affective term, as the evaluation principle in forming associations. Effectively, instincts would be constituted and conserved by the genetic system acting both as control system and memory in the broad sense. Search would be accomplished by mechanisms of mutation, sexual recombination, crossing over, etc., and selection ultimately would be physical. Habits, conceived as associations between perceptions and actions, would then result from a psychological control system evaluating new interaction rules formed from instinctual elements in terms of whether they satisfy a need. Here search would involve assimilating new situations to old schemes or fitting existing schemes together. Finally, intentional behaviors would result from the goal-oriented composition of instinctual and associational elements using the evaluative principle of minimizing distances in problem space. Although this leaves vague how goals are set and monitored, it appears that on this point Cellérier is generally compatible with Pugh.

The *fourth component* in Pugh's list (i.e., a method for assigning values) is central to affective theory. Pugh contends that evaluation is accomplished by specific evaluative "processors" that forward information to a central decision system where action is composed. In his model, this evaluative output is experienced as feelings the quality and intensity of which are determined by the processor. Affective data are, therefore, much like sensory data processed by perceptual processors and experienced as perceptions. Both feelings and perceptions become conditions for productions. One strength of Pugh's analysis is that it explores the innate human value system in some detail. Another is that its notion of secondary values provides a foundation on which a theory of affective development might be constructed. Its greatest weakness, perhaps, is that it does not specify the mechanisms by which values are assigned at any level.

By contrast, although Cellérier accepts the idea of innate values when he speaks of needs, he does not develop this idea fully and does not explicitly connect it with affectivity. In fact, he appears to fuse Pugh's fourth and fifth components and concentrates on how evaluation operates after a need is recognized and intentional action undertaken. This places the evaluative activities with which he deals within the decision system rather than within affective processors external to it. For Cellérier and Pugh to be brought together, Cellérier's "needs" and the *Criteria of Progress* establishing the order of importance in his table of connections would have to be placed within Pugh's affective processors. But Cellérier's model would still not account for how new heuristics (i.e., Pugh's secondary values) are developed.

Pugh's *fifth component* (i.e., the decision mechanism for selecting best valued alternatives) is part of a central control system where intentional actions are composed. Essentially, Pugh equates central control with the conscious system conceived as a serial processor using input from perceptual, mnemonic, and affective parallel processors to set goals, explore action alternatives, and evaluate which ones are better. As such, it includes Cellérier's control structure but goes considerably beyond it to make decisions on at least two levels, one the level of goal selection, the other the level of means selection relative to that goal. Undoubtedly this system would also regulate attention, perceptual centration, etc., but these are subjects left unanalyzed by both Cellérier and Pugh.

Finally, let us only recognize that Pugh's *sixth* and optional *component* (i.e., procedures for creating and refining world models) was extensively dealt with in our discussion of Cellérier's epistemic transformation. There is, therefore, no need to elaborate it further.

Although the model that emerges from integrating Cellérier and Pugh is incomplete and somewhat hazy, still it moves us closer to understanding the role affective evaluation plays in constructing adapted actions and extracting knowledge structures from them. What is needed now is to establish an empirical base from which to pursue the theory.

SOME APPLICATIONS

Although the main thrust of this chapter has been theoretical, it seems wise to ask, even in a very preliminary way, what empirical ramifications integrating Pugh's and Cellérier's conceptions might have. No studies of our own having yet been undertaken, such speculation must be based on existing data. Whereas the examples that follow are not exhaustive, they do indicate three areas in which the notions developed here may prove useful.

Genevan Studies of Procedures

The Genevan school's switch from the study of structures to the study of procedures was officially announced during festivities honoring Piaget's 80th birthday in 1976 (Inhelder, Ackermann-Valladao, Blanchet, Karmiloff-Smith, Kilcher-Hagedorn, Montangero, & Robert, 1976), and considerable empirical work was done either before Cellérier's (1979a, 1979b) synthesis or before Inhelder and Piaget's (1979) *"Procédures et structures."* As Alex Blanchet (1987, p. 252) points out, while Genevans' investigations of problem-solving strategies have produced better understanding of how goals and means become coordinated, how ascending and descending control interact, and how children reconcile different descriptions of an object with one another, they have neglected the role that values play. Our purpose in examining one such inquiry is, therefore, to see whether affective factors have crept undetected into the data.

In a study focusing on relationships of ascending and descending control, Boder (1978) asked children to load a truck with colored blocks so that they could drive along a road and deposit blocks on loading docks. They were instructed that the block deposited had to be the same color as the dock. The truck was of a size that blocks could only be stacked one on top of the other, and the direction of the route was indicated. Because blocks had to be unloaded in top-down order and because backing up or turning around was not allowed, it was necessary that the blocks be placed in the truck in reverse order to the order in which loading docks would be encountered. Children from ages 4 to 8½ years old were studied.

Boder found that one reaction of children from 4 to about 5½ years of age (*Group 1*) was to load the blocks in essentially arbitrary fashion. Although these subjects seemed to try to coordinate color, they did so in a peculiar way. When they had a block in hand they appeared to match it to a particular loading dock, but they did not consider the loading docks once only or consider them in order. Consequently, they loaded several blocks for some loading docks and none for others. This resulted not only in a lack of correspondence between the order of the blocks loaded and the order of the loading docks but also in lack of correspondence between the number of blocks in the truck and the number of loading docks along the road. Boder does not report what happened when mismatches occurred during unloading.

Other children in this group (*Group 2*) understood that it was necessary to organize how the blocks were loaded but still did not arrange loading to correspond to unloading. These subjects usually put the correct number of blocks in the truck and often the correct number of each color. Oddly, however, they put all the blue blocks in first, the yellow second, or vice versa, even though this violated the unloading order.

A third group (*Group 3*) indicated progress toward coordinating loading with unloading but without complete success. One child, for example, noticed that somewhere along the route there were two blue loading docks together. He began, therefore, by putting two blue blocks into the truck, explaining, "I start there because there is another blue and that's not hard." Sometimes subjects in this group also reversed the direction in which the truck was going, a violation of instructions, in order to achieve better correspondence.

A fourth reaction appearing in this group and one that persisted into later ages (*Group 4*) was to alternate loading blue and yellow blocks without keeping count of the number loaded or making that number correspond to the number of loading docks. In consequence, both the order of the colors and the number of blocks loaded proved incorrect. Apparently, alternation seemed the most significant aspect of the situation.

In children 5½ to 8½, the notion that the loading docks dictate both the number and order of the blocks to be loaded becomes stable, but the need for inversion presents problems. A subgroup of these children (*Group 5*) put a block corresponding to the first loading dock into the truck first, a block corresponding to the second dock second, etc. This, of course, puts the block for the first dock on the bottom of the pile and makes it impossible to unload it first. Subjects in this group could not correct their strategy.

Some children who made this mistake, however, came to understand that their error consisted in reversing the unloading order and began to correct it (*Group 6*). This was done by inverting the order of only two or three elements at first, but in certain individuals it eventually led to complete inversion and success.

Because the task involved is highly intellectual and relatively easy, it might be thought that affective approximating devices would not be needed. That assumption is strengthened by the fact that Boder's analysis has to do with ascending and descending control and makes no mention of values or affectivity. Nevertheless, his minute descriptions of the children's struggles reveal that, even in activity of supposedly so rational a nature, affectivity is at work at every turn.

One place that affective mechanisms are evident is in the goal's pursued by subjects at various stages in their activity. Because no protests are recorded, it appears that all the children wanted to follow the instruction. This is an affective phenomenon. Moreover, once taken, this affectively determined decision establishes an evaluative hierarchy for all ensuing behavior. It is the child's continuing wish to cooperate with the investigator that makes it *important* for him to load blocks in the truck, that makes him *interested* in matching order, color, and number, that makes him *feel* he has done something wrong if he turns the truck around or backs it up, etc. Moreover, the entire motivational framework is constantly open to revision. The child may become tired, lose interest, or be distracted by more interesting possibilities, depending on reassessments in terms of interest, fatigue, frustration, etc.

A second evidence of affective regulation is seen in the order in which sub-goals are selected. Why, for example, did *Group 1* subjects begin with the subgoal of matching color, whereas the somewhat more successful *Group 2* subjects began with number? It appears that affective preferences determine such decisions.

A third affective manifestation has to do with Pugh's "intellectual values." These play the cost of computation off against the degree of accuracy desired. For example, "Vla" in *Group 3* says explicitly that he put two blue blocks in the truck first because he could see that there were two blue loading docks together and that that part of the problem was easy. And the alternating loading pattern of the *Group 4* subjects is based on similar considerations. Because there were five blocks and only two of like color together, this strategy could lead to 80% accuracy with very little cost of calculation. Although making decisions on this basis may seem stupid or lazy when tasks are simple and total accuracy is achievable, it becomes acceptable in many real-life situations. The IRS, for example, fails to collect billions of dollars each year because of the tremendous cost of accuracy. Faced with millions of complicated tax reports, shortcuts of the type employed by *Group 3* children become quite reasonable.

Finally, affective mechanisms determining when action should be terminated can be discerned in Boder's data. Because the majority of his subjects did not succeed and because there is no reason to believe that they are still working on the problem, something in them or Boder must have turned them off (cf. Janet's termination regulations). Either they felt hopeless, lost interest, complied with Boder's own hopelessness or satisfaction and his resulting request that they stop, or gave up for other no doubt affective reasons. In at least one case, the affective nature of termination decisions is clear. A 5½-year-old who had finally figured out that he would have to put the block corresponding to the first dock on top became distressed by the thought that it would be first off the truck but last onto it. He concluded, therefore, that the task could not be done. The exclamation point embellishing his final answer must be read as an affective marker.

Examples from Decision Science

As mentioned in footnote 9, the index to Kahneman, Slovic, and Tversky's (1982) book, *Judgment Under Uncertainty: Heuristics and Biases*, contains no references to affective terms of any kind even though article after article refers to affective processes. Nevertheless, it is instructive to examine the articles to see how affectivity comes into play. I consider only a single example here.

In a paper entitled "Facts versus Fears: Understanding Perceived Risk," Slovic, Fischhoff, and Lichtenstein (1982) point out that even when considerable statistical evidence is available as a basis for deciding important protection issues: "facts can only go so far toward developing policy. At some point, human judgment is needed to interpret the findings and determine their relevance" (p. 463). Let us take this problematic opposition of facts to human judgment to be the authors' way of marking a distinction between *rational decisions* based on probabilities calculated from systematically established information and *irrational, "heuristic" decisions* based on criteria of another kind. The point is that the studies cited support the basic thesis that risk assessment is "inherently subjective" and that knowing the limitations of such assessments is "crucial to effective decision making."

The first group of results presented by the authors have to do with "judgmental biases in risk perception." Essentially, the authors argue that people are usually forced to make estimates of risk without systematic information, and that in doing so they employ "very general inferential rules" that have been brought to light by psychological investigations. For example, people often assume that the likelihood of some disastrous event is directly proportional to the ease with which examples come to mind (*availability bias*). In support of this contention the authors cite data from three sources: studies on how people estimate the risk of floods; studies on the relationship of earthquakes to sales of earthquake insurance; and studies on the reaction to public discussion of the risks of recombinant DNA research. In the first instance, it has been shown that despite the availability of good evidence to the contrary, people tend to believe that future floods will not exceed in extent or severity the flood most recently experienced. In the second instance, it is known that the sale of earthquake insurance increases sharply after an earthquake and decreases as "memories fade." In the third instance, it was found that initial praise for scientists' announcement of possible benefits of recombinant DNA experiments soon transformed into outrage as speculation escalated and scenarios became more "scary."

It is interesting to compare the way Slovic et al. explain these finding with Pugh's ideas about decision making. To begin with, Slovic and his colleagues argue that ease of remembering becomes a criterion of probability: The facility with which the most recent flood is remembered gets translated into the probability of what the next flood will be like. This takes on affective significance when one remembers that ease is a feeling and that Pugh links it explicitly to intellectual values. Moreover, this significance is considerably increased by evidence that affective experience influences how memory is organized, so that ease of remembering may well be linked to other kinds of feelings. Secondly, Slovic et al. invoke another principle of memory to explain the finding that fading memory of an earthquake leads to decreasing sales of earthquake insurance. Assuming they are correct, the question then becomes, "What causes memories to be vivid and then to fade?" There seems little doubt, moreover, that it is not the memory itself that faded. Subjects asked to recall the earthquake no doubt could recall its major features, although some details might eventually be lost. The fading factor that motivates insurance purchases would much more reasonably be identified with subjects' fear (i.e., with fading feelings). Not only would this make affective evaluation a central feature in the decision process, but it would also illustrate Pugh's principle of "time dependence" as part of any value structure. Finally, Slovic and his colleagues invoke "heat" and "scariness" to explain the recombinant DNA example. However, they do not, as Pugh would, speak of affectivity or go on to interpret affects as heuristic evaluation mechanisms. The affective nature of heuristic mechanisms remains implicit in their work.

A second example of Slovic et al. missing the affective aspect of decisions concerns what they call the "it won't happen to me" heuristic. To illustrate this decision strategy, they cite studies showing that most individuals believe themselves to be better than average drivers, to be more likely than average to live past 80, and less than likely to be harmed by the products they employ. Their explanation of these judgments is based on the notion that people are poor statisticians. For example, they (Slovic et al., 1982) suggest that the reason people think they are such good drivers has to do with the fact that "despite driving too fast, tailgating, etc., poor drivers make trip after trip without mishap. This personal experience demonstrates to them their exceptional skill and safety. Moreover, their indirect experience via the news media shows them that when accidents happen, they happen to others (p. 470)." In consequence, they have good statistical evidence on which to base decisions. For students of human motivation, however, this explanation seems very partial. Surely the need to see oneself in a certain way, to impress, to experience the thrill of speed, etc., along with one's defenses in handling the fear of death, one's conscious goals such as a need to hurry, etc. play roles in determining behavior. It cannot be only a rational, statistical affair.

In the end, Slovic and his colleagues (1982) appear to agree implicitly with the central premise underlying the work of Pugh. This is illustrated by the following excerpt having to do with technical obstacles impeding rational estimation of how probably serious nuclear accidents are: "The technical reality is that there are few 'cut-and-dried facts' regarding the probabilities of serious reactor mishaps. The technology is so new and the probabilities in question are so small that accurate risk estimates cannot be based on empirical observation. Instead, such assessments must be derived from complex mathematical models and subjective judgments" (p. 486).

The Axiology of Science

As a final illustration, let us turn from studies conducted on the microgenetic time scale to examine an account of historical construction. As Garcia (1983) has pointed out, such studies are no less empirical than "experimental" microgenetic studies, although the nature of the data is quite different. Their importance is that they illustrate how Pugh's secondary values evolve and how Cellérier's epistemic transformation operates historically.

The text at issue is Laudan's (1984) *Science and Values*. In this work, Laudan is concerned with two puzzles concerning science. On the one hand, there is the puzzle of how, in a social world of such diversity, scientists ever can agree. On the other hand, there is the puzzle of how the disagreement or dissensus increasingly recognized in science can be explained, because the defining feature of science is adherence to methods that produce consensus.

Laudan begins his analysis by considering the best known theory of how consensus is formed. This he summarizes in what he calls "The Simple Hierarchical Model of Rational Consensus Formation." Essentially, this model holds that disagreement can occur and be resolved on three hierarchized levels. The first level of disagreement is *factual*, the lowest level in the hierarchy. According to this theory, disagreements of this kind are settled by second-level evidentiary rules to which all scientists adhere. However, *methodological* disagreements at this level in the form of disputes about the rules of evidence or rules of procedure used to settle factual disputes and how they should be applied must be resolved on a still higher level (i.e., that of axiology). The reason for this is that methods are means of achieving scientific goals and can, therefore, be evaluated in terms of their effectiveness in realizing scientific or cognitive ideals. Here, however, the strategy of resolving problems on one level at the next higher level in the hierarchy breaks down. *Axiological* disputes, that is disagreements about the aims and goals of science, are either held not to exist on the grounds that all scientists share identical values, or, if they are admitted to exist, they are held to be incapable of resolution.

Particularly relevant to our purposes are Laudan's examples concerning the supposedly unrevisable nature of scientific goals. Reichenbach, he points out, believed that goals in general, including scientific goals, are not rationally negotiable. He quotes Reichenbach as follows: " 'If anyone tells us that he studies science for his pleasure [as opposed to his doing science because he wants to know the truth], . . . it is no statement at all but a decision and everybody has the right to do what he wants. . . . [When we propose an aim for science, we cannot] demand agreement to our proposal in the sense that we can demand it for statements which we have proven to be true' " (p. 49). Similarly, Laudan cites Popper's belief that realism and instrumentalism are both internally consistent accounts of science and that which account one chooses "ultimately reduces to an irresolvable matter of taste." Laudan (1984) sums up: "The thrust of such arguments [is that if] a certain set of cognitive ends or values is internally consistent, then there is no scope for a rational evaluation of those aims or for a rationally grounded comparison of those aims with any other (consistent) set. We may or may not like a certain set of goals; we may or may not share them. But these are emotive matters, quite on a par with other subjective questions of personal or sexual preference" (p. 49).

Laudan, of course, believes that the unrevisability of goals is false and denies the hierarchical model. In its stead he erects "The Triadic Network of Justification," where theories, methods, and aims form a triangle and influence one another mutually. The relationships envisioned by Laudan specify that theories must be consistent with aims and constrain methods whereas at the same time being justified by them. Conversely, methods justify theories and realize aims whereas being constrained by theories and justified by aims. And finally, aims must be in harmony with theories whereas at the same time both justifying methods and being realized by them. All of this is illustrated in Fig. 17.3.

What makes it possible for Laudan to bend what was formerly a straight line into a triangle is his demonstration that scientists' goals are open to criticism and revision. This destroys the hierarchy. As evidence, he cites many 18th-century scientists' realization that the aims of empiricist science, formulated in the wake of Newton, were no longer desirable. Too many phenomena had been discovered that were unamenable to explanations limited to observable entities and processes. Successful theories of electricity, of embryology, and of chemistry had to invoke unobservable factors for progress to occur. During this epoch also,

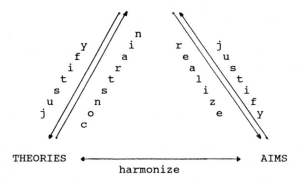

FIG. 17.3.   The triadic network of justification. From Laudan (© 1984, The Regents of the University of California) p. 63.

Lesage's chemical and gravitational theories, Hartley's neurophysiological ideas, and Boscovich's conception of matter were all criticized, not on grounds of theory or method, but because they deviated from empiricist axiology (i.e., from the ambition or goal of explaining nature in terms of observations).

Laudan identifies two criteria on which such criticism and revision can be rationally based. The first or "utopian" criterion is leveled against goals that, however desirable, cannot be realized or that cannot be known to have been accomplished even should that be the case. Although not cited by Laudan, an example might be the abandonment of Hilbert's search for a finitistic absolute proof of consistency for arithmetic when Gödel's theorem showed that it was essentially impossible to achieve (Nagel & Newman, 1968). The second or "shared archetype" criterion is leveled against scientists who do not practice what they preach or, in other words, who pursue contradictory goals. As an example, Laudan points out that Newton, despite stressing "hypotheses non fingo," had, in fact, used hypotheses. Under attack, Lesage employed this fact to defend his own use of hypothetical entities and to argue against complete observability as a scientific aim. As history has shown, Lesage won; empiricist aims were gradually abandoned.

This brief précis of Laudan's conception of consensus and dissensus in the development of scientific knowledge not only provides an excellent illustration of Pugh's notion of secondary values but also illustrates how values operate in Cellérier's epistemic transformation. Out of primitive intellectual values (i.e., feelings regulating intellectual activity in terms of interest, fatigue, satisfaction with success, disappointment with failure, etc.), complex secondary values are constructed. When these are discovered to be inconsistent with primary intellectual values, as in the example of Lesage abandoning empiricism's aspirations, they must be rejected. But the primary values are not themselves open to revision. Scientists will always value intellectual activity and success, will always husband intellectual resources, and will always devalue inconsistency and failure. Their goals as well as their theories and methods must reflect those values. If they do not, they will eventually be corrected, unless the primary value structure, because of its surrogate nature, is inadequate to the problem or unless competing values outweigh the goal of rationality and lead to irremediable disaster before reason can prevail.

CONCLUSION

Selecting the evaluative aspect of affectivity for analysis, I have argued that the internalization of organic evolution to form the intellectual system required devising some means of selecting behavioral variations and that the selective mechanism devised was the affective system. From that perspective it is possible to relate Pugh's conception of value-driven decision systems and his account of affective mechanisms to Cellérier's analysis of the pragmatic and epistemic transformations. Tenuous as the resulting model may be, it gives a picture more complete than other models of the role that affective evaluations play in adapting action and in constructing knowledge. In a preliminary way, it also allows us to bring together empirical data on problem solving, on decision making, and on the evolution of scientific thought. Further study is needed to determine whether these promising beginnings can mature into a full-blown theory including other aspects of affectivity.

ACKNOWLEDGMENTS

This work was conducted in part while the author was Clinical Research Training Fellow in Adolescence in a program sponsored by the Institute for Psychosomatic and Psychiatric Research and Training, Michael Reese Hospital and Medical Center; the Committee on Human Development, Department of Behavioral Science, University of Chicago; Department of Psychiatry, University of Chicago; and the Adolescent Program of the Illinois State Psychiatric Institute. The program is funded by grant 5 T32 MH14668-10 from the National Institutes of Mental Health.

REFERENCES

Anderson, J. (1980). *Cognitive Psychology and Its Implications*. San Francisco: W. H. Freeman.

Blanchet, A. (1987). Rôle des valeurs et des systèmes de valeurs dans la cognition. *Archives de Psychologie* (Geneva), *54*, 251–270.

Boder, A. (1978). Étude de la composition d'un ordre inverse: Hypothèse sur la coordination de deux sources de controle du raisonnement. *Archives de Psychologie* (Geneva), *46*, 87–113.

Brooks, D., & Wiley, E. O. (1986). *Evolution as entropy*. Chicago: University of Chicago Press.

Brown, T., & Weiss, L. (1987). Structures, procedures, heuristics, and affectivity. *Archives de Psychologie* (Geneva), *55*, 59–94.

Cellérier, G. (1979a). Structures cognitives et schèmes d'action, I. *Archives de Psychologie, 47*, 87–106.

Cellérier, G. (1979b). Structures cognitives et schèmes d'action, II. *Archives de Psychologie, 47*, 107–122.

Darwin, C. (1964). *On the origin of species*. Cambridge, MA: Harvard University Press.

Depew, D., & Weber, B. H. (1985). *Evolution at a crossroads*. Cambridge, MA: MIT Press.

Fraisse, P. (1968). The emotions. In P. Fraisse & J. Piaget (Eds.), *Experimental Psychology: Its scope and method. V. Motivation, emotion, and personality*. New York: Basic Books.

Garcia, R. (1983). Psychogenesis and the history of science. In D. de Caprona, J.-J. Ducret, O. Rod, M.-C. Rosat, & A. Wells (Eds.), *History of sciences and psychogenesis* (Cahiers de la Fondation Archives Jean Piaget, No. 4). Geneva: Fondation Archives Jean Piaget.

Hubbard, B. A. F., & Karnofsky, E. S. (1982). *Plato's protagoras*. Chicago: University of Chicago Press.

Inhelder, B., Ackermann-Valladao, E., Blanchet, A., Karmiloff-Smith, A., Kilcher-Hagedorn, H., Montangero, J., & Robert, M. (1976). Des structures cognitives aux procédures de découverte. *Archives de Psychologie*, (Geneva), *44*, 57–72.

Inhelder, B., & Piaget, J. (1979). Procédures et structures. *Archives de Psychologie*, (Geneva), *47*, 165–176.

Kahneman, D., Slovic, P., & Tversky, A. (1982). *Judgment under uncertainty: Heuristics and biases.* Cambridge: Cambridge University Press.

Laudan, L. (1984). *Science and values.* Berkeley: University of California Press.

Moore, J., & Newell, A. (1974). How can Merlin understand? In L. Gregg (Ed.), *Knowledge and cognition.* Potomac, MD: Lawrence Erlbaum Associates.

Nagel, E., & Newman, J. R. (1968). *Gödel's proof.* New York: New York University Press.

Newell, A., & Simon, H. A. (1972). *Human problem solving.* Englewood Cliffs, NJ: Prentice-Hall.

Nuttin, J. (1968). Motivation. In Paul Fraisse and Jean Piaget (Eds.), *Experimental psychology: Its scope and method. V. Motivation, emotion, and personality.* New York: Basic Books.

Piaget, J. (1952). *The origins of intelligence in children* (Margaret Cook, Trans.). New York: W. W. Norton. (First published in 1936.)

Piaget, J. (1974). *Réussir et comprendre.* Paris: Presses Universitaires de France.

Piaget, J. (1977). *Recherches sur l'abstraction réfléchissante. (Tomes I et II).* Paris: Presses Universitaires de France.

Piaget, J. (1978). *Recherches sur la généralisation.* Paris: Presses Universitaires de France.

Piaget, J. (1980). *Adaptation and intelligence* (Stewart Eames, Trans.). Chicago: University of Chicago Press.

Piaget, J. (1981). *Intelligence and affectivity* (T. A. Brown & C. E. Kaegi, Trans.). Palo Alto, CA: Annual Reviews. (First published in 1953–54.)

Piaget, J. (1985). *The equilibration of cognitive structures.* (Terrance Brown & Kishore Julian Thampy, Trans.). Chicago: University of Chicago Press.

Piaget, J. (1987). *Possibility and necessity: Volumes 1 and 2* (Helga Feider, Trans.). Minneapolis: University of Minnesota Press.

Prigogine, I. (1980). *From being to becoming.* San Francisco: W. H. Freeman.

Prigogine, I., & Stengers, I. (1984). *Order out of chaos.* Toronto, Canada: Bantam Books.

Pugh, G. E. (1977). *The biological origin of human values.* New York: Basic Books.

Scherer, K. R. (1984). On the nature and function of emotion: A component process approach. In K. R. Scherer & P. Ekman (Eds.), *Approaches to emotion.* Hillsdale, NJ: Lawrence Erlbaum Associates.

Skinner, B. F. (1984). Selection by consequences. *The Behavior and Brain Sciences, 7,* 477–510.

Slovic, P., Fischhoff, B., & Lichtenstein, S. (1982). Facts versus fears: Understanding perceived risk. In D. Kahneman, P. Slovic, & A. Tversky (Eds.), *Judgment under uncertainty: Heuristics and biases.* Cambridge: Cambridge University Press.

Zajonc, R. B. (1980). Feeling and thinking. Preferences need no inferences. *American Psychologist, 35,* 151–175.

Zinchenko, V. P., & Davydov, V. V. (1985). Foreword. In James V. Wertsch, *Vygotsky and the social formation of mind.* Cambridge, MA: Harvard University Press.

Author Index

448 AUTHOR INDEX

Subject Index

Action, 3, 7–8
Action, words for
  in children, 283, 285–286, 289
  in parents, 288–289
Activation Theory
  see Arousal Theory
Adaptive Priming, Theory of, 152–161
  dimensionality of emotion, 157–159
  limbic memory, 152–155
  memory access, 159–161
  primitive adaptive priming, 155–157
Affect, 21–23, 27, 34, 75, 215–242
  effects on children with Down syndrome,
    365–367
  effects, 76, 89–91
  expression, 216, 223, 225–236
    beliefs and desires in children, 234–236
    cognition, 239–240
    negative affect, 230
    neuropsychological considerations, 240–
      241
    neutral affect, 224, 228–229, 231–232
  hemispheric dysfunction, *see* Left or Right
    Hemisphere Dysfunction
  neuropsychological models, 109–110
    in children with Down syndrome
  inductions, 91
  influence on word learning, 222–229
  organization of material, 78
  origins, 76, 87–88

see also Developmental psychopathology
  structuring studies, 78
Anger, 64–71, 387–388
  animate agent, 69
  definition, 65
  socialization, 65
  cross-cultural variations, 396–399
Anger, concept of, 298–301
Anger, development of, 301–304
Anger, expression, 247–279
  in infants
    crying, 270
    directionality, 275–277
    elicitation, 252–254
    facial expression, 250–252, 255, 257–
      260, 261, 262, 271–274
    flushing, 277
    restraint, 261–267
    social targets, 267–268
    tears, 277
    vocalic expression, 261, 269–270, 278
  in young children, 304
  socialization, 304–306
Anger, in mothers, 306–307
Anger, naturalistic approach, 300–303
Anger, in young children, 297–308
  response to anger, 301–304
Appraisal, 4, 5–6, 8–9, 12–15
  primary, 5
  secondary, 5